All-In-One

MCSE NT 4.0

Certification Exam Guide

Brian Schwarz
Total Seminars

McGraw-Hill
New York • San Francisco • Washington, D.C. • Auckland
Bogotá • Caracas • Lisbon • London • Madrid • Mexico City
Milan • Montreal • New Delhi • San Juan • Singapore
Sydney • Tokyo • Toronto

McGraw-Hill

A Division of The McGraw·Hill Companies

Copyright © 1999 by The McGraw-Hill Companies, Inc. Printed in the United States of America. Except as permitted under the United States Copyright Act of 1976, no part of this publication may be reproduced or distributed in any form or by any means, or stored in a data base or retrieval system, without the prior written permission of the publisher.

1 2 3 4 5 6 7 8 9 0   AGM/AGM   9 0 4 3 2 1 0 9

P/N 0-07-038299-9
PART OF ISBN 0-07-913739-3

The sponsoring editor for this book was Michael Sprague and the production supervisor was Clare Stanley. It was set in Century Schoolbook by D&G Limited, LLC.

Printed and bound by Quebecor/Martinsburg

DEDICATION

To my wife, Libby, for putting up with me.

ACKNOWLEDGMENTS

Producing this book was a group project in every way. Mike Meyers, Scott Jernigan, and Libby Ingrassia Schwarz and I collaborated on every aspect of this project: writing, rewriting, editing, rewriting, graphics, rewriting . . . their names could have just as easily gone on the cover of this book. They and all my friends at Total Seminars deserve my heartfelt thanks for putting up with me when I put on my "prima donna persona." Special thanks go out to Cassandra, Bob, Janelle, Roger, and Dudley.

Last but not least, I want to thank all of my family and friends for sticking with me over the last four years, while my travel and teaching schedule has prevented me from paying you the attention you deserve.

CONTENTS

Contents

Contents

INTRODUCTION

So, you think you're ready to get *Microsoft Certification Systems Engineer* (MCSE) certified? Well, my friend, you've come to the right place. Sit right down on the bookstore floor and read on, because the world will soon be yours for the taking. Getting an MCSE is like getting your first driver's license; you finally have *freedom*. Becoming a Microsoft Certified Systems Engineer is not going to make you smarter, taller, or sexier, but certification just might be the ticket to a better life.

Certifications are the key to the competitive *information technology* (IT) marketplace. You might be a crack system administrator, but if you walk into a potential employer's office, how do you prove it? "Umm . . . well, yes, I have a degree in fine arts, but I'm good, honest." That's just not going to fly, is it? Certifications prove to employers that you know how to do the job that they need done, regardless of whether your background is in computer science, poetry, or auto mechanics.

Microsoft Certified Systems Engineers are in extremely high demand right now. Windows 95/98, Windows NT 4.0, and the soon-to-be Windows 2000 (NT 5.0) control the lion's share of the *Operating Systems* (OS) market, and Microsoft's application software dominates business environments. Employers need capable and qualified people to develop and maintain their enterprises using Microsoft software. That's where you come in. When you have an MCSE to tag onto your business card and the skills to go with that title, you, too, will be in demand. That demand translates into higher salaries, better benefits, and possibly a better life.

Are you ready?

Microsoft Certification Programs

Microsoft offers four major technical certification programs: *Microsoft Certified Professional* (MCP), *Microsoft Certified Solution Developer* (MCSD), *Microsoft Certified Trainer* (MCT), and *Microsoft Certified Systems Engineer* (MCSE).

MCP

The Microsoft Certified Professional designation acts as the stepping stone to all other technical certifications offered by Microsoft. Becoming an MCP requires that you pass any one of the current Microsoft Certification exams, *with the exception of Networking Essentials* (exam 70-058). Microsoft had previously limited the MCP designation to those who had passed an operating system exam but changed the requirement to any exam except Networking Essentials as of October 1, 1998.

NOTE: *For most MCSE candidates, taking the Networking Essentials exam first makes sense. Many of the other MCSE exams assume a strong understanding of how networks work. Unfortunately, because it is the only exam that does not by itself make you an MCP, many MCSE candidates leave the Networking Essentials exam for their last exam.*

Unless you have a specific deadline for becoming an MCP, I encourage you to take the Networking Essentials exam first. Although not technically a prerequisite of the other exams, Networking Essentials provides a strong foundation for many of the other exams.

Most MCSE and MCSD candidates view the MCP designation as the first step toward ultimate certification, giving them something to add to their resume and business cards in the meantime. Microsoft has added other intermediate certifications that can be earned on the way to the full MCSE or MCSD title: MCP +Site Building and MCP +Internet.

MCP +SITE BUILDING The MCP +Site Building certification demonstrates the capability in building and developing solutions for Internet sites. Candidates for this level of certification must take two of the following approved exams: Designing and Implementing Web Sites with Microsoft FrontPage 98 (Exam 70-055), Designing and Implementing Commerce Solutions with Microsoft Site Server 3.0, Commerce Edition (Exam 70-057), and Designing and Implementing Web Solutions with Microsoft Visual InterDev 6.0 (Exam 70-152). Because these exams can also apply toward the MCSD requirements, the MCP +Site Building designation will appeal to MCSD candidates.

MCP +INTERNET The MCP +Internet designation requires the candidate to pass three exams: Internetworking Microsoft TCP/IP on Microsoft Windows NT 4.0 (Exam 70-059), Implementing and Supporting Microsoft Windows NT Server 4.0 (Exam 70-067), and either Implementing and Supporting Internet Information Server 3.0 and Microsoft Index Server 1.1 (Exam 70-077) or Implementing and Supporting Microsoft Internet Information Server 4.0 (Exam 70-087). Because all three of these exams can apply to the MCSE requirements, the MCP +Internet designation will appeal to MCSE candidates.

MCT

The Microsoft Certified Trainer program certifies instructors to deliver the official Microsoft curriculum through Microsoft's *Authorized Technical Education Centers* (ATECs). For details, check Microsoft's Web site at **http://www.microsoft.com.**

MCSD

The Microsoft Certified Solution Developer program certifies programmers and developers as qualified to build and design applications using Microsoft products such as SQL Server, Visual Studio, and Transaction Server.

Microsoft redesigned the MCSD certification track in late 1998, refocusing its exams on newer technologies, especially Internet and Web-based technologies.

MCSE

According to Microsoft, a Microsoft Certified Systems Engineer should be "qualified to effectively plan, implement, maintain, and support information systems in a wide range of computing environments using the Microsoft Windows NT Server and the Microsoft BackOffice integrated family of server products." Plus, every MCSE exam demands that you understand how Microsoft products function within a networked environment. Although the MCSD certification is intended for developers and programmers, it also targets system administrators, architects, and troubleshooters. The specific requirements for MCSE certification are discussed later in this chapter.

NOTE: *The MCSE designation is probably more critical for system administrators than the MCSD is for programmers. Programmers can prove their skill to employers with sample programs they have built. A system administrator's contributions are often more intangible. In fact, the goal of a system administrator should be invisibility — the systems run so smoothly that end-users never even notice that there is a system administrator. Programmers get noticed for the problems they solve; system administrators get noticed for the problems that they prevent.*

In addition to the basic MCSE, Microsoft enables MCSEs specializing in Internet technologies to earn an additional certification: MCSE +Internet.

MCSE +INTERNET   MCSE +Internet requires a total of nine exams. In addition to the four core MCSE requirements, MCSE +Internet candidates must take the TCP/IP exam (70-059), one of the IIS exams (70-087 or 70-077), the Internet Explorer Administration Kit exam (70-079), and two electives.

The two electives can include exams covering SQL server, Microsoft Exchange, Microsoft Site Server, Microsoft Proxy Server, or Microsoft SNA server. See Microsoft's Web site, **www.microsoft.com**, for exam numbers and other details.

What Exams Should I Take To Become an MCSE?

NOTE: This book covers the MCSE NT 4.0 track. Although Microsoft continues to offer an MCSE Windows NT 3.51 certification track, I recommend that candidates pursue the more current certification, which has greater market value and will remain valid longer.

You must pass six exams to earn the MCSE designation: four core exams and two electives. The core exams include the following: Networking Essentials (Exam 70-058), Implementing and Supporting Microsoft Windows NT Server 4.0 (Exam 70-067, often referred to as simply "the Server exam"), Implementing and Supporting Microsoft Windows NT Server 4.0 in the Enterprise (Exam 70-068, often referred to as simply the "Enterprise exam"), and an exam covering an approved Microsoft client operating system (see Figure I–1).

Six exams, three of which Microsoft has retired and no longer offers, can fulfill the client operating system requirement. See Figure I–2.

Unless you have already taken one of the other client exams, I recommend that you take the Implementing and Supporting NT Workstation exam (Exam 70-073). Microsoft often allows older, retired exams to be used to meet current requirements. When Microsoft announces its Windows NT 5.0 certification track at some point in the future, chances are good that the NT Workstation exam will meet some requirement within the new program. Although Microsoft will eventually retire all of the current client exams, I suspect that the Windows NT Workstation 4.0 exam will remain current longer than the other exams. Microsoft tests much of the same material on the Workstation exam as on the Server and Enterprise exams. If you must take those exams anyway, studying for all three as a group makes sense and saves work.

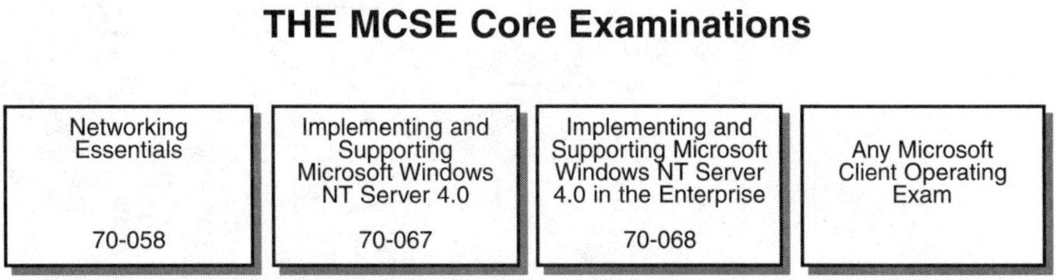

THE MCSE Core Examinations

Figure I–1
To earn your MCSE designation, you must pass four core exams.

Acceptable Client Operating System Examinations (choose 1)

Figure I–2
These six exams can fulfill the client exam requirement.

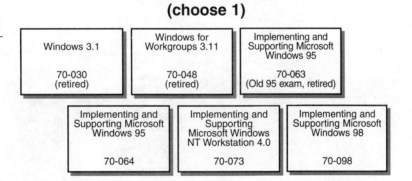

Microsoft requires two elective exams for the MCSE (see Figure I–3). They also offer eleven elective choices, with some having different tests for different versions of the software covered by the exam. For example, Microsoft offers exams in both Internet Information Server 3.0 (Exam 70-077) and Internet Information Server 4.0 (Exam 70-078). Although you are free to take and pass both exams, only one can count toward your MCSE requirements.

Microsoft has kept many of the older exams in place because the products they cover continue to be used. As a general rule, take the exam covering the most recent version of the software unless you currently use or have extensive experience with the older version. What exams should you choose for your elective if you don't have extensive experience in a particular product?

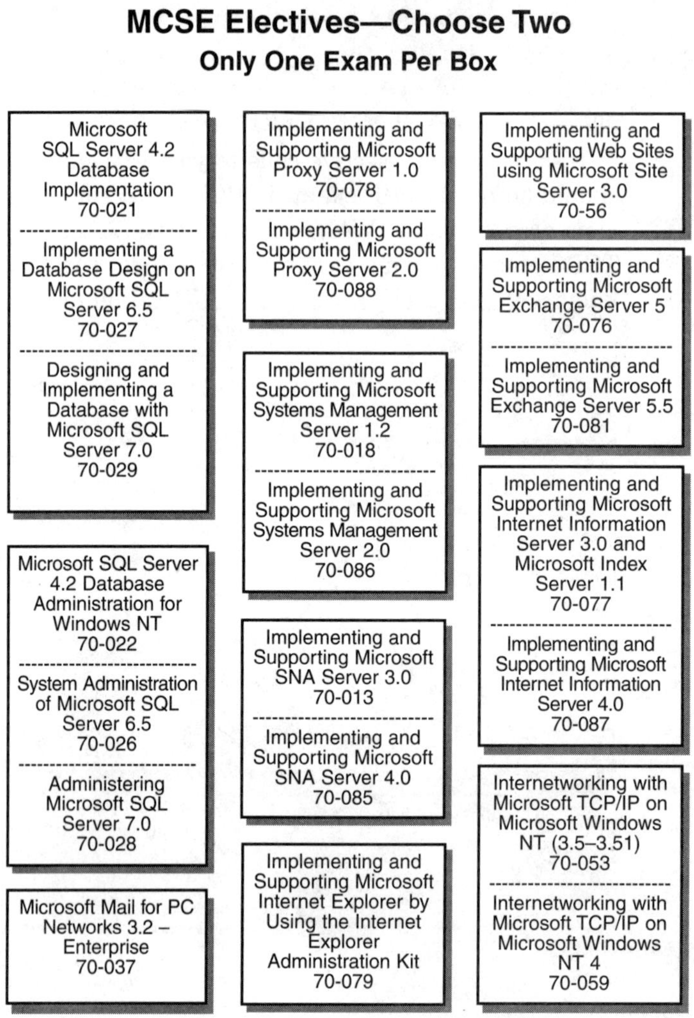

Figure I–3
The MCSE electives.

MCSE Electives—Choose Two
Only One Exam Per Box

Microsoft SQL Server 4.2 Database Implementation 70-021	Implementing and Supporting Microsoft Proxy Server 1.0 70-078	Implementing and Supporting Web Sites using Microsoft Site Server 3.0 70-56
Implementing a Database Design on Microsoft SQL Server 6.5 70-027	Implementing and Supporting Microsoft Proxy Server 2.0 70-088	Implementing and Supporting Microsoft Exchange Server 5 70-076
Designing and Implementing a Database with Microsoft SQL Server 7.0 70-029	Implementing and Supporting Microsoft Systems Management Server 1.2 70-018	Implementing and Supporting Microsoft Exchange Server 5.5 70-081
Microsoft SQL Server 4.2 Database Administration for Windows NT 70-022	Implementing and Supporting Microsoft Systems Management Server 2.0 70-086	Implementing and Supporting Microsoft Internet Information Server 3.0 and Microsoft Index Server 1.1 70-077
System Administration of Microsoft SQL Server 6.5 70-026	Implementing and Supporting Microsoft SNA Server 3.0 70-013	Implementing and Supporting Microsoft Internet Information Server 4.0 70-087
Administering Microsoft SQL Server 7.0 70-028	Implementing and Supporting Microsoft SNA Server 4.0 70-085	Internetworking with Microsoft TCP/IP on Microsoft Windows NT (3.5–3.51) 70-053
Microsoft Mail for PC Networks 3.2 – Enterprise 70-037	Implementing and Supporting Microsoft Internet Explorer by Using the Internet Explorer Administration Kit 70-079	Internetworking with Microsoft TCP/IP on Microsoft Windows NT 4 70-059

Try to choose two exams that are related to each other and that cover skills you are likely to use. Do not treat certifications as a chore to be completed and forgotten. Certifications provide a useful roadmap for developing new skills.

For example, I chose to take the NT 4.0 TCP/IP exam (70-059) and the IIS 4.0 exam (70-087), because the IIS 4.0 exam requires knowledge of TCP/IP. Although the TCP/IP exam is not a prerequisite for the IIS exam, knowledge of TCP/IP is critical to passing the IIS exam. Preparing for both exams at the same time saved time and allowed me to develop a complementary set of skills.

Other elective exam combinations complement each other as well. Someone with a database or programming background should take Designing and Implementing Databases with Microsoft SQL Server 7.0 (Exam 70-029) and Administering Microsoft SQL Server 7.0 (Exam 70-028).

If no particular elective calls to you, I suggest that one of the electives should be the TCP/IP exam. TCP/IP has become the standard protocol for *wide-area networks* (WANs), including the Internet. Working knowledge of TCP/IP makes you more competitive in today's job market. In addition, some knowledge of TCP/IP is critical for success on many of the other exams.

Signing Up for the Exams

To sign up for any of the Microsoft exams, call Sylvan Prometric at (800) 755-EXAM. Sylvan Prometric will help you find the closest testing center to you. Testing centers are often located at companies offering official Microsoft courses. If you have taken one of those classes, you probably already know the location of a testing center.

The "All in One" Approach

In this book, we cover three of the core exams: NT Workstation (Exam 70-073), NT Server (Exam 70-067), and NT in the Enterprise (Exam 70-068).

 NOTE: *For the sake of brevity, we will refer to these exams as Workstation, Server, and Enterprise in the rest of this book.*

Anyone who has taken these three exams will tell you they cover many of the same topics. All three test your knowledge of Windows NT in a networking environment, each from a different perspective.

The Workstation exam emphasizes the internal details of the Windows NT operating system and how NT functions as a network client. Key topics include the following:

■ Choosing operating systems—Windows 95 versus NT Workstation versus NT Server

■ Windows NT application support

- NT boot process
- File systems

The Server exam emphasizes NT's role as a server. Key topics include the following:

- Network security
- Network monitoring
- Microsoft networking
- Interoperability with Novell NetWare
- Users, global groups, and local groups

The Enterprise exam emphasizes NT's role in a large, "enterprise" network. Key topics include the following:

- Managing trust relationships
- Domain models
- WAN design

Although each exam emphasizes a different aspect of NT, the three exams require knowledge of many of the same topics. For example, all three exams ask questions about fault tolerance. (See Chapter 7, "Managing NT Server Partitions.") Virtually identical fault tolerance questions can appear on all three exams. Other topics are covered with varying degrees of depth on each exam. For example, the Workstation exam requires knowledge of how to join a domain; the Server exam requires you to know how to create one; and the Enterprise exam requires the knowlege of managing multiple domains.

This book covers the NT concepts tested for on all three exams. Most exam guides limit themselves to a particular test, leaving out important information not covered on a particular exam. An NT Workstation guide, for example, might give a brief definition of a domain and describe the process by which an NT Workstation joins a domain, but not discuss NT domain issues such as trust relationships. Studying these topics exam by exam can leave gaping holes in your knowledge.

Covering all three exams (Workstation, Server, and Enterprise) avoids the awkward exclusions required by an exam-by-exam approach. This book attacks the Windows NT domains in detail, covering everything you need to know for all three exams, with a sprinkling of "real world but not covered by the exams" information for seasoning.

You should approach the MCSE exams with two goals in mind: first, passing the exams to attain your certification; second, and more importantly, gaining real-world knowledge in learning how to use Windows NT. These goals are shared by all candidates. Approaching NT on a topical basis is the best way to meet those goals.

Taking the Tests

Many people spend all their time studying the topics covered on the exam and spend little or no time preparing for the exam itself. That is a *big mistake*. You may know everything there is to know about NT but still miss questions on the exams if you are not ready for the exam format.

Multiple-Choice

For many MCSE candidates, the MCSE exams represent the first multiple-choice exams that they have taken since high school. Many people who fail the exams do so because they have not taken the time to understand Microsoft's exam format. To prepare for the exams, remind yourself how to take multiple-choice tests, familiarize yourself with Microsoft's test design goals, and review the Microsoft "company line." Test taking is a skill. Before taking the exams, make sure to practice with the exams on the CD-ROM that accompany this book.

When taking any multiple-choice exam, look for answers that can be immediately eliminated. Most multiple-choice exams list four or five possible answer choices. Test writers usually include one or two throwaway answers that they feel will be obviously wrong to anyone who has actually studied. In the MCSE exams—like many multiple-choice exams—there is no penalty for guessing. So be sure to answer every question. You can count on guessing the correct answer about 20–25 percent of the time, even if you have no idea what the right answer is. Eliminating even a single possibility greatly increases the chance of guessing the right answer. The following sample question illustrates the principle of "intelligent guessing."

SAMPLE QUESTION #1   You are building a small, local area network with 10 Windows 95 machines, all located in the same small building. Which networking protocol would allow you to set up the network with the least complex network configuration?

Select the best answer.

    a. NetBEUI

    b. TCP/IP

    c. IDE

    d. DHCP

Correct Answer: a—NetBEUI

In this question, answer C, IDE, can be eliminated immediately because IDE is not a networking protocol. IDE is used to connect hard drives to the system. Answer D, DHCP can also be eliminated; DHCP is an additional protocol used in TCP/IP networks to allow for centralized administration of TCP/IP settings.

That leaves two answers, giving you a 50/50 chance if you guess at this point. Of course, if you know that TCP/IP networks require a great deal more configuration of each machine than NetBEUI networks, then this particular question would pose no problem. (For more information about protocols, see Chapter 10, "Networking Protocols.") But, even if you didn't know the right answer, knowing that even one of the answers was wrong greatly increases your chances of guessing the right answer.

Another problem with multiple-choice exams is that they force you to use somebody else's answer. For example, the following sample question lists a possible answer to the question, but may not be the answer you would come up with in the real world or on a fill-in-the-blank test.

SAMPLE QUESTION #2 You manage a TCP/IP-based network. The Windows NT Workstation ACCOUNT4 cannot access any of the file shares on the Windows NT Server ACCT_SERV. The network has recently been rewired, and you suspect a physical cabling problem. How would you determine whether a physical cabling problem exists between the two Windows NT machines?

    a. Check the Windows NT event viewer for cable errors.

    b. Use the PING utility to test the connection.

    c. Use the IPCONFIG /TEST utility to test the connection.

    d. Use the NBTSTAT utility to test the connection.

Correct Answer: b—Use the PING utility to test the connection.

Although PING would be an excellent tool to use in this situation, it is not the only possible right answer. In real life, you might want to ask a few additional questions. For example, could the two machines communicate before the rewiring took place? Have either of the machines changed their TCP/IP configuration? Are the link lights on the hub and the network card lit?

In the real-world, PING would not be the only option in checking for a bad physical connection, but these exams do not enable you to give a free-form answer. They ask you to choose the "best answer" from those given. In the scenario described in Sample Question #2, double-checking the IP address information of each machine with the IPCONFIG utility might not be a bad idea. Unfortunately, the option listed (/TEST) is not a valid option for the IPCONFIG utility, and IPCONFIG itself has nothing to do with testing physical connections.

Regardless of whether or not PING would be the first tool you would use to try to fix the problem, it is the best choice among the options given in this question.

Test Formats

With the MCSE exams, Microsoft has begun the transition from traditional multiple-choice exams to adaptive testing. In a traditional multiple-choice exam, test takers are free to move back and forth through the exam, which enables them to skip questions and return to them later or come back and double-check for mistakes. In adaptive testing, the questions that you get later in the exam are determined by your success or failure on earlier questions. After you have selected your answer, therefore, you may not alter it later. Microsoft will not tell you prior to the exam which style of test you will take on a given day. Because the same types of questions and content are covered on both exams, Microsoft claims that it should not matter to the MCSE candidate which type of exam they are given.

TRADITIONAL TESTING The traditional multiple-choice exams include 50 to 70 items, with the average duration lasting 90 minutes. Passing scores vary but usually fall in the 70 percent range. The exact passing score will be included in the information given to you when you sit down to take the test. When taking traditional format exams, keep the following tips in mind:

- All questions count exactly the same, and there is no penalty for guessing. Go through the exam quickly at first, answering all the easy questions. Do not spend so much time on a difficult, complex question that you fail to finish before the end of the exam. Quickly answer complex questions, but be sure to review them after going completely through the exam.

■ Microsoft treats a skipped question as a wrong answer. Because there is no penalty for guessing, answer every question, even if you have no idea what the right answer is.

ADAPTIVE TESTING: THE FUTURE OF MICROSOFT TESTING

In adaptive testing, the questions that you get later in the exam are determined by your success or failure on earlier questions. The test will start off with a question of medium difficulty. If you answer correctly, then the next question will be more difficult. If you answer incorrectly, the next question will be easier. To pass an adaptive test, you must answer a sufficient number of **DIFFICULT** questions, not simply a **SET NUMBER** of questions. Getting all the easy ones right will not cut it. Adaptive format exams tend to be shorter than traditional exams in both time and the number of questions.

NOTE: *One of Microsoft's goals with adaptive testing is to cut the cost of test development. Microsoft wants to test MCSE candidates' understanding of NT, not their ability to memorize test questions. Unfortunately, those complex questions take more time to create. Traditional testing requires Microsoft to have a huge pool of these questions to ensure that no candidate sees the exact same question when retaking a failed exam. In adaptive testing, most MCSE candidates failing the exam will never see the more difficult questions, because they will fail to answer the less difficult questions correctly.*

When taking an adaptive test, keep the following tips in mind:

■ Answer each question carefully, because there is no going back. In an adaptive test, you cannot go back and double-check your answers, because the answers to earlier questions determine the later questions that you are asked.

■ Get to the tough questions. The first time many people hear about adaptive testing, they think "Hey, I'll just get the first few wrong intentionally to make sure that the rest of the test is easier." You cannot pass an adaptive test that way. If you do not answer enough of the easier questions correctly to get to the tough questions, you cannot pass.

■ There is still no penalty for guessing. If you do not know the answer, give it your best guess and move on.

REMEMBER THE MICROSOFT COMPANY LINE   Microsoft bases their exams on particular versions of their own software. Unless otherwise specified, all questions assume that only Microsoft software is in use. Sample Question #3 provides a typical example of this focus.

SAMPLE QUESTION #3   NTFS Partitions can be converted into FAT partitions using which of the following utilities?

 a. Disk Administrator

 b. FDISK

 c. CONVERT

 d. NTFS partitions cannot be converted to FAT partitions.

Correct answer: d—NTFS partitions cannot be converted to FAT partitions.

 Microsoft does not care if you have a third-party utility that can convert from NTFS to FAT. No Microsoft utility can convert an NTFS partition to FAT. As far as the Microsoft exams are concerned, if it did not come from Microsoft, it does not exist. Remember, you are being tested on the Microsoft company line. Even if you disagree with Microsoft's opinion, you need to know the company line in order to do well on the tests.

UPDATES AND SERVICE PACKS.   The current exams do not cover service packs, option packs, and other updates. For example, the original release of Windows NT 4.0 supported only one IP routing protocol: RIP. Microsoft subsequently released OSPF routing support for NT 4.0 (code name: Steelhead). Because of the differences between the original Windows NT 4.0 release and a real Windows NT 4.0 installation with all the current service packs and updates, questions like Sample Question #4 can present problems.

SAMPLE QUESTION #4   Windows NT 4.0 Server can be used as an IP router. Which of the following routing protocols does Windows NT 4.0 support?

 a. IGRP

 b. RIP

 c. OSPF

 d. EIGRP

Correct answer: b—RIP

Even though Microsoft has released an update that adds support for OSPF, they do not consider OSPF to be a part of the "core" product. When taking any Microsoft exam, take care to remember which features exist in the "core" product.

IMPORTANT: *The Windows 95 test has been updated once. The original exam (70-063) has been retired and replaced by a new exam (70-064) based on Windows 95 OSR2.*

QUESTION FORMATS Test questions on the Microsoft exams come in a few basic formats. The first type is the simple, factual "you know it or you don't" question, like Sample Question #5.

SAMPLE QUESTION #5 The _____ protocol is not routable. Select the best answer.

    a. TCP/IP

    b. NetBIOS

    c. NetBEUI

    d. NWlink

Correct answer: c—NetBEUI

TCP/IP and NWlink (also known as IPX/SPX) are both routable protocols, and NetBIOS is an upper-layer protocol that can be routed with either TCP/IP or NWlink.

When approaching factual questions, first try to eliminate unlikely answers. In this example, TCP/IP is the most common protocol used on the Internet and is clearly a wrong answer. NWlink, also known as IPX/SPX, is the default routable protocol used by Novell 3.X and 4.X networks. The "tricky" part of this question is in remembering the distinction between NetBIOS and NetBEUI. NetBIOS is a "higher level protocol" used by all Microsoft Networking applications to manage connections between machines. NetBEUI is a simple, easy-to-use transport level protocol that lacks routing capability. (For a detailed discussion of the protocol issue, see Chapter 10, "Networking Protocols.")

Other questions test your ability to diagnose and respond to certain situations.

SAMPLE QUESTION #6   A Windows NT 4.0 Server is installed with two mirrored hard drives for fault tolerance. The first hard drive fails. To boot to the second hard drive, you must

a. Edit the **CONFIG.SYS** and **AUTOEXEC.BAT** files.

b. Run Disk Administrator and change the boot partition.

c. Modify the startup options in the control panel.

d. Edit the **BOOT.INI** file and change the ARC path name.

Correct answer: d—Edit the **BOOT.INI** file and change the ARC path name.

The ARC path name specified in the **BOOT.INI** file specifies the partition containing the operating system. The **CONFIG.SYS** and **AUTOEXEC.BAT** files control the DOS boot process and are not used in Windows NT, and therefore this answer cannot be correct. The Disk Administrator program, although involved in setting up disk mirroring, can be run only from within the Windows NT graphical interface. The control panel likewise cannot be used outside of the Windows NT graphical interface. In this example, there is one right answer, one clearly wrong answer, and two answers that are wrong but related to the question closely enough to catch the unaware.

The third type of question is the most dreaded: the "primary objective, secondary objective" question that Microsoft uses to test your ability to analyze more complex situations.

SAMPLE QUESTION #7   The Bayland Widget Company wants to upgrade a Windows NT server's hardware to ensure the safety of the company's database. The Bayland Widget Company also wants to improve server performance.

Required Result

▪ No data must be lost in the event of a single hard drive failure.

Optional Results

▪ Increase hard disk performance.

▪ Reduce the frequency of hard disk access.

Proposed Solution

▪ Install a stripe set. Upgrade the server's RAM from 64MB to 128MB.

Select the best answer

    a. The proposed solution produces the required result and both optional results.

    b. The proposed solution produces the required result and one of the optional results.

    c. The proposed solution produces the required result but neither of the optional results.

    d. The proposed solution does not produce the required result.

Correct answer: d—The proposed solution does not produce the required result.

In this question, increasing the server's RAM would decrease the frequency of disk access, meeting one of the optional results. Installing a stripe set would definitely increase performance, meeting the other optional result. A stripe set without parity, however, cannot protect against data loss in the event of a hard drive failure. Therefore, the proposed solution does not meet the required result. (See Chapter 7, "Managing NT Server Partitions," for details on striping and other fault tolerance methods.)

Be careful when reading these scenario-based questions. Be sure to distinguish between required and optional results.

Conclusion

Becoming an MCSE requires mastery of the Windows NT operating system. By avoiding the artificial division imposed by Microsoft's exams, this book will teach you what you need to know in the real world and help you prepare for three of the core MCSE exams in record time.

1

Windows NT Overview

The MCSE exams test your knowledge of the entire Microsoft line of network operating systems, from the obsolete to the cutting edge. Microsoft expects an MCSE to be able to choose the correct operating system for a given situation. The Workstation exam, for example, will ask you to compare Windows 95 and Windows NT and choose the appropriate operating system. Microsoft also expects MCSEs to understand how Windows NT can function in both Microsoft and non-Microsoft networks. For the Server and Enterprise exams, prepare to be tested on the various types of client operating systems that can access an NT server, and on techniques for including NT servers in environments that include Novell NetWare and UNIX servers as well. All three of the exams covered here require an understanding of the basic features and capabilities of the Microsoft operating systems.

Microsoft Operating Systems

Microsoft's foray into the *Network Operating System* (NOS) arena began long before Windows NT 4.0. Microsoft LAN Manager, Windows for Workgroups, Windows 95 (and 98), and earlier versions of Windows NT remain a part of many networks. Microsoft continues to have a vested interest in supporting its older product lines, and continues to test MCSE candidates on their knowledge of those products.

MICROSOFT LAN MANAGER Microsoft made its first serious attempt at networking with Microsoft LAN Manager in the late 1980s. Microsoft LAN Manager introduced many features that continue to exist in Windows NT, including NetBIOS support and domain security. All Microsoft client and server software share the same Microsoft LAN Manager roots and can communicate with each other, which explains why Windows for Workgroups, Windows 95, and Windows NT workstation clients can all function within a Windows NT domain.

Microsoft introduced LAN Manager during its partnership with IBM. Because of that partnership, LAN Manager was usually installed on top of IBM's OS/2 operating system. Questions mentioning Microsoft LAN Manager rarely appear on the exams, because it is both obsolete and in little use today.

MICROSOFT WINDOWS FOR WORKGROUPS 3.11 Windows for Workgroups—Microsoft's first Windows based network operating system—provides basic peer-to-peer networking capabilities, including file and print sharing. Windows for Workgroups clients can access any other Microsoft server, including Windows for Workgroups, Windows 95, Windows 98, Windows NT 3.1, and Windows NT 4.0. In a large part because of this versatility and compatibility, Windows for Workgroups maintains a fairly large installed base. Companies often leave their Windows for Workgroups network intact, even while adding new NT servers and 95/98 clients.

Windows for Workgroups' primary virtue in today's world is its extremely low hardware requirements. Windows for Workgroups runs many applications well, even on i386-based systems with as little as 8MB of RAM. Still, businesses rarely install Windows for Workgroups in any new or upgraded network. Windows for Workgroups does not support plug-and-play, and offers very weak network security—features that most administrators have come to expect.

WINDOWS 95 Windows 95 refined the Windows-based networking which was introduced with Windows for Workgroups. Windows 3.X programs had to be "fooled" into accessing network resources by "mapping" network resources to local names. For example, a database directory stored on a network server would be mapped to drive G:, allowing programs to access that directory as though it were stored on a local hard drive.

In Windows 95, Microsoft introduced applications that were "network aware." Instead of fooling programs into treating network resources as though they were local, Windows 95-compliant applications can access network resources with *Universal Naming Convention* (UNC) names such as `\\SERVER1\ACCOUNT\SALES.XLS`.

Windows 95 also features plug-and-play support. Instead of manually assigning IRQs, I/O addresses, and other resources to each device, Windows 95 can negotiate with plug-and-play hardware devices, automatically assigning resources. In theory, plug-and-play can prevent the hardware conflicts that have made past hardware installation a potential nightmare.

NOTE: *Unfortunately, for plug-and-play to work as advertised, all hardware in the system must support plug-and-play, especially the motherboard. While plug-and-play generally works well, be wary of the problems that non-plug-and-play hardware can cause. Plug-and-play works best with a plug-and-play operating system, 100 percent plug-and-play devices, and a plug-and-play motherboard.*

Microsoft includes support for hardware profiles in Windows 95. With older operating systems such as Windows for Workgroups, laptop users would often get error messages for hardware not currently connected to the system. For example, a driver for a device in a docking station would attempt to load and discover that the device in question was not present. Hardware profiles create separate lists of device drivers to be loaded for different hardware configurations. When a user chooses a hardware profile option from a boot menu, only the appropriate device drivers load (see Figure 1–1).

Windows 95 also boasts relatively low hardware requirements. Officially, Microsoft lists the system requirements for Windows 95 as a 386DX or higher processor, 4 MB of RAM, and 40 MB of free disk space. A 486 or Pentium system with 16 MB of RAM would be more realistic as a minimum, and Windows 95 does not really start to fly with less than 32MB.

Windows 95 does not offer any meaningful degree of security, a serious drawback in some environments. In situations that do not require high

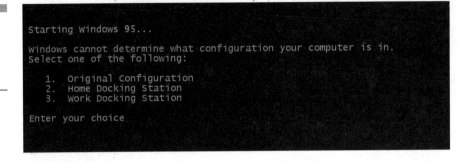

```
Starting Windows 95...

Windows cannot determine what configuration your computer is in.
Select one of the following:

    1.  Original Configuration
    2.  Home Docking Station
    3.  Work Docking Station

Enter your choice
```

levels of security, however, Windows 95's lack of security can actually be a benefit, keeping administrative costs down. Because high levels of security create administrative overhead, the lack of security in Windows 95 keeps costs down in environments where security is not critical.

Windows 95's key features include

■ Compatibility with older applications, including DOS and Windows 3.X software

■ Compatibility with existing hardware

■ Hardware profiles

■ Low system requirements

■ Plug-and-play support

■ FAT16 file system (or FAT32 with Rev. B/OSR2)

WINDOWS 98   Windows 98, Microsoft's replacement for Windows 95, offers some upgraded features, such as better support for FAT32 (see Chapter 6, "File Systems," for more details), tighter integration of Internet Explorer into the operating system (see the Justice Department brief for more details), and faster load times for applications. The NT Server, Workstation, and Enterprise exams, however, do not currently include questions about Windows 98 or FAT32.

WINDOWS NT 3.51   Windows NT 3.51 machines can coexist with Windows NT 4.0 machines on the same network. The most obvious difference between Windows NT 3.51 and 4.0 is their user interface. NT 3.51 mimics the Windows 3.X user interface, while NT 4.0 uses the Windows 95 user interface. Microsoft offers a separate NT 3.51 MCSE track with a separate set of exams. Unless you will reap guaranteed financial benefits for NT 3.51 mastery and certification, skip it and learn NT 4.0.

WINDOWS NT WORKSTATION 4.0   NT Workstation 4.0 and Windows 95 share the same user interface, making the transition between Windows 95 and NT Workstation 4.0 easy for the end-user. While on the screen, Windows 95 and NT Workstation 4.0 look identical, Windows NT Workstation supports advanced features, including local and network security, advanced file system support, and improved operating system stability and scalability. Microsoft presents Windows NT Workstation 4.0 as a high powered alternative to Windows 95 for use as either a stand-alone system or as a workstation in a networked environment.

NT Workstation 4.0 supports both local and network security. Administrators can tightly control what operations users can perform on their PC. In addition, when using the NTFS File system NT Workstation 4.0 can restrict access to files to particular users.

While NT Workstation 4.0 supports the FAT16 file system used by Windows 95, file level security relies on the *NT File System* (NTFS). In addition to security, NTFS also provides a safer, more efficient file system. For more information about NTFS, see Chapter 6, "File Systems."

NT Workstation 4.0 also provides a more stable and powerful platform for running applications. While Windows 95 can pre-emptively multi-task most applications, NT Workstation 4.0 pre-emptively multi-tasks all applications. This means that the operating system alone controls the allocation of resources to applications, rather than letting the applications decide on their own how much resources they need (as in cooperative multitasking). This makes NT very stable. NT Workstation 4.0 also supports multiple processors, allowing it to scale up to meet higher demands on processor time.

Finally, Windows NT is a portable operating system, meaning it can run on multiple platforms, including Intel x86-based systems and RISC-based systems such as DEC Alpha-based servers.

NT Workstation 4.0's key features include

- Local and Network Security
- NTFS file system
- Pre-emptive Multi-tasking of all applications
- Operating system stability
- Multiprocessor support
- Hardware profiles
- Portability

CHOOSING BETWEEN NT WORKSTATION 4.0 AND WINDOWS 95

From an end user perspective, NT Workstation 4.0 and Windows 95 look much the same. Windows 95 offers greater support for older hardware and supports plug-and-play. If support for plug-and-play and for older hardware is not a critical concern, Microsoft recommends NT Workstation 4.0 because of its superior performance, reliability, and security.

WINDOWS NT SERVER 4.0   Microsoft optimized Windows NT Server 4.0 for use as a file, print, and application server, while using the same user interface as Windows 95 and NT Workstation 4.0. Among other things, this means that NT Server places a higher priority on serving requests it receives through the network than on serving the requests of a user sitting at the server keyboard. However, a Windows NT Server can run any Windows NT application, including Microsoft Office.

NOTE: The term "server" causes confusion in the Microsoft world because it can mean several things. A server is any machine that can share anything over the network. Servers usually share files, printers, and applications. Windows for Workgroups, Windows 95 and 98, NT Workstation, and NT Server machines can all act as servers on a Microsoft network.

NT Server is a particular Microsoft operating system that has been optimized for use as a server.

In addition to subtle internal differences, NT Server comes with additional, special purpose server software, including:

- Domain security—Microsoft's NT security model relies on Domain Controllers to maintain a centralized database of user and machine accounts. Only NT Servers can be domain controllers.
- TCP/IP server capabilities—Microsoft also included a number of TCP/IP server software packages for NT, including Web services, FTP services, WINS, DNS, and DHCP.
- *Remote Access Server* (RAS)—RAS allows users to connect with a network remotely via phone lines or the Internet.
- Scalable connections—While NT Workstation is limited to 10 simultaneous incoming connections, NT server can accept as many incoming connections as you are willing to pay for. See Chapter 2, "Installing NT," for a discussion of the licensing options available for NT.

■ *Gateway Service for NetWare*—A Windows NT Server can act as a "gateway" to NetWare servers, allowing Microsoft client computers to access files and printers on a NetWare network without installing Novell client software. See Chapter 11, "NT and Novell," for a full discussion of GSNW.

■ Services for Macintosh—Used in conjunction with the Appletalk protocol, Services for Macintosh allows Macintosh clients to access NT Server file shares and shared printers.

■ Routing—NT server can act as a router for both IP and IPX traffic.

Microsoft chose to include these additional software packages with Windows NT Server. If you were to remove these options and impose a 10-network connection limit on Windows NT Server, guess what you get? NT Workstation. The difference between NT Workstation and NT Server is like the difference between a bare bones Ford Explorer and the Eddie Bauer Edition Ford Explorer. One provides basic functions while the other comes with all the bells and whistles.

Interoperability with Other Operating Systems

NT server competes with other server operating systems, notably Novell NetWare and UNIX. MCSEs must be able either to replace these other operating systems with NT Servers or to integrate NT Servers into existing networks.

NOVELL NETWARE Novell NetWare has traditionally offered stiff competition to Windows NT Server. NetWare enjoys a large installed base and a reputation for speed and efficiency as a file and print server.
See Chapter 11 for a more detailed discussion of Novell NetWare.

UNIX UNIX is not actually a single operating system. The name UNIX refers to a variety of commercial operating systems that evolved from the original UNIX operating system developed by Bell Labs. The various "flavors" of UNIX share enough similarities that they can be usefully discussed as a group. Like Windows NT, UNIX can be used as both a server and a workstation operating system. UNIX relies on TCP/IP for networking, and most Windows NT TCP/IP utilities mirror the functions of their UNIX equivalents. See Chapter 10, "Networking Protocols," for a more detailed discussion of Windows NT and TCP/IP.

To communicate with UNIX servers and clients, a Windows NT machine must be running TCP/IP. Windows NT comes with most of the utilities required to communicate with UNIX servers, including the Internet Explorer Web browser and a command line FTP utility. To share files with UNIX clients, Windows NT machines must install appropriate server-side software: Peer Web Services for Workstation or Internet Information Server for Server. See Chapter 13, "Internet and Intranet Services," for more detail.

Questions

1. To enjoy the benefits of NT security fully, you must

   a. Install the Microsoft Security Manager.

   b. Use the NTFS file system instead of FAT16.

   c. Install TCP/IP.

   d. Install fault tolerant disk mirroring.

2. Windows NT includes built in features that support which of the following network operating systems? (Choose all that apply)

   a. Novell NetWare

   b. Banyan Vines

   c. UNIX

   d. Artisoft LANtastic

   e. Microsoft Windows for Workgroups

   f. Apple Macintosh

   g. Microsoft Windows 95

3. Reasons to choose Microsoft Windows 95 instead of Windows NT Workstation include (Choose all that apply)

   a. Compatibility with older hardware

   b. Improved Security

   c. Plug-and-play support

   d. Hardware profiles

4. You are asked to install a network server at a client site. The new server will store the company's tax database. Of the 50 accountants at the client site, 35 use Windows 95 for their desktop operating system and 15 use Windows NT Workstation. The new server must support disk fault tolerance to ensure the safety of the database. Why should you choose to use Windows NT Server instead of Windows NT Workstation as the operating system for the new server? (Choose all that apply)

   a. Windows NT Server is optimized for acting as a network server, while Windows NT Workstation is optimized for use as a desktop operating system.

   b. Windows NT Workstation cannot share files across a network.

   c. Windows 95 clients can connect to NT Server machines, but cannot communicate across the network with NT Workstation machines.

   d. Windows NT Workstation limits incoming network connections to 10.

   e. Windows NT Workstation does not support fault tolerance.

Answers

1. b—Use the NTFS file system instead of FAT16.

   Answer a refers to a utility, the Microsoft Security Manager, which does not exist. Answer c is also wrong. Although certain security measures can be implemented with TCP/IP, they are not specific to Windows NT security. Answer c refers to fault tolerance. While fault tolerance is a Windows NT feature, it has nothing to do with security. Therefore answer d is wrong. Windows NT file security relies on NTFS; therefore b is the correct answer.

2. a, c, e, f, g—While third parties are free to add additional support features to Windows NT, Windows NT has no built-in support for either Banyan Vines or Artisoft LANtastic.

3. a, c—Answer b is incorrect because Windows NT Workstation offers better security than Windows 95. Answer d is also incorrect. While it is true that Windows 95 does support hardware profiles, so does Windows NT Workstation.

4. a, d—Answers b, c, and e are false statements.

IMPORTANT: *There is no "partial credit" on Microsoft exams. On a "choose all that apply" question, if you select two correct answers out of three, the question will still be marked incorrect.*

Installing Windows NT

The process of installing Windows NT can be compared to playing chess. The individual components of NT, like the individual chess pieces, are not too complicated. But without proper planning and a solid overview of the big picture, one can easily lose at chess—and easily be overwhelmed with the NT installation process. This chapter builds on the overall concept of the organization of NT networking and makes sure the reader understands how the individual components of NT "move" during the progression through an example of installing both NT Server and Workstation.

This chapter is broken into three main sections: Overall Planning Issues, Installing NT Server, and Installing NT Workstation. Each of these sections gives an understanding of the overall picture of NT networking, as well as supplies enough information about the individual components to enable the reader to say, "Checkmate" every time Windows NT Server or Workstation is installed. In addition to the main sections, this chapter also ad-dresses some special issues, such as upgrading and automatic installations.

Overall Planning Issues

Setting up a stable and secure NT network requires careful planning in two areas: hardware and organization. We must look at hardware requirements and hardware compatibility issues to make sure that we have stable systems that can handle the rigorous demands of Windows NT. We need to conduct a quick study of organizational components, such as workgroups and domains, and find out how servers and workstations fit into these organizations. Finally, we must take a "Network Cards 101" lesson to make sure you understand some of the basics of installing and configuring network cards.

Hardware Requirements

The inherent power of Windows NT makes it one of the most demanding operating systems in terms of hardware. Windows NT has truly "raised the bar" in terms of minimum and recommended processors, amount of RAM, and hard drive space. Microsoft has provided minimum and recommended hardware requirements to help determine whether a particular system is capable of running Windows NT. These requirements are the same for both NT Server and NT Workstation.

NOTE: *These minimum and recommended requirements have changed over the years. The requirements listed in this book are the original requirements stated by Microsoft back in 1996 and are the ones you should know for the exam.*

MINIMUM REQUIREMENTS FOR NT CPU: Intel 80486/25, MIPS R4x00, Digital Alpha Systems, or PowerPC

RAM: 12MB for NT Workstation on Intel, 16MB for NT Server on Intel, and 16MB for others

Disk space: IDE, SCSI, or ESDI drive with 128MB for Intel, and 158MB for others

Other: VGA monitor, CD-ROM, mouse, floppy drive, and keyboard

Of course, these items are minimums. A more accurate statement might be that NT can "crawl" with these minimum levels, as opposed to "run." Microsoft itself recommends at least an Intel Pentium processor and 32MB of RAM or more. These levels are considered laughably small today and would be unacceptable for a real-world NT machine. Given the fact that even a standard desktop computer today has 64MB of RAM, a Pentium II processor, and a multiple-gigabyte hard drive, one would have difficulty even finding a machine that hits near these older, minimum requirements.

FINDING THE RIGHT SERVER   Ignore these requirements when it is time to find a real NT machine. Due to the ongoing collapse of PC prices, the hardware is not really as big of a concern as it once was when considering speeds and capacities. Instead of worrying about "size" and "speed," think about "load," "compatibility," and "safety."

LOAD   NT Servers and Workstations work hard for a living and have to carry a heavy load in terms of CPU processing and program size. When looking for a server, people want as much CPU firepower as they can afford and as much RAM as their wallets can handle. Workstations tend to have a lower hardware demand but still need to be carefully considered. First, let's address the issue of RAM requirements. Hundreds of books exist that come up with many formulas to help users determine their RAM requirements, based on numbers of users, concurrent connections, or who knows what kind of silliness. Ignore these formulas. What really determines the amount of RAM that NT Server needs is the application(s) that will be running on the machine. NT Server might be running many different applications, such as Internet Information Server (Microsoft's Web server), Lotus Notes, Oracle, or some homemade application. These applications all have their own clearly documented RAM needs and are the primary determination of the RAM needs for an NT Server. Certainly, the NT operating system itself has a base RAM requirement. A good starting point is to double Microsoft's recommendation and use 64MB. To calculate the RAM requirements, use the 64MB starting point and then add the requirements for the applications that will be on that particular server to come up with a proper amount of RAM. NT Workstations should also start with 64MB, but it is common to see NT Workstation systems with 128MB to 256MB of RAM.

NOTE: *Most people underestimate their RAM requirements. Make sure you have a system with a motherboard that enables you to double the amount of RAM from your first guess. Most better workstation motherboards can take up to 1GB of RAM. Specialized server motherboards can handle 2GB or more. Purchasing motherboards*

that severely limit the total amount of RAM they can handle is still easy, and this determines how much that motherboard can meet future needs. Select motherboards that can handle the inevitable increase in operating system and application size. NT2000, remember, is due in late 1999. Plan ahead, and spare yourself some grief later.

Second is the issue of CPUs. Given the massive firepower of NT and the fact that newer, faster CPUs are coming out faster than anyone can possibly keep track of them, it makes it impossible to recommend a particular CPU. A better route is to consider what is the best, versus what is affordable. Additionally, there is the issue of multiple processors. NT 4.0 can support up to four CPUs, which enables systems that use older Pentium and Pentium Pro CPUs in groups to perform extremely well. For most uses, Pentium IIs should be considered the lowest common denominator. The only down side to the Pentium II is that it can support only two CPUs, and older Pentium IIs (smaller than 333 MHz) can support only 512MB of RAM. Newer Pentium IIs can support up to 4 GB of RAM. Most serious servers are quickly moving to the Intel Xeon CPU, because it can handle up to eight CPUs—assuming that the wallet can handle the price tag.

COMPATIBILITY Windows NT must be able to "speak the language" of all the system hardware to run properly. NT speaks to the system via device drivers. One of the greatest problems with NT is its relatively limited support of hardware, as compared to Windows 95 and Windows 98. The reason for this limited support is simple. Many hardware manufacturers do not write device drivers for Windows NT. Their motivation is simple— Windows NT is designed to be a high-end operating system. In concept, high-end operating systems are not going to be running fancy graphic cards or sound cards. As a result, a company that makes sound cards, for example, may not make an NT driver—or may make a limited NT driver. Now that NT 4.0 has been in existence for about three years, good hardware drivers are more common but are still far less common than for Windows 95 or 98.

To help answer the great question of whether a certain piece of hardware works under NT 4.0, Microsoft has provided its famous *Hardware Compatibility List* (HCL). A badly dated copy of the HCL is on the NT installation CD-ROM in the **\SUPPORT\HCL.HLP** directory. Do not use this list—just be aware that it is on the CD-ROM. Instead, access the latest HCL on Microsoft's Web site. This constantly updated HCL will help determine whether a particular piece of hardware is compatible with NT. The current location for the HCL is **http://www.microsoft.com/isapi/ hwtest/hcl.idc**, but Microsoft is notorious for changing its location. Be prepared to go to **http://www.microsoft.com/** and do a search for "HCL."

While the HCL can help greatly, the HCL also has some quirks—so beware. First of all, just because two devices are listed on the HCL, there is no guarantee that the two devices will work together under NT. For example, I was recently involved with a powerful server (listed on the HCL) that locked up whenever it was used with a certain network card (also on the HCL). Second, when a new piece of hardware comes out, it usually takes a while before it is placed on the HCL. Unless a user is simply dying to use a new piece of equipment, it is usually a better idea to simply wait or select another device that is on the HCL. The one exception to that rule is when the user has the luxury of exhaustively testing the device in a working system—and has the opportunity to return it if it does not work.

Microsoft provides a special program called the *NT Hardware Qualifier* (NTHQ) that is supposed to determine any possible hardware incompatibilities. The NTHQ is located on the NT Installation CD-ROM in the **\SUPPORT\HQTOOL** directory. That directory contains a batch file called **MAKEDISK.BAT,** which will create a bootable floppy with the NTHQ tool. The idea is to create this bootable floppy—which Microsoft calls the NTHQ Disk—and to boot the machine to be tested with the NTHQ disk. Figure 2–1 shows the NTHQ in action.

Figure 2–1

The NT Hardware Qualifier tool in action

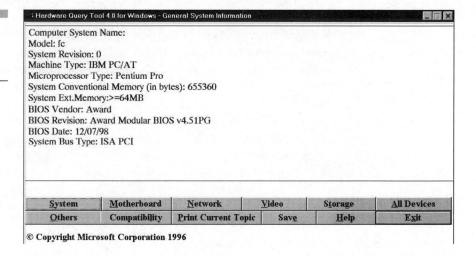

```
Hardware Query Tool 4.0 for Windows - General System Information          _ □ ✕

Computer System Name:
Model: fc
System Revision: 0
Machine Type: IBM PC/AT
Microprocessor Type: Pentium Pro
System Conventional Memory (in bytes): 655360
System Ext.Memory:>=64MB
BIOS Vendor: Award
BIOS Revision: Award Modular BIOS v4.51PG
BIOS Date: 12/07/98
System Bus Type: ISA PCI




┌───────────┬──────────────┬───────────────────┬────────┬──────────┬─────────────┐
│  System   │  Motherboard │      Network      │ Video  │ Storage  │ All Devices │
├───────────┼──────────────┼───────────────────┼────────┼──────────┼─────────────┤
│  Others   │ Compatibility│ Print Current Topic│  Save  │   Help   │    Exit     │
└───────────┴──────────────┴───────────────────┴────────┴──────────┴─────────────┘
```

© **Copyright Microsoft Corporation 1996**

SAFETY The most important goal of any NT system, especially for NT Server systems, is to keep the data safe. At this level, keeping data safe does not include addressing issues such as hackers and viruses—important issues that will be covered later—but rather keeping the data safe from hardware failures. Only one system crash due to a bad hard drive or power supply is necessary to reinforce this most basic of concepts. Unfortunately, no one has yet to develop the perfect hard drive, power supply, etc., that never dies; so it is not really a matter of "if" your system crashes, but "when" your system decides to die. This failure will invariably happen at the least opportune moment.

Fortunately, Microsoft has armed NT with many tools to help prevent data loss. One of the most powerful tools is NT's built-in support for *Random Array of Inexpensive Devices* (RAID). RAID is discussed in detail later in the book, but fundamentally RAID enables the system to spread data across multiple drives to enable faster disk access and/or safety of data. RAID comes in five different "levels," numbered one through five, which provide increasingly powerful levels of disk access and security. Due to NT's built-in and easy-to-configure RAID support, RAID commonly appears on NT Servers that cannot afford to lose data. RAID can be as simple as multiple EIDE hard drives in the system, or it can be as complicated as massive external "RAID Arrays" that handle large numbers of drives that can be removed and replaced without disturbing the running system. Before purchasing a system, be up-to-speed on RAID in order to decide on the level of RAID necessary for the system and to buy the hardware that best fits your needs.

Systems that contain their own safety features independent of the operating system can also be purchased. A popular option is dual power supplies. These systems add a second power supply that can kick in when the first power supply fails. Dual power supplies are popular on systems that are never shut down. Because servers are the most common types of systems that are constantly "up," dual power supplies tend to be installed mostly on servers—although the occasional workstation may benefit from them as well.

No matter how many power supplies are in a system, if the power is shut down the computer is going to turn off. If the system must stay running, there must be an *Uninterruptible Power Supply* (UPS) with the system. A UPS is little more than a glorified battery, but this item is absolutely essential. Not only will a UPS provide backup power in the case of power loss, but a good UPS will also "condition" the power and protect the system from power spikes and sags. UPSs have become so inexpensive that they have become an integral part of most NT systems, both for servers and workstations. If an NT system is going to be installed, the system is going to have a UPS—especially if the system is an NT Server system.

No matter how hard one tries and no matter how much fancy hardware one installs on a system, eventually data loss will occur. When the data is gone, the only source for recovery is a solid backup. NT supports a wide variety of backup hardware options, including tape, optical, and removable media. The type of backup hardware used is, for the most part, a function of the amount of data that needs to be backed up. Smaller networks will use Iomega Zip or Jaz drives, while medium-to-large networks tend to use tape or magneto-optical media. Regardless of size, there is no such thing as a good NT Server installation without some type of backup hardware.

MAKE IT EASY Buying an arbitrary system and hoping that it will run NT is often a frustrating experience. Save a lot of unnecessary hassle by doing what most folks do today and purchase systems designed for Windows NT. These systems have been extensively tested by the manufacturers to verify their load, compatibility, and safety features. Most PC manufacturers divide their systems into distinct desktop and server lines. The server systems will be on the HCL and are stocked with components that are not only on the HCL themselves, but have also been tested with the system to ensure full compatibility. Server systems will usually come with extra drives, tape backups, dual power supplies and many other options to ensure that NT will run efficiently and safely. Some of the more popular manufacturers of server systems are Dell, Compaq, IBM, and AST. Purchasing a system to run an NT workstation is much easier than buying a system for an NT server. The vast majority of desktop systems sold today are fully Windows NT Workstation compatible, but they will not have the extras that most servers need.

Network Organization Issues

Before we start this section, let's take a moment and get back to some of the basics of networking—and then use that knowledge to answer a number of questions that come up in the organization process. This "Network 101" portion of the section is not on any of the MCSE exams, but this information is absolutely necessary for understanding the "whys" of NT, as opposed to just the "hows."

The goal of any network is to provide users access to shared resources. Examples of resources are hard drives, modems, printers, etc. The *network operating system*, better known as the NOS, is the software element that enables those resources to be shared. Now that the hardware is established, it is time to decide which resources to share and to create the environment that enables them to be shared. The process of sharing is fairly involved, but breaks down into four discrete components: physical, protocols, network, and shared resources.

NOTE: *These four discrete steps are not on any exam, but they are an excellent way to visualize the steps of making a network "go." Please do not confuse this with the OSI seven-layer model discussed later in the book.*

Physical—There must be a physical medium for moving bits between computers. Classically, a copper cable of some type is strung between computers, although fiber optics, infrared, laser, and radio signals can also be used. There must be a *Network Interface Card* (NIC) in the computer that can send and receive those signals. The physical layer includes issues such as topologies, hubs, routers, etc.

Protocols—The protocol is the language of the network. Every device on the network must speak the same language—i.e., use the same protocol—to communicate. Fortunately, there are only a few types of protocols commonly used in networks. They have names like NetBEUI, IPX/SPX, Appletalk, DLC, and the most famous of all, TCP/IP. NT provides native support for all of these protocols. At some point in the process of installing NT, the system will need to be told which protocol(s) to use. Each protocol has its own unique configuration issues that need to be handled when the protocol is installed.

Network—To share resources, a computer must have two items: a name that other machines on the network can refer to, and the software capability to share information. When you install NT—or any NOS, for that matter—on a computer that will share resources, one step will require you to name the computer. For most NOSs, including NT, the names are similar to "Server1," "Accounting Server," "Mike's Computer," or some other fairly clear name. The concept of naming is fairly simple.

The concept of software capability is much more complex. In NT, both NT Workstation and NT Server machines can share resources. This feature is a major departure from older network NOSs such as the old Microsoft LAN Manager, where only a machine configured as a "server" could share resources. The other machines, called "workstations," could only access the shared resources of server machines. This concept is an area of great confusion, especially for users with previous network experience who then decide to learn NT. To clarify this confusion, we will need to understand the many concepts of network security, including user accounts, rights, and permissions, and how these items are controlled by a mysterious little item known as the *domain*. We will clarify this topic in the next section.

Shared Resources—Once certain machines are capable of sharing, they must then "offer up" those shared resources in such a way that the other machines can see them. This process is handled by giving the shared resource a name on the network. For example, a system's C:\FRED folder could be shared as "FRED." The share name of the serving machine and the shared device can then be used by other machines to "map" or "connect" to that shared resource.

NT Network Security

Of the four steps previously described, Network is by far the most complex. The reason for this complexity is because the process of sharing a resource, in particular a drive or folder with important data, requires some level of security. The most important job of a network is ensuring that those shared resources 1) are protected from unauthorized access and 2) provide levels of access to those authorized, to minimize the chances of data corruption.

So how does a serving machine protect data? Well, there has to be a way to lock resources so that you can give access to particular resources to certain people and deny access to others. Over the years, there have been hundreds of methods to perform this procedure. First is the concept of passwords. A resource is locked unless the correct password is selected. The down side to this is that you must know the passwords to all of the resources you wish to access. An improvement or addition to passwords is the concept of user accounts. A user is given an account on a system.

Such an account—usually nothing more than a database listing of names —shows that a particular user has access to the system. The user "logs in" to a system, which then knows the shared resources that the user can access on the system.

In many cases, large numbers of users will have the same access on the same system. The process of setting access for each user can be rather tedious, so there is a strong motivation to simplify the process. To help, most NOSs utilize the concept of groups. Administrators can create a common set of accesses and save them collectively as a group. Users can then be assigned as members of these predefined groups, giving the user the same level of access to shared resources as the other members of the group. Invariably, users can be members of more than one group, and groups can be members of groups—enabling powerful flexibility in network security.

There are many methods by which passwords, user accounts, and groups can be used individually or combined to provide security for a system. Within the world of PCs, the use of these methods has been separated into two different groups of NOSs known as "Peer-to-Peer" and "Client/Server."

When reading the next few paragraphs, stop thinking about Windows NT and forget that you know anything about the words "NT Server" and "NT Workstation," because Microsoft has done a really good job of confusing terms such as "workstation" and "server." For the moment, think of a server as any machine that can share resources; whereas a workstation is a machine that cannot share resources but can access shared resources from a server.

PEER-TO-PEER In a Peer-to-Peer NOS, any computer can be a server or a workstation. A machine that is a server can also access other servers' shared resources. A machine configured as a workstation can easily be configured as a server—and vice-versa—by adding a little software or clicking on a few configuration screens. Most peer-to-peer NOSs only offer the most rudimentary security. The most famous of all peer-to-peer NOSs is Microsoft Windows 95 and 98. The only difference between a server and a workstation system is a little extra software that is added when a configuration checkbox is clicked, as shown in Figure 2–2. Simply checking or unchecking these boxes can change a system.

Windows 95 and 98 can have one machine, a few machines, or all of the machines on the network configured as servers. Once a resource has been shared, that resource can have a password assigned to it to determine who has access to that resource. The level of access can be full or read-only. See Figure 2–3.

Figure 2–2
Enabling File and
Print Sharing in
Windows 95

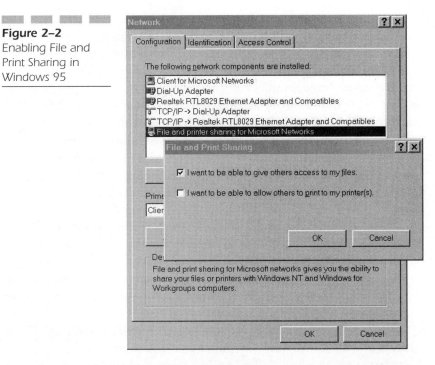

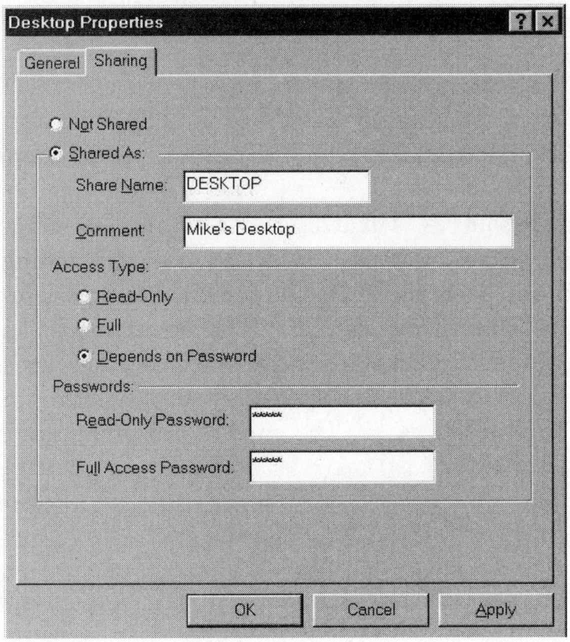

Figure 2–3
Setting the level of
access to a file share
in a Windows 95
Peer to Peer network

User accounts tend to be quite basic in peer-to-peer and usually enable access to just the local system or the network. In Windows 95 and 98, failure to provide the proper account and password will still give the user access to the local machine, but they will not be able to see any other computers on the network.

A peer-to-peer NOS is excellent for smaller networks, where defined levels of security are not needed. As a network becomes more complex, peer-to-peer begins to break down. Because all systems are designed to act as both a server and a workstation, significant amounts of NOS overhead must be used to support applications as well as serve shared resources. A serving machine, therefore, runs poorly on heavy use.

CLIENT/SERVER Á Client/Server NOS is designed for larger networks that require higher levels of security. A client/server NOS usually has two totally separate software packages: a server and a client (the word "workstation" is rarely used). The most popular, true client/server NOS is probably Novell NetWare. The Novell NetWare server has its own operating system, as well as a NOS, and runs on a dedicated machine that does nothing more than share resources. The server does not run DOS or Windows of any form. Because the server never acts as a client, the system can be optimized for resource-sharing through specialized file structures, massive disk caches, and many other features that would be difficult, if not impossible, to run on a peer-to-peer NOS. Figure 2–4 shows a configuration screen in NetWare 3.12.

The clients in client/server are not really NOSs. They usually have just a little extra software that runs "on top of" the client's existing operating system to provide the necessary access to the server. This extra software can manifest itself as TSRs in DOS or a few DLLs in Windows 95 and 98. In the case of NetWare, the client software is usually free. Novell makes its money by designing the server to enable only a limited number of connec-

Figure 2–4
A NetWare 3.12
Server's AUTOEXEC.
NCF file, one of its
key configuration
files

tions. Customers can purchase NetWare for different numbers of connections. The more connections a user wants, the more the user pays.

Client/server NOSs invariably provide a much higher level of security than peer-to-peer NOSs. The clearest example of this idea is in the concept of "permissions." Users, the people who actually get on the machines to get work done, are given "accounts" with permissions. In the earlier example of Windows 95 and 98, we saw that the only permissions were read-only and full. While these permissions may be acceptable for small networks, larger, more complex networks may require much more control over how users can access those shared resources. For example, Windows NT enables the following permissions to shared files or folders:

1. Read (R)

2. Write (W)

3. Execute (X)

4. Delete (D)

5. Change permissions (P)

6. Take ownership (O)

NT not only has permissions, but it also has something called "rights" that are completely different. An NT permission might be something such as Read and Write to the `c:\ACCOUNTING\DATA` folder. Some examples of rights in NT are Log on Locally, Shutdown the System, and Access the Computer from the Network. This separation of rights and permissions is unique only to Windows NT.

NOTE: *Do not panic about understanding permissions—yet. For now, completely ignore rights and just appreciate that the NT permissions are more powerful than the "full" and "read-only" permissions we saw for peer-to-peer. Rights and permissions will be discussed in much more detail in Chapter 6, "File Systems."*

User accounts in client/server are vastly more powerful than in the typical peer-to-peer NOS. In client/server, all user account information is usually stored on the file server and is the cornerstone for access not only to the network, but also for individual shared-resource access.

WORKGROUPS AND DOMAINS One cannot pigeonhole Windows NT into either client/server or peer-to-peer. Microsoft has taken the best from both of these models and blended them together to make what could be described as a "Super Peer-to-Peer" NOS. First, NT can act exactly like a peer-to-peer NOS. NT Servers and NT workstation machines can co-exist

Figure 2–5
Workgroups break up the "Network Neighborhood" into smaller units for browsing

with Windows 95 and 98 clients—each machine a fundamental equal to all the others, optionally acting as both servers and workstations. Microsoft calls this peer-to-peer function a "workgroup." This workgroup is a loosely associated group of computers that shares a common name called the "workgroup name." This name has no function other than to organize how the other machines on the network visualize the network. Network browsing demonstrates the function of browsing. If there are a number of computers on a network separated into three workgroups, Windows Explorer will show the network broken down by workgroup name, as shown in Figure 2–5.

Workgroups have no function in network security. From a security standpoint, each PC is an island, only in control of its own security. As mentioned earlier, workgroups are a poor way to provide security, because each user is required to know how and where to access shared resources. If any of those resources are password-protected, the user must know the password.

While NT has complete backward compatibility with workgroups, NT has a far more robust and flexible security model known as a domain. Basically, a *domain* is a group of computers that share a common security database known as the *Domain Security Accounts Manager* (Domain SAM). The Domain SAM stores all of the domain's security information, including user accounts, groups, and rights. The Domain SAM is stored on a designated NT Server called the *Primary Domain Controller* (PDC). Each domain can have only one PDC, but can have many *Backup Domain Controllers* (BDCs) that store backup copies of the Domain SAM.

NOTE: *Every NT machine—server and workstation—has a SAM that contains the security information for that computer, such as user accounts, permissions, passwords, etc. The Domain SAM contains information about domain-level security*

and local security for every domain controller, PDC, and BDCs. Just to make all this confusing, most documentation simply calls all these different databases SAMs and does not distinguish between domain and local.

Once a domain has been established, other computers running NT Server, NT Workstation, Windows 95 and 98, and even old Windows 3.X and DOS machines (running the DOS client) can then log onto the domain via the PDC (or a BDC, if the PDC is not available). The domain controls the security not only for NT Servers but also for NT Workstations and Windows 95 and 98 machines. If a machine is not a member of the domain, the machine automatically becomes a member of a workgroup.

NOTE: *A network must have at least one system running NT Server to have a domain. NT Workstation cannot support domains.*

Server Roles

Many different types of server machines can exist on the network. These types are PDCs, BDCs, member servers, and stand-alone Servers. Let's look at each of these to understand how they function in the NT network.

PDC The PDC holds the Security Accounbts Manager for the domain. As previously mentioned, there is only one PDC in an NT domain. If you are installing only one server, that server will be the PDC. A PDC can easily handle the administrative functions of being a PDC, while also handling the usual server functions.

BDC The BDC is a backup copy of the PDC. If there are two or more servers in a domain, it is a good idea to make one of the extra servers a BDC. The BDC can take over and authenticate logins if the PDC is not available. There are two situations where a BDC is helpful. First and most obvious is when the PDC is not working. Without a domain controller, no one can log into the domain—making the entire network practically useless. A BDC is a nice way to enable the administrator to take the PDC down without disrupting users. The second reason for a BDC is when the domain is dispersed around widespread locations. Imagine two offices in different cities with networks connected by an ISDN line. The PDC is in one city. Every time a user logs into the domain, the ISDN line is used to transfer the authentication to the PDC in the other city. This process is a terrible waste of ISDN bandwidth, and will clog it up with authentication requests. Plus, if the ISDN line goes down, one entire side of the network will not even be able to log into the network. The right answer is to place a BDC at every remote location.

MEMBER SERVER   A member server is not a BDC or a PDC. If a domain has a sufficient number of PDCs and BDCs, all other servers that are members of the domain without being either a PDC or BDC are member servers. A typical use for a member server is a server designated for heavy demand use. By removing the need to make the server a PDC or BDC, the machine will have less overhead and will be able to perform its job more efficiently.

STAND-ALONE   Some cases exist where a server will be installed that is not a member of the domain. These servers are known as *stand-alone servers*. A stand-alone server is used when there is no need for authentication. Because all computers that are not members of a domain automatically become members of a workgroup, the system is visible to all users on the network. Some good examples of stand-alone servers are machines that are used for system development—or systems that are running a specific application and do not need security.

Protocols

One of Windows NT's great strengths is its native support for all of the most common network protocols. The type of protocol the administrator decides to use will be based on the type of NT network being created. Most NT networks use either TCP/IP or NetBEUI. Refer to "Networking Protocols," Chapter 10, for a full discussion of protocols and the criteria for determining the protocol needed.

   In the previous sections, we presented an overview of the many concepts that need to be taken into consideration for the overall network when planning an NT installation. Be sure to read through the many chapters referenced to make sure these many concepts are clear before putting an install CD-ROM into a system. In particular, be sure you are comfortable with domains and user accounts, because it will make the installation much easier.

Installing NT Server Issues

Now that the overall issues for the network have been addressed, we need to look at a few issues that are unique to NT Server before we can begin the actual install process. For the rest of this chapter, we will assume that we are installing a completely new NT network. Currently, there are no machines. All of the machines in this network will be running Windows NT. There will be multiple servers, all running Windows NT Server, and all of the workstations will be running NT Workstation.

NOTE: *Many situations exist where NT will be installed as an upgrade to an existing network. We will cover the many issues in upgrading later in this chapter.*

Role of the Machine

Before a system has NT installed, it is imperative that you have decided the role for the server. The first machine to be created in this network will be an NT server. As this will be the first server for the system, it must be the PDC. Then, as other servers and workstations are created, they can be set up during their installations to log onto the PDC. If a machine is going to be a BDC, that machine must be connected to the PDC via a LAN connection. Member servers and stand-alone servers do not require a network connection.

File Systems

Choosing the type of file system to be used on an NT server is a critical step—and one that really needs to be decided before installing any NT Server. The file system is the organizational structure for data on drives. The PC world has many different types of file systems, including FAT16, FAT32, HPFS, and NTFS. Both NT Server and NT Workstation support many different types of file systems, providing incredible security, flexibility and cross-platform support. Unfortunately, once a file system is in place, the system usually requires erasing part or all of the hard drive to change to another file system. Let's take a moment to make sure we understand file systems before we explore the power, and the few pitfalls, of NT's use of file systems.

FAT16 When DOS was invented way back in the early 1980s, DOS included a new type of file system called FAT16. Compared to earlier file systems, FAT16 was extremely powerful. FAT16 stored all of the file information in groups of drive sectors called clusters. The contents of each cluster were tracked via a special data structure called a *File Allocation Table* (FAT) that could store information on up to 2^{16} or 65,536 clusters (that is where we get the "16" of FAT16). FAT16 had support for multiple drive letters and subdirectories and even provided some basic redundancy in the case of a drive failure by making two copies of the FAT.

FAT16 was and still is a popular file system. Yet it became obvious, even by the late '80s, that FAT16 had some serious limitations. The first limitation is that FAT16 is extremely wasteful of hard drive space as drives become larger than 400MB, because clusters are groups of sectors. As the individual drive letters, more correctly known as the partitions, grow larger, more sectors are grouped together to form individual clusters. A large partition (2GB) can waste 25 percent to 40 percent of the hard drive. Secondly, FAT16 does not provide any type of security functions. No method exists to give permissions to users or groups to enable levels of access to files or directories. DOS had no security features, after all, so there was no motivation to create any type of security in FAT16. Additionally, providing security makes the operating system bigger and takes up drive space. An original IBM PC with 256K of RAM and two floppy drives simply could not support any significant type of security. By the late '80s, the onset of networking within the PC environment made security important. The file system is an obvious place to add that security. If the file system is already tracking the contents of sectors and the location and organizational structure of files and directories, it would make sense to have the file system also track permissions for those files and directories. The early client/server NOSs, such as Novell NetWare, placed powerful security on their servers using proprietary file systems. In client/server NOSs, only the server shares data—so implementing security is fairly easy. The workstations can continue to run DOS or whichever operating system they normally use.

An advanced operating system such as Windows NT, however, has a much tougher job. In an NT environment, potentially every system can share files and directories, not just the servers. So a need developed to create a new file system that could be installed on all the systems to enable security on every machine. One of the first attempts at an improved file system was the *High Performance File System* (HPFS), implemented in IBM's OS/2 in the late '80s. Although HPFS was an excellent file system, the lack of interest in OS/2 sent HPFS to the file system graveyard.

NTFS   Microsoft took a much "higher" view of the needs of a file system. Microsoft knew that NT would need security, safety, and better efficiency than FAT16. To achieve these lofty goals, Microsoft started with the concept that security would not simply be a network function, but also a stand-alone function. In Microsoft's view, a system should have user accounts, groups, and permissions, even when the system is not on a network. The other machines in a network should respect these securities without regard to whether the machine is on a network or exists by itself. This idea was the cornerstone for a totally new file system developed for NT called *NT File System* (NTFS).

NTFS SECURITY   NTFS provides powerful system security. With NTFS, each file and folder has its own tiny database of permissions called an *Access Control List* (ACL). The ACL is nothing more than a list of users and groups that have permissions to the folder or file. The ACL not only defines who has permissions, but the ACL also defines which permissions those users and groups have to the resource.

NOTE: *NT can operate on both NTFS and FAT16 partitions. Any partition that uses FAT16, however, will not have the security of NTFS. If the data needs to be secure on a particular partition, that partition must be NTFS. If a partition is FAT16, the only security options are full and read-only, just as though the system were a Windows 95 and 98 machine.*

Providing security to every machine on the network creates a serious conceptual problem. What if there are three or four machines on the network, each with their own security? In concept, an administrator would have to go to each machine and set up permissions for each user or group. This process is where the domain really begins to shine. NT creates two levels of users and groups: local and global. Local users and groups are designed for just the machine. When an NT machine is running stand-alone, or when the machine is a member of a workgroup, there are only local users and local groups. Global users and groups exist only as part of the domain.

Fortunately, these issues do not have to be determined at installation time. See "Microsoft Networking," Chapter 9, for an in-depth discussion of local and global issues.

NTFS EFFICIENCY   NTFS uses hard drive space far more efficiently than FAT16. NTFS's equivalent to a FAT is not limited to 65,536 addresses and can therefore put fewer sectors in each cluster, thus resulting in much less waste.

NTFS SAFETY   The last big motivation for NTFS is its powerful safety features. In particular, NT has the capacity to check file writes and hot-fix errors. Every time a file is written to a drive, the write is verified before the part of the file currently being written is taken from memory. If a problem is noticed, NT will automatically write that portion to another part of the drive. NT's hot-fix can be best described as a permanent "scan disk," constantly checking the drive for bad sectors and repairing on the fly.

NOTE: *This section for NTFS is designed to motivate the reader to use NTFS in NT Server installation. All of these issues are covered in much greater detail in Chapter 7, "Managing NT Server Partitions."*

The one down side to NTFS is that in the case of a substantial system failure, an administrator cannot boot to a C: prompt. Most real-life NT systems will have a small (300MB–400MB) DOS-bootable FAT16 partition as the C: drive and all other drive letters as NTFS. Later, we will see that NT can be installed in such a way that the system can be booted to either DOS or NT. In the extremely rare situation where the system fails, the ability to boot to DOS to edit certain files can be a lifesaver.

BEWARE OF FAT32   Later versions of Windows 95 and 98 use FAT32, an excellent improvement from FAT16. While FAT32 is a fine file system, FAT32 was created after NT 4.0 and is completely incompatible and unreadable by NT. Do not attempt to install Windows NT on a FAT32 system—it will not work. If planning to install NT on a system with FAT32, use FDISK to wipe out the FAT32 partition and replace it with a small FAT16 partition. Third-party disk utilities, such as PowerQuest's Partition Magic, can also be used to convert FAT32 to FAT16 without losing data. Just remember to make the FAT16 partition small and leave the rest of the drive unpartitioned. NT will handle partitioning NTFS during the install process.

NETWORK CARD   Isn't it funny how just because you are comfortable with one aspect of computing, you are thought to be an expert at everything in the world of PCs? Users, customers, and bosses seem to assume that simply because you understand the nuances of, say, configuring Windows 98, you are also experts at writing Visual Basic macros in Microsoft Word. Nowhere is this phenomenon more apparent than in the world of networking. Installing, configuring, and administrating Windows NT is only one part of the overall network. An entirely separate area, the network hardware—NICs, cabling, hubs, switches, and routers—is an area where it is usually assumed that someone is as much of an expert as they are in Windows NT.

One of the exams necessary to pass the MCSE is the Networking Essentials Exam (70–58). Networking essentials covers the hardware of networking and the basic functions of the networking software without being NT-specific. People commonly take this exam last for a number of reasons, most often because networking essentials is the only MCSE examination that does not award a *Microsoft Certified Professional* (MCP) certification. While this reason is valid, it is probably far better to take networking essentials first, because networking essentials will present a much stronger concept of the overall networking picture—and the learner will have a much more solid understanding of why he or she is doing many of the tasks within NT. The reality is, however, that many people will still continue to do networking essentials last. Accepting this reality, and assuming that you will probably try to do an NT installation without the benefit of the networking essentials exam, this section has been added to help you through some of basic hardware concepts of network card installation.

The only exam that cares about NIC details, such as IRQs, I/O addresses, etc., is the networking essentials exam. NT Server and NT Workstation exams, however, assume that you know how to install cards and understand these terms.

People with experience installing cards, including network cards, into Windows 95 and 98 systems often get a rather nasty shock when installing cards into NT. Those wonderful *Plug and Play* (PnP) features that enable network cards to come to life automatically in Windows 95 and 98 simply do not exist in Windows NT. NT's lack of PnP means that installing a network card requires dealing with two related issues—determining available system resources and setting the network card to use those system resources.

First, the card must be configured with an acceptable I/O address, IRQ, and possibly a memory address. Collectively, Microsoft calls them the system resources (or resources). Virtually every part of the computer requires an I/O address and an IRQ. The I/O address can be considered the "telephone number" of the device. The CPU dials the I/O address to talk to a particular device. No two devices can share the same I/O address. If they did, it would be like two people with the same phone number. I/O addresses have values that look like "330h" or "6500h" (h is for hexadecimal). The *Interrupt Request* (IRQ) is the "doorbell" that devices use to get the CPU's attention. PCs have 16 IRQs numbered from zero to 15. Finally, a few NICs use "Memory Addresses," which are stored memory areas, to enable on-board ROMs to operate. Like I/O addresses, no two devices should share IRQs or memory addresses.

So how do you know which IRQs, I/O addresses, and possibly memory addresses are available for the network card? The starting point is to know which of the system resources are already used. All NICs come with pre-set resources. If you install a PCI network card, the I/O address and memory address will not be an issue, because PCI can use tens of thousands of addresses—and every manufacturer usually has unique addresses. If installing an old ISA card, on the other hand, the chances of I/O address or memory conflict is much higher, although still not too bad. The IRQs will drive you crazy, especially on a machine loaded with sound cards, SCSI host adapters, modems, and the like. The trick is to get rid of all the extra cards temporarily and know what the classically available IRQs are. Start an NT installation by yanking out all the superfluous cards. Leave only the network card, floppy, CD-ROMs, hard drives, mouse, keyboard, and video. These devices all use standard IRQs; they never change from machine to machine. You can then know by process of elimination which IRQs are available. The available IRQs will almost always be IRQs 2/9, 10, 11, and 12. (IRQ 2/9 is one IRQ—it just has a funny name.) Say to yourself, "I'm going to try IRQ X," and write it down.

NOTE: *A good network support person always tries to use the same system resources for every network card in the network, which sure makes troubleshooting a lot easier.*

After picking an IRQ, set up the card. A few NICs still use jumpers, although they are rare today. Most cards have a floppy diskette that has a program called "setup" or "install" that can talk directly to the card and set the system resources. This program will not only configure the NIC, but the program will also provide the capacity to test the NIC to verify it is in good operating condition. Remember when we talked about making a small FAT16 partition? A great trick is to make it a DOS bootable partition, boot to the C: prompt, and copy this program onto the drive. If the partition is ever needed again, it is on the C: drive—and you are not digging for diskettes. If a FAT16 partition is not made, or if the drive is not yet prepared, these programs can easily be run using a bootable floppy. Figure 2–6 shows a typical program of this type.

These programs differ dramatically from card to card, but basically all of them carry the same information. Note the I/O address and IRQ.

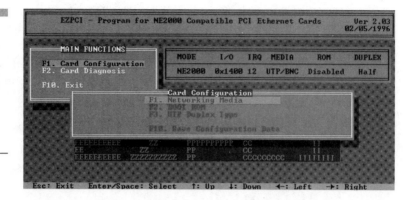

Figure 2–6
A typical NIC setup program. Because Windows NT does not allow programs to access hardware directly, most setup programs must be run from DOS

Another trick to verifying whether the system resources are acceptable is by running this program. If the setup program has difficulty, cannot find a card, or locks the system, usually there is a resource conflict. If all of the cards are removed as described, this situation almost certainly will never happen. Once the system resources have been determined, document them. Documentation will be needed once we begin to install NT Server.

The last critical item for NICs is the NT device driver. Without a device driver written especially for NT 4.0, the chances of getting the system to recognize and use the NIC is near zero. NT comes with a large selection of NIC drivers, yet most of these are 1996 technology—and your brand-new NIC probably will not be listed. The same floppy that holds the SETUP files for the NIC should also contain NT drivers. If you have a brand-name card such as Intel or 3COM, you can pretty well guarantee that the NT drivers are present. If you like to buy cheap, no-name NICs from your local PC parts supplier, then you better check the installation diskette to verify whether NT drivers exist—or you will be wasting your time with that particular card.

NOTE: *Good technicians find a make and model of NIC that they like and stick with it. Every new model of NIC supported means more support disks and more quirks to memorize.*

There is a lot of work involved before you can even begin to pick up an NT Server installation CD-ROM. First of all, you have created a smallish (300MB or so) FAT16 Primary partition on your boot hard drive, have made it DOS bootable, and have a DOS CD-ROM driver and MSCDEX running so that the system can recognize the CD-ROM. You ran the setup program for your NIC and have configured its resources. If you are good, you will put a copy of the NIC's installation floppy on the C: partition you created.

You are now ready to start the installation of the first NT Server system. Grab the NT Server installation CD-ROM, and let's get started.

NOTE: *You can make a text-mode Windows 95 and 98 partition; just be sure to use the LOCK command before running WINNT.*

The NT CD-ROM

The NT Server CD-ROM has all of the tools needed to get NT up and running for all of the different platforms that NT supports. The different installation programs each have separate directories:

\ALPHA—for DEC Alpha systems

\I386—for Intel x86 systems

\MIPS—for MIPS systems

\PPC—for Power PC systems

In our demonstration, we will use the **\I386** directory, because Intel is by far the most common platform for NT systems. The NT Server installation CD-ROM also has many other directories that contain a number of helpful programs, such as the NTHQ program mentioned earlier. We will see many more of these handy programs throughout the rest of this chapter.

Installing NT Server

When you buy Windows NT (Server or Workstation), you receive the NT Installation CD-ROM and three floppy diskettes. These floppy diskettes, commonly called the boot diskettes, can be used to boot the system, recognize the CD-ROM, and install NT onto a completely unformatted hard drive. While this process works perfectly, the process is rarely done in the real world. Most NT CD-ROM installations are handled by one of three processes. First, you could directly boot off the NT Server CD-ROM. The NT CD-ROM is fully bootable. If the system that is being installed has a bootable CD-ROM option in CMOS, you can simply insert the CD-ROM, reboot, and begin the installation process. Second, you could boot to DOS on the C: drive after installing a DOS CD-ROM driver and the venerable MSCDEX, so that you can access the CD-ROM. You then install from the CD-ROM directly. We will use this method as we march through the installation process example in this section. Third, you could do a slight variation on the second option: do exactly as above, but instead of installing from the CD-ROM, copy the entire contents of the \I386 directory to the C: drive. This option is an attractive one in that if you ever need to access the install CD-ROM in the future (and you will), you will not have to scramble for the CD-ROM disk. Or, you could copy all of the installation files from the CD-ROM to a server of some type. This method is often done in upgrade scenarios where some type of network software already exists.

How do you install NT on a machine that is physically connected to the network, yet has no software? If you are the intrepid type, the NT Server CD-ROM has a wonderful subdirectory called \CLIENTS\MSCLIENT. There are three subdirectories called DISK1, DISK2, and NETSETUP. You can create a DOS-level network client that will enable you to access LAN Manager, Windows for Workgroups, Win95 and 98, or NT machines on a network. This client is easy to use and is a common trick for installing NT on "blank machines." Just make bootable network client diskettes and have them access a shared CD-ROM or folder with the NT installation files, and you are installing over the network. Although slow, this method works well. If you already have an existing NT Server machine, you can easily create installation disks with the Network Client Administrator (NCADMIN.EXE) program. Figure 2–7 shows NCADMIN in action. Without NCADMIN, you need to run the DOS level install programs. Good thing you kept that old copy of DOS!

NOTE: *Network Client Disks are not just for installing NT. You can use them to install any operating system, but the most common use is to install Windows 95 and 98. You do it the same way you install NT. Copy the install files to a shared directory, or just share a CD-ROM. Boot with the network client, access the shared folder or CD-ROM, and install.*

Figure 2–7
The Network Client
Administrator
program

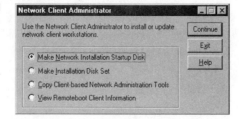

It All Starts with WINNT

The program to start the installation of Window NT Server (and Work-station) is called **WINNT**.

The fact that Microsoft calls this program **WINNT** has always been a source of irritation. Microsoft got us all hooked on installation programs being called **SETUP**, then for Windows NT, Microsoft changed it from **SETUP** to **WINNT**. Why? Well, because Microsoft is Microsoft, and it is bigger than both of us put together. The company can do whatever it wants. So resist your previous inclination to type **SETUP**, and get used to **WINNT**. The **WINNT** program has a number of switches, all of which you need to know for the test—and some that you might actually use. Here is the complete list in alphabetical order:

```
/B - floppyless operation
```

This is probably the most commonly used switch. If you do not use it, the installation process will force you to make boot diskettes. If you run the **WINNT /?** (help) option, this switch says that the **/S** option is required. If you run **WINNT** from the **\I386** directory—and where else would you run it—the **/S** option is not needed at all.

```
/C - Skip free space check on boot floppies
```

When NT makes boot floppies, it first verifies that the floppies are blank formatted. NT will not erase any existing files. If for some reason you want to keep a few files on a boot floppy, use this switch. Be aware that if your files do not leave enough space, NT will give you an error screen and you will have to start over!

```
/E:<command line> - Specifies command to be executed at the
        end of the GUI setup
```

This option is mostly used by OEMs who need to tweak the NT instal-lation to run some of their own applications.

```
/F - No verify of boot floppies
```

Makes sure that the files copied to the boot floppies are in good shape. Basically, it is the old DOS command **COPY /V** option. Not really neces-sary given the quality of today's floppies but the only benefit to turning it off is a slightly faster creation of the bootable floppies. Do not use it.

```
/I:<path of INF file> - Specifies the location of the
        installation's INF file.
```

Used for automated setups. If this switch is not used the system will use the default INF file called **DOSNET.INF**. See automated setups at the end of this chapter for details.

/O - Create boot floppy disks only

This command is obsolete in NT 4.0, but you are expected to know it for the exam.

/OX - Create boot floppies for CD-ROM installation

Creates boot floppies for CD-ROM installation only. Does not install NT.

/R - Specifies optional directory to be installed

Unused, not on the exams. Ignore this one.

/RX - Specifies optional directory to be copied

Unused, not on the exams. Ignore this one.

/S:<path to install files>-Defines path to the installation files

By default, **WINNT.EXE** will prompt for the location of the NT installation files. If this option is used, **WINNT.EXE** will not prompt for the location of the install files.

/T:<drive letter>-Defines the drive to store temporary files

WINNT.EXE copies the entire contents of the **\I386** directory into a temporary file. Use this option to change the location for the temporary files.

/U:<filename> - Location of unattended installation files

See automated setups at the end of this chapter for details.

/UDF:ID,<database file name> - Location and ID for the UDF file.

This specifies the ID and the name of the *Uniqueness Database File* (UDF), used in unattended installations. See automated setups at the end of this chapter for details.

/X - Do not create Setup boot floppies, still requires original setup floppies.

A rarely used option.

NT Installation—Step-by-Step

Once **WINNT** has been started, the installation of Windows NT can be separated into five distinct steps. First, copy the temporary installation files and establish NT on the boot drive. Second, create and format the boot partition, and then create the **\WINNT** directory. Both of these steps are in text mode. Third, determine and set up the critical configuration information, including the role of the server, the name of the machine, and licensing information, as well as a few other steps. Fourth, set up and configure the networking components: configure the network card, install the protocols, and define the name of the domain. Fifth and last, reboot the machine and follow the final configuration steps.

COPYING THE FILES For the purposes of this example, we will assume that you have run the **WINNT** command with the **/B** option. Keep in mind that different switches, location of the install programs, type of hardware, etc., may make your screens look different, but the overall process will be the same. The install process begins with NT prompting for the location of the installation files as shown in Figure 2–8. If you use the **/S** option, this step will be skipped.

Once you have specified the location of the installation files, go find something else to do for at least fifteen minutes. At this point NT begins to copy the contents of the **\I386** directory into a temporary directory on your hard drive and it seems to take forever (Figure 2–9). On a slower machine (Pentium 133 on down) or a machine with a small amount of RAM (16MB or less), the copying can take an hour! At least they are kind enough to give you a status bar so that you can see the percent complete.

After the installation files have been copied, the NT installation will reboot itself and begin the second step of the installation process. From this point forward, the installation is robust. You can turn off the system and turn it back on and the installation will usually simply pick up where it left off.

INSTALLING NT FILES   When the machine reboots, it is now running Windows NT, but in a primitive character mode. Figure 2–10 shows the main welcome screen.

From this screen we usually press Enter to continue, although using the "R" to repair a botched installation is helpful for those times when the installation program is not as robust as we would like! After we press enter, NT looks for mass storage devices on the system. NT is good at finding just about any IDE or SCSI devices.

Figure 2–8
Windows NT Setup
prompts for the
location of the
installation files

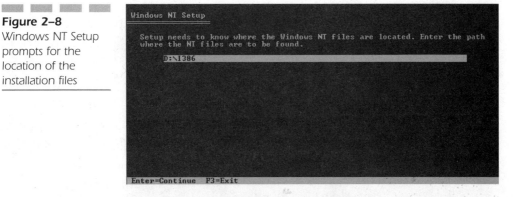

Figure 2–9
Windows NT Setup
copies files to the
hard drive

Figure 2–10
Windows NT Setup
following the first
reboot

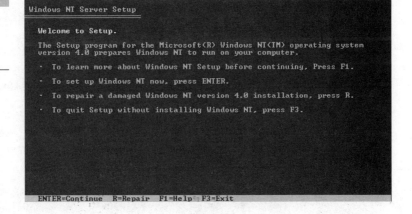

NOTE: *Although most SCSI devices are easy for NT to find, many SCSI host adapters and SCSI devices have "quirks" that make them challenging. One exception seems to be Adaptec SCSI Host adapters. It almost seems as though Adaptec has some secret relationship with Microsoft that guarantees they work well every time. I strongly recommend Adaptec SCSI host Adapters!*

Figure 2–11 shows an NT installation recognizing a standard IDE CD-ROM. This is the most common view when using only EIDE mass storage devices.

It is a trivial process to add other devices. NT is ready to support a broad cross-section of SCSI and proprietary controllers; press **s** to see the selection of controllers that NT can support natively (Figure 2–12). More advanced controllers and drive arrays will often come with their own controller device drivers. They can be added here by selecting the "Other (Requires disk provided by a hardware manufacturer)" option. This option is the last option on the list and is not visible in the figure.

Many times NT may not be able to detect a device. If that happens, hit the **s** and see whether the device is listed. If it is, select the device. Some devices supported by NT may not always be detected.

After hitting Enter, you are then prompted to sign your life away by agreeing to the *End User License Agreement* (EULA). Do not read it. You'll just get sick to your stomach. Press Page Down repeatedly until you can exit the screen by pressing F8 to get to the next hardware screen. This screen (Figure 2–13) shows what NT thinks you have in terms of the most critical components of your computer. If you have any Win 95 and 98 experience, this screen will look familiar. If you have a unique system, key-

Figure 2–11

Windows NT detects EIDE devices, such as CD-ROM drives

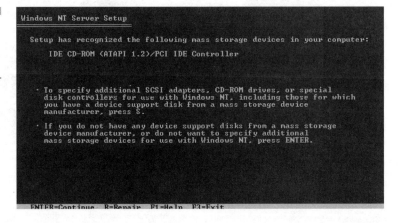

Figure 2–12
Specifying additional
SCSI adapters during
setup

```
Windows NT Server Setup

You have asked to specify an additonal SCSI adapter, CD-ROM drive,
or special disk controller for use with Windows NT.

   • To select a mass storage device from the following list,
     use the UP or DOWN ARROW key to move the highlight to
     the mass storage device you want, and then press ENTER.

   • To return to the previous screen without specifying an additional
     mass storage device for use with Windows NT, press ESC.

┌─────────────────────────────────────────────────────────────────┐
│ Adaptec AHA-151X/AHA-152X/AIC-6X60 SCSI Adapter                   │
│ Adaptec AHA-154X/AHA-164X SCSI Host Adapter                       │
│ Adaptec AHA-174X EISA SCSI Host Adapter                           │
│ Adaptec AHA-274X/AHA-284X/AIC-777X SCSI Adapter                   │
│ Adaptec AHA-294X/AHA-394X/AIC-78XX SCSI Controller                │
│ AMD PCI SCSI Controller/Ethernet Adapter                          │
│ AMIscsi SCSI Host Adapter                                         │
│ BusLogic SCSI Host Adapter                                        │
│ BusLogic FlashPoint                                               │
│ Compaq 32-bit Fast-Wide SCSI-2/E                                  │
│ Compaq Drive Array                                                │
│ Dell Drive Array                                                  │
│ DPI SCSI Host Adapter                                             │
│ Future Domain TMC-7000EX EISA Host Adapter                        │
│ Future Domain 8XX SCSI Host Adapter                               │
│                                                    <More ↓>       │
└─────────────────────────────────────────────────────────────────┘
Enter=Select   F3=Exit   ESC=Cancel
```

Figure 2–13
The Windows NT
Setup hardware
summary screen

```
Windows NT Server Setup

Setup has determined that your computer contains the following hardware
and software components.

           Computer: Standard PC
            Display: Auto Detect
           Keyboard: XT, AT, or Enhanced Keyboard (83-104 keys)
    Keyboard Layout: US
     Pointing Device: Microsoft Serial Mouse

        No Changes: The above list matches my computer.

If you want to change any item in the list, press the UP or DOWN ARROW
key to move the highlight to the item you want to change. Then press
ENTER to see the alternatives for that item.

When all the items in the list are correct, move the highlight to
"The above list matches my computer" and press ENTER.

Enter=Select   F3=Exit   ESC=Cancel
```

board, or mouse, now is the time to whip out any special disks that may have come with that component. There is no need to select any Display information, the Auto Detect option works great. Most of the time this screen is ignored and it is time to hit Enter once again.

The partitions screen is probably the single most important screen in the entire installation. The function of this screen is to determine the partition where Windows NT will be installed and to format that partition with the correct format for your needs. Invariably, this means NTFS. After NT is installed, there are other tools to format other partitions. Once a partition is created and NT is installed on that partition, the only way to change it is to reinstall NT, so get it right the first time! In Figure 2–14,

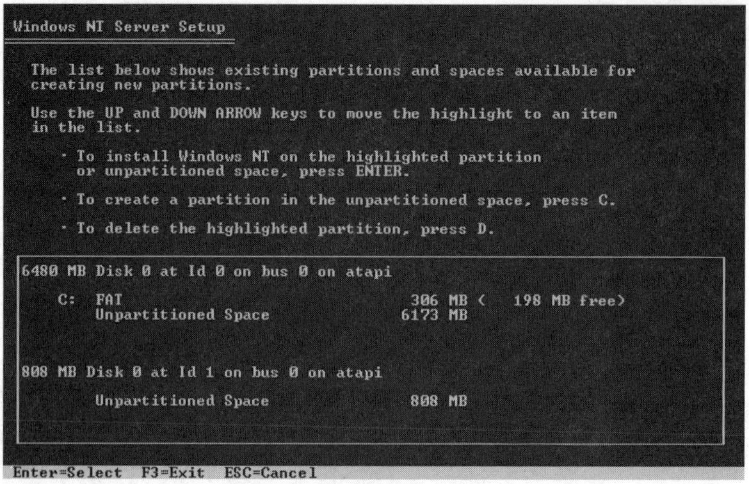

Figure 2–14
Drive partitioning
during Windows NT
Setup

Figure 2–14
Drive partitioning
during Windows NT
Setup

```
Windows NT Server Setup

   The list below shows existing partitions and spaces available for
   creating new partitions.

   Use the UP and DOWN ARROW keys to move the highlight to an item
   in the list.

      • To install Windows NT on the highlighted partition
        or unpartitioned space, press ENTER.

      • To create a partition in the unpartitioned space, press C.

      • To delete the highlighted partition, press D.

   6480 MB Disk 0 at Id 0 on bus 0 on atapi

      C:  FAT                                  306 MB <   198 MB free>
          Unpartitioned Space                 6173 MB


   808 MB Disk 0 at Id 1 on bus 0 on atapi

          Unpartitioned Space                  808 MB


Enter=Select  F3=Exit  ESC=Cancel
```

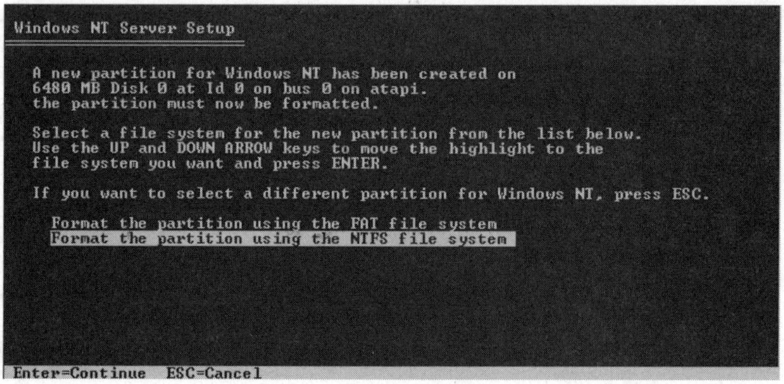

Figure 2–15
Formatting a
partition during
Windows NT Setup

```
Windows NT Server Setup

   A new partition for Windows NT has been created on
   6480 MB Disk 0 at Id 0 on bus 0 on atapi.
   the partition must now be formatted.

   Select a file system for the new partition from the list below.
   Use the UP and DOWN ARROW keys to move the highlight to the
   file system you want and press ENTER.

   If you want to select a different partition for Windows NT, press ESC.

        Format the partition using the FAT file system
        Format the partition using the NTFS file system


Enter=Continue  ESC=Cancel
```

the system has two hard drives. We can see the small FAT16 partition created before the NT installation process began. It also shows all of remaining unpartitioned space on the first drive and the second drive. Our goal is to make the unpartitioned space on the first drive an NTFS partition and to install NT on that partition.

To do so, select the unpartitioned space and press Enter. If you wish to create multiple logical drives in that unpartitioned space, press **c** and select the amount of space to partition for the NT install. Either way, you will then be prompted for the type of format to use (Figure 2–15). The format of choice is NTFS.

Formatting the drive NTFS takes about the same amount of time as it would to format a FAT16 drive. Once the drive is formatted, you are prompted for the name of the directory where NT will be installed. Any name is fine, including the default (Figure 2–16).

Figure 2–16

Windows NT setup
prompts you to
specify the directory
in which to install the
NT operating system

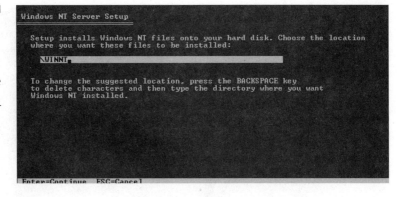

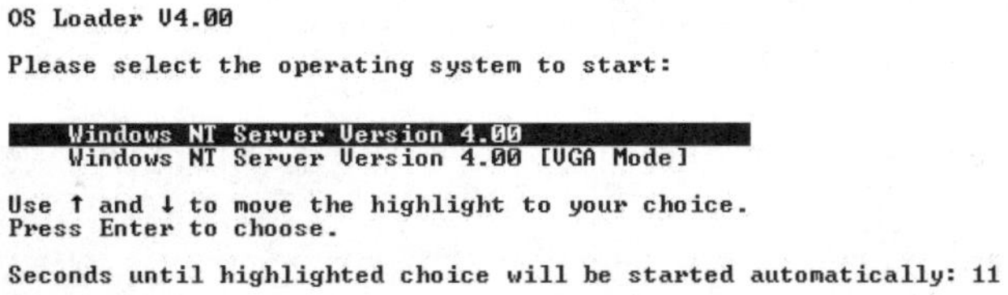

Figure 2–17

The Windows NT OS
Loader startup menu

```
OS Loader V4.00

Please select the operating system to start:

    Windows NT Server Version 4.00
    Windows NT Server Version 4.00 [VGA Mode]

Use ↑ and ↓ to move the highlight to your choice.
Press Enter to choose.

Seconds until highlighted choice will be started automatically: 11
```

At this point, Windows NT copies a few files to the new directory and reboots, starting the third step of the installation, the critical configuration options.

INSTALLATION CONFIGURATION   When the machine reboots, you see the NT startup menu for the first time. Figure 2–17 shows the first startup menu.

This menu enables an NT system to support many other operating systems and is highly customizable, as will be shown in Chapter 4, "NT Boot Access." For now, just select the first option to continue the setup. From this point forward, the installation will progress in graphic mode. The appearance of Figure 2–18 shows a successful boot into graphic mode. Click Enter—this is a good time to check the mouse!

Enter your name and organization name (Figure 2–19). This is not to be confused with the name of the computer or the domain name. Only a name is required.

After you have entered a name and an organization, Windows NT will prompt you for the CD key. Enter it to see the licensing modes screen, as shown in Figure 2–20. NT has two licensing modes options: Per Server and Per Seat. With Per Server, you tell the system the number of concurrent connections enabled. For example, if you bought a 10-user license,

Figure 2–18
Windows NT Setup
begins the graphical
part of the NT
installation

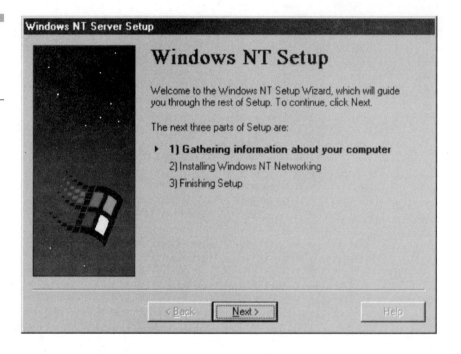

Figure 2–19
Windows NT Setup
prompts you for
user name and
organization name

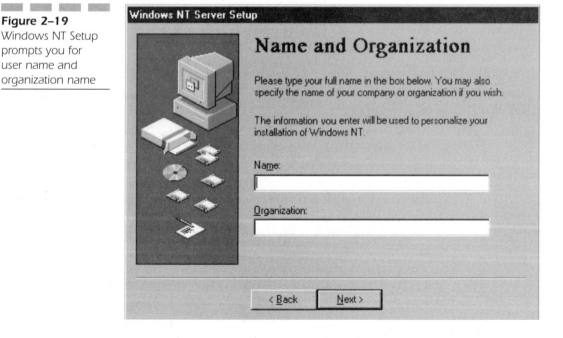

Figure 2–20

Windows NT Setup prompts you to choose between Per Server and Per Seat licensing

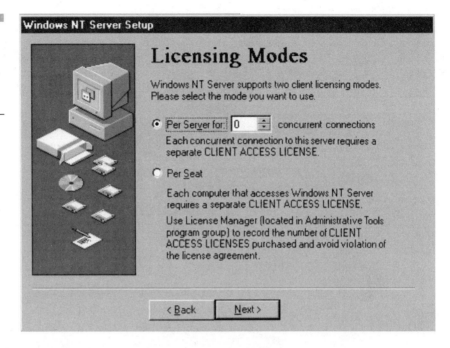

you would click the Per Server radio button and type a 10 for the number of concurrent connections. A single machine with multiple connections to a server is only considered to have one connection as far as the license is concerned. If one more than the allowed number of concurrent connections is made, NT will not enable that extra user access to the server. Per Seat says that Microsoft will trust you to purchase a *Client Access License* (CAL) for every machine that accesses the server.

Most people select the Per Server option initially. If for some reason in the future you desire to go to Per Seat, there is an option in the Control panel that enables for a one-time, one-way conversion from Per Server to Per Seat. Once this is done it can never be returned to Per Server except via a reinstall.

In single server cases, Per Server is the way to license. If more than one server will be installed on the network, Per Seat makes more sense. Consider a situation where there are ten systems accessing one server. If you need to add another server, you have the choice of buying another ten CALs or simply configuring both servers as Per Seat.

There is a big temptation for network administrators to steal from Microsoft by buying, for example, a five-user license and configuring the Server as Per Seat, thus enabling any number of concurrent connections.

Apart from the obvious illegality, there is a strong business reason for not doing this. Before NT became so prevalent, the NOS of choice was Novell NetWare. NetWare had only Per Server licensing back then. This would drive network administrators and company accountants crazy, because you had to buy a lot more access than you usually needed. Microsoft's Per Seat licensing eliminates this extra cost. Give them a break and do not cheat Microsoft.

After selecting the licensing mode, give the computer a name (Figure 2–21). This name is important, as it is the one that will show up when browsing the network. The name can be any alphanumeric up to fifteen characters including spaces, but cannot use the following characters: / \ [ ] " : ; | < > + = , ? *. You should try to give the computer a name that gives some description of its function or location. Keep in mind, however, that the computer's name can easily be changed in the future to a more descriptive name.

Next, you need to determine the role of the server. As this machine is the first machine in the network, the choice is simple—it will be a Primary Domain Controller. (See Figure 2–22.) Remember that if you are going to make it a BDC, it must be already connected to the network! If you want to make a member server, select Stand-Alone Server now and you will be prompted for a domain name.

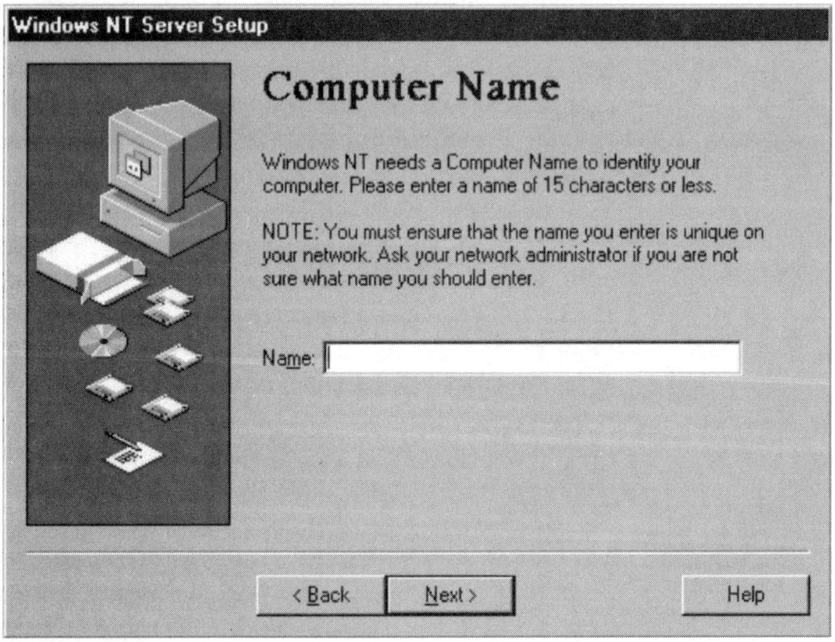

Figure 2–21

Windows NT Setup prompts you to enter the computer name

Windows NT Server Setup

Computer Name

Windows NT needs a Computer Name to identify your computer. Please enter a name of 15 characters or less.

NOTE: You must ensure that the name you enter is unique on your network. Ask your network administrator if you are not sure what name you should enter.

Name:

< Back   Next >   Help

Figure 2–22

Select the role of the NT server—PDC, BDC, or Stand-Alone Server

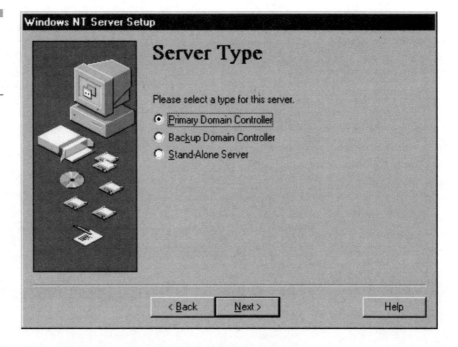

Every NT domain has one "administrator" account, a "super account" that can do anything on the domain. When the PDC is first established, it must create this super account. The administrator account will be used on the initial login to the new server and will be the account that will create all of the other accounts on the domain, or at least will create the accounts that let others create all of the other accounts on the domain. You can create other accounts just as powerful as administrator later. Figure 2–23 shows the screen that prompts you to give the administrator account a password. This account is all-powerful and must be protected with a strong password. This can be up to 14 characters and should include both alphabetic and numerical characters. The password will even accept punctuation marks and it is case sensitive.

More sophisticated NT networks avoid using the administrator password altogether. The one down side to NT is that the administrator account can never be deleted, so every hacker already knows the default name to an account on your domain. Take two steps to secure the administrator account. First, give the administrator account some phenomenally difficult password like "No12W4&&aY4g," use it to create a new account with the same power as the administrator account, then put the password in an envelope and place the envelope in a safe place. If someone gets a hold of

Figure 2–23
Specify the
Administrator
account's password

the administrator password, they can do anything they want to your NT network. Second, rename the administrator account so that hackers will no longer know the name of the most powerful account on your system. (User accounts can be renamed using the User Manager for Domains program, discussed in Chapter 8, "NT User Management.")

Once the password is established, the next screen, shown in Figure 2–24, asks if you wish to create an *Emergency Repair Disk* (ERD). The ERD is a powerful utility that stores critical information about your system on a floppy disk.

You want to make an ERD. It will save you in the case of a system crash where you cannot boot NT. The ERD is itself not bootable. Should you ever be in a position where you need to recover a crashed NT system, you will need your three bootable NT floppies to access the system.

The ERD is only as good as the information it holds. As users are created and hardware is added to the system, the ERD will need to be updated. NT provides a special program called **RDISK.EXE** that enables you to create a new ERD or update an old ERD. See Chapter 4, "The NT Boot Process," for an in depth look at the ERD.

The last step in the Configuring and Installing part of the NT installation is the selection of optional components. A person with Windows 95

Figure 2–24
Windows NT Setup
prompts you to
create an Emergency
Repair Disk (ERD)

and 98 experience will find this screen familiar. The most important point is that none of these optional components are needed by the server to do its job. By default, NT Server only selects a small number of these components, and that is too many for most folks. See Figure 2–25. Select what you want for the server to use and move on to the next big step in installing NT—the Networking Component.

NETWORKING COMPONENT The networking component handles all of the necessary details to get the network established on Windows NT Server. If a network is already established, then the networking component gets the system linked into the network. The networking component begins with another welcome screen, shown in Figure 2–26.

The first screen in the networking component of the Windows NT installation process determines how the server will connect to the network. The two choices, displayed in Figure 2–27, are Wired to the network and Remote access to the network. Choose the correct option(s) for your installation.

The computer will ask you whether you wish to install the *Internet Information Server* (IIS). IIS is the Microsoft Web server software, select the checkbox if you wish to install IIS. For more detail on IIS, see Chapter 13, "Internet and Intranet Services."

Figure 2–25
Select the optional
components to install

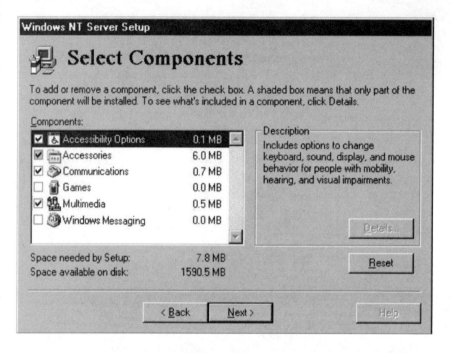

Figure 2–26
Windows NT
Setup begins the
installation of
the networking
component

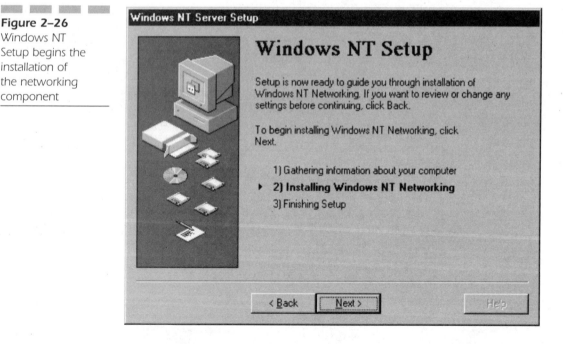

It is now time to install the drivers for the *Network Card* (NIC). Windows NT has a primitive NIC locator function that attempts to locate the network card automatically. This feature is not to be confused with *Plug and Play* (PnP), although it certainly seems to act as though it were PnP. While not true PnP, it does a moderately good job at locating NICs installed in the system. If NT is successful at locating a NIC, the screen in Figure 2–28 will appear.

Unfortunately, the system is not perfect and in many cases will not find a NIC. In that case, you need to load the proper driver manually. NT has a broad selection of built-in device drivers, but unfortunately, the majority of these are now badly dated. In most cases, we click the Have Disk button and load the drivers that came with the card (Figure 2–29).

This only installs the driver. Depending on the NIC, you may then have to set IRQs, I/O addresses, etc. to finish the card configuration. The NIC manufacturers have a lot of power here and can make card installation easy or difficult. Read all of the documentation that comes with a NIC to determine whether there is a certain method for installing the card.

Now that the card is installed, the next screen enables you to select the protocols to be used. NT easily supports multiple protocols on the same system. On this screen (Figure 2–30), Windows shows the "Big Three"

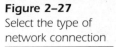

Figure 2–27
Select the type of
network connection

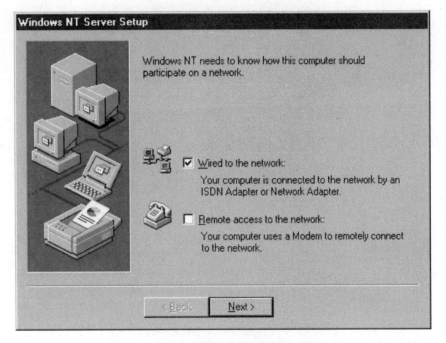

■■ ■■ ■■ ■■
Figure 2–28
Windows NT Setup
displays any Network
Adapters that it has
detected

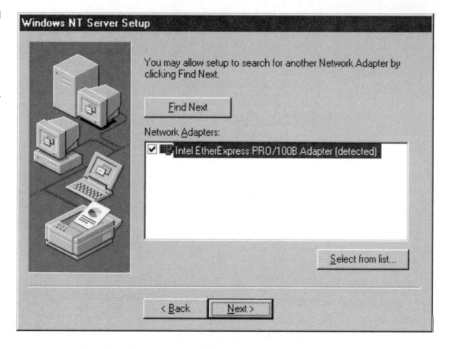

protocols, TCP/IP, IPX/SPX and NetBEUI. You can also select other protocols by clicking the Select from list... button. Note that of the "Big Three," some of these may already be selected or selected and grayed out. NT will try to use TCP/IP by default and will always have it selected. If you choose to install IIS, the TCP/IP option will be selected and grayed-out as IIS must have TCP/IP in order to work.

You should select IPX/SPX only if you intend to link into a network with Novell NetWare servers. The NetBEUI protocol is often handy to install in a new network as it is much easier to configure than TCP/IP and is a good way to get a network started quickly to make sure everything works. You can then turn off NetBEUI once you know the network is in good working order.

NOTE: *There is nothing wrong with NetBEUI in smaller networks. You still get all of the security and power of NT with NetBEUI. You need TCP/IP for only three reasons: Internet access, in-house use of TCP/IP services such as web browsing (an Intranet), and routing. If you do not need any of these three options, NetBEUI is trivial to configure compared to TCP/IP.*

Figure 2–29
Use the Have Disk
button to install and
unlisted or updated
device driver

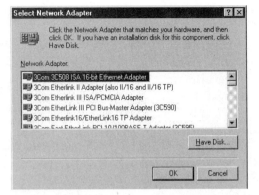

Figure 2–30
Select the network
protocol(s) to use

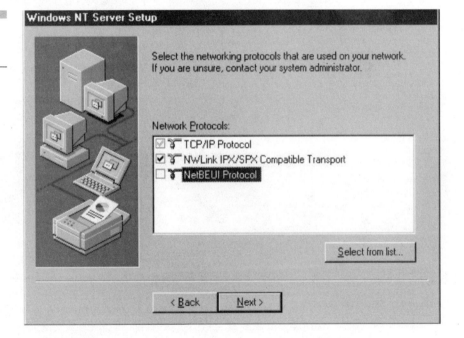

The nicest part about protocols is that you can always add and remove them. Just remember that any machines that want to talk to each other must use the same protocol.

After the protocols have been added, we move to the next screen to load the Network Services. A *service* is a program that is constantly running, providing a necessary network function. By default, NT will install four necessary functions: *Remote Procedure Call* (RPC) configuration, NetBIOS Interface, Workstation, and Server (Figure 2–31). You may need quite a few other services, especially if you are running TCP/IP. These other services will be discussed as needed throughout the rest of this book.

When you press Enter, NT then brings up the bindings screen (Figure 2–32). Bindings are the links between the network cards and the protocols and the protocols and the services. A classic example would be an Internet dial-up network connection. A system is on a small network. The network runs NetBEUI. In order to access the Internet, the system must also install TCP/IP. A binding would be established between the modem and the TCP/IP protocol and the network card and NetBEUI. TCP/IP would not be bound to the network card and NetBEUI would not be bound to the modem. These bindings are usually correct at this point and should not be edited.

After pressing Enter, NT then asks for the name of the domain (Figure 2–33). As this machine will be the PDC, we must now create a domain name. Domain names can be up to fifteen alphanumeric characters long and must not contain any spaces or punctuation marks. Keep domain names as simple as possible while still being descriptive.

Figure 2–31
Windows NT Setup allows you to add and remove network services during installation.

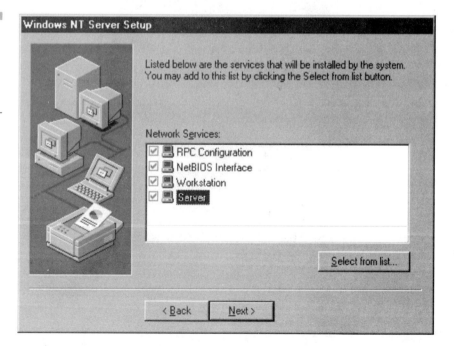

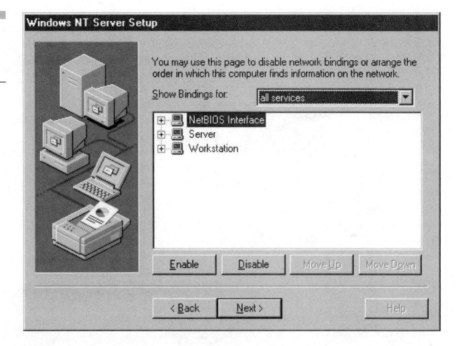

Figure 2–32
The Windows NT
Setup bindings
screen

NOTE: *If you are making a member server, you need to enter the domain name. You can also simply set it up as a workgroup and add it to the domain later.*

After selecting the domain name, NT then installs all of the necessary software for the network and starts the network. You are asked to select the time zone and then to configure the display adapter (Figure 2–34). Most NT Servers run with the standard VGA driver, simply because there is little need for a higher resolution display and video drivers are often a little problematic. If you have the video driver, you can install it at this time and adjust the sliders for the color depth and resolution you desire. Be sure to use the Test button to verify your drivers. If you get a lockup at this point, you can reboot and select the VGA mode text option (as shown way back in Figure 2–17) to get NT to boot and change the video driver or video configurations.

If you decided to make an Emergency Repair Disk, NT will now prompt for a floppy and make the ERD. The floppy will be formatted in the process, so it does not have to be formatted or even blank. Just make sure the floppy is not write protected.

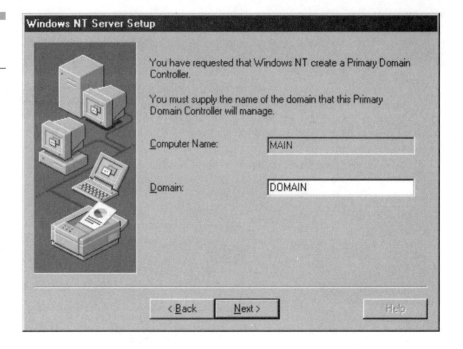

Assuming all is done well, NT reboots and starts. NT Server is installed and ready to work. There will be some configuration issues that need to be addressed, but basically the machine is ready to go. Be sure to first log in as administrator and create a new account with the same capabilities as the administrator. Use that account instead of the administrator account for your daily work.

Installing NT Workstation

The process of Installing NT Workstation is similar to the installation of NT Server. In this section, we will not run through the entire installation process. Instead, we will look at the installation screens that are different and understand their functions and how to use them. The single biggest thing to keep in mind as you install NT Workstation is that it is not designed to control a domain. It can be used stand-alone. It is not NT

Figure 2-34

Setting the Display
properties

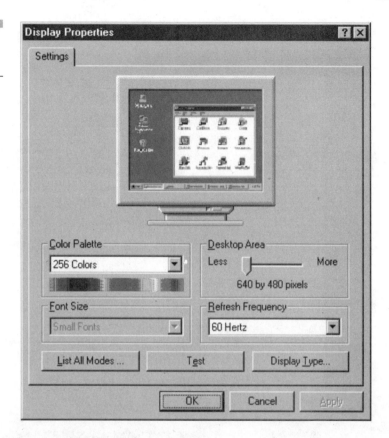

Server. Before going any further we will know that certain screens that we saw in NT Server installation process simply will not show up in NT Workstation. For example, we know there will not be a screen to ask whether the system will be a PDC, BDC or Stand-alone server. Let's look at the NT Workstation installation process.

Installing NT Files

The first step of the installation of Windows NT Workstation is absolutely identical to the process of NT Server. You still use **WINNT.EXE** with all of the same switches. The creation and formatting of partitions is exactly the same.

Installation Configuration

The first screen of the installation configuration step is different in NT Workstation. NT Workstation makes a Windows 95 and 98 look by prompting for an installation type (Figure 2–35). Your four choices are Typical, Portable, Compact, and Custom. These options are roughly similar to Windows 95 and 98 and do not affect any aspect of the network installation. Which choices you use is a matter of personal preference. When in doubt, choose Custom and select the options individually.

The rest of this installation step is again identical to NT Server with the exception that NT Workstation will not give screens for Licensing mode (Figure 2–20) or Role of the server (Figure 2–22). These are options unique to NT Server.

Networking Component

As might be expected, the networking component of NT Workstation installation has a few differences from NT Server. In particular, NT Workstation may be stand-alone so the first screen gives you the option of skipping the networking component altogether. (Figure 2–36).

Figure 2–35
Setup options when installing Windows NT Workstation

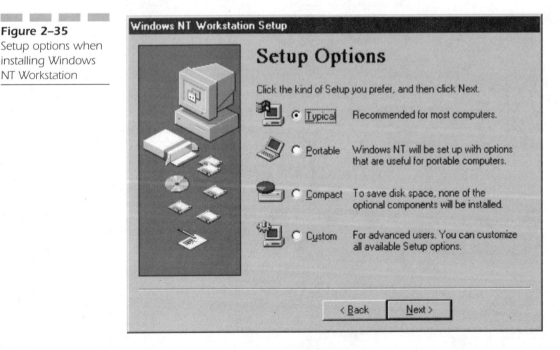

Figure 2–36
Windows NT
Workstation Setup
gives you the option
to "not connect this
computer to a
network at this time."

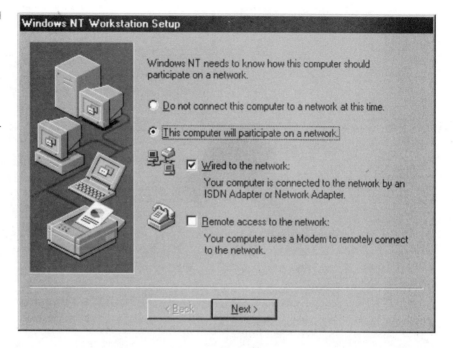

NT Workstation installs the protocols, but does not have the bindings screen or the network services screen of NT Server. NT Workstation does not assume a domain as our PDC installation example earlier. Instead, you see the screen shown on Figure 2–37.

This screen enables you to select a Domain or a Workgroup. If you select a domain, the system must be able to access the PDC for the domain. You must also have an account already established on the domain. You can also optionally configure a computer account on the domain but you must have access to that domain in order for this to operate.

NT Workstation does not prompt for the installation of Internet Information Server. Instead, you have the option to install the Peer Web Services. It is an interesting note that NT Workstation can easily run IIS but it has been hobbled by Microsoft by only enabling 20 concurrent connections. There is no way to change this.

The rest of the NT Workstation process is identical to NT Server. Once the system reboots, it is ready to join the domain, workgroup, or to act as a stand-alone.

As we can see, the processes of installing NT Server and NT Workstation are much the same. The exams are not interested in your ability to quote the exact order of screens, but it is helpful for you to be sure that

Figure 2-37
Select either a
Domain or a
Workgroup for
your Windows NT
Workstation
computer

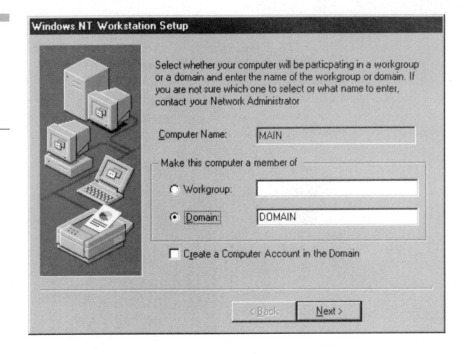

you understand the basic differences between the two. Use a little common sense, remember the differences between NT Server and NT Workstation, and you'll have no problems on the exams.

Patches and Service Packs

Windows NT has been around since 1996. In that time, hundreds of problems have surfaced that have compelled Microsoft to provide free replacement software. The replacement software is packaged in downloadable
components called "patches." Over time, as a number of patches develop,
Microsoft will combine them into a "pile o' patches" called a "Service Pack."
Service Packs fix so many problems that they have become absolutely necessary. Administrators often ignore patches until they are combined into
a Service Pack, although any good NT administrator watches for the latest announcement from Microsoft and will decide for themselves whether
the patch is necessary. Patches come out almost monthly and Service Packs
about once a year. The latest Service Pack is Service Pack 4.

NOTE: *Microsoft often refers to patches as "updates."*

As a rule, always install the latest Service Pack—after checking around the Internet to be sure there are not any nasty problems with it. A good example would be Service Pack 2. It actually did more damage than good! Let someone else test the service packs and only install them after a couple of weeks have passed. By then, all of the NT Web sites and newsgroups will say it is O.K.—or not.

Service Packs are not additive. In other words, you do not have to install Service Packs 1 and 2 before you install Service Pack 3. Just grab the latest and you are in good shape. A Service Pack, however, will only update installed components. For example, if a system does not have *Internet Information Server* (IIS) installed, and if the Service Pack has fixes for IIS, they will not be installed. If IIS is then installed on a "Service Packed" system, it will not have the updates. Fortunately, simply installing the Service Pack again will update any recently installed components.

Installing a Service Pack is usually a fairly simple process. First make sure you know what Service Pack has been installed. Go to any Explorer Window and Click Help/About. The screen shown in Figure 2–38 will appear, telling the Service Pack version.

The actual install process usually consists of running a single .EXE file. The system then reboots with the Service Pack installed.

NOTE: *The entire issue of patches and service packs is ignored on the exams. However, using Service Packs and patches is absolutely critical for real-world NT support!*

Figure 2–38
Checking the Service
Pack version

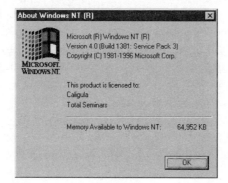

Troubleshooting NT Installations

NT has an amazingly robust installation process. Compared to other NOSs, NT installations are usually a simple and easy process. There are certain problems, however, that do take place in the installation process frequently enough to warrant listing. These problems break down into two groups: Hardware and Networking.

Hardware Problems

The single biggest headache, perhaps the only headache, to NT installations is hardware-related problems. These manifest themselves in many different ways during the NT installation process, usually in the form of a system crash or the inability for the installation to progress due to NT not locating a device or a device not having enough resources/space/speed.

AN OUNCE OF PREVENTION ...   The best way to deal with hardware problems is to avoid them in the first place. Use the *Hardware Compatibility List* (HCL) to make sure that every component is truly NT compatible, especially if the system is homemade. If you buy a complete system, make sure the system, in the configuration you purchased, is NT compatible. Once you have determined that the system is on the HCL, take a few moments on the Internet to poke around the manufacturers' sites to see whether any component has a quirk that might cause problems. It seems that every system and component has a quirk that can generate significant hair loss unless you know about it ahead of time. It is rare to be at the "bleeding edge" of technology. Whatever you are doing to a computer has invariably been done by someone else in the past. It would be nice to have that person next to you when it happens. They are out there! Try a company's Web site, e-mail tech support, and use USENET newsgroups. A good place to start is all of the newsgroups that start with `COMP.OS..MS-WINDOWS.NT`. These active newsgroups have bailed me out of a number of issues, due simply to the fact that I was able to find the person who had suffered from the same problem.

Here is a classic example. I was building up a high-end server system for a client. The system was on the HCL. The client requested to use a special high-speed NIC—also on the HCL—in the server. Not only were both the server and the NIC on the HCL, but they had been tested together and approved for use by the manufacturer of the server. I had all of the correct, latest drivers. Everything seemed set for an easy installation.

Well, I installed the NIC and the moment that NT tried to determine the NIC, the system froze up. After three reinstalls, new NICs, and a new server with the exact same result at the exact same time, I decided to call tech support from the manufacturer of the server. After three days of the usual finger pointing and denials that tech support folks are so good at doing, I cried for help on the newsgroups. Two other people had the exact same setup of NIC and system, yet had not experienced any problems. One gave me his telephone number and we compared every part of the computers. We determined that the only difference was that I installed the NIC into a secondary PCI bus slot (the system had two PCI busses) and the other guys put the NIC on the primary PCI bus. I moved the NIC to the primary and instantly had success. Well, maybe sometimes you ARE on the "bleeding edge" of technology.

TROUBLE WITH MASS STORAGE   Mass storage devices can cause a lot of trouble during the install process. The first problem is surface defects on a drive. This is usually manifested by NT screaming that it cannot read from a drive, or by freaky reboots and spectacular system lock-ups. If you experience these, stop trying to install NT and run a serious diagnostic utility. I will start with Norton's Utilities and then move to powerful utilities such as Microhouse's DrivePro and Gibson Research's Spinrite.

Another drive problem during installation is when NT cannot recognize any controllers in the first step of the setup. This is most prevalent with old and new controllers. If the card is old, check with the manufacturer to see whether an NT compatible device driver for the controller has been written or replace the controller with one that is on the HCL. If the controller is new, there is probably a new (and downloadable) driver written to correct some problem with the controller. This is most common with SCSI host adapters. If NT does not recognize an IDE/EIDE controller, manually install the ATAPI 1.2/PCI IDE Controller. It works almost every time.

When you format a partition you have just created on an EIDE drive, sometimes you get an error saying that the partition is too large to format. This is not NT's fault. The problem is traced to some older (pre-1998) motherboards that cannot support partitions greater than 4GB. To fix it, upgrade the BIOS, replace the motherboard, or keep your partitions under 4GB.

NT does not require a massive amount of drive space relative to the multi-gigabyte drives used today. But sometimes, particularly during an upgrade (see Upgrading to Windows NT 4.0, next section), the drives can run out of space. When you do not have enough space, first try to move the temporary file to another drive using the **WINNT /T:<drive>** option. If that does not work, try moving off some of the files to another drive. If you do not have another drive, add one. The last option is to create larger partitions. This will require wiping out data, so be sure to back up first.

TROUBLE WITH OTHER HARDWARE   Mass storage devices are not the only problem hardware devices. Virtually any piece of hardware on your system can cause problems during the NT install. Here are a few good rules of thumb.

1. Do not install hardware you do not need, particularly with servers. Do not waste your time with sound cards and high-end video. The fancier and more powerful the device, the better the chance that it will not work under NT.

2. Know your resources. Know your I/O addresses, IRQs, and DMAs. Do not let basic resource conflicts cause you trouble.

3. Get the right device driver. Check with the manufacturer for updates.

Network Problems

Getting the installation to bring up the network is always an interesting process. Buckling the pieces and installing the hardware is fine, but until that moment when the Network Neighborhood sees the other machines on the network, the tension is palpable. Here is a sample of the more common problems during and after the networking component is installed.

1. Unable to find Network card. Two words for this one: resources and drivers.

2. Inability of a Service to start. Certain services need the support of other software such as protocols or of hardware such as the NIC. Make sure that the devices and programs that the service needs are running properly.

3. Inability to connect to Domain PDC. Did you type the domain name correctly? Do you have the correct administrator account? Is the PDC on? Are you connected to the PDC?

Most NT errors in the network component can be traced to an installation error. Take your time on the networking component and avoid silly mistakes.

Upgrading to Windows NT 4.0

Many times Windows NT will be installed on top of another operating system. The term "upgrading" is misleading. Upgrading implies that an existing program is in some way improved. Windows NT does not improve an existing operating system, it completely replaces it. But in the most technical sense, it is still considered an upgrade. Windows NT is designed to install over DOS, Windows 3.X, Windows 95 and 98, and older versions of Windows NT, in particular NT 3.51. Not only will NT install, it will preserve the older operating system and enable you to boot to that older operating system via its boot menu. In this section, we will look at some of the tricks involved with upgrading to Windows NT 4.0 from various operating systems.

Upgrading DOS & Windows 3.X

This is probably the easiest of all the upgrades. As mentioned earlier, many "clean" NT installations will begin by installing DOS onto the boot drive and creating a small partition. NT is then installed on a separate NTFS partition. NT can run on the same partition as another operating system but it will not be able to use NTFS and still enable the other operating system to survive. NT does not change any of the operating system files. This enables the machine to boot to both DOS as well as NT. When NT is installed over a DOS system, the NT boot menu will give a DOS menu option that will enable the user to boot selectively to DOS or to Windows NT. Windows 3.X is not truly an operating system, so from the view of NT, Windows 3.X is simply a program on the drive that runs on top of DOS.

 NOTE: *If NT notices a copy of Windows 3.X or Windows 95, it will ask to install into the same directory. Do not do this for 95 and only do it for 3.X if you are sure you will never have to uninstall NT in the future.*

Windows 95 and 98

The Windows 95 and 98 upgrade is basically identical to the DOS upgrade. Like DOS, Window NT does not use any of Windows 95 and 98.

Although NT *looks* a lot like 95 and 98, an NT install cannot access the 95 and 98 Registry or use any current settings. Two features can make a Windows 95 and 98 upgrade a little tricky. First, NT cannot support FAT32. If the boot partition is FAT32, you will have to wipe it—and Windows 95 and 98—out in order to load NT. If you do have a FAT16 partition, make sure to run the **LOCK** command to prevent Windows 95 and 98 from stopping NT from installing.

Previous Versions of NT

NT 4.0 can easily upgrade an earlier version of Windows NT. In this case it is a true upgrade in that NT 4.0 will read the older NT's information and copy the type of machine, accounts, and other information. When upgrading an older copy of NT Server to NT Server 4.0, the role of the machine cannot be changed without reinstalling NT and wiping out the old copy. So if the server was a PDC under the old Windows NT, it will be a PDC under the new NT.

To upgrade an older version of NT from within the graphical NT interface, use the command **WINNT32** rather than **WINNT**. (See Figure 2–39.) **WINNT32** uses the same switches as **WINNT** and it cannot be used with any other operating system other than Windows NT. You can also use **WINNT32** to reinstall Windows NT 4.0 over a previous copy of NT 4.0.

The only way to do a fresh install on a machine with an older version of NT is to run **WINNT** from a DOS prompt and make sure not to install it into the same directory as the old Windows NT. If you run **WINNT** and select the old directory, it will still act as an upgrade and keep all the settings.

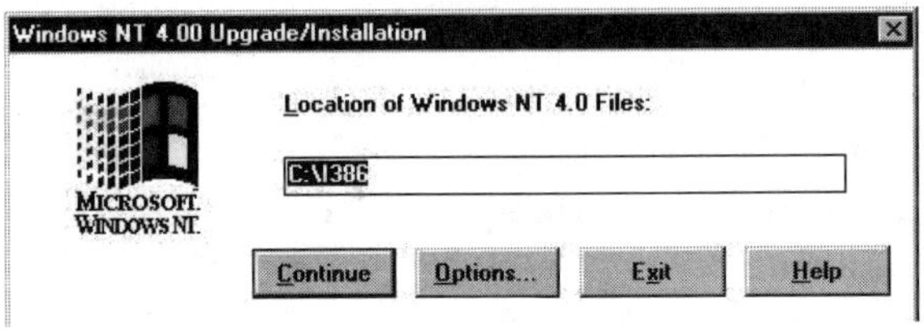

Figure 2–39
Upgrading NT using
WINNT32 instead of
WINNT

Windows NT 4.00 Upgrade/Installation

Location of Windows NT 4.0 Files:

C:\I386

MICROSOFT.
WINDOWS NT.

Continue   Options...   Exit   Help

Dual Boot

When NT installs over a previous operating system, it will automatically add that operating system to a hidden text file called **BOOT.INI**, which resides in the root directory of the boot partition. This ability to boot more than one operating system is often mistakenly called the "dual boot." The reason that dual boot is an improper term is the fact that **BOOT.INI** can boot many different OSs. It can even enable you to make multiple versions of Windows NT. See Chapter 4 for a detailed description of **BOOT.INI**.

Unattended (Automated) Installation

Marching through the many screens of the NT installation shows us that in order to load NT, you need to know the answers to a large number of questions that are asked by the multitude of installation screens. In the real world, we are often exposed to installation situations that would swamp a support person who was forced to install 30 or 40 systems. Most of the time in multiple system installations, the computers and the software to be installed are close to or exactly identical. In these situations, a more automatic installation would be helpful. To help automate the installation process, Microsoft gives the NT installation the ability to read data files for the answers it needs. This process is known as unattended installation. Unattended installation is accomplished by using switches with **WINNT** or **WINNT32** to read three different types of data files: Answer Files, Uniqueness Database Files, and the **SYSDIFF** utility. Each of these files performs a different function in the installation process and can be used separately or together. Let's look at each of these files and understand their respective jobs.

Answer Files

The answer file is a text file that holds the setup information for the system. This is the most common of the unattended installation files. Microsoft has provided an example file on the NT CD-ROM called **UNATTEND.TXT**. Here is a part of the **UNATTEND.TXT** file:

```
[Unattended]
OemPreinstall = no
ConfirmHardware = no
NtUpgrade = no
Win31Upgrade = no
TargetPath = WINNT
OverwriteOemFilesOnUpgrade = no
[UserData]
FullName = "Your User Name"
OrgName = "Your Organization Name"
ComputerName = COMPUTER_NAME
[GuiUnattended]
TimeZone = "(GMT-08:00) Pacific Time (US & Canada);
     Tijuana"
[Network]
Attend = yes
DetectAdapters = ""
InstallProtocols = ProtocolsSection
JoinDomain = Domain_To_Join
```

The answer file has a straightforward organizational structure. Major topics are divided into groups. Each group has a group name that is identified by square brackets such as "[UserData]" or "[Network]." Underneath each group are keywords and values. Microsoft predefines the groups and keywords; the values are what you want for those keywords.

The **UNATTEND.TXT** file is simple compared to what a real answer file would look like. While one could use the example **UNATTEND.TXT** file and edit it for their purposes, it is far more common to use the **SETUPMGR.EXE** program to create the answer file (see Figure 2–40).

Figure 2–40
The Windows NT
Setup Manager

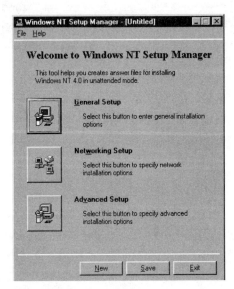

The Setup Manager is broken into three sections: General, Networking, and Advanced. The General section covers user information, display, directories, role of machine (not just role of server), Domain/Workgroup name, and licensing. The Networking section handles NICs, protocols, services, etc. Advanced has settings for converting file systems, display and keyboard drivers, as well as a few advanced settings that are used only in rare and specific situations.

NOTE: *Setup Manager also runs great on Windows 95 and 98. Handy for situations where there are not any NT systems.*

After running the Setup Manager, save the file. You can use any legal filename for the file, although you should pick an extension that lets you know they are answer files. The most practical extension is .TXT. If you stick with .TXT, Setup Manager will easily enable you to reload an answer file for editing. Here is a copy of a real-life answer file. The example is a little lengthy, but it really gives you an idea of the power of a true answer file.

NOTE: *Microsoft refers to the answer file as* **UNATTEND.TXT**.

```
[Unattended]
OemPreinstall = yes
NoWaitAfterTextMode = 0
NoWaitAfterGUIMode = 0
FileSystem = ConvertNTFS
ExtendOEMPartition = 0
ConfirmHardware = yes
NtUpgrade = no
Win31Upgrade = no
TargetPath = \WINNT
OverwriteOemFilesOnUpgrade = no
[UserData]
FullName = "Mike Meyers"
OrgName = "Total Seminars"
ComputerName = ACCT03
ProductId = "427-7777777"
[GuiUnattended]
OemSkipWelcome = 0
OEMBlankAdminPassword = 0
TimeZone = "(GMT-06:00) Central Time (US & Canada)"
[Display]
ConfigureAtLogon = 0
BitsPerPel = 8
XResolution = 640
YResolution = 480
```

```
VRefresh = 60
AutoConfirm = 1
[Modem]
InstallModem = ModemParameters
[ModemParameters]
COM1 = "USR 56K," "3COM"
[Network]
DetectAdapters = DetectAdaptersSection
InstallProtocols = ProtocolsSection
InstallServices = ServicesSection
JoinDomain = Total
[DetectAdaptersSection]
LimitTo = AM1500T2
AM1500T2 = AM1500T2ParamSection
[AM1500T2ParamSection]
InterruptNumber = 10
IOBaseAddress = 300
!AutoNetInterfaceType = ISA
!AutoNetBusNumber = 0
[ProtocolsSection]
NBF = NBFParamSection
TC = TCParamSection
[NBFParamSection]
[TCParamSection]
DHCP = yes
[ServicesSection]
RAS = RASParamSection
[RASParamSection]
PortSections = PortSection1
DialoutProtocols = TCP/IP
[PortSection1]
PortName = COM1
DeviceType = Modem
PortUsage = DialOut
```

To use an answer file, run the **WINNT** or **WINNT32** program:

```
WINNT /S:<location of installation files> /U:<path and name
    of answer file>
```

You have to use the /S option when you are using the /U. Here is a real-world example:

```
WINNT /S:E:\I386 /U:C:\IFILES\ACCT3.ANS
```

Uniqueness Database Files

The problem with answer files is that they contain a lot of information that is unique only to one machine. Some of the unique items are things like the username and name of the computer, meaning that every computer is going to need its own answer file. Creating a unique answer file for each computer would still be faster than manually installing NT, but this process would require creating one answer file, then editing it and saving it under a different name for each machine. It would be nice to use an answer file, but to have another file that holds the unique information for each computer. This second file would have to be more like a database, because it would really be a list of the variables you want to change. You would have to load this file with the **WINNT** command, but you would also say which set of variables you would want to use.

These files do exist, and they are known as *Uniqueness Database Files* (UDF). UDFs are text files, just like answer files. They are designed to store the information that is specific to individual systems. The only down side to UDFs is that there is no handy application to create them. They have to be made in a text editor. The best way to understand how UDFs work is to give an example. Let's say that there are 60 computers that need to have NT Workstation installed. All of the machines are identical, except for the username and the computer name. They will be installed using the real-world answer file described earlier. In the answer file, the two variables that will change from machine-to-machine are under the [UserData] group:

```
FullName = "User Name"
ComputerName = Name of Computer
```

All UDFs should start with a [UniqueIds] group. **WINNT** uses the [UniqueIDs] group to determine which set of data to use. Under this group, each ID is defined by any variable you want to use, although most everyone uses a short, sequential, alphanumeric variable, such as **a1**, **a2**, **a3** . . . , or **id1**, **id2**, **id3**, . . . This variable is followed by an equal sign and the answer file groups that need to be changed for that entry. In our example, the only group that is being changed is the UserData group, so the [UniqueIds] group in the UDF will look like this example:

```
[UniqueIds]
id1 = UserData
id2 = UserData
id3 = UserData
id4 = UserData
   . . .
id60 = UserData
```

For each Unique ID, a group has to be made for every group in the answer file that you want to change. Because we are only changing the UserData group, the rest of the example UDF will look like the following example.

```
[id1:UserData]
FullName="Brian Schwarz"
ComputerName= ACCT01
[id2:UserData]
FullName="Laura Trefil"
ComputerName= ACCT02
[id3:UserData]
FullName="Mike Meyers"
ComputerName= ACCT03
 . . .
[id60:UserData]
FullName="John Phelps"
ComputerName= ACCT60
```

To use a UDF, run the **WINNT** or **WINNT32** program:

```
WINNT /S:<location of installation files> /U:<path and name
     of answer file> /UDF:<ID Number>,<path and name of
     UDF file>
```

Again, you have to use the /S option when you are using the /U. Here is a real-world example:

```
WINNT /S:E:\I386 /U:C:\IFILES\ACCT3.ANS
     /UDF:ID2,C:\IFILES\ACCT.UDF
```

SYSDIFF.EXE

While answer files and UDFs are great for installing NT, there are situations where you would like to make a new install of NT that mirrors exactly an existing machine. In particular, any NT installation will have a number of applications installed after the installation. It would be nice to have a copy of all the files and registry settings to make a new NT installation have all of the same applications, settings and files that another NT system has installed.

Microsoft provides a fascinating tool called **SYSDIFF** that can be used to take a "snapshot" of an existing NT installation. A snapshot is a binary file that stores all of the aspects of an NT installation, including complete applications, registry settings, etc. As you may imagine, because the snapshot contains copies of these files and settings, it can be massive. **SYSDIFF** can compare that snapshot to another NT machine's installation—including applications that have been installed—and create a "difference" file that can be applied to other NT installations to make them identical. **SYSDIFF.EXE** can be found on the NT CD-ROM in the **\SUPPORT\DEPTOOLS\I386** directory. **SYSDIFF** only works on Windows NT.

It takes usually three steps to use **SYSDIFF** successfully. First, run **SYSDIFF** to create a snapshot of a basic NT installation. Second, install the desired applications on the same system and run **SYSDIFF** a second time to create a difference file. This difference file will hold all of the files and registry settings of the applications. Third, copy the difference file to other basic NT installations and use **SYSDIFF** to apply the difference file to the basic NT installations. This process will, in essence, instantly install all of the applications from the original system. Optionally, **SYSDIFF** can create an INF file that will enable these applications to be installed during the installation of NT, during either a manual or an unattended install.

To perform these many different functions, **SYSDIFF** can be run in five different ways: **SNAP**, **DIFF**, **APPLY**, **INF**, and **DUMP**. These items are run as switches after the **SYSDIFF** command. Running **SYSDIFF** without switches is meaningless.

SNAP   `SYSDIFF /SNAP [/log:<name of logfile>] <snapshot file>`

This command creates the snapshot of the system and records it to the snapshot file. Snapshot files can have any legal filename, but try to avoid known filenames such as TXT or REG to prevent confusion. I usually do not give snapshot files an extension. The **/LOG** switch is optional and rarely used in the real world. Here is a real-world example:

`SYSDIFF /SNAP D:\SNAPS\BASIC`

DIFF   `SYSDIFF /DIFF [/c:title] [/log:<name of logfile>]`
`<snapshot file> <difference file>`

The **DIFF** function makes a difference file by creating a second snapshot of the system, comparing it to an existing snapshot, and removing all of the registry settings and files that are the same. The **/c:title** gives the difference file a title that can sometimes be handy when you are dealing with a number of difference files. The **/c** switch is optional. Here is a real-world example of **DIFF** in action:

`SYSDIFF /DIFF D:\SNAPS\BASIC C:\SNAPS\DIFF1`

APPLY   `SYSDIFF /APPLY /m [/log:<name of logfile>] <difference`
`file>`

The **APPLY** function applies a difference file to a system, placing all of the files and registry settings into the system. The **/m** option tells NT to place all of the per-user differences into the Default user profile as opposed to the profile of the currently logged in user.

```
SYSDIFF /APPLY /M G:\SNAPS\DIFF1
```

INF   SYSDIFF /INF /M [/U] <difference file> <OEM Root>

The **INF** switch is used to apply differences during the installation of a new system, as opposed to using the **/APPLY** after the installation. The **/U** option says to make the INF file Unicode text as opposed to the usual ANSI text. When this line is run, two files are created, the INF and a **CMDLINES.TXT** file. These files are placed into a directory called **\OEM**. The OEM Root is the location of the directory where the **OEM** directory will be placed.

```
SYSDIFF /INF /M D:\SNAPS\DIFF1 C:\NTINSTAL
```

The INF file will take on the name of the difference file. You can then use the INF file with **WINNT** or **WINNT32**:

```
WINNT /I:<name of INF file>
```

DUMP   SYSDIFF /DUMP <difference file> <dump file>

The **DUMP** switch is used to create a dump file that lists the changes to be found in a difference file. The dump file is a text file and can be handy as long as the differences are not so great that it becomes unreadable. This option is rarely used. Here is a typical **DUMP** line:

```
SYSDIFF /DUMP D:\SNAPS\DIFF1 D:\SNAPS\DUMP1.
```

IMPORTANT: Before you use the extremely powerful (and thus extremely dangerous) **SYSDIFF** *command, make sure that you have* **SYSDIFF.INI** *in the same directory as* **SYSDIFF.EXE**. **SYSDIFF.INI** *defines all the things* **SYSDIFF** *should exclude when it creates a difference file. By default,* **SYSDIFF.INI** *excludes all the registry settings, system files, and hardware settings from the difference file. If you do not have* **SYSDIFF.INI** *in the same directory as* **SYSDIFF.EXE**, *that difference file will contain all those normally excluded files and settings. Imagine how devastating it would be to apply incorrect hardware and system settings to a new machine when you had only meant to put a copy of Microsoft Office on it. This action would totally trash the new system, requiring you to spend the time to rebuild NT on that new machine.* **SYSDIFF** *is designed to speed up software installations on different machines, but without* **SYSDIFF.INI** *in the same directory as the executable,* **SYSDIFF** *will cost you many hours of frustrating rebuilding.*

Uninstalling NT

Uninstalling Windows NT is a rather brutal but simple affair. There is no pretty uninstall program as there is for Windows 95 and 98. If you want to get rid of Windows NT, you wipe it out and replace it with another operating system. This removal process has basically four steps. First, back up any desired data. Second, delete any NTFS volumes. Third, delete the **WINNT** directory. Fourth, delete the boot files and add a new operating system.

Backing Up

No such thing exists as a computer that has no important data, with the exception of a machine that has just been set up. Do not forget to poke around for data files for applications, templates, special fonts, address books, mail folders, and the like. Most users do not think about these things until they get the new system and realize they are gone.

Removing an NTFS Volume

Removing an NTFS volume requires you to purchase and use third-party software utilities or run through the tedious floppy disk swapping procedure built into NT. You cannot simply boot to a floppy and run FDISK. The FDISK utility that comes with DOS and Windows 95 and 98 cannot delete NTFS logical drives in an extended partition.

The easiest way to wipe out an NTFS partition is with third-party utilities. My personal favorite is Partition Magic by PowerQuest, due to its ease of use and the fact that it is fully aware of NTFS. A good second choice is DrivePro by Microhouse—but stay away from DrivePro unless you are familiar with partition tables. This program is a little on the "techie" side.

If you do not have a third-party utility, you can use the NT boot floppies. Boot to Disk 1 and insert Disks 2 and 3 when prompted. When you get to the partitions screen, select the NTFS partition and press **D** to delete it. Press **L** to confirm the delete and press **F3** twice to exit setup. The NTFS partition will be gone, and you probably will not be able to boot to NT unless you installed NT on a FAT partition.

Delete the NT Directories

If the **\WINNT** directory was not on an NTFS partition, you will have to
delete it now. If it was, it is already gone and you can skip this step. Here
is where you need a DOS or a Windows 95 and 98 bootable floppy. Make
sure the bootable floppy also has the following programs:

FORMAT

FDISK

SYS

DELTREE

ATTRIB

Boot to the floppy, locate the **\WINNT** directory and use **DELTREE** to eliminate it. Do not forget to get the Program Files directory (**PROGRA~1** in
short name) and the hidden **RECYCLER** directory.

NOTE: *To see hidden files or directories, type* **DIR /AH**. *To unhide them, type*
ATTRIB -r -s -h <name of hidden directory or file>.

Delete the NT Boot Files and Add a New Operating System.

If your boot partition is FAT, you will have to remove the NT boot files.
Use the **ATTRIB** and the **DEL** commands to remove:

NTLDR

NTDETECT.COM

BOOT.INI

PAGEFILE.SYS

BOOTSEC.DOS

NTBOOTDD.SYS (may not be there, only used by SCSI devices without
boot ROMs)

After the files are deleted, use the **SYS c:** command to add the new
operating system. NT is gone.

Questions

1. Windows NT can create and run on what type of formats (choose all that apply)?

   a. NTFS

   b. HPFS

   c. FAT16

   d. FAT32

2. You have 30 systems that need to have NT Workstation installed unattended. You are told to use the **WINNT /U** command. What type of file must be used with the **/U** switch?

   a. **SYSDIFF.EXE**

   b. UDF

   c. **WINDIFF.EXE**

   d. Unattended Answer File

3. Which is not a valid switch for the **SYSDIFF.EXE** program?

   a. **/APPLY**

   b. **/DUMP**

   c. **/CLEAR**

   d. **/DIFF**

4. You have been given the job of installing NT and a set of applications on 50 identical systems. These systems will be on the network and must be able to log into a domain. What three files do you need?

   a. An INF file

   b. The **SYSDIFF.EXE** program

   c. A file called **UNATTEND.TXT**

   d. A UDF file

5. **SYSDIFF** is used to automate the installation of

   a. Applications

   b. The NT operating system

   c. Hardware devices

   d. Device drivers

6. You have 17 computers on which you need to install NT Workstation; there are three different models of systems. All of the systems have 4GB hard drives, divided into 500MB boot partitions and 3.5GB extended partitions, formatted as FAT16. The systems can boot to Windows 95. There are four different applications that must be installed on every system. You must use an unattended installation. It would be nice if you could: 1. Get the users on the same domain, 2. Convert the FAT16 partitions to NTFS, and 3. Get the applications installed. You install NT workstation on one machine, create an **UNATTEND.TXT** file and create a UDF for usernames and domain. You take a snapshot on the installed machine, install the applications, then create a difference file. This process will result in

   a. The required result and two of the optional results

   b. The required result and one of the optional results

   c. The required result and none of the optional results

   d. None of the required results

7. You have an NT Workstation system (System A) with a CD-ROM drive. An NT Server installation CD-ROM is in System A's CD-ROM drive. The Workstation system is connected to a brand-new machine (System B) that has no operating system or CD-ROM drive. You have decided to install NT Server on System B. Which of the following would not be an acceptable option? (Choose all that apply):

   a. Share System A's CD-ROM. Use a Network Client Disk to boot System B and access System A's CD-ROM. Run **WINNT /B** from the **\I386** directory of the shared CD-ROM.

   b. Share System A's CD-ROM. Use a Network Client Disk to boot System B and access System A's CD-ROM. Run **WINNT /OX** from the **\I386** directory of the shared CD-ROM.

   c. Install DOS on System B. Configure DOS's built-in networking software. Share System A's CD-ROM. Access System A's CD-ROM and run **WINNT /B** from the **\I386** directory of the shared CD-ROM.

   d. Install Windows 95 on System B. Configure Windows 95's built-in networking software. Share System A's CD-ROM. Access System A's CD-ROM and run **WINNT /B** from the **\I386** directory of the shared CD-ROM.

8. Which of the following cannot be achieved with **UNATTEND.TXT**?

    a. Change a FAT16 partition to NTFS

    b. Set the domain name

    c. Set the username

    d. **UNATTEND.TXT** can do all of the above

9. The first step to removing NT from a system is to

    a. Delete the primary partition

    b. Backup the registry

    c. Backup any data you want to keep

    d. Run **ROLLBACK.EXE**

10. According to Microsoft, how much RAM is required for an Intel-based NT system?

    a. 8MB

    b. 12MB

    c. 16MB

    d. 24MB

Answers

1. a, c—NT can read HPFS, but it cannot create it. NT 4.0 is completely incompatible with FAT32 and it certainly cannot create it.

2. d—Only unattended answer files are used with **/U**—There is no such thing as **WINDIFF**.

3. c—There is no switch for **SYSDIFF** called **/CLEAR**.

4. b, c, d—You do not need to make an INF file. Just use **SYSDIFF** **/APPLY** on each machine. Remember, Microsoft refers to all answer files as **UNATTEND.TXT**.

5. a—**SYSDIFF** is used to automate the installation of applications only.

6. d—This one is fraught with errors, but the biggest one is the fact that you only created one **UNATTEND.TXT** file for three different models. That alone will prevent any of the results.

7. b, c—**WINNT /OX** will not install NT; it only makes boot diskettes. DOS does not have any built-in networking software.

8. d—**UNATTEND.TXT** can perform all of these functions. Run Setup Manager and see for yourself.

9. c—Backup data you want to keep. Note **ROLLBACK.EXE** is a dangerous program on the NT Workstation CD-ROM and is designed to wipe out the registry for reinstalls. Never run this program.

10. b—Microsoft says that you need 12MB for Intel and 16MB for RISC-based systems.

CHAPTER **3**

The Control Panel and Registry

The real work of Windows NT comes after the operating system is installed. Every NT installation is unique in one way or another—different CPUs, amounts of RAM, number of drive partitions, different cards and software, etc. Each piece of hardware and software might need specialized "tweaking" to make sure the particular component is running optimally. Certainly, Microsoft does a heroic job of making as many of these "tweaks" and "configurations" as automated as possible. But every NT installation will require some amount of manual configuration. These configurations will vary from system-to-system, but they include issues such as adding a new piece of hardware, optimizing hard drive performance, or customizing the desktop or system sound events.

Properly configuring Windows NT requires mastery of two separate items: the control panel and the registry. Although most configuration work is handled by the control panel, both areas control certain aspects of configuration, and both are required to accomplish all the tasks of configuration. In this chapter, we will take an exhaustive tour of the control panel, followed by a quick look at some configuration tricks that need to be performed by direct manipulation of the registry.

Control Panel or Manual—It Is Always the Registry

All of the NT system's settings are stored in the registry. The *registry* is a single database containing the values that define the working environment for the Windows NT operating system and any service or device installed on the computer. The registry might be a single database but consists of a number of files in the **\WINNT\SYSTEM32\CONFIG** folder that are read into memory by NT on startup to create the registry. When NT is configured in any way, the configuration is performed by editing settings in the registry. The registry can be directly edited through the use of one of two programs: **REGEDT32.EXE** or **REGEDIT.EXE** (see Figure 3–1), but this method is rarely done. (We will see these programs again at the end of this chapter).

Direct manipulation of the registry can be a daunting task. The registry is a phenomenally complicated database, difficult to navigate and completely non-intuitive (see Figure 3–2).

For a safer and certainly easier manipulation of the registry, Windows NT provides a series of specialized mini-programs called *applets*, which are stored as a group into a special folder called the Control Panel. Each applet is designed to handle a specific aspect of the configuration of an

Figure 3–1
REGEDIT.EXE

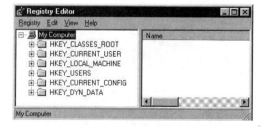

Figure 3–2
The registry is complicated.

NT system. The registry itself will be discussed in detail in the registry section later in this chapter. For now, we will stick to the easy way to edit the registry—the Control Panel.

Control Panel

The Control Panel folder contains applets for configuring the Windows NT operating system. Each applet contained within the Control Panel folder manipulates the registry to achieve a specific function. The applets provide a *Graphical User Interface* (GUI) to the registry, thus enabling much easier configuration changes to be made to the Windows NT operating system. This section will cover the applets on which the test-taker will potentially be tested. The Control Panel discussion focuses on the Windows NT Server, but the configuration options apply to both NT Server and NT Workstation. The differences are minimal, with NT Server having a few extra—but no fewer—applets.

To open the Control Panel folder, click the Start menu, point to Settings, and then click the Control Panel (see Figure 3–3). Examples of some of the tasks that can be accomplished through the Control Panel folder include the following:

■ Enabling users to configure their own desktop environment

■ Installing new hardware

■ Controlling the configuration for each Windows NT-based workstation, regardless of which user is logged on

No special order exists for the icons in the Control Panel, nor is there a particularly good way of organizing their discussion. So, for the sake of convenience, we will simply start at the top and work our way down through the icons as they are placed by a default NT installation.

Figure 3–3
Control Panel

NOTE: *Remember that these are the applets seen in most NT installations. Individual installation might have less—probably more—applets.*

Accessibility Options

The Accessibility Options applet enables the user to configure some keyboard and mouse settings, sound events, and more. Some of these options are downright handy, so take note. The Keyboard tab enables a user to specify how the Shift, Alt, and Control keys respond, among other settings. The Sound tab enables the configuration for visual warnings and displaying captions for speech and sound. The Mouse tab provides the capacity to control the pointer with the numeric keypad. The General tab configures automatic reset for turning off accessibility features after a specified idle time, notification for sound, and support for "SerialKey" devices that enable alternative access to keyboard and mouse features (see Figure 3–4).

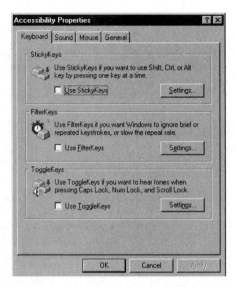

Figure 3–4
Accessibility options

Add/Remove Programs

The Add/Remove Programs applet in the Control Panel enables administrators to add and remove application software and Windows NT components. The operation is fairly straight-forward. To add a program, select the Add/Remove button under the Install/Uninstall tab. The tab will automatically scan the floppy and CD-ROM drives for executable programs called `setup` or `Install`. If the application is elsewhere or has a non-standard name, use the browse feature. Similarly, to uninstall a program that was previously installed, select the program in the application list and click the Add/Remove button. Only programs that were installed using the Add/Remove Program applet *and* the Install/Uninstall *Application Programming Interface* (API) will appear on the installed application list. Any program that is not on the list must be removed manually, i.e., by deleting the files and folders in Windows Explorer or from the command prompt, as shown in Figure 3–5.

Components of Windows NT can be added or removed by selecting the Windows NT Setup tab. Installed components show up with a check mark in the little boxes on the left. White checked boxes mean that all components within the heading have been installed. Gray checked boxes mean

Figure 3–5
Add/Remove
Programs

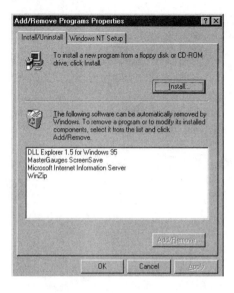

Figure 3–6
Add/Remove
Windows NT
components

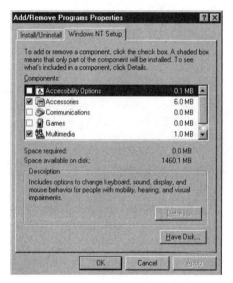

that some programs available under that heading have been installed. White unchecked boxes mean that none of the programs available under that heading have been installed. To change items, simply check or uncheck components and click OK (Figure 3–6). This process might require a Windows NT CD-ROM or shared network installation files if the user has not copied the **I386** folder to the hard drive.

Console (MS-DOS)

The Console applet enables the configuration of the default appearance of character-based windows and command prompt windows. Once configured, all newly created console windows will inherit the settings. Four tabs are available: Options, Font, Layout, and Colors (Figure 3–7).

This screen can also be accessed for a specific, character-based application by starting the application, bringing it to a window, right-clicking the MS-DOS icon and selecting Properties. This action enables different, character-based applications to have their own unique settings.

Date/Time

This applet controls the settings for the system date and time. The two tabs available are Date and Time and Time Zone. Under the Time Zone tab is the option for automatically adjusting for Daylight Savings Time (see Figure 3–8).

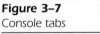

Figure 3–7
Console tabs

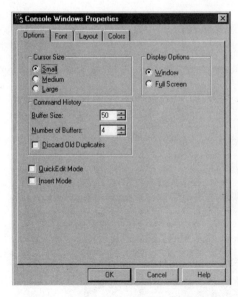

Display

Located in the Control Panel, the Display applet's Settings tab enables the configuration of the number of colors, the video resolution, font sizes, and the refresh frequency (Figure 3–9). Also available for configuration are Background, Screen Saver, Appearance, and Plus! settings tabs.

Figure 3–8
Date/Time properties

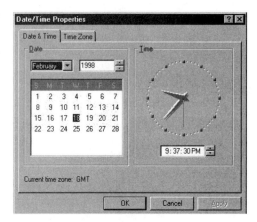

Figure 3–9
The Display applet

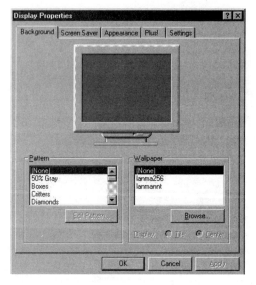

The following options are configurable through the Display applet:

1. *Color Palette*—Lists the color options for the display adapter

2. *Desktop Area*—Enables the configuration of the desktop size used by the display. The larger the desktop area, the smaller the icons will appear on the monitor.

3. *Font Size*—This option sets the smaller or larger display font sizes.

4. *Refresh Frequency*—This option configures the frequency of the screen refresh. Only use this option for high-resolution drivers. Always choose the lower refresh rate if unsure of the proper setting for the driver, to avoid potentially damaging the monitor.

5. *List All Modes* (button)—This option simultaneously configures color, desktop, and refresh.

6. *Test* (button)—This option provides testing for a video driver when the old and new drivers do not conflict. For example, the VGA driver cannot be installed with the SVGA driver because of conflict with the VGA driver.

7. *Display Type* (button)—Use this option to load or unload the display device drivers. You must have the user right to "load and unload device drivers" to perform this function. By default, only the Administrators group has this capability.

Fonts

This applet is used to install, remove, change, or view fonts for the Windows NT system. The four tabs available under the Options . . . View menu for configurations are Folder, View, Tile Types, and TrueType Fonts (Figure 3–10).

Internet

This applet is used to determine which server will be utilized for access as a proxy server for Internet access. The proxy server can be named, and the user can also name computers, domains, and ports to skip over the proxy. This option is handy for accessing an Internet server that is on the LAN (Figure 3–11).

Figure 3–10
Fonts applet

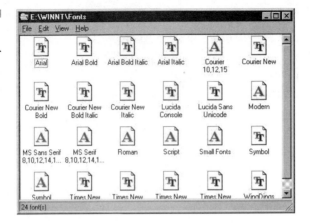

Figure 3–11
Internet applet

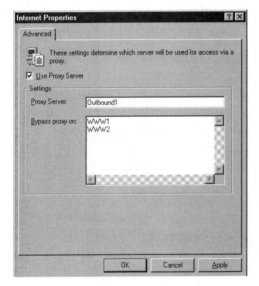

Keyboard

This applet configures the settings for the keyboard and how the keyboard reacts to use. Three option tabs, Speed, Input Locales, and General, are available. Under the Speed tab, the user can configure the character rate and the cursor blink rate. The Input Locales tab provides support for different countries. Various countries have different standard keyboard layouts. Compared with the U.S. keyboard layout, for example, the French keyboard layout supports characters specific to the French language, such as accented letters, and some keys are in different positions. The "z" and "w" are reversed, for example, relative to their position on the U.S. keyboard. Whenever NT utilizes a different script, such as Russian or Greek, the user must change the keyboard layout. The General tab specifies the physical keyboard device type itself. If the user wants to change the keyboard device, he or she will be required to supply the device drivers for the installation process. Before changing to a different keyboard device, verify that it is compatible with the Windows NT 4.0 operating system (see Figure 3–12).

Licensing

The Licensing applet is used to add or remove licenses from the Windows NT server. The choice exists of adding licenses on a Per Server or Per Seat basis. In Per Server licensing, each client's access is assigned to a particular server and is enabled on one concurrent connection to that server. Specify the amount of Client Access Licenses for concurrent connections that have been purchased for that server. The Per Seat mode requires a Client Access License for each workstation that will access the Windows NT server. Because you license the workstation, the workstation can access any Windows NT server on the network at no additional charge. This mode is more practical if users are required to access a multitude of

Figure 3–12
Keyboard applet

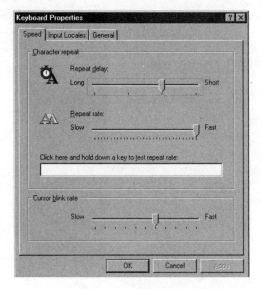

Windows NT servers. The Per Server license agreement enables you to change to a Per Seat mode later. This function does not work in reverse, however. You cannot change from a Per Seat mode to a Per Server mode. So if you are uncertain which mode to choose, select the Per Server mode, thus enabling a later conversion to Per Seat mode. The Replication button enables you to set how the computer replicates licenses to a master server or to an enterprise server (Figure 3–13).

Another important tool for licensing is the License Manager. While not a Control Panel applet, its use with the Licensing applet warrants its discussion here. The License Manager enables administrators to track license use to stay within Microsoft's legal license requirements. The License Manager can keep track of all licenses within any domain to which it has access. A particular PDC is defined as the *master server*. The master server receives replicated license information from the other PDCs, creating a single license database. The License Manager is also used to set how often the other PDCs report to the master server (Figure 3–14).

For the License Manager to operate, the License Logging Service must be running. Check the Services applet to make sure it is running (see Figure–15).

Figure 3–13
Licensing applet

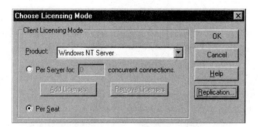

Figure 3–14
License Manager

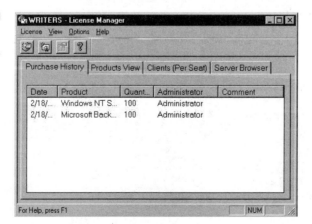

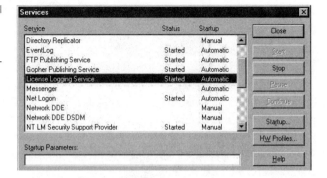

Figure 3–15
License Logging
Service

Figure 3–16
Mail applet

Mail

The Mail applet adds and configures profiles for use with messaging applications. The General tab is for Microsoft Exchange Profiles. The default profile for starting Windows messaging is selected at the bottom of the window (Figure 3–16).

Modems

This applet is used to automatically detect modem devices attached to the computer and to configure modems already installed (Figure 3–17). Three basic choices exist here: choosing from a built-in list of modem device drivers, supplying your own driver if the modem does not appear on the list, or supplying your own driver to replace an older modem driver.

Figure 3–17
Modem applet

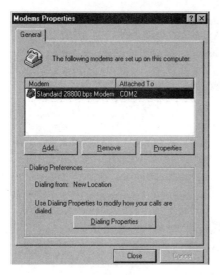

Figure 3–18
Mouse applet

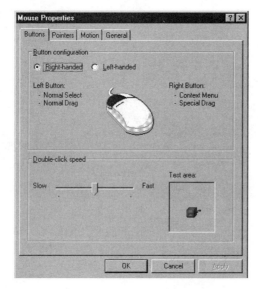

Mouse

This applet configures the mouse device in various ways: for right-handed or left-handed use under the Buttons tab, the type of pointer desired under the Pointers tab, and the pointer speed under the Motion tab. The General tab is where the user can install a different device driver for a different, compatible mouse device (Figure 3–18).

Multimedia

This applet configures sound parameters for audio, video, MIDI, CD music, and devices. The Audio tab provides control over the volume for the speaker and the microphone, with the capacity to switch to a preferred recording device and type of quality. The Video tab provides the capacity to present videos in a Window or Full screen mode preference. The MIDI tab is for setting up the MIDI output port to a MIDI input device. The CD Music tab sets the drive letter of the CD-ROM device and the headphone volume. The Devices tab lets the user configure new multimedia device drivers and remove or verify the properties of a specific device driver (Figure–19).

Network

The Network applet is one of the more popular applets used frequently within the Control Panel, which is where the following configurations are made:

■ *Identification tab* (Figure 3–20)—This tab changes the name of the Windows NT server and the domain name in which it resides. To change either option, click the Change button under the Identification tab, make the appropriate change to the Computer Name field and/or Domain Name field, and click OK. The system should be shut down and restarted for the changes to take effect.

Figure 3–19
Multimedia applet

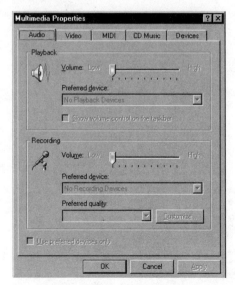

■ *Services tab* (Figure 3–21) —This tab enables the user to add or remove properties, determine properties of a particular network service, or update a network service. Clicking on the Add button displays a list of available services. You must supply the drivers for the desired service to be installed. Usually, these drivers will be on the Windows NT CD-ROM.

Figure 3–20
Identification

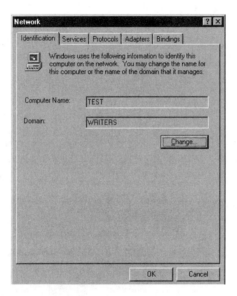

Figure 3–21
Services

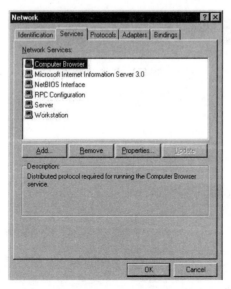

■ *Protocols tab* (Figure 3–22) —This tab enables the user to add or remove, determine properties of, or update a specific protocol. The wise administrator will not add any additional protocols within this window. The protocols that are installed are bound to the *Network Interface* (NIC). By adding unnecessary protocols, it requires more service out of the NIC. By clicking the Add button, a list of available protocols is displayed. The user is required to supply the necessary driver for the protocol to be installed. Usually, this would be the Windows NT CD-ROM. Any protocols that are installed will require the system to be shut down and restarted for changes to take effect.

■ *Adapters tab* (Figure 3–23)—This tab enables you to add or remove, determine properties, or update any network adapter or NICs that are physically installed on the system. By clicking the Add button, a list of available network adapters is displayed. You are required to supply the necessary driver for the network adapter you want to install. Usually, this would be the Windows NT CD-ROM. Any network adapter that you install will require the system to be shut down and restarted for changes to take effect. This process enables the adapter to initialize and the installed protocols to bind to the newly installed adapter.

Figure 3–22
Protocols

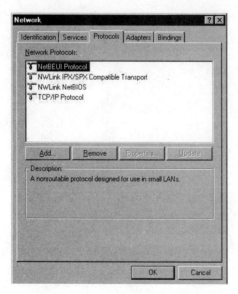

■ *Bindings tab* (Figure 3–24)—This tab enables you to set the precedence in which the protocols are bound to the network adapter. For better performance within the networking environment, always place the most utilized protocol first for communication purposes. You can move a protocol for a specific service by highlighting it and clicking the Move Up button to the desired order. Any changes made will require that the system be shut down and restarted.

ODBC

This applet stores the information on how to connect to the data provider. The six tabs that are available are User DSN, System DSN, File DSN, ODBC Drivers, Tracing, and the About tab. The acronym "DSN" stands for data-source name. The User data source is only visible to you and can only be used on the current machine. The System DSN stores the information about how to connect to the indicated data provider and is visible to all users on the computer, including NT services. The File DSN tab can be shared by users who have the same drivers installed locally. The ODBC Drivers tab allows ODBC-enabled programs to obtain information from ODBC data sources. The Tracing tab can be useful in troubleshooting ODBC communication problems to a data source. To verify which version of the ODBC drivers are being utilized by the system, check under the About tab (as in Figure 3–25).

Figure 3–23
Adapters

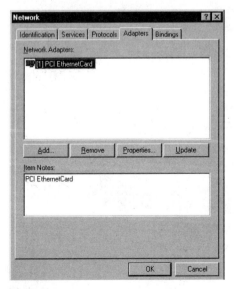

Figure 3–24
Bindings

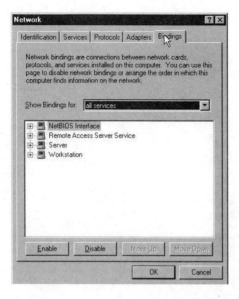

Figure 3–25
ODBC applet

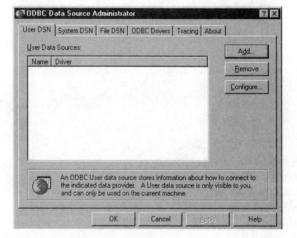

PC Card (PCMCIA)

The *PC Card* (PCMCIA) applet, located within the Control Panel, shows which PCMCIA devices are installed on the server and which socket(s) they occupy (Figure 3–26).

The Controller tab will give you the information of Input/Output Range and the Memory Range of the highlighted PC Card (Figure 3–27).

Figure 3–26
The PC Card
(PCMCIA) applet

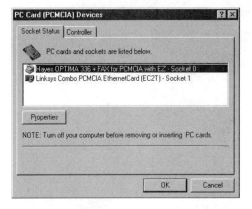

Figure 3–27
The Controller tab

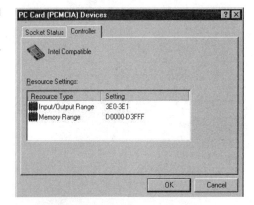

Figure 3–28
The Properties button

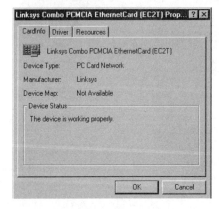

The Properties button contains information for CardInfo, Driver, and Resources of the highlighted PC Card device (Figure 3–28).

All the information obtained from the PC Card applet can be useful in troubleshooting device conflict. Always remember to shut down the server when adding or removing any PC Cards. Windows NT recognizes changes to all connected devices.

Ports

The Ports applet in the Control Panel enables you to assign COM ports to serial ports and devices (Figure 3–29). The Ports icon offers the following options:

- Settings—This option is used to configure the port settings, such as flow control and baud rate.
- Add—This option enables up to 256 COM ports to be added to the server.
- Delete—This option simply enables the deletion of a COM port.

Ports show up only when they have free resources. If a device is connected to a serial port, or if a device is using the same IRQ required by a port, the port will not be available—nor will it even appear on the port list. For example, a typical system will have two built-in serial ports that get the default resources of COM 1 and COM 2 (IRQs 4 and 3, respectively). If you have a mouse attached to Serial 1 and it is set to COM 1, only COM 2 would appear as an available port. Access the registry through **REGEDT32.EXE** to determine what device is using an unlisted serial port. The location of the subkey is

```
HKEY_LOCAL_MACHINE\HARDWARE\Description\System\Multifunction
     Adapter
```

or

```
HKEY_LOCAL_MACHINE\HARDWARE\Description\System\EisaAdapter\0
     \SerialController
```

Figure 3–29
Ports applet

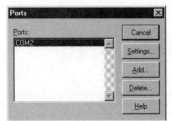

Located under the SerialController key are the subkeys for each port within the system. COM 1 would be specified with 0 continuing in ascending order for the next COM port. When a mouse is attached to the port on the system, a subkey for \PointerPeripheral will be visible. When another device is attached to this port or is using the same IRQ, the port is being utilized by another device.

Printers

The Printers applet configures all printing within the system. By double-clicking on the Add Printer icon, you will be prompted in a Wizard format to setup a new printer. Once a printer is installed you can reconfigure its properties and control the printing functionality as desired (Figure–30).

Regional Settings

The Regional Settings icon enables support for international setting for numbers, currency, time, date, and input locales (Figure 3–31).

SCSI Adapters and Tape Device Configuration

The SCSI Adapters applet and Tape Devices applet in the Control Panel enable the configuration and detection of new devices, including installing the driver software and starting the appropriate driver for the new device. After installing a SCSI device, the computer must be rebooted in order for the new device driver to initialize. Tape device installations do not require the computer to be rebooted. Otherwise these applets are virtually identical in form and function. Compare them side by side (Figure 3–32).

Figure 3–30
Printer applet

Figure 3–31
Regional settings

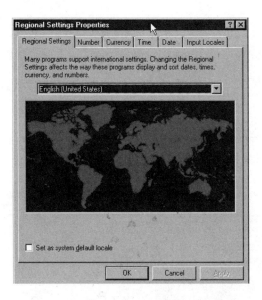

Figure 3–32
SCSI adapters and
tape devices

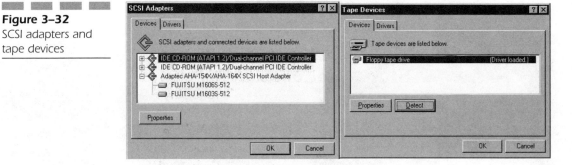

Both utilities have two option tabs: Devices and Drivers. The Detect button on the Devices tab is used to detect Tape device drivers automatically (Figure 3–33).

The Properties button in either applet will give descriptive information about the device, such as SCSI host adapter, firmware, and SCSI ID number. This information is useful when configuring multiple SCSI devices to avoid conflicts such as two devices sharing the same SCSI ID number (Figure 3–34).

The Add and Remove buttons on the Drivers tab removes device drivers. This option is also available within both applets (Figure 3–35).

Figure 3–33
Tape devices applet,
Detect button

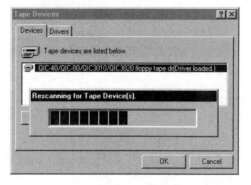

Figure 3–34
Properties button for
SCSI adapter

Figure 3–35
Add and Remove
buttons

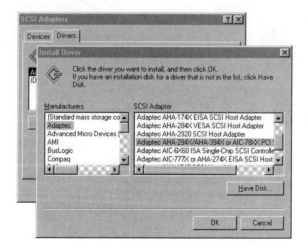

Server

This applet is used to view the server usage. You can also view the currently connected users to the Windows NT server, the shared resources, and files that are in use by a specific user. The server applet will enable you to disconnect users, shares, and files, selectively (Figure 3–36).

The Replication button enables you to configure the replication or copying of logon scripts for authenticating users and for redundancy to a Windows NT domain (See Chapter 8, "NT User Management," for details on directory replication). A master collection of logon scripts is maintained usually by the network administrator in the export directory. The default path for the export directory is **\WINNT\SYSTEM32\REPL\EXPORTS\SCRIPTS** and any of its subdirectories. This master collection is then distributed throughout the domain. The directory where the servers receive the copies is **\WINNT\SYSTEM32\REPL\IMPORTS\ SCRIPTS**. All files and subdirectories of the export directory are replicated or copied. This function helps balance the loads between the servers. If you have many users who need to receive the same file periodically, for example, you can replicate the file directory to several computers to prevent any one server from becoming overburdened. You can even replicate directories between servers/computers located in different domains. Export servers can export to domain names, and import computers can import from those domain names. This is a convenient way to set up directory replication for many computers. Each export server and import computer needs to specify only a few domain names for export or import, rather than a long list of many computer names (Figure 3–37).

The Alerts button is configured to send warning messages to a list of users and computers when the network thresholds are reached. When using this utility, the Alerter and Messenger services must be running on the destination computer. To verify that these two services are started, open the Services applet in the Control Panel.

Figure 3–36
Server applet

Figure 3–37
Directory replication

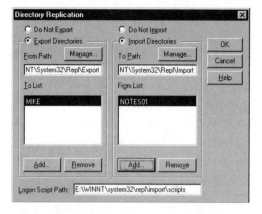

Figure 3–38
Services applet

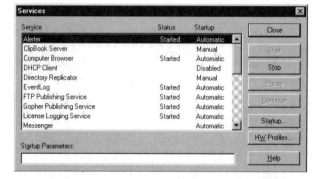

Services

The Service applet enables you to start and stop services selectively. A service is a background application used by other applications. Windows NT uses many different services. A default NT Server installation will have around thirty services running, as shown in Figure 3–38.

For example, when discussing the Licensing Applet earlier in this section, you were told to start the License Logging Service. The License Logging Service runs invisibly in the background, updating the License database. Individual services can be configured to run at startup, to show an interface on the desktop, and to run either in the system account (always runs) or only when a particular user is logged in (Figure 3–39).

Figure 3–39
License Logging
Service settings

Figure 3–40
Sounds applet

Sounds

This applet enables you to change the sounds that the Windows NT system uses for various functions. You can use the Windows NT Default scheme, no sounds, or you can add your own sound scheme to the system (Figure 3–40).

System

The System Applet is a hodgepodge of totally unrelated, but very important, functions separated into six tabs. The functions of these tabs vary from purely informational (the General tab) to handy personalizations (User Profiles tab) to critical system configuration and optimization (Performance tab). Most of these tabs are either on the MCSE exams, are critical to practical NT administration, or both. Let's begin with the most important of these, the Performance tab.

PERFORMANCE   Configuring virtual memory in Windows NT is almost a matter of doing nothing at all: NT handles most of the settings automatically and periodically updates itself. Windows NT maps a portion of the hard drive to make it think it is RAM, thus enabling more programs to be in memory than the actual system RAM would allow. The swapfile thus created on the hard drive is called **PAGEFILE.SYS**.

When first installed, NT creates a **PAGEFILE.SYS** on the hard drive, the size of which is based on the amount of system RAM plus 12MB. If the available free space on the drive is less than what it wants, NT will scale down all the way to 2MB for the **PAGEFILE.SYS**. That would also be a very big clue for you to get another hard drive.

The virtual memory settings can be checked and tweaked under the Performance tab in the System applet in the Control Panel, as shown in Figure 3–41. Select the Change button if you want to make changes, one of those rare instances of truth in advertising. If you change virtual memory settings manually, you need to shut down and restart the server for the changes to take effect.

Figure 3–42 shows the various options available for manipulating virtual memory.

NOTE: *You should occasionally check out the registry size located at the bottom of the Virtual Memory window as the Windows NT server is used over a period of time. If the current registry size swells beyond the maximum registry size, users might have problems logging into the server. Adjust the maximum registry size accordingly.*

Once a paging file is created, the registry size will not shrink below its original size. Any extra space within **PAGEFILE.SYS** will be available to the Virtual Memory Manager. If you create a paging file with the wrong amount of space, the Windows NT system will automatically open the System applet within the Control Panel after a user logs on, prompting you to reconfigure the Virtual Memory definition.

Figure 3–41
Virtual Memory,
Change button

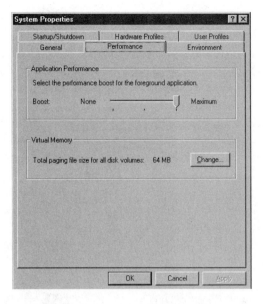

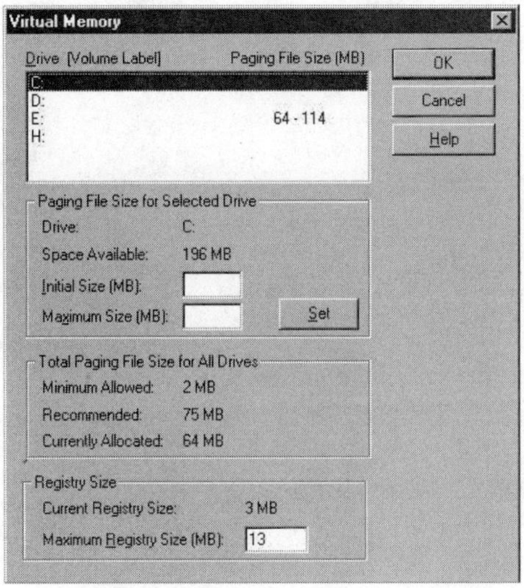

Figure 3–42
Virtual Memory
Definition

To enhance system performance when multiple disks are available, consider creating a paging file for each disk. Distribution of multiple paging files can increase system performance considerably. You can also improve system performance by moving the paging file off the `\WINNT_ROOT` directory, to avoid conflict between read or write requests to the disk. You might need to move the paging file off the boot partition to make more disk space available. If this action is necessary, be aware that this process blocks NT's capacity to create a **MEMORY.DMP** file in case of server recovery. In addition to the performance enhancements listed earlier, set the initial size of the paging file to the optimal size required by the system. By setting this option, you relieve the operating system of the task of enlarging the file on its own. All changes to virtual memory are NOT dynamic. You must reboot the system for changes to take effect.

The Performance tab also has a slider bar called Boost. This bar is used to change the amount of time given to the application running in the foreground. See Chapter 5, "NT Application Support," for details on how to use the Boost slider.

HARDWARE PROFILES   Hardware profiles define the devices and services that will load on startup. Hardware profiles can be altered to accommodate individual, user-specific needs, such as whether the user's laptop is docked or undocked. Creating a hardware profile for this type of scenario would prompt the user upon boot-up to choose between a docked or undocked laptop, loading only the necessary hardware drivers for that session. Three applets in the Control Panel—System, Devices, and Services—enable you to define hardware profiles.

A default hardware profile always exists within the Available Hardware Profiles list and is created when you install the operating system. Select the Hardware Profiles tab under the System applet in the Control Panel to view and manipulate the profiles (as in Figure 3–43).

Figure 3–43
Available hardware profiles

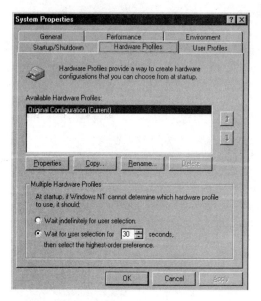

Using the Copy option button can easily create a new profile. This feature creates an exact copy of the default hardware profile that you can then modify. After you have created a new profile, you can determine the order in which the events will be executed. Simply use the up-and-down arrows to move the desired profile to the top of the list. In addition, when there are multiple hardware profiles available, you can require the user to select a profile or make the profile at the top of the list execute after a specified amount of time (in seconds). To override the automatic selection, press the space bar when prompted.

The Devices and Services Applets can also be used to modify hardware profiles. Each program has a Hardware Profiles button for configuration of a specific hardware profile (see Figure 3–44).

STARTUP/SHUTDOWN   The configuration properties for starting up or shutting down the Windows NT system are located in the System applet within the Control Panel, under the Startup/Shutdown tab. Two sections exist for configuring the operating system in the Startup/Shutdown tab. The top section, System Startup, configures which operating system will execute after a default time of 30 seconds without user intervention (see Figure 3–45). When Windows NT is the only operating system installed on the computer, the drop-down box for the Startup option will have the following options:

```
"Windows NT Server Version 4.00"
"Windows NT Server Version 4.00 (VGA mode)" /basevideo /sos
"MS-DOS"
```

When you view these settings, you are actually viewing the **BOOT.INI** file. If you have installed Windows NT on the same partition as MS-DOS and have converted that partition to NTFS, booting to an MS-DOS partition is no longer possible. The option in the Startup/Shutdown tab, however, will remain until the option has been edited out of the **BOOT.INI** file. See Chapter 4, "NT Boot Process," for more information.

Figure 3–44
Devices—HW Profiles
button

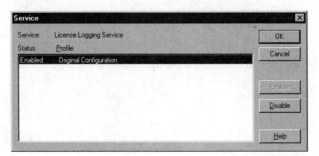

Figure 3–45
System startup

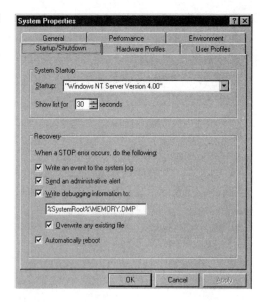

Several options are available under the Recovery section at the bottom of the Startup/Shutdown tab for configuring Windows NT. These options define how Windows NT recovers from an illegal interruption to the operating system and indicate which tasks should be performed. The following items are the available options:

■ Write an event to the system log—When enabled, this option logs an event in Event Viewer . . . System Log with interruption details, which can be interpreted with the help of a Microsoft systems engineer.

■ Send an administrative alert—When this option is enabled, the Windows NT system will send an alert to the administrator notifying him or her that the error has occurred.

■ Write debugging information to:—When selected, this option enables you to specify a filename to which the Windows NT system can write the contents of the system memory dump when a stop error occurs. Then, this file can be examined to diagnose what caused the system interruption.

■ Overwrite any existing file—This option is available when the "Write debugging information to:" option is enabled. This command enables you to overwrite any pre-existing file that was created by a previous memory dump utilizing the filename specified in the earlier option. If this checkbox is disabled, the

Windows NT system will create a new memory dump file if a file with the specified name already exists.

■ Automatically reboot—When enabled, this option causes the Windows NT system to reboot automatically when a stop error occurs.

Generally, if the Windows NT system illegally shuts down, you will want as much information as possible about the event. Check all of these options. At a bare minimum, check both the "Write debugging information to:" option and the "Overwrite any existing file." By default, the **MEMORY.DMP** file will be created in **%SYSTEM_ROOT%\MEMORY.DMP**, as long as the page file is also in there with at least 1MB more than the amount of physical RAM in the system—and enough available disk space to write the memory dump file. Because the amount of RAM dictates the size of the **MEMORY.DMP** file, you could run out of disk space while the system is creating a new **MEMORY.DMP** file. This event would prevent Windows NT from providing necessary information to a technical support person (assuming you are not wearing that hat as well) for troubleshooting the illegal shutdown.

ENVIRONMENT VARIABLES Two types of NT environment variables can be configured: System and User. These variables are located within the System applet in the Control Panel, under the Environment tab. System environment variables can only be set by an administrator. User environment variables are set by the user and by any application that might require environment variable settings. Environment variables contain information for items such as drive, path, or filename. Both system and user environment variables are displayed under the Environments tab for the user currently logged on (see Figure 3–46).

By default, Windows NT sets any environment variables dictated by **C:\AUTOEXEC.BAT**, if one exists. If **C:\AUTOEXEC.BAT** does exist, Windows NT will append the path statement automatically to the system path every time the system is booted. Environment variables are set in the following order:

1. **AUTOEXEC.BAT** variables

2. System environment variables

3. User environment variables

Because the environment variables load in this order, any variable that is set by the **AUTOEXEC.BAT**—but is also defined by the system environment variable—will be overwritten by the system environment variable.

Figure 3–46
Environment
variables

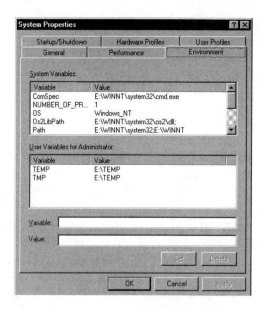

If that system environment variable is defined within the user environment variable, the system variable will be overwritten in turn by the user environment variable. Instances occur, therefore, where you might need to stop Windows NT from scanning the **AUTOEXEC.BAT** file for settings. To disable this function, edit the following registry parameter:

```
\HKEY_CURRENT_USER\Software\Microsoft\Windows
        NT\CurrentVersion\Winlogon\ParseAutoexec REG_SZ=0
```

You can also use the System Policy Editor in Administrative Tools to disable this function. Choose Windows NT System, located under the Local User hierarchy, and select the Parse Autoexec.bat checkbox (as in Figure 3–47).

GENERAL　The General tab is purely informational. This tab gives the NT installation type and the registration information, as well as details on the CPU and RAM (as in Figure 3–48).

USER PROFILES　The User Profiles tab is for saving and copying user profiles. This tab is discussed in detail in Chapter 8, "NT User Management."

Figure 3–47
Parse Autoexec.bat

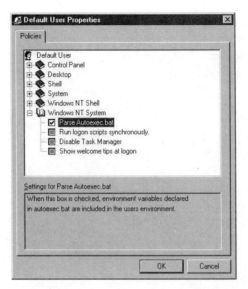

Figure 3–48
General tab

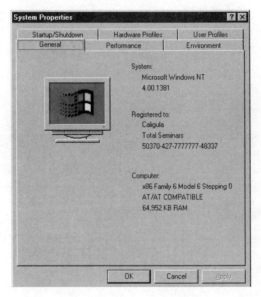

Telephony

The Telephony applet enables you to configure different dialing locations and their specific parameters when Dialup Networking is used. Also, third-party dialing applications exist that will take advantage of these configurations. You can be specific with setting up the dialing template,

Figure 3–49
Telephony applet

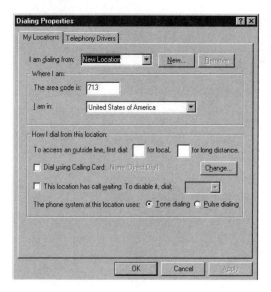

or you can be more general. An example of how to set up this applet would be to base it on the area codes to which you will need to dial, with or without a "9" for an outside line (see Figure 3–49).

UPS

A UPS will support a system for a period of time when there is an electrical power outage. UPS also will protect a system from various unstable electrical services, such as brownouts and power surges. The batteries for a UPS are kept charged, while the main power supply is available. The settings for the UPS are located in the UPS applet within the Control Panel (see Figure 3–50).

The job of the UPS service during a power failure is to keep the system running by communicating with the UPS device until there is a power restore, until the system is gracefully shut down, or until the UPS signals a low battery. During a power outage, the UPS pauses the Server service so that new user connections are unable to authenticate to the failing server. The UPS then sends out a broadcast message notifying all connected users of a possible server system shutdown—and telling them to log out of their session. The UPS service does a graceful shutdown of the system when it receives the signal to shut down. If power is restored, a broadcast message will alert users that normal operation has resumed.

Figure 3–50
UPS applet

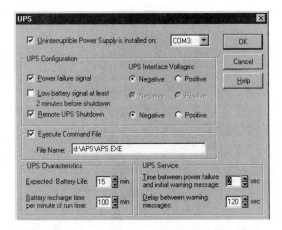

The UPS requires a special cable that can communicate through the serial port because of the difference in the pin-outs, although the UPS communicates through a standard serial port. You will be required to use a cable specifically for UPS connectivity to your system. Once you have connected the UPS to the serial port and started up the server, **NTDETECT.COM** sends out a signal to all ports to determine whether new devices have been added to the system. Once the server comes up, verify that the UPS is configured properly. Some UPSs do not respond to the **NTDETECT.COM** signal. If this situation happens, use the /NoSerialMice switch within the **BOOT.INI** to stop the **NTDETECT.COM** signal going to the serial port. The following list describes the available options within the Control Panel to configure UPS:

■ Power failure signal—The UPS can send a message in case of a power outage. This option directly corresponds to the *clear to send* (CTS) pin signal on the serial port connection.

■ Low battery signal at least two minutes before shutdown—The UPS can send a warning message when batteries are low. This option directly corresponds to the *data carrier detect* (DCD) pin for the serial port connection.

■ Remote UPS Shutdown—The UPS can receive a signal from the UPS service to initiate a server shutdown. This option directly corresponds to the *data terminal ready* (DTR) pin for the serial port connection.

NOTE: *The options mentioned earlier can be utilized with either positive or negative voltages within the UPS applet. The default is set to Negative. Refer to the UPS owner's manual for the required voltage setting.*

- Execute Command File—This option is used for the system to execute a command file, either *.CMD, *.BAT, *.COM, or *.EXE, before server shutdown. The command file will be given 30 seconds to complete its task.

- Expected Battery Life—The default for this option is two minutes —the duration that a server is allowed to run on a battery—and can be set within the range of two to 270 minutes.

NOTE: *When selecting Power Failure Signal and not Low Battery Signal, be sure to select Expected Battery Life and Battery Recharge Time.*

- Battery Recharge Time—The default for this option is 100 minutes for the amount of time needed for battery recharge. This option can be set within a range of one to 250 minutes.

- Time between power failure and initial warning message—The default for this option is five seconds to send a broadcast message to users notifying them of power failure. The range for this option can be set between zero and 120 seconds.

- Delay between warning messages—The default for this option is 120 seconds to send a broadcast message to users notifying users of a possible server shutdown. The range for this option can be set between five and 300 seconds.

Microsoft Mail Postoffice

This applet is used to administer an existing Postoffice workgroup or to create a new workgroup. This applet will be visible only if Microsoft Mail has been installed on this system.

CONTROL PANEL SUMMARY

Using the Control Panel is the best way to configure a Windows NT system. The MCSE exams expect you to be able to discuss every applet in considerable detail. Some situations exist, however, where it becomes important to be able to access the registry directly to make configuration changes. Let's take a look at the registry to understand its organization, and then we will see how Registry Editors can be used to make changes.

Registry

The registry contains many values that define the working environment for Windows NT. The registry also contains specific settings that are created whenever you install a service or application or add a physical device to the server computer.

Understanding the Registry

The primary tool for understanding the registry is the Registry Editor program **REGEDT32.EXE**. **REGEDT32.EXE** enables you to inspect and modify the configurations that are encoded within the registry. You can start **REGEDT32.EXE** from the Start/Run menu on the desktop tool bar. This action will open the registry, as shown in Figure 3–51. **REGEDT32.EXE** is located in the **\WINNT_NT\SYSTEM32** folder by default upon installation.

   REGEDIT.EXE is another registry editing tool installed by NT's Setup. If you installed NT over a Windows 3.X installation, Setup installs a version of **REGEDIT.EXE** that is compatible with Windows 3.X. In all other cases, NT's Setup installs the Windows 95 version of **REGEDIT.EXE**. In

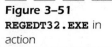

Figure 3–51
REGEDT32.EXE in
action

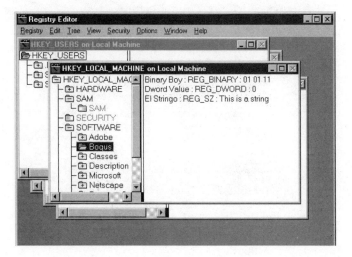

either case, the real message is NOT to use **REGEDIT.EXE** to edit your NT registry. **REGEDIT.EXE** does not have a security menu or a Read-Only mode and does not allow editing of certain data types, so it is therefore insufficient for Windows NT registry editing.

The NT Registry Editor (**REGEDT32.EXE**) is an extremely powerful tool for direct editing. Because of the capabilities you have within the Registry Editor, it is highly recommended that, while studying, you set the registry to "Read-Only Mode," located on the Options menu. See Figure 3–52.

This action will help prevent any accidental changes to the registry that you do not want to make. Incorrect or invalid registry changes can cause serious damage to the system and require a reinstallation of the Windows NT operating system. Some registry changes, however, require you to use the Registry Editor. The purpose of the Registry Editor is to help with troubleshooting. Portions of the registry can be saved to diskette to be viewed on another computer for further analysis. The registry can also be opened and viewed over a network.

By default, administrators have Full Control over the registry, whereas other users have Read-Only access. An administrator can change the permissions to the registry with the Security menu in the Registry Editor.

While **REGEDT32.EXE** is definitely the tool to use when editing the registry, **REGEDIT.EXE** has one "ace in the hole" that makes the program handy. **REGEDIT.EXE** has a "find" option that searches for both keys and values. REGEDT32, on the other hand, can only search for keys—and only on a "root key-by-root key" basis. In other words, REGEDT32 can only search one root key at a time. Keep **REGEDIT.EXE** around for searching the registry, but use REGEDT32 for actual editing.

The Registry Editor commands are on the registry and view menu of the Registry Editor. The following list shows the available registry commands and their functions:

FIND KEY This command is used to search for a specific key within the registry. Keys are located on the left side of the window. A search will begin when the current key is selected, searching throughout the subordinate keys. Searches will include only the subtree in which you are

Figure 3–52
Registry—Read-Only mode

located. For example, **HKEY_LOCAL_MACHINE** searches will not go into **HKEY_CURRENT_USER**.

SAVE KEY   This option enables you to save a specific portion of the registry in binary format. Because the file is in binary format, you have the ability to restore the registry using the Restore command, in case you need to reload a set of values after testing.

RESTORE   This command will load data in the selected file under the currently highlighted key. The Registry Editor will overwrite the key with the values in the file if the highlighted key was saved in the data file.

SAVE SUBTREE AS   The command will save the entire subtree and all of its subkeys in a text file. After saving, you can use a text editor to review the file and make modifications.

Select Computer

This option enables you to connect to and access a remote server's registry. A Windows NT Workstation enables remote access by any valid user account. Windows NT Server restricts remote access to the Administrators group. You may modify the remote access permission for either platform under the following registry key:

```
HKEY_LOCAL_MACHINE\CurrentControlSet\SecuredPipeServers\
    winreg
```

The type is **REG_DWORD** with a value of one.

Registry Hierarchical Structure

The registry is structured in a folder/file fashion, similar to folder/files on a disk.

The following information describes the components of the registry hierarchy:

- *Subtree*—This component is analogous to the root folder of a disk and can also be called a subtree key. Five predefined subtrees exist: **HKEY_LOCAL_MACHINE**, **HKEY_USERS**, **HKEY_CURRENT_USER**, **HKEY_CLASSES_ROOT**, and **HKEY_CURRENT_CONFIG**.

■ *Hive*—A hive has a corresponding registry file and ***.LOG** file located in the **\WINNT_ROOT\SYSTEM32\CONFIG** directory. The ***.LOG** file records all changes to the registry to keep the registry accurate. A hive is a combination of keys, subkeys, and their values.

■ *Keys and subkeys*—Every hive can contain keys and subkeys, which is similar to a folder containing subfolders.

■ *Values*—Three entries to a value exist: the name, data type, and a configuration parameter. Values would be equivalent to a file of a folder.

■ Value Data Types:

1. **REG_DWORD**—Only one value can be assigned, and the value must be a hexadecimal string between one and eight.

2. **REG_SZ**—Only one value can be assigned, and the value is interpreted as a string to be stored.

3. **REG_EXPAND_SZ**—The text for this value type can be replaced by a variable.

4. **REG_BINARY**—Only one value can be assigned, and the value must be a combination of hexadecimal numbers. Each pair of hexadecimal numbers is translated as a byte value.

5. **REG_MULIT_SZ**—You might have multiple values for this data type. Values are considered strings and are translated as a component of the **MULTI_SZ**. Entries are separated by the null character.

The Five Root Keys

The registry is divided into individual sections, or headings, called *root keys*. You can access all registry keys through one of the five root keys shown in Figure 3–53.

Figure 3–53
The five root keys

HKEY_LOCAL_MACHINE—This root key contains all configuration information about the local computer system. Applications, device drivers, OLE-enabled applications, and the operating system for computer configuration all use this information. Some of the stored information is used to boot Windows NT. This information is static and does not change on a per-user basis. This root key has five subkeys: Hardware, SAM, Security, Software, and System. The Security, SAM, Software, and System subkeys are also considered hives because of the files located in the **\WINNT_ROOT\SYSTEM32\CONFIG** folder. Install applications will search all five subkeys for information, although they can only add information to the Software and System subkeys. The following list describes the **HKEY_LOCAL_MACHINE** subkeys:

Hardware—This value is built from information obtained each time the computer system boots, and this subkey is volatile. Installed applications examine this information to determine the type and the state of the physical devices connected to the computer. This key does not map to a file on the disk because of the key's volatility. Each time the system boots, information is again obtained about the system. Use this subkey to determine whether you have the appropriate drivers installed for a specific hardware device—and whether a device driver is failing to load because it is undetected, due to a conflict with a pre-existing device.

SAM—This hive maps to the **SAM.LOG** files in the **\WINNT_ROOT\ SYSTEM32\CONFIG** folder and is the directory database for the computer. Applications require the appropriate APIs to query the SAM, and it is also a copy to **HKEY_LOCAL_MACHINE\SECURITY\SAM**. When in a domain model, the SAM database contains the domain user account database.

Security—This subkey contains all of the security information for the computer. This subkey cannot be modified by an application. Applications can only query security APIs. The Security hive points to the Security and **SECURITY.LOG** files located in the **\WINNT_ROOT\SYSTEM32\CONFIG** folder.

Software—This hive contains information about the installed software on the computer and contains information such as version numbers and manufacturers of software. The hive is independent of per-user configuration. This hive points to the Software and **SOFTWARE.LOG** files located in the **\WINNT_ROOT\SYSTEM32\CONFIG** folder and also contains the file associations and OLE information.

System—This hive contains information about the devices and services available to the computer system. This hive points to the System and **SYSTEM.LOG** files located in the **\WINNT_ROOT\SYSTEM32\CONFIG** folder. A backup copy of this information is kept in the **SYSTEM.ALT** file.

HKEY_USERS—Only two subkeys exist: DEFAULT and the *security identification number* (SID) of the currently logged-on user. The DEFAULT contains the information about the operating system default profile and is visible at the point of the CTRL+ALT+DEL logon prompt.

HKEY_CURRENT_USER—This root key contains the information of the currently logged-on user. When a user logs on, a copy of the account is stored in **\WINN_NT\PROFILES\USERNAME**. This subkey corresponds to the data located under **HKEY_USERS\SID_of_the_currently_logged_on_user**. This subtree also has priority over **HKEY_LOCAL_MACHINE**.

HKEY_CLASSES_ROOT—This subtree contains information about installed applications.

HKEY_CURRENT_CONFIG—This key provides information about the current hardware configuration profile and is a combination of the SOFTWARE and SYSTEM hives.

The separate files in the **\WINNT\SYSTEM32\CONFIG** folder correspond to particular parts of the registry. Any part of the registry that is a complete part of an actual file is called a "Hive." For example, **HKLM\SECURITY** is a hive that corresponds to the file **\WINNT\SYSTEM32\CONFIG\SECURITY**.

NOTE: *The registry is phenomenally complicated. You are not expected to memorize the hundreds of registry details or even the six root keys. You are expected, however, to understand the layout and organization and be able to navigate through the registry. We will see more of this at the end of this chapter.*

Any of the root keys can be opened so they can see subkeys. Note that when another subkey is pressed, values show up on the right-hand side of the screen. This feature is the cornerstone of the registry: keys and values. Values have a name and data. The value's data must be of a string, binary, or *double word* (DWORD) value. In Figure 3–54, we see the key **HKLM\SOFTWARE\Bogus**. Do not look for this key in your PC—because this

Figure 3–54
Example values

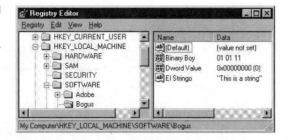

key really is bogus. The key has four example values of each data type, plus the always present [Default] value—which is in every key and cannot be removed.

NOTE: *Dealing with the registry directly is always a game of chance. As mentioned earlier, messing up the registry can force a complete reinstallation of Windows NT. To prevent this danger, make sure that there is always a backup copy of the registry. You can always take the risk that the "Last Known Good Configuration" will work, but it is better to make a backup of the registry hives to tape. Make sure that if you need to restore, you will be able to read the tape. You can also use the ERD if necessary.*

Questions

1. John's NT workstation does not have any of the games that come with NT. He wants to add them. He puts in his installation CD-ROM and

   a. Runs **SETUP /U**

   b. Runs Windows NT Setup under the Add/Remove Programs applet in the Control Panel

   c. Runs the Windows Install applet in the Control Panel

   d. Runs **REGEDIT32**, locates the **ACTIVE_GAMES** key, and changes it to one

2. Pepe wants to prevent his machine from being used by others when he is away from his desk. He does not want to log off or reboot the system. He could

   a. Password-protect a screen saver

   b. Password-protect the desktop

   c. Use NT's Password applet to protect the entire system

   d. Do nothing—he cannot do this in NT

3. The Control Panel Display applet can also be accessed by

   a. Start/Run **DISPLAY.EXE**

   b. System/Device Manager applet

   c. Services applet

   d. Right-click/Properties from Desktop

4. Which Control Panel applet can be used to edit the **BOOT.INI** file?

   a. Services

   b. System

   c. Network

   d. Boot

5. If an NT system is booted with an **AUTOEXEC.BAT** file, it will

   a. Overwrite all environment variables and only use the **AUTOEXEC.BAT**'s environment variables

   b. Ignore the environment variables in **AUTOEXEC.BAT**

   c. Append the environment variables in **AUTOEXEC.BAT** to its own environment

   d. NT does not use environment variables.

6. Josh wants to install a new sound card in his system. Which Control Panel applet is used?

   a. Devices

   b. Multimedia

   c. Sounds

   d. Services

7. Which of the following is not an NT registry root key?

   a. **HKEY_LOCAL_MACHINE**

   b. **HKEY_CURRENT_USER**

   c. **HKEY_CLASSES_ROOT**

   d. **HKEY_PROFILES_SYSTEM**

8. The correct Registry Editor to use when editing an NT system is

   a. **REGEDIT.EXE**

   b. **REGEDIT32.EXE**

   c. **REGEDT32.EXE**

   d. **REGEDT.EXE**

9. John installs a new UPS on his NT Workstation. Upon booting, the UPS does not seem to respond to the system, thus making the system think it is not working and preventing the bootup. What should John do first?

   a. Reinstall the UPS

   b. Erase the **BOOTSEC.DOS** file

   c. Use the /NoSerialMice switch in **BOOT.INI**

   d. Replace the **NTDETECT.COM** with **IDETECT.COM**

10. Florence wants to install a modem to access the Internet. She will have to use the _____ applet to install it.

   a. Telephony

   b. Modem

   c. Internet

   d. Network

Answers

1. b—Windows NT Setup under the Add/Remove Programs applet in the Control Panel enables the addition or removal of individual NT components.

2. a—Password-protect a screen saver.

3. d—Right-click/Properties from Desktop.

4. b—The Startup/Shutdown Tab in the System Applet enables changing the default startup option.

5. c—Append the environment variables in **AUTOEXEC.BAT** to its own environment.

6. b—The multimedia applet.

7. d—There is no root key called **HKEY_PROFILES_SYSTEM**.

8. c—**REGEDT32.EXE** is the only editor to use when editing a registry file in NT. **REGEDIT.EXE** is good for searching but should never be used for editing.

9. c—Use the /NoSerialMice switch in **BOOT.INI**.

10. b—The Modem applet.

The NT Boot Process

Understanding the boot process in Windows NT requires you to take your knowledge of the boot process for DOS and Windows 95/98 and throw it out the window. Windows NT, unlike Microsoft's other operating systems, can live happily on more than just Intel x86 hardware. An NT CD-ROM contains, for example, all the necessary files to install and boot NT on RISC-based systems, including DEC Alpha and Power PC. An NT machine can be set up to boot to several different operating systems, including DOS, Windows 95/98, UNIX, etc. Basically NT can coexist with any other OS that can run on the same architecture. Further, NT can coexist with other installations of NT on the same machine, allowing you the option of which version or variation you want to boot to at that moment. Finally, even though NT bears a surface resemblance to Windows 95/98, that resemblance is truly only skin deep. NT differs radically from 95/98 in the way that NT boots.

This chapter discusses the differences between NT and other Microsoft operating systems and covers what you should know about the NT boot process. We discuss the various boot files, boot and system partitions, ARC naming, and many other exciting things. You will be taught how to create a multi-boot machine and, perhaps most importantly, how to troubleshoot when something goes wrong in the boot process. Read on!

Older Microsoft operating systems can only run on Intel x86 compatible processors—a rather serious limitation. Being "processor specific," however, has one advantage. Both DOS and Windows 95/98 require only a simple set of files to boot the operating system to a C: prompt—**IO.SYS**, **MSDOS.SYS**, and **COMMAND.COM**.

Windows NT, in contrast, can happily run on machines based on either Intel x86 compatible processors (i.e. Intel Pentium and Pentium PRO, AMD K6, etc.) or RISC chips such as the DEC Alpha. Because the hardware of x86 compatible processors and RISC chips find their operating system in different ways, different files and configurations must be used for each type of system.

Another limitation to DOS and Windows 95/98 is that they do not support multiple bootable partitions on one hard drive. FDISK, the popular partitioning program that comes with DOS and Windows 95/98, only allows the creation of one bootable partition on a hard drive. FDISK calls bootable partitions "Primary" partitions. Multiple bootable partitions on one drive allow a system to boot multiple and totally unique operating systems. True, Windows 95/98 has a primitive "dual-boot" option that allows a Windows 95/98 system to boot DOS, but that is done through a rather strange file-swapping process which is only possible due to the fact that the boot files for DOS and Windows 95/98 are very similar. The Windows 95/98 type of dual-booting is useless with any other operating systems other than Windows 95/98 and DOS. This is due to the fact that other operating systems—like Windows NT, OS/2, and UNIX—have very different, very incompatible formatting and boot files than DOS and Windows 95/98. To allow very different operating systems to boot off of the same hard drive, they must all exist on their own bootable partitions. Each separate partition can then be formatted in that operating system's preferred format, and can have it's own boot files. NT does an excellent job at supporting multiple operating systems, although as a rule, the other operating systems need to be installed before NT.

Booting Up Versus Going Graphical

Windows 95/98 and Windows NT share a surface resemblance—they are both graphical operating systems. Inside, however, they differ significantly. Further, with both 95/98 and NT, there is a big difference between booting up the operating system and "going graphical." Both NT and 95/98 have primary boot files that start the operating system. Once these files have started the system, a completely different set of files starts the graphical user interface (GUI). The boot files are usually quite small in size and there are very few of them, compared to the size and the number of the GUI files. The distinction between OS and GUI files is sharp in 95/98, but much muddier in NT.

In Windows 95/98, there is a very clear distinction between the boot files and the GUI files. This can be easily shown at boot. Next time you boot a Windows 95 machine, wait until the system says "Starting Windows 95 . . ." and quickly press the F8 key. In Windows 98, reboot and hold down the Ctrl key to get the same result. You will get a text "Startup" menu. Select "Command Prompt only." This will prevent the operating system from loading the GUI files. Type **VER**, hit Enter, and you will see that it really is Windows 95 or 98, but with only the boot files loaded. The boot files in and of themselves can create a fully functional command line interface. Type **WIN** and hit Enter to load the graphical portions of Windows 95/98.

In Windows 95/98, the boot files must be loaded onto the C: partition, but the GUI files can be loaded onto any other drive letter. Of course, most installations place the GUI files in a directory called **\WINDOWS** on the C: drive, but this is not at all required. The boot files and the GUI files are totally separate issues in Windows 95/98.

Windows NT also has separate boot and GUI files. Like Windows 95/98, the boot files must be on the boot partition and the GUI files can be anywhere else. Unlike Windows 95/98, however, the boot and GUI files are closely linked. There is no way to boot NT to a command prompt only, as is possible in Windows 95/98. The boot files only start the operating system and then pass control to the GUI. The only way to get to C: prompt in NT is after the GUI is started.

That is about where the comparisons between Windows 95/98 and NT end. Windows NT has a vastly more complicated boot file structure and organization. Additionally, Microsoft uses some terms very differently than other authorities, requiring a little bit of unlearning and accepting the "Microsoft Way" of defining different aspects of the boot process. The best way to understand the NT boot process is to begin with an overview of the different files used in the boot process. On the way, terms will be defined the "Microsoft Way," while making sure the concepts are understood.

The Boot Files

The NT operating system itself consists of **NTOSKRNL.EXE** (the Windows NT kernel), the **\WINNT\SYSTEM32\CONFIG\SYSTEM** file (which controls the loading of device drivers), and the device drivers themselves. While these files are the core of the NT operating system, they are not capable of booting the system. They can reside on any partition, in any directory in the system. How does a computer find those files so that they can be run to start the operating system? The answer is that NT needs boot files that can "point" to these critical files (see Figure 4–1).

Time for a little Microsoft terminology. The **NTOSKRNL.EXE**, **SYSTEM**, and device driver files that make up the operating system are stored on the *boot partition*. The files that will help us find the operating system when the system boots up are stored on the *system partition*. That is not a typo. In Microsoft's terminology, the partition that you boot from, the bootable

Figure 4–1
Which partition on which drive has the operating system files?

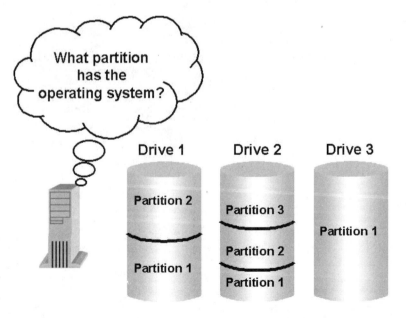

partition, is the *system partition*. The partition that holds the actual NT operating system is call the *boot partition*. It's backwards, everyone knows that it's backwards, and it's too late to change it. In an NT system, there will be only one system partition. There can be more than one boot partition, but only if NT needs to exist with other operating systems that require special formatting. NT can coexist with DOS or Windows 95/98 on the same boot partition. The boot partition and the system partition can also be the same partition.

NOTE: *A computer boots from the system partition. The operating system is stored on the boot partition.*

While we are at it, we need to take a moment to define one other term that is relevant to partitions—*active partition*. In a computer, it is possible to have many primary partitions, either on one or more drives. How does the PC know which primary partition to access when there are more than one primary partitions? All PCs require that one of the primary partitions be set as active. The first primary partition set as active is the drive that the system will attempt to boot from. Active partitions are handy tools only for multiple-OS systems. With the right operating system or third-party utility, a small primary partition is set as active, starting a boot menu under the control of whatever operating system or program created this boot menu. When the user selects a particular operating system from the menu, the controlling operating system then points to the partition of the selected operating system. This is how operating systems such as Linux, OS/2, and third-party utilities like System Commander allow multiple operating system to exist on one system. As the overwhelming majority of PCs use only one operating system, the first primary partition is simply set to active and this issue is completed.

NOTE: *NT dual-boot capabilities are handled in a different way than just described. Read on to appreciate these differences!*

It would be nice at this point simply to list all of the boot files used by NT and explain their functions. Well, that cannot happen . . . yet. The reason lies in the fact that Windows NT is designed to run on different platforms: Intel x86, MIPs, Alpha, PPC, etc. Fortunately, all of the different platforms can be separated into two groups: the Intel x86 group and all of the other platforms lumped together in what we will call the RISC group.

How the system partition is organized and which files make up the boot files are determined by the hardware platform NT is installed on. Each platform has a specific method for finding its operating system, so these two groups need to be discussed separately. Let's start with the far more popular Intel x86 group and then move to the RISC group. The MCSE exams concentrate heavily on the Intel x86 group and require only minor knowledge about the RISC group, so the emphasis here will be on the Intel x86 group.

INTEL X86   Intel x86 compatible processors require the following files on the system partition:

- **NTLDR**

- **NTDETECT.COM**

- **NTBOOTDD.SYS** (Only for SCSI controllers that don't have their own ROM BIOS)

- **BOOT.INI**

When the system boots up, the **NTLDR** program launches. The **NTLDR** program then launches either Windows NT or another operating system. In order to find the available operating systems, the **NTLDR** program must find the **BOOT.INI** configuration file. To accomplish this, the **NTLDR** program loads its own minimal file system, which allows it to read a **BOOT.INI** file off a system partition formatted with either NTFS or FAT.

RISC   The MCSE exams, due to their stress of the Intel x86 group and the variance in files on RISC systems, do not expect you to know the system files for RISC group systems. Both RISC and Intel x86 systems, however, share one system file: **BOOT.INI**. The **BOOT.INI** file tells **NTLDR** the locations of the boot partition and the operating system.

BOOT.INI FILE   The **BOOT.INI** file is a text file that lists the operating systems available to **NTLDR**, and tells **NTLDR** where to find the boot partition (where the operating system is stored) for each of the operating systems. The **BOOT.INI** file has sections defined by section headings enclosed in brackets. A typical **BOOT.INI** file would look like this:

```
[boot loader]
timeout=30
default= multi(0)disk(0)rdisk(0)partition(1)\WINNT
[operating systems]
multi(0)disk(0)rdisk(0)partition(1)\WINNT="Windows NT
```

```
        Server Version 4.00 "
multi(0)disk(0)rdisk(0)partition(1)\WINNT="Windows NT
        Server Version 4.00 [VGA mode]" /basevideo /sos
C:\="Microsoft Windows"
```

Such a **BOOT.INI** would result in the boot menu that appears in Figure 4–2.

THE [BOOT LOADER] SECTION The **[boot loader]** section tells **NTLDR** how to do its job, specifying how long to keep the boot menu on the screen at boot up and what default option should be used if no user intervenes. The **[boot loader]** section on an Intel x86 based system contains only two options, **timeout=** and **default=**.

NOTE: *The* **[boot loader]** *section for RISC-based systems offers many additional options, but these are not covered by the Workstation, Server, or Enterprise exams.*

The timer is set with the option:

timeout = x

The x equals the number of seconds to keep the boot menu on the screen. In the example above, the timeout is set as:

timeout= 30

This gives a 30-second display of the NT boot menu before the default operating system starts.

The default is set with the option:

Default = arc naming path

The default option specifies which operating system to use as a default. In the example above, the default = option is set as:

default= multi(0)disk(0)rdisk(0)partition(1)\WINNT

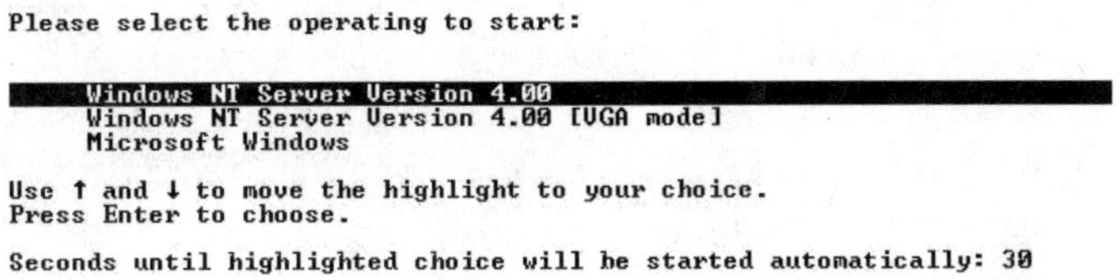

Figure 4–2
The Windows NT
Boot Menu

```
Please select the operating to start:

  Windows NT Server Version 4.00
  Windows NT Server Version 4.00 [VGA mode]
  Microsoft Windows

Use ↑ and ↓ to move the highlight to your choice.
Press Enter to choose.

Seconds until highlighted choice will be started automatically: 30
```

This specifies that the operating system can be found in the \WINNT subdirectory on the first partition on the first hard drive. The format of `multi(w)disk(x)rdisk(y)partition(z)` for describing partitions is known as the *Advanced RISC Computing* (ARC) convention. Understanding ARC is imperative both for passing the exams and supporting NT.

ARC NAMING CONVENTION The ARC naming convention shown above tells **NTLDR** how to locate the system partition and the subdirectory with the operating system files. Both Intel x86 and RISC processor computers use the ARC naming convention. The syntax for the ARC name has two formats:

```
scsi(w)disk(x)rdisk(y)partition(z)
multi(w)disk(x)rdisk(y)partition(z)
```

The format that starts with "scsi" will be called the SCSI ARC format. The format that starts with "multi" will be called the MULTI ARC format.

The ARC format used depends on the type of drive being accessed. The **SCSI** option is used for SCSI drives that do not have ROM BIOS support. The *Basic Input/Output System* (BIOS) is the collection of programs that allow the CPU to communicate with the hardware in the system. For IDE controllers, the BIOS is located in the ROM BIOS chip on the motherboard. SCSI controllers can use a ROM BIOS chip built into the SCSI controller (a.k.a. host adapter) card. If there is no ROM BIOS on the host adapter, or if the ROM BIOS on the host adapter is disabled, a device driver must be loaded to access the SCSI hardware.

The **MULTI** format is for all other drives, in particular EIDE/IDE drives and SCSI drives with ROM BIOS support. In the PC world, there are two situations where ROM BIOS supports SCSI. First are the SCSI host adapters with ROM BIOS. Second are motherboards with onboard support for SCSI—in essence a motherboard with a built-in host adapter.

The ARC format must be always use lower case in **BOOT.INI**. If any of the ARC values other than the one used in the default= option are set to uppercase, NT will fail to boot. **MULTI** and **SCSI** will be capitalized in the book for clarification, but don't let that confuse you! All of the examples will show the proper lower-case format.

The ARC naming convention is a general-purpose tool that can be used on a wide variety of hardware platforms. As a result, while there will always be either `scsi(w)disk(x)rdisk(y)partition(z)` or `multi(w)disk(x)rdisk(y)partition(z)`, the meaning of these values and the numbers each one holds varies dramatically between the **SCSI** and the **MULTI** options. Let's look at each portion of the ARC name.

MULTI   The **MULTI** option determines the controller that controls the drive containing the boot partition. The **MULTI** version of the ARC naming path follows the format:

```
multi(w)disk(x)rdisk(y)partition(z)
```

The **MULTI** option is used for IDE, EIDE, ESDI, and SCSI hard drives that are supported by ROM BIOS in an IDE system.

NOTE: *The* **MULTI** *option is not used on RISC-based symptoms.*

The **MULTI** option determines the number of the hard drive controller, starting from zero. In theory, as you add more controllers, the **MULTI** option could change, but in practice, the **MULTI** option will always be set to zero. It is true that almost all PCs have a Primary and a Secondary controller, each running up to two drives, but the ARC format considers this as only one dual-purpose controller. Additionally, even though SCSI drives will also have their own separate controllers, they respond to the same **Int13h** calls as the IDE drives, making all of the drives act as one big controller. Therefore, if the system has only IDE/EIDE drives and SCSI drives under ROM BIOS, the **MULTI** value will always be **0**.

DISK   The **DISK** option is not used in the **MULTI** version of ARC naming paths and should also be set to **0**.

RDISK   The **RDISK** option specifies which hard disk on the controller holds the boot partition. The numbers for the hard disks are numbered ordinally, starting with zero (0). The **RDISK** value that a particular hard disk receives depends on the drive's boot order and what drives are present. For PC systems, the boot order is as follows:

1st First hard drive on primary IDE controller (Primary Master)

2nd Second hard drive on primary IDE controller (Primary Slave)

3rd First hard drive on secondary IDE controller (Secondary Master)

4th Second hard drive on secondary IDE controller (Secondary Slave)

5th First hard drive on first SCSI host adapter (Usually **SCSI ID0**)

6th Second hard drive on first SCSI host adapter (Usually **SCSI ID1**)

And so on for the rest of the SCSI drives and SCSI host adapters.

The boot order is not the **RDISK** value! The boot order only determines the **RDISK** value. The **RDISK** value starts with the first drive it finds in the boot order and calls it **rdisk(0)**. The next drive in the boot order is **rdisk(1)**, the third is **rdisk(2)**, etc. If a system has one IDE drive and one SCSI drive, for example, the IDE drive will be **rdisk(0)** and the SCSI drive will be **rdisk(1)**. If a system has an IDE drive set as Primary Master, another IDE set as Secondary Master, and two SCSI drives (on the same controller) set to SCSI ID2 and SCSI ID5 respectively, the Primary Master IDE drive will be **rdisk(0)**, the Secondary Master will be **rdisk(1)**, the SCSI ID2 drive will be **rdisk(2)**, and the SCSI ID5 drive will be **rdisk(3)**.

NOTE: *Some systems have a CMOS option that allows the SCSI drives to boot before the EIDE/IDE drives. If the SCSI drives boot first, the boot order changes first to the SCSI drives and then to the EIDE/IDE drives. If that is the case, use the same boot order shown above, but put the IDE drives at the end of the list.*

PARTITION The **PARTITION** parameter specifies the boot partition on the disk that holds the operating system to be booted. An NT boot partition can be a system (bootable) partition or an extended partition. Just to be confusing, the partition number starts with one, not zero. Therefore the first system partition would be **partition(1)**. Keep in mind that PCs have a limit of no more than four partitions on a drive, so **PARTITION** will always be from **partition(1)** up to **partition(4)**.

DIRECTORY The directory specifies the directory that stores the boot files. In most NT systems, the NT boot files are stored in the **\WINNT** directory. There is no space between the **partition(z)** and the directory name. If the boot files are in the root directory of the partition, no directory is used.

MULTI EXAMPLES Some examples of ARC naming for EIDE and BIOS controlled SCSI will help solidify our understanding of the ARC naming conventions.

Example 1: IDE Primary Master with two boot partitions, IDE Primary slave with one boot partition:

■ To boot to the **\WINNT** folder of the second partition on the IDE Primary Master: **multi(0)disk(0)rdisk(0)partition(2)\WINNT**.

■ To boot to the **\WINNT** partition on the IDE Primary Slave: **multi(0)disk(0)rdisk(1)partition(1)\WINNT**.

Example 2: IDE Primary Master with one boot partition, One SCSI hard drive set to SCSI ID3 with two boot partitions. All boot files are in a directory called **WINNT**.

- To boot to the partition on the IDE Primary Master:
  `multi(0)disk(0)rdisk(0)partition(1)\WINNT.`
- To boot to the second partition on the SCSI drive:
  `multi(0)disk(0)rdisk(1)partition(2)\WINNT.`

Example 3: Three SCSI hard drives on the same host adapter, all with two partitions, set to SCSI IDs of 1, 2, and 3. All boot files are in a directory called **WINNT**.

- To boot to the first partition on the SCSI drive with the SCSI ID of 2: `multi(0)disk(0)rdisk(1)partition(1)\WINNT.`
- To boot to the second partition on the SCSI drive with the SCSI ID of 1: `multi(0)disk(0)rdisk(0)partition(2)\WINNT.`
- To boot to the first partition on the SCSI drive with the SCSI ID of 3: `multi(0)disk(0)rdisk(2)partition(1)\WINNT.`

The **MULTI** option is very common in PC systems running NT, and is the one most likely to be seen in systems. When using SCSI drives without ROM BIOS support, however, the SCSI option is used.

SCSI The **SCSI ARC** option is used only for SCSI drives that do not have ROM BIOS support. The **SCSI** option determines the controller for the drive containing the boot partition. The **SCSI** version of the ARC naming path follows the format:

`scsi(w)disk(x)rdisk(y)partition(z).`

The **SCSI** option works very similarly to the **MULTI** option. Three values, the `scsi(w)` value, the `partition(z)` value, and the `directory` value are identical. Only the function of the `disk(x)` value and the `rdisk(y)` value differ from their usage in the **MULTI** option.

One big difference between the `scsi(w)` and the `multi(w)` values is that while **MULTI** may see multiple controllers as only one controller, this rarely happens with the `scsi(w)` option. If there are two SCSI host adapters, there will be a `scsi(0)` and a `scsi(1)`.

DISK Whereas **DISK** is unused in the **MULTI** option, it is heavily used in the **SCSI** option. The **DISK** option is the SCSI ID for the drive. If a drive is set to SCSI ID 4, then its **DISK** value will be `disk(4)`.

RDISK   Just as **DISK** is always set to **disk(0)** with the **MULTI** format, the **RDISK** option is always set to **rdisk(0)** for the **SCSI** format.

SCSI EXAMPLES   Example 1: Two SCSI drives on the same controller, one drive set to SCSI ID0 and the other drive set to ID2. Both drives have two boot partitions:

■ To boot to the **\WINNT** folder of the second partition on the SCSI ID0 drive: **scsi(0)disk(0)rdisk(0)partition(2)\WINNT**.

■ To boot to the **\WINNT** folder of the first partition on the SCSI ID2 drive: **scsi(0)disk(2)rdisk(0)partition(1)\WINNT**.

Example 2: Two SCSI drives on 1st controller, first drive set to SCSI ID0 and second drive set to ID1. Two SCSI drives on 2nd controller, first drive set to SCSI ID5 and second drive set to ID6. All drives have one boot partition:

■ To boot to the **\WINNT** folder of the partition on the SCSI ID0 drive on the first controller:
scsi(0)disk(0)rdisk(0)partition(1)\WINNT.

■ To boot to the **\WINNT** folder of the first partition on the SCSI ID6 drive on the second controller:
scsi(0)disk(2)rdisk(0)partition(1)\WINNT.

The ARC formats exist in only one place in all of NT, the **BOOT.INI** file. It is important to be comfortable with ARC naming conventions and how they are used by **BOOT.INI**. Certainly, the MCSE exams will expect you to know them, but far more importantly the **BOOT.INI** is used for dual-booting and for a number of troubleshooting issues, as we will see in the next sections. Now that we understand ARC, let's go back and examine the default **BOOT.INI**.

THE DEFAULT BOOT.INI   The default **BOOT.INI** splits information into two sections—**[boot loader]** and **[operating systems]**—as shown below. Each section defines the different boot options available.

```
[boot loader]
timeout=30
default= multi(0)disk(0)rdisk(0)partition(1)\WINNT
[operating systems]
multi(0)disk(0)rdisk(0)partition(1)\WINNT="Windows NT
     Server Version 4.00 "
multi(0)disk(0)rdisk(0)partition(1)\WINNT="Windows NT
     Server Version 4.00 [VGA mode]" /basevideo /sos
C:\="Microsoft Windows"
```

The **[boot loader]** section defines the boot drive and the boot partition(s). **The default= line** is set to the following:

```
multi(0)disk(0)rdisk(0)partition(1)\WINNT
```

The **MULTI** option shows that the drive is controlled by ROM BIOS; **DISK** is always set to **disk(0)** under **MULTI**; **rdisk(0)** shows the first drive in the boot order; and **partition(1)** shows the first boot partition on the drive.

The three lines under the **[operating systems]** section list the operating systems available. The first line defines the NT boot partition. The second line also defines the NT boot partition, but with two special switches: **/basevideo** and **/sos**. These kick NT into a sort of safe mode, which we will discuss later in this chapter. The third line allows the computer to boot to a previously installed version of Windows 95. When NT is installed onto an existing 95/98 machine, it creates a **BOOTSEC.DOS** file that contains the information necessary to boot to Windows 95/98. NT also adds the simple non-ARC line **C:\="Microsoft Windows"** to the **BOOT.INI** file to describe the location of the **BOOTSEC.DOS** file. The line above, for example, would translate to "Hey NT! You'll find the **BOOTSEC.DOS** file for Microsoft Windows 95 in the root directory of the C:\ drive."

Dual-Booting with BOOT.INI

Several reasons exist why a machine may need to be able to boot to more than one operating system. A system may need to run an application that is incompatible with the current operating system. The system may have different roles that compel it to act in two totally different ways, requiring certain aspects of two operating systems. It may be desirable to load a new operating system but to keep the old one until the new operating system has proven itself. The most common motivation for dual-booting in the NT world is to allow the system to boot to a more basic operating system, in particular DOS, to effect repairs in the event of system crashes.

The term "dual-booting" is something of a misnomer. "Dual" implies only "two." While it is most common to have NT boot only to itself and one other operating system, usually DOS, there is nothing to prevent many more operating systems from booting off the same machine. Dual-booting in NT would probably be better known as "Multi-booting," but everyone uses the term dual-boot. So even if a system can boot five different operating systems, it is still a "dual-boot" machine.

Many other operating systems such as OS/2 and the popular UNIX clone Linux also have dual-boot features. Surprisingly, these dual-boot capabilities are far superior to the NT dual-boot. These dual-boot operating systems create a special partition that always boots first. This boot partition contains a menu that then points to the selected partition. The boot partition is not the system partition. There are no operating system specific files in this partition. It only contains enough programming to start its menu and then "points" to a partition based on the menu selection.

Sadly, NT does not have this powerful capability. NT does not have a separate, non-operating system specific partition. Instead, NT uses its own system partition to store special files that contain the information necessary to boot another operating system. These files reside in the root directory of the system partition along with **NTLDR**, **NTDETECT**, and **BOOT.INI**. Microsoft has limited NT's dual-boot capability to DOS, Windows 95/98, and other copies of Windows NT. Perhaps Microsoft assumes that once a system has had NT installed, these will be the only operating systems that anyone would have any interest in dual-booting. Maybe Microsoft is right, but if a system needs to boot any other operating system, it will have to use the dual-boot capabilities of the other operating system, because NT will not support dual-booting anything that isn't made by Microsoft.

The process of making a system dual-boot is very simple—let NT do the work. Install DOS or Windows 95 on the system partition first before you install NT. Make sure that the drive is formatted with FAT16, because NT cannot read a 95/98 installation with FAT32. When NT installs, it will recognize the existing operating system, create the special file for that operating system (the file is called **BOOTSEC.DOS**, even if the other operating system is Windows 95/98), and add a line to the **BOOT.INI** file to add the operating system to the boot menu.

NOTE: *Without* **BOOTSEC.DOS**, *attempting to select the DOS or Windows 95/98 operating system will give a "system files" error.*

ADDING DUAL-BOOT TO AN EXISTING NT INSTALL   Two processes exist for adding a new operating system to an existing installation of Windows NT. The first process is adding another installation of NT. You might do this if you needed a single machine to boot as a stand-alone NT Server or as a Primary Domain Controller. The second process is adding either DOS or Windows 95/98. Adding another copy of NT is very easy.

Adding a copy of DOS or Windows 95/98 can be a little challenging and is sometimes impossible without wiping out the NT installation.

NOTE: *In theory, it is impossible to add both a DOS and a Windows 95/98 boot. You can have either one or the other. But there is a way to "triple boot" between DOS, Windows 95/98, and NT. It's way outside the scope of this book and it certainly isn't on the exams, but if you want to try it, locate the Microsoft Knowledge Base article # Q157992. It is not supported by Microsoft and doesn't always work, but it sure is neat! Use it at your own risk!*

ADDING DOS DUAL-BOOT   The ability to boot to DOS on an NT system is a very handy option when troubleshooting boot problems. Arguably the best way to install NT is to create a small, DOS-bootable 300–500MB FAT16 partition on the system partition before installing NT. In doing so, NT will make the DOS boot option for you. Should there be a boot problem, it is simply a matter of selecting **MS-DOS** when the menu appears to get to a C: prompt. If DOS needs to be installed after NT, however, follow the process outlined below.

First, verify that the system partition is FAT16. If the system partition is NTFS, the system cannot be configured for dual-boot. Windows NT has no facility for converting an NTFS system partition to FAT16, although there may be a third party utility with that capability. If the system partition is FAT16, then it can be made to dual-boot.

1. Make sure you have a current Emergency Rescue Disk for the NT installation. See the next section, "Dealing with Boot Failures," for details on the ERD.

2. Create an NT boot floppy. Again, see the next session on how to make an NT boot floppy.

3. Make sure you have the three NT setup disks. They can be the originals or the copies made by NT.

4. Boot to a DOS floppy disk. Run the **SYS C:** command to make the system partition DOS bootable. Copy any extra DOS files.

5. Remove the DOS floppy and verify that the system boots successfully to DOS. Insert the first NT setup disk and reboot. Add the other setup floppies as the system calls for them.

6. At one point, the NT Install welcome screen will appear and prompt you to hit Enter to continue or to hit **R** to "repair a damaged Windows NT version 4.0 installation." Press **R** and you will see four check boxes. Select only the "Inspect boot sector"

checkbox. This will "repoint" the hard drive's boot sector to **NTLDR**
and add the MS-DOS option.

ADDING WINDOWS 95/98 DUAL-BOOT   The process of installing
Windows 95/98 to an existing installation of NT is virtually identical to
the DOS process. There are a few special issues that need to be addressed.
In step four, make sure to create a Windows-bootable floppy that can
access the CD-ROM. In fact, it does not even have to be a Windows-
bootable floppy—a DOS one will be fine—as long as it can see the CD-
ROM. Install Windows 95/98 as the last step of step four.

A dual-boot of Windows 95/98 and NT does not affect the Windows 95
boot menu. You can have a boot to Windows 95/98 that then allows the
option to boot to Previous Version of MS-DOS. Do not use Windows 95
OSR2, because this version does not support the Previous version of MS-
DOS option. Oh sure, it will show up in the Windows 95 boot menu, but
it will also screw up your system and keep it from booting.

ADDING ANOTHER NT DUAL-BOOT   Compared to adding DOS or
Windows 95/98, adding another copy of Windows NT is a cakewalk. Run
WINNT32 and install as normal. At one point, NT will see the previous
installation and ask you if you want to install over that installation or if
you want to make a new installation. If you select new installation, you
will march through a standard installation. Just make sure to create a
new partition for the new NT installation. The new installation will add
two new lines to the **BOOT.INI** file, allowing the choice between the two
installations. The following example shows two copies of NT Server
installed on two different EIDE drives.

```
[boot loader]
timeout=30
default= multi(0)disk(0)rdisk(0)partition(1)\WINNT

[operating systems]
multi(0)disk(0)rdisk(0)partition(1)\WINNT="Windows NT
     Server Version 4.00 "
multi(0)disk(0)rdisk(0)partition(1)\WINNT="Windows NT
     Server Version 4.00 [VGA mode]" /basevideo /sos
multi(0)disk(0)rdisk(1)partition(1)\WINNT="Windows NT
     Server Version 4.00 "
multi(0)disk(0)rdisk(1)partition(1)\WINNT="Windows NT
     Server Version 4.00 [VGA mode]" /basevideo /sos
C:\="Microsoft Windows"
```

NOTE: Installing multiple copies of NT on one machine is a great way to practice for the MCSE exams. Not only do you get to try dual-booting, but you also get one machine with as many different versions of NT as you need to practice.

There is one small problem with the this earlier example. Two copies of NT server have been installed: One installation is configured as a PDC and the other is a stand-alone server. The problem is they look identical on the boot menu. To fix this, simply change the text in parentheses to something more readable.

```
[boot loader]
timeout=30
default= multi(0)disk(0)rdisk(0)partition(1)\WINNT

[operating systems]
multi(0)disk(0)rdisk(0)partition(1)\WINNT="NT Server PDC"
multi(0)disk(0)rdisk(0)partition(1)\WINNT="NT Server PDC
      [VGA mode]" /basevideo /sos
multi(0)disk(0)rdisk(1)partition(1)\WINNT="NT Server Stand
      Alone"
multi(0)disk(0)rdisk(1)partition(1)\WINNT="NT Server Stand
      Alone [VGA mode]" /basevideo /sos
C:\="Microsoft Windows"
```

Dual-booting is a handy and powerful feature of Windows NT. Dual-booting, as well as the rest of the boot process, is, for the most part, a robust process. But, from time to time, problems can take place in the NT boot process. NT has a number of tools to help when these little nasties take place on a system. Let's take a look at the most common ones—the ones you should know for the exams.

Boot Failure Tools

A boot failure in NT is any problem that prevents the system from getting to the system's desktop. These failures range from bad sectors on drives through corrupted and missing files. To help when things go wrong at boot, NT provides a number of handy tools. The most common of these tools are **BOOT.INI** troubleshooting switches, the ERD, bootable floppy disks, and the Last Known Good Configuration.

TROUBLESHOOTING SWITCHES FOR BOOT.INI   When Windows NT is installed in a system, the installation will always place two menu options for that installation in the **BOOT.INI** file.

```
[operating systems]
multi(0)disk(0)rdisk(0)partition(1)\WINNT="Windows NT
      Server Version 4.00 "
multi(0)disk(0)rdisk(0)partition(1)\WINNT="Windows NT
      Server Version 4.00 [VGA mode]" /basevideo /sos
```

The first menu option starts the standard installation, set by default in the **[boot loader]** section. The second option is identical to the first option with the exception of two switches, **/basevideo** and **/sos**. In a way, this option can be seen as the "Safe Mode" of Windows NT. While these switches do perform a few of the features of Windows 95/98 Safe Mode, they are a far cry from a true Safe Mode. For example, these switches do not turn off virtual memory or 32-bit disk access as does the Windows 95/98 Safe Mode. This second option is used in only two different situations: Troubleshooting video problems and troubleshooting boot drivers.

TROUBLESHOOTING VIDEO   Two different problems can take place with the video software. First is a corrupted or an incorrect video driver. During the installation of NT, it is way too easy to install an old, buggy, or just plain wrong video driver. The second problem is to configure a video card to do a resolution that needs a refresh rate that the monitor can't handle, resulting in a blank screen at boot. One of the most common manifestations of this is the inability to boot to the NT desktop. The **/basevideo** switch tells the system to use only standard VGA drivers. You can then attempt to reinstall a driver, reconfigure video settings, etc.

TROUBLESHOOTING DRIVERS   NT loads a large number of drivers at boot. Once in a while, a driver can become corrupted or get erased, preventing the system from booting properly or from booting at all. It would be nice to see the drivers as they load to help zero in on the culprit driver. That's where the **/sos** switch comes into play. During a normal boot the loading of these drivers is hidden behind a screen that looks like this:

```
OS Loader V4.00



...
```

When the **/sos** option is loaded, this screen shows each driver as it loads:

```
OS Loader V4.00

      multi(0)disk(0)rdisk(0)partition(2)\WINNT\System32\nto
      skrnl.exe
```

```
multi(0)disk(0)rdisk(0)partition(2)\WINNT\System32\hal.dll

   multi(0)disk(0)rdisk(0)partition(2)\WINNT\system32\con
   fig\system

   multi(0)disk(0)rdisk(0)partition(2)\WINNT\system32\c_1
   252.nls
```

EMERGENCY REPAIR DISK   An *Emergency Repair Disk* (ERD) is probably the single most important tool for recovering from boot failures. An ERD is a floppy diskette that contains critical system information, including details on the Registry, account and group information, passwords, including the administrator password, partitions, and copies of the all of the installed files on the system. This is identical to the information stored in the **\WINNT\REPAIR** directory. The ERD is the first line of defense for correcting a number of errors in NT.

CREATING AN ERD   An ERD can be created in two different ways. The first way is during the install process. As mentioned in Chapter 2, "Installing NT," the NT installation process prompts you to create an ERD, as shown in Figure 4–3.

Figure 4–3
Creating an ERD
during Windows NT
Setup

The other way to create an ERD is through the **RDISK** program. This program is not on the Start menu, you need to run it via the Start/Run command (see Figure 4–4). Select Create Repair Disk to make an ERD. The floppy does not need to be blank or formatted, because **RDISK** formats the floppy as it runs.

The information on the system that the ERD backs up changes constantly. Virtually anything done to the system—Installing new files, adding new hardware, etc.—requires creating a new ERD. The test may refer to this process as "updating" the ERD. There is really no way to "update" an ERD. The update process is to insert an old ERD, run **RDISK**, and overwrite the old ERD with new information. That is not updating, that is creating a new ERD. But the term everyone uses is updating so we will use it here.

UPDATING AN ERD   Keeping an updated copy of the ERD is critical. Good NT administrators will make a point to update their ERD every time they update their system. Unfortunately, real-world systems don't really get updated that often; they get configured and spend months, even years, never being touched. One time where systems get their ERDs updated quite a bit is during the initial configuration. Most NT configurations are a multi-step process of adding hardware and applications one at a time. There's no absolute rule on updating the ERD. Stick to the old standard —"When in doubt, update the ERD."

Use the command **RDISK** to update the ERD. The process of updating the ERD with **RDISK** requires two steps. When **RDISK** starts, Update Repair Info is already selected. This will update the information in the system's **\WINNT\REPAIR** directory. After the information has been updated on the system, the system then prompts for creation of an ERD. Insert either the old ERD floppy or a new floppy to make the new ERD.

CREATING A BOOT DISK   An ERD is very important. If a system refuses to boot, getting the information off of the ERD and onto the system will repair a large number of boot problems. But if the system doesn't boot, how will this information get to the system? The ERD holds information

Figure 4–4
The Repair Disk Utility
(RDISK)

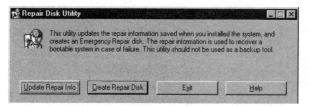

that the system needs, but it is not bootable. To get the system started so that you may use the ERD requires some type of boot floppy. To create a bootable diskette, format a floppy under NT by running **FORMAT A:** from a command prompt or by right-clicking the floppy icon under My Computer and selecting Format. The floppy must be formatted under Windows NT— a DOS formatted floppy doesn't have the capability to start NTLDR. Copy the following files onto the newly formatted floppy:

```
NTLDR
NTDETECT.COM
BOOT.INI
```

If the system is configured for dual-boot, be sure to copy the **BOOTSEC. DOS** file. If there are any SCSI drives without ROM BIOS support, **NTBOOTDD. SYS** is also needed. You now have a bootable NT floppy. Boot to the floppy to verify that it works.

LAST KNOWN GOOD CONFIGURATION After every successful boot, NT stores critical information about the configuration of the system in a special backup. During the system boot, NT will prompt the user with

```
OS Loader V4.00
...
Press spacebar NOW to Invoke Hardware Profile/Last Known
       Good menu
```

Selecting this option shows a Recovery Menu that allows the user to select the earlier configuration. This option is very handy for errant hardware drivers. By selecting the Last Known Good Configuration, the system can be brought to the point before the device was installed, allowing the installation to be tried again.

Common Boot Problems

The secret to handling boot problems is to understand the boot process, make backups of every level of the boot process, and know how to read the errors to determine the correct backup to use. Armed with these tools (plus a few more that will be discussed next), the process of recovering from a problem at boot is a relatively easy and painless task. The following is a list of the more common problems, starting at the "bottom"—hardware— and moving up through the different boot files.

HARDWARE WOES A good MCSE understands disk hardware. This includes drives, jumpers, proper connections, terminations (if SCSI), and CMOS/BIOS settings. This chapter could be filled with stories about MCSEs who can talk about `BOOT.INI` and ARC all day long, but who don't know how to plug in an EIDE or SCSI hard drive, or who couldn't punch their way out of a wet CMOS setup with both hands. This is really embarrassing. Too many MCSEs haven't taken the time to understand such trivial hardware basics. Sure, you can get an MCSE without this knowledge, but a real-world environment assumes you know this stuff.

IMPROPER DISK INSTALLATIONS The one nice part about disk problems is that most improper disk installations give basically the same type of error:

```
DISK BOOT FAILURE, INSERT SYSTEM DISK AND PRESS ENTER
```

or

```
NO ROM BASIC, SYSTEM HALTED
```

When these errors show up, it is time to check the hardware and CMOS/BIOS settings. Without going into an entire chapter on disk hardware, here's a checklist of disk configuration issues:

EIDE/IDE

1. Do the drives have power? Are they properly connected?
2. Are the Master/Slave settings correct on all drives?
3. If the CMOS has an Autodetect feature, does it see the drives? If not, check the first two again.

SCSI

1. Any IRQ or I/O address conflicts with the host adapter?
2. Power to all drives?
3. Unique SCSI IDs?
4. Proper Termination?
5. Cabling correct?
6. ROM BIOS enabled `/NTBOOTDD.SYS` in root of system partition?
7. Does the drive require a special option like "Send Start Command," etc.?

All Drives

1. Is the CMOS allowing the drive you wish to be the boot drive first in the boot order?

2. Any onboard controller active that should not be active, or vice-versa?

CORRUPTED MASTER BOOT RECORD   The first drive in the boot order needs to have a Boot Sector. The boot sector requires both a *Master Boot Record* (MBR) and a Partition Table. The Master Boot Record is the first code read off of the hard drive and is very standardized. If the MBR is corrupted, it can be fixed by booting to a DOS floppy and running the `FDISK /MBR` command.

There are two situations where using `FDISK /MBR` will not fix a corrupted MBR. The first situation is when a drive overlay is in use. Drive overlays are special MBRs used by third-party software programs (with names like OnTrack Disk Manager) to allow systems with older BIOS to accept larger (greater than 2G) hard drives. If you are using an overlay, you were provided a program that allows you to make a bootable disk to replace that overlay. You must use that disk. If the disk wasn't created, you're probably going to have to reinstall everything from scratch. All data on the drive will be lost. The second situation is with boot sector viruses. A boot sector virus lives in the MBR, corrupting files as they are loaded. Yes, `FDISK /MBR` will erase a boot sector virus, but many boot sector viruses will move file information to another spot on the drive. If you delete the boot sector virus, you lose all the data on the drive. If you suspect that you have a virus, boot to a floppy, run a good anti-virus program, then use a boot floppy to start NT and copy the system files. You can also rerun the setup from the setup floppies and select the "Repair a previous installation," as described earlier.

CORRUPTED PARTITION TABLES   The partition tables are also part of the boot sector. The partition tables tell where the partitions start, stop, and the type of partitions. Unfortunately, NT has no facility for saving the partition table. Use a good backup tool like Microhouse's Drive-Pro to save the partition table.

CORRUPT SYSTEM FILES   Corrupt system or boot files can generate a number of different errors. Usually there will be a clue that the system is trying to boot but can't work. Some examples are:

```
BOOT: Couldn't Find NTLDR
Please insert another disk
```

NTLDR is missing or corrupt. Boot to an NT bootable floppy and copy NTLDR to the root directory of the system partition.

```
Windows NT could not start because the following file is
     missing or corrupt:
<winnt root>\system32\ntoskrnl.exe.
Please reinstall a copy of the above file.
```

Usually this error points to a bad or missing **BOOT.INI** file. It will be necessary to boot to a bootable floppy. If it works, copy the **BOOT.INI** on the floppy to the root directory of the system partition. If booting to a boot floppy does not work, either the partition values have been changed due to adding or taking away drives/partitions or the **NTOSKRNL** is truly corrupt. If drives have been added or removed, use the boot order chart to determine the correct **rdisk(y)** and **partition(z)** values and manually edit them on the boot floppy. If the problem is still there and you know you have the correct ARC formats in the boot floppy's **BOOT.INI**, run the setup floppies and perform a repair install.

```
NTDETECT V4.0 Checking Hardware . . .
NTDETECT failed
```

NTDETECT.COM is missing or corrupt. Boot to an NT bootable floppy and copy **NTDETECT.COM** to the root directory of the system partition.

Fixing system file problems without an NT boot disk requires an alternative boot disk and the NT installation CD-ROM. Boot to a DOS or Windows 95/98 floppy that has support for the CD-ROM. If the bad file is **NTDETECT.COM** or **NTLDR**, copy the file off the CD-ROM into the system partition. If the file is **BOOT.INI**, inspect the **BOOT.INI** file in the system directory and edit it or recreate it.

CORRUPT BOOT AND OPERATING SYSTEM FILES While the errors are different, the easy fix is always the same. Boot from the setup disks and run the Repair install, using the ERD. If you do not have a recent ERD, the next choice is to reinstall NT and restore from backup.

Questions

1. An NT system has two IDE drives, a Primary Master and a Secondary Master. Both drives have only one bootable partition. NT Server is installed on the Primary Master. You install a copy of NT Workstation on the Secondary Master. Both copies are installed into a directory called **\WINNT**. What will the ARC name for the Secondary Master look like in the **BOOT.INI** after the copy of NT Workstation is installed?

   a. `multi(0)disk(0)rdisk(0)partition(2)\WINNT="Windows NT Workstation Version 4.00"`

   b. `multi(0)disk(1)rdisk(0)partition(1)\WINNT="Windows NT Workstation Version 4.00"`

   c. `multi(0)disk(0)rdisk(1)partition(1)\WINNT="Windows NT Workstation Version 4.00"`

   d. `multi(0)disk(0)rdisk(0)partition(1)\WINNT="Windows NT Workstation Version 4.00"`

2. Which of the following is not stored on the ERD?

   a. Passwords

   b. Master Boot Record

   c. Hardware

   d. Installation Files

3. You have two copies of Windows NT installed on a system. The system always boots to one of the installations unless the other installation is selected from the boot menu. What must be changed in the **BOOT.INI** to make the other installation boot automatically?

   a. `[boot loader]`

   b. `C:\="Windows NT Server . . . "`

   c. `Default=`

   d. `Auto=`

4. An NT system locks up at boot with an "Error loading NTLDR" message. You only have a recent ERD and the Windows NT installation CD-ROM. Which of the following options has the best chance of success?

    a. Boot to the ERD and run **WINNT32**; use the setup repair option

    b. Go into CMOS and make the system boot first to a CD-ROM. Boot to the CD-ROM and use the setup repair option

    c. Reboot the system and create a boot floppy and copy **NTLDR** to the root directory of the system partition

    d. None of these options can possibly work

5. A system with ROM BIOS supported SCSI host adapters must have a file that other NT systems will not need. This file is

    a. **NTBOOTDD.SYS** in the root directory of the boot partition

    b. **NTBOOTDD.SYS** in the root directory of the system partition

    c. **NTOSKRNL.EXE** in the boot partition

    d. **NTOSKRNL.EXE** in the system partition

6. Which of the following ARC formats could be valid for a SCSI drive with ROM BIOS support?

    a. **multi(0)disk(1)rdisk(0)partition(4)**

    b. **scsi(0)disk(0)rdisk(1)partition(2)**

    c. **multi(0)disk(0)rdisk(1)partition(1)**

    d. **scsi(0)disk(1)rdisk(0)partition(3)**

7. An NT boot floppy must have (Choose all that apply)

    a. **NTLDR.SYS**

    b. **NTDETECT.COM**

    c. **BOOT.INI**

    d. **BOOTSEC.DOS**

8. You decide to upgrade the video card in your NT Workstation. After the upgrade, the system seems to boot, but the monitor goes blank before you get to the desktop. Which of the following would be the best procedure to fix this problem?

   a. Run setup floppies

   b. Boot to ERD and restore the original video settings

   c. Select the VGA Mode boot option

   d. Select the Last Known Good Configuration at boot

9. If an NT system can dual-boot to DOS or Windows 95, you know that

   a. A file called **BOOTSEC.DOS** is in the system partition.

   b. A file called **BOOTSEC.DOS** is in the boot partition.

   c. A file called **NTLDR** is in the system partition.

   d. A file called **NTLDR** is in the boot partition.

10. The error **DISK BOOT FAILURE, INSERT SYSTEM DISK AND PRESS ENTER** would point to

    a. Hard Drive not properly installed

    b. Corrupt or incorrect **BOOT.INI**

    c. Corrupt or missing **NTLDR**

    d. Corrupt or missing **NTDETECT.COM**

Answers

1. c—**multi(0)disk(0)rdisk(1)partition(1)**—**rdisk(1)** shows it is the second drive in the boot order and **partition(1)** shows it is the first partition.

2. b—The ERD does not store the *Master Boot Record* (MBR)

3. c—The **Default=** option in the **[boot loader]** section must be changed to show the location of the partition to be automatically started. The location must be in ARC format.

4. b—Try to boot from the CD-ROM if the system has that capability. The ERD is not bootable (b) and if the system can't boot you can't create a boot floppy (c).

5. b—**NTBOOTDD.SYS** must be in the system partition. **NTOSKRNL** in the boot partition (c) is needed by all NT installations.

6. c—The SCSI format is never used for drives with ROM BIOS support (b,d). When using the **MULTI** option, the **DISK** value will always be **disk(0)** (a).

7. b, c—There is no file called **NTLDR.SYS** (a). **BOOTSEC.DOS** is only needed if the system dual-boots (d).

8. c—The driver is probably fine, it is just that the monitor is being pushed too hard. Running setup disks would totally reinstall NT (a). You can't boot to an ERD (b). Last Known Good Configuration would work, but it wouldn't allow you to fix the problem. VGA mode would allow you to set the resolution down to something the system could handle.

9. a—**BOOTSEC.DOS** must be in the system partition, not the boot partition (b). **NTLDR** is always in the system partition, the fact that the system dual-boots is meaningless (c, d).

10. a—A general rule for NT system file errors is that the error message that appears will reflect the file name. The generic "DISK BOOT FAILURE" message means the computer cannot find an operating system at all. Check the hard drive installation.

NT Application Support

Information technology folks sometimes forget why operating systems exist. All operating systems exist for only one reason: to support application programs. A typical PC user does not want to be an MCSE. To the typical user, the PC is simply a tool for getting work done. When asked to define the term "operating system," a typical user would probably be able to tell you the name of the OS he or she uses, but the user would not be able to provide an acceptable definition. This situation is good. The ideal OS should be invisible. Sure, a user may use aspects of the interface when clicking the Start button or dragging a file from one window to another, but users should not worry about issues of device drivers, file structures, or any of the thousands of functions performed by the OS. The typical PC user walks up to the PC, fires it up, and starts an application. The applications—spreadsheets, databases, and word processors—make PCs valuable. Without the applications, the OS is useless.

Windows NT excels in its support for applications. To appreciate the beauty of NT's application support, let's first define the goals of application support.

The following list describes the basic goals for supporting applications:

1. To provide all resources needed for the applications to do their jobs

2. To enable applications to run safely, minimizing any threat of failure

3. To enable applications to run quickly

In addition, more modern, multi-tasking operating systems have additional goals:

1. To enable multiple applications to run simultaneously in an efficient fashion

2. To prevent, or at least minimize, the damage from an errant application

3. To distribute limited resources evenly to applications and ensure the return of unused resources from applications that no longer need them

While not directly associated with application support, any OS should accomplish three other goals:

1. The OS should be shielded from the details of different hardware.

2. The OS should be able to run on different CPUs (i.e., "multi-platform").

3. The OS should support applications from other Operating systems.

NT addresses all of these issues. This chapter details the internal structure of NT to show how NT achieves these goals and why it is a powerful and safe OS.

NT Building Blocks

Microsoft developed Windows NT with support for applications as the primary goal. To this end, Microsoft developed NT around the concept of a "Client/Server" OS. Just to add confusion, this idea does *not* mean client/server in terms of networking. Figure 5–1 shows that in this context, client/server means layering·the functions of the OS in such a way that applications are treated as client programs, each one being serviced by server programs that provide the necessary resources for the application to run.

NOTE: *Keep in mind that in the NT world, the term "application" does not always refer only to user programs such as Microsoft Word or Netscape Communicator. An application can also be printing functions, virtual machines (see NTVDMs in this section), and many other "higher-level" programs.*

In addition to the client/server model, NT is an "object-oriented" OS. In classic "linear" programming, a program has a large, main chunk of code with a start and a finish. This large chunk of code contains all of the primary functions of the OS, as shown in Figure 5–2. The main program, often referred to as the "kernel," starts and then continually loops, calling subprograms as needed. The danger of linear programming is that if the main code breaks down at any point, the entire program crashes.

In an object-oriented program, the program is divided into many small objects, each being serviced by another object. If one object breaks down, the rest of the program should not be affected (see Figure 5–3). NT, as an object-oriented OS, differs dramatically from older Operating systems which tend to be linear and incorporate most of the functions of the OS into the main code.

Figure 5–1
The client/server
relationship

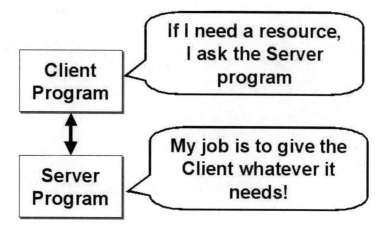

Figure 5–2
Linear OS

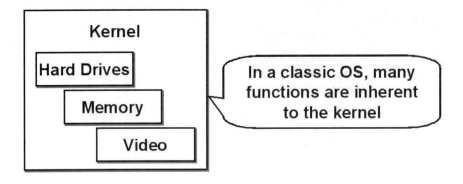

Figure 5–3
Object-oriented OS

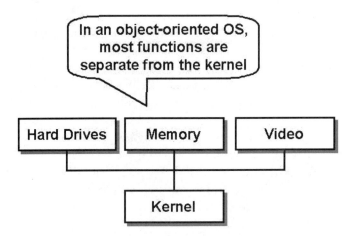

All Intel processors use a "ring" concept for protected-mode operation. In ring-based protected mode, every program running is assigned a privilege level—also known as a ring level—to define which programs can access that particular program. Intel has defined four ring modes, numbered Ring 0 through Ring 3. Ring 0 is the most protected mode; no program with a higher ring number can access a Ring 0 without going through a rather involved process. As shown in Figure 5–4, any program with a higher privilege—a lower Ring number—can easily access programs with a lower privilege—a higher Ring number.

OS designers are not required to use all four rings. When designing NT, Microsoft decided to use only two ring levels to improve system speed and

Figure 5–4
Protected mode ring
levels

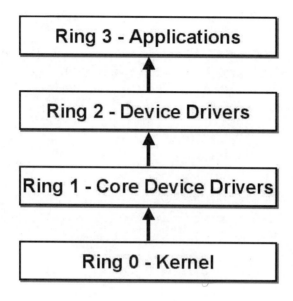

Figure 5–5
NT protection modes

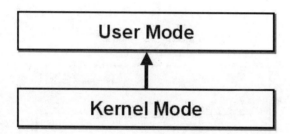

simplicity. NT divides all the functions of the OS into Ring 0 and Ring 3. Ring 0 programs are called "Kernel Mode," and Ring 3 programs are called "User Mode" (see Figure 5–5).

The goal for Microsoft was to place as many functions as possible into User Mode. This idea would enable the system to protect the Kernel Mode functions as much as possible, thereby improving system stability. This separation of Kernel and User modes also enables NT to achieve many OS goals, such as platform independence and the capacity to support applications from many different operating systems. Let's dismantle the NT Kernel to see in more detail how these goals are achieved.

Kernel Mode—The NT Executive

All functions of NT kernel mode are encompassed in the "NT Executive." The NT Executive is not a single program, but rather a group of program objects that work together to provide the base OS needed by higher-level functions. The NT Executive has three major components:

1. The Microkernel

2. The Hardware Abstraction Layer (HAL)

3. The Executive Services

Figure 5–6 displays the organization of the Kernel mode components. The layering of the figure shows the relative communication paths.

The Microkernel

The Microkernel, sometimes referred to as the "kernel," is the heart of the NT OS. It is known as the microkernel as opposed to the kernel to reflect the fact that while it is very important, it is very small and delegates all

Figure 5–6
NT kernel mode
applications

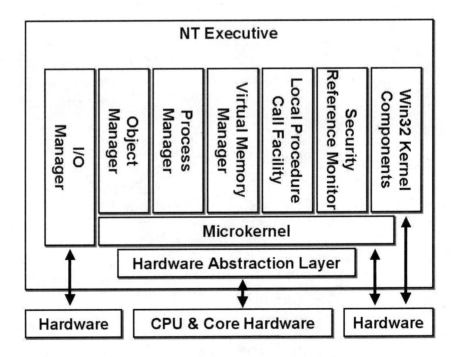

but the most critical of OS functions to other parts of the OS. It might even be better to call the microkernel the "boss," rather than the "heart," because it does little more than direct other parts of the NT Executive.

The microkernel directs other parts of the NT Executive through "thread processing." In an NT system, a running program, or part of a running program, is called a "process" and a process is composed of one or more threads. A large number of threads run simultaneously from many different processes on an NT system. For example, a well-written word processing program may have one thread updating the screen as keys are pressed, another checking the grammar, and another performing a background save. The microkernel uses a built-in priority system to determine which threads run at any given moment. The threads then pass to the Hardware Abstraction Layer for processing.

The Hardware Abstraction Layer

The *Hardware Abstraction Layer* (HAL) of the NT Executive gives Windows NT the ability to operate on more than one type of computer platform. All other Windows Operating systems (3.X, 95, 98) are designed to operate only on Intel x86 processors like the 486, Pentium, and Pentium II. While this is fine for the majority of systems on desktops and laptops, it keeps Windows from entering into the large number of UNIX-based systems that run on other CPUs, such as the DEC Alpha, MIPS, and PowerPC. The HAL provides the interface between the CPU, the core machine components (cache, RAM, etc.), and the OS. No matter what type of CPU is installed in a system, other parts of the Executive talk to the HAL in the exact same way. Every type of CPU that NT supports requires its own specific HAL. Using the HAL to separate the OS from the CPU type makes NT very portable. To make NT work on another CPU requires only the recompiling of the HAL.

 NOTE: *Actually both the HAL and the microkernel need to be recompiled for different Operating systems. The Windows NT CD-ROM comes with separate HALs and microkernels for x86, MIPS, and DEC Alpha CPUs. When NT is installed, there is no obvious compiling being performed. The person installing NT simply picks the proper "setup" program from the proper subdirectory on the NT CD-ROM.*

The HAL also enables NT to work in computers with more than one CPU—a process better known as *Symmetric Multiprocessing* (SMP). When NT runs on a system with more than one processor, the HAL informs the microkernel of the status of every CPU and sends threads to the CPU as dictated by the microkernel.

Somebody is bound to ask: "If there is symmetric multiprocessing—then there must be *asymmetric* multiprocessing, right? What's the difference?" Well, there is such an animal as asymmetric multiprocessing. In asymmetric multiprocessing, certain processors can only handle certain code. In symmetric multiprocessing, on the other hand, each CPU can handle all supported types of code. Almost all CPUs are designed to run SMP, because it is regarded as superior to asymmetric.

Executive Services

The workhorses of the NT Executive are the "Executive Services." The executive services are seven functions within the NT Executive that have very specific, very separate functions. They are (in no specific order)

1. I/O Manager
2. Local Procedure Call Facility
3. Object Manager
4. Process Manager
5. Security Reference Monitor
6. Virtual Memory Manager
7. Win32 Core Components

I/O MANAGER   The I/O Manager receives all of the resource requests for devices under its control and accesses those resources via the appropriate device driver. The I/O manager handles all of the hardware in the system, with the exception of the CPU and other core components described in the HAL section. This includes hard drives, network cards, and any SCSI devices; making I/O Manager clearly the hardest working component of all the Executive Services. In the earlier diagram of the NT Kernel, do you see how the I/O manager directly accesses the system hardware? This implies that the I/O Manager does not need either the HAL or the microkernel. While the I/O Manager most certainly can access the system hardware without the HAL, it makes direct access of the hardware under the direction of the microkernel.

One of the more exciting aspects of device drivers under Windows NT is the capacity to load and unload device drivers dynamically, without the need to restart the computer. (Ah, if only Windows 95/98 could do that.) Device drivers are loaded via installation programs and, at least until Windows NT 5.0 with Plug-and-Play support comes along, must be modified from one of many different icons within the control panel window. Figure 5–7 shows a typical Windows NT control panel. Note that there are icons for Networking, SCSI, Multimedia, etc.

Once device drivers are installed, they can be loaded or unloaded via the Devices icon in the Control Panel. Figure 5–8 displays a common Devices window showing a number of devices loaded.

Figure 5–7
NT control panel

Figure 5–8
NT devices

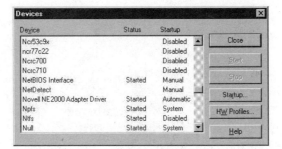

Note that some of the devices are running while others are not. This is normal in NT—many device drivers are loaded by default, regardless of whether or not the system actually needs them. The Devices applet not only enables the device drivers to be loaded and unloaded, it is used to determine how the device drivers are loaded.

An OS is only as good as its device drivers. Due to the I/O Manager's direct access to hardware, a poorly written device driver can completely lock up an NT system. To avoid such headaches, Microsoft makes device drivers for many products and provides a testing method for third-party device drivers to ensure that device drivers will operate properly under NT.

LOCAL PROCEDURE CALL FACILITY   Programs, or more correctly the threads created by programs, often need to communicate. In a client/server OS such as Windows NT, the client—or server—must be able to enable their threads to communicate in a safe, efficient manner. This is the job of the Local Procedure Call Facility. Let's say we have two threads running in a memory function. One thread accesses the memory address for one object while another thread calculates a value that will be based on the results of the first thread. Clearly, the first thread must inform the second thread when it has the result, so the second thread can finish the calculation of the value. It must be done quickly and without messing up any other code. The Local Procedure Call Facility process enables the information to run from the first thread to the other as quickly as possible without creating problems for any other threads.

OBJECT MANAGER   Everything in the world of Windows NT manifests itself as an object. An *object* is a data structure, stored in memory, that defines its attributes, values, and capabilities. For example, a data object for storing last names might be something like

```
fieldname = LNAME(23)
Data type = string
Max Length = 20
Language = English
Value = Meyers
```

Objects are not limited to defining only data. An object can define physical aspects of the computer as well. Whenever a program uses a serial port in NT, for example, the Object Manager creates an object in memory and names it so that whatever program needs access to that port actually accesses the data ports' object. When the program needing the serial port finishes, the Object Manager erases the serial port object from memory. An object can also be used to define another program or part of another program. Using the earlier database example, there could be another object called RECORD(23) that looks like

```
Name = RECORD(23)
Number of fieldnames = 4
Fieldname1 = FNAME(23)
Fieldname2 = LNAME(23)
Fieldname3 = ADDRESS(23)
Fieldname4 = PHONE(23)
```

Note that the RECORD object does not store the data, it simply points to subobjects—like LNAME(23)—that hold the data. In NT, objects are the way things are done and, as you can imagine, when NT is running, there are LOTS of objects!

This is great, but something has to keep track of these objects. This is the job of the Object Manager. The Object Manager creates and erases objects. Using the earlier example of the serial port, a communication program calls to the Object Manager for access to a serial port. The Object Manager will first see whether that particular device already has an object created—perhaps another communications program is active, for example. If the object is not created, the Object Manager then calls to the I/O Manager to verify the existence of the resource (the serial port) and to determine the characteristics of that resource. The Object Manager then uses this information to create the object for the serial port and gives the object a name. This name, known as a "handle," is used by the Object Manager and by the programs accessing the object to refer to the serial port.

PROCESS MANAGER   Just as the Object Manager tracks objects, the Process Manager tracks the many processes and threads that are passed to and from the microkernel. The Process Manager keeps all of the important information associated with a process or thread. Keep in mind that a process or thread is code: it has a memory location, a list of associated objects, and a security device called a "token" (see Security Reference Monitor, below). When the microkernel decides to process a particular thread, it accesses the Process Manager for information on the thread to run the process. When the microkernel is finished processing the thread, it updates the thread information via the Process Manager before moving to another thread.

SECURITY REFERENCE MONITOR   The Security Reference Monitor determines whether or not a user has the proper rights to access objects. The Security Reference Monitor is, therefore, the cornerstone of NT security. NT security is based on the concept of users and groups who are given certain rights to objects. When a user logs on to an NT system, a special token called the *Security Access Token* (SAT) is created. Within the SAT is an encoded *Security Identifier* (SID) that identifies the user and any groups to which the user belongs. Every process initiated by that user contains the SID. As requests to access objects come into the Object Manager, the Object Manager queries the Security Reference Monitor to determine whether the user's process has access rights to that object and which types of accesses the user's thread can perform.

VIRTUAL MEMORY MANAGER   The Virtual Memory Manager enables an NT machine to utilize its memory capability, even when it does not have the maximum possible RAM. Windows NT can access up to 4 GB of memory addresses, which is certainly well beyond the scope of today's systems. No computer (currently) actually has 4 GB of RAM, leaving most of the address space unused. The Virtual Memory Manager enables NT to use those extra addresses to map portions of the hard drive as RAM. When the system runs out of RAM, programs can be temporarily stored—although not run—on permanent storage, almost always a hard drive. The process of using a drive to store the contents of RAM temporarily is called "virtual memory."

The NT memory model splits the 4 GB of address space into two 2-gigabit sections. The first two gigabytes are reserved for applications. Programs such as Word, Lotus 123, and Internet Explorer run in this area. The upper two gigabytes are reserved for all of the Kernel-mode components. Windows NT uses a "demand-paged memory model"—the entire 4 gigabytes of memory are broken down into 4096 byte chunks called "pages." As programs request memory, NT gives it to them in pages.

WIN32 CORE COMPONENTS   Both Windows 95/98 and NT share a common set of program elements (i.e.—fonts, icons, scroll bars) needed to run their programs. The Win32 Core Components, often referred to as WIN32K, handle the basic program elements needed by Windows programs. Keep in mind that WIN32K does not provide everything needed to run Windows programs—only the most common. In particular, the Win32 Core components include the GDI functions—the basic functions that enable creation of the many different graphical elements.

Environment Subsystems

At first swipe, it would seem silly not to put ALL of the Windows components into the NT Executive. What is Microsoft's motivation? The answer is simple: Windows NT is designed to run a broad cross-section of programs from a number of other Operating systems. Windows NT can run programs designed for the following Operating systems:

Windows 95/98 and NT applications (32-bit Windows)

OS/2 (character-based and 16-bit Presentation Manager up to version 2.1)

POSIX (Portable Operating System Interface)

Windows 3.X (16-bit Windows)

MS-DOS

The method for supporting multiple operating systems is based on the concept of "Environment Subsystems." Each type of OS supported has its own Environment Subsystem, which is in essence a "pseudo-operating system" running in User Mode. The Environment Subsystem creates the environment, allocates memory, and provides all other resources necessary to enable the particular application to think as though it were running in its native OS environment. The Environment Subsystems access resources in the form of requests to the Executive Services (see Figure 5–9).

Figure 5–9
NT environment subsystems

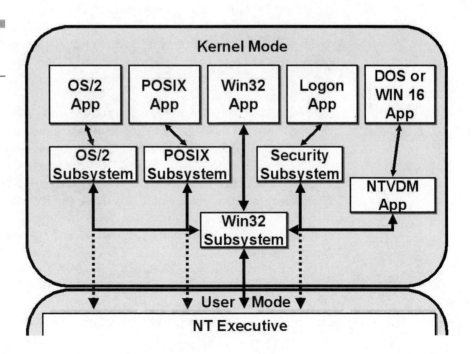

The separation of the Environment Subsystems from the Executive Services enables Windows NT to be extremely modular, providing a number of advantages. First, each Environment Subsystem runs in a separate, protected memory space. Should one subsystem fail, it will not affect the other ones. Second, this separation prevents the need to duplicate services for each subsystem. Third, should Microsoft decide to provide support for another operating system's applications, it would be simply a matter of creating the new Environment Subsystem and updating a few aspects of the Executive Services. Let's look at each of the Environment Subsystems.

Win32 Subsystem

Win32S creates a pseudo-OS for 32-bit Windows applications and provides support for all other subsystems. The other subsystems do little more than translate non-Win32 requests into the Win32 language (which is better known as API). Some cases exist where a non-Win32 subsystem can talk directly to the Executive Services, but such cases are rare exceptions. The Win32 subsystem also handles and tracks all mouse, keyboard, and screen updates across the system. Win32S clearly is the most important of all the Executive Services. Figure 5–10 shows the Win32 subsystem working with an OS/2 subsystem.

The Win32 subsystem provides all of the benefits of 32-bit Windows to 32-bit Windows applications. First is the provision for each 32-bit Windows application to have its own separate 2GB address space. Secondly, the subsystem provides support for multi-threaded applications.

SUPPORT FOR DOS APPLICATIONS   The Win32 subsystem provides all of the support for DOS applications. Microsoft built DOS support into NT from the beginning to support the vast majority of programs on the market at the time. To support a DOS application, Win32 runs a built-in application called the *NT Virtual DOS Machine* (NTVDM). The NTVDM is not a subsystem. Take a close look at the earlier subsystem figure—the NTVDM is shown as an application, not a subsystem. Everything that the NTVDM requests goes through the Win32 subsystem—with a few rare exceptions. Figure 5–11 shows an NTVDM creating a DOS environment.

The DOS environment provided by the NTVDM is an extremely high-quality environment and is similar to the excellent DOS support provided by Windows 95. One good example is in memory management. The NTVDM provides built-in support for all types of memory a DOS application might

Figure 5–10
WIN32S supporting
an OS/2 subsystem

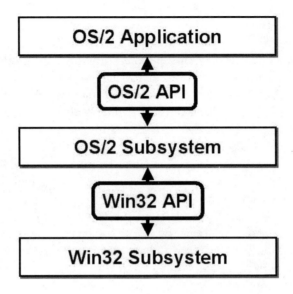

Figure 5–11
NTVDM creating a
DOS environment

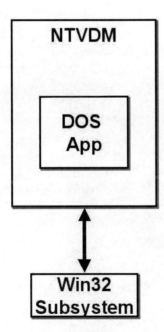

need, including Conventional, *High Memory Area* (HMA), *DOS Protected Mode Interface* (DPMI), *Expanded* (EMS), and *Extended Memory* (XMS). These values are automatic or can be set for a particular DOS application simply by right-clicking the DOS program's icon, selecting the Memory tab in Properties, and changing them, as shown in Figure 5–12. For the majority of DOS applications, the default memory settings will work well.

The DOS NTVDM also provides built-in support for many items that would normally require a device driver in a true DOS system. The two biggest examples would be the CD-ROM and the mouse. Any calls by a DOS application to either of these pieces of hardware is "redirected" by the NTVDM to the appropriate Windows drivers. In essence, the DOS applications receive the benefits of these devices (and others) without the need to eat up any of the memory provided to them. Should a DOS application require a **CONFIG.SYS** and **AUTOEXEC.BAT**, the application can use the default **CONFIG.NT** and **AUTOEXEC.NT**—or the application can have its own **CONFIG.SYS** and **AUTOEXEC.BAT**. This situation is also handled in the DOS application's Properties window . . . Program tab . . . Windows NT button (See Figure 5–13). The NTVDM also has built-in support for serial ports, parallel ports, etc. All of these supported devices have a virtual device driver, which is the one limitation to the NTVDM. The NTVDM cannot support any DOS application that needs to or even tries to access hardware that is not supported by a virtual device driver. As a result, a small percentage of DOS applications will not work on Windows NT.

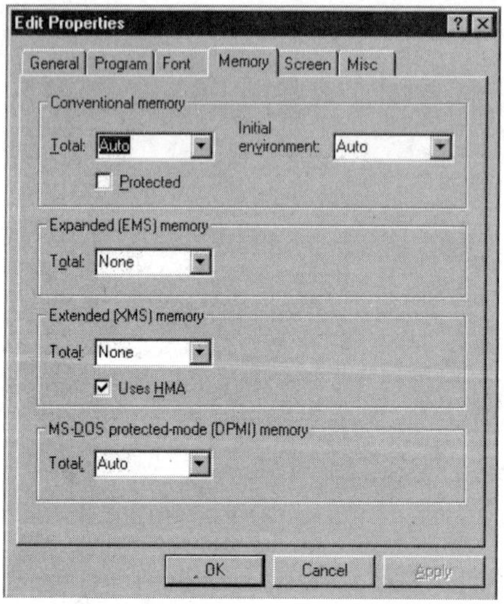

Figure 5–12

Configuring the memory for an NTVDM

Figure 5–13
Special boot files for
an NTVDM

NOTE: *DOS applications are designed to run in Conventional Memory, which is limited to only 655,360 bytes (640K) before any program, including the OS itself, is loaded. In a true DOS machine, losing 100K or more of memory to the OS, to device drivers in the* **CONFIG.SYS** *file, and to the* **Terminate and Stay Resident** *(TSR) programs in* **AUTOEXEC.BAT,** *is not uncommon. In NT, DOS programs have by default about 635,300 bytes (620K) of free memory.*

Another big benefit provided by the NTVDM is in network support. An NTVDM provides complete support for shared network drives and printers. A user can access a drive or printer as easily as if it were in the NT desktop. The only caveat is that drives should be mapped to local drive letters, and printers should be mapped to local LPT ports. Again, in a DOS world, a huge amount of memory is used to provide network support. This situation is virtually eliminated with an NTVDM.

In many ways, running a DOS application in an NTVDM is better than running that application in DOS itself. As mentioned earlier, an NTVDM handles the memory more efficiently, thus enabling more DOS programs to run. Many devices commonly used by DOS applications have built-in support. Because a DOS program runs in an NTVDM, more than one program can be run at one time. When multiple DOS programs are running, each DOS application runs in a separate NTVDM, enabling NT to pre-emptively multi-task each DOS application and to protect each application from the other DOS applications, as shown in Figure 5–14. Try doing that on a pure DOS machine.

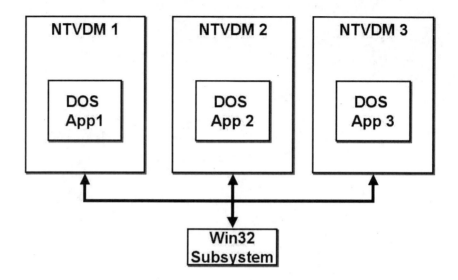

Figure 5–14
Multiple, pre-empted
NTVDMs

PROGRAM INFORMATION FILES Selecting a DOS application's properties by right-clicking its icon creates a special file called a *Program Information File* (PIF). By default, the PIF file is located in the same directory as the DOS application to which it is associated. The PIF file contains all of the information necessary for the NTVDM to create the correct DOS environment for that particular application. To edit a PIF file, right-click the icon for the PIF file or its DOS application and select Properties.

NOTE: *PIF files are only for DOS applications.*

The Properties window for a PIF file has six tabs. The General tab simply provides details on the file's size, dates, and attributes. The Program tab shows the path to the DOS application and provides options for the startup (working) directory and command line parameters. The Windows NT button discussed earlier appears on the Program tab. The Font tab selects the font size for the application. The Memory tab has already been discussed earlier in this chapter. The Screen tab options offer the selection of full-screen or windowed and the number of default lines on the screen, as well as a few other options. The number of default lines is a helpful tool for people who spend a lot of time at a C: prompt, enabling them to increase the number of lines from 24 to something larger. The Miscellaneous tab is well-named. This tab covers all the options that do not readily fit into one of the other categories, which would include the following items: whether the application can work with the Windows NT screen saver and whether the application can run in the background, Idle sensitivity, and shortcut keys.

SUPPORT FOR 16-BIT WINDOWS APPLICATIONS Before Windows NT and Windows 95/98, there were a series of versions of Microsoft Windows known generically as Windows 3.X. These versions of Windows were the following

Windows 3.0

Windows 3.1

Windows for Workgroups 3.1

Windows for Workgroups 3.11

Windows 3.11

Unlike its descendants NT and 95/98, Windows 3.X was not a true OS at all. Windows 3.X actually ran "on top of" DOS. A user would boot the machine into DOS, go to the **\WINDOWS** directory, and start Windows by running the WIN command from a DOS prompt. Of course, many machines had the WIN command in the **AUTOEXEC.BAT** file, which made the Windows 3.X machine seem like an OS from the user's point of view.

NOTE: *Although these versions of Windows are referred to in the past tense, there are millions of machines still running Windows 3.X.*

The Win32 subsystem supports 16-bit Windows (Win16) applications, also known as Windows 3.X applications. As with DOS applications, WIN32S creates an NTVDM to support the Win16 applications. The NTVDM that runs Win16 programs is identical to the ones that run DOS applications. The Win16 NTVDM, however, loads a special process called *Win16 on Win32* (WOW), designed to enable the NTVDM to support the Win16 applications.

One major difference between Windows 3.X and Windows 95/98 is the fact that Windows 3.X is cooperative and multi-tasking, while Windows 95/98 is pre-emptive and multi-tasking. In cooperative multi-tasking, the amount of time that each application runs is up to the applications themselves. Each application is designed to take a certain amount of the processor total time—a "timeslice"—and then release itself so that the next application can run. This problem was big in the early days of Windows 3.X, because some applications refused to give up their timeslice.

When these programs ran, the rest of the system grinded to a halt. Over time, Win16 programmers learned proper etiquette to make well-behaved programs. Windows 95/98 and NT are pre-emptive, multi-tasking operating systems. A pre-emptive, multi-tasking OS keeps control of the times-licing. The OS tells the applications when to start and stop.

Some Win16 applications use a portion of Windows 3.X cooperative multi-tasking called "shared memory." In Win16, the applications can "see" other applications. Many Win16 applications count on this shared-memory model as a way to communicate with other programs. Because of cooperative multi-tasking and shared memory, Windows NT runs all Win16 applications in a single NTVDM. Within the NTVDM, the Win16 applications perform cooperative multi-tasking and share the same memory space.

Through WOW, Win32S provides emulators for the three major components of Windows 3.X: GDI, USER, and KRNL386. When a Win16 application makes a resource request to one of these components, the emulators pass the 16-bit requests to the NTVDM—just like Windows 3.X passes requests to DOS. The Win32 subsystem then "thunks" the 16-bit calls into 32-bit calls before they are passed down to the Executive Services. *Thunking* is the process of turning 16-bit commands into 32-bit commands, and vice-versa.

The unfortunate side of this method is that all of the down sides of the old Win 3.X OS are still present. If one program locks up, that program will almost certainly crash the other Win16 applications running within the same NTVDM. The Win16 applications also cooperatively multi-task within the NTVDM. If all of the applications are well-behaved, this situation is not a problem; but if one application does not play well with the others, the entire NTVDM will run slowly. Furthermore, the entire Win16 NTVDM is pre-emptively multi-tasked with any other NTVDMs and other subsystem applications, which makes the relative timeslice for all the Win16 applications relatively small.

This problem can be reduced—or often eliminated—by having Win16 applications run in their own separate NTVDMs. Each separate NTVDM will have its own separate WOW servicing the single Win16 application. Any Win16 application can be configured to run in its own NTVDM and WOW in a number of ways. The most common way is to create a shortcut for the Win16 application. After creating the shortcut, access the Properties for the shortcut. Select the Run in Separate Memory Space checkbox (Figure 5–15) to enable the application to use its own NTVDM.

Figure 5–15
Making a WIN-16 application run in its own memory space

NOTE: *You can only select the Run in Separate Memory Space checkbox if the shortcut is for a Win16 application. The Windows NT shortcut inspects the EXE file and automatically determines whether the program is a DOS, Win16, or Win32 program. If the application is not Win16, the option will be grayed.*

Two other ways exist to start a Win16 application in a separate NTVDM. The first method is from the Start/Run button. As with shortcuts, select the Run in Separate Memory Space checkbox to enable the application to have its own NTVDM. The second method is from a C: prompt. Type the following command:

```
START /SEPARATE <name of the Win16 program>
```

Advantages and disadvantages exist to running Win16 applications in separate NTVDMs. Some of the more important benefits are the following

1. Eliminates the risk of one Win16 application locking up other applications in the same NTVDM

2. Eliminates the effects of cooperative multi-tasking by eliminating the need to multi-task with other Win16 applications in the same NTVDM

Some of the negatives are as follows

1. Windows programs that take advantage of the shared resource model will not operate properly. Fortunately, these programs are relatively few in number. Programs that use OLE or DDE will operate correctly.

2. Multiple NTVDMs take up more memory.

3. When an NTVDM is closed, the memory is not returned to the system. To return the memory to the system, you must use the Task Manager and close the NTVDM process or log off and log back on. If an NTVDM is shut down and then another is requested, the new 16-bit process will use the NTVDM created earlier—and not create a new NTVDM.

Only one shared NTVDM/WOW exists. For example, if there were four Win16 applications: Application A, Application B, Application C, and Application D, there is no way to have Applications A and B share one NTVDM while another shares Applications C and D. If a Win16 application is started without requesting a separate address space, the application goes into the default shared NTVDM. If a Win16 application is started with the separate address space, it will go into its own NTVDM/WOW.

OS/2

Windows NT is not a new OS. While Windows NT has only been around since 1993, development of the product began in the late '80s. Keep in mind that before 1990, Microsoft and IBM had a cross-license relationship that gave them access to each others' codes. In the first years of NT development, most people assumed that the primary interface for Windows NT would be the OS/2 Presentation Manager. After all, OS/2 was the OS to match at that time. In the author's opinion, IBM began to ladle more and more functions into OS/2 that Microsoft felt were unnecessary. A good example would be 3270 (an IBM mainframe terminal) emulation. As a result, in 1990, Microsoft and IBM had the "Great Divorce"—and the cross-license relationship ended.

Microsoft, however, is nothing but pragmatic. Even well after the "divorce," Microsoft realized it had the code for OS/2 and that at the time, OS/2 had a relatively large support base. As a result, it was easy and prudent for Microsoft to create an OS/2 subsystem. This OS/2 subsystem has been in Windows NT since the original version 3.1.

Some fairly strong shortcomings exist in the OS/2 subsystem. In particular, the OS/2 subsystem can only run character-mode, OS/2 version 1.2 programs. For a price, an "Add-On for Presentation Manager" can be added to Windows NT (4.0 only) that will enable the system to support 16-bit Presentation Manager applications. Also, only the Intel (x86) version of Windows NT can support OS/2 applications.

Outside of these limitations, the OS/2 subsystem runs OS/2 applications quite well. Each application has 4GB of memory, is pre-emptively multi-tasked, and has complete support for networking.

POSIX

If you want to sell anything to the United States federal government, you often find yourself doing strange things. Microsoft wants to sell NT to the Feds. The Feds, like any large organization, like to keep things as standardized as possible. To that end, the U.S. government pushed hard for support of a new set of standards to enable portability of UNIX applications across a broad cross-section of many different "flavors" of UNIX that were then (and still are) in use. The idea was that an application written for, say, SCO UNIX could also run on IBM's AIX. The idea was great in concept. The *Institute of Electronic and Electrical Engineers* (IEEE) created the *Portable Operating System Interface* (POSIX), a set of specifications for operating systems and applications. A number of levels of POSIX exist, called POSIX.0, POSIX.1, etc. through POSIX.12, and each level is more sophisticated than the next. Windows NT jumped on the government POSIX bandwagon and gave Windows NT a rudimentary POSIX.1 compliance. This move, more than anything else, made Windows NT a little bit easier to sell to the U.S. government but does not really provide much added function. (While this opinion is only the author's, the idea is one shared by many others who are familiar with the NT OS.)

NT Application Cross-Platform Compatibility

In the perfect Microsoft world, any application written for any OS would be able to run on any platform using the NT OS. Microsoft has not yet reached that goal. Currently, NT only supports DOS, Win16, Win32, OS/2, and POSIX applications. Windows NT also supports the Intel x86, MIPS, Alpha, and PowerPC platforms. The problem is that not all applications run with all platforms.

The modular design of Windows NT is a powerful step towards the goal of complete cross-platform compatibility. Yet, despite Microsoft's best efforts at modularity in Windows NT, some applications for some platforms are simply incompatible due to their dependence on certain aspects of one OS or platform. For example, do not even think about trying to run Norton Utilities on a UNIX machine. Any program can be made to work on any platform, but the program must first be recompiled using a compiler for that platform. Programmers write programs in "source code" using computer languages such as C, C++, and Visual Basic. An example of source code might look like the following lines:

```
while(1)
    {
       if(PeekMessage(&msg, NULL,0,0,PM_NOREMOVE))
       {
          if(!GetMessage (&msg, NULL, 0, 0))
              return msg.wParam;
          TranslateMessage (&msg);
          DispatchMessage (&msg);
       }
       else
       {
           // do critical game stuff
          gcScheduler();
       }
    }
```

A compiler takes the source code and creates an executable file. In the DOS/Windows world, executable files are distinct by their EXE extension. An EXE file is a binary file—all ones and zeros that only a particular CPU can understand. Microsoft has many different compilers to support the different platforms supported by Windows NT. For example, you can purchase a C++ compiler for Intel, MIPS, or Alpha processors that are running NT. So, while a particular application may not run on another NT platform, you can easily take the source code of that application, recompile it with a compiler for another platform, and create a new executable file that will run on the other platform.

This concept boils down to the fact that there are two levels of cross-platform portability: binary (the EXE will run across all platforms as is) and source (the source code needs to be compiled for each platform). Here is the breakdown.

DOS	Binary
Win16	Binary
Win32	Source
OS/2	Binary (bound programs only; otherwise Source)
POSIX	Source

To interpret this list, any DOS or Win16 application will run on any platform, regardless of the platform upon which the application was compiled. All the others need to be recompiled for them to work properly. A few exceptions exist. Character Mode OS/2 applications compiled as "Bound" applications can work with either the OS/2 subsystem or in a DOS NTVDM. Because all platforms support DOS, a bound OS/2 application will run on a platform that does not have OS/2 support by noticing that there is no OS/2 subsystem (Windows NT only has an OS/2 subsystem on x86 based systems) and requesting a DOS NTVDM.

Setting Priorities

In any multi-tasking system, there may be applications that need more of the timeslice than other applications that are running simultaneously. To achieve this end, Windows NT gives every process a "Priority Level" to determine how much timeslice the application receives relative to the other processes. The NT priority levels are numbered zero through 31. A process with a higher priority level is run before a process with a lower priority level. By default, all applications are given the priority level of eight. Windows NT can change the priority level of a process, but users have a small amount of control over the priority level.

One area where the priority levels are important to users is with foreground applications. By default, the foreground application gets a priority of 10. Open the System applet in the control panel and choose the Performance tab. On this tab, slide the Application Performance slider to change the priority of the foreground application. The left is eight; the middle is nine; and the right is 10 (as in Figure 5–16).

Windows NT enables an application to be started at one of four different priority levels using the START command, followed by a special switch. The four switches and their corresponding priority levels follow on the next page.

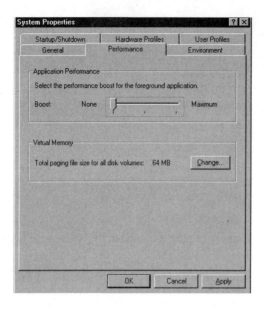

/low	priority level four
/normal	priority level eight
/high	priority level 13
/realtime	priority level 24

For example, to run the program **COOL32.EXE** at priority level 13, the following command would be executed from the C: prompt:

```
START /HIGH COOL32.EXE
```

Once an application is running, its priority level can be changed to one of the four previously described levels by using the Task Manager. To access the Task Manager, press Ctrl-Alt-Delete and click the Task Manager button. Once the Task Manager opens, right-click the process or application and select Set Priority to change the priority level for any process (in the Process tab) or application (in the Application tab). Keep in mind that only users with administrative privileges can change priority levels (see Figure 5–17).

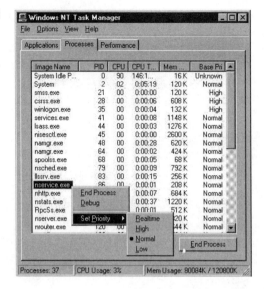

Figure 5–17
Changing priorities
from Task Manager

Application Failures

Applications fail—no matter how robust, how modular, or powerful the OS. Windows NT is no exception to this rule. An application failure manifests itself in a thousand different ways in NT, ranging from simple, recoverable errors (error messages saying the program cannot find a DLL) to massive system failures (the famous "Blue Screen of Death"). A large portion of the average NT person's day involves dealing with application failures, especially if an application is new and is not yet fully understood. Microsoft provides two powerful tools for dealing with application failures: the NT Application Event Log and the ever-present Dr. Watson.

Application Event Log

Windows NT provides powerful auditing functions for OS events (such as a service failing to start), security events (such as a person failing to log in), and applications. Chapter 6, "File Systems," and Chapter 8, "NT User Management," will explain auditing in detail, but one aspect of auditing—the auditing of applications—needs to be clarified. Windows NT enables (but does not require) programmers to create "events" that can be reported to a special file called the Application Event Log. The programmers can generate an event for anything they feel is worth reporting. A good example would be a communications program that reported an event each time a connection was started or stopped.

To observe the results of the application's events, use the Event Viewer application. The Event Viewer can be set to show one of three different types of events: System, Security, or Application. Click the Log menu pull-down and select Application to see the application event log, as shown in Figure 5–18.

The application event log is not a perfect tool. First of all, not all programs provide reporting to the log. The program must have been written to generate events, or this screen would look blank. Fortunately, most programs written for NT do a pretty good job of reporting events (although not the case even a year ago) and can give handy information. The second problem with the application event log is that the information it provides often needs a little interpretation. On one application, a failure is clearly documented by a line in the event log. In another application, the event log may only provide the last event that took place before the error. In another application, an error may not be manifested in the application event log at all. Although the log is not a perfect tool, it makes sense to give the log a peek when application errors take place.

Dr. Watson

When a serious application error takes place, NT looks for a program called a handler. In concept, a *handler* is a program that knows how to deal with the application error. In reality, most serious application errors do not have special handlers. When NT does not have a special handler for the application error, NT sends the error to the venerable Dr. Watson (shown in Figure 5–19).

For years, Dr. Watson has been the "handler of last resort" for Windows 3.X, 95/98, and NT. The Dr. Watson that comes with NT is designed specifically for NT and should not be confused with the Windows 95/98 Dr. Watson that also comes with NT. The average NT support person receives no benefit from Dr. Watson, but Dr. Watson has a few nuances that can, on

Figure 5–18
Application event log

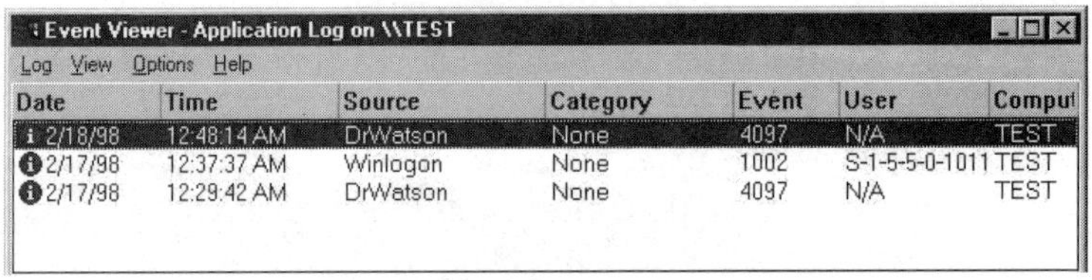
Event Viewer - Application Log on \\TEST
Log View Options Help
Date Time Source Category Event User Comput
2/18/98 12:48:14 AM DrWatson None 4097 N/A TEST
2/17/98 12:37:37 AM Winlogon None 1002 S-1-5-5-0-1011 TEST
2/17/98 12:29:42 AM DrWatson None 4097 N/A TEST

occasion, be more helpful for higher-level technical support. To see these nuances, run the program **DRWTSN32.EXE**, which should be in the **WINNT\ SYSTEM32** folder. This action brings up a configuration screen, as shown in Figure 5–20.

Most of these settings simply tell Dr. Watson what to store into one of two files: **DRWTSN32.LOG** and the Crash Dump File. **DRWTSN32.LOG** stores detailed information about an application error—far more than is registered into the application event log. The contents of this log can be customized slightly. The technical support person will usually tell you what he or she needs. The Crash Dump File is a special binary file that can be loaded into a debugging program to help determine the cause of the application error.

Fortunately, the MCSE exams ignore the conceptual aspects of NT application support and concentrate on the more practical aspects, such as the procedures for running DOS and Win16 programs in different

Figure 5–19
Typical Dr. Watson error message

Figure 5–20
Dr. Watson for NT

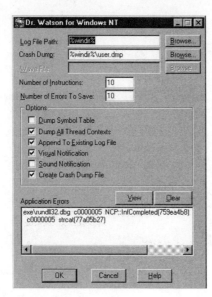

memory spaces or tweaking Dr. Watson. While the MCSE exams do not require you to be able to explain the different NT subsystems, any good NT support person should at least understand the basic concept of NT's modular subsystems and know NT's limits, in terms of cross-platform support, types of platforms, and applications.

Questions

1. The NT Executive runs in _____ mode and is composed of three major components: the microkernel, the Hardware Abstraction Layer, and the _____.

2. The HAL is the interface between the OS and the _____.

3. Object security is handled by which two executive services?

4. True or False: "Once a device driver is loaded, it can be started or stopped, but not unloaded."

5. Each type of OS supported by NT has its own _____ running in _____ mode.

6. Each DOS application runs in a separate _____.

7. How is a DOS application's PIF file edited?

8. All Win16 applications in the shared NTVDM perform _____ multi-tasking.

9. True or False: "All Win16 applications must run in a single WOW."

10. DOS applications are _____ level cross-platform portable.

Answers

1. kernel, Executive Services

2. CPU (Hardware would also be an acceptable answer.)

3. Security Reference Monitor and the Object Manager

4. False—It can be completely unloaded.

5. environment subsystem, user

6. NTVDM

7. By right-clicking the DOS application or the DOS application PIF file and selecting Properties

8. cooperatively

9. False—They can be configured for separate NTVDM/WOWs.

10. binary

CHAPTER **6**

File Systems

Windows NT 4.0 supports two major file systems: *File Allocated Table* (FAT) and *New Technology File System* (NTFS). By supporting both the antiquated FAT system and the new, more powerful NTFS system, Microsoft meets two important goals: providing users access to all of their older files and offering new file system capabilities, such as security and increased storage efficiency. NT does not support the file systems of the other major operating systems in the marketplace—Microsoft's FAT32, IBM's HPFS, or any UNIX file system. The MCSE exams require thorough understanding of the basic behaviors of NTFS and FAT and their appropriate uses.

FAT16

The FAT16 file system was the first DOS file system designed for hard drives. At the time of its creation, FAT16 revolutionized mass file storage with its capacity to support large drives. Of course, for the early '80s, "very large" meant perhaps a whopping 20MB drive. Although FAT16 has been modified and upgraded over the years, FAT16 has begun to show its age. By modern standards, the FAT table system for organizing hard drives is inadequate, offering no security features, primitive repair capabilities, and inefficient use of disk space. FAT16 still remains an important choice in the PC world today, simply because the system has been around for so long. FAT16's longevity implies proven technology, solid support, and a large installed base of applications that count on this technology. Great danger exists, however, in trying to replace any technology with such a large installed base. Will the new technology make the applications that relied upon the old technology obsolete? The watchword in the PC world for many years has been "backward compatibility." Users may clamor for the latest and greatest products, but they still want all of their old "stuff" to work. That point raises some complications for the people at Microsoft. They want to offer new capabilities, but not if those new capabilities prevent users from using their old "stuff." To that end, they made NT backwardly compatible to FAT16.

How FAT Works

Formatting a hard drive as a FAT volume creates two data structures: the directory structure and the FAT. The directory structure contains a list of files on the hard drive, pointers to any subdirectories and/or folders, and a few pieces of pertinent information, such as the file's name, extension, size, date of creation, and time of creation. The directory structure also contains the volume label and indicates whether an entry is a file or a directory. To see this information from a command prompt, simply type the **DIR** command.

```
C:\data>dir
Volume in drive C has no label
Volume Serial Number is 1F3C-07E2
Directory of C:\data
     .        <DIR>                08-06-98 10:21a  .
     ..       <DIR>                08-06-98 10:21a  ..
```

```
CONFIG          SYS     30        07-20-98   1:39p  CONFIG.SYS
AUTOEXEC        BAT     66        07-20-98   3:46p  AUTOEXEC.BAT
FILESEC         VXD     23,029    05-11-98   8:01p  FILESEC.VXD
15_16W95        VXD     29,827    11-04-97   9:40a  15_16W95.VXD
DINPUT          VXD     16,986    05-11-98   8:01p  DINPUT.VXD
DSOUND          VXD     87,487    05-11-98   8:01p  DSOUND.VXD
FIOLOG          VXD     10,720    05-11-98   8:01p  FIOLOG.VXD
ENABLE2         VXD     25,159    05-11-98   8:01p  ENABLE2.VXD
ENABLE4         VXD     21,634    05-11-98   8:01p  ENABLE4.VXD
DCAPVXD         VXD      9,001    05-11-98   8:01p  DCAPVXD.VXD
BIOS            VXD     30,193    05-11-98   8:01p  BIOS.VXD
ISAPNP          VXD     21,281    05-11-98   8:01p  ISAPNP.VXD
        12 file(s)          275,413   bytes
         2 dir(s)     2,075,729,920   bytes free
```

To see the same information in a Windows 95 or Windows NT environment, use Windows Explorer (Figure 6–1).

Two pieces of information exist in the directory structure that do not appear by default with either the DIR command or through Windows Explorer: attributes and the starting cluster for each file. Every file on a FAT volume has some number of additional attributes to which it is assigned. *Attributes* on a FAT volume are simply individual bits—little on/off switches in the directory entry for each file that specify whether the file is a read only, system, hidden, or archived file. (Backup programs use the archive bit to determine whether a file has been changed since the last backup.) These file attributes can be displayed and changed with the ATTRIB command or by using Windows Explorer. In Windows Explorer,

Figure 6–1

File information in Windows Explorer

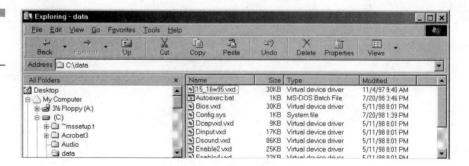

select a file or directory and choose the Properties option from the right-click menu, as displayed in Figure 6–2.

The directory structure contains information about the starting cluster for each file. FAT volumes are divided into equally sized storage sections called *clusters*. Cluster sizes vary according to the size of the volume (but never vary within a volume). Files start in a cluster and either finish in that cluster or spill over into the next available cluster(s). Each cluster can contain information from only one file, so a partially filled cluster is as completely used up as a fully filled cluster.

The FAT keeps track of the status of each cluster in a volume. For example, the FAT defines whether the cluster is in use. Think of the FAT table as a two-column spreadsheet. The left-hand column designates the number of the cluster (in hexadecimal), and the right-hand column specifies whether the cluster is "in use," "available," a "bad cluster—do not use," or "this file continues in cluster x." The problem with FAT16 is that the FAT table can only have 216 (or 65,536) entries. As the size of the volume increases, so must the size of the clusters (Table 6–1).

Table 6–1

FAT16 cluster sizes

Size of the FAT partition	Cluster Size
16–127.9MB	2K
128–255.9MB	4K
256–511.9MB	8K
512–1023.9MB	16K
1024–2048MB	32K

Wasted Drive Space

Every file saved on a FAT volume will waste some amount of space. Unfortunately, the amount of space wasted by a given file increases with the size of the volume. A 17K file saved on a 400MB volume (8K clusters) wastes 7K, for example, while the same 17K file stored on a 900MB volume wastes 15K, as displayed in Figure 6–3. FAT volumes of more than 1024MB will usually waste between 25 percent and 40 percent of their total capacity. This inefficiency when dealing with large hard drive volumes makes FAT16 an inappropriate choice for larger hard drives.

Figure 6–2
File attributes in
FAT16

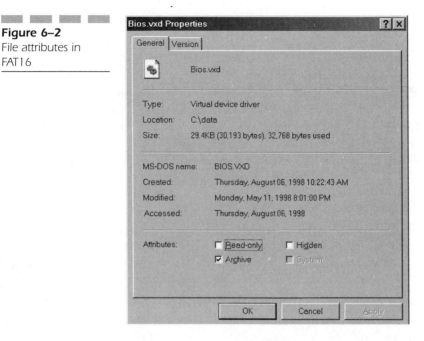

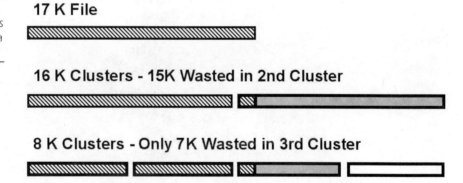

Figure 6–3
Saving a 17K file uses
more disk space on a
larger FAT partition

Lack of Security

The designers of FAT16 never intended for the system to be used in a network environment. FAT16 was created for stand-alone systems where security was not supposed to be an issue. As a result, the FAT16 system does not have any methods for file system security. Any user with physical access to the system can access any file. Data stored on a FAT volume can only be secured through network access restrictions. A true network file system, however, needs much more robust and flexible security than simple network access restrictions.

No Self-Repair Capabilities

The primary function of a file system is to create a fast and safe method for saving and retrieving files. If the file system fails to perform this function, the entire motivation for using a computer is lost. Data is king. Data loss is bad in a stand-alone system and is unacceptable in a network environment. FAT has few built-in protections against data loss. Repair utilities such as SCANDISK or Norton Disk Doctor must be run to catch and repair file system errors. Stopping a stand-alone system to run repair utilities is a pain. Stopping a network server to run these utilities is unacceptable. A network-based file system needs to have the capacity to check and fix file systems errors without taking the system down. FAT has no such "fix-it-on-the-fly" functions.

Long Filenames and Aliases

The designers of the FAT system worked in an era when hard disk storage was expensive. To cut down on the amount of space the FAT table and directory structure information itself would take, they limited the names of files to eight characters, with three-character file extensions. These 8.3 character names (pronounced "eight-dot-three") restricted end users to obscure filenames such as `Q1SALHOU.XLS` for files that they would have preferred to refer to as "Houston Sales Report for Quarter 1." As hard drive prices dropped and capacities soared, saving a few bytes here and there became trivial. Each character in a filename, after all, only takes up one byte of storage. Microsoft wanted to enable users to use more sensible, human-language filenames while still supporting FAT16.

To break the 8.3 filename restriction, Microsoft created a new way to store files on FAT16 partitions, called *Long Files Names* (LFN). LFN supports filenames up to 255 characters. Microsoft could not radically change the way filenames were handled without completely rewriting the file system (which they did with NTFS), and thus lose backward compatibility. LFN provided a workable compromise. LFN creates a long filename by using unused directory entries. Those entries get the rather strange attribute combination of Hidden, System, Directory, and Volume Label. This attribute combination assures that DOS will ignore these entries. To support older applications and operating systems, all files would continue to have an 8.3 filename. While a file might be saved with the name **Houston Sales Report for Quarter 1.DOC**, its 8.3 name would be **HOUSTO~1.DOC**. The FAT system creates the 8.3 character name by taking the first six characters of the name, adding a tilde (~) and a number. The file extension remains the same.

What if more than one filename begins with the same six characters? Then they will be numbered sequentially, beginning with number one. For example, if you create another file in the same directory as **Houston Sales Report for Quarter 1.DOC** and call the file **Houston Sales Summary**, the new file's 8.3 character name would be **HOUSTO~2.DOC**.

Accessing files with long filenames from a command prompt requires you to use the 8.3 name or enclose the whole, long filename in quotations. This process is required because spaces in a command line often have special, preassigned meanings. To edit the file **Houston Sales Report for Quarter 1.DOC** from a command line, for example, either of the following would work:

```
edit HOUSTO~1.DOC
```

or

```
edit "Houston Sales Report for Quarter 1.DOC"
```

Be aware that although long filenames "remember" the case in which they were entered, they are not case-sensitive. The following lines would be treated as functionally equivalent:

```
edit "Houston Sales Report for Quarter 1.DOC"
edit "HOUSTON SALES REPORT FOR QUARTER 1.DOC"
edit "houston sales report for quarter 1.doc"
```

Why Keep FAT Around?

Microsoft keeps FAT around for three reasons: backward compatibility, dual-booting, and support for smaller drives. First, despite FAT's limited capabilities compared to more modern systems such as NTFS, FAT remains a widely used file system. Because FAT was one of the first PC-based file systems, most operating systems today, including Windows NT 4.0, support FAT partitions. Microsoft watched other powerful operating systems such as OS/2 fail to become popular, due in part to their failure to completely support FAT16. In other words, Microsoft hedged its bets. The second reason for supporting FAT is that booting multiple operating systems on the same PC and having each OS read the data files created under the other OS is often possible. Without support for FAT, Windows NT systems could not dual boot.

NOTE: *Why dual boot? In some cases, booting up a system in an OS other than Windows NT 4.0 can be helpful. For example, many NICs come with diagnostic and setup programs that cannot be run from within NT. Windows NT prevents programs from directly accessing hardware. To set up these NICs under NT, you must boot to DOS—either by booting to a floppy or having a dual boot system set up. Dual booting with DOS is only possible if at least one volume (C:\\) has been formatted as a FAT partition. Booting to DOS can also be helpful when you have to edit the* **BOOT.INI** *file directly.*

Finally, a FAT file system requires less hard drive space than an NTFS file system, making FAT an attractive choice for smaller hard drives. Floppy disks and volumes smaller than 50MB do not have enough storage space to justify NTFS's overhead. On larger volumes, the greater efficiency of NTFS makes up for the extra overhead of the system.

Key Features of FAT for the Exams

1. FAT volumes can be read by many operating systems, making FAT a good choice for dual-boot systems.
2. Large volumes formatted with FAT make inefficient use of disk space. Officially, Microsoft recommends NTFS instead of FAT for all volumes larger than 400MB.

3. Floppy diskettes formatted in NT or Windows 95 will be formatted with FAT. No room exists on the floppy for the NTFS file system.

4. FAT supports no security features. Anyone with physical access to the machine can access all files.

FAT32, Windows 98, and Windows NT 4.0

With Windows 95 Version B (also called *OEM Service Release 2*, or OSR2) and Windows 98, Microsoft has introduced FAT32, a FAT system that uses a 32-bit FAT instead of the 16-bit table in FAT16. The number of entries in the FAT table becomes flexible, enabling large volumes to continue using small clusters. By using smaller clusters, FAT32 eliminates the majority of the waste created on large volumes by FAT16 formatting. Unfortunately, FAT32 changes the file system in such fundamental ways that FAT16 disk utilities no longer function and can sometimes be dangerous.

On the current MCSE exams, *you do not need to know this*. FAT32 is not mentioned on the NT Workstation or NT Server in the Enterprise exams. All references to FAT that appear on the exam refer to FAT16. Because FAT32 had not yet been released, the test writers did not feel the need to specify the version of FAT to which they were referring.

Only two current operating systems can read FAT32 volumes: Windows 95 OSR2 and Windows 98. Windows NT 4.0 cannot read FAT32 volumes. To upgrade to NT on a machine with FAT32 volumes, you must back up all data, reformat the drives, install NT, and restore the backup data files. If the machine had been formatted with FAT16, on the other hand, NT can be installed on the existing volumes without reformatting (and can be installed with the option of converting to NTFS). Table 6–2 describes the steps for upgrading from Windows 95 or 98 to Windows NT.

While not covered on the exams, understanding that Windows NT 4.0 cannot read FAT32 volumes is critical for planning NT upgrades. Microsoft currently plans to support FAT32 in Windows NT 5.0 (a.k.a. Windows 2000), but exactly how that support will be implemented is unclear.

Table 6–2

FAT vs. NTFS

Upgrading from Windows 9X to Windows NT 4.0— Differences Between File Systems	
Windows 9X installed on FAT16 volumes	Windows 9X installed on FAT32 volumes
1. Run the Windows NT setup program.	1. Back up all data files.
2. Leave the current FAT16 file system in place, or convert to the NTFS file system.	2. Delete existing FAT32 volumes using FDISK or a similar program.
	3. Run the Windows NT setup program.
	4. Create FAT or NTFS partitions.
	5. Restore data files to a new partition.

NOTE: *FAT32 is not covered on the NT 4.0-based exams.*

HPFS

Earlier versions of NT supported *High-Performance File System* (HPFS), the OS/2 file system. Microsoft discontinued support for HPFS volumes in NT 4.0, but Microsoft does supply a utility for converting from HPFS to NTFS (called CONVERT).

NOTE: *HPFS is not a supported file system under Windows NT 4.0, although it was supported in Windows NT 3.51.*

Key Features of HPFS for the Exams

1. Windows NT no longer supports HPFS.
2. Microsoft supplies a utility to convert HPFS volumes to NTFS.

Because Microsoft has discontinued support for HPFS as a file system option in NT, the exams do not require knowledge of its inner workings.

NTFS

Clearly, the FAT file system is a poor choice for a powerful network-centric operating system such as NT. The need for more advanced features motivated Microsoft to create NTFS especially for the NT operating system. The support in NTFS for advanced features such as file-level security, self-repair, and compression makes NTFS the file system of choice for Windows NT 4.0. Many NT features, in particular security features, depend on NTFS to provide secure and reliable access to files.

Key NTFS features

NTFS supports the following key features:

1. Compression—The capacity to compress individual files safely
2. Recoverability—The capacity to recover from failures without loss of data
3. Security—The capacity to control access to directories and individual files
4. Auditing—The capacity to determine which user accessed certain objects and when he or she accessed those objects

Compression

NTFS supports compression on individual folders and files. Unlike file compression schemes for FAT (such as Drivespace and Doublespace), NTFS file compression is integrated into the file system and is considered a safe means of conserving disk space. Files can be compressed by using either the **COMPACT.EXE** command line utility or Windows Explorer. When using Windows Explorer, check the box labeled "compression" under Properties. The files will be compressed immediately upon closing the file (as in Figure 6–4).

Figure 6–4
Compressing
a file in NT

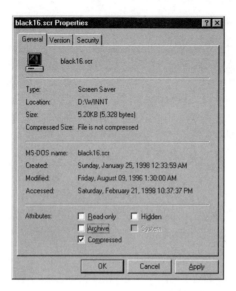

The **COMPACT.EXE** program supports the following options (from the **COMPACT.EXE** help screen):

```
COMPACT [/C | /U] [/S[:dir]] [/A] [/I] [/F] [/Q] [filename
        [...]]
   /C          Compresses the specified files. Directories
               will be marked so that files added afterward
               will be compressed.
   /U          Uncompresses the specified files. Directories
               will be marked so that files added afterward
               will not be compressed.
   /S          Performs the specified operation on files in
               the given directory and all subdirectories.
               Default "dir" is the current directory.
   /A          Displays files with the hidden or system
               attributes. These files are omitted by
               default.
   /I          Continues performing the specified operation
               even after errors have occurred. By default,
               COMPACT stops when an error is encountered.
   /F          Forces the compress operation on all
               specified files, even those which are
               already compressed. Already-compressed files
               are skipped by default.
   /Q          Reports only the most essential information.
   filename    Specifies a pattern, file, or directory.
```

Used without parameters, COMPACT displays the compression state of the current directory and any files it contains.

NOTE: *Why bother with a command line utility when you can do the same thing through the graphical interface with Windows Explorer? One reason is because many system administration tasks can be automated with batch files and created and executed at the command line. On the MCSE exams, you probably will not need to know all of the switches for the* **COMPACT.EXE** *program, but make sure that you know* **COMPACT.EXE** *is the command line utility that handles NTFS file compression.*

DO I REALLY WANT TO COMPRESS MY FILES?   While compression in NTFS is safe and reliable, you may not always want to compress your files. File compression saves space at the cost of system performance. Every time the compressed file is accessed, the file must be decompressed and then recompressed if changes are made to the file. To maintain system performance, frequently accessed files should not be compressed.

Recoverability

System failures, program errors, and power outages can prevent the system from properly recording changes to files and directories. To handle these issues, NTFS uses a *Transaction Tracking System* (TTS). NTFS's TTS logs all changes to files and directories automatically. TTS will detect incomplete changes when the system restarts and "back them out," going back to the last successfully saved copy. NT continually checks NTFS volumes for errors, automatically fixing most problems before the end user notices them. You rarely need to run disk repair software such as SCANDISK on an NT machine.

File Security

NTFS provides a crucial element of NT security. In NTFS, each file is a separate object, with a far more extensive set of attributes than those provided by FAT. As seen in Figure 6–2 earlier, files in NTFS support the same basic file attributes that FAT supports (i.e., System, Hidden, Read-Only, Archive), plus a Compression attribute. NTFS files also support a more extensive set of security attributes, because NTFS is an object-oriented file system.

WHAT DOES OBJECT-ORIENTED MEAN?   In FAT, the files themselves contain only the most basic of file attributes because of the restrictions of FAT file structure size—and the fact that nobody was thinking about things like security or compression when FAT was invented. Microsoft could have redesigned FAT with some security functions, but Microsoft would risk backward compatibility or marketplace failure.

In NTFS, each file is its own object, meaning that the file itself contains its own complex attributes without regard to the directory structure that points to the file. An object is similar to a little database of attributes. Each piece of data has a name and a value. When a program "calls" to any object, the program does not really go into the object. Instead, the program observes the state of the object via calls to variable names. How the data is stored in an object is unimportant, as long as there is a mechanism for programs to call to it and see the results of their calls. Because NTFS is object-oriented, there is no programming limit to the number of variables any object—including files and folders—can hold. Because each file contains practically unlimited space for attributes, the files can be given a much more detailed set of attributes.

NOTE: *In NT, everything is an object. An object combines data and the functions required to manipulate the data into a single unit. In NT, programs never access data directly; instead, they access the object's functions. For files, these functions would include reading data, writing data, deleting data, etc. For other object types, different functions would exist such as resizing, maximizing, or minimizing a window. Think of an object as a restaurant with a drive-through window. When you pull up to the window, you can only order things that are on the menu. (If the designer of the object did not include the function, you cannot perform that function.) In addition, as long as you receive your food and it is hot and tasty, you really do not care exactly how the kitchen is laid out. (How an object performs its functions is not our concern; rather, we just want the object to do its job.)*

SECURITY UNDER NTFS: THE *ACCESS CONTROL LIST* (ACL)
The cornerstone of security in NTFS is a series of special security attributes known as permissions. In addition to the basic attributes that NTFS shares with DOS, each file and directory on an NTFS volume contains an *Access Control List* (ACL). The ACL lists both the users and groups that can access a file or directory and the specific permissions associated with each user or group.

The permissions that can be granted to files or directories are listed on the following page.

1. *Read* (R)

2. *Write* (W)

3. *Execute* (X)

4. *Delete* (D)

5. *Change permissions* (P)

6. *Take ownership* (O)

Understanding these permissions is critical to understanding NT security. The function of these permissions may vary depending on whether the permission is being assigned to a file or to a directory. The Execute permission is a good example. If a user has Execute permission to a file, the user will be able to run the file. If a user has Execute permission to a directory, the user will be able to open that directory. Some of the permissions are obvious. If a user has the permission of Delete for a particular file or directory, the user will be able to delete that file or directory.

NOTE: *Permissions can apply to any "object," not just NTFS files and directories. For example, a person might have "Change Permissions" for a particular printer, enabling them to modify the list of users who are allowed to use the printer. What a particular permission means depends on the object to which it refers. Objects in NT can be many things, such as files, printers, memory, windows, etc. On the MCSE exams, permissions are covered with respect to files and printers. While programmers may have to worry about permissions in other contexts, the MCSE exams do not require extensive knowledge of those other areas.*

These permissions are usually referred to as individual, or special, permissions, because they are not normally assigned directly to users or groups. NTFS designers realized that a user would rarely need to write to a file that he or she did not also need to read from time-to-time. In NTFS, these special permissions are grouped into sets of permissions called the "standard permissions." Instead of assigning individual "special permissions," an administrator would assign a standard permission to a user. Tables 6–3 and 6–4 list the standard permissions that can apply to NTFS files and directories.

Permissions are cumulative. If a user has been assigned Read access to a directory as a member of the Domain Users global group—and Change access to the same directory as a member of the Accounting global group—the user receives the sum of the special permissions contained in those standard permissions. Read Access includes *Read* (R) and *Execute* (X), while

Table 6–3

The standard
permissions for files

Standard Permission	Special Permissions	Effect
Read	(RX)	User can read the contents of a file and execute the file if it is an application.
Change	(RWXD)	User can read, modify, and delete the file.
Full Access	(RWXDPO)	User can read, modify, and delete the file, as well as change other users' permissions and take ownership of the file.
No Access	No Permissions	Overrides all other permissions —the user has no access.

Table 6–4

Standard
permissions for
directories

Standard Permission	Special Permissions On Directory	Special Permissions on Files in the directory	Effect
List	(RX)	( )	User can list the files in this directory and change to subdirectories of this directory. User cannot access files in this directory without being granted additional permissions.
Read	(RX)	(RX)	Same as List, but the user can also read the contents of files in the directory and execute programs in the directory.
Add	(WX)	( )	User can add files to the directory, but cannot view the contents. Note: All that the execute (X) on a directory does is enable you to open the directory. It does not enable you to execute programs in that directory.
Add and Read	(RWX)	(RX)	User can add files to the directory and read files that already exist, but the user cannot change the contents of existing files.

Standard Permission	Special Permissions On Directory	Special Permissions on Files in the directory	Effect
Change	(RWXD)	(RWXD)	User can read and add files and change the contents of existing files.
Full Control	(RWXDPO)	(RWXDPO)	User can read and change files, add new files, change other users' permissions for the directory and for individual files within, and take ownership of the directory and any files within that directory.
No Access	No permissions	No permissions	Overrides all other permissions; the user has no access.

Change Access includes *Read* (R), *Write* (W), *Execute* (X), and *Delete* (D). The user, therefore, receives RWXD, also known as Change Access.

NO ACCESS AND TAKE OWNERSHIP   Tables 6–3 and 6–4 explain the *Read* (R), *Write* (W), *Execute* (X), *Change Permissions* (P), *Delete* (D), and the standard permissions that group these items into standard packages for easy assignment by administrators. The No Access standard permission and the Take Ownership special permission, however, require further examination.

The No Access standard permission is the sole exception to the rule that permissions are cumulative. By adding a user or group to the No Access list in the ACL of a file or directory object, the Administrator prevents that user or group from having any permissions to that object, no matter how many other ways that user would ordinarily have permissions. No Access always overrides all other permissions.

NOTE: *No Access overrides all other permissions. If a user has been "granted" No Access to a file or directory, that user cannot under any circumstances access that file or directory.*

The Take Ownership special permission (granted as part of Full Access or Full Control) enables a user to become the owner of a file. An owner is normally the creator of the file. The owner of a file can always modify the ACL, changing the permissions assigned to users and groups. The *Take Ownership* (O) permission does not automatically grant ownership; rather, it merely gives the user the capacity to take ownership through the Ownership option on the Security tab on the Properties screen for a file (see Figure 6–5).

The distinction between Full Control/Full Access and Ownership lies in the capacity to take ownership of a file or a directory for which a user currently has no permissions. In NT 4.0, members of the Administrators group always have Take Ownership permission to every file—even files for which they have No Access. This feature gives an administrator a back door into all files on an NTFS partition. For example, imagine that user BSMITH has left on vacation, and only BSMITH has access to a file that must be accessed today (e.g., a pending sales contract). Because the Administrators group can always take ownership of the file and then grant permissions to other users, the data can be accessed. Ownership can only be taken, however, and not given. By preventing a user who has taken ownership of a file from return-

Figure 6–5

Taking ownership of a file

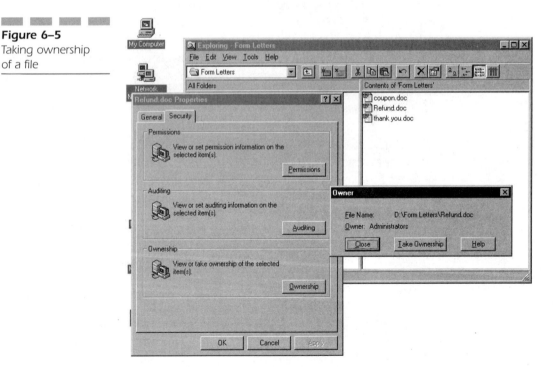

ing ownership, NT makes it more difficult for a dishonest network administrator to cover his or her tracks after accessing files that he or she should not have accessed. BSMITH, upon returning from his vacation, will be able to tell by checking the ownership of the file that a member of the Administrators group has taken ownership of his file. Take Ownership ensures that administrators can always gain access to a file—while still holding them accountable for doing so.

NOTE: *Ownership can only be taken. It cannot be given.*

ASSIGNING PERMISSIONS USING WINDOWS EXPLORER The usual tool for determining and assigning permissions is Windows NT Explorer. Any users with the Change Permissions special permission to a particular file or directory can change the ACL. A user generally has Change Permissions because the user has been granted the standard permission Full Access (RWXDPO) to a file or Full Control (RWXDPO) to a directory. Right-click a file or directory, select Properties, then select the Security tab (Figure 6–6).

Click Permissions to see a screen similar to Figure 6–7, which shows users and groups that have been assigned permissions for the file or directory.

Clicking the Add button brings up a dialog box, as shown in Figure 6–8, which enables users with the Change Permission special permission to grant additional users permissions to the file or directory. This dialog box

Figure 6–6
Security tab

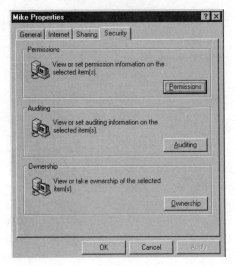

Figure 6–7
Adding Permissions
to a folder

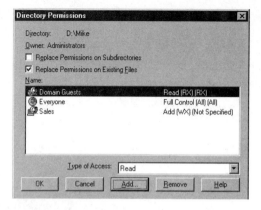

Figure 6–8
Selecting standard
permission

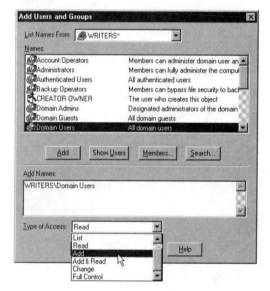

is not organized well and is always under criticism by NT users. The problem is that you select a Standard Permission (for some reason, Microsoft calls it "Type of Access" on this dialog box), and then select all of the Groups (and Users, if the Show Users button is clicked) that are to be assigned that standard permission. The Add dialog box can only be used to assign standard permissions, not special permissions.

After the users and groups are added, their permissions can be modified from the Permissions screen. Note that the Permissions screen enables you to select both standard and special permissions. In Figure 6–9, the user MICHAELM is getting special permissions for the directory **D:\MIKE**.

Figure 6–9
Setting special
permissions

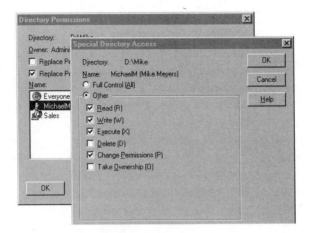

NOTE: *When a resource is first shared, everyone has full control until the administrator changes those permissions.*

NTFS File Auditing

A number of situations exist where an administrator would like to know "who is doing what" to systems, files, and folders. People want to know details about access. For example, if someone opened a particular database file, what did they do? Were they successful in reading the file? Did they write anything to the file? How long was the file opened? Possibly an administrator would like to see whether user permissions have been changed on a directory. Tracking this type of information is known as *auditing* and is one of NT's most handy administrative tools. Auditing includes far more than tracking file and directory access. Auditing on an NT system also includes tracking who is logging on and off, who is restarting the system, etc. In this section, we discuss only the auditing of files and folders. Refer to Chapter 8, "Managing Users in Windows NT," for a more detailed description of auditing other events.

File auditing only works on—you guessed it—NTFS volumes. FAT has no file auditing functions. File auditing is based on special permissions: tracking the reads, writes, executes, etc. File auditing provides for the tracking of both successful permissions and failures. In other words, this feature will tell you not only whether someone tried to read a file, but also whether he or she succeeded. Last, file auditing is based on groups and users. You have to tell NT who to audit and then set the events to be audited.

Auditing files and folders requires three steps. First, through User Manager, tell NT that you want to audit (auditing does not happen by default). Second, access the auditing screen for the object you wish to audit and select the special permissions you wish to audit. Select also the users and groups you wish to associate with this audit. This process is all done in the object's Properties dialog box. Third, use Event Manager to track auditing events.

Auditing is a bit of a double-edged sword. The information gleaned from auditing can certainly be powerful, but be warned that auditing can take significant resources. Auditing takes CPU processing, and if not implemented sparingly, auditing can bring a system to its knees. Auditing also makes massive log files that can take up a lot of drive space. These files must be carefully managed, as discussed later. Last, auditing can provide massive data overload. Do not try to audit more than can be tracked, or the entire auditing process is a waste of time.

SETTING UP FILE AUDITING   To set up file auditing, open User Manager from the Start/Programs/Administrative Tools menu. Select Policies . . . Audit, as shown in Figure 6–10.

This action opens the Audit Policy dialog box, as shown in Figure 6–11. In this figure, note that there are many more types of auditing than File and Object Access. Again, refer to Chapter 8 for a discussion of these other auditing features. Be sure to select both Success and Failure on this screen, regardless of what you actually want to audit.

Now that auditing is enabled, you should begin adding auditing to individual files and folders. In this example, we wish to audit a Microsoft

Figure 6–10

Accessing the
Auditing dialog box

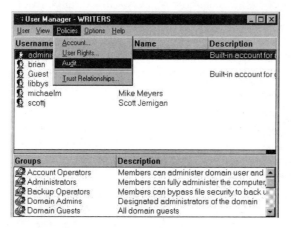

Access database file called **D:\PROSPECTS\PROSPECTS.MDB**. Only the Mailing group has Read access to the file. No other group except Administrators has any access to this file at all. We want to know two things: Who in the Mailing group is reading the file, and when are they reading it— and is anybody, not just users in the Mailing group, trying to do something that they should not—such as writing, changing permissions, taking ownership, or deleting the file?

Let's first deal with the folks in the Mailing group. Right-click the **PROSPECT.MDB** file, select Properties, and then select the Security tab, just as though we were going to set permissions. Then, click the Auditing button (Figure 6–12). At first, no auditing is set, producing a rather blank-looking screen.

Figure 6–11
Audit Policy
dialog box

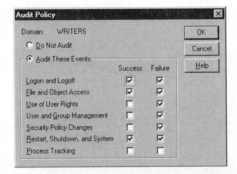

Figure 6–12
Initial File Auditing
screen

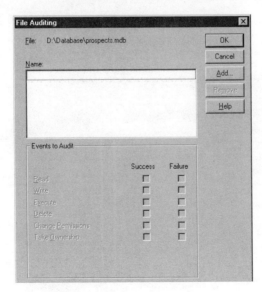

Auditing on a directory will look a little different, as shown in Figure 6–13. Note the addition of the Replace Auditing on Subdirectories and the Replace Auditing on Existing Files checkboxes.

We then click the Add button to add an audit to the file. Here, we locate the Mailing group (Figure 6–14) and select Add.

Note how similar this screen is to the Permissions Add screen shown earlier. More groups and users could be added if desired. We then click OK to open the next dialog box, File Auditing (Figure 6–15).

Figure 6–13
Directory auditing screen

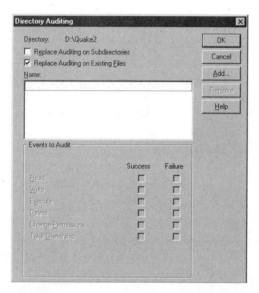

Figure 6–14
Adding a group for auditing

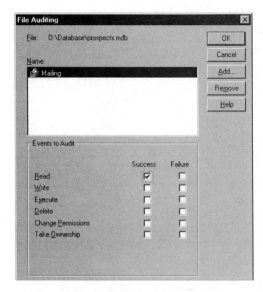

Figure 6–15
Setting Auditing
events

In this case, we want to know who in Mailing is reading this database and when they are doing it. Because everyone in the Mailing group has Read permission, the chances of a failure to read is small, so only the Success checkbox under Read is selected. There might be a temptation to click the Failure checkbox at this point to track potential problems. While this idea is a good one, the second audit we will set up later makes this redundant.

Setting up the second audit is similar to setting up the first. After clicking the OK button to return to the Security dialog box, we again click the Auditing button to start the process again for the second audit. Here, we will select Everyone (Figure 6–16).

This time, we want to track all Failures. The motivation is based on the idea that only Administrators have any access to the file, other than the Mailing group's Read access. Therefore, anyone trying to access this file should fail (we completely trust our administrators—gulp!), so we select only Failure checkboxes in the File Auditing dialog box (Figure 6–17).

The MCSE exams test extensively on all aspects of auditing, including File Auditing. Be sure to go through a number of scenarios to make yourself think about HOW auditing should be enacted in a particular scenario. Do not forget that while setting auditing on directories, you can also change subdirectories and existing files.

Figure 6–16
Adding everyone
for auditing

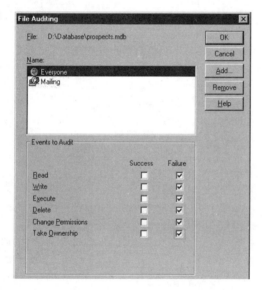

Figure 6–17
Setting Everyone
auditing events

USING FILE AUDITING   Once auditing has been established, simply go to Event Viewer to view the events. The default view for the Event Viewer is the System view. Be sure to select Log/Security to view the file and directory audit file (Figure 6–18).

Reading any audit log is always a little confusing. Fortunately, reading file and directory accesses from the Security Log is one of the more clear features. Just select the event you wish to inspect by double clicking it from the list. In Figure 6–19, an event has been selected, showing the detail screen.

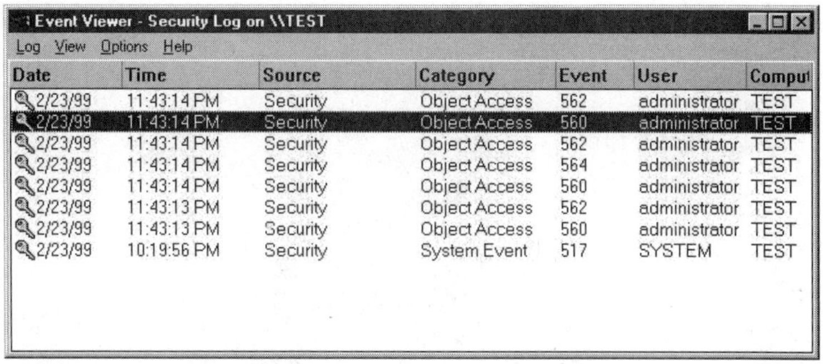

Figure 6–18
Event Viewer

Figure 6–19
Event details,
top section

This screen shows that the Administrator has accessed the **D:\DATABASE\ PROSPECTS.MDB** file. Scrolling down, we can see the administrator has deleted the file (Figure 6–20).

One big challenge with auditing is keeping up with the data. The audit log may store thousands of different audit events, and you are only looking for one particular item. To assist in location of that item, the Event Viewer allows for moderately powerful filtering of log events. From the main screen, select View/Filter events to bring up the Filter dialog box (Figure 6–21).

The filtering options are extremely helpful, especially the Time and Date, Types, User, and Computer fields. Once a filter is set, the Event Viewer will keep that filter, even if the filter is closed and then reopened. But once a filter is changed, it must be recreated every time. No way exists to make a filter and then to save it for later use.

Figure 6–20
Event details,
lower section

Figure 6–21
Filter dialog box

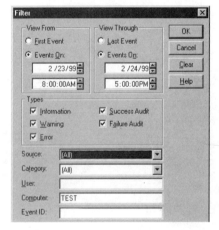

The last important issue for auditing is the Event Log Settings, selected from the Log/Log Settings menu in the Event Viewer (Figure 6–22). This dialog box determines the maximum size of each log file and how that file is to be overwritten when the file reaches its maximum size.

Relationship with Network Security

NT includes another level of security called "Network Security." Network security and NTFS security work together to create a multi-level, redundant security environment. Network security is discussed in depth in

Figure 6–22
Event Log Settings
dialog box

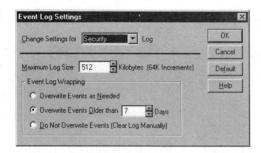

Chapter 9, "Microsoft Networking," but a brief discussion of the interaction between network security and NTFS is relevant here.

The permissions granted by network security and those granted by NTFS security are not cumulative. In NT networking, four *share* permissions can be assigned: Read, Change, Full Control, and No Access. These permissions are handled not by NTFS but by the networking security provided by NT. Unlike NTFS permissions, share permissions can be applied to subdirectories but not to individual files. Because share permissions do not rely on the file system, they can be applied to both NTFS and FAT volumes. When applied to NTFS directories, share permissions add an extra layer of security between network users and the data they want to access.

Applying both share permissions and NTFS permissions can severely restrict access to (and thus protect) that data. Imagine a building with a security guard at the front door (Figure 6–23). Accessing a file through share permissions is similar to entering the building and showing your ID to the security guard. The guard will give you a pass, enabling you to enter whichever parts of the building his master list says you can. Imagine NTFS permissions as a list that every person in the building keeps, which describes to whom they can talk. If an individual in the building has a list that indicates that individual can talk to you, but the security guard will not let you into that part of the building, then you will not be able to talk to that individual. By the same token, if the security guard lets you enter a particular part of the building, but the individuals in that part of the building do not have you on their list of people to whom they can talk, then you will also not be able to talk to those individuals.

In NT, imagine that we have shared the NTFS directory **D:\CONTRACTS** as CONTRACTS. The user FREDL has Full Access to the Contracts share, but he has Read Access to the **D:\CONTRACTS** directory. While the networking component of NT gives him Full Access to the share, NTFS prevents him from deleting a file because his NTFS permissions limit him to *Read Access* (RX). Another user, ASHLEYS, has Read Access to the CONTRACTS share but has Full Control over the NTFS directory

Figure 6–23
Network and NTFS
security are different.

Share Permissions   **NTFS File Permissions**

**Just because the share permissions let you in does not
mean that the NTFS File Permissions will let you have access**

`D:\CONTRACTS`. If ASHLEYS accesses the directory through the network share, her effective permissions will be Read Access—by the time she accesses the file, the share permissions have already restricted her from changing or deleting files. (If, however, ASHLEYS logs on locally to the machine where `D:\CONTRACTS` is stored, she would not have to go through the networking security software and would have Full Access as defined by her NTFS permissions).

The recommended practice in NT-based networks is to share all NTFS drives with Full Access to the Everyone group—and to restrict access based on the NTFS permissions. You should only implement restrictions on network access for FAT volumes, because they do not offer file-level security.

Moving and Copying Files in NT

Moving and copying files in NT raises complex issues because of the nature of the NTFS file system. In NTFS, each file is an object with its own ACL. What happens to the ACL of a file that is copied or moved? What permissions apply? Because NTFS supports file permissions but FAT does not, what happens when you move or copy files to or from NTFS and FAT? Each of these questions has important security ramifications in an NT environment.

NOTE: *How file permissions are affected when a file is copied or moved is covered in detail on the NT exams. Pay careful attention to this section when preparing for the exams.*

FAT to FAT

FAT partitions, as mentioned previously, have no file permissions at all. Copying or moving files between two FAT volumes or within a single volume does not affect file security—there is nothing to affect!

NTFS to FAT

When copying or moving files from an NTFS partition to a FAT partition or floppy disk, all permissions are lost. NTFS supports file permissions through the use of the ACL, which is attached to the file itself. FAT partitions have no capacity to retain that extra information, so the ACL simply disappears into the great "bit heaven" in the sky. The same phenomenon applies to floppy disks. Floppy disks are not large enough to support the overhead required by NTFS. The only file system that NT uses on floppy disks is FAT. NTFS files copied or moved to floppies lose all file-level permissions.

FAT to NTFS

Files created in FAT have no file permissions at all. When copied to an NTFS partition, however, they pick up the default permissions of the destination directory.

NTFS to NTFS

The effects of copying and moving files in NTFS depends on whether the action occurs within a single NTFS partition or between two NTFS partitions. Within a single partition, moving and copying do exactly what they denote: move and copy. Between two partitions, on the other hand, the commands do not always respond as advertised. A **MOVE** will copy—not move—a file, and then delete the original.

The effects of all this moving and copying and running about on the ACLs attached to the files—and the permissions that go along with them—vary according to whether the action occurs within an NTFS partition or between two partitions. Three rules govern this process:

1. Moving a file within a volume does not create a new file. Moving only changes file system pointers to the file, with no effect on the file itself. The file retains its original ACL. The permissions granted to users and groups for that file, therefore, also do not change.

2. Copying a file creates a new file. Its ACL inherits the default permissions for the directory in which it is created.

3. Files can only be moved within a volume. Moving a file between two volumes actually copies the file and then deletes the original. The ACL of the new file inherits the default permissions of the destination directory.

Let's see how this rather non-intuitive process works.

NTFS TO NTFS WITHIN A SINGLE VOLUME   Each file in NTFS contains its own ACL, detailing the permissions granted to various users and groups. Because NTFS stores the ACL within the file object, the permissions travel with the object regardless of where the object is stored. NTFS thus provides file-level security by virtue of being object-oriented.

Moving and copying file objects in NTFS plays havoc on those file-level permissions. Moving a file changes the pointers to that file but leaves the file object itself intact. A moved file, therefore, retains its original ACL and resulting permissions, regardless of the permissions that have been set for the destination directory. Copying a file, on the other hand, creates an entirely new object. The new object inherits the default permissions of the directory in which it is created. The following examples illustrate the effects of moving and copying on a file's permissions.

ERINR *moves* the file **BAGWELL.DOC** from **D:\CONTRACTS** to **D:\CONTRACTS\COMPLETED**. The local group SALESMEN has Full Access to all files in the **D:\CONTRACTS** directory (including **BAGWELL.DOC**) and has Read Access to files in the **D:\CONTRACTS\COMPLETED** directory. The moved file, **BAGWELL.DOC**, retains its original ACL—and thus all the permissions contained therein, as illustrated in Figure 6–24. Despite its location in the **D:\CONTRACTS\COMPLETED** directory, therefore, the local group SALESMEN has Full Access to the file **D:\CONTRACTS\COMPLETED\BAGWELL.DOC**.

Figure 6–24
Moving a file in NTFS

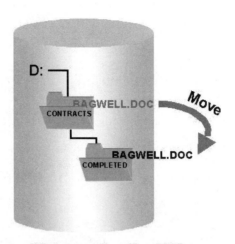

A moved file carries its ACL, keeping all its original permissions

KARYNB *copies* the file **JOHNSON.DOC** from **D:\CONTRACTS** to **D:\ CONTRACTS\COMPLETED**. The local group SALESMEN has Full Access to all files in the **D:\CONTRACTS** directory and has Read Access to files in the **D:\CONTRACTS\COMPLETED** directory. The copied file, **JOHNSON.DOC**, receives a new ACL based on the default ACL for the directory in which it is created, as illustrated in Figure 6–25. The local group SALESMEN, therefore, has only Read Access to the file **D:\CONTRACTS\COMPLETED\ JOHNSON.DOC**, because the group only had Read Access to the directory in which it was created.

NOTE: *Remember that the ACL for each file is stored in the file object, NOT in the directory structure. A file's ACL may not match the ACL of the directory in which the file is stored.*

NTFS TO NTFS BETWEEN TWO VOLUMES Moving or copying files between two NTFS volumes always creates new files. The ACLs for the new files take on the default ACL of the destination directory, losing all previous permissions. To "retain" the permissions for a moved file means that you must manually reset those permissions in the new location.

A file copied to another NTFS volume takes on the ACL of the directory in which it is created. Copying, therefore, works the same way between volumes as it does within a single volume.

Figure 6–25
Copying a file
in NTFS

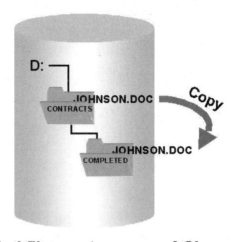

**A copied file creates a new ACL,
permissions are taken from new directory**

Moving a file between two NTFS volumes actually copies a file and then deletes the original. Although the user sees this action as a "move," the process is actually two actions: a copy and a delete. Because this creates a new file, the new file *takes on the default permissions of the destination directory*, losing its original permissions. Let's look at an example of moving a file between volumes.

DIANEC moves the file **MCGUIRE.DOC** from **D:\CONTRACTS** to **E:\CONTRACTS\CANCELLED**. The local group SALESMEN has Full Access to all files in the **D:\CONTRACTS** directory (including **MCGUIRE.DOC**) and has Read Access to files in the **E:\CONTRACTS\CANCELLED** directory. Moving the file **MCGUIRE.DOC** between volumes actually created a new file object with a new ACL, based on the default ACL of the **D:\CONTRACTS\ CANCELLED** directory. The original **MCGUIRE.DOC** object is then deleted, as illustrated in Figure 6–26. The local group SALESMEN, therefore, ends up with only Read Access to the (new) file, **D:\CONTRACTS\CANCELLED\MCGUIRE.DOC**.

NOTE: *Moving files between partitions always copies the file and deletes the original.*

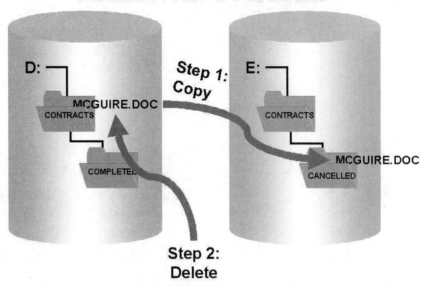

"Move"
Between NTFS Partitions

D:

Step 1:
Copy

E:

MCGUIRE.DOC

CONTRACTS

CONTRACTS

MCGUIRE.DOC

COMPLETED

CANCELLED

Step 2:
Delete

Converting FAT to NTFS

Windows NT 4.0 will safely convert FAT volumes to NTFS, without damaging the data. You should always back up all critical data before making major changes to a system, of course, but the process of converting a volume from FAT to NTFS does not require the restoration of files from backup. (All references to FAT here, as well as on the MCSE exams, assume FAT16, not FAT32.) See Figure 6–27.

The **CONVERT.EXE** program can either be run during the initial Windows NT setup or from the NT command prompt. When run from the command prompt, **CONVERT.EXE** supports the following options:

```
CONVERT drive: /FS:NTFS [/V]
   drive     Specifies the drive to convert to NTFS. Note
             that you cannot convert the current drive.
   /FS:NTFS  Specifies to convert the volume to NTFS.
   /V        Specifies that Convert should be run in verbose
             mode.
```

Figure 6–27
FAT to NTFS

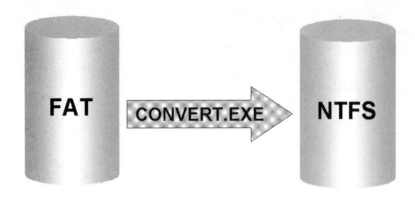

CONVERT.EXE converts FAT volumes into NTFS in a single step

For example, to convert drive F: from FAT to NTFS, type the command:

```
CONVERT F:  /FS:NTFS
```

The convert utility will actually execute following the next reboot of the system. The **/v** option forces the **CONVERT** utility to list each file as it converts the files to the NTFS format.

Converting NTFS to FAT

Converting from FAT to NTFS is a one-way process. There is no Windows NT utility to convert from NTFS to FAT. To "convert" an NTFS partition to a FAT partition, you must back up all data, reformat the partition, and then restore the data (see Figure 6–28). While Microsoft documentation occasionally refers to this process as a "conversion," restoring a full backup is a much more time-consuming process than running a conversion utility such as **CONVERT.EXE**.

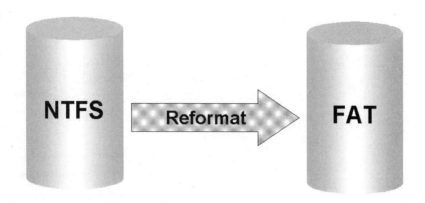

Figure 6–28
NTFS to FAT

Changing a volume from NTFS to FAT requires reformatting the drive - all data is lost and must be restored from backup

Summary

Windows NT 4.0 supports two file systems: FAT and NTFS. FAT support exists primarily for two purposes: formatting floppy disks and supporting other operating systems. NTFS must be used to take full advantage of Windows NT 4.0 as a secure, efficient, and reliable operating system. Features such as compression, automatic recovery, and file-level security make NTFS the file system of choice for NT systems.

Questions

1. Ashley moves a file called **PAYROLL.XLS** from her D: drive, an NTFS partition, to a floppy disk. Ashley had Full Access to the file, and the ACCOUNTING global group had Read Access to the file. What permissions will Ashley and the ACCOUNTING group have to the file on the floppy?

   a. All permissions are retained. Ashley will have Full Access, and the ACCOUNTING global group will have Read access.

   b. Ashley will have Full Access, and the ACCOUNTING global group will have No Access.

   c. All users will be granted Full Access.

   d. All file-level permissions are lost.

2. Fred moves the file **D:\RECENT\DATA.XLS** to **D:\BACKUP\DATA.XLS**. Drive D: is formatted as an NTFS volume. The ACCOUNTING global group has Full Access to the file **D:\RECENT\DATA.XLS**, and the group has Read Access to the **D:\BACKUP SUBDIRECTORY**. What permissions will the ACCOUNTING global group have to the file **D:\BACKUP\DATA.XLS**?

   a. Full Access

   b. Read Access

   c. No Access

   d. All permissions are lost and must be reset.

3. The global group TEACHERS has Full Access to the file **F:\STUDENT\REGISTRATION.DOC**, while the global group STUDENTS has No Access. The global group STUDENTS has Read Access to the **F:\STUDENT\FORMS** subdirectory. Drive F: is an NTFS volume. Basil copies the file **F:\STUDENT\REGISTRATION.DOC** to the **F:\STUDENT\FORMS** directory. What permissions do the STUDENTS global group have to the file **F:\STUDENT\FORMS\REGISTRATION.DOC**?

   a. Full Access

   b. Read Access

   c. No Access

   d. All permissions are lost.

4. The global group TEACHERS has Full Access to the file
   `F:\STUDENT\REGISTRATION.DOC`, while the global group
   STUDENTS has No Access. The global group STUDENTS has
   Read Access to the `F:\STUDENT\FORMS` subdirectory. Drive F: is an
   NTFS volume. Paula moves the file `F:\STUDENT\REGISTRATION.DOC`
   to the `F:\STUDENT\FORMS` directory. What permissions do the
   STUDENTS global group have to the file `F:\STUDENT\FORMS\`
   `REGISTRATION.DOC`?

   a. Full Access

   b. Read Access

   c. No Access

   d. All permissions are lost.

5. The global group TEACHERS has Full Access to the file
   `F:\STUDENT\REGISTRATION.DOC`, while the global group
   STUDENTS has No Access. The global group STUDENTS has
   Read Access to the `D:\STUDENT\FORMS` subdirectory. Both drives D:
   and F: are NTFS volumes. Robert moves the file `F:\STUDENT\`
   `REGISTRATION.doc` to the `D:\STUDENT\FORMS` directory. What
   permissions do the STUDENTS global group have to the file
   `D:\STUDENT\FORMS\REGISTRATION.DOC`?

   a. Full Access

   b. Read Access

   c. No Access

   d. All permissions are lost.

6. The global group TEACHERS has Full Access to the file
   `F:\STUDENT\REGISTRATION.DOC`, while the global group
   STUDENTS has No Access. Drive F: is an NTFS volumes. Robert
   copies the file `F:\STUDENT\REGISTRATION.DOC` to the `D:\STUDENT\`
   `FORMS` directory. Drive D: is a FAT volume. What permissions do
   the STUDENTS global group have to the file `D:\STUDENT\FORMS\`
   `REGISTRATION.DOC`?

   a. Full Access

   b. Read Access

   c. No Access

   d. All permissions are lost.

7. The user PATRICIAS has been granted Add access to the NTFS directory `G:\SCHEDULE`. What special permissions will PATRICIAS have by default to new files created in that directory? (Choose all that apply)

   a. Read

   b. Write

   c. Execute

   d. Change Permissions

   e. Take Ownership

   f. Delete

   g. None of the above

8. The user KIMG is a member of three global groups: DOMAIN USERS, WEATHER, and OPERATIONS. Both WEATHER and OPERATIONS belong to the local group FLIGHTS. KIMG has been assigned Full Access to the file `H:\REPORTS\EMPLOYEE.DOC` on an NTFS partition. The local group FLIGHTS has been granted No Access to the file `H:\REPORTS\EMPLOYEE.DOC`. What will KIMG's effective permissions be to the file `H:\REPORTS\EMPLOYEE.DOC`?

   a. Read

   b. Full Access

   c. Change

   d. No Access

Answers

1. d—All permissions are lost. Because NT only supports the FAT file system for floppy disks, a file on a floppy disk cannot have file-level permissions.

NOTE: *Exam questions will often include irrelevant information. In this question, the permissions possessed by the user ASHLEYS and the group ACCOUNTING have no relevance, nor does the filename. The key piece of information in this question is the fact that you are copying or moving the file to a floppy disk. Windows NT always formats floppy disks with FAT, and FAT does not support file permissions. The rest of the question is irrelevant.*

2. a—Full Access. In NTFS, a file is an object that contains its own ACL. When moving a file within an NTFS partition, the pointer to the file changes but not the object itself or its ACL. Regardless of the permissions of the destination directory, the file's original permissions are retained.

3. c—Read Access. Copying a file always involves the creation of a new file. New files take on the permissions of the directory where they are created. Because the global group STUDENTS has Read Access to the directory **F:\STUDENT\FORMS**, they will also have Read Access to the new file **F:\STUDENT\FORMS\REGISTRATION.DOC** created in that subdirectory.

4. c—No Access. Moving a file within an NTFS volume does not create a new file; rather, it merely changes the pointer to that file object. The file retains its original ACL. Therefore, despite the fact that the STUDENTS group has Read Access to the directory, they have No Access to **F:\STUDENT\FORMS\REGISTRATION.DOC**.

5. b—Read Access. Files cannot truly be moved between NTFS volumes. Instead, when a user "moves" a file to a different NTFS volume, the file is actually copied to the new location, then deleted from its original location. Because a new file is created, the file inherits the permissions of the destination directory.

6. d—All permissions are lost. FAT volumes do not support file-level permissions. Therefore, all permissions are lost.

7. g—None of the above. The Add standard permission gives Write and Execute permission to the directory but no permissions to the files in that directory. Notice that not giving any permissions to files in the directory is not the same as giving the standard permission No Access, which would prevent the user from being granted access in any way.

8. d—No Access. No Access always overrides all other permissions.

7

Managing NT Server Partitions

To manage an NT server successfully, you must make proper use of the hard disk space available on that server. In the bad old days of DOS, Windows 3.X, and even Windows 95 and 98, the tools for disk manipulation were FDISK—a rather cryptic command-line utility—and FORMAT, a command-line utility in DOS and Win3.X but a graphical utility in Windows 95 and 98. NT uses a single graphical tool, Disk Administrator, for all the mundane disk management tasks, such as creating, formatting, and deleting partitions and labeling and formatting volumes. But Disk Administrator goes far beyond the mundane tasks, enabling us to create volume sets, striped drives (with or without parity), and mirrored drives, which are all features once reserved for higher-level SCSI hardware RAID solutions.

In addition to setting up and playing with hard drives, NT administrators must regularly back up the precious data on their servers. NT comes with a well-meaning, but sadly limited, backup utility that is appropriately called NT Backup. Backup, which works only with tape drives and no other media, enables us to back up some or all of an NT machine's data, including data stored on mirrored drives and stripe sets —and even the registry.

Hard Drive Terminology

This chapter deals heavily with hard drive terminology. We covered most of this subject in detail in Chapter 2, "Installing NT," and in Chapter 4, "NT Boot Process," but for a refresher (or in case you are reading out of order—you rebel!), here is a quick list. The few new terms (volume sets, mirroring, duplexing, and striping) will be covered in this chapter.

- Partition—A *partition* is an area of disk space that functions similarly to an individual hard disk. Partitions are referred to as either *primary* or *extended*.

- Primary partition—A primary partition is an area of a physical disk that is reserved for the OS. NT enables four primary partitions on a single, physical drive or up to three primary partitions if an extended partition is present. Primary partitions can not be sub-partitioned.

- Extended partition—An extended partition is the extra free space on a hard disk that can be sub-partitioned into logical drives. As noted earlier, an extended partition counts as one of the four partitions available for a single drive. Each drive can have only one extended partition, with or without any primary partition(s).

- Logical drive—Extended partitions must be subdivided into *logical drives*. Each logical drive gets a drive letter and is formatted separately.

- Active partition—Any primary partition can store an OS. By setting a partition as the *active partition*, you tell the system to use that partition's OS.

- Free space—*Free space* describes unused and unformatted hard disk space that can be partitioned or sub-partitioned. If the unused or unformatted free space is within an extended partition, you can create logical drives. If the unused/unformatted free space spans several disks, you can create Volume Sets or other types of volumes for fault tolerance. Unused or unformatted free space that is not within an extended partition can be partitioned as well. NT enables only four partitions per physical disk.

- Volume—A *volume* is a set of disk space that is set aside as a unit and is formatted by a file system. In Windows NT, volumes are assigned drive letters.

- Volume set—A *volume set* is a volume that spans multiple physical devices.

- Stripe set—A *stripe set* describes the technique of saving data across partitions of the same size on different drives. Stripe sets come in two varieties: with and without parity. Stripe sets without parity improve performance, while Stripe sets with parity improve performance and provide fault tolerance.

- Fault tolerance—*Fault tolerance* is the technique of ensuring that data can be retrieved in case of disk failure.

- Disk mirroring—In *disk mirroring*, two drives of the same size connected to the same controller store the same data. In the event of a single drive failure, no data is lost.

- Disk duplexing—In *disk duplexing*, two drives of the same size connected to two different controllers store the same data. In the event of either a disk or controller failure, no data is lost.

- System partition—This partition incorporates the **NTLDR**, **OSLOADER.EXE**, **BOOT.INI**, and **NTDETECT.COM** files needed to launch Windows NT.

- Boot partition—This partition incorporates the actual Windows NT OS files. These files are located by default in the **\WINNT** and **\WINNT\SYSTEM32** directories.

Disk Administrator

The Disk Administrator enables us to manage hard drives through a graphical, easy-to-use interface. To access Disk Administrator, go to Start ... Programs ... Administrative Tools and select the program. Disk Administrator opens with a small, customizable window, as shown in Figure 7–1.

Figure 7–1

Disk Administrator

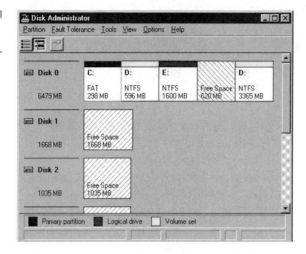

In the same screen, Disk Administrator provides data about all the physical hard drives and how they are set up and enables us to manipulate the drive settings. Simply right-clicking a volume, for example, enables you to change the size of a partition, format it, make it active (and thus potentially bootable), and even assign a non-contiguous drive letter. This sure beats FDISK! The pull-down menus reveal the other functions of Disk Administrator, including mirroring and striping. This chapter examines in detail the capabilities of Disk Administrator.

REFERENCE LIST OF DISK ADMINISTRATOR FUNCTIONS   Here is a list of the capabilities of the Disk Administrator utility. These items are useful for studying and quick reference. In Disk Administrator, you can do the following actions:

■ See the status of the available hard drives, such as partition sizes and the amount of free (unpartitioned) space available

■ See information about the Windows NT volumes for drive letter assignment, volume label, file system type, and size

■ Create or delete partitions on the hard disk and logical drives within an extended partition

■ Select and mark which partition will be active

■ Change and create drive letter assignments

■ Save and restore drive letter assignments, volume sets, and stripe set configuration information to-and-from a floppy diskette

- Migrate disk configuration information from one version of Windows NT to another
- Create and delete volume sets
- Create and delete stripe sets

Creating, Formatting, and Deleting Partitions

To store information on a hard drive, either EIDE or SCSI, requires four specific steps: physical installation, BIOS support, partitioning, and formatting. Some SCSI drives also require a "low-level format" before partitioning. Let's look at each of these items in turn.

EIDE Step One: Physical installation. Physical installation of EIDE has three components: jumper settings, cabling, and power. Most systems come with two separate EIDE controllers built into the motherboard, called the *primary and secondary controllers*. The basic rule is to plug the drive you plan to boot to into the primary controller, although this process can be finessed with some motherboard BIOSs. Each controller can handle two physical drives, which are distinguished as the master and the slave. Set the jumpers on the drives so that you have only one master and one slave on a controller. Two masters or two slaves on the same controller make for a bad day. Also, make sure the controller is enabled—which is usually done in CMOS (or, on an expansion card, with a jumper). With cabling, the rule is to plug one end of the 40-pin ribbon cable into a controller and the other end into a hard drive, aligning pin one (the red stripe) with pin one on both the controller and the drive. Reversing the cable on one end will not cause damage; the cable just will not work. Finally, plug in the power connector. Hard drives do not play well without electricity.

Step Two: Securing BIOS support. After successfully installing the EIDE drive in the system, you must introduce the drive to the System BIOS. Most commonly, this process is a matter of booting up, going into CMOS, and auto-detecting the drive. If a drive does not auto-detect, the drive is either dead (unlikely) or you missed some physical installation step. Check your cabling and jumper settings, and then try again. If you have no auto-detect feature built into the motherboard, you will have to input the drive geometry parameters manually (i.e., type the number of cylinders, heads, and sectors per track in the main CMOS screen). Manufacturers usually print these numbers directly onto the hard drive casing.

Step Three: Partitioning. In a new installation, during the install NT will prompt you to set up the partitions on the drive, as discussed in great

detail in Chapter 2, "Installing NT." In an existing NT installation, partitioning a new drive is as simple as firing up Disk Administrator, selecting a "Free Space" section on a drive, and choosing "Change" from either
the pull-down "Partitioning" menu or by right-clicking the drive. See Figure 7–2. NT gives you the opportunity to set the size of the partition, as
shown in Figure 7–3. By default, Disk Administrator assumes that you
want to use the entire space for a single, primary partition.

   To create an extended partition, either choose "less than the whole" for
the primary or select "create extended" from either the pull-down Partitioning menu or by right-clicking the free space of the drive, as shown in
Figure 7–4. Right-clicking the free space again and selecting "Create" will
enable you to make a logical drive, which can then be formatted and used
for data storage. See Figure 7–5.

Figure 7–2
Right-clicking Free
Space will display the
option for creating a
new primary
partition.

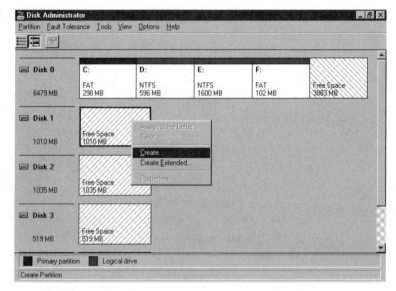

Figure 7–3
Disk Administrator
enables you to set
the size of the new
primary partition.

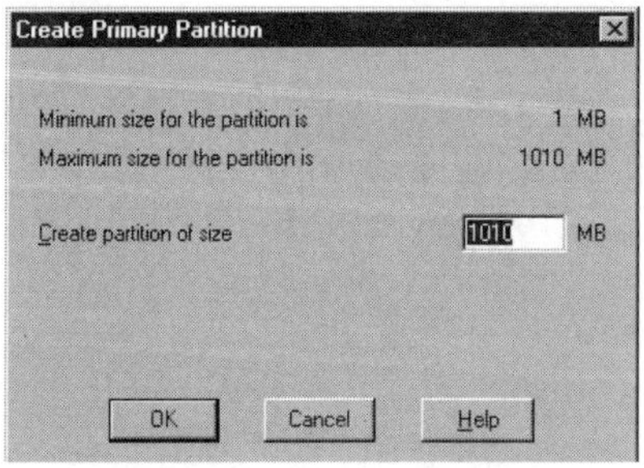

Figure 7–4
Right-clicking Free Space will display the option for creating a new extended partition.

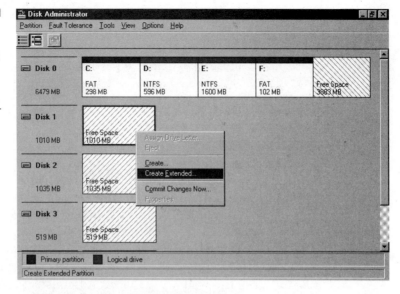

Figure 7–5
Setting the size of the logical drive

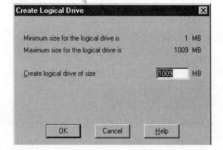

At this point, you should save your work. One more time, right-click the newly created primary partition or logical drive and select "Commit Changes Now . . . ." NT will update itself and let you go to the next step, which is formatting.

 NOTE: *Whenever you save in Disk Administrator, NT suggests that you update the Emergency Recovery Diskette. See Chapter 4, "The Boot Process," for information about creating and updating the ERD.*

If you want to be a serious Luddite, you can opt to use the MS-DOS utility FDISK, rather than Disk Administrator, to partition your drive. You probably will not be able to access all of your hard disk space using the

FDISK utility, however, because FDISK can only read up to 4GB. Depending on the geometry, you might only be able to access 1GB, because MS-DOS cannot access volumes that go beyond cylinder 1023. If you have the choice, use Disk Administrator to partition your drives.

NOTE: *On a RISC-based system, use the program* **ARCINST,** *which is on the Windows NT Server CD.*

All the programs that make the initial partition—either primary or extended—on a disk also create the *Master Boot Record* (MBR) and write it to the first sector on the disk (cylinder 0, head 0, sector 1). The MBR contains the information about each defined partition on the hard disk. When you create, delete, or format the hard disk, information about those changes is stored in the Partition Table within the Master Boot Record.

Step Four: Formatting. Formatting a newly created primary partition or logical drive is equally easy in Disk Administrator. Right-click the new drive (or select the drive from the menu), and select format. NT has two built-in formats available, FAT16 and NTFS, as discussed in Chapter 6, "File Systems." Keep in mind here that the size limit of FAT16-formatted partitions is only 2GB. Bigger drives have to use NTFS. Selecting NTFS also enables you to change the default cluster size for the drive, and if for some bizarre reason you want to do this, click the arrow under Allocation Unit Size to set the cluster size manually. Finally, you can name the newly born partition by typing something for Volume Label. Once you have formatted the primary partition or logical drive, you are ready to start filling up the drive with data.

SCSI   Disk Administrator and NT do not recognize any differences between SCSI and EIDE drives. A hard drive is a hard drive. From a software side, therefore, getting a SCSI drive ready for data is the same as for EIDE. Steps 3 and 4, in other words, are the same for SCSI as for EIDE. The big differences come from the first two steps—physical installation and BIOS—and from the sometimes-used step in-between 2 and 3, which is low-level formatting.

Step One: Physical installation. Four issues exist when physically installing SCSI drives: SCSI ID, termination, cabling, and power. SCSI controllers can handle many more drives than EIDE controllers—as many as 7 or even 15. To differentiate between the drives, each drive must have a unique SCSI ID. Furthermore, many controllers assume that a bootable SCSI drive will have an ID of zero. Second, you must terminate the ends of the SCSI chain. If it is the last device in the system, then the chain must be terminated (by jumpers, terminating resistors that plug into the drive, or by an external resistor that connects to the SCSI cable). Cabling is essentially the same as for EIDE. Connect one end of the 50- or 68-pin ribbon cable to the controller and the other end to the drive, aligning pin one on the cable with pin one on the drive. Be careful here. Reversing one end of a SCSI cable can destroy both your drive *and* your controller. An expensive mistake you will likely not make twice. Finally, plug the power cable into the drive.

Step Two: Securing BIOS support. SCSI drives need BIOS support just like EIDE drives. The difference here is that most motherboards do not have built-in SCSI controllers, and therefore they have no support in System BIOS. Many better SCSI controllers will have their own BIOS built into a ROM chip on the card itself. Make sure the BIOS is enabled if you plan to use the SCSI drive for the system partition.

Step Two-and-a-Half: Low-level formatting. Low-level formatting scans a drive, creates the tracks on the disks, and then verifies whether each sector is good or bad. The low-level format marks the individual sectors accordingly. Generally, there is no reason to low-level format a drive unless the drive keeps coming up with bad sectors or if the manufacturer recommends low-level formatting. In the latter case, the manufacturer will usually provide a diskette with a low-level formatting utility. Use the provided diskette or the built-in formatting feature of some SCSI host adapters. Low-level formatting a SCSI drive does no damage.

NOTE: *Do not low-level format EIDE drives. This process can destroy the drive. Such formatting is done once at the factory by trained professionals. Do not try this at home, kids.*

Once you have installed, given BIOS support for, and, if necessary, low-level formatted the SCSI drive, fire up Disk Administrator and partition and format the drive, as in the earlier example with EIDE.

DELETING PARTITIONS   Perform the following steps to delete a partition, volume, or logical drive (Figure 7–6):

- Select the desired partition to delete by clicking it within Disk Administrator.
- On the menu bar, click Partition, then click Delete.

Figure 7–6
Deleting a partition
using Disk
Administrator

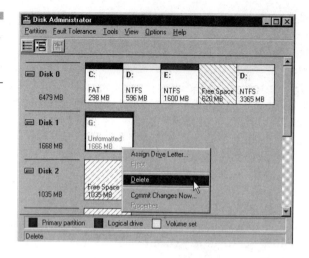

You will receive a message window warning you that all data will be lost if you continue. Click Yes to confirm your actions. The space will become free space again.

You will need to click Commit Changes Now . . . from the Partition menu on the menu bar or quit Disk Administrator to finish the partition deletion process. Also, NT requires you to delete all logical drives or other volumes in an extended partition before you can delete that extended partition.

NOTE: *On an x86-based system, Windows NT will not allow you to delete a partition with the system files on it or delete individual partitions that are part of a set without deleting the entire set first. On a RISC-based system, however, you can delete the system partition—so be careful.*

ASSIGNING DRIVE LETTERS Perform the following steps to assign a drive letter to a partition or to a logical drive:

- Within the Disk Administrator applet, select the partition or logical drive to which you wish to assign a letter.
- From the menu bar, click Tools, then click Assign Drive Letter (Figure 7–7).
- In the Assign Drive Letter window, click Assign drive letter and select the appropriate letter.
- Click OK to finish the process.

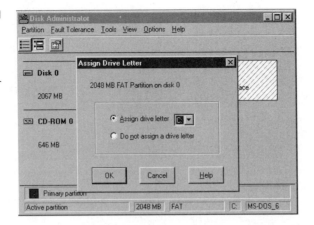

Figure 7–7
Assigning a drive
letter using Disk
Administrator

NOTE: *Be aware when creating drive letter assignments that many MS-DOS and Windows programs make references to or have pointers to specific drive letters. You may have to change the command line or working directory or completely reinstall the application for proper functionality. When assigning a letter to the CD-ROM drive, you may receive an error message if that drive letter is being accessed by another application. To work around this problem, close the application and try the command again.*

Windows NT does enable static drive mapping assignment on volumes, partitions, and CD-ROM drives, which means that a drive letter can be permanently assigned to a specific hard drive, partition, volume, or CD-ROM. Adding a new hard disk to the system will not affect static drive mapping assignments.

Spreading Data onto Multiple Partitions

Windows NT enables you to do some cool things with partitioning and formatting, beyond creating traditional partitions. Through a special fault tolerance driver called **FTDISK.SYS**, Windows NT gives you several methods for making two or more partitions into one single logical drive. Depending on the method you choose, some of these techniques can also provide performance enhancements or fault tolerance. Specifically, NT has four separate partitioning levels for combining multiple partitions into a single logical drive: volume sets, mirrored drives, stripe sets, and stripe sets with parity. These partitioning levels—with the exception of volume sets—provide software solutions equivalent to RAID levels 0, 1, and 5.

RAID Some years ago, several people at the University of California—Berkeley came up with the idea that using bigger and bigger hard drives to store data was both too expensive and too dangerous. What happens to the data if one of those giant drives fails? You better hope you purchased and used that unbelievably slow tape backup drive the night before, right? Would it not make more sense to use several smaller drives, each storing a piece of the data or even the same data? That way, if one drive fails, all is not lost. The Berkeley folks wrote out a set of levels for this *Redundant Array of Inexpensive Disks* (RAID), which provide more or less degrees of data redundancy, data protection, and increased data access speed by utilizing multiple disk drives.

RAID 0 combines two or more disks into one larger, logical drive through a process called "striping." *Striping* divides the drives into equal blocks and then interlaces stored data. Cluster one is on drive one, cluster two is on drive two, cluster three is on drive one, cluster four is on drive two, etc. This process can lead to better performance, because mechanical access times are reduced. RAID 0 does not provide any data *redundancy*, however, so it only marginally qualifies as true RAID.

RAID 1 takes two separate drives and mirrors the data exactly. Disk mirroring provides an instant backup. If one drive fails, all the data is intact on the other drive. Better yet, a good RAID system immediately sends all reads and writes to the backup drive, which makes the transition relatively transparent to users. Disk mirroring will typically slow down system performance, because data must be written to and acknowledged by both drives.

An alternative to disk mirroring is "disk duplexing." *Disk duplexing* keeps duplicate data on two drives, each governed by their own controller. Disk mirroring, on the other hand, uses a single controller for both drives. Both mirroring and duplexing provide redundancy. Disk duplexing provides greater fault tolerance, protecting data against either controller or drive failures—but at an increased cost.

RAID 2 provides a degree of data security by requiring multiple drives with several parity drives as well. No one uses RAID 2, so ignore it.

RAID 3 and 4 use at least two data drives and a dedicated parity drive (using *Error Correcting Code*, or ECC). Data is striped between the drives, but the size of the data blocks differ. RAID 4 uses bigger blocks than RAID 3, which makes the former marginally faster. Regardless, each change to a drive requires writing ECC data to the parity drive, which slows things down.

RAID 5 is similar to RAID 3 and 4 but distributes the ECC information among all the drives. This feature gives a nice performance boost and good protection for data. In addition, RAID 5 reduces ECC data redundancy to 25 percent, thus using less hard drive space.

RAID 6 is just like RAID 5 with the added capability of asynchronous and cached data transmission. RAID 6 is the last official level in the RAID specification.

Most servers implement RAID solutions in one of two ways: through hardware or software. Hardware solutions generally use specific SCSI controllers or hardware boxes with a RAID controller and built-in drive bays. Windows NT provides software versions of RAID 0, 1, and 5, as well as a strange hybrid called volume sets. Let's deal with the hybrid first.

VOLUME SETS   NT can take multiple partitions (between one and 32) and combine them into a single "volume set." A *volume set* acts precisely like a single, logical drive. Volume sets can span multiple drives, even drives of different types—EIDE, SCSI, and ESDI. The limitations to volume sets are that you cannot place the NT system partition into one, and you must format the volume with a single file system, FAT16 or NTFS. Furthermore, volume sets are not part of the RAID levels because they do not provide any protection from data loss or corruption. When one of the partitions goes down, they all go down.

Even without fault tolerance, a volume set could be a useful solution for an NT machine with multiple small drives or free volumes scattered on several drives. When upgrading some business to NT Server, for example, do you have to toss those five 540MB drives into a drawer to gather dust, because they are too small to be useful or take up too many drive letters? Making them into a single volume set would give you a decent-sized drive and would take only one drive letter, which is a rather elegant use for older drives.

To create a volume set, perform the following steps:

■ Within the Disk Administrator applet, select two or more areas of available free space on up to 32 hard disks by pressing the CTRL key and clicking the desired free space areas. See Figure 7–8.

■ From the menu bar, click Partition and then select Create Volume Set.

■ The Disk Administrator displays the minimum and maximum sizes available for the volume set.

■ Within the Create Volume Set window, type the desired size of the volume set and click OK.

Figure 7–8
Creating a
Volume Set

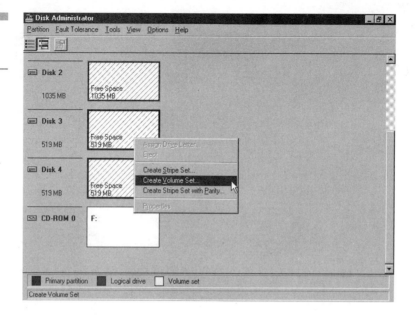

If you choose less than the total amount of space, Disk Administrator divides the total size by the number of disks to create almost equal-sized, unformatted partitions on each of the hard disks. This process can lead to even more fragmented drives and should be used with care. Disk Administrator then assigns a single drive letter to the collection of partitions that make up the volume set.

NT also gives you the capacity to *extend* a volume set, meaning that if you run out of space on a partition—when an application is too big to load, for example—you can add to the size of the partition by grabbing free space elsewhere. This feature could be useful in situations where drive letters are scarce or time is more important than clean solutions (i.e., just add a little to the partition rather than repartition the whole drive, reload NT, etc.). To extend the size of a partition into a volume set, simply select the partition and a free space partition in Disk Administrator. Right-click (or go to the Fault Tolerance menu) and select "Extend Volume Set . . . ." Remember that the system partition cannot be part of a volume set. Disk Administrator will let you select the system partition here but later gives you a nice error message.

If you need to delete a volume set for some reason, perform the following steps:

- Back up all of the data on the volume set.
- Within the Disk Administrator applet, select the volume set you wish to delete.
- Select Partition from the menu bar and then choose Delete Volume Set. Click Yes to confirm the action.

NOTE: *When you delete a volume set, you also delete all of the information stored in the volume set.*

STRIPE SETS *Stripe sets* combine areas of unformatted free space on two or more (up to 32) physical hard disks into one large logical drive. Each area of the stripe set must be on a different physical hard disk of identical size, which is RAID 0. Stripe sets, like volume sets, can combine areas of disk space on different types of drives, such as SCSI, ESDI, and EIDE. Also, a stripe set cannot contain the Windows NT system partition. Having the data striped—or "interlaced"—between two or more physical disks permits the execution of concurrent I/O commands, thus increasing throughput and performance. Stripe sets, however, similar to hardware RAID 0 solutions, provide no fault tolerance.

NOTE: *If the Windows NT system is a dual boot system with another OS that does not support stripe sets, that other OS will not be able to see the stripe set.*

MIRROR SETS A *mirror set* has two physical drives, each containing an exact copy of all the data in the other drive. This idea is NT's software RAID 1 solution. All data written on one partition is identically written to the mirror set in another partition. This event results in 50 percent disk space utilization and complete data redundancy—and thus, excellent data protection. Both the original partition and the copy of the original partition are continuously updated by Windows NT. NT sometimes refers to the copy of the original partition as a shadow partition, or shadow disk.

In the event that one of the drives in a mirror set fails, the fault tolerance driver **FTDISK.SYS** kicks in to save the day. In case of a read failure to one of the disks, FTDISK reads the data from the shadow disk. When a write failure occurs, FTDISK uses the remaining available disk space for all accesses.

To make mirror sets even more robust, many administrators will use two drives, each on their own controllers. We know and love this as disk duplexing. NT makes implementing duplexing or mirroring as simple as selecting two partitions on the different controllers, or on the same controller.

To mirror, select the partition in Disk Administrator that you want to mirror, hold the CTRL key, and click a free space of equal or greater size. Select "Create Mirror" from the Fault Tolerance menu or by right-clicking the selected partitions, as shown in Figure 7–9. Disk Administrator then does the rest.

All partitions can be mirrored, including the system and boot partitions. You are not required to select a shadow partition of the original partition's exact size (or number of tracks and cylinders). This feature enables you to replace a failed hard disk with a disk that is not identical. You cannot, however, select a shadow partition smaller than the original partition. If you select a shadow partition that is larger than the original partition, the extra disk space on the shadow partition is left as free space. That free space can be configured as another additional partition—but only when there are fewer than four partitions on that physical hard disk. When you configure the system partition as a part of a mirror set, it is always best to use identical, physical hard disks and the same disk geometry. The boot partition can also be part of a mirrored set, which will

Figure 7–9
Establishing a
Mirror Set

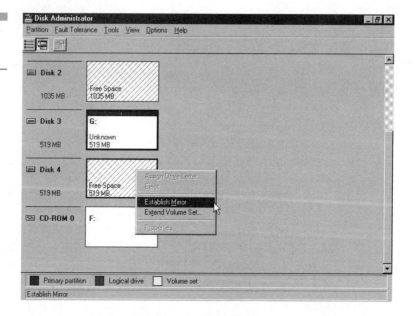

significantly reduce the time required to recover Windows NT in case of failure. Once again, the system partition is the location of space on the hard disk that contains the hardware-specific files and support files required for booting Windows NT.

If you make a mirror set for the system or boot partition on x86-based systems, make sure to create a Windows NT startup floppy disk so you can restart the system in case of failure. The **BOOT.INI** file points to the first drive, not the mirrored drive. If the primary drive goes down, you may not be able to boot to the second drive, although all the information is still intact. See Chapter 4 for more information about **BOOT.INI** and creating bootable floppies.

STRIPE SETS WITH PARITY   A *stripe set with parity* defines three or more (up to 32) hard drives as a single volume, distributing data and parity information evenly across all of the hard disks within the group. Each drive contains data and ECC, but not the ECC for its own data, as shown in Figure 7–10. If any one drive dies, the other two have the information necessary to rebuild the stripe set with parity. This idea is Windows NT's software RAID 5 solution.

Implementing a stripe set with parity requires a minimum of at least three hard drives (but can handle as many as 32 drives). The hard disks do not need to be physically alike. The unpartitioned space available, however, must be equal-sized blocks. The hard disks can reside on the same controller or on different controllers. Unfortunately, you cannot add another physical hard disk to a pre-existing stripe set with parity if you need to expand the volume space. This restriction is also true for stripe sets without parity.

Figure 7–10
Stripe Set with parity
Organization

To create a Stripe Set with parity, select three or more equal-sized free spaces in Disk Administrator. Right-click the partitions, or go to the Fault Tolerance pull-down menu and select "Create Stripe Set with Parity . . . ," as shown in Figure 7–11. Choose the size you want, hit OK, and then save your work. You are ready to format.

When there is a hard drive failure within a stripe set with parity, all data integrity remains. Data can even be read from the drive, although performance will degrade significantly because the system will have to reconstruct the lost data on the fly. A read operation that is required from the failed hard disk will be retrieved from the other valid remaining stripes. Through the miracles of higher binary mathematics, the missing data is reformulated. When a write operation is required on a hard disk that has failed, the write operation reads the other data stripes and the parity stripe and then reconstitutes the missing data stripe. Changes that are required to the parity stripe can then be properly calculated and created. Only the parity stripe can be written to when the data stripe is bad. For a read operation on a failed hard disk that contains the parity stripe, no effect results. Parity stripes are not needed for a read operation unless there is a failure in a data stripe. Also, when the hard disk with the parity stripe fails, the system does not write or calculate a parity stripe if there is no change required.

Figure 7–11

Creating a Stripe Set with Parity

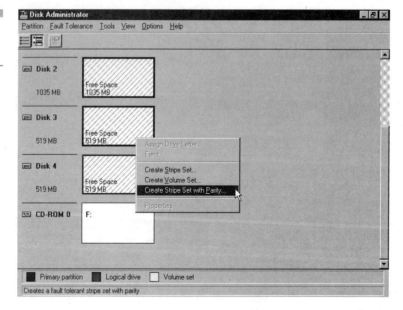

DUELING RAID: MIRROR SETS VERSUS STRIPE SETS WITH PARITY   Mirror sets and stripe sets with parity both accomplish the goal of disk redundancy—they provide a backup and recoverable solution for your data. What are the relative merits or disadvantages of the two? Mirror sets provide the following benefits that stripe sets with parity lack:

- Mirror sets are less expensive, because you are only required to have two physical hard disks versus three physical hard disks for a stripe set with parity.
- A mirror set is less taxing on system resources.
- If there is a hard disk failure, a mirror set will show less performance degradation to the user.

Stripe sets with parity provide the following benefits:

- In most implementations, stripe sets with parity give better system performance than mirror sets. Database applications that can execute random read operations, for example, work best with the load-balancing abilities of a stripe set with parity.
- Stripe sets with parity are excellent, cost-efficient, fault-tolerant solutions. They are more cost effective than mirror sets when a large number of hard disks are involved in the system environment. Parity storage monopolizes 1/x of disk space, where "x" is the number of hard disks. If you have three 4GB hard drives with a total disk space of 12GB, for example, the parity information would monopolize 1/3 of the total disk space (4GB of disk space), or one complete hard disk. You would be left with 8GB of actual disk storage for data. The same total size in a Mirror Set, on the other hand, accomplished with two 6GB hard drives, would leave only 6GB of data storage space.

Each of the multiple partition solutions within Windows NT serves different purposes. As a system administrator, you must decide which solution works for your environment. For creative use of hard drive space, try volume sets. When fault tolerance takes a back seat to performance, choose stripe sets without parity, which give the best performance boost. If secure data is important, use either mirror sets or stripe sets with parity. A little thought about solutions at the beginning can save a lot of work later.

Backing Up in Windows NT

I once took a rock climbing course in college. This course was a "technical climbing" class, in that we used special devices called "cams." Cams are little metal nuts that you can shove into cracks in the rock, and they will hold you if you fall. When the instructor told us that we had to put cams in the rock to tie off our ropes, I asked how often and how far apart I should put those nuts. She casually looked me in the eye and responded with, "Well, how far would you like to fall?" Ouch.

Performing backups on your NT systems is a lot like rock climbing. The down side is not falling but rather having a system crash and losing data. Just as falling is a guarantee with climbing, data loss is a guarantee with computers. No way exists to ensure that your system will never fail. You must take steps to ensure that when your systems fail, you can restore them. Certainly, good systems people take many steps to help insure against system failure. Some of this insurance takes the form of a UPS, dual power supplies, disk mirroring/duplexing, and the many advanced RAID options, such as disk striping with parity. Be aware, however, that all of these excellent technologies will eventually fail. When this happens, your only hope of survival is to have a backup that you can restore from tape. The only question you should ask yourself is, "How far do I want to fall?"

Think about how much work you have done to create your nice, stable NT servers, workstations, and domains. Imagine how many hours your users have spent creating data and storing that data on those servers. Now imagine a virus that deletes critical files or the registry on your hard drives. As you can also imagine, this situation is not good either for your blood pressure or for your job security. What Microsoft recommends, and what common sense dictates, is that you create backups of your data. In addition, backups are useless if you only make them once. You are not doing any good when you restore a file or registry that has been changed for three weeks since the last time it was backed up. You should therefore create a regularly scheduled backup that ensures that your data is backed up regularly and can be restored easily. Keep your "fall" as short as possible.

WHAT DOES NT PROVIDE FOR BACKUPS? NT provides backup software to make this part of your job easier to accomplish. The backup software is called **NTBACKUP.EXE** and is accessible from the menus by choosing Start . . . Programs . . . Administrative Tools . . . Backup. This tool will enable you to meet the minimum requirements of backing up your systems, although this tool does have some significant limitations.

NOTE: *NTBACKUP is not your only backup option. Many excellent third-party backup programs are available today that provide many options not available in NTBACKUP.*

WHAT ARE THE ADVANTAGES AND DISADVANTAGES?   The biggest advantage of the NTBACKUP utility is that it is free and included with your NT software, which means you will have it easily at hand to install. In addition, because NTBACKUP is a native NT utility, the chances are excellent that it will actually work correctly with NT with no conflicts or other issues. You will have the important ability to back up and restore from FAT and NTFS, because these are the two supported file systems. Again, the utility is native to NT, rather than transported from UNIX or DOS. Last, NTBACKUP knows about the registry and makes backing it up easy. You can completely back up the local registry "on the fly" without stopping services.

On the disadvantages side, however, NTBACKUP only supports one type of media for backup and restore: tape drives. Forget about newer technologies such as rewriteable CDs, Jaz, or Bernoulli drives. If the machine you want to back up has no tape drive, you cannot even look at the backup dialog box in NTBACKUP to learn how to use the utility. Some other disadvantages of NTBACKUP include the fact that there is no way to do an unattended backup from within the utility. We will discuss a way to work around this issue by using the Windows scheduler (**AT.EXE**), but this problem is a significant drawback. Additionally, you do not have the ability to back up the registry of remote machines. While you do have the ability to back up files over a network share, if you choose to backup the registry, you can only back up the registry of the machine running the backup utility, not the remote machine.

The advantages and disadvantages of NTBACKUP are fairly well-matched. What it means in the real world is that if you are part of a smaller environment that wants to have backups but does not want to spend any money for convenience or for an enterprise-type backup solution, you will probably be fine using NTBACKUP. If you work in a large, multi-domain, multi-server environment, however, invest in a more advanced, third-party backup tool.

NOTE: *There is no universal, standard format for backing up data on tapes. A backup done with NTBACKUP will not be readable by another backup program.*

USING NT BACKUP The NTBACKUP utility is fairly straightforward to use for backups and restores. To start, ensure that you have installed a tape backup device in the machine from which you want to run backups. In some cases, because you cannot back up registries remotely, you might need more than one tape backup device. To install the tape backup device drivers, use the Tape Devices applet in the Control Panel (described in Chapter 3). You should also ensure that you have a blank (or erasable) tape in the drive before you begin the backup process.

After the tape device is installed and working, start the NTBACKUP utility by selecting Start . . . Programs . . . Administrative Tools . . . Backup. NT will display the Backup utility, focusing on the drives available. Selecting any drive will open more windows. Also, a window will be available for the tape device(s). This window gives details on the status of the tape drive and the tape currently being used. Figure 7–12 shows the Tape and the Drives windows, as well as another window detailing the C: drive. Other applications, such as Microsoft Exchange, might also add their own windows to provide easier backup of critical files.

The menu options across the top of NTBACKUP are straight-forward. The "Operations" menu option is the only menu where some discussion may be needed. Figure 7–13 shows the Operations menu in action.

■ The Backup and Restore options correlate with the large Backup and Restore buttons on the main window. Note that one or the other is always grayed, which is simply a function of which window is active. If the Tape window is active, NTBACKUP assumes that you want to restore—so the Restore option is active and the Backup

Figure 7–12
NT Backup utility
showing different
windows

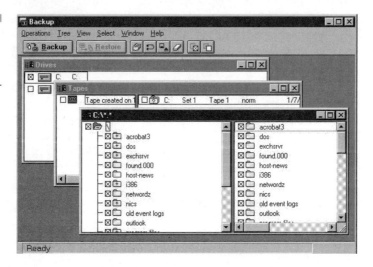

Figure 7–13
Operations menu

option is grayed. If the Drives window is active, NTBACKUP
assumes that you want to back up, so the Backup option is active
and the Restore option is grayed.

■ The Catalog menu option is simply a way to tell NTBACKUP,
"Show me what is on this tape without actually restoring it." The
big problem with tapes is that they are streaming data media. To
access requested data requires constant winding and rewinding,
which makes them slow. We put up with the slowness because
tapes are still the cheapest way to store large amounts of data.
Visualize a situation, however, where a file becomes corrupt on a
hard drive and needs to be restored from tape. In most cases, there
will be a large number of backup tapes from which to choose.
Which one has the file you need? Imagine the nightmare of having
to run through each tape, trying to find a certain file. That option
is unacceptable. Instead, we should have the backup program
create a list of filenames that are stored on a particular backup. If
a backup spans more than one tape, the list is stored on the last
tape. These lists are called Backup Sets. Backup Sets are created
automatically when a backup is performed. The catalog is the
visual display of the backup set. When catalog is pressed, this
option shows the contents of the backup set.

The rest of the options under Operations have to do with tape maintenance.

■ Erase Tape does exactly what it sounds like: erases the tape. Most
of the time, backups simply overwrite older information, so erasing
is not commonly done. There are two types of erasing: Quick and
Secure. Quick erase simply erases the tape header and takes only
a minute or two. Secure erase literally erases the entire tape.
Secure is a long, multi-hour process and should be avoided unless
necessary.

■ Retension tape is for certain types of tape (quarter-inch or QIC) that tend to not tension tightly around the reels after 15–20 backups. Retensioning rewinds the entire tape evenly around the takeout reel, ensuring faster data reading and writing. If NT detects a type of tape that does not require retensioning, this option will be grayed.

■ Eject tape will eject the tape, if the hardware supports software ejection.

■ Format tape formats the tape with NTBACKUP's formatting. Formatting is often done to make an unreadable tape readable again. Not all tapes will require formatting by NTBACKUP. If this option is grayed, you can usually assume that the tape will function without formatting.

To perform a backup in NTBACKUP, use the slightly Windows Explorer-like interface to select the files you want to back up and click the big Backup button. To restore, insert the correct tape and hit the big Restore button. The interface is easy, but there are a number of nuances to backing up that need to be understood to ensure good, easy-to-restore backups. Let's start by going through the process of backing up a system.

BACKING UP To begin the backup process, select the drives, folders, and/or files you would like to back up. In many cases, you will simply select an entire drive by placing a check mark in the box to the left of the drive letter. If there are easily reinstalled programs or other non-essential files, however, you may want to back up more selectively. This process will speed up the back up and require less tape. To back up specific files and folders, double-click the drive to display the tree and directory for that drive. If you were familiar with File Manager in Windows 3.X, selecting files from the NTBACKUP window will seem familiar as well, as you can see in Figure 7–14.

After you have selected the appropriate files and there is a tape in the drive, either choose Operations . . . Backup from the menu or click the Backup button on the toolbar. NTBACKUP displays the Backup Information dialog box, shown in Figure 7–15.

This dialog box enables you to select the options for your backup procedure and gives you some information about the tape installed in the drive. The following list describes the options and other fields on the Backup Information dialog box.

Figure 7–14
Selecting files to
back up

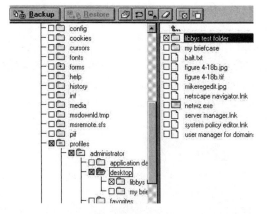

Figure 7–15
Backup Information
dialog box

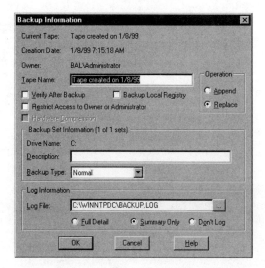

■ The Current Tape field displays the name of the tape, if applicable. Or, if the tape in the drive is blank, the Current Tape field displays that information. That field will also tell you whether there is a tape in the drive.

■ The Creation Date field displays the date that the first backup was made to the current tape. If the tape is blank, this field is blank.

■ The Owner field shows the name of the user who created the backup on the tape. If the tape is blank, this field is blank.

■ The Tape Name field gives you the opportunity to name a blank tape. In addition, if you choose the Replace radio button, you can rename the tape. If you choose the Append radio button, this field is unavailable. The default name of a tape is "Tape created on *today's date*."

■ The Operation section gives you the choices of Append or Replace. Append means that you will add the newly backed-up information to the end of the tape, without erasing anything else on the tape. This process will create a new backup set on the tape. If you choose the Replace option, the tape will rewind to the beginning and the new backup will write over the data currently on the tape.

■ The Verify After Backup checkbox enables you to require NTBACKUP to perform a check on the backed-up data. After the backup is performed, NTBACKUP will compare the backed-up data to the original data. Be aware that this option adds a significant amount of time to the backup process. In addition, if you back up data over a network, this option sends more traffic over the network.

■ The Backup Registry option enables you to create a backup of the entire registry database. When you choose to back up the registry, you will back up all the files contained in `%systemroot%\system32 \ config`. To select this option, you must select at least one other file on the system partition of your local system. Keep in mind that NTBACKUP can only perform registry backups on the local registry.

■ The Restrict Access to Owner or Administrator option, which is only available when you select the Replace radio button, indicates in the header of the backup tape that access should be restricted. Keep in mind, however, that there is no encryption or other security being added to the tape, which means that you should keep your tapes in a secure location.

■ The Hardware compression checkbox will enable you to store more data on a tape. If your tape device does not support hardware compression, however, this option will be grayed.

■ The Backup Set section enables you to see the drive being backed up and how many sets are being backed up. In addition, you have the ability to give a description to the backup, such as, "Backup of Total server."

■ The Backup Type box enables you to choose the way you want files backed up. This issue is important and will be discussed in the next section.

■ The Log File is a text file that documents the backup process. The log can be Full Detail, which shows the file, or it can be Summary Only, giving only the main steps of the backup process.

Figure 7–16
Figure 7–16
Backup in progress

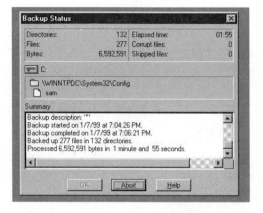

To begin the backup process, simply click the OK button, and the backup begins (Figure 7–16).

WHAT ARE THE TYPES OF BACKUPS?   The goal of backing up is to ensure that whenever a system dies, there will be an available, recent backup to restore the system. At first thought, backing up can be visualized as simply backing up the complete system at the end of each day—or whatever interval the administrator feels is prudent to keep the backups "fresh." But complete backups can be a tremendous waste of time and materials. Most files do not change that often—so why back them up? Instead of backing up the entire system, let's take advantage of the fact that files do not always get changed. NTBACKUP has a series of backup options available other than Complete (usually called Full or Normal) backup.

The cornerstone to understanding backups, other than the full backup, is a little fellow called the Archive attribute. All files have little, one-bit storage areas called *attributes*. The most common attributes are Hidden (does not show when DIR is typed), System (shows critical files for the system), Read-Only (cannot erase it), and the Archive bit. These attributes were first used in FAT formatted drives (DOS) but are still completely supported today by all file formats, including NTFS. The archive bit basically works as such: whenever a file is saved, the archive bit is activated. Simply opening a file will affect the current state of the archive bit. A backup program will turn off the file's archive bit when it is backed up. In theory, if a file's archive bit is turned off, there is a good backup of that file on some tape. If the archive bit is activated, that means that the file has been changed since the last backup (Figure 7–17).

Figure 7–17
Two files; one has
the archive bit set

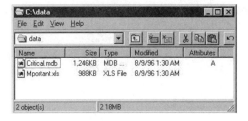

Figure 7–18
Backup Type options

NOTE: *Microsoft calls archive bits "markers." You will see statements such as, "This file was marked that it was backed up." This sentence shows bad terminology, but Microsoft is bigger than we are—so there.*

Archive bits are the tools we use to perform backups that are not full backups. Let's refer to the Backup menu again, in particular the Backup Type option. When this option is selected, a number of options are available from which to choose (see Figure 7–18).

■ *Normal* is a full backup. Every file selected will be backed up. The archive bit will be turned off for every file backed up. This option is the standard "back it all up" option.

■ *Copy* is identical to Normal with one big exception: the archive bits are not changed. This feature is used (although not often) for making extra copies of a previously completed backup.

■ *Incremental backups* only back up the files that have the archive bit activated. An incremental backup only copies the files that have been changed since the last backup, then turns off the archive bits.

■ *Differential backups* are identical to incremental backups, but they do not turn off the archive bits.

■ *Daily*, better known as *Daily Copy*, makes a backup of all of the files that have been changed that day and does not change the archive bits.

The motivation for having both the incremental and differential backups is not always clear. They seem so close that they would be basically the same. At first, incremental seems the better option. If a file is backed up, you would want to turn off the archive bit, right? Well, maybe. But one scenario exists where that action might not be too attractive. Most backups do a big, weekly Normal backup, followed by daily incremental or differential backups at the end of the business day. Let's look at the difference in Figure 7–19.

Notice that a differential backup is a cumulative backup. Because the archive bits are not set, the differential backup keeps backing up all changes since the last Normal backup. Clearly, the backups will become progressively larger through the week as more files are changed. The incremental backup only backs up the changes since the last backup. Each incremental backup will be small and also will be totally different from the previous backup. Let's assume that the system is wiped out during the day on Thursday. How will the system be restored? Well, with an incremental backup, you need to restore the weekly backup first, then the Tuesday

Figure 7–19

Incremental versus differential backups

Incremental

MON	TUE	WED	THU	FRI
Full Backup	All Tuesday Changes	All Wednesday Changes	All Thursday Changes	All Friday Changes

Differential

MON	TUE	WED	THU	FRI
Full Backup	All Changes Through Tuesday	All Changes Through Wednesday	All Changes Through Thursday	All Changes Through Friday

backup, and then the Wednesday backup before the system is restored. If you use a differential backup, on the other hand, you only need the weekly backup and then the Wednesday backup to restore the system. The greater the distance between Normal backups, the more incremental backups you need to restore the system. A differential will always be only two backups to restore (Figure 7–20). Suddenly, the differential backup looks better than the incremental.

A number of backup strategies are available for use, and each one makes incremental or differential backups more attractive than the other. One big benefit of incremental over differential is backup size. Differential backups will be massive compared to incremental. The type of backup you perform will determine the type of backups you do. The MCSE exams are not worried about what strategy you use, but they do expect you to be able to restore a system based on the type of backup strategy used.

AUTOMATIC BACKUPS Windows NT Backup utility (**NTBACKUP.EXE**) does not include any scheduling functions; rather, all backups must be started manually. Fortunately, Windows NT includes the handy **AT.EXE** program that enables us to run any program or batch file at a specified time each day.

Figure 7–20
Restoring comparison

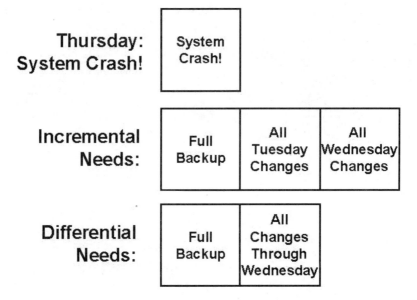

The Scheduler Service To use the **AT** command to schedule programs to run at specific times, you must first start the Scheduler service. To start the Scheduler service, double-click the Services tab in the Control Panel. Highlight the Scheduler service and change its startup option to automatic, as shown in Figure 7–21.

The **AT** command uses the following syntax:

```
AT time [options] [program name]
```

Running the **AT.EXE** command with no options displays the scheduled commands, their ID numbers, and their scheduled time, as shown in Figure 7–22.

The **AT.EXE** command supports the following options:

- **\\computername**—Enables **AT.EXE** command to remotely execute commands on another machine on the network.

- **Id**—Specifies the ID number of the previously scheduled command to be modified. (This option is usually used to delete commands from the schedule.)

- **/delete**—Deletes a scheduled job. If a job ID is not specified, this option deletes all of the scheduled commands.

- **/interactive**—Shows real-time network activity.

- **/e:<date>, . . .**—Sets date for command to run.

- **/next:<date>, . . .**—Sets next day of the month for the command to run.

Figure 7–21
Starting the schedule service

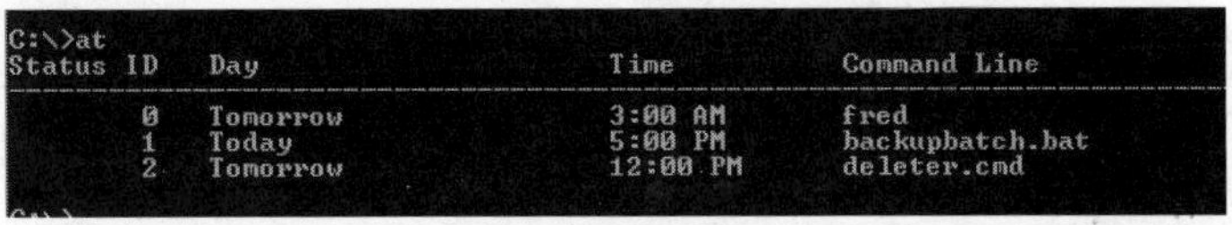

Figure 7–22
AT.EXE command status

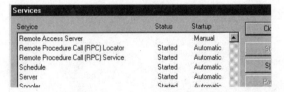

NTBACKUP Command Prompt Options   The **AT** command simply starts other programs. You will find it useless to start the NTBACKUP automatically, unless the program has the capability to do what it needs to do without your intervention. If the **AT.EXE** command starts NTBACKUP at 2 A.M., and all that NTBACKUP does is show up on the screen waiting for user input, the program is useless. Fortunately, Microsoft has armed NT-BACKUP with a number of command line options to enable the program to run completely unattended. Here is the command line syntax:

```
NTBACKUP <BACKUP | EJECT > <options>
```

The only option ever used is **BACKUP**. The **EJECT** command is never used. You cannot perform unattended restores with **NTBACKUP**. Table 7–1 shows the NTBACKUP command line options. A typical NTBACKUP command line might look something like the following:

Table 7–1

NTBACKUP command line options

Option	Description
/a	Append backup to existing tape; if not used, the backup will overwrite data on the tape
/v	Verifies data on tape after the tape is written
/r	Restricts access to this backup to Administrators, Backup Operators, and the Owner
/d "text"	Backup description
/b	Backup Registry
/hc: <on | off>	Hardware compression on or off
/t < normal | copy | incremental | differential | daily >	Backup type
/l "filename"	Name of logfile
/e	Exceptions only in logfile
/ tape: <0 to 9>	Number of tape drive to use

```
NTBACKUP BACKUP /d "Nightly Backup" /b /t incremental
      /tape:0
```

LOGGING THE BACKUP AND READING THE BACKUP LOG   After you have configured a backup to run, and especially after you have configured the backup to run unattended by using the scheduler, you will want some extra assurances that the backup is actually running. Obviously, the best way to receive these assurances is to occasionally spot-test the backup tapes by restoring elements of the backup to a different location and making a comparison. On a more regular basis, however, you will find it more convenient to check the backup logs. Backup logs are created by NTBACKUP by default, based on the options in the Backup Information dialog box. In the Log Information section of the dialog box, shown in Figure 7–23, you have the ability to view or change the default name and location of the backup log. By default, the backup log is called **BACKUP.LOG** and is stored in the **C:\WINNT** directory.

NOTE: *If Windows NT is installed in a different directory, the default location will vary.*

You also have the ability to decide how much information is logged in this file. Your options are Do not Log, Summary Only, and Full Detail. Summary Only logging is usually sufficient for normal work. Full Detail provides good data for troubleshooting if you are experiencing some problems with the backups. Logging verifies that the backup has occurred.

If you open the **BACKUP.LOG** file using any text editor, you will see text and information similar to the excerpt shown in Figure 7–24. This excerpt shows the information logged with Summary Only logging activated. Keep in mind that the log will grow fast, especially with large backup operations or with Full Detail logging. Periodically copying the data out of your log file into another document or location will create a potentially useful permanent record. Then, you can clear the **BACKUP.LOG** file and enable the next set of data to continue writing to the default file. Alternatively, you can give each day's backup log a different name.

Figure 7–23
Log information

Log Information	
Log File:	C:\WINNTPDC\BACKUP.LOG

○ Full Detail   ● Summary Only   ○ Don't Log

Figure 7–24
Excerpt of
BACKUP.LOG,
Summary Only

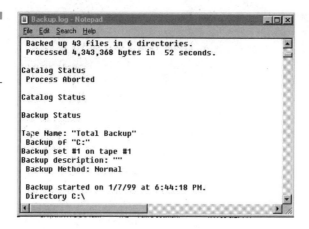

```
Backup.log - Notepad                              _ □ ×
File  Edit  Search  Help
Backed up 43 files in 6 directories.
Processed 4,343,368 bytes in  52 seconds.

Catalog Status
 Process Aborted

Catalog Status

Backup Status

Tape Name: "Total Backup"
 Backup of "C:"
Backup set #1 on tape #1
Backup description: ""
 Backup Method: Normal

 Backup started on 1/7/99 at 6:44:18 PM.
 Directory C:\
```

RESTORING A BACKUP Immediately after completing your first backup of data, you should complete your first restoration of data. If you tell the company at-large that you are performing backups, the company will expect you to be able to restore data when the server crashes. If you have never tested the integrity of your data or the process of restoring files and the registry, your ability to complete this task is sadly weakened. To begin the restore process, place the tape with the appropriate data in the tape drive. Suddenly, you understand why you should keep good logs of the backup and label the tapes carefully. Next, access the Tapes window of NTBACKUP to select the data to be restored, as shown in Figure 7–25.

You can select the elements to restore at various levels—from the entire tape to a backup set, or to a directory or file. You can select an entire tape or an entire backup set directly from the Tapes window. To select a directory or file, you must expand a set, as shown in Figure 7–26. To select levels below the tape level, you must sometimes wait for NTBACKUP to perform a catalog operation. The catalog operation displays the contents of a set.

After you have selected the data to be restored, click the Restore button to display the Restore Information dialog box, shown in Figure 7–27. Use the Restore Information dialog box to set any restore options and to determine where the files will be restored, if restoring to a different drive or location. The following list shows options on the Restore Information dialog box.

- The Tape Name field displays the name of the current tape. You should compare this name with your backup logs to ensure you are using the correct tape to restore the necessary data.

Figure 7–25
Tapes window

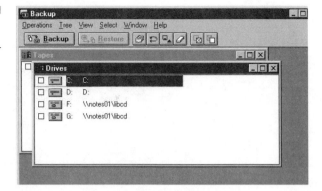

Figure 7–26
Expanded data
to restore

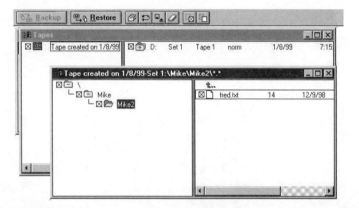

Figure 7–27
Restore Information
dialog box

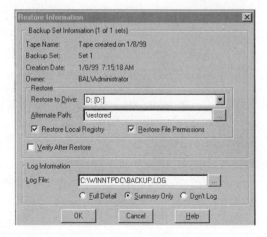

- The Backup Set field displays the number of the backup set. If you have backed up data from multiple volumes or drives, you will have multiple sets. This number will be the one from which you have chosen to restore files.

- The Creation Date field displays the date that the current set was created.

- The Owner field displays the username of the person or service that created the backup.

- Use the Restore to Drive field to select any currently available drive as a location to restore data. This drive may be a local or mapped drive. By default, the data will be restored to the same directory structure.

- Use the Alternate Path field to specify a restore location that is different from the original directory structure. Use this option to test your restore process without overwriting your current data.

- Use the Restore Local Registry checkbox to restore the system registry to the local machine. This option will only be available if you are restoring files from the system partition of the local machine.

- Use the Restore File Permissions checkbox to restore the ACL information of files that were backed up from an NTFS partition. You must also restore to an NTFS partition to maintain the ACL.

- Use the Verify After Restore checkbox to make a comparison of the restored data to the data on the tape. Keep in mind that this process significantly increases the time required for the operation and adds significant network traffic when restoring over a network.

- Use the Log File field to verify or change the name of the backup log file.

- Use the Full Detail, Summary Only, and Don't Log radio buttons to determine how much information about the restore process gets written to the log file.

After selecting the appropriate options for the restore job, choose OK to start the restore process. While the restore process runs, NTBACKUP displays the Restore Status dialog box, shown in Figure 7–28, to enable you to monitor the restore events. If you need to stop the restore process at any time, you can select the Abort button on this dialog box. The restore process will prompt you to decide whether the program should complete the restoration of the current file.

Figure 7–28
Restore status
dialog box

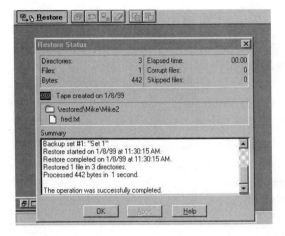

Note that if you are restoring the data to the same location from which the data was backed up, you may be prompted to enable NTBACKUP to overwrite any duplicate files. Be certain before accepting this choice that the backup data is the correct version of the file—and that no further need exists for the current file. In addition, if the restore is being performed by a batch file, the restore process might stop and wait for user input. To avoid this problem, choose to restore your data to an alternate location when appropriate.

NTBACKUP RIGHTS AND PERMISSIONS The NTBACKUP program is extremely sensitive to rights and permissions. This sensitivity is based on two separate areas. First, which rights and permissions does the person doing the backup or restore need? Second, how does the backup or restore process affect the existing permissions? A few interesting tricks are available here that can make the backup/restore process much easier. Let's approach each of these questions, starting with the first question.

RIGHTS AND PERMISSIONS NEEDED TO BACK UP AND RESTORE The bottom line for backing up is that a user only needs Read permissions to back up a file. But setting up permissions in that fashion can be confusing and difficult. Microsoft fixes this issue by creating two special rights called *Backup Files and Directories* and *Restore Files and Directories*. These rights will override all other rights and permissions. If you want someone to do your backups, give them the Backup Files and Directories option. If you want them to be able to restore, give them the Restore Files and Directories right. To make the job even easier, Microsoft has created a special local group called *Backup Operators*. Backup Operators have both the Backup and Restore rights, as well as the Log on Locally and Shutdown the System rights. The normal process is to make a Global group called "Backups," add the backup people to that group, and then add that group to the Backup Operators local group on the systems that you wish the group to back up and restore. See Chapter 8, "Managing Users in Windows NT," for more information about all these local and global groups.

NOTE: *Be careful with handing out Backup operator rights. The Restore, Log on Locally, and Shutdown rights are dangerous in the wrong hands. Many administrators simply give Read rights to the folder and files they want the backup people to actually back up.*

THE EFFECT OF BACKING UP AND RESTORING ON FILES AND FOLDERS Once users have the proper rights for backing up information, the actual permissions are of little consequence to the backing up and restore processes—due primarily to the fact that the correct rights supersede all permissions. This idea is wonderful and certainly makes the backup and restore process easier. Now, the question needs to be reversed—sort-of —by asking, "What does backup and restore do to existing permissions?" This question is relatively simple. First, you have only file permissions to worry about if you back up files from an NTFS partition. Similarly, to retain any of these permissions, you must also restore to an NTFS partition. If you are restoring to a FAT partition instead, you will lose all the permissions because they are NTFS-specific. When you restore to an NTFS partition, however, you can retain your file permissions by selecting the Restore File Permissions checkbox on the Restore Information dialog box.

Backup Strategies

Now that you have the information necessary for doing backups and restores, we should discuss the strategies necessary for doing backups and restores in your actual environments. The most important issue is ensuring that you can back up all the necessary information from all the necessary machines. This process can include both servers and workstations. Backing up multiple machines can be a factor both of hardware and of time. Another issue to take into consideration when planning your backup strategy is what to do with the all-important tapes. You must realize that you are protecting your environment not only against viruses and other computer-related catastrophes, but also against fire, flood, and warfare.

No hard and fast rule exists for minimum hardware requirements when using NTBACKUP—other than a tape backup device. What you may notice in larger environments, however, is that your backups begin taking too long as you add data, servers, and workstations to the backup mix. You may have backups scheduled to begin at 11 P.M. to ensure that all your users are gone and have closed their files. When you arrive at 8 A.M., however, you may notice that your backups are still running or have just finished, which could hinder the network and server performance for users who are just arriving. In this case, you should begin adding tape devices to other machines until your backups are taking an acceptable amount of time. Your tape devices should be located on the servers that have the most important registries, such as your PDCs and BDCs, so that their registries can be backed up. If you are backing up many workstations and servers—both domain controllers and member servers—you may want to consider the following options:

- Using a tape drive on the PDC to back up all data on the domain controllers and to back up its own local registry. Use an additional tape device on a BDC to back up all data on the member servers and workstations.

- Using a logon script (discussed in Chapter 8) to copy user data and registry information from the workstations to a server location. This process would enable backups to run locally, rather than across the network, which would speed up the process and give users more flexibility in how they use their workstations— without hampering the backups.

- Having your users store their data in a home directory (discussed in Chapter 8) located on a server. Again, this process enables backups to proceed locally, rather than across a network, and gives users more flexibility.

After you have backed up all your data, you should give some thought to data integrity on the backup tapes as well as to the safekeeping of those tapes. To verify data integrity, test restore procedures on a regular basis by doing restore on some of the files from a tape to an alternate location, then compare the data to make sure the information is usable and correct. In addition, tapes do wear out. If you have used the same tapes for a long period of time, splurge on some new ones. Set a schedule for taking tapes out of production and either archiving them or destroying them and replacing them with new tapes.

Speaking of archiving tapes, have you given any thought to where you are going to store the tapes? If you said "at my desk," or "in the server room," think again. You should always store backups off site, in a secure location. Imagine that your building has a fire. You want the backup tapes as far as possible from the servers they are backing up. Similarly, you do not want to store all your backups on a single tape. You should rotate tapes so that you always have the tapes necessary to do a full restore procedure back to your last full backup. Depending on the type of backup you have chosen to do, this process may entail having a full week's worth of tapes that you rotate—or even a month's worth of tapes that you rotate.

Questions

1. Fidel's NT Server has three hard drives configured as a stripe set. One of the hard drives fails. To recover the data on his hard drive, Fidel must (Choose the best answer):

   a. Install a new hard drive, then run Disk Administrator to restore the stripe set

   b. Install a new hard drive, run SCANDISK, and restore the stripe set

   c. Install a new hard drive, run Disk Administrator to recreate the stripe set, and restore from backup

   d. Replace the drive. Windows NT will automatically restore the stripe set

2. The Bayland Widget Company hires Marty as its new NT administrator. As his first assignment, Marty must update the fault tolerance on one of the company's NT file servers. Required results: No data must be lost in the event of a single hard drive failure. Optional result: Hard disk performance must be improved. Proposed solution: Create a stripe set with parity. The proposed solution

   a. Achieves both the required result and the optional result

   b. Achieves only the required result

   c. Fails to achieve the required result and does not work

3. The minimum hardware requirements for disk duplexing are the following

   a. One hard drive controller and three hard disks

   b. Two hard drive controllers and three hard disks

   c. One hard drive controller and two hard disks

   d. Two hard drive controllers and two hard disks

4. Isabelle has three SCSI hard drives in her NT Server. One of the hard drives has a capacity of 4.2GB, while the other two have capacities of 3.2GB each. What is the usable capacity of the largest stripe set that she can make using these three hard drives?

   a. 10.6GB

   b. 9.6GB

   c. 6.4GB

   d. 3.2GB

5. Ferdinand has three SCSI hard drives in his NT Server. One of the hard drives has a capacity of 4.2GB, while the other two have capacities of 3.2GB each. What is the usable capacity of the largest stripe set with parity that he can make using these three hard drives?

   a. 10.6GB

   b. 9.6GB

   c. 6.4GB

   d. 3.2GB

6. Christopher has three SCSI hard drives in his NT Server. One of the hard drives has a capacity of 4.2GB, while the other two have capacities of 3.2GB each. What is the usable capacity of the largest volume set that he can make using these three hard drives?

   a. 10.6GB

   b. 9.6GB

   c. 6.4GB

   d. 3.2GB

7. Nicholas replaces the failed hard drive in a mirror set. What must he do before he can regenerate the mirror set?

   a. Stop the Fault Tolerance service in the Control Panel

   b. Reformat the remaining drive and restore from backup

   c. Break the mirror set using Disk Administrator

   d. Break the mirror set using FDISK

8. Reggie's Windows NT server has five SCSI hard disks configured as a stripe set with parity. One of the five disks fails. Reggie replaces the failed disk. What must he do next?

   a. Nothing; NT will automatically regenerate the stripe set

   b. Use Disk Administrator to regenerate the stripe set

   c. Use FDISK to regenerate the stripe set

   d. Restore from backup

9. The Bayland Widget Corporation hires Melissa to upgrade a file server that lacks sufficient speed or storage capacity to handle the corporation's primary database. Required results: The total capacity of a single volume must be 15GB or greater. Optional results: No data must be lost in the event of a single hard drive failure. Hard disk performance must be improved. Proposed Solution: Create a stripe set with parity using four 4GB SCSI hard drives. The proposed solution

   a. Achieves the required result and both optional results

   b. Achieves the required result and one of the optional results

   c. Achieves only the required result

   d. Fails to achieve the required result and does not work

10. Ethel wants to use NT backup to make a backup copy of the registry files on her Windows NT Server. She must (Choose all that apply):

   a. Select differential as the backup type

   b. Select the "Backup Registry" checkbox in NT Backup

   c. Use the Windows NT backup program from a remote Windows NT Server computer only

   d. Specify at least one file to be backed up on the volume that contains the registry in NT Backup

11. You have a PDC, a BDC, and 75 workstations. You currently have a tape device on your PDC for backups. You have created a scheduled backup using **AT.EXE** and NTBACKUP. The backup starts at 2 A.M. When you arrive in the morning, your backup log indicates that the backup finished at 7:45 A.M. Unfortunately, users sometimes arrive by 7 A.M. to start their work. What can you do to make the backup finish more quickly?

   a. Turn on hardware compression in the Backup Information dialog box

   b. Add another tape device to the BDC. Back up the servers using the tape device on the PDC. Back up the workstations using the tape device on the BDC.

   c. Turn on the Verify After Backup option on the Backup Information dialog box

   d. Set up disk striping with parity on both the PDC and BDC. Use the **AT.EXE** utility to copy the BDC's registry to the PDC. Run the backups as scheduled.

12. Which of the following is a valid NTBACKUP command argument?

   a. **NTBACKUP backup /a /g /t normal**

   b. **NTBACKUP backup /d "Backup 33" /l "TEST.LOG" /t incremental**

   c. **NTBACKUP restore /a /d "Backup 33" /t "Today"**

   d. **NTBACKUP eject /a /d "Backup 33" /t division**

Answers

1. c—The data must be restored from backup, because stripe sets (unlike stripe sets with parity) do not provide fault tolerance.

2. a—Achieves both the required result and the optional result. stripe sets with parity prevent data loss in the event of a single hard drive failure and improve hard disk performance.

3. d—Two hard drive controllers and two hard disks.

4. b—9.6 GB. Every partition used to make a stripe set must be of equal size. Because no drive is set aside for parity, the entire capacity of all three drives is available for storage.

5. c—6.4GB. Every partition used to make a stripe set with parity must be of equal size. Because a partition is set aside for parity, the entire capacity of one partition is used for parity and is not available to store data.

6. a—10.6GB. The partitions used to create a volume set do not have to be the same size. The entire capacity of the three partitions can be combined and used for data storage.

7. c—Break the mirror set using Disk Administrator.

8. b—Use Disk Administrator to regenerate the stripe set.

9. d—Fails to achieve the required result and does not work. A stripe set with parity using 4–4GB hard drives creates a volume with only 12GB of usable storage, which is insufficient to meet the required disk capacity of 15GB.

10. b, d—The "Backup Registry" checkbox in NT Backup cannot be selected until at least one other file on that volume has been selected to be backed up.

11. b—Adding an additional tape device is the only valid method of speeding up the backup process. If the Verify option is activated, backups will take longer. You can turn off Verify to speed the process.

12. b—Only this option has valid arguments. Restore is not a valid operation. Eject is a valid operation, but the arguments are incorrect for this option. In addition, /g is not a valid argument in answer a.

CHAPTER **8**

Managing Users in Windows NT

Once you have an NT environment up and running—complete with servers, workstations and installed applications—don't forget to let real people have access to these systems and the data they hold. After all, it's nice to get some work done around the office. But you don't want just anyone rummaging through your network. The thought of letting the unwashed masses run rampant across the pristine world of your new NT environment should horrify any network administrator. Fortunately, we have the power to prevent that.

The most time-consuming aspect of any NT system is the determination of *what* type of access is provided to *who* to allow work to get done—and then actually setting it all up. Allowing access to a system's resources is not, after all, a simple "open the gate and let them flood in" type of function. Different users and groups must be allowed different levels of access to shared resources in order to get work done. The amount of access users and groups are given to a particular shared resource is an area of significant thought and planning. A good administrator is constantly torn between the desire to provide as much access as users and groups request and the need to protect the network from accidental and intentional harm. Additionally, the level of access granted to each user and group must change periodically to reflect changes in the organization, personnel, or business of the system. This process of creating and managing is referred to as "user management."

The goal of user management is to create an efficient, orderly, and safe process of allowing users to access the resources they need. These aspects can be broken down into two major parts. First is the initial setup: Creating users, creating groups, and assigning users and permissions to groups. Second is the ongoing maintenance of the access: Adding, editing, and deleting users and groups; changing a particular right or permission; and assigning/removing users, rights, and permissions to groups. Each of these tasks, along with the tools to perform them, will be discussed individually to illustrate the power, flexibility, and unfortunately, complexity of NT User Management.

The NT View of Networks

There should be a sign placed on the wall of every network administrator's office, saying, "The primary function of all networks is to let users access shared resources." It's funny how the same people who are supposed to provide that service forget such a basic concept! One group that has never forgotten this is Microsoft. Microsoft developed NT to give administrators phenomenal control and flexibility over the access of shared resources. Unfortunately, with control and flexibility comes complexity, and NT user management can easily become complex in very short order. To reduce complexity, Microsoft has forwarded a model of user management that is widely used (but not required) in NT systems.

The cornerstone of user management is the user account. Every person who wants to access an NT machine, whether that machine is on a network or stand-alone, must have an account. NT administrators create user accounts (just say "users;" nobody says "user accounts") with the User Manager program. The user account identifies to the system the user currently in front of the keyboard and determines the permissions to be granted—at least until that user logs off and another user logs into the system. A user account is nothing more than a line in a database that gets compared to the values typed into a dialog box, as shown in Figure 8–1.

Once the user account exists, the user can be assigned permissions to shared resources, as shown in Figure 8–2. For more information about permissions, review Chapter 6, "File Systems."

EARLY CLIENT/SERVER NETWORK SECURITY In the earliest network operating systems (NOSs), there were only users and permissions. It became obvious fairly early on, however, that many users had identical, or at least similar, permissions to many of the resources on the system. It seemed silly to create users and keep setting the same permissions. So, long before NT was a twinkle in Bill Gates' eye, network operating systems developed the concept of "groups." A group was nothing more than a group of user accounts that could be assigned permissions to a resource *en masse*.

Figure 8–1
An account is just a database entry!

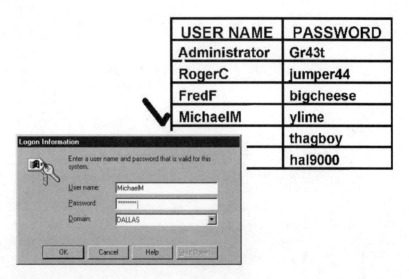

Figure 8–2
Accounts get rights and permissions

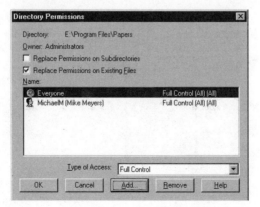

With groups, an administrator could create a group, assign permissions to the group, and then assign users to the group. Life was good. Each computer that shared resources had its own database of users and groups. This system worked great if you only owned one server. If you owned more, then each server would have its own user and group information. In the early days of networking, owning multiple servers was rare enough that this was not a big issue. This system of each server storing its own user and group information was the cornerstone of popular client/server network operating systems such as Novell's NetWare 3.X. (See Figure 8–3.)

PEER-TO-PEER NETWORK SECURITY The first peer-to-peer NOSs had a problem with security. Peer-to-peer networks were designed to be smaller, friendlier NOSs. They were supposed to get away from the administrative overhead of client/server NOSs, at the cost of reducing security and speed. Since peer-to-peer networks tend to have many systems serving shared resources, the idea of users and groups on each system was dropped, almost from the very beginning of the concept of peer-to-peer networks. The administration of users and groups on multiple servers was completely outside the scope of peer-to-peer. Users and groups did not exist. Instead, security on most peer-to-peer networks consisted (and still does) of nothing more than the password protection of systems and shared resources (see Figure 8–4). Anyone who knew a password could access a shared resource.

Some later peer-to-peer networks such as Artisoft's LANtastic took advantage of more advanced network features such as groups and permissions, but they were the exception. Microsoft's peer-to-peer NOSs—LAN Manager, Windows for Workgroups, and Windows 95/98—remained extremely limited in terms of security.

Figure 8–3
Older Network Operating Systems (NOSs) stored account information on each server

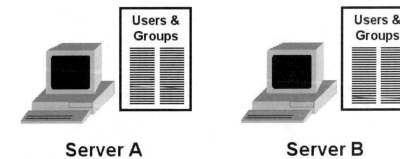

Server A   Server B

Figure 8–4
Peer-to-peer
networks have
little security.

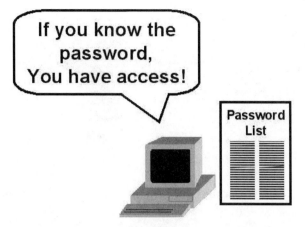

Sharing Peer to Peer system

NT SECURITY   Microsoft designed NT to take advantage of both the power and security of client/server and the flexibility and ease of use of peer-to-peer. But to enjoy the power of both types of networks creates a problem. The One Million Dollar Question: How can each system have its own users and groups while allowing a person to make one login, on any machine in the network, that will determine the access for a number of shared resources on multiple systems? How can User X, in other words, log in on System A and have access to specific resources on System A, System B, and System C? Microsoft uses "Domains" to provide the answer.

WORKGROUPS VS. DOMAINS   NT networks can operate two ways: As conventional peer-to-peer networks, through use of "workgroups," or as special "super peer-to-peer" networks, through the use of domains. This was discussed in Chapter 2, "Installing Windows NT," but bears repeating here. Any NT system—NT Server or NT Workstation—can be a member of a workgroup. In order to have a domain, at least one machine on the network must have NT Server installed and configured as a *Primary Domain Controller* (PDC). Whether a system participates in a domain or in a workgroup is determined when the system first has NT installed. Again, refer to Chapter 2 for the installation step of Domain vs. Workgroup.

In an NT workgroup, each system has its own "local" users and groups (Figure 8–5). In a workgroup, therefore, a user must have a user account and password for every NT system he or she attempts to access. (Figure 8–6).

Figure 8–5
In a workgroup,
each system has its
own users and
groups.

NT Workgroup

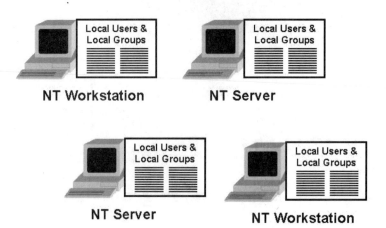

Figure 8–5
In a workgroup,
each system has its
own users and
groups.

Figure 8–6
Logging into another
system

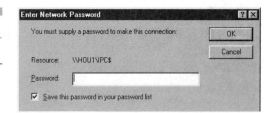

A domain, in contrast, has a system configured as a PDC that stores all of the information about a totally different set of users and groups: Global Users and Global Groups. Think of global users and global groups as the domain-level users and groups. When an NT domain is used, a person need only log in once. The PDC determines at that point all accesses. (See Figure 8–7.)

In a Microsoft NT domain, there can be local users and local groups as well as global users and global groups. Local user accounts are rarely used, except for relatively uncommon administrative tasks. (The local Administrator user account, for example, might be used to change an NT Workstation from one domain to another.) In a domain, local user accounts have few uses. Users typically log in to a domain user account in order to access all resources within the domain.

Figure 8–7
In a domain, the
PDC controls all
accesses.

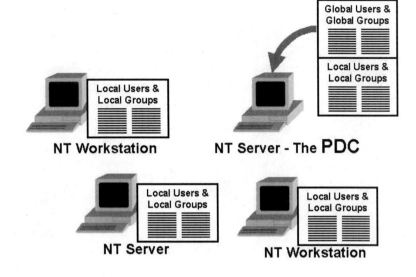

In the world of domains, therefore, there are only users, global groups, and local groups. To understand the interrelation between these three, just memorize the famous "Microsoft Mantra." Are you ready? Here it is:

"Users go into Global Groups, which go into Local Groups, which get Rights and Permissions."

NOTE: *The Microsoft Mantra is not a law of physics. It is an organizational recommendation from Microsoft that most NT administrators support. While there are exceptions, the Microsoft exams assume that administrators follow the "mantra."*

Let's go through each portion of the mantra.

Users . . .

Remember, we're talking about domains here. Microsoft means global users. You can never make local users in a domain. Local users are only for workgroups.

. . . go into Global Groups . . .

Global groups can only contain global user accounts. A typical global group would be something like "Accountants," "Salespeople," or "Print

Operators." Again, only users go into global groups! You cannot add Local groups or other global groups to a global group.

. . . which go into Local Groups . . .

Every NT system that shares its resources will have local groups. These local groups will have names such as "Accounts" or "Sales." These names usually refer to the resources available to the local groups.

. . . which get Rights and Permissions.

Each local group is given the necessary rights and permissions to access those shared resources. For example, assume that a server named SERVER14 has a database in the `D:\ACCOUNTING\LEDGER` directory that all the accountants need to access and keep up to date. On SERVER14, the "ACCOUNTS" Local group might get Add and Read permissions to the `D:\ACCOUNTING\LEDGER` directory. The accountant Kim Rhodes has a (global) user account KRHODES in the domain, which belongs to the global group ACCOUNTANTS, which is a member of the local group ACCOUNTS on SERVER14. Kim would therefore get Add and Read permissions to the `D:\ACCOUNTING\LEDGER` directory and be able to do her job (Figure 8–8).

Figure 8–8
The "Microsoft Mantra"

Users ...

Go into Global Groups ..

Which go into Local Groups ...

Which get Permissions ...

C:\Accounting	= Add &Read
C:\Mail	= Read
D:\Users\EmilyJ	= Full Control

To perform the Microsoft Mantra, we need to (not necessarily in this order):

1. Create Local groups on individual systems and give them rights and permissions.
2. Create Global groups.
3. Create Users and add them to the proper global groups.
4. Add Global groups to local groups.

Let's look at the tools that allow us to perform these tasks.

THE TOOLS NT primarily uses two tools to do most of the work in managing resources: User Manager and Server Manager. User Manager —called User Manager for Domains in NT Server —allows you to set rights, permissions, and profiles for users and groups of users. Server Manager allows you to introduce new machines and servers and handle all the fun chores of synchronizing account information, promoting domain controllers, and managing shared directories.

In the rest of this chapter, we will first discuss creating and managing users, describing the tools we use and the steps involved. Second, we will discuss user and system policies in detail. Finally, we will cover how to create and manage servers and workstations within a domain.

Creating and Managing Users

NT domains, servers, and workstations require a user to log in and be authenticated (recognized and approved) by the computer or domain before gaining access to resources. You will therefore need to create user accounts for all the people that will use your NT environment. During this process, you can also set user properties related to which machines they can use and the hours during which they can log on. Further, NT comes with a few built-in accounts that you should deal with soon after creating the network. Finally, certain aspects of user management apply to the network as a whole. You set these aspects—such as password policies—through creating account policies. To do all of these creating and managing tasks requires only one tool—User Manager.

USER MANAGER AND USER MANAGER FOR DOMAINS The User Manager utility allows you to manage users and groups in NT. (There are other ways, but User Manager is the most common.) User

Manager comes in three varieties: User Manager, designed for NT Work-station—this version contains the fewest functions; User Manager for Domains (for non-domain controlling NT Servers)—essentially the same as User Manager, but allows remote administration of other servers and domains; and User Manager for Domains (for Domain Controllers)—this contains many more functions than either other version and allows remote administration of other servers and domains.

NOTE: *User Manager makes changes to the Security Accounts Manager (SAM) database. The SAM contains all the information about user accounts and group memberships for every single user on a machine. On a domain controller, the SAM contains all the information about all the domain user and group accounts, as well as its own local account information. See Chapter 9, "Microsoft Networking," for a more detailed analysis of the SAM.*

To access User Manager (whichever version), choose Start . . . Programs . . . Administrative Tools (Common) . . . User Manager (or User Manager for Domains), as shown in Figure 8–9.

The users, either on your machine or in your domain, are listed at the top of the application. The bottom pane of the application displays the groups, again either on your machine or in your domain. This includes both built-in groups and the groups you or other administrators have created. Groups and their creation and management will be discussed later in this chapter. The difference between user manager and user manager

Figure 8–9
User Manager for
Domains

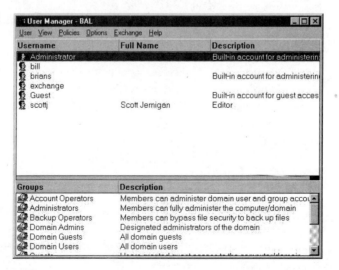

for domains—user manager is missing some options that are visible in user manager for domains. As Figure 8–10 shows, the User Properties is more detailed in User Manager for Domains next to User Manager—note the lack of options on the left.

CREATING USERS   To create a new user, choose User . . . New User from the menus. This displays the New User dialog box, as shown in Figure 8–11.

In the Username field, place a user logon name that is unique for the machine or domain. The Username field can be up to 20 characters, in either upper or lower case. The following characters are not allowed in the Username field:

" / \ [ ] : ; | = , + * ? < >

To make user names unique and meaningful, it is helpful to design a naming convention or standard for your environment, whether that is a

Figure 8–10
User Manager versus
User Manager for
Domains

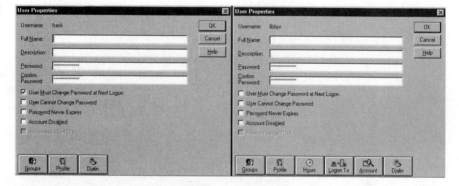

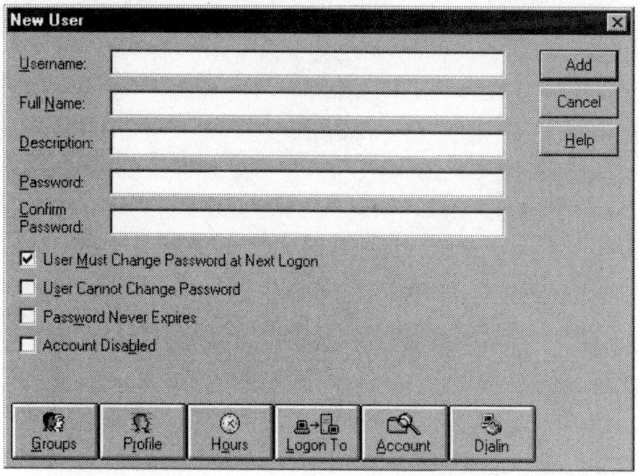

Figure 8–11
New User dialog box

single machine or a domain. Naming conventions can be in a wide variety of formats, such as LibbyS or LSchwarz or LNSchwarz, for example. In larger environments especially, it is important to take into consideration the possibility of similar names. If you have a user named David Smith, for example, neither DavidS nor DSmith is likely to be unique. A Username like DJSmith (including a middle initial) is more likely to allow for uniqueness so users do not have to deal with DavidS1 and DavidS2 or something similar. The most important things to remember when creating your naming convention are that all your user names must be unique and the names should be something memorable and simple for your users. The Username field is required to create a user.

In the next field, the Full Name field, place the user's full name. You should establish a convention here too, to determine whether you will list names last name first (Schwarz, Libby) or first name first (Libby Schwarz), and whether you will include the middle initial (Schwarz, Libby N.). It is important to be consistent here, because you will have the ability to display the users sorted by their full name. Inconsistency will make your lists more chaotic and thus less useful. Note that the Full Name field is not required.

The Description field allows you to write a few words about the particular user. While not required, a clear, concise description will give other administrators useful information quickly. Almost anything goes in the description, although for security reasons, avoid discussing which accounts have administrator privileges or are guest accounts. Also be aware that other people will most likely see the user description at some point. A bit of sensitivity here will avoid hurt feelings (and those fun defamation of character lawsuits!) later. Don't describe JohnS as "John with the Big Nose," in other words, unless, of course, John is inordinately proud of his proboscis.

The next two fields allow the administrator to determine the password for the user account. The password must be entered in both the Password and Confirm Password fields to be valid. The password can be up to 14 characters and is case sensitive. To enhance security, use multiple types of characters in passwords, such as lower-case letters, upper-case letters, numbers, and other characters, such as asterisks or exclamation points. If you have specified an account policy (discussed later in this chapter) that requires a minimum length for passwords, you must follow this policy when setting the password for the user.

NOTE: *Account Policies allow you to define certain aspects of your whole network, such as passwords and lockouts. Through account policies, you can set expiration times, minimum character length, and user controls over passwords. Also, account policies allow you to lock accounts in case someone tries to hack their way in. You can lock an account after a certain number of wrong passwords, for example. Account policies, therefore, provide an important tool for network security. Account policies are discussed in detail later in this chapter, but are referenced several times along the way.*

The four check boxes below the main fields define specific qualities of the password for an account or disable the account completely. The User Must Change Password At Next Logon option must be enabled or disabled. If enabled, the user will be forced to change their password immediately upon their next logon. This is especially useful when you have used a default password for that user that other users may know. Disable this option if you take the time to give each user a unique and secure password. You can also lockout the user's ability to change the password on the account by enabling the User Cannot Change Password Option. This is usually enabled for shared accounts, such as the guest account. The Password Never Expires option overrides the Password selections in the Account Policies settings (discussed later in this chapter). This option is usually only enabled when you are creating an account for use as a service account or an account that a software product such as Exchange will use to log on to your environment. You can, however, enable this option for any user account, although this may make it less secure. Finally, you can select the Account Disabled option. This prevents a user from accessing your Domain or machine using this account. Any user account with the exception of the built-in administrator account can be disabled. Disabling accounts can be useful when creating user templates (discussed later in this chapter), for disallowing use of NT's built-in "guest" account, or for disabling an account for a user that has left your environment.

If you open an existing account, you will also see an option for Account Locked Out. If an account becomes locked out due to violating an account policy, this option enables an administrator to unlock the account. An administrator cannot lock out an account using this option, however; they can only unlock an account. To prevent a user from logging on using a particular account, an administrator will have to disable the account using the option discussed above.

TIP: *The exams expect you to be able to distinguish between the Account Disabled option and the Account Locked Out option, especially regarding what role an administrator plays with each option. To review, an administrator can disable or enable an account for use with the Account Disabled option. An administrator can only unlock an account with the Account Locked Out option, however, as the locking out process occurs automatically based on the account policies.*

The buttons at the bottom of the dialog box allow you to set more options for the account. In User Manager for Domains, the following buttons are available:

- Groups
- Profile
- Hours
- Logon To
- Account
- Dialin

NOTE: *Only the Groups, Profile, and Dialin options are available in the Windows NT Workstation User Manager.*

The Groups button displays the Group Memberships dialog box, as shown in Figure 8–12. This dialog box allows you to assign group memberships to the user account.

The Profile button displays the User Environment Profile dialog box, shown in Figure 8–13. This dialog box allows the administrator to assign the following elements to a user account: User profile, logon script, and

Figure 8–12
Group Memberships
dialog box

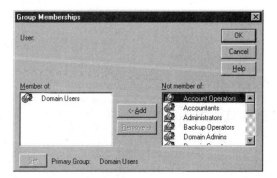

Figure 8–13
User Environment
Profile dialog box

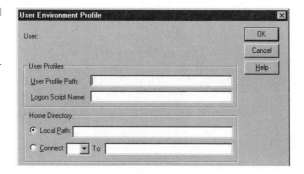

home directory. The *user profile* stores information such as the contents of the Start Menu and the user's desktop settings. Profiles are local, roaming, or mandatory. User Profiles are discussed in more detail later in this chapter.

A *logon script* allows an administrator to create automatic drive mappings or assign network printer settings for a user. This is especially useful for users of non-Windows NT or non-Windows clients. Even Windows or Windows NT clients, however, may be assigned logon scripts as an easy method for creating these settings. Logon scripts and user profiles are similar, but unlike a profile, a logon script does not add any settings for the desktop. A logon script usually has a .CMD, .BAT, or .EXE extension. If you are in an NT domain environment, the logon script should be stored on both the PDC and the BDCs for the domain, so that a user will activate the logon script regardless of where their logon occurs. To make logon scripts available for export to the BDCs in the domain, they should be stored in the **\Winnt\System32\Repl\Export** directory. Exporting and replicating directories around the domain will be discussed later in this chapter. You may also store a logon script locally on a workstation, although this is not required if logging on to a domain.

A *home directory*—usually residing on a server—stores a user's files. If you assign a home directory, the other Microsoft products that the user has will use this as the default directory in the File Open and File Save As dialog boxes. One of the benefits of using a home directory for a user is the ease of finding the user's files when performing backups.

You have the option in this dialog box to locate the home directory either locally or remotely. If you locate the home directory locally, specify the path, such as **C:\Users\LibbyS**. If you locate the home directory remotely, this dialog box allows you to map a drive to a server. Use a UNC name to describe the path to the home directory; for example: **\\NTServer\Users\LibbyS**. To specify a home directory when you define multiple users, you can use the variable %username% in place of the folder name; for example: `\\NTServer\Users\%username%`. Most of the time, when you specify a home directory on a server using User Manager for Domains, you can specify the directory and NT will create it for you automatically. If NT gives you an error at this point, create the directory manually and then specify the path using this dialog box.

NOTE: *When creating home directories, be aware that users still using MS-DOS clients or Win 3.1 clients cannot access long share names.*

Choose the Hours button to specify the hours during which the user is allowed to log on to the environment. The Logon Hours dialog box, shown in Figure 8–14, allows the administrator to add some security to the environment to prevent logon during off-hours for users such as temporary workers that should not have access to the system all the time. In addition, this setting allows an administrator to prevent logon during hours necessary for backup of the servers. To change logon hours, select a block of time by clicking and dragging, and then click either the Allow or Disallow buttons. If a blue line covers the time slot, it is a time during which the user may log on. When a user is currently logged on at a time when they are disallowed, they can either remain logged on without being allowed to make new connections or they may be disconnected. This option is determined in the Account Policy settings, discussed later in this chapter.

The Logon To button allows the administrator to limit the workstations to which the user account has access. The Logon Workstations dialog box,

Figure 8–14
Logon Hours dialog box

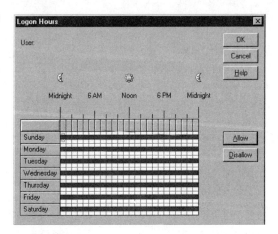

shown in Figure 8–15, allows the administrator to determine whether the user can access all workstations or up to eight specific workstations. If you have created an environment where users do not share machines, and do not need to share machines, this can be a useful setting to link a user to a particular machine.

The Account button displays the Account Information dialog box, shown in Figure 8–16. This dialog box allows the administrator to define two main issues about the account: Expiration date and type. The Account Expires option allows the administrator to set an expiration date for a user account. If an expiration date is set for an account, the account will expire at the end of the specified day. If a user is logged on when the account expires, they will not be logged off. They will not be able to log in again after they have chosen to log off, however, nor will they be able to connect to any new resources. If the user is connected to one share on the server, for example, they can continue to access that particular share, but they cannot access a different share. This option is particularly useful when you have temporary users in your environment. You can set the last date of their assignment as their expiration date. The administrator can change the expiration date at any time.

Figure 8–15
Logon Workstations
dialog box

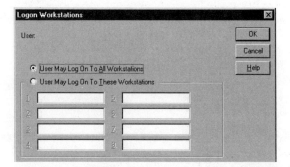

Figure 8–16
Account Information
dialog box

The Account Type section of the dialog box allows the administrator to determine whether the account is a global account or a local account. A global account is simply a standard account that exists in the domain. A local account, in contrast, exists only on a particular local machine.

NOTE: *Remember that a domain is a group of servers and users that share common security information. In addition, the accounts within a domain are administered from the same SAM database, on a PDC or BDC (primary or backup domain controller) for that domain.*

In most cases, if a user from another domain needs access to resources in this domain, the domain administrators would set up a trust relationship between the domains, allowing administrators in one domain to assign rights and permissions to users in the other. (Trust relationships and domains are described in great detail in Chapter 9, "Microsoft Networking.") In cases where a trust relationship does not exist, administrators can choose to create a "Local" account for users from the non-trusted domain. Users with local accounts cannot log in *interactively*, meaning that they cannot sit down and log in to machines within the domain. They must log in to a machine in their own domain (or workgroup) and access machines within this domain via the network.

NOTE: *An interactive logon occurs when a user types their logon information into NT's Logon dialog box. A remote logon occurs when a user is already logged in to an account and makes a remote connection to a shared resource.*

A global account is the most common setting for a normal user account that exists within the domain, and is the default. All users that will be in your domain should have a global account.

The final button available on the dialog box is the Dialin button. Click the Dialin button to access the Dialin Information dialog box shown in Figure 8–17. This dialog box allows the administrator to grant Dialin permission to a user and to determine the user's Call Back rights. Dialin permissions give the user the ability to connect using a modem or other non-WAN/LAN connection. The user may only use remote access services if they are granted the Dialin permission in this dialog box. RAS and Dialin connections are discussed more fully in Chapter 14. Call Back rights determine whether the caller or the server will pay for remote access. The three Call Back options are as follows:

Figure 8–17
Dialin Information
dialog box

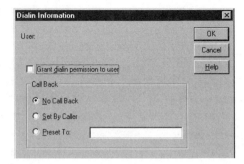

- *No Call Back*. This option forces the remote caller to initiate and maintain the call. The remote caller dials in to the server and pays all connection charges.

- *Set By Caller*. This option allows the user to call the server, connect, and specify a number where the server will call them back. This allows the user to avoid paying some of the call charges. It can also be a security loophole, however, as the server can be directed to call non-authorized users.

- *Preset To*. This option gives the administrator the convenience of predetermining who is paying for the charges, as well as setting the number the server should call. It also allows the administrator to set the security features.

After you create a user, choose Add to place the user's information in the *Security Accounts Manager* (SAM) database for either the machine or the domain. When you create a new user, you create at the same time a unique identifier for that user called a *Security ID* (SID). The SID is stored in binary format in a database called the SAM. Each user, group, and machine has a SID that is unique not only to its particular SAM, but to all SAMs everywhere. The SAM will either be located on a Primary or Backup Domain Controller for a domain or located on the local machine for stand-alone servers and workstations.

You can edit the user account any time by selecting it in the User Manager window and choosing User . . . Properties from the menus. This displays the User Properties dialog box, with the same options available as in the New User dialog box.

USER TEMPLATES User Templates simplify the process of creating users, by providing common information for each new user automatically. User Templates are simply disabled user accounts that you can copy and edit to create new users with the same options. This speeds up the process of creating multiple users in large environments by allowing administrators to copy information that will be the same, rather than having to re-enter all the data for each user individually. To create a User Template, create a new User account, as described above. The Username should have a pound sign (#) or other symbol at the beginning of the user name to separate it from real users, such as `#SalesTemplate`. In addition, a clear description, such as Sales User Template, makes it easier to recognize and use the User Templates. You should then give the template account membership in the appropriate groups. Also, set the times that the user can log on and the machines he or she can log on to. Finally, give the account a home directory by specifying the `%username%` variable.

To use the template after creating it, simply select the appropriate template and choose User . . . Copy from the menus (or press the F8 key). This creates a copy of the account and opens the property dialog box for you to give the account a unique name and make any additional changes necessary.

NOTE: *When you make a copy of another account or template, the Username and Full Name fields are cleared automatically to force the administrator to create a unique name for the user.*

BUILT-IN ACCOUNTS   Installing a server or workstation automatically creates two accounts in User Manager: Administrator and Guest. The Administrator account allows complete management of the machine or domain. The Guest account allows domain visitors to log on to the machine or the domain. At creation, the Administrator account is automatically enabled and has all possible rights assigned, such as creating and deleting user accounts, sharing resources, creating and formatting partitions, and setting account policies. The Administrator account is automatically placed in the following groups: Local Administrators, Domain Admins, and Domain Users. These groups and the rights associated with them will be discussed later in this chapter.

To enhance network security, you should immediately rename the Administrator account and give it an extremely complex password. The problem with built-in accounts is that every hacker knows the name of two accounts on your server. The Administrator account poses a giant security risk. You cannot delete or disable the Administrator account, nor can you remove it from the Local Admin group. Worse, Administrator accounts let you do *anything* in an NT network. Don't mess around here.

Copy the Administrator account to the few users who need administrative access; give the original a terribly difficult password composed of letters, numbers, and symbols; and rename the thing. Write all this down, stick it in a safe, and forget about it.

The Guest account, on the other hand, is automatically disabled at creation time and has no rights to the environment. The Guest account allows the administrator to define certain limited rights for visitors that need to access the domain or the workstation. Many administrators either disable or rename this Guest account for security purposes. To use the Guest account, the user would specify Guest as the Username when logging on to the workstation, server, or domain. The Guest account may or may not have a password. The user would then get whatever privileges the administrator has given to the Guest account. The Guest account is automatically added to the Domain Guests group, which will be discussed later in this chapter.

NOTE: *Neither of the two built-in accounts can be deleted. They can be renamed, but if you try to delete them, you will receive an error message.*

DELETING AND RENAMING ACCOUNTS When a user leaves your organization, your first impulse might be to delete that user's account. Restrain that impulse! User accounts are unique. If you delete the account, it is gone forever, even if you create a new account with the same name. They are different accounts. Let's see how this works. Each user gets a *Security Identifier* (SID) upon creation. The Security Accounts Manager database stores the unique SID for every user account. NT uses the SID for all its internal processes, such as authentication and granting of user rights. If you delete an account, that SID is gone. Creating a new account, even with the same name and password, creates a new SID. This might not be a big deal, but could lead to unnecessary work for an administrator. The lead project artist Terrell, for example, gets in an argument with his boss Sydney, and ends up either quitting or getting fired. You, as the dutiful administrator and assuming such action is permanent, delete Terrell's account. The next day, however, the boss and the artist make amends and she rehires him. Oops. Merely creating an account with Terrell's name and password will not recreate that deleted account. You have to figure out all his groups, rights, permissions, etc., a potentially time consuming chore. Better to disable his account at first and then delete it later. NT can handle an outrageous number of users, so letting one account linger will not hurt.

To disable a user account, open the account in User Manager and place a check mark in the Account Disabled option. When an account is disabled, it still appears in the User list, but no users can log in to the environment using that account. An account can be re-enabled at any time by removing the check mark from the Account Disabled option. If you do decide to delete an account, simply select the account and press the Delete key on your keyboard. You will receive an error when you try to delete an account, as shown in Figure 8–18, which reminds you of all the issues with deleting an account that we have discussed here. To finish deleting the account, click OK in this dialog box.

User Manager also lets you rename accounts, an ability useful for enhancing security and cutting down administration time. The built-in Guest and Administrator accounts, for example, should be renamed for security purposes, as discussed above. In addition, renaming, rather than deleting, an account preserves all the rights and permissions for that account. Take the artist and boss scenario above, for example. If Sydney hired a new, less temperamental artist to replace Terrell, renaming Terrell's account to reflect the new project artist would ensure that the new artist had the same rights and group memberships as the old artist. To rename the account, select the account and then choose User . . . Rename from the menus. This displays the Rename dialog box, as shown in Figure 8–19. You cannot rename accounts using the Account Properties dialog box.

USER MANAGEMENT   Now that we have created and configured the user accounts in your NT environment, we must do some additional tasks: Determine user account policies, specify user rights, and configure user profiles. In addition, we must track the changes made to accounts and other events that occur with accounts, through the process called auditing.

Figure 8–18
Deleting a User account

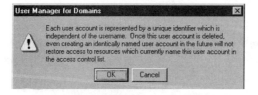

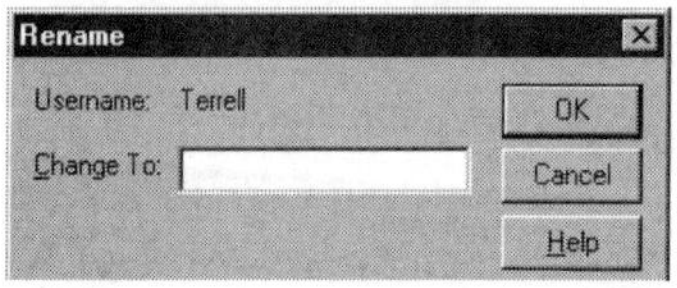

Figure 8–19
Rename dialog box

ACCOUNT POLICIES Account Policies provide two essential ingredients of a successful network: Security for your data and servers, and control over people who access those servers. Account policies allow you to define user password properties, such as expiration, minimum character length, and whether or not a user can reuse one or even set their own. Further, you can lock out accounts here, either because someone has blown a password or if someone has left the organization. Together, passwords and lockouts stop unscrupulous access of servers or use of accounts, thus protecting the most precious commodity in a network—data. Account policies also offer a degree of control over the users of the accounts, by allowing you to forcibly disconnect users when their logon hours expire. We set the logon hours earlier, when we first created the user account. Here is where you decide whether people can work overtime or possibly access the server when you have other tasks scheduled, such as backups and the like. Account policies apply throughout the domain, and therefore represent powerful tools for security and control over your network.

To access the Account Policy dialog box, shown in Figure 8–20, choose Policies . . . Account from the menus.

In this dialog box, you will first determine the password restrictions for the accounts. The first setting is the maximum password age. The maximum password age is the amount of time a password can be used before NT requires the user to change it. Your options for the maximum password age can be from 1 to 999 days or you can set the Password Never Expires option to allow the password to age indefinitely. This option

Figure 8–20
Account Policy dialog box

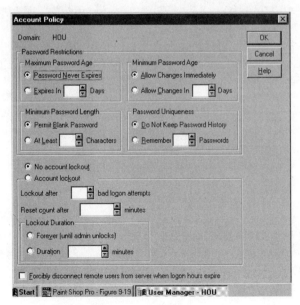

affects all user accounts in the SAM. If you want to prevent a particular account from having its password expire, you can choose the Password Never Expires option for that particular account.

The next option in the Account Policy dialog box is for the minimum password age. Setting the minimum password age allows the administrator to require that a user wait a certain period of time before resetting their password. The options for the minimum password age can be from 1 to 999 days or you can set the Allow Changes Immediately option. This option is most useful in combination with the Password Uniqueness option. If you require passwords that differ from the passwords the user has used in the past, you will need to set the minimum password age to an appropriate length to make the user keep the new password for a sufficient length of time.

The next option allows the administrator to choose a minimum length for passwords in the environment. You can choose to permit a blank password or to set a minimum from 1 to 14 characters. You should require a minimum length of 6 to 8 characters for security purposes in most environments.

The Password Uniqueness option allows the administrator to require that a user's new password be different than the password they were just using. The administrator can require between 1 and 24 passwords before a password can be reused. If you want to allow a user to reuse passwords immediately, choose Do Not Keep Password History. Bear in mind that this option should be used in combination with the minimum password age option to require both a number of passwords to remember and a minimum number of days between changes.

The next section of options in the Account Policy dialog box relates to account lockout options. An account can be locked out based on bad logon attempts, where a user tries to use an incorrect password to log on. You may choose No Account Lockout, to allow continuous retries for password attempts, but this option leaves your environment exposed to password-guessing programs. If you select the Account Lockout option, specify how many attempts can be made before the account is locked out. In the Lockout after option, you can select between 1 and 999 failed attempts before the account is locked out.

The count for the number of lockout attempts can be reset based on the setting in the Reset count after __ minutes option. Place a number between 1 and 99999 minutes in this field. If the account lockout is set to 5 and the reset is set to 15 minutes, and a user tries to log in incorrectly 4 times in 5 minutes and then waits 15 minutes before trying again, the counter will have been reset.

The next option relates to the amount of time that an account remains locked out. The administrator can choose to lock the account forever (which means it will remain locked until an administrator unlocks it) or the administrator can choose to lock it for a specified number of minutes between 1 and 99999. If you place a duration in this field, the account will automatically unlock after that number of minutes, although an administrator can still unlock it before that amount of time expires. Locking the account forever requires more work on the part of the administrator, but it is also more secure, as it gives the administrator the opportunity to investigate any locked accounts before allowing access.

The final two options in the Account Policy dialog box are the Forcibly disconnect users when logon hours expire option and the Users must log on in order to change password option. The Forcibly disconnect users option works with the logon hours set for each user in the user account. When the logon hours are exceeded, selecting this option disconnects the user from all open connections to the servers. If this option is not selected, users who exceed their logon hours will not be able to open new connections, but they will not be forcibly disconnected from the current connections. This option can stop abuse—such as unsanctioned overtime—and conflict, such as accessing data during a backup.

Finally, you have the ability to require users to log on to the server, domain, or workstation before changing their password. If this option is selected, users that allow their passwords to expire will need to contact an administrator to have their passwords changed. They will only be able to change their own passwords if they do so before the original password expires.

The options configurable in the Account Policy dialog box relate to the security of your environment. The policies set here govern the default settings for all accounts in the SAM that you are administering. Consider the security of your environment fully. The more secure options for the settings discussed above usually require more administrative intervention, but they contribute significantly to the security and data safety in your environment. Also remember that none of the account policy settings exist in a vacuum—you must take into consideration not only the account policies individually, but also all account policies as a group, and any exceptions to account policies that you set in individual accounts.

USER RIGHTS   User Manager lets you define user rights for individuals and groups, a key ingredient in data security. User rights define a person or group's access to systems in an NT network, granting such things as the ability to log on locally or over a network, backup and restore files and directories, shut down the system, etc. You might give the artists group, for example, the right to access a server from the network and backup files and directories, but not the ability to shut down the system or load device drivers. Rights work hand-in-hand with permissions (discussed in Chapters 6, 9, and 15) to grant only the kind of access to users and groups that maximize security and productivity at the same time.

User rights are accessible from the User Manager using the Policies . . . User Rights menu choice. This displays the User Rights Policy dialog box, shown in Figure 8–21.

The User Rights policy dialog box allows you to determine what rights have been granted to a particular user (or group) as well as to assign a right or set of rights to a user or group. To determine which rights are assigned to each user or group, click the Right: drop-down arrow and select a right. The users and groups that are granted this right are displayed in the Grant To: field. For example, if you select the *Access this computer from the network* right, you should see Administrators and Everyone groups granted this right by default. These groups will be described in more detail later in the chapter. You can click the Add . . . button to grant users or groups a particular right. When you click the Add . . . button, the Add Users and Groups dialog box is displayed, as shown in Figure 8–22. By default, only Groups are displayed in this dialog box. To display users in addition, click the Show Users button.

Microsoft recommends that you assign rights to groups rather than directly to users. Unless you have a very small amount of users or derive great satisfaction from excessive and tedious work, go with the default and apply rights to groups rather than users. Trying to keep track of who has what rights on an individual basis is a nightmare. Plus, it opens up huge security holes. What if you grant someone the right to log on to a certain system and then they change jobs within the company? They no longer need to or should access that system, but might retain access because they got lost

Figure 8–21
User Rights Policy
dialog box

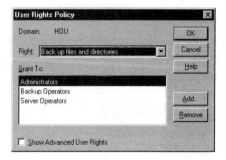

in the shuffle. In the hands of a careless or unscrupulous employee, this can lead to trouble.

At the top of this dialog box, you should see the List Names From drop-down list. You should have the ability to add users and groups from your domain, any trusted domains, or your stand-alone server or workstation SAM. The default domain or machine that you are administering will appear with an asterisk in this list. If you cannot find the group or user account that you need, click the Search button. This displays the Find Account dialog box, as shown in Figure 8–23.

Choose the SAM or SAMs in which you want to search and then type in the Group or User account. The group or user account name must be typed in correctly and completely to find the account using this feature. When the account is located, the domain and account name will be listed in the Search Results field.

After finding the appropriate group or user account, select that user or group and choose Add . . . This will grant the currently selected user right to the group or user account. You can also choose the Remove button to revoke a right from a user or group.

The user rights that you can grant in this dialog box are listed in Table 8–1, below. Additionally, if you select the Show Advanced User Rights checkbox, you will see additional rights, also listed in Table 8–1. In the table, these Advanced rights are indicated with an asterisk (*). Be aware that most of the Advanced user rights are necessary and useful for programmers that create NT applications.

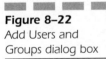

Figure 8–22
Add Users and Groups dialog box

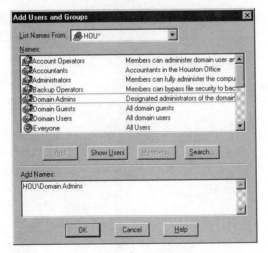

Figure 8–23
Find Account
dialog box

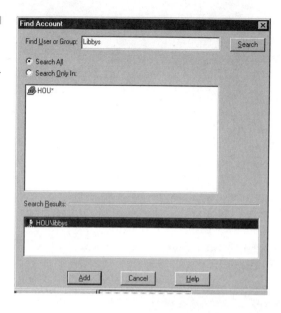

Table 8–1

NT Rights

User Right	What this allows you to do	Default Members
Access this computer from network	Users and groups with this right can open a connection to this machine over a network. If you are in the Domain SAM, this applies to all domain controllers. If you are on a standalone server or a workstation, this right applies only to that machine.	Administrators, Everyone
Act as part of the operating system*	Users and groups with this right can perform as a secure, trusted part of the operating system. Some subsystems are granted this right.	
Add workstations to domain	Users and groups with this right can create a workstation account in the domain using the Server manager tool. This allows the workstation to use the domain's user and global group accounts and those of trusted domains.	Although it does not display in the Grant To field, this right is given to Administrators and Account Operators groups by default. This right cannot be taken away from these groups and they can grant this right to other users.

User Right	What this allows you to do	Default Members
Back up files and directories	Users and groups with this right can back up files and directories. This right allows the user to read all files. This right supersedes file and directory permissions, and also applies to the registry. If you are in the Domain SAM, this right applies to all domain controllers. If you are on a standalone server or a workstation, this right applies only to that machine.	Administrators, Backup Operators, Server Operators
Bypass traverse checking*	Users and groups with this right can change directories and navigate through a directory tree, even if the user has no permissions for those directories. If you are in the Domain SAM, this applies to all domain controllers. If you are on a standalone server or a workstation, this right applies only to that machine.	Everyone
Change the system time	Users and groups with this right can change the time for the internal clock of a computer using the NT interface. If you are in the Domain SAM, this applies to all domain controllers. If you are on a standalone server or a workstation, this right applies only to that machine.	Administrators, Server Operators
Create a page file*	Users and groups with this right can create a paging file.	Administrators
Create a token object*	Users and groups with this right can create access tokens. Only the Local Security Authority can do this.	

continues

Table 8–1

Continued.

User Right	What this allows you to do	Default Members
Create permanent shared objects*	Users and groups with this right can create special permanent objects, such as \Device, which are used within the Windows NT platform.	
Debug programs*	Users and groups with this right can debug various low-level objects such as threads.	Administrators
Force shutdown from a remote system		Administrators, Server Operators
Generate security audits*	Users and groups with this right can generate security audit log entries.	
Increase quotas*	Users and groups with this right can increase object quotas (not available in this version of Windows NT Server).	Administrators
Increase scheduling priority*	Users and groups with this right can boost the priority of a process.	Administrators
Load and unload device drivers	Users and groups with this right can install and remove device drivers using the Control Panel applets. If you are in the Domain SAM, this applies to all domain controllers. If you are on a standalone server or a workstation, this right applies only to that machine.	Administrators
Lock pages in memory*	Users and groups with this right can lock pages in memory so they cannot be paged out to a backing store such as PAGEFILE.SYS.	
Log on as a batch job*	Users and groups with this right can log on using a batch queue facility for delayed logons.	

User Right	What this allows you to do	Default Members
Log on as a service*	Users and groups with this right can access the system as a service. This right is used to administer the Directory Replicator service as well as create service accounts for applications such as Microsoft Exchange. If you are in the Domain SAM, this applies to all domain controllers. If you are on a standalone server or a workstation, this right applies only to that machine.	
Log on locally	Users and groups with this right can log on to a specific machine locally. If you are in the Domain SAM, this applies to all domain controllers. If you are on a standalone server or a workstation, this right applies only to that machine.	Account Operators, Administrators, Backup Operators, Print Operators, Server Operators
Manage auditing and security log	Users and groups with this right can determine the auditing for resource access, such as File access. They can also view and clear the security log in the NT Event Viewer. Be aware that this right does not allow a user to set auditing for the system, using the Policy... Audit in User Manager for Domains. Only the Administrators group has this ability.	Administrators
Modify firmware environment variables*	Users and groups with this right can modify system environment variables. (Users can always modify their own user environment variables).	Administrators
Profile single process*	Users and groups with this right can use Windows NT platform profiling (performance sampling) capabilities on a process.	Administrators

Table 8–1

Continued.

User Right	What this allows you to do	Default Members
Profile system performance*	Users and groups with this right can use Windows NT platform profiling capabilities on the system. (This can slow the system down.)	Administrators
Replace a process-level token*	Users and groups with this right can modify a process's security access token. This is a powerful privilege used only by the system.	
Restore files and directories	Users and groups with this right can restore files and directories. This right allows the user to write to all files. This right supersedes file and directory permissions, and also applies to the registry. If you are in the Domain SAM, this applies to all domain controllers. If you are on a standalone server or a workstation, this right applies only to that machine.	Administrators, Backup Operators, Server Operators
Shut down the system	Users and groups with this right can shut down a Windows NT Server. If you are in the Domain SAM, this applies to all domain controllers. If you are on a standalone server or a workstation, this right applies only to that machine.	Account Operators, Administrators, Backup Operators, Print Operators, Server Operators
Take ownership of files or other objects	Users and groups with this right can take ownership of files, directories, and other objects on a computer. If you are in the Domain SAM, this applies to all domain controllers. If you are on a standalone server or a workstation, this right applies only to that machine.	Administrators

NOTE: *Rights apply to a system as a whole. Rights are assigned and used differently than permissions, which relate to specific resources, such as folders, files, and printers. Permissions are discussed in Chapters 6, 9, and 15.*

USER PROFILES Users like to customize their systems. They like to have their own colors, messy desktops, and shortcuts. In a multi-user operating system such as NT, this can be tough. If John logs into a system, he wants his customized settings, and when he logs off and Betty logs in, all those settings need to change to fit Betty's desired customizations. In Windows 95, Windows 98, and Windows NT, this is achieved through the use of User Profiles. User profiles allow users to make changes to many elements of their desktop, applications, and start menu; these changes are stored—either locally or on a server—and will then be available the next time the user logs on. If the profile information is stored locally, it can only be used when the user logs on to that specific machine. This is called a Local User Profile. If you store the profile information on a PDC or BDC server, however, that user can access it from any machine in the domain. In this case, it would be called a Roaming User Profile. In addition, you can use the profiles as a measure of consistency and security in your environment by making the profile required at logon. This is called a Mandatory User Profile. When you make a mandatory user profile, you remove the ability of the user to change their profile. Only an administrator can make changes to a mandatory profile. In this section, we will first describe local user profiles and how they are created. In addition, we will discuss what is stored in these profiles. Next, we describe the use and administration of roaming user profiles, so that you can allow your users to log on to multiple machines in your environment. Finally, we describe the use and administration of mandatory user profiles, to allow you to limit what elements of their environment your users can affect.

NOTE: *Keep in mind that while the name and intention of user profiles remains constant among 95, 98, and NT, NT creates and stores user profiles differently than 95 or 98.*

USER PROFILE STRUCTURE The first time a user logs on to a Windows NT machine, the machine creates and stores a configuration file for that user called a user profile. This profile contains information that restores a user's desktop and start menu configuration each time that user logs on to that machine, as well as options for other applications and settings. This snapshot of settings is saved when a user logs off and automatically restored when the user logs back on to the workstation.

NTUSER.DAT   A User Profile is contained in a Windows NT registry hive and a set of profile directories. Below, we describe what elements of the profile are stored in which location. This information will be important for troubleshooting profiles as well as for making detailed and specific changes prior to implementing mandatory profiles.

The registry, which we have described earlier, is the internal database that stores all the settings for the computer, including settings for the machine, for the user, and for the applications. A hive is a portion of the registry that contains information related to a particular topic. The hive that contains the information for the User Profile is the **HKEY_CURRENT_USER**. Each user that has logged on to a machine will have a subkey, or portion, of the hive related to their user account that stores their information. The SID, or security identification number, relates the subkey to the user account. The hive data related to the profile is written to the file **NTUSER.DAT**. The **NTUSER.DAT** portion of the user profile stores the information required for the user's environment. When editing elements of the profile stored in the registry, therefore, you will need to open the registry for editing. Run **REDEDT32.EXE** and highlight the appropriate key under **HKEY_CURRENT_USER**, as shown in Figure 8–24. Then, choose File . . . Load Hive to add in and access the information stored for a particular user. When prompted for a Key Name, it is easiest to type the Username for the user whose profile you are editing. Make a note of whatever you use in this case, as you will need it again when unloading the particular user. You will then select **NTUSER.DAT** (or possibly **NTUSER.MAN**). You will then have the ability to edit the necessary profile information in the registry. The list below describes the settings stored in the **NTUSER.DAT**. In addition to the registry entries, the profile directories, which are also listed below, contain the information required to maintain a user's application and desktop settings.

NOTE: While we are describing the method to edit the registry directly, keep in mind that it is not a recommended practice unless absolutely necessary, as you can make your machine unusable by changing settings incorrectly or inappropriately. You should back up the registry regularly and especially before editing it. When possible, edit the registry by using the Control Panel applets or other GUI interfaces.

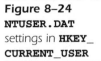

Figure 8–24
NTUSER.DAT
settings in **HKEY_**
CURRENT_USER

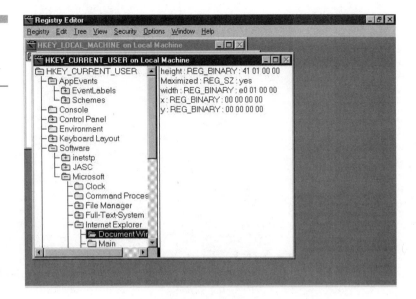

The following settings are stored in the **NTUSER.DAT**:

■ *Program Manager, File Manager, and Windows NT Explorer*. All user-definable settings for Windows NT Explorer, such as folder and view options, as well as persistent network connections (i.e., mapped drives that reconnect at logon) are stored in the registry hive.

■ *Taskbar*. All customizations made to the Start menu, all programs added or removed from the Start Menu, all personal program groups and their properties, all program items and their properties, and all taskbar settings are stored in the registry hive.

■ *MS-DOS Command prompt*. All of the MS-DOS command prompt options and settings, such as color, font, usage, and memory are stored in the registry hive.

■ *Print Manager*. All network printer connections and settings, such as default printer, are stored in the registry hive.

■ *Control Panel Applet options*. All user-defined settings made in the Control Panel, including keyboard and mouse settings, for example, are stored in the registry hive.

■ *Accessory options*. All user-specific application settings, such as the clock, that may affect the Windows NT environment, are stored in the registry hive.

■ *Online help bookmarks*. Any bookmarks placed in the Windows NT Help system by the user are stored in the registry hive.

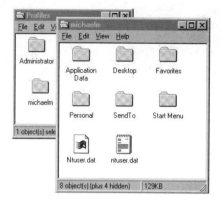

PROFILE DIRECTORIES Similarly to the registry hive, the profile directories stored on the NT machine contain more settings for applications and user specific options. Figure 8–25 shows an example of the directories stored in the Profiles directory on a Windows NT machine.

The profile directories contain the following configuration settings:

- *Application data.* Application-specific data, such as a custom dictionary for a word processing program, is stored in this folder. Application vendors, such as the makers of Microsoft Word, decide what to store in this directory.

- *Desktop.* Any items placed on the Desktop, including files, the briefcase, and shortcuts, are stored in this directory.

- *Favorites.* This directory stores shortcuts to anything that has been designated as a favorite in Windows Explorer or Internet Explorer, including program items, favorite URLs, and favorite folders.

- *NetHood.** Shortcuts to Network Neighborhood items.

- *Personal.* Shortcuts to program items. Also a central store for any documents that the user creates. Applications should be written to save files here by default.

- *PrintHood.** Shortcuts to printer folder items.

- *Recent.* Shortcuts to the most recently used items.

- *SendTo.* Shortcuts to document storage locations and applications.

- *Start Menu.* Shortcuts to program items.

- *Templates.** Shortcuts to template items.

* These directories are hidden by default. To see these directories, change the View Options.

LOCAL USER PROFILES   Windows NT Workstations and servers automatically create local profiles. When a user logs on, a new profile is created, based on the information contained in the Default User profile. Each of the choices that user makes to the desktop and other preferences are stored in the new profile. When a user logs off, the profile information is stored in the registry and in the profile folder. When the same user logs on again, the workstation recognizes the user and loads the appropriate profile. Local profiles are computer specific: Settings made at one workstation are not available when the user logs in at another workstation. This type of profile is created automatically and does not require administrator intervention. In addition to the individual user profiles, NT also has the following types of local-based profiles:

- The *system default* profile, which is used when no user is logged in. The only settings that are affected by the system default profile are the wallpaper and background colors.

- The *user default* profile, which is stored on a per workstation basis and is loaded when one of the following types of users log in or when a user logs in under the following conditions. First, a user account that does not have a profile assigned to it will use the user default profile. This occurs the first time a user logs on, although after this initial logon the user will keep his own profile with his own specific settings. Second, if the user's server-based profile is not available—for example, if the server is down—NT uses the default profile. Finally, the default user profile is used if a user logs in using the Guest account.

SERVER-BASED PROFILES   With user accounts in the domain, an administrator can also create server-based profiles. Server-based profiles provide the following advantages to administrators:

- A user can access and use the same profile at multiple workstations (these are known as Roaming profiles).

- A group of users can share the same profile, better known as Group profiles—useful when multiple users log on to the same machine or when multiple users need the same settings.

- A profile can be created that restricts the user's access to aspects of a user's machine, called a Mandatory profile. This is useful in security-intensive environments.

These server-based profiles require an administrator's intervention to be created and implemented. They can take the form of either Roaming profiles or Mandatory profiles.

Roaming Profiles A roaming profile, unlike a local profile, is stored on a network drive (often the user's home directory) and can therefore be accessed from any machine from which the user can log on. This allows your users to maintain their information and preferences on any computer in the environment. The roaming profile allows users to share computers and continue to maintain their own desktops, Start menus, and other preferences. Keep in mind that with roaming user profiles, changes made by the user will be added to the profile and used the next time the user logs in. There are a number of methods to implement roaming user profiles. The easiest way is simply to add a profile path to each user account.

To add the profile path, edit a user in User Manager. In the User Properties dialog box, click the Profile button. This displays the User Environment Profile dialog box. Add a path to the User Profile Path field by typing in the name of the server, the share name of the directory containing the profile, and the user name. This is called the UNC name (see Chapter 9 for more information on UNC naming conventions), as shown in Figure 8–26. If you want to store a profile for ErinR on server Nero, and the profiles are stored in a directory with a share name of Profiles, for example, you would use the following path: **\\Nero\Profiles\ErinR**. Create a Profile directory —if one does not already exist—on the machine on which you store profiles, and share that directory with the Everyone group.

When a user logs in for the first time, NT creates a new profile if no profile exists in the user's folder. The user can make whatever changes he or she wants to their desktop. These changes are stored in their user profile and will appear at the next logon. Another option for creating Roaming user profiles is to copy a user profile that has already been configured

Figure 8–26
A full path using the UNC name

into the directory. If you choose this method, the user will be given a set of preferences as defaults that the user can then change, by altering their desktop, etc. To copy an existing profile so that you can reuse it for another user, open the System applet from the Control Panel. In the System Properties dialog box, select User Profiles, highlight the user profile and select Copy To . . . to copy the profile to the shared location (see Figure 8–27).

Group Profiles   A Group profile is a Roaming profile shared by a group of users. All the users in the group will log on to identical desktops, Start menus, and application options. The serious downside to this standardization is that every change made by every user affects every user in the group. Imagine the outcry if late one night, Bob decided that fluorescent green and purple made his desktop perfect! To create a group profile, point the User Profiles path for each user to the same profile. Group profiles are rarely used, as you might imagine. Administrators prefer instead a special type of group profile called a Mandatory profile.

Mandatory Profiles   Mandatory profiles are Roaming profiles that cannot be changed by their users. Mandatory profiles are handy for standard profiles to be used by a group. A good example would be 500 accounts receivable systems where each system had to look exactly the same. Another good use for Mandatory profiles would be in a high security situation, perhaps an inventory lookup system in the middle of a sales floor. The process

Figure 8–27
Copying a profile

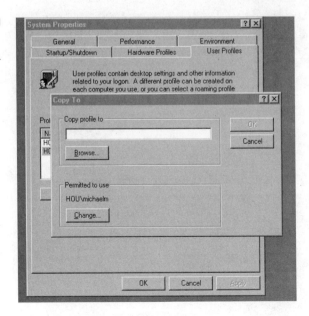

of creating a Mandatory profile begins by creating a Roaming profile. Add a user profile path to each user account, copy a pre-configured user profile to the user profile path specified in each user account, and then rename the **NTUSER.DAT** file to **NTUSER.MAN** in the user profile path specified in each user account. This creates a mandatory user profile.

When you need to work with a large number of accounts simultaneously, you can create a User Template with the proper User Profile settings and create the users based on that template. If the users already exist, simply select the users you wish to edit while holding down the shift key to make multiple selections (Figure 8–28). Yes, this works for any of the user settings, not just User profiles!

Managing User Profiles   The primary tool for managing user profiles is the User Profiles tab in the System Properties Control Panel applet. Earlier we saw how this is used to copy profiles to a shared location to make it a roaming profile. This is also where bad or no longer needed profiles are deleted and where profiles can be changed from roaming to local, as shown in Figure 8–29. A local profile cannot be converted into a roaming profile unless the local profile was once a roaming profile. This makes sense. It is easy to convert a roaming profile to a local profile; just tell the system to use the local copy and ignore the profile on the PDC or BDC. A local profile cannot be converted into a roaming profile so easily. It needs a UNC path to the shared profile folder. Converting local to roaming profiles is the job of the Copy to . . . button, not the Change To button.

The User Profiles Tab has another handy feature for assigning users or groups to a particular User Profile. Click on the "Copy to . . . " button and notice the option "Permitted to use" and the "Change" button (see Figure 8–30). Clicking the Change button allows you to choose users and groups selectively to use this profile. A nice touch for quick Group profiles!

Figure 8–28

Making multiple selections in User Manager

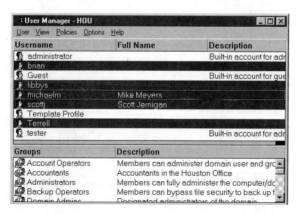

Figure 8–29
Changing a profile in
system properties

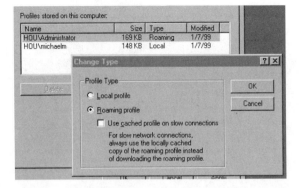

Figure 8–30
Adding a group
profile

The last aspect of User Profiles is the concept of Logon scripts, handled back in the User Profiles dialog box in User Manager (Figure 8–31). This allows users to create logon scripts that run every time a user logs in. Logon scripts can be DOS batch files, NT CMD files, or executable files.

Logon files are designed primarily for backward compatibility with Novell NetWare systems. The use of startup folders and persistent drive mappings in NT has made Logon scripts rather unnecessary and Microsoft likes to stress just how unnecessary on the exams. Watch out for questions that deal with Startup folder versus Logon file type questions!

While user profiles are handy customization tools, they are very poor tools for security. When it comes time to get serious about security, NT turns to a powerful tool called a system policy.

Figure 8–31
Logon Script setting
in User Profiles

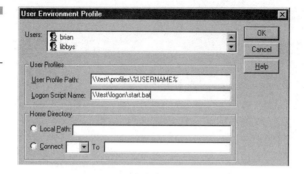

SYSTEM POLICIES   A System Policy is a set of registry settings that defines the computer resources available to a group of users or an individual. Policies define the many various facets of the desktop environment that a system administrator needs to control, such as which applications are available, which applications appear on the user's desktop, which options appear in the Start menu, who can change attributes of their desktops and who cannot. A User Profile defines a user's environment and preferred settings, but a system policy defines both the default environment and the user's ability to shape that environment. Bob might want a fluorescent green desktop, in other words, but if the system policy says no green, Bob is out of luck.

The User Profile is actually built both from System Policy settings (for example, those things that a user has access to and those things that the user can and cannot change) and also from saved changes that a user makes to customize his or her desktop.

A system policy is manifested as a special binary file with the extension POL. This file, usually named **NTCONFIG.POL**, is stored on individual machines or on a PDC in the domain. On boot, this file is read into the Registry along with the User Profiles, setting all of the security functions. Each POL file is highly flexible. It can contain all of the security information for one user or many groups, a single system or an entire domain —it's simply a matter of configuring the POL file to do what is desired.

CREATING POLICIES   POL files are created and edited with the System Policy Editor (**POLEDIT.EXE**). The System Policy Editor is a graphical program that allows administrators to select the desired security options for computers, users, and groups (global groups only). Figure 8–32 shows a typical POLEDIT screen. Notice the different icons for computers, users, and groups. The individual security options for users, systems, and groups are also known as policies. Don't let this confuse you! Let's say it again:

Figure 8–32
Sample system policy

"The System Policy file contains policies for users, groups, and individual computers." Looking again at Figure 8–32, we see that this system policy has policies for two users, three groups, and one system. Also, note that there are two special "Default User" and "Default System" policies that cover the "if it isn't in a special user or computer policy, then this is how it is" policy settings.

The security options for users and groups are identical. The security options for computers are totally different. Some typical security options for computers are:

■ Remote Update of System Policies

■ Autostart Programs

■ Create Hidden Shares

■ Customizing User Environment

■ Do not display last logged on user name

■ Delete cached copies of roaming profiles

■ RAS autodisconnect

Here are some sample security options for users and groups:

■ Hide Screen Saver Tab

■ Set wallpaper

■ Hide Network Neighborhood

■ Disable shutdown

■ Disable Registry Tools

■ Custom Startup Folder

■ Remove File Menu from Explorer

POLEDIT can create a new POL file, edit an existing one, or directly edit any registry to which it has access. In most cases, there is only one

NTCONFIG.POL file in a domain. After this file is created, it is copied to the **NETLOGON** share on the PDC, forcing all users to load the **NTCONFIG.POL** file on startup.

If you plan to use directory replication, be sure to copy the **NTCONFIG.POL** file to the **%systemroot%\system32\repl\Import\Scripts** directory so that it will be copied to the BDCs in the domain.

Administrators can also create policies from policy template files. These files, distinct by their ADM extension, contain basic information for the creation of System policy files. Templates are stored in the **%system root\INF** folder and can be selected in **POLEDIT** by choosing Options\Policy Template (see Figure 8–33).

Managing Policies   It is possible, even common, to have conflicts in policies and profiles, especially between a user and a group policy or between a policy and a profile. The user JOHHNYB, for example, has a user policy that allows him to use Registry access tools. (Under the System Policy editor, the JOHNNYB\System\Restrictions\Disable Registry editing tools option would not be checked.) But JOHNNYB is also a member of the AUDITING group that has a group policy. The AUDITING group policy has the Disable Registry editing tools option checked. When two polices conflict, there is a definite "pecking order." First, *policies* always take precedence over *profiles*. Second, *specific* profiles take precedence over *default* profiles. Third, if there are conflicts between multiple groups, the group with the highest priority takes precedence. The group's priorities are set in **POLEDIT** under Options\ Group Priority, as shown in Figure 8–34.

Last, as in the example, if there is a conflict between a group and a user policy, the user policy takes precedence. So, for our example, JOHNNYB will still be able to use Registry editing tools.

NOTE: *Be sure to review the different functions of Computer vs. User/Group policies!*

Figure 8–33
Policy Template

> Current Policy Template(s):
> D:\WINBDC\INF\COMMON.ADM
> D:\WINBDC\INF\WINNT.ADM
>
> OK
> Add...
> Remove
> Cancel
>
> You must close all active policy files before adding or removing new policy templates.

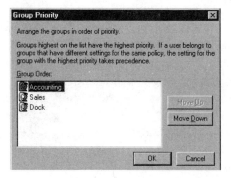

Figure 8–34
Group Priority

Profiles and Policies are an important function of any NT system and are very commonly seen on real-world installations. Be prepared for Policy/Profile questions on every one of the core exams! The inherent conflicts between the functions, creation and management of profiles and policies (they even sound the same!) make them a prime candidate for those "Geez, if I had only read the question more carefully!" type of mistakes. Make sure that you understand the function of both policies and profiles and can create/edit either as needed.

Creating and Managing Windows NT Groups

Groups allow administrators to organize users who need the same types of rights and permissions into manageable units. A group can be given rights and permissions. Users assigned to a group take on the rights and permissions of that group.

Groups, if set up correctly, save NT administrators a lot of time. Administrators need not perform the tedious task of assigning the same rights and permissions over and over again to users who have similar access needs. To give FredA and GingerR individual *Read, Write, Execute, and Delete* (RWED) access rights to the server DANCEHALL seems like a minimal amount of work, but what happens when GeneK, BenV, and CarmenM join the firm? It makes more sense to create the group DANCERS, assign it RWED access to the server DANCEHALL, and then add all five users to the group. If someone leaves or joins, the administrator simply removes or adds them to the group.

TYPES OF GROUPS   NT allows administrators to create two types of groups: Local groups and global groups. With an NT workstation or server, administrators can create only local groups. In a domain, on the other hand, administrators can create both local and global groups. Further, when you install a new server, workstation, or domain, NT creates several groups automatically and gives them default rights, as mentioned above. This section will describe the types of groups, the creation and uses of these groups, and the uses of the default groups provided with NT.

Local groups are created for (and reside on) individual NT systems. According to the "Microsoft Mantra," Local groups are given permissions to resources such as files, folders, and printers. On an individual system, this is the only type of group that you have the ability to create and the only groups you will see listed in the bottom pane of the User Manager application.

Global groups, in contrast, are groups associated with the entire domain and stored on the Primary Domain Controller. You will recognize a local group by the icon, which looks like a computer as the background rather than the globe as the background, as shown in Figure 8–35.

CREATING LOCAL GROUPS Local groups can contain Global groups— when you administer a domain—and users. Administrators can add groups and users from the local machine SAM, the Domain SAM, or from trusted domains. To create a new local group, choose User . . . New Local Group from the menus in the User Manager. This displays the New Local Group dialog box, as shown in Figure 8–36.

First, type in a unique name for the group. This name can be up to 256 characters, including any upper and lower case alphanumeric characters,

Figure 8–35
Local Groups and
Global Groups

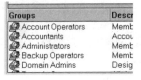

Figure 8–36
New Local Group
dialog box

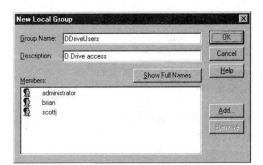

except the backslash (\). The backslash is used to indicate the domain in which an account is stored, and therefore can not be used as another aspect of the name. After you name and save the group, the name cannot be changed without copying or recreating the group. Next, enter a description for the group. While this field is not required, it will be useful when you are administering a large organization with many users and groups. The Show Full Names button allows you to display the full names of the members of the group. If you have not selected this button, only the User Name of the members is displayed. The advantage to only showing the User Name is that it may display faster, especially in cases where you have users from many domains in a group. If you choose to show the full name, you can verify which users from which domains are listed as members of each group. To add users or global groups to the local group, click the Add . . . button. This displays the Add Users and Groups dialog box to allow you to choose users and groups from the SAM to add to this group. You may also click the Remove button to remove users and groups from the Local group. Bear in mind that a group has a SID, just like a user. If you delete a group, you cannot restore access to resources that had this group listed just by creating a new group with the same name, because the new group will have a different SID. When you try to delete a group, NT forces you to verify multiple times that you actually want to delete the group.

CREATING GLOBAL GROUPS Administrators create Global groups to group together certain user accounts from a domain. You can then place these global groups into the local groups so that the users contained in the global groups have access to the necessary resources. To create a global group, choose User . . . New Global Group from the menus in User Manager for Domains. The New Global Group dialog box, shown in Figure 8–37, gives you the opportunity to type a name and description for

Figure 8–37
New Global Group
dialog box

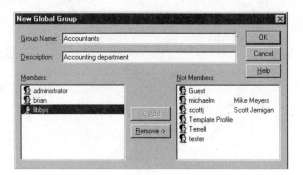

the new group, as well as to add members from the list of users in your domain that are currently Not Members of the group. The Members and Not Members dialog boxes give you information on the users that are in the group and can be added to the group. The Add and Remove buttons allow you to control the membership in the group.

GROUPS AND RIGHTS   There is an important clue that will help in conquering local and global group usage for the exams. If you can remember the Microsoft Mantra and apply it to scenarios, you have the answer to many of the questions on the NT exams. Just in case you have forgotten it, here it is one more time: Users go into Global groups, which go into Local groups, which get rights and permissions. While it may be possible to add users directly to local groups, or while it may be possible to give rights and permissions to Global groups, Microsoft recommends neither. In addition, Microsoft expects you to put Users into Global groups, put Global groups (from either your domain or other domains) into Local groups, and then assign rights and permissions to the Local groups. Stick to the Mantra.

When you want to apply the rights discussed above to users, assign the rights to local groups rather than global groups or individuals. If you want to assign the Change System Time or Load and Unload Device Drivers rights, for example, you should create a Local group that relates to those rights and assign the rights to that local group. Then create a global group (or multiple global groups) that contain the users that need this right. Place the global group or groups inside the local group. This saves time—always a precious commodity for a harried NT administrator. Further, be aware that you may place a global group from a trusted domain into the local group, allowing a central administrator to perform these actions outside his or her own domain. Best practices for global and local group usage will be discussed again in Chapter 9, to show the relationships of groups to permissions and sharing, especially among multiple domains.

MANAGEMENT OF GROUPS   The vast majority of group management is handled at the user level. For example, there is no such thing as a Group equivalent to a User Profile. It is impossible to set a policy geared to a particular group. The overwhelming majority of group management has administrators adding and deleting users from global groups and adding and deleting rights and permissions from local groups. Fortunately, these are both very straightforward processes that can be handled from the User Manager.

PRE-DEFINED GROUPS When you first open the User Manager, you will see some default, pre-created groups already in existence. The paragraphs below list these built-in groups. Tables 8–2 and 8–3, below, list the available rights and abilities that these groups are given by default. Stand-alone or member servers and workstations contain the following local groups by default:

- Administrators
- Backup Operators
- Users
- Guests
- Replicator
- Power Users

Table 8–2

Rights and Pre-made Groups in Domains

Rights and Abilities	Groups granted this right on Domain Controllers
Log on Locally	Administrators, Server Operators, Account Operators, Print Operators, Backup Operators
Access this computer from network	Administrators, Everyone
Take Ownership of Files	Administrators
Manage auditing and security log	Administrators
Change the system time	Administrators, Server Operators
Shut down the system	Administrators, Server Operators, Account Operators, Print Operators, Everyone
Force shutdown from a remote system	Administrators, Server Operators
Backup Files and Operators	Administrators, Server Operators, Backup Directories
Restore Files and Operators	Administrators, Server Operators, Backup Directories
Load and Unload device drivers	Administrators
Add workstations to domain	Administrators*, Account Operators*
Create and manage user accounts	Administrators, Account Operators**
Create and manage global groups	Administrators, Account Operators**

continues

Table 8–2

Continued.

Rights and Abilities	Groups granted this right on Domain Controllers
Create and manage local groups	Administrators, Account Operators,** Users***
Assign user rights	Administrators
Managing auditing of system events	Administrators
Lock the server	Administrators, Server Operators, Everyone****
Override the lock of the server	Administrators
Format server's hard disk	Administrators
Create common groups	Administrators, Server Operators
Share and stop sharing directories	Administrators, Server Operators
Share and stop sharing printers	Administrators, Server Operators, Print Operators

*—This is a built-in ability for Administrators and Account Operators and cannot be taken away. These groups can grant the right to other groups and users.

**—Account operators are limited in their ability to create and manage Administrators in terms of their user accounts, local groups such as Administrators, Server Operators, Backup Operators, Account Operators, Print Operators, the global Domain Admins group, and any other global groups that are members of the listed local groups.

***—The Users group can only create Local groups if they also have the right to log on locally or have access to User Manager for Domains.

****—The Everyone group can only actually lock the server if they are allowed to log on locally.

NT Servers that are domain controllers contain the following local groups by default:

- Administrators
- Backup Operators
- Server Operators
- Account Operators
- Print Operators
- Users
- Guests
- Replicator

Table 8–3

*Rights and
Pre-made Groups
in Member and
Stand-alone Servers
and Workstations*

Rights and Abilities	Groups granted this right on Member or Stand-alone servers and workstations
Log on Locally	Administrators, Power Users, Users, Guests, Everyone, Backup Operators
Access this computer from network	Administrators, Power Users, Everyone
Take Ownership of Files	Administrators
Manage auditing and security log	Administrators
Change the system time	Administrators, Power Users
Shut down the system	Administrators, Power Users, Users, Backup Operators, Everyone*
Force shutdown from a remote system	Administrators, Power Users
Backup Files and Directories	Administrators, Backup Operators
Restore Files and Directories	Administrators, Backup Operators
Load and Unload device drivers	Administrators
Create and manage user accounts	Administrators, Power Users **
Create and manage local groups	Administrators, Power Users, *** Users****
Assign user rights	Administrators
Managing auditing of system events	Administrators
Lock the server	Administrators, Power Users, Everyone
Override the lock of the server	Administrators
Format computer's hard disk	Administrators
Create common groups	Administrators, Power Users
Share and stop sharing directories	Administrators, Power Users
Share and stop sharing printers	Administrators, Power Users

*—Note that the Guests group does not have the explicit ability to shut down the system; however, unless you remove them from the Everyone group, they will be given this right through their membership in the Everyone group.

**—Power Users can create accounts but can only edit the accounts that they have created.

***—Power Users cannot modify the Administrators or Backup Operators local groups.

****—Users can create local groups but can only edit the local groups that they have created.

On the Domain Controllers in the environment, you will also see the following predefined Global groups:

- Domain Admins
- Domain Guests
- Domain Users

When users are created in domains, they are automatically added to the Domain Users global group. This group is then placed automatically in the local Users groups in each machine. Users that are members of the local Users group directly cannot necessarily log on locally at servers without being placed in the global Users group or the group local to that server. Users have the ability to run applications, use and manage files, create and manage groups in a limited fashion, maintain a personal profile on a machine, and connect to other computers over the network.

The Power Users group allows users that are logged on to a workstation or server to perform more administrative functions. In addition to all the tasks and rights given to a user, a power user can share directories, install and manage printers, and create, modify, and delete user accounts.

A member of a local administrators group has complete control over that local system. By default, the Domain Admins group will be placed in the local administrators group for all machines in a domain. This group allows a user to have all the rights that a power user has, and to do the following things in addition:

- Modify and delete group and user accounts created by anyone on the system, not just themselves.
- Determine membership of the default groups.
- Administer and use administrative shares, unlock a locked workstation.
- Format or partition the disks on workstations or servers.
- Determine and assign user rights.
- Determine the audit policy for a system.
- Perform all tasks necessary for backing up and restoring workstations or servers.
- Take ownership of objects on the workstation or server.

Backup Operators are given rights to open, backup, and restore all files and folders, regardless of the other NTFS or sharing permissions on those folders. While any user could backup or restore objects to which they had been given access, only members of this group can perform these tasks on objects to which they are not given access.

A Guest can log on locally to a workstation or to a domain's built-in Guest account over the network. Users logged in as Guests have limited abilities and no rights at domain servers.

Account Operators are given rights in User Manager for domains to create and manage user and group accounts. Account operators groups would be appropriate when you want to give a user the ability to create and manage user accounts without giving the ability to manage other administrative accounts. The account operators account can also log on locally to domain servers, shut down domain servers, and add computer accounts to a domain.

Print Operators have administrative rights to printer shares in a domain. The members of this group can create, edit, and delete any printer shares on the domain controllers. They also have the ability to log on locally to these machines as well as shut them down.

Members of the Server Operators group have the ability to manage the domain controller machines in a domain. They can manage printer and file and folder shares on PDCs and BDCs, for example, as well as tasks such as backing up and restoring, locking and unlocking, formatting and partitioning, and shutting down.

In addition to the groups listed above, you may see the following special groups created by the system to refer to special sets of users. These groups may not be available in User Manager itself, but may be visible in dialog boxes that allow you to give permissions and rights to groups. The following is a list of special sets of users:

- *Everyone.* This group contains the name of everyone using a computer either remotely (over a network) or locally.

- *Interactive.* This group contains the name of everyone using a computer locally—which means physically sitting at the keyboard of that machine.

- *Network.* This group contains the name of everyone using a computer remotely—which means everyone that is using the network or a network share to access the computer.

- *System.* This group refers to the operating system itself.

- *Creator Owner.* This group allows permission to be transferred to users based on the objects they have created. If a specific permission to delete a print job is given to the Creator Owner group on a printer, for example, the user that created a particular print job inherits those rights, as she is the creator and owner of that print job.

AUDITING USER ACCOUNTS   Auditing user accounts is a powerful feature to track the creation, change, use, and deletion of user accounts and groups. It can track every time an account logs in or out and every time a particular user right (other than logon or logoff) is used. In this section, we will look at file auditing and take a moment to review all of the audit options that can be set in the User Manager.

The auditing of User accounts is somewhat similar to the auditing of folders and files seen in Chapter 6. You have to tell NT who to audit and then set the events to be audited in the User Manager. You can then observe the events with the Event viewer. User auditing, like any other type of auditing, can require significant resources, demand excessive CPU processing power, and make massive log files that can take up a lot of drive space. Only audit events that are necessary!

SETTING UP USER AUDITING   To set up user auditing, open User Manager from the Start/Programs/Administrative Tools menu. Select Policies . . . Audit, to open the Audit Policy dialog box, as shown in Figure 8–38.

The one major difference between file auditing and user auditing is that with file auditing, only the File and Object Access option would be checked (Success, Failure, or both, depending on what you want to audit). Then every different file or folder that you wished to audit would be configured for the permissions you wished to audit. In User Auditing, everything is done from the Audit Policy dialog box. Let's look at all of the auditing options:

- *Logon and Logoff.* An event is written if a user logs on or off, or tries to log on or off unsuccessfully.
- *File and Object Access.* An event is written when a user tries, either successfully or unsuccessfully, to open a file or directory that has additional auditing enabled on it using its security properties or to send a print job to a printer that has additional auditing enabled.

Figure 8–38
Audit Policy dialog box

Audit Policy			
Domain: HOU			OK
○ Do Not Audit			Cancel
● Audit These Events:			Help
	Success	Failure	
Logon and Logoff	☑	☑	
File and Object Access	☑	☑	
Use of User Rights	☐	☑	
User and Group Management	☐	☑	
Security Policy Changes	☐	☑	
Restart, Shutdown, and System	☑	☑	
Process Tracking	☐	☐	

■ *Use of User Rights.* An event is written any time a user tries to use a right given in the User Rights dialog box, with the exception of those rights related to logging on and off.

■ *User and Group Management.* An event is written if a user or group account is created, edited, or deleted. In addition, if changes such as renaming, disabling, enabling, or changing or setting a password are attempted or completed, an event is written.

■ *Security Policy Changes.* An event is written if a change is made to the following types of policies: User rights policy, audit policy, or trust relationships policy.

■ *Restart, Shutdown, and System.* An event is written when a user restarts or shuts down a computer being audited for this event. In addition, if any event occurs that would be written to the security log or might affect system security, an event is written.

■ *Process Tracking.* Events are written for process tracking to enable administrators to track programs being activated, certain types of object access, and other internal processes.

Again, it is a good idea to limit the day-to-day auditing of your system depending on the security necessary in your environment. A very secure environment will require more auditing. In most organizations, however, you can usually limit logging to the events that you suspect a problem with or those that your organization has a special interest in tracking, such as unsuccessful logon attempts.

NT Server Management

Some of the administration that you will be required to do will be accomplished with the NT Server Manager tool. This tool allows you to do the following administrative tasks:

■ View the machines in your domain

■ Add workstation and server accounts to the domain

■ Synchronize the SAM among PDCs and BDCs in your domain

■ Monitor and manage shared directories and services on machines in your domain

■ Send messages within the domain

■ Promote BDCs to PDCs when necessary

The sections below describe many of these administrative tasks. The tasks that you can accomplish using the Server Manager tool are discussed throughout this book. Refer to Chapter 16, for example, for monitoring and managing shared directories in your domain.

USING SERVER MANAGER   To open Server Manager, choose Start . . . Programs . . . Administrative Tools (Common) . . . Server Manager. This will display Server Manager for your current domain, as shown in Figure 8–39. This dialog box will list all of the machines in the domain—including domain controllers, other servers, and workstations—that have accounts in the domain. You can limit the types of machines visible using the View menu.

You may choose to view Server Manager for a different, trusted domain by selecting Computer . . . Select Domain from the menus. All trusted and available domains will be listed in the Select Domain dialog box, as shown in Figure 8–40. You can also specify a particular computer by typing in the computer name in the UNC format: **\\computername**. If you want to display a workgroup, type the workgroup name in the Domain field.

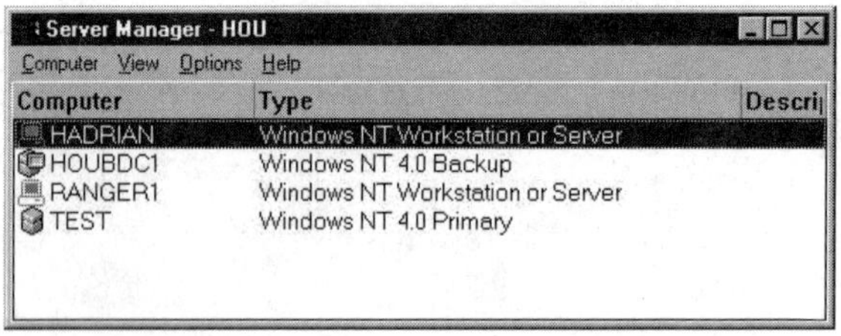

Figure 8–39
Server Manager

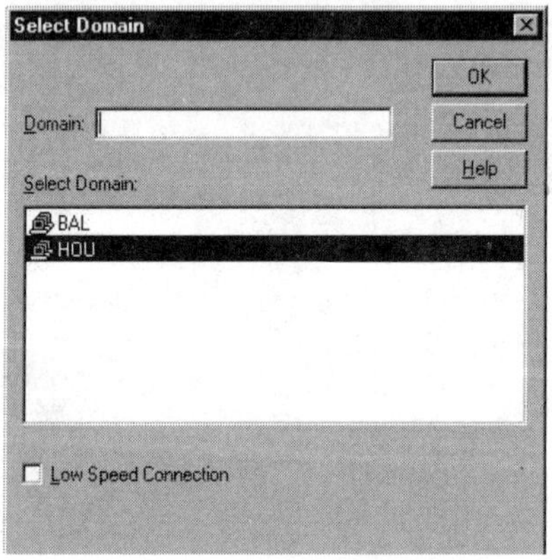

Figure 8–40
Select Domain
dialog box

Note that in this dialog box you also have the ability to specify that you are connecting over a Low Speed Connection, such as a slow WAN link. This selection prevents automatic refreshes from occurring during use of Server Manager.

MACHINE PROPERTIES   After selecting a domain, workgroup, or machine to administer, you may select a particular computer from the list. If you double-click or select Computer . . . Properties, you will see the Properties dialog box for this machine, as shown in Figure 8–41. This dialog box shows you information such as open user sessions, files open on the machine, and open connections to the machine.

You may select the following buttons for more information or administrative abilities:

■ *Users.* Clicking the Users buttons displays the User Sessions dialog box, as shown in Figure 8–42. This dialog box lists the currently connected users, with information about the number of open resources, the computer from which they are connecting, and the amount of time the session has been in use. You may also see information about how long the session has been idle and whether

Figure 8–41
Properties dialog box

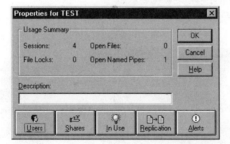

Figure 8–42
User Sessions
dialog box

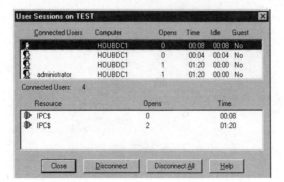

the user is connected using their own account or as a Guest. You can also view how many users are connected to the machine. If you select a particular user, you can see what type of resource the selected user is connected to, such as a shared folder, a named pipe, a shared printer, or an unrecognized resource. From this dialog box, you can forcibly disconnect a single, selected user, or all users using the Disconnect and Disconnect All buttons.

■ *Shares.* Clicking this button displays the Shared Resources dialog box, as shown in Figure 8–43. This dialog box lists the shared resources on the machine, the users connected to the shared resources, and the path to the shared resource. The Disconnect and Disconnect All buttons are available to forcibly disconnect users from specific connections.

■ *In Use.* The In Use button allows the administrator to view the resources in use on the machine in yet a different manner. The In Use dialog box, shown in Figure 8–44, shows the number of open resources, the number of file locks, and which users have resources opened. For each user, the dialog box lists the purpose of the open

Figure 8–43
Shared Resources
dialog box

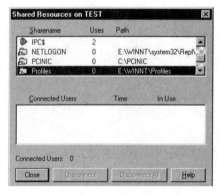

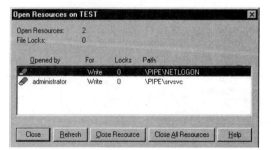

Figure 8–44
In Use dialog box

resource, such as read or write, the locks on the files, and the path to the shared resource. This dialog box allows the administrator to close a single resource or all resources, using the Close Resource and Close All Resources buttons. To refresh the view of the opened resources, click the Refresh button or press F5. This is especially necessary if you are connected to the machine using a Low Speed Connection.

■ *Replication.* The Replication button displays the Directory Replication dialog box, shown in Figure 8–45. This feature of NT allows files or folders, such as logon scripts or user profiles, to be available not only when the user logs on to the PDC, but also when the user logs on to the BDC. In addition, use of Directory Replication allows changes made to the profiles in one location to be updated in all locations. The three requirements for Directory Replication are export computers, import computers, and the directories that should be replicated. Any NT server can be an Export computer. Any Windows NT machine can be an import computer. The export and import directories are stored in the **%systemroot%\system32\repl** directory under subdirectories located in either Export or Import. Please note that a subdirectory under the Export or Import is required—information stored in the root of the Export directory, for example, will not be replicated. There is no need, however, to create the subdirectories under the Import directory, as these will be created by the replication process.

■ In the Directory Replication dialog box, the left-hand pane is devoted to export and the right-hand pane is devoted to import. The Do Not Export and Do Not Import radio buttons prevent

Figure 8–45
Directory Replication
dialog box

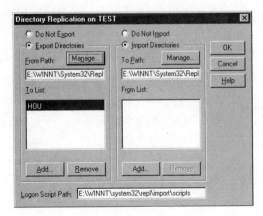

directories from being exported from or imported to the machine you are administering. To enable Export, select the Export Directories radio button and ensure that the information that you want to Export is under the correct path, usually `C:\WINNT\ System32\Repl\Export`. To determine which computers will receive the Exported information, click the Add . . . button under the To List: field. This displays the Select Domain dialog box to allow you to select machines with which to replicate. Similarly, if this machine will receive imported information, select the Import Directories radio button and ensure that the correct information is in the To Path field. You can select which machines to receive information from by clicking the appropriate Add . . . button under the From List: field.

To ensure that replication occurs in the manner you expect for both Export and Import, you can select the Manage button. This displays the Manage Exported Directories dialog box, shown in Figure 8–46, or the Manage Imported Directories dialog box, which has many of the same elements. The Manage dialog box allows you to manage the replication of the subdirectories of this path. To add a subdirectory to be managed, click the Add . . . button and type in the name of a subdirectory in the path. This subdirectory will then appear in the list under Sub-Directory. By default, there are no locks on the subdirectories. To add a lock, click the Add Lock button. No replication will occur for that subdirectory until this column has a zero value. This prevents any incomplete replication. If a particular user is making changes to the information in a subdirectory, they might place a lock on it. If another user also begins making changes, they might also add a lock. Both users would need to remove their locks by clicking the Remove Lock button before that subdirectory and its contents would replicate. If a Lock has been placed on a subdirectory, the Locked Since column

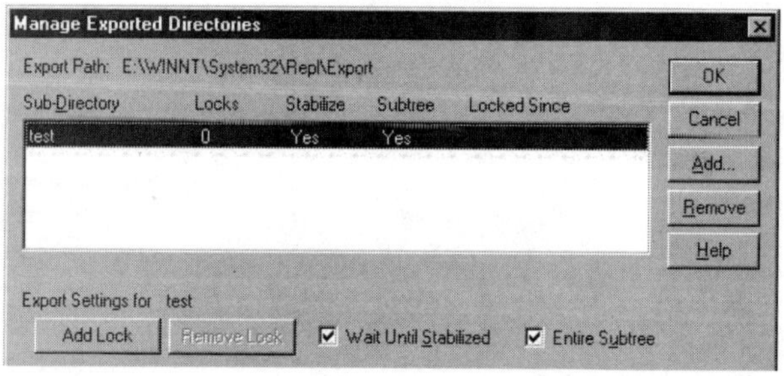

Figure 8–46
Manage Exported
Directories dialog
box

displays the amount of time the lock has been enabled. The Stabilize column either has a Yes or No value, determined by the checkbox Wait Until Stabilized. If this is set to Yes, no replication will occur for this subdirectory until it has not been changed for 2 minutes. This prevents incomplete replication. By default, export is configured to occur using broadcasts from the export server every five minutes when there are changes in the files or directories to be replicated. This interval can be set to anywhere from 1 to 60 minutes, using a registry entry. The Stabilize setting is a way to effect this default. In addition, the Stabilize interval, called the GuardTime, can also be changed in the registry and should be if the Interval is changed. The Subtree column also has either a Yes or No value and is determined by the Entire Subtree checkbox. If the value is Yes, any subdirectories under this subdirectory will also be replicated. In the Manage Imported Directories, you can only manage Locks. Another column of information visible in this dialog box is the Status of the directory, which tells an administrator three things: Whether the subdirectory is OK, which means it is receiving regular updates; whether there is No Master, which means that the subdirectory is not receiving any updates; and No Sync, which means that the subdirectory has received some updates in the past, but that the data is not current and updated. This dialog box will also display the last updated date and time, and any information on how long a Lock has been in place.

■ Finally, the Logon Script Path field at the bottom of the dialog box allows the administrator to indicate where the logon scripts for the computer are stored. If a server allows a user to authenticate and that user's profile indicates that the user has a logon script, the server will look in this directory to find the appropriate logon script. On Domain Controller machines, all logon scripts should be stored in a specific replication export directory. This directory should be exported to all other domain controllers and servers in the domain, to ensure that users have the appropriate logon script when they try to authenticate.

■ For any replication to take place, the directory replicator service must be started, using the Services applet in the control panel. The directory replicator service must also have a user account to allow it to log on and that account must have the appropriate access to the export and import directories. Create an account using User Manager, and ensure both that it does not have to change the password, and that this password never expires. Use the Services applet to configure the Directory Replicator service to start automatically using this account. Use the NTFS permissions or Sharing permissions to ensure that the account has full access to the Import and Export directories. Also place the account in the default local group Replicator on each machine that will be participating. As long as you are within a single domain, or trusting domains, you can use one user account for all directory replication.

- *Alerts.* The Alerts dialog box, shown in Figure 8–47, allows the administrator to determine which Users and computers NT notifies when system-generated administrative alerts occur. Administrative alerts usually warn about security or access problems, problems with directory replication or printing, and any problems that include power loss or shutdown. The events that trigger an administrative alert are selected and configured internally by Windows NT. An administrator would probably decide to configure the alerts to increase the knowledge they have about the system on a real-time basis. If an administrator only finds out about problems with the machines by examining the Event Log, it may take longer to solve problems that damage productivity. If an administrator has configured alerts to be delivered to the appropriate administrators, however, some problems can be seen and corrected more quickly.

- To configure the Alert, add a computer account name or a user account name to the appropriate field and click Add . . . These users or machines will then receive a broadcast alert when one of the pre-determined events occurs on the system. You can also configure alerts directly through the Control Panel . . . Server applet. Note that the Alerts are sent out by a service running under NT called the Alerter service. When you make changes to

Figure 8–47
Alerts dialog box

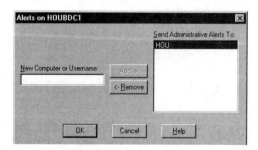

this field for who should receive alerts, you should stop and restart the Alerter service using the Control Panel . . . Services applet. You will also need to restart the Server service on the computer for which you are configuring the Alerter service, as the two services are connected.

CREATING COMPUTER ACCOUNTS   Administrators can also use the Server Manager to create computer accounts in the domain or workgroup. All NT-based machines need computer accounts in the domains they try to access in order to use the domain level security and user accounts from the Domain SAM. A computer account can either be added using the Server Manager Computer . . . Add to Domain menu choice, or it can be added when the server or workstation is being installed, if the installer has the correct administrative rights in the domain. To add a computer using the Add Computer to Domain dialog box, shown in Figure 8–48 below, first select whether the computer being added is a Backup Domain controller or a workstation or server using the appropriate radio buttons. Next, type in a unique name for the computer in the Computer Name field. To add the computer to the Domain SAM, click the Add button. This creates a unique SID for the computer in the Domain SAM and allows the computer to participate in domain security and be managed from within the domain.

SYNCHRONIZING THE DOMAIN   When you make changes to the SAM for a domain, using either the PDC or a BDC, you must replicate those changes to the other domain controllers in the environment. This will usually occur automatically as changes are made to the user accounts. If you notice that user passwords or access tokens (discussed in Chapter 9) are having problems, one technique to troubleshoot this problem is to synchronize the domain manually. To do this, use the Computer . . . Synchronize Entire Domain menu choice in Server Manager. You should receive a warning, shown in Figure 8–49, below, that the process of synchronizing takes a few minutes. Click Yes to continue the process. This allows the account manager

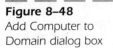

Figure 8–48
Add Computer to
Domain dialog box

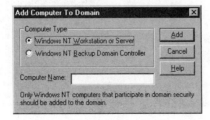

Figure 8–49
Computer
Synchronization
Warning

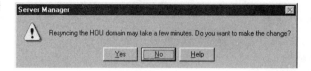

database (the SAM) to be updated on all domain controllers so that any changes will be available to all users connecting. Keep in mind that the larger your domain, and the more spread out your backup domain controllers, the less likely you will want to do this during the day.

PROMOTING A BDC   If you need to take the PDC out of service for a time for maintenance, you should promote a BDC to fill the position first. To promote a BDC, first synchronize the entire domain, as discussed above. This ensures that any changes that have been made in the Domain SAM will be available to all BDCs. Then select the BDC that you would like to promote using the Server Manager list of machines. After selecting the BDC, choose Computer . . . Promote to Primary Domain Controller from the Server Manager menus. If it is possible for NT to make the change, the original PDC will be demoted to a BDC, and the selected machine will be promoted to be the PDC.

MONITORING AND MANAGING SERVICES REMOTELY   In many cases, you will administer many machines in a domain from a single workstation or server. You might need to monitor or manage the services running on a specific machine. You may need, for example, to verify that your Alerter service is running on a machine that you have configured to send out administrative alerts. You may also need to verify that services such as the Directory Replicator are running when configuring replication. You may also need to start and stop services remotely when troubleshooting. To work with services on your local machine, you will probably select the Services applet in the Control Panel. To administer services on another machine, however, select the appropriate machine from the Server Manager list and then select Computer . . . Services from the menus. The Services dialog box, shown in Figure 8–50, displays the services installed on the machine, their current status, and what type of startup the service uses.

A service will display *Started* under status if it is currently running. If it not running, it will be blank. You may also see a status of *Paused* for a service that can be paused. From the buttons on the right-hand portion of the dialog box, you can start a service that is currently not running, stop a service, or pause some of the services. Not all services can be paused. If

Figure 8–50
Services dialog box

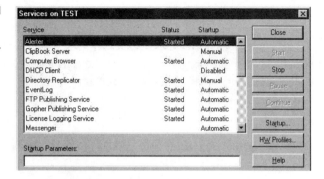

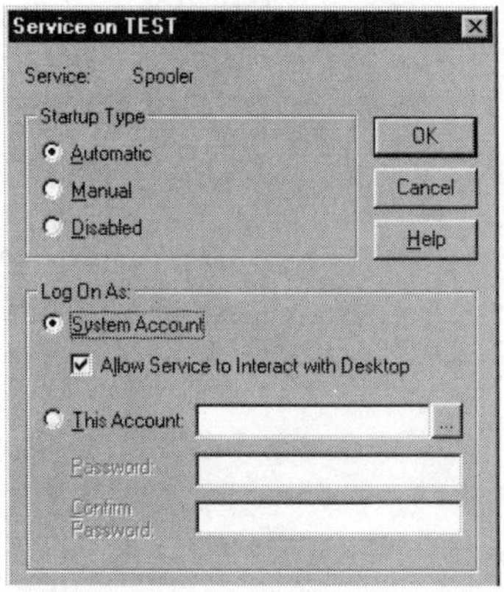

Figure 8–51
Service dialog box

you pause a service, you can then continue it or stop it completely. You may also select how the service should be started, using the Startup button. When you select the startup button for a particular service, the Service dialog box shown in Figure 8–51 is shown to allow you to choose whether the service should be started automatically at startup of the machine, manually when necessary, or whether it should be disabled.

You will also use this dialog box to select an account for the service to use for logon. The service can either use the system account or another user account created specifically for the service. For most default NT services, they will log on using the system account. Two examples of NT services that require a separate user account for logon are the Directory Replicator service and the Schedule service. Other examples will include other Microsoft products, such as Microsoft Exchange, that may require the ability to act as a service. If you select to allow the service to use the system account, you must select the Allow Service to Interact with Desktop checkbox if the service needs to be available to a user interface at the desktop. If you choose to create a specific account for this service, create the account using User

Manager for Domains first. Ensure that you do not require the user to change the password and that you set the password never to expire. You will also want to assign the user account to the appropriate groups and give it the logon as a service user right. In the Service dialog box, either type in or select the appropriate account and then type in and confirm the account password.

Administration—The Thankless Task

Becoming comfortable with User Manager and Server Manager guarantees that you will become a very unpopular person in your network. The business of administration has never been known to ingratiate you with your fellow co-workers. The administrator invariably is the one whose phone is constantly ringing off the hook with users requesting new rights, new permissions, lost passwords, and profile changes. When everything is running properly, you're the Maytag repairman. Administration is an absolutely critical function in any NT network and is also absolutely the most thankless task you will ever endure.

Questions

1. Joan wants to create a user template that creates the users home directory on the PDC (Server1) as `\\Server1\Users\(Name of User)`. If Joan creates a user **JOHNNYB**, then his home directory should be: `\\Server1\Users\JohnnyB`. Can a template be created to do this? If it can, what needs to be done in the template file?

   a. Yes, Set the Home Directory in the User Environment Profile to connect to `\\Server1\Users\%username%`

   b. No, The home directory will need to be created each time.

   c. Yes, Set the Home Directory in the User Environment Profile to Local Path `\\Server1\Users\%username%`

   d. Yes, Set the Home Directory in the Group Environment Profile to Local Path `\\Server1\Users\%username%`

2. All User templates should be saved with a ____ at the beginning of the username or it won't be a template.

   a. #

   b. *

   c. %

   d. Doesn't matter

3. Which of the following is not a built-in NT local group?

   a. Backup Operators

   b. Admins

   c. Users

   d. Replicator

4. FreddyK, the head of the Sales department, has just angrily announced he is quitting—and walking out—today. The best way for an NT administrator to handle this will be to _____ his account.

   a. shutdown

   b. delete

   c. disable

   d. change the password on

5. Which of the following functions cannot be performed in the User Manager?

    a. Audit Use of User rights

    b. Set Group Priority

    c. Create New User

    d. Add Users to a Group

6. Steve creates a new policy for the group Players that removes the Run command from the Start menu. The new policy works perfectly for all member of the Players group with one exception. Joyce, a member of the Players group, can still use the Start/Run command, even after rebooting. This is true on every machine she logs in on. What could be the problem?

    a. Joyce is an administrator

    b. Joyce has a User Profile allowing her to use the Start/Run command

    c. Joyce is not using the System Policy

    d. Joyce has a User Policy that allowing her to use the Start/Run command

7. "Log on Locally" is an example of a:

    a. Right

    b. Policy

    c. Permission

    d. Profile

8. Which built-in group does not have the right to restore files and directories?

    a. Administrators

    b. Backup Operators

    c. Server Operators

    d. Account Operators

9. The file **NTUSER.DAT** contains the _____ .

    a. User Policy

    b. User Rights

    c. User Profile

    d. User Passwords

10. Scott tries to change his desktop's background color but it always returns to Windows default whenever he logs on. This is most probably due to:

    a. A roaming profile

    b. A group policy

    c. A mandatory profile

    d. A system policy

11. According to the "Microsoft Mantra," a global group should only be comprised of:

    a. Rights

    b. Local groups

    c. Permissions

    d. Users

12. Timmy, an administrator on the MAIN domain, has to add four NT stand-alone systems to the domain. To do this, he can:

    a. Reinstall NT and add them to the Main domain

    b. Use Server Manager

    c. Go to each machine and use the Network Control Panel Icon to add them.

    d. All of the above

Answers

1. a—Set the Home Directory in the User Environment Profile to connect to `\\Server1\Users\%username%`.

2. d—It doesn't matter what you name a template. There is no difference between a template and any other user account. However, using a # sign or other character is a good way to separate a template from a real account.

3. c—There is no built-in local group called Admins. There is a built-in global group called Domain Admins.

4. c—Disabling the account allows the administrator to keep all of the rights and permissions without having to create from scratch —besides, Freddy might come back in an hour after he cools off!

5. b—There is no Group Priority features in User Manager. This is a function in System Policy Editor.

6. d—Joyce has a User Policy that allows her to use the Start/Run command. User policies take precedence over group policies.

7. a—Log on Locally is an NT right.

8. a—Account Operators do not have the right to Restore files and directories.

9. c—`NTUSER.DAT` contains the user profile

10. c—Preventing a person from changing their desktop's background is handled by a mandatory profile.

11. d—"Users go into Global Groups, which go into Local groups, which get rights and permissions."

12. d—All of the above.

9

Microsoft Networking

At this point in our Windows NT network, we have users who have been placed into groups, and we have groups to which we have given rights and permissions (this concept is discussed in Chapter 6, "File Systems," and Chapter 8, "Managing Users in Windows NT"). Now, we need to share resources (the actual point of a network, after all) and give the proper people access to those resources. Plus, we need to deny access to users who should not receive those resources. The goal is to make sure that Jane in Engineering and John in Accounting each have access to the files and other resources they need to do their respective jobs. If we set the network up correctly, Jane and John would never have to leave their desks—except to get some coffee and answer nature's call. This idea sounds pretty straightforward, but several different ways exist to organize a network in NT—and thus several different ways to set up sharing and security.

On the most basic level, NT enables machines to be servers, clients, or both. In a client/server network setup, servers share resources, and clients access resources. In a peer-to-peer network, machines can both share and access resources. (See Chapter 2, "Installing Windows NT," for more discussion about client/server and peer-to-peer network operating systems.) NT muddies these distinctions.

In an NT network, we group machines—clients and servers—into workgroups, or domains. A *workgroup* is a loosely associated group of computers that shares a common name called the "workgroup name." This name has no function, other than to organize how other machines on the network visualize the network. In a workgroup, NT Servers and NT Workstation machines can coexist with Windows 95 and 98 clients, with each machine equal to all the others—optionally acting as both servers and workstations. A workgroup is simply a peer-to-peer network.

In a workgroup, users log in locally and then try to access resources on the other machines. Each machine has a list of all the users (and their passwords) who can access that particular machine. Users must know the password(s) for every single machine they wish to access. In a bigger network, such a scheme is called *share-level access control* and creates chaos for users and administrators.

A domain is a group of Microsoft clients and servers that share a common security database, called the Domain SAM. The Domain SAM is stored on a special NT Server called a *Domain Controller*. In that database, each user will have an account that identifies them to all machines within the domain. Because every computer in the domain can distinguish User A from User B, the users only have to remember the password for their user account, not a password for each resource on the network that they access. This scheme—called *user-level access control*—makes sense for bigger networks.

To share and access resources in NT, we have to understand six ideas. First, we need some way to refer to machines that have resources we want. The Universal Naming Convention determines how we say, "Hey, Server Zed, give me a file." Second, we need a way to navigate between machines. Browsing enables us to find the machines and resources we need to do our jobs. Third, we need to share resources. Fourth, we need to access resources. The procedures for sharing and accessing—literally only a mouse click or two—are the same for both workgroups and domains. Fifth, we need to provide security for the resources on the servers. The security tools and techniques differ among stand-alone machines, workgroups, and domains, with domains providing much greater flexibility and strength of security. Finally, once we master all the sharing, accessing, and securing of resources in a single machine, workgroup, and domain, we need to delve deeply into bigger network issues and work with multiple domains. This last section requires mastery of such arcane terms as trust relationships and Domain Models. Getting Jane and John to spend their time working, rather than wandering over to the server with a floppy disk, takes quite a bit of work on our end.

Universal Naming Convention

For users to access resources on other machines in a network, they must have some consistent way to refer to these other machines. While a user will find it easy to say, "Hey, save that on Bob's machine," or, "Put that file on the server," computers require more precision. The *Universal Naming Convention* (UNC) provides that precision.

UNC defines a simple set of rules for naming network resources. UNC names can refer to a computer, a share, a subdirectory of a share, or a file. A *share* is a directory on a server shared by that server under a particular name. A server named KNIGHT, for example, might share a directory called `c:\DATA\SALES` as SALES. UNC names use the format `\\computer name\share name\subdirectory\file name`. Let's look at some examples.

- The server named SQUIRE would have the UNC name `\\SQUIRE`.

- To refer to a share on the server called PROJECTS, Jane would type the UNC path name `\\SQUIRE\PROJECTS`.

- Assuming that the PROJECTS share refers to a subdirectory called `D:\PROJ`, to refer to a file stored on the server as `D:\PROJ\STATUS.DOC`, John would type the UNC path name `\\SQUIRE\PROJECTS\STATUS.DOC`.

- A file stored on SQUIRE as `D:\PROJ\COMPLETE\SUMMARY.DOC` would have the UNC path name `\\SQUIRE\PROJECTS\COMPLETE\SUMMARY.DOC`.

NOTE: *In this example, notice that the share name (PROJECTS) and the subdirectory name (`D:\PROJ`) are not the same. While the name of a directory and the name under which the directory is shared will often be the same, NT does not require them to be the same.*

Browsing

When you look in the Network Neighborhood and see a list of servers available to you on your network, you are taking advantage of the browsing function of either Windows 95 or Windows NT. The "browse list" you see contains all of the machines on the network that your machine currently knows. Windows machines generate this list of servers, called the *browse list*, by listening for browser announcements. Such announcements could theoretically come from all servers at regular intervals, but that would waste network bandwidth. Microsoft uses instead a single, elected "Browse Master" machine to maintain the list of available servers. Let's look at each stage of the process.

Browser Announcements

One can readily imagine the first network design team brainstorming ideas and deciding that it would be cool—and useful—if users could "browse" the network to see a list of servers and their resources. The inevitable follow-up question must have been, "How do we make that happen?"

Each server on the network could periodically "announce" its presence, broadcasting a message that said, "Hi, I'm a server, my name is _____, and I am sharing the following resources:", then each machine could listen to these broadcasts and maintain its own list, as in Figure 9–1. In such a scheme, should machines broadcast frequently or infrequently?

With frequent broadcasts, say every 30 seconds or so, a machine joining the network would quickly have a complete list of network servers. Unfortunately, the broadcast traffic would flood the network, making it difficult to get real work done, as shown in Figure 9–2.

Infrequent broadcasts, on the other hand, where servers instead announce themselves every 10 minutes, would reduce the traffic to a more manageable level—but this idea causes a new problem. A machine coming onto the network might not "see" some of the servers in the network for as long as 10 minutes, assuming the machine joined the network right after the last announcement. People could still access the new machine as long as they knew its name (the "Find Computer" option on the Start menu in Windows 95, 98, and NT, for example, enables this function). Most users, however, would not even know the new server was online. Microsoft networks solve the frequency dilemma through use of a "Browse Master."

■■ ■■ ■■ ■■
Figure 9–1
PC making a browser
announcement

■ ■■ ■■ ■■
Figure 9–2
Network flooded
with browser
announcements

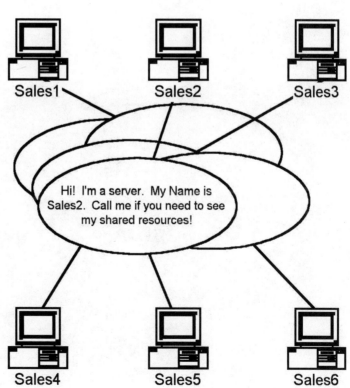

Browse Masters

Microsoft's "Browse Master" in 95, 98, and NT provides a compromise solution that avoids both excessively frequent broadcasts that bog down a network and infrequent broadcasts that delay access to newly online servers. A *Browse Master* is a machine on the network that maintains a list of the available servers on the network. Instead of having each machine maintain its own list of available resources, the Browse Master listens to the network for server announcements. Each time a server boots into the network, the server sends out a special broadcast to any Browse Masters on the network and says, "I'm a server, and here are my resources." The Browse Master adds that information to the master browse list.

When a client machine logs into the network, the machine sends out a message that says, "Hey, Browse Master, send me a list of the servers." The Browse Master sends back the list, and everybody is happy. Clients receive a complete list of available resources, and servers announce their presence only once every 12 minutes or so. See Figure 9–3.

Figure 9–3
Browse Master returning a browse list to an MS client

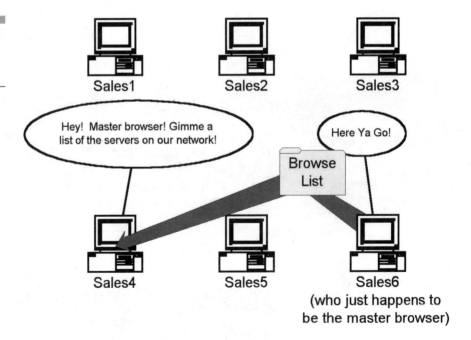

NOTE: *Microsoft actually requires the servers to announce their presence on a set schedule. A server must announce itself at least once every 12 minutes.*

The Browse Master system provides a good balance, keeping an accurate browse list without flooding the network with traffic. Unfortunately, Microsoft made the Browse Master system automatic. Instead of forcing the network administrator to select a machine as the Browse Master, Microsoft networks use *browser elections*.

Browser Elections

When a machine boots up, the machine sends out a broadcast that says, "If there is a Browse Master that can hear me, please send me a list of available resources." If no master browser responds back, as illustrated in Figure 9–4, the user receives the message, "Unable to Browse the Network." The machine, unable to find a Browse Master, sends out an "election packet," which broadcasts to the network a message that says, "I can't find a Browse Master. I'll become the new Browse Master, unless there is someone out there with a higher priority to do the job." Who has a higher priority? The first criterion is the OS. Windows NT servers always have

Figure 9–4
A PC cannot find the master browser.

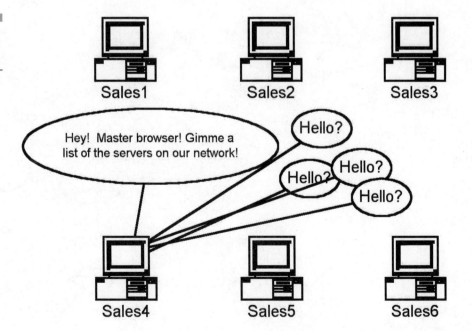

a higher priority to become master browsers than Windows 3.X or Windows 95 machines (which have equal priority). If there are multiple NT machines, then the more recent OS version wins. A Windows NT 4.0 machine, therefore, has a higher priority than a Windows NT 3.51 machine. If there are multiple Windows NT 4.0 machines, then a primary domain controller has priority over all other machines on the network. If the network has multiple machines with equal priority, then the machine that has been running on the network the longest has priority.

Once the servers elect a new master browser, that browser builds up its own list of available resources. Each client will be able to browse the network again. Notice that the end user does not have to do anything. The server machines decide themselves who will be the master browser. The problem with this system is that elections generate a lot of unnecessary traffic—called "broadcast storms"—on the network.

BROADCAST STORMS AND ELECTIONS The broadcast storms caused by these browser elections can cause significant "traffic jams" on the network, as shown in Figure 9–5. Every browser-capable machine (by default, every Microsoft machine with "File and Print Sharing for Microsoft Networks") responds to the call for a new master browser. Worse yet, if multiple protocols are installed, separate browser elections can occur for each protocol.

Figure 9–5
Broadcast storm
caused by browsing

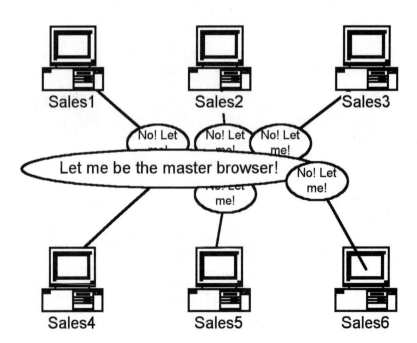

To avoid such a waste of bandwidth, network administrators should try to minimize both the number of elections and the number of machines that participate in those elections. To minimize the impact of browser elections, limit the network to as few protocols as possible. Not only does this action cut down on the number of potential browser elections, limiting the network also cuts down on network traffic in general. When the client machines need to browse the network, they only need to contact a single Browse Master, rather than a Browse Master for each protocol. Further, in larger networks, turn off the Browse Master function of most of the machines. Having 100 machines vying to become Browse Master, after all, can slow a network to a crawl.

The process to disable the Browse Master function differs with each Microsoft OS. To disable the Browse Master function of an NT machine, edit the REGISTRY key **\SYSTEM\CurrentControlSet\Services\Browser\Parameters** and change the value of MaintainServerList from "Yes" to "No." In a Windows 95 or 98 machine, right-click Network Neighborhood and select Properties. Double-click "File and Print Sharing for Microsoft Networks" in the list of installed network components. This action displays the sharing properties, as shown in Figure 9–6. In a Windows for

Figure 9–6
Browse Master
option in
Windows 95

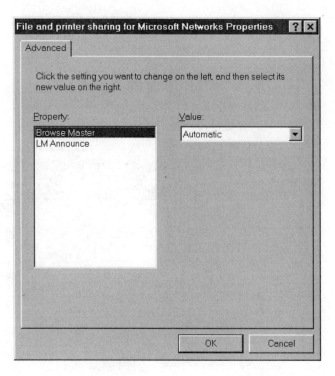

Workgroups machine, edit the **SYSTEM.INI** file and add the following line to the network section:

```
[network]
MaintainServerList=no
```

Allowing fewer machines to act as master browsers minimizes the impact of browser elections when they do occur. In some cases, network administrators decide to turn off all browsing features to minimize traffic. Shared resources still remain available (through their UNC names), and network traffic flows without the burden of a browse election. See the following discussion about accessing shared resources for more discussion of alternatives to browsing.

Browsing in NT provides a useful tool for users, and if properly managed, browsing only marginally impacts network performance. Browsing enables users to surf to shared resources with a mere click or two of the mouse. Let's look now at the process of sharing resources to see both how to share and access resources and how to secure those resources against undesirable access.

Sharing Resources

To share resources in NT literally requires a mouse click or two. Open Windows Explorer, right-click the folder you want to share, and select the sharing option as shown in Figure 9–7. The Sharing tab appears for that folder, as shown in Figure 9–8.

Figure 9–7
Sharing a folder

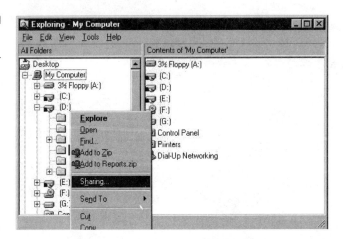

Figure 9–8
Sharing options for a folder

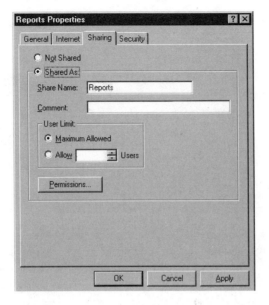

The share name defaults to the name of the subdirectory—in this case, REPORTS. The Comments field can describe the share but is often left blank. In this example, you could add the comment "accounting info" to clarify that these reports belong to the accounting department. The Comments field has no effect on any other networking behavior and does not affect the UNC name of the shared resource.

The User Limit option enables you to limit share access to a specified number of users. In some cases, you will use this feature to limit the amount of server resources devoted to sharing a particular resource. You might, for example, store a large file—such as a training video—on a server. If all 400 employees attempt to access the training video at the same time, the server's performance will plummet. By limiting the number of users who can access the share, you can ration access to the resource and ensure a reasonable level of performance. The User Limit option can also enable you to ensure compliance with the licensing requirements of some pieces of software, limiting access to the number of users for whom your organization has purchased licenses.

Accessing Shared Resources

NT provides three distinctly different ways to access shared resources: browsing, shortcuts, and mapped drives. Each method relies on the UNC name for the shared resource but gives users graphical tools to see those resources. If browsing in the network is disabled, shortcuts and mapped drives enable users to access shared resources—as long as users know the UNC name for that resource.

Browsing

The simplest way to access a file on a shared resource is through the "Network Neighborhood" option within Windows Explorer or the dialog boxes of a Windows 95-, 98-, or NT-compatible program. Windows Explorer puts a graphical front end on the use of UNC names such as **\\NERO\PROJECTS\ WORKING\OUTLINE.DOC**. A 95-, 98-, or NT-compatible program will also accept complete UNC path names in any dialog box that points to a particular file. Figure 9–9, for example, shows that in a Save As dialog box, Microsoft Word will accept the full UNC path name in the File Name field.

Shortcuts

Shortcuts are graphical links to resources, either on the local machine or on another machine somewhere on the network. The UNC path defines

Figure 9–9
Save a file using a UNC name

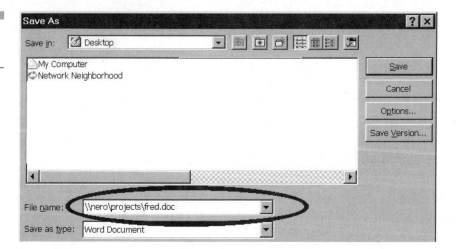

shortcuts for network resources, as shown in Figure 9–10. Shortcuts can refer to servers (**\\SQUIRE**), shares (**\\SQUIRE\PROJECTS**), directories (**\\SQUIRE\PROJECTS\COMPLETE**), or individual files (**\\SQUIRE\PROJECTS\COMPLETE\SUMMARY.TXT**).

Mapped Network Drives

Mapping network drives provides a third way to access shared resources. To map a network drive means to assign a local name, such as D:, to a network share such as **\\SQUIRE\PROJECTS**. Older programs that do not understand UNC path names often require a mapped network drive to work. Many older programs, especially DOS-based programs, have no clue that networks exist. Mapped network drives enable Windows to "lie" to older programs, fooling them into treating a networked resource as a local hard drive. This feature saves us from having to trash or redesign that program. Both NT and Windows 95 will indicate that a drive letter refers to a network share, rather than a local hard drive, by using a different icon, as shown in Figure 9–11.

Figure 9–10
Use a UNC path name for a shortcut

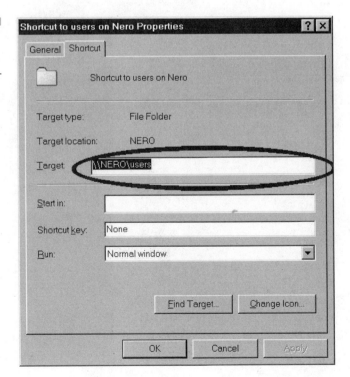

Figure 9–11
Mapped drives in
My Computer

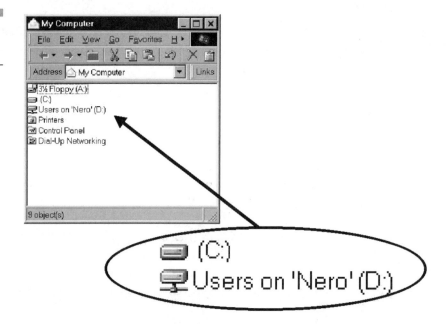

NOTE: *Mapped drives must refer to network shares. Shortcuts can refer to servers, shares, directories, or individual files.*

NT Networking Security

Although the true goal of networking is to share resources, part of the job of an NT administrator is to make sure that people access only the resources that they should access. In other words, administrators must implement network security.

Two sets of permissions and a complex authentication process comprise the bulk of network security in Windows NT. Users log in—locally or remotely—and receive, as part of this authentication process, an "Access Token," which is basically a big stack of ID cards telling who the user is and to which groups the user belongs. When a user attempts to access a resource, NT compares that stack of ID cards against the lists of Share Permissions and/or NTFS Permissions on that resource to determine which level of access—from none at all to total—the user receives for that resource. Administrators need to understand how the permissions applied to resources will affect the various users and groups in NT, both in stand-alone machines and networked machines. Let's look at each piece of the network security puzzle, starting with permissions and then going into authentication and access of resources locally, in a workgroup, and in a domain.

NOTE: *Rights, discussed thoroughly in Chapter 8, "Managing Users in Windows NT" and thus not discussed here, impact network security in two basic ways. Administrators can set the rights on accounts (users and groups) to force a user to log on locally or remotely. The former means that John has to get up and walk over to the server to change things. The latter means that Jane can only log into the machine over the network, which brings all the network security to bear on what she can do.*

Permissions

Two separate sets of permissions—Share and NTFS—determine the availability of resources in NT. Share Permissions apply strictly to networked (not local) resources. NTFS Permissions, in contrast, apply to local and networked resources, as long as the resources reside on a drive formatted with NTFS and not FAT. To access a particular resource on a server, a user must have the proper permissions set at both the Share and NTFS levels.

SHARE PERMISSIONS NT has four Share Permissions: Full Control, Read, Change, and No Access. The permission names accurately describe the level of access granted to a user. Full Control permission to the share **KNIGHT**, in other words, means that Jane can read, write, edit, delete, and play games with that share. Table 9–1 outlines the permissions and their

Table 9–1

Share Permissions revealed

Permission	Users Can . . .
No Access	Do nothing. No Access means users cannot read, edit, delete, or commune with a file or folder.
Read	Read a file or the see the contents of a folder and execute programs
Change	Create new files and folders, and edit or delete existing files and folders. Change permission includes Read permission as well.
Full Control	Do all of the above, plus change file-level (NTFS) permissions and take ownership of the file or folder

meanings. Permissions are stored in the share's ACL. NT enables you to set the type of permission on a share and to specify which users and groups may access that share. Better still, NT does this function in a single screen.

Open up the properties for a particular resource that you want to share, select the Sharing tab, and click the Shared As radio button, just like we did earlier. Click the Permissions button to define permissions for the share and specify which users and groups may access the share. See Figure 9–12 and Figure 9–13.

Share Permissions apply all the way down a directory structure, granting the same level of access to all subfolders and files in the main share. Sharing a subfolder of the main share and giving that new share different permissions than the main share can create some huge holes in security. Users directly accessing the shared subfolder will run into the subfolder's Share Permissions. Users accessing the subfolder share through the main share, on the other hand, will have the level of permission granted by the main share.

Consider the following example. John shares drive D: on Server KNIGHT with the share name of KD, giving Full Control to Everyone. Remembering suddenly that he has files in the folder **D:\JOHNQP** on the server that he would rather not have changed, read, or deleted, he shares the JOHNQP folder as XXX with No Access to Everyone. This action, he mistakenly thinks, will stop anyone from accessing his folder through the network, as illustrated in Figure 9–14.

Figure 9–12
Share Permissions

Figure 9–13
Add Users and
Groups to the ACL

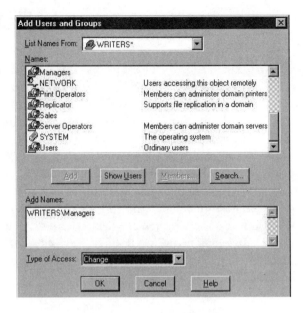

Figure 9–14
Share Permissions on
subfolders

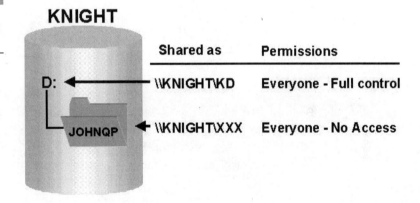

Bob, part of the Everyone group, notices the new shares `\\KNIGHT\KD` and `\\KNIGHT\XXX`. Being curious, he attempts to access the share to John's personal folder, `\\KNIGHT\XXX`, but he is denied due to the No Access permission. Bob then clicks the `\\KNIGHT\KD` share and sees, among other folders, the JOHNQP folder. He clicks the folder, and lo and behold, John's personal files are there for reading, deleting, etc. Share Permissions work only according to how a user accesses that share. By sharing two levels in the directory structure, John created a gaping back door. Most administrators avoid this whole mess by giving all their shares Full

Control, and to implement file and folder security, they turn to the second level of permissions, NTFS.

NTFS PERMISSIONS NTFS Permissions enable an administrator or user to restrict access to resources—shared or otherwise—on drives formatted with NTFS. Each file and folder maintains in its ACL a list of every user and group that is provided access to the file or folder—and all the levels of access available for each user and group. Because NTFS treats users and groups as similar entities, most administrators set permissions only on the group level. This action saves much pulling of hair, gnashing of teeth, and changing individual permissions later in the network's life. An administrator will find it easier to move people in and out of groups than to redo a bunch of permissions in a network.

NTFS Permissions come in six basic varieties called "special permissions," which are grouped together for convenience into several "standard permissions." The special permissions granted to files or folders are the following:

1. Read (R)
2. Write (W)
3. Execute (X)
4. Delete (D)
5. Change Permissions (P)
6. Take Ownership (O)

Administrators rarely assign these individual or special permissions directly to users or groups. The designers of NTFS realized that a user would rarely need to write to—but not read—a file. In NTFS, these special permissions are grouped into sets of permissions called "standard permissions." Instead of assigning individual "special permissions," administrators usually assign a "standard permission" to a user.

Permissions are cumulative. If a user has Read access to a directory as a member of the Domain Users global group and Change access to the same directory as a member of the Accounting global group, the user receives the sum of the special permissions contained in those standard permissions. Read access includes Read (R) and Execute (X), while Change access includes Read (R), Write (W), Execute (X), and Delete (D). The user, therefore, receives RWXD—also known as Change access—to the directory. See Chapter 6, "File Systems," for a much more detailed analysis of NTFS Permissions.

To set NTFS Permissions, right-click a resource and select Properties. Select the Security tab and click Permissions. This action will bring up the File or Directory Permissions dialog box, as shown in Figure 9–15. From this window, you can set the various standard or special permissions for that file or folder.

NOTE: *Windows NT can share files on both FAT and NTFS volumes. Because FAT does not provide any security on its own, the only security present when sharing files on a FAT volume are the permissions set on the share and the rights of a user to access the machine.*

PERMISSION TANGO   When determining the actions a particular user can take on a particular file through the network, the user must pass through two checkpoints: Network security and file security (if accessing a share on an NTFS volume). Share Permissions and NTFS Permissions work independently, but both affect a user's ability to access resources in NT. For example, Jane has Full Control permission to the share **\\SQUIRE\LANCE**, but she has No Access to the folder **D:\SQUIRE\LANCE** set

Figure 9–15
NTFS Permissions

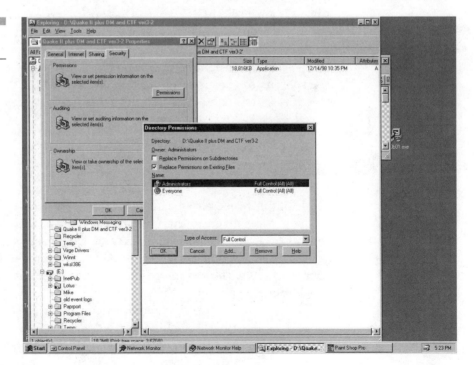

in the NTFS Permissions. When she tries to access LANCE, she receives the dreaded "Access is denied" dialog box. The NTFS permission trumped the share permission. The reverse action might do the same—but only if Jane had no higher access to the host share **SQUIRE**, as discussed earlier. As we layer NTFS Permissions and Share Permissions in an NT world, determining whether a user can access a particular resource can become confusing. To understand how to dance the Permission Tango, we need to understand the authentication process.

Authentication and Access to Resources

When a user logs in to a machine or domain, the user goes through the authentication process. Three pieces define the authentication process: SIDs, SAMs, and Access Tokens. Each user and group account has an SID, a unique number that identifies that user or group to the machine or domain. The SAM database stores the SIDs. When a user logs in, the SAM issues that user an Access Token, which contains all the SIDs for the user and the groups to which the user belongs. The Access Token becomes the key that lets the user succeed or fail when accessing resources.

When a user attempts to access a resource, NT checks the user's Access Token against the ACL of both the share and the file system for that resource. If the user's SIDs are contained in both sets of permissions, the user receives the resource. If either or both sets of permissions deny access, on the other hand, the user is out of luck. This process remains transparent to the user. Bob either gets in when he tries to access a shared resource, or he receives a cruel "Access is denied" dialog box on his screen. Let's look at each stage of this process.

Access Token

The login process creates an *Access Token* for each user, which is a collection of SIDs given to the user at login. When the user logs in (either remotely or locally) with a valid username and password, the NT machine consults the SAM and constructs an Access Token. The Access Token contains the SIDs of the user account and the SIDs of any group to which the user belongs, as shown in Figure 9–16.

With the Access Token in hand, the user can now identify himself to the objects on the NT machine (such as NTFS files or network shares) that use ACLs. A user named John Smith, for example, logs in to an NT

Figure 9–16
Generic Access Token

The Access Token

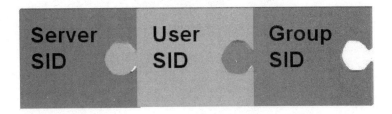

Figure 9–17
John Smith's Access
Token

**John Smith's Access Token
after logging in to NERO**

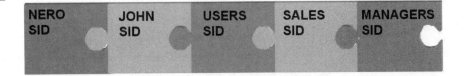

Server named NERO with the user account JOHN. JOHN belongs to the USERS, SALES, and MANAGERS groups. John's Access Token contains the SIDs of the user account JOHN, the groups USERS, SALES, and MANAGERS, and the computer NERO. When John tries to access any object on NERO, the objects know that he logged in to NERO and that NERO believes him to be the user JOHN, who is a member of the groups USERS, SALES and MANAGERS. As long as the object trusts NERO to give out valid Access Tokens, users now have a way to prove their identities to the objects. Figure 9–17 shows John Smith's Access Token.

Each NT object maintains its own ACL, which contains the SIDs of each user and group that can access the object. Use Windows Explorer to view the file or folder properties, which show the ACL of an NTFS object.

NOTE: *For a more detailed look at NTFS, see Chapter 6, "File Systems."*

Figure 9–18 shows the ACL for the NTFS directory REPORTS. While nowhere on the screen do the words "Access Control List" appear, the list of names under the heading "Name:" corresponds to the various SIDs

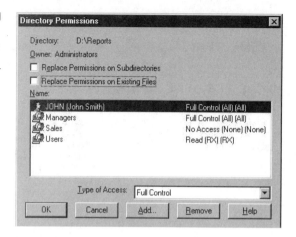

Figure 9–18
Directory permissions
for **D:\REPORTS**

contained in the directory's ACL. In this case, assume that John Smith logs in and attempts to access the REPORTS directory. Because the REPORTS directory is an NTFS object, the system will compare the Access Token that John Smith received at logon to the SIDs in its ACL. In this case, John would receive No Access, because the No Access permission has been assigned to the group SALES, and the SID for SALES is part of the Access Token that John received when he logged on.

Once you understand the nature of the Access Token, the behavior of Windows NT makes more sense. Assume that John Smith has been transferred to the marketing department. John's user account, JOHN, should be removed from the SALES group and added to the MARKETING group. After using User Manager for Domains to make that change, Jane, the administrator, contacts John and discovers that he can still access everything that a member of SALES can access—but he cannot access the files that he should have access to as a member of MARKETING. Why? John still has the old Access Token. Because NT assigns the Access Token at logon, John will not receive a new Access Token until he logs off and then logs on again.

Applying Access Schemes in NT Environments

Now that we understand the processes of sharing, permissions, authentication, and accessing of resources, let's turn to five different sets of NT environments and apply this information. Administrators need to understand how the security process works with accounts—users, local groups, and global groups—on a local machine and on machines networked without a domain, within a domain, and among multiple domains.

Groups in NT

Each level of security and accessing resources has added complexity to our understanding of NT. Groups make up the last element to throw into the mix, so we will review groups briefly here and then see how they affect —or are affected by—the different NT environments.

NOTE: *Chapter 8, "Managing Users in Windows NT," covers groups and User Manager—the tool that creates users and groups and assigns users to specific groups—in detail.*

NT contains two types of groups: Local groups and global groups. Administrators create local groups on all NT systems—workstations, member servers, and domain controllers—to give access to resources. Administrators create global groups, in contrast, to organize users.

Global groups are all about users. Administrators place users with similar needs and responsibilities into a global group. With 40 accountants in an organization, for example, an administrator should create an ACCOUNTANTS global group and place each accountant's user account in that group.

Local groups, on the other hand, are all about resources. Administrators can create an ACCOUNTING_PRINTER local group, for example, to give administrative permissions to the special accounting printer. The administrator would then place the ACCOUNTING_PRINTER local group in the ACL for the printer. The ACCOUNTANTS global group would then become a member of the ACCOUNTING_PRINTER local group. In addition, most administrators would also want to place the ADMINISTRATORS global group in the ACCOUNTING_PRINTER group, which ensures that they have the appropriate rights to this resource.

While NT enables you to add global groups and accounts directly to the ACL of any object (files, printers, etc.) in the domain, Microsoft encourages you to put the local group between your global groups and individual resources.

Local groups exist in the individual SAM database of each NT Server and Workstation in the domain. For machines that are not part of a domain, this local group is the only level available. Administrators will place users on the local workstation or server directly into the local group and give access rights to printers, files, or other resources to those groups. In a domain, however, the situation is a little more complex. Global groups exist in the Domain SAM. Administrators will therefore place the domain users into the global groups. Administrators of the workstations and servers that are members of a domain can add the domain's global groups directly into the local groups, as shown in Figure 9–19.

To give Jane, a member of the ENGINEERS global group, access to local resources on a domain member machine, you could create an individual account for her on that machine. When she wants to access those local resources, she logs in and conducts her business. When she needs access to another machine's resources, however, you will have to create an account for her again. What a waste of time for both you and Jane. You could instead add Jane's global user account into the local group that has access to the resources that she needs. That way, Jane could log in to the domain and have access to those resources without having to log in again. What if you wanted all the engineers, however, not just Jane, to have access to those local resources? Adding each one individually does not make sense. Instead, put the whole ENGINEERS global group into that local group. All the engineers would have access to those local resources as soon as they logged in to the domain. This layering of global groups into local groups provides an efficient way to organize resources and users in a domain.

Figure 9–19

Adding a Global group into a Local group

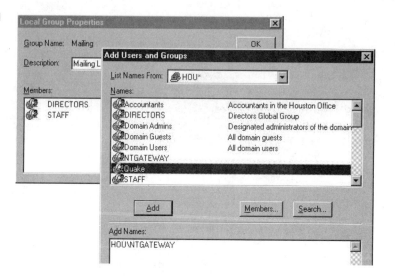

NOTE: *Memorize the following NT mantra before taking any of the NT tests:*

Users go into global groups,

Global groups go into local groups,

And local groups receive rights and permissions.

This seemingly strange way of assigning rights gives an information technology department in a large organization the capacity to delegate responsibility. The administrator in charge of the user accounts does not need to concern herself with every resource on the domain. Instead, she makes sure that every user belongs to the global groups that are appropriate to their job responsibilities. Typical global groups would include ACCOUNTANTS, SALES, MARKETING, SUPERVISORS, etc. The administrator in charge of the users would leave assigning rights and permissions to the administrators of each individual server.

The individual member server's administrator would be in charge of creating local groups on that server. Each local group would typically correspond to a common set of resources. A server might contain, for example, several directories that contain engineering databases. The local administrator would create a local group called ENGINEERING and put the global group ENGINEERS in that local group. After assigning the appropriate permissions to the local group ENGINEERING for the various engineering related files and directories, members of the global group ENGINEERS could access those files. Sounds like a bunch of work, right? Why go to all this trouble when you could have assigned permissions directly to the global group ENGINEERS? This action enables you to divide tasks between the two administrators. The local administrator does not have to concern herself with who belongs in which global groups; rather, she trusts the administrator of the domain user accounts to assign people to the appropriate groups based on their job functions. Likewise, the administrator of the domain user accounts does not concern herself with the resources on every member server; instead, she relies on the administrator of each server to give every global group the appropriate access to resources.

Accessing Resources Locally

NTFS Permissions determine access to local resources. The user must have the right to log on to that local machine, but once the user is logged on, only NTFS Permissions apply. Share Permissions apply to resources accessed remotely, not locally. Every NTFS file and folder possesses its own ACL. NTFS handles security based on individual ACLs, file-by-file, folder-by-folder. Local machines contain only user accounts and/or local groups. Administrators can grant permissions to the NTFS resources to each user account, but more often—in this domain-challenged environment—they would grant permissions to local groups and then put users into those groups.

Whenever a user attempts to access an NTFS file, the file compares the Access Token of the user (which contains the user's SID and the SIDs of any groups to which the user belongs) to its own ACL and grants the user the appropriate level of access. If the user's Access Token contains several SIDs that have access to the file, NTFS grants the user the highest level of access.

Bill's user account, BILLM, is part of both the SECURITY and USERS groups. For a file called **PHONE.DOC**, the SECURITY group has Full Control, and the Users group has Read access. When Bill tries to access the **PHONE.DOC** file, the file compares the SIDs in his Access Token to its ACL and determines that Bill is a member of both SECURITY and USERS. Bill will receive Full Control access to the file **PHONE.DOC**, because NTFS grants him the sum of the permissions to which he is entitled. When combining the NTFS Permissions that a user receives from various sources, NTFS always grants the user the highest level of access to which he or she is entitled.

NOTE: *One exception exists, however. The No Access permission overrides all other permissions. If Bill's user account, BILLM, or any group to which he belongs, had been "granted" the No Access permission, he would have been denied access to the file. No Access trumps all the other permissions.*

When accessing files and folders locally, only the NTFS Permissions apply. Once you access files and folders through the network, the dance of NTFS and Share Permissions begins.

Accessing Resources Remotely without Domains

Accessing resources remotely brings both NTFS and Share Permissions into play. As long as the resources reside on NTFS-formatted machines, users—or the groups to which they belong—must have the correct permissions to access a resource. Without a domain, the user must also have an account on the remote machine. That account could then also go into various local groups on the remote machine. To access resources remotely requires the user to have Share permission as well. Without both sets of permissions, the user cannot access the remote resource. Each set of permissions acts like a door. A user shows the Share doorman his Access Token, and the doorman checks the ACL for the level of access that user has. The user then passes through the door with the permission to do whatever was set in the ACL. The NTFS doorman goes through the same process but cannot grant the user anything more than the user already has. If the Share door lets only Read permission through, the NTFS doorman cannot grant Write permission. The reverse is also true.

Jane needs to add some data to the `c:\ENGINEERING\PROJECTS` folder stored on Bill's machine. For Jane to access that data remotely, Bill needs to do several things. First, Bill needs to grant Jane access to the local machine, so he creates a user account called JANE. Bill then shares the project folder, which then receives the UNC name of `\\BILL\PROJECTS`. He sets the Share permission to Full Control for the user account JANE. Bill had previously set the NTFS Permissions for the projects folder to Read access for Everyone, however, because he did not want someone to accidentally delete anything important. What happens when Jane browses over and tries to write a file to the PROJECTS folder? At the Share level, she has no problem getting in and doing anything at all. At the NTFS level, on the other hand, she can only Read and Execute—not Write. As an automatic member of the Everyone group, Jane has Read access according to the NTFS Permissions, but nothing else. She is out of luck until Bill changes the NTFS Permissions, as illustrated in Figure 9–20. The reverse would also be true. If Jane's access to the share is limited to Read, even if the NTFS Permissions were set higher, Jane would only have Read access.

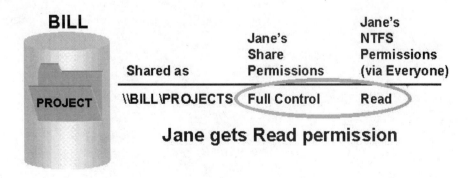

Figure 9–20
Jane cannot write, because Bill blew the permissions.

Accessing Resources Remotely within a Domain

Domains enable users to log in once and then access resources all over the domain without logging in again. Likewise, administrators do not need to create accounts for users on every single machine. Instead, administrators can create domain-level user accounts (called *global accounts*) that are stored on a central database, the Domain SAM. They can assign those accounts to global groups. Local administrators can then assign global groups to their local groups, which contain all the resources. Jane logs into the domain and can access shared resources on every machine within the domain. Life is sweet. NTFS and Share Permissions still apply to every resource, but the login process is simplified. Let's look first at the Domain Controllers and then at what happens when users access Domain Controllers, Member Servers, and Workstations within an NT domain.

DOMAIN CONTROLLERS   In a domain, one NT Server is designated to serve as the PDC. The PDC makes its SAM database available to other machines when they join the domain. When other NT Server and NT Workstation machines become members of the domain, they gain the capacity to refer to Security IDs contained in the PDC's SAM. When assigning permissions to objects (files, printers, and shares) on the machines that have joined the domain, the administrator can grant permissions to users whose user accounts exist in the Domain SAM database, stored on the PDC. In addition, users can now log into the domain, obtaining a single Access Token from the domain controller. That Access Token is valid throughout the domain. In essence, the machines in the domain trust that the domain controller will only give out valid Access Tokens.

What if the PDC fails? NT enables you to designate additional NT Servers to serve as BDCs. The BDCs hold an exact duplicate of the PDC's Security Accounts Manager database, enabling the BDC to authenticate users and hand out Access Tokens. As we will see later, machines do not log in to the PDC; rather, they log in to the domain. Whether a PDC or a BDC services the logon request is irrelevant to the user logging in, because they use identical SAM databases to create their Access Tokens.

NOTE: *When installing BDCs, the PC must have a useable network connection to the PDC during installation, or the installation will fail. Part of the install process for a BDC requires copying the Domain SAM. See Chapter 2, "Installing Windows NT," for more detail on installing NT.*

Because PDCs and BDCs are interchangeable from the point of view of the member servers and workstations, the member server or workstation never needs to know the names of the domain controllers. When they need to talk to the domain controller, they will send out a broadcast saying, "Hey, I need to talk to a domain controller for the SALES domain." For more information about the use of broadcasts for this purpose and other purposes, see the discussion of NetBIOS names in Chapter 10, "Networking Protocols."

NOTE: *Terminology note:*

PDCs are Primary Domain Controllers.

BDCs are Backup Domain Controllers.

Member Servers are servers that have joined the domain.

Member Workstations are workstations that have joined the domain.

JOINING A DOMAIN While BDCs must be connected to the network, NT machines that simply want to join a domain do not have to be physically connected at installation. To join a domain, bring up the Network Control Panel applet and select the Identification tab, as shown in Figure 9–21.

Figure 9–21
Network
Identification Tab

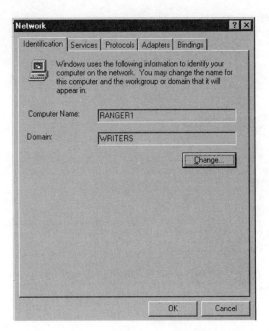

Click the Change button, and the screen shown in Figure 9–22 appears.

Select the radio button for Domain under the "Member of . . . " section, and type the name of the domain. Warning! A common mistake here is to type the name of the PDC instead of the name of the domain. A workstation or server in a domain does not care about the names of the domain controllers; rather, the workstation or server simply needs to know the name of the domain.

When adding an NT machine to the domain, the checkbox for Create a Computer Account on the Domain will be available. NT machines joining a domain must have a computer account. Creating a computer account adds the SID of the machine joining the domain to the domain's SAM database. From that point forward, the domain controllers can identify that machine. The SID of each machine can be used for a variety of security and auditing features. For example, users can be restricted to logging in from specific machines, as discussed in Chapter 8, "Managing Users in Windows NT."

NOTE: *Windows 95 machines do not have computer accounts or SIDs. The only way for NT to distinguish one Windows 95 machine from another is by its name. The capacity to be identified by computer accounts and to have the accompanying level of security is one advantage of Windows NT Workstation over Windows 95 in a domain environment.*

Figure 9–22

Changing domains

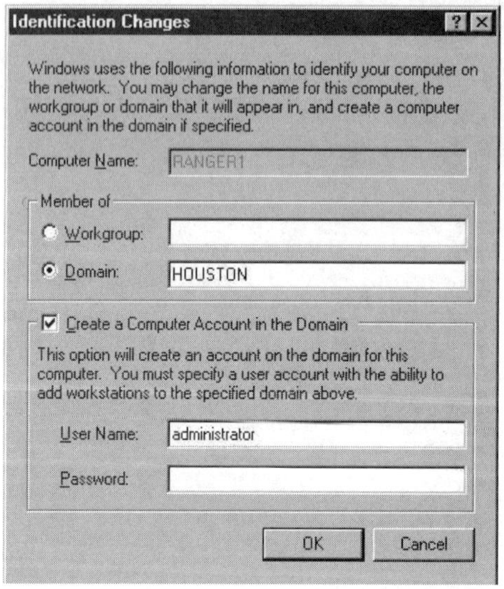

> **Identification Changes**   ? ✕
>
> Windows uses the following information to identify your computer on the network. You may change the name for this computer, the workgroup or domain that it will appear in, and create a computer account in the domain if specified.
>
> Computer **N**ame: [RANGER1   ]
>
> ┌ Member of ─────────────────────────────────
> │ ○ **W**orkgroup: [   ]
> │
> │ ◉ **D**omain: [HOUSTON   ]
> └──
>
> ┌ ☑ **C**reate a Computer Account in the Domain ───
> │ This option will create an account on the domain for this
> │ computer. You must specify a user account with the ability to
> │ add workstations to the specified domain above.
> │
> │   **U**ser Name: [administrator   ]
> │
> │   **P**assword: [   ]
> └──
>
>   [OK   ]   [Cancel]

To create a computer account, you must enter a user account and password with the authority to do so. By default, the Domain Administrators and Account Operators groups can add computer accounts to the domain. (Additional users can be granted that right with User Manager for Domains.)

ACCESSING SHARED RESOURCES ON A DOMAIN CONTROLLER   Accessing resources on a domain controller amounts to little more than logging in to the domain and browsing the shared resources. NTFS and Share Permissions still apply, doing their tango with great gusto. Most commonly, the administrator has given permissions for local resources to local groups, created users, placed those users into global groups, and then put those global groups into the local groups.

When a user logs in to the domain, the PDC checks the Domain SAM and gives the user an Access Token that contains the SIDs for the user's global account, as well as for any global groups or local groups to which the user belongs. When a user accesses a share on the PDC, the machine checks the Share ACL against the Access Token and then the NTFS ACL against the Access Token. If the user's Access Token contains local and/or global groups that have the necessary permissions assigned in the ACLs, the user can access resources.

Arturo, who recently switched from sales to accounting, wants to access the **D:\TAXES** folder on the PDC (named NERO). Arturo's user account, ARTUROO, is a member of the global groups SALESPEOPLE and ACCOUNTANTS. The Domain Administrator has shared the **D:\TAXES** folder as **\\NERO\TAXES**, granting Read permission on the Share for the local group SALES and Full Control permission on the Share for the local group ACCOUNTS. The NTFS Permissions, however, grant No Access to the local group SALES and Full Control to the ACCOUNTS local group. The SALESPEOPLE global group is a member of the SALES local group, whereas the ACCOUNTANTS global group is a member of the ACCOUNTS local group, as shown in Figure 9–23. What happens when Arturo tries to access that TAXES database?

When Arturo first logged into the domain, the PDC issued an Access Token identifying him as ARTUROO, member of SALESPEOPLE and ACCOUNTANTS, and in turn issued a token identifying him as a member of SALES and ACCOUNTS. Armed with this nice, shiny set of ID badges, Arturo browses to the share **\\NERO\TAXES**. At the Share level, Arturo readily passes through—maintaining the highest-level access of his group membership (in this case, Full Control). When he hits the NTFS level, on the other hand, the file system checks his Access Token against the folder's ACL and discovers that Arturo is a member of the dreaded

Figure 9–23
Arturo and the share

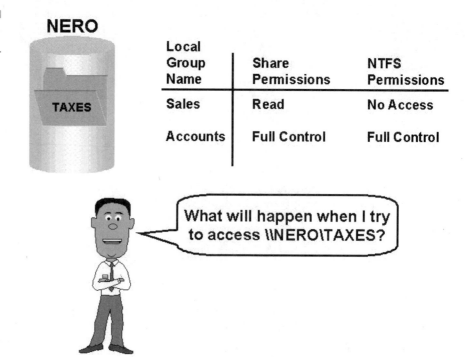

Local Group Name	Share Permissions	NTFS Permissions
Sales	Read	No Access
Accounts	Full Control	Full Control

SALES local group. Regardless of the fact that as a member of the ACCOUNTS local group (via the ACCOUNTANTS global group) he has Full Control, the No Access for SALES stops him cold. Figure 9–24 shows NTFS Permissions stopping Arturo from accessing the file.

Changing permissions on the share or at the file level or changing group affiliations will completely change the outcome of the scenario. To give Arturo access to the **\\NERO\TAXES** share, the Domain Administrator must remove Arturo from the SALESPEOPLE global group, remove the SALESPEOPLE global group from the SALES local group, or change the NTFS permission for SALES to anything but No Access. Conversely, if the administrator set the NTFS Permissions so that ACCOUNTS and SALES had Full Control access to the database but made the Share Permissions Read access for both ACCOUNTS and SALES, Arturo would have only Read access to the database. Each set of permissions can only narrow, not expand, levels of access.

ACCESSING SHARED RESOURCES ON A MEMBER SERVER OR WORKSTATION Accessing shared resources on a member server or workstation in a domain adds a layer of behind-the-scenes complexity to the process, although that layer is never visible to the user. When a user

Figure 9–24
Arturo stopped at the NTFS level

accesses a resource on a non-domain controller machine that is a member of a domain, the machine checks the user's Access Token and issues a new Access Token based on the user's memberships in the local SAM. (Technically, the member server issues a separate badge, called a UID, but nobody cares outside of programmer land.) The process of logging in to the member server or workstation occurs without user interaction.

Arturo wants to access the **D:\TAXES** database, as in the earlier example. But this time, the database is stored on a member server (CLAUDIUS) and not on a domain controller. With permissions exactly as the initial example, the result of Arturo clicking the share **\\CLAUDIUS\TAXES** is the same: No Access. The underlying process, however, is not the same.

When Arturo logs into the domain, the domain controller consults the Domain SAM and issues an Access Token containing the user account ARTUROO, the global groups SALESPEOPLE and ACCOUNTANTS, and the local groups for the domain controllers. When Arturo browses over to the member server CLAUDIUS, CLAUDIUS consults its SAM to see whether Arturo's accounts (his global account and his global groups) belong to any local groups. In this case, CLAUDIUS appends the SIDs for the local groups SALES and ACCOUNTS to Arturo's Access Token. That Access Token then is compared to the Share ACL for **\\CLAUDIUS\TAXES** and the NTFS ACL for **D:\TAXES**. Because the local administrator had set No Access permission at the NTFS level for the SALES local group, Arturo once again is blocked. See Figure 9–25.

Figure 9–25
No Access is always
followed.

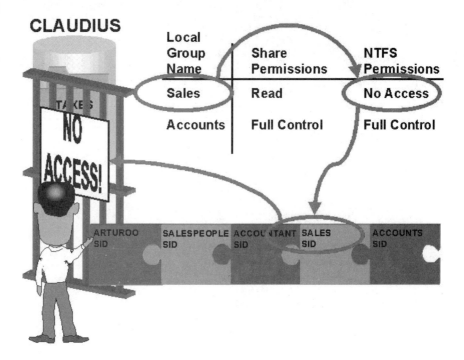

Multiple Domains

Accessing resources across domains requires resolution of all the issues within each domain. Administrators must set Share and NTFS Permissions for resources, place users into global groups and global groups into local groups, and assign permissions for resources to the local groups. Also, establishment of trust relationships between the domains must occur. Administrators also need to implement a model for a multi-domain environment that enhances the efficiency of the network. Once administrators set up the domains properly, users can open Network Neighborhood, browse happily to machines in the other domain(s), and while away the hours accessing resources. Let's look first at some reasons to have multiple domains. Then, we will examine trust relationships. Finally, we will analyze four different domain models.

Multiple domains enable organizations to split up their networks into two or more coherent pieces. This feature enables large organizations to reduce each domain to manageable sizes and lets all organizations decentralize their networks.

Some organizations require more than one domain, because they have so many users, groups, and computers that their domain database becomes unmanageably large. No rule defines the maximum size for a domain, but Microsoft recommends that the Domain SAM remains smaller than 40MB. Let's look at the numbers to determine the size of a Domain SAM. Every user account requires 1K; every group account requires 4K; and every computer account requires 0.5K. A domain with 28,000 user accounts, 24,000 computer accounts, and 300 group accounts, for example, would result in a Domain SAM of 39.7MB, which is just under the suggested limit, as shown in Table 9–2. Only the largest organizations need to worry about the Domain SAM database growing too large.

More commonly, organizations divide their networks into multiple domains for organizational purposes. For medium and large organizations, a single domain that contains all machines becomes cumbersome. One group of administrators has to handle all administrative tasks in a single domain environment. For a company that spans multiple cities, for example, having a single administrative staff for all network functions is impractical. Large organizations also tend to have individual departments that prefer to maintain some degree of control over their own resources. Enabling each department to have its own domain gives the departments that control.

If an organization has multiple domains for whatever reason, users will still want to access resources throughout the entire network. Administrators will not, however, want to deal with the headaches of maintaining separate user accounts on each domain for each user. Ideally, a user should log in once and immediately have access to all of his or her resources, regardless of the domain where the resources reside. To deal with the need for a single login with multiple domains, Microsoft uses trust relationships.

Table 9–2

SAM database size

Number of Accounts	Size of Accounts	Total Addition to SAM Database
28,000 User Accounts	1K each	28,000K = 27.3MB
23,000 Computer Accounts	0.5K each	12,000K = 11.2MB
300 Group Accounts	4K each	1200K = 1.2MB
Total size of SAM database:	39.7MB	

TRUST RELATIONSHIPS   Trust relationships enable users in one domain to access resources in another domain. A *trust relationship* is a special, one-way connection between two domains, enabling one domain to place a second domain's user and global group accounts in the first domain's ACLs. As a one-way connection, the trust only gives access in a single direction. Two trust relationships must exist for both parties to have access to each other's resources.

The Bayland Widget Company has offices in Houston and Baltimore. To match the two locations, the MIS department for BWC created two domains: an HOU domain and a BAL domain, as shown in Figure 9–26.

The Baltimore office handles only retail sales. The Houston office takes care of all the company's accounting and managerial functions. The global group ACCOUNTING in the HOU domain needs access to the sales figures stored on a server in the BAL domain. No user in the BAL domain needs access to the HOU domain. Without a trust relationship, all of the accountants in the Houston office would need two user accounts: one in HOU, and one in BAL. Both users and administrators dislike multiple user accounts for individual people, because users must remember mul-

Figure 9–26
HOU and BAL
domains

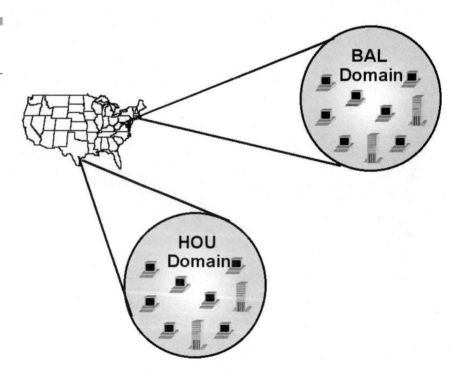

tiple user account names and passwords—and the already-overworked
MIS department has to work harder.

To avoid creating multiple accounts for each user, the MIS department
creates a trust relationship that states that BAL trusts HOU, as shown in
Figure 9–27. This relationship makes BAL the *trusting domain* and HOU
the *trusted domain*. Administrators in the trusting domain can assign
rights and permissions to users in the trusted domain. Notice that the
administrators *can* assign rights and permissions—but they do not have to
assign them. Establishing the trust relationship does not automatically
assign any rights or permissions to users in the trusted domain. Here,
"trust" means that the domain controllers in the trusting domain "trust" the
domain controllers in the trusted domain to give out Access Tokens. Now,
machines in the trusting domain will accept Access Tokens that contain
either their own domain SID or Access Tokens that contain the SID of the
trusted domain. The easy way to remember how the relationship works is
to memorize this mantra: *I trust you, so you can use my stuff.*

Figure 9–27
BAL trusts HOU.

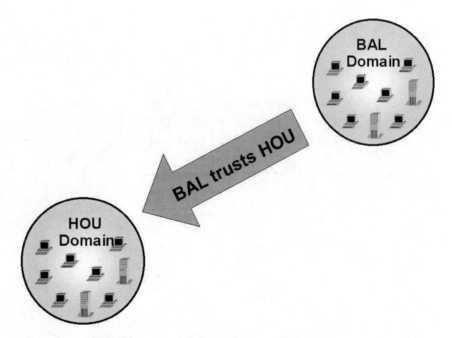

**The BAL domain trusts the HOU domain, allowing servers
the BAL domain to grant rights and permissions
to users in the HOU domain.**

Trust relationships work only in a single direction, not both ways. BAL trusts HOU; therefore, HOU can access BAL's stuff. BAL cannot access HOU's stuff. Creating reciprocal access requires two trust relationships.

NOTE: *Memorize the trust relationship Mantra: I trust you, so you can use my stuff.*

TERMINOLOGY ALERT   The evil terminology of trust relationships can quickly warp the minds of small animals. Read terms carefully to understand the direction of the trust. The *trusted domain* contains users who need to access resources in the *trusting domain*. The *trusting domain* trusts users from the *trusted domain* to have access to the *trusting domain's* resources. Many questions on the Server and Enterprise exams will require you to be clear on the distinction. Figure 9–28 illustrates the trust relationship.

CREATING A TRUST RELATIONSHIP   Creating a trust relationship requires that you first set up the trusted domain and then set up the trusting domain. Trying this action in reverse order generates nothing but an error message.

Figure 9–28
Trusted and trusting
domains

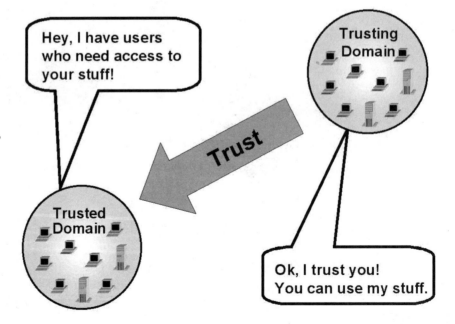

SETTING UP THE TRUSTED DOMAIN To create the trust relationship between BAL and HOU, configure the HOU domain as the trusted domain. In User Manager for Domains, select the Policies menu, as shown in Figure 9–29. Selecting Trust Relationships displays the Trust Relationships dialog box, as shown in Figure 9–30. This dialog box contains two areas: The Trusted Domains on top and the Trusting Domains below. Each area has an Add button. Click the lower Add button to bring up the Add Trusting Domain dialog box, as shown in Figure 9–31. Here you can inform HOU, the trusted machine, of the domains that HOU can access.

Figure 9–29
Policies Menu, trust
relationships

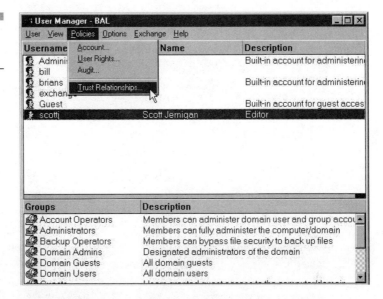

Figure 9–30
Create a trust
relationship

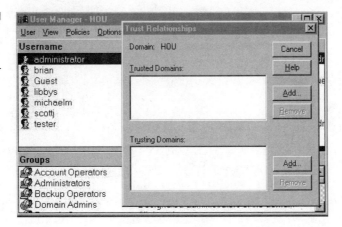

Figure 9–31
Add a trusting
domain

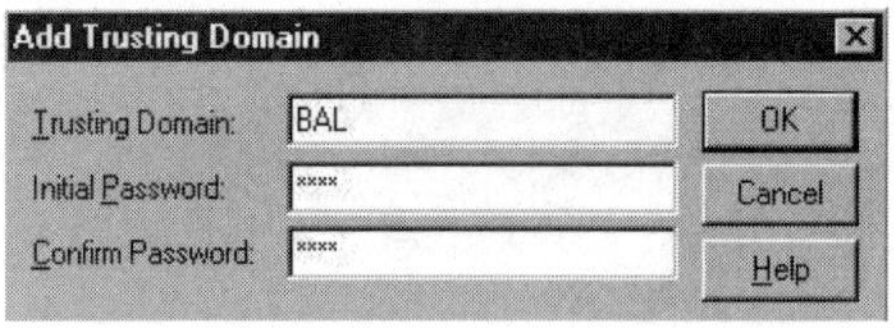

Figure 9–32
Add a trusted
domain

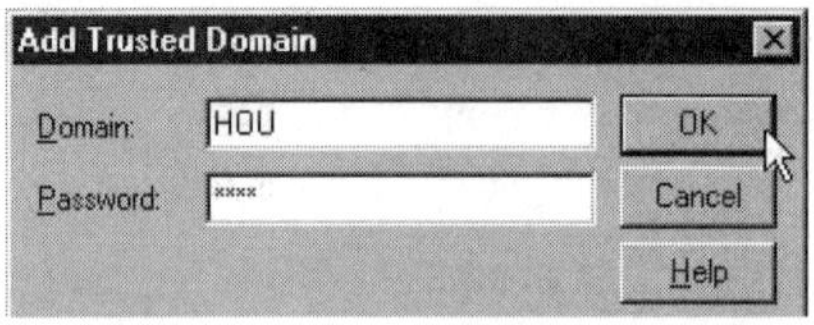

Figure 9–33
Trust failure error
message

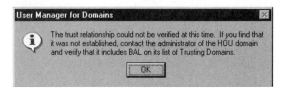

Specify BAL as the name of the trusting domain, and type and confirm the "Initial Password." NT uses the initial password to establish the trust relationship. Once the trust has been established, the two domains refer to each other internally using their SIDs. The password used here has no further use. Remember this password, however, because you need the password when you set up the trusting domain.

SETTING UP THE TRUSTING DOMAIN After configuring the trusted domain, log in to the trusting domain, BAL, to establish its side of the trust relationship. Run User Manager for Domains and select Policies . . . Trust Relationships. Click Add to add a domain to the Trusted Domains box. Specify HOU as the trusted domain, and type the password that was used when you configured the trusted domain earlier, as in Figure 9–31. Refer to Figure 9–32 to see the configuration of the trusting domain.

Creating the trust relationship requires a password on the trusting side, because the trusting domain (BAL) gains access to the SAM database of the trusted domain (HOU). You would not want to give that information out to just anybody, would you? If you attempt to configure a trust relationship and the trusted domain has not been configured, you will receive the error message shown in Figure 9–33. If you have properly set up the trusted domain, however, you will receive a success message, as shown in Figure 9–34.

Figure 9–34
Successful trust
relationship

TRUST RELATIONSHIPS: AN ANALOGY   In some ways, the trust relationships resemble the relationship of a bank with the various state governments in the U.S. If a man walks into a bank in Baltimore, Md., and wants to access his account, the bank teller will certainly accept a Maryland driver's license as proof of his identity. But he does not have a Maryland driver's license; rather, he has a Texas driver's license. That is okay. The Maryland bank teller "trusts" the state of Texas to issue valid driver's licenses. Notice that just because he has proven his identity does not mean that he is permitted to do anything. The bank has to decide what to permit the man to do. Can he make a withdrawal, order new checks, and make a deposit? The "trust" relationship between Maryland and Texas enables the man to prove his identity with a Texas-issued ID card, but the relationship does not automatically give him any access to the "resources" of the bank.

NOTE: *Trust relationships between domains enable servers in one domain to grant access to users from another domain. The trusting domain has the resources. The trusted domain has the users who need access.*

ASSIGNING PERMISSIONS TO A GROUP FROM A TRUSTED DOMAIN   Once the trust relationship has been established, the trusting Domain Administrator must go through the same steps to share resources that she shared within her own domain. She must share the specific resources and decide which groups or users receive which sets of permissions. In this case, however, she has access to a whole new set of groups and users: Those from the trusted domain.

To assign permissions to a group or a user from a trusted domain, bring up the Permissions window for the resource (file, folder, or printer). Select the drop-down box for domain, as shown in Figure 9–35. If the trust relationship exists, usernames from the trusted domain appear in the dialog box, as shown in Figure 9–36. Notice that groups and users added are listed in the format *domain/group name*. In this example, the ACCOUNTING group from the domain HOU is listed as HOU/Accounting. Once the administrator assigns permissions to the trusted users and/or groups, those users

Figure 9–35
Selecting a trusted
domain

Figure 9–36
Adding groups from
a trusted domain

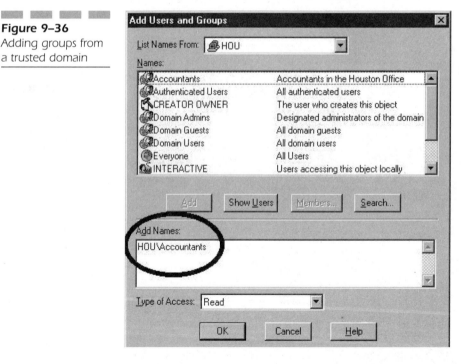

can access the resources on the trusting machine. Jane in Houston opens
up Network Neighborhood and can access the BAL domain just as readily
as she can access her own HOU domain.

TWO-WAY TRUST RELATIONSHIPS Although NT documentation will often refer to "two-way" trust relationships, in Windows NT 4.0, all trust relationships are one-way. Just because BAL trusts HOU, HOU does not necessarily trust BAL.

To create a "two-way" trust relationship, you must actually create two one-way trust relationships, as shown in Figure 9–37. A company has two major divisions, SALES and SHIPPING, each with its own domain. Some users in the SALES domain will need access to resources in the SHIPPING domain, and some users in the SHIPPING domain will need access to resources in the SALES domain. In a two-way trust relationship, users in either domain can be assigned rights and permissions in the other domain.

Trusts Are Not Transitive Trust relationships are not transitive. If Domain A trusts Domain B and Domain B Trusts Domain C, Domain A does not trust Domain C. See Figure 9–38.

The Bayland Widget Company opens a new office in Dallas and adds a DAL domain. A two-way trust relationship already exists between the BAL and HOU domains (we know this relationship is actually *two* one-

Figure 9–37
A "two-way" trust relationship

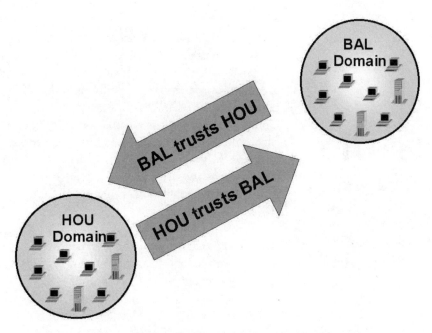

To create a "two-way" trust relationship,
create two one-way trust relationships.

Figure 9–38
Trust relationships are
not transitive.

Domain Trusts Relationships.

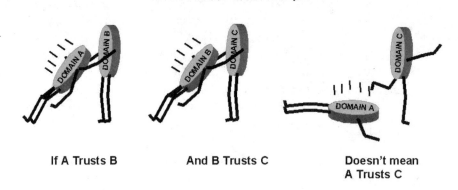

| If A Trusts B | And B Trusts C | Doesn't mean A Trusts C |

way trust relationships). The administrators of the HOU and DAL domains set up a two-way trust relationship between HOU and DAL. In this scenario, DAL does not trust BAL, and BAL does not trust DAL. The BAL and DAL domains have no relationship with each other whatsoever. Although they both have a two-way trust relationship with the HOU domain, the BAL and DAL domains do not trust each other, as shown in Figure 9–39.

Trust relationships give users in one domain the capacity to access resources in another domain. Trust relationships must have two components: a trusted domain and a trusting domain. Users in the trusted domain can access resources in the trusting domain. These trust relationships do not, however, grant permissions to resources. Administrators in the trusting domain must still set those permissions for users and groups.

Trust relationships only grant trust at the most limited level. Trusts are only one-way and are never transitive. Two one-way trust relationships make one "two-way trust relationship." Furthermore, just because A trusts B and B trusts C does not mean that A trusts C. Trusts only go one step in one direction.

DOMAIN MODELS   Microsoft advocates designing networks to fit one of four domain models: Single Domain, Complete Trust Domain, Master Domain, or Multiple Master Domain. Do not look for settings for these domain models in User Manager for Domains or any other administrative program. They do not exist. The domain models are schemes for organizing your network and are not an actual part of the software itself. Let's look at each model.

Figure 9–39
BAL and DAL trust
HOU, but they do
not trust each other.

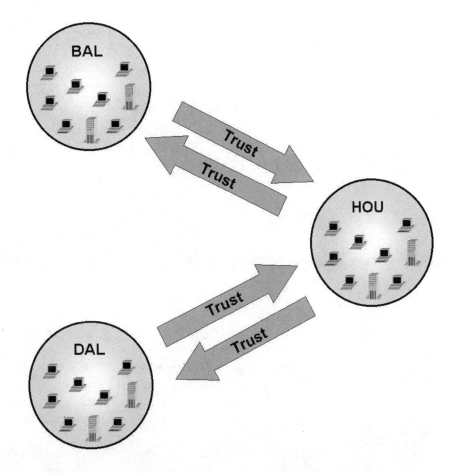

SINGLE DOMAIN MODEL In a Single domain model, all users, groups, and resources exist within a single domain, and no trust relationships exist, as illustrated in Figure 9–40. Single domains require less planning and effort for administrators than more complex domain models that involve trust relationships. The Single domain model works best for smaller organizations where most users and computers sit in the same physical location. This setup enables the same administrator(s) to manage all users and resources, and the lack of trust relationships simplifies administration.

Larger organizations should not use the Single domain model. Performance in the Single domain model decreases as the number of accounts grows, because the domain database grows out-of-hand—and more users attempt to log in to the same domain controllers. To some extent, introducing additional BDCs and faster domain controllers can mitigate these performance problems. Also, because all user accounts exist in the same

Figure 9–40
Single domain model

Single Domain Model

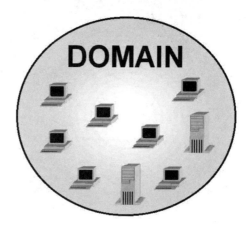

domain, individual departments have no control over their own users and resources. All administrative changes must go through some centralized information technology department. To deal with these problems, Microsoft proposes three decentralized domain models that use trust relationships to connect the domains: the Complete Trust domain model, the Master domain model, and the Multiple Master domain model.

COMPLETE TRUST DOMAIN MODEL   In the Complete Trust domain model, all domains trust all other domains, as illustrated in Figure 9–41. In this model, all domains have a "two-way" trust relationship with all other domains. Because every domain trusts every other domain, administrators can assign rights and permissions to any user or group from any of the domains. The Complete Trust domain model enables the administrators in each domain to control their own resources and user accounts, while enabling users to log in once and access resources in any of the domains within the enterprise.

NOTE: *The term "enterprise" is often used to refer to large-scale networks. In this context, "within the enterprise" refers to the entire network, including all domains.*

A single company with divisions in three cities might use the Complete Trust domain model. Go back to the example of the Bayland Widget Company, with operations in three cities: Baltimore, Houston, and Dallas (see

Figure 9–41
Complete Trust
model

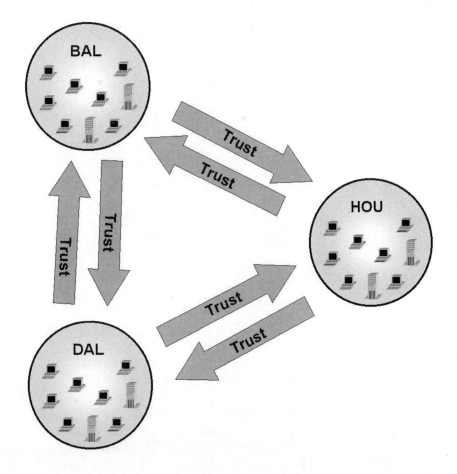

Figure 9–42). The administrators in each city control their own user accounts and resources but can assign rights and permissions to users and groups from the other two domains.

The salespeople in Houston need to be able to see whether an item they have run out of is in stock in Dallas. The administrators of the DAL domain might put the global group SALES from the HOU domain (HOU/SALES) into the local group INVENTORY on a server in the DAL domain. They could then grant that local group permissions to the inventory database stored on that server, enabling the salespeople to check the inventory of a particular type of widget.

One possible down side to this setup is that the DAL administrators must trust (in the normal sense of the word) the administrators in the HOU domain to put only the right people in the HOU/SALES group. The

Bayland Widget Company

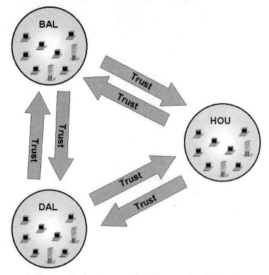

Complete Trust Domain Model

two sets of administrators must communicate with each other effectively, or they will fail to grant the proper level of access to the right users.

The Complete Trust domain model has several other disadvantages. The chief disadvantage is the exponential growth of the number of trust relationships that have to be established and maintained as the network grows. Creating a Complete Trust domain model with three domains for the Bayland Widget Company only required six trust relationships, but a network with 20 domains would require the establishment of 380 distinct trust relationships.

To calculate the number of trust relationships required for a particular number of domains, use the following formula:

```
Domains X (Domains-1)=trusts
```

For example, if you use the Complete Trust domain model with 15 domains, you would require [15 × (15–1)] trusts, or 210 trusts.

In addition, no centralized management of user accounts exists, which creates the possibility of inconsistent naming standards and account policies. These problems are manageable with three or four domains but become increasingly difficult as the number of domains increases.

The Complete Trust domain model can work well for three or four domains, but setting up and keeping track of the trust relationships grows increasingly difficult as the number of trust relationships increases. Managing a larger number of domains requires a greater degree of centralized management.

MASTER DOMAIN MODEL The Master domain model provides a more centralized approach to account management. Instead of having each domain maintain its own user accounts, all user accounts are created and maintained in the "Master" domain. The other domains, known as *resource domains*, contain only computer accounts and resources. Each resource domain trusts the master domain, as shown in Figure 9–43.

Figure 9–43
Master domain
model

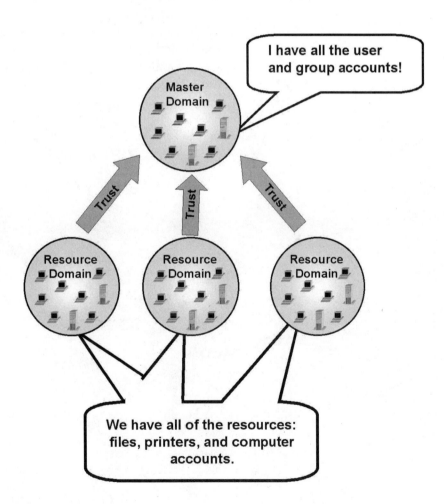

NOTE: *The master domain is the domain that contains all of the user and group accounts.*

The resource domains can correspond to departments, cities, projects, or any other organizational unit. The Master domain model enables one group of administrators to concentrate on the users while enabling each department (or project, or city) to manage its own resources. The Master domain model provides a good balance of centralized user management with distributed resource management.

Remember that domains do not necessarily correspond to geographic locations, as seen in Figure 9–44. In the Master domain model, a particular domain might have domain controllers in several locations. The earlier diagram shows a BDC for the USERS domain at each site. Maintaining a BDC for the Master domain at each site guarantees that users will be able to log in, even if the WAN links fail.

Rico, the administrator for the Bayland Widget Company, sets up the company servers again—this time using a Master domain model. Rico creates four domains: the master domain USERS and three resource domains—HOU, DAL, and BAL—which correspond to the locations of the company offices in Houston, Dallas, and Baltimore, respectively. He establishes trust

Figure 9–44
Domains do not
imply location.

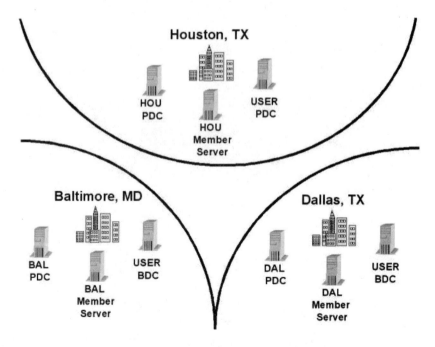

Figure 9–45
Master domain
model for the
Bayland Widget
Company

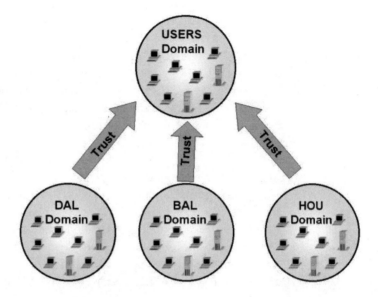

relationships between the four domains, making each of the resource domains trust the USERS domain, as shown in Figure 9–45.

Because all user accounts exist in the USERS domain, all users must log in to either a PDC or a BDC in the USERS domain. Rico, a smart administrator, decides it would be a bad idea to put all of the domain controllers for USERS in the Houston office, because that would require the login traffic from Dallas and Baltimore to go out over the slower WAN links between the cities. In addition, should one of those links fail, no user in the affected city could log in. Placing a BDC in each city guarantees that users can log in, even if the WAN links fail, and cuts down on traffic across those WAN links.

A Master domain model solves many of the problems associated with multiple domains. Local administrators manage resources, while central administrators manage users and groups. If set up logically with BDCs at each remote location, users can log in at any location and access all the resources on the network. Furthermore, expanding to new locations does not greatly increase the amount of administration required for the network. When the Bayland Widget Company opens its San Diego office, Rico simply adds a new resource domain—SAN—and puts a BDC at the new office to handle user logins. With such a smooth operation, he can spend the majority of his time relaxing on the beach. Life is good.

The Master domain model holds up for all but the largest organizations needing multiple domains. Some large enterprises run into the suggested

40MB limit for the Domain SAM, as discussed earlier, and have to turn to the Multiple Master domain model.

MULTIPLE MASTER DOMAIN MODEL A Multiple Master domain model handles the needs of large organizations by splitting the single master domain into several pieces. Each master domain contains a unique set of user and group accounts, thus reducing the size of each Domain SAM to something manageable. All of the master domains trust each other in two-way trust relationships, and all of the resource domains trust all of the master domains, as shown in Figure 9–46. In all other respects, the Multiple Master domain mirrors the master domain model.

The Multiple Master domain model accepts a theoretically unlimited number of users, yet retains the advantages of the simpler master domain model. Resources can be controlled and administered separately from user and group accounts. This separation provides for the delegation of administrative tasks and enables individual departments (or projects, locations, or other organizational units) to control access to their own resources.

DOMAIN MODELS: MAKING CHOICES The Enterprise exam covers the domain models in detail. Unfortunately, many experienced NT administra-

Figure 9–46
Multiple Master
domain model

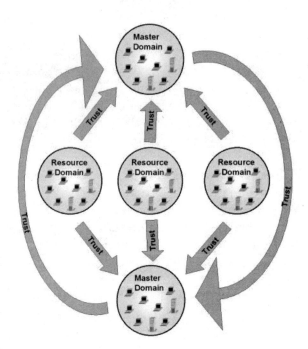

tors have little experience with domain planning. They may not have worked for their organization when the network was being built. In many cases, all of their experience has been with the single model used in their own environment. To make matters worse, the domain models that Microsoft proposes are not always followed in real life. Real networks often grow and develop without the kind of advanced planning that Microsoft stresses on the Enterprise exam. For the purpose of the Enterprise exam, remember that you are being tested on the Microsoft company line. Be prepared to choose the appropriate domain model for a given situation. Table 9–3 summarizes some of the key points to remember.

With Windows NT, Jane and John can work all day long, accessing resources locally or at any company location without missing a beat. To create a seamless network setup requires mastery of many facets of NT, from user, global, and local accounts to domains, workgroups, trust relationships, and domain models. Regardless of the size or geographical dispersion of a company, NT can provide a network setup that enables Jane and John to receive whatever resources they need through a simple click in Network Neighborhood. Memorize the two mantras discussed in this chapter, and

Table 9–3

Selecting the right domain model

	Single Domain Model	Complete Trust Domain Model	Master Domain Model	Multiple Master Domain Model
No trust relationships to manage	λ			
Limited Number of User Accounts	λ			
Scalable to enable a unlimited number of users		λ		λ
Centralized Management of User and Group Accounts			λ	λ
Department Level Control of Resources		λ	λ	λ
Fewer trust relationships to manage than with Complete Trust Domain Model	N/A		λ	λ

your world will be a better place (or at least your test-taking ability will dramatically improve). Recite the mantras one more time for the Gipper:

Mantra One: Domain Organization

Users go into global groups;

Global groups go into local groups;

Local groups receive rights and permissions.

Mantra Two: trust relationships

I trust you, so you can use my stuff.

Questions

1. When configuring her NT network, Lois chose to set it up as a workgroup. On her local NT workstation, she has a resource shared as **\\LOIS\NEWNEWS**. If her colleague, Clark, wants to access this resource from his NT workstation, what must Lois do?

   a. Add Clark's computer account from the Domain SAM to the Share ACL and the NTFS ACL for the resource

   b. Add Clark's global user account from the Domain SAM to the Share ACL and the NTFS ACL for the resource

   c. Create a computer account for Clark's NT workstation. Add the Computer account to a local group that is in the Share ACL and the NTFS ACL for the resource

   d. Create a local user account for Clark. Add the user account to a local group that is in the Share ACL and the NTFS ACL for the resource

2. Hank is a member of the global groups TRAININGDEPARTMENT, TRAININGACCOUNTS, and MANAGERS. The TRAININGDEPARTMENT global group is a member of the TRAININGRESOURCES local group. The TRAININGACCOUNTS global group is a member of the TRAININGSUPERRESOURCES local group. The MANAGERS global group is a member of the ACCOUNTS local group. Hank is trying to access the **\\TRAIN01\ACCOUNTS** share, to which the ACCOUNTS local group has Full Control NTFS permissions and Full Control Share permissions. The TRAININGRESOURCES local group has No Access NTFS permissions and Full Control Share permissions. The TRAININGSUPERRESOURCES local group has Read and Write NTFS permissions and Full Control Share permissions. Can Hank access the **\\TRAIN01_ACCOUNTS** resource, and which level of access will he have?

   a. Hank cannot access **\\TRAIN01\ACCOUNTS**.

   b. Hank can access **\\TRAIN01\ACCOUNTS**, and he is given Full Access and Control of the resource.

   c. Hank can access **\\TRAIN01\ACCOUNTS**, and he is given Read and Write permissions of the resource.

   d. Hank can access **\\TRAIN01\ACCOUNTS**, and he is given Read Only permissions to the resource.

3. On her NT server named ABILENE, Jolene shares her `c:\`
   `MyDocuments\Reviews` folder as REVIEWS. She saves a text
   document to that folder, naming the file `MOVIE.TXT`. While sitting
   at another PC, which UNC path should she type to open the file?

   a. `\\ABILENE\%systemroot%\MyDocuments\Reviews\movie.txt`

   b. `\\ABILENE\JOLENEC\MyDocuments\Reviews\movie.txt`

   c. `\\ABILENE\MyDocuments\NT_JOLENE\Reviews\MOVIE.TXT`

   d. `\\ABILENE\Reviews\MOVIE.TXT`

4. John Bob is trying to access the shared resource
   `\\NERO\NEROC\REPORTS`. He is currently a member of the SALES
   and MANAGEMENT groups. The SALES group has Read access
   to the share, and the MANAGEMENT group has Full Control
   access to the share. What access does John Bob have to the share?

   a. No Access

   b. Read access

   c. Change access

   d. Full Control access

5. Pepe is trying to access the shared resource `\\SRV1\USERS`. The
   groups USERMANAGERS and ACCOUNTANTS have access to
   this resource. The administrator for SRV1 places Pepe in the
   ACCOUNTANTS group, but Pepe discovers that he still does not
   have access to the resource. What might the administrator suggest
   to Pepe?

   a. Pepe must map a drive using the UNC name. The browse list
      has not been updated.

   b. Pepe must log out and then log back in. He needs to receive a
      new Access Token.

   c. Realign the tachyon field emitters and reboot the forward
      deflector grid.

   d. Pepe must log out and log back in using the login name
      ACCOUNTANTS.

6. All the machines in the office were spontaneously rebooted by a friendly neighborhood power surge. After rebooting a few of the machines, you notice that the network is busy and you cannot use Network Neighborhood to locate and select shared resources. What might be happening to cause this problem?

   a. Rebooting the machines caused all the mapped network drives to be unmapped. Each machine is trying to remap the drives to access the resources.

   b. Rebooting the machines caused all the mapped network drives to be unmapped. The Browse Master is trying to remap the drives.

   c. The machines are having browser elections to elect a new master browser. The shares will be visible in Network Neighborhood when the browse list is complete.

   d. The PDC has not yet been turned on, and only PDCs can become master browsers.

7. Mickey needs to share his `c:\RESULTS` folder with his colleagues. He is using an NT workstation with an NTFS partition. What should he do to share `c:\RESULTS` and give permissions to the TESTERS local group?

   a. Open the Network Control Panel applet and choose Sharing. Add the `c:\RESULTS folder` to the list of shared resources. Add the TESTERS local group to the ACL of `\RESULTS`.

   b. Open User Manager. Choose Policies . . . Sharing. Add the `c:\RESULTS` folder to the list of shared resources. Add the TESTERS local group to the ACL of `\RESULTS`.

   c. Right-click the `c:\RESULTS` folder and choose Properties. Click the Share As button to share the folder. Click the Change ACL button to add the TESTERS local group to the Share ALC of `\RESULTS`.

   d. Right-click the `c:\RESULTS` folder and choose Sharing. Click the Permissions button to add the TESTERS local group to the Share ACL of `\RESULTS`.

8. The Fielding Manufacturing Company currently uses a single domain model for its single office environment. The company is about to expand into five different states, with a total of nine offices and 250 employees. The employees in the offices in each state want to be able to manage their own files, folders, and printers, but they understand that the central information technology department wants to manage the users and groups in the environment. Assuming that Fielding Manufacturing Company hires you to design its NT implementation within its new WAN environment, what would you recommend?

   a. Continue to use the single domain model. Add BDCs to each new office.

   b. Move to the Complete Trust model. Make each office its own domain, with two-way trusts configured among the each of the different offices.

   c. Move to the Master domain model. Make each office its own resource domain. Create one user domain, administered by the central information technology department. Place a BDC for the user domain in each office. Have each of the resource domains trust the user domain.

   d. Move to the Multiple Master domain model. Make each office its own resource domain. Create a user domain for each state to accommodate the large number of users. Place a BDC for the appropriate state's user domain in each office in that state. Have each resource domain trust each user domain.

9. There are two domains: SFA and LAX. SFA trusts LAX. LAX contains a printer that users from the SFA domain need to use for printing their marketing materials. The local group MARKETINGPRINTER has access to the shared printer on the Market server in the LAX domain. What do you need to do to give the SFA/MARKETINGUSERS global group access to this printer?

a. In LAX's User Manager for Domains, add SFA/MARKETINGUSERS to the MARKETINGPRINTER local group.

b. In SFA's User Manager for Domains, add the LAX/MARKETINGPRINTER group to the SFA/MARKETINGUSERS group.

c. In LAX's User Manager for Domains, configure LAX to trust SFA. Add the SFA/MARKETINGUSERS global group to the MARKETINGPRINTER local group on the Market server.

d. In SFA's Server Manager, configure LAX to trust SFA. Add the SFA/MARKETINGUSERS global group to the MARKETINGPRINTER local group on the Market server.

10. There are three domains: SFA, LAX, and ORD. ORD trusts LAX. SFA trusts ORD. LAX trusts SFA. Which users can use resources in which domains?

a. Users in LAX can use resources in ORD. Users in ORD can use resources in SFA. Users in SFA can use resources in LAX.

b. Users in ORD can use resources in LAX. Users in SFA can use resources in ORD. Users in LAX can use resources in SFA.

c. Because of the transitive properties of trust, users in ORD and LAX can use resources in SFA. Users in SFA can use resources in ORD and LAX.

d. All users can use resources in all domains.

Answers

1. d—If Lois has chosen to configure her network as a workgroup, then her PC is not a member of a domain and can therefore not obtain user or computer accounts from a Domain SAM. User accounts are placed into groups to receive permissions, not computer accounts.

2. a—If No Access is given to a user through any group membership, No Access will override all other permissions—and the user is given No Access to the resource.

3. d—The format for the UNC name is `\\computername\share name\file name`.

4. d—When determining the share access of a user, he receives the cumulative access of all his group memberships.

5. b—The browse list would be affected by machines being rebooted, not by changes to the groups and ACLs. Do not confuse group accounts with user accounts. Group names do not enable logons.

6. c—When the Browse Master is turned off, the other machines on the network need to elect a new master browser, which then needs to compile a browse list. Until this process occurs, the machines will not be visible in Network Neighborhood—although you could access them by using Find Computer.

7. d—The Network applet and User Manager will not enable you to create shares. Going to either the Properties dialog box or the Sharing dialog box will enable you to create a share, but there is no Change ACL button. Use the Permissions button to add users or groups to the share ACL.

8. c—Microsoft recommends that when you move into a multi-office enterprise environment, you should separate out users and resources—which enables decentralized administration of the resources but provides centralized administration of the users.

9. c—The clue lies in the direction of the trust. Remember the mantra, "I trust you, so you can use my stuff." If users in the SFA domain want to use resources in the LAX domain, LAX has to trust SFA. Trust relationships are configured in User Manager for Domains.

10. a—Again, the key is in the direction of the trust relationships and the idea that trust is NOT transitive.

10

Networking Protocols

The entire PC network industry has in its power the ability to eliminate world hunger completely in one week if it so desired. The process to do this is simple. Just make every networking person donate 25 cents to World Hunger Relief Fund every time they misuse the word "Protocol." The money would roll in by the billions and everyone on earth would have their fill of Ding-Dongs, filet mignon, pepperoni pizza, etc.

The goal of this chapter is massive: To define the many protocols used in general networking, followed by a detailed tour of the use of these protocols under Windows NT. The problem with this goal is that the word "protocol" is so horribly abused that it requires a significant definition before we can even begin.

What's a Protocol?

The first step to understanding protocols is to *stop thinking about computers* for a moment! Let's go back to 1933 and ask that same question. Back then, if you asked someone qualified to answer this question, they would probably say something to the effect of: "A protocol is the organized process of ceremony and etiquette used by diplomats and heads of state when they meet." That makes sense—when the King of Bratislava calls the President of France on the telephone, there are very established processes of who talks first, what they say, how the other person responds, etc. This ensures an orderly process of communication. The protocols define the process of communication between two entities—Bratislava and France. The King and the President are just two parts of this big communication. Underneath them are all of the lower people and equipment that are used to make the communication work. There are ministers, policy directors, cabinet members, telephones, and so on—all working together to make this communication work.

Let's make a hypothetical conversation between France and Bratislava. The President of France wants to trade wine for wine barrels. He calls the King of Bratislava, but the king is clueless about trade. Although it is the King and the President who will make the agreement, in reality, the President of France talks to the French finance minister, who takes the President's idea and adds a few technical details that would be important to the Bratislavan finance minister. The French finance minister calls the Bratislavan finance minister on the telephone; the latter removes the technical stuff that the king doesn't need and then talks to the King. Even though the King and the President don't actually speak to each other, they are having a conversation (see Figure 10–1). In this communication, each level talks to their equals on the other side—the King of Bratislava communicates with the President of France and the Finance Minister of Bratislava talks to the Finance Minister of France, each very careful to respect the protocols of communication. Only the telephones actually talk to each other. The king and president and the finance ministers are having "virtual" conversations through the people and devices below them. In reality, there is not one protocol, but actually many layers of protocols, all working together.

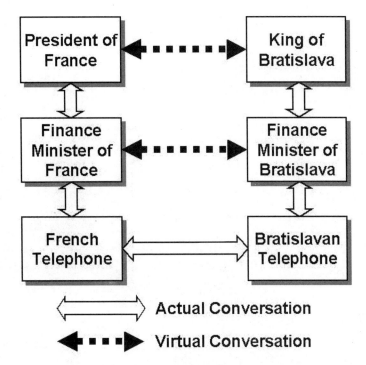

Figure 10–1
A conversation
between France and
Bratislava

Actual Conversation

Virtual Conversation

Protocols are Just a Means to Transport Data

It would not be too far of a stretch to take the conversation between Bratislava and France and turn it into a conversation between two computers. Just as in diplomacy, there can be many different protocols all working together to allow a successful conversation. Imagine that one computer called "France" wants to send a file to another computer called "Bratislava." For the sake of simplicity, pretend that only two processes need to take place on each machine. One process—call it the "Transport Protocol"—breaks down outgoing files into small (about 1000 bits) chunks and assembles incoming chunks back into files. The second process—call it the "Data Link Protocol"—moves the chunks from one machine to the other. The combined work of these two processes gets the file from one system to another, as shown in Figure 10–2.

This analogy is fairly close to reality. In the computer networking world, there really are processes (programs and hardware) that do these jobs. These programs and hardware were designed with preset rules to allow an orderly process of communication. These preset rules are called

Figure 10–2
Computer
conversations
between France and
Bratislava

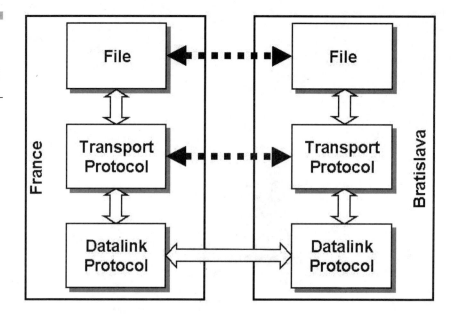

Protocols. In the network business, the different protocols have different names, depending on their function. For example, all networks really do have a Data Link protocol that moves the chunks from one system to another. Datalink protocols have names like Ethernet, Token Ring, and PPP. Equally, there really are Transport protocols, with names like Net-BEUI, TCP/IP and IPX/SPX. The term "Networking Protocols" is used when talking about any protocol of any type used in networks.

NOTE: *A protocol is a set of rules for communication between two systems.*

A system will have many protocols.

Protocols are organized in layers that work together to ensure orderly communication.

ORGANIZING NETWORKING PROTOCOLS Armed with this basic knowledge of networking protocols, we can turn to another analogy to understand the many types of networking protocols and how they are organized. In this analogy, think of the transport protocol as a box, as shown in Figure 10–3.

We can use this box regardless of which shipping service we use, be it via United Parcel Service, Federal Express, or the U.S. Postal Service. In

Figure 10–3
Think of the transport
protocol as a box.

Figure 10–4
Think of the datalink
protocol as the
shipping service.

this analogy, the datalink protocols (which are not the main focus of this chapter) such as Ethernet, Token Ring, or a PPP link, would be analogous to the shipping service we use, as shown in Figure 10–4.

The shipping services do not care what is in the box (unless it's ticking); their job is just to move it from point A to point B. The box can also be used to ship all types of goods, such as clothing, machine parts, or canned goods. (In this analogy, the contents of the protocol package might be a file transferred by Microsoft File and Print Sharing, a print job, or a Duke Nukem "you are about to get a rocket in the back of the head" message.) By standardizing on one or a few types of boxes, we can guarantee that packages can be shipped efficiently throughout the world. By standardizing on a limited number of networking protocols, we guarantee that messages sent from one machine to another could be reliably interpreted and acted upon.

Travis has a large machine to move from one city to another, as illustrated in Figure 10–5. It is unlikely that it can fit into a single box, so Travis has to break it up into many pieces and pack those pieces in separate boxes.

Travis's company, Large Machines, Inc., has rules that describe how to break the machine down and package it. Travis has to label the boxes with an address and include instructions for how to reassemble the pieces at the other end, along with information that might help the people at the receiving end. Finally, Travis needs to track the boxes, to ensure that they all arrive at the destination. Figure 10–6 illustrates Travis's tasks.

The transport "boxes" are loaded onto datalink "trucks" for delivery to the proper system, as shown in Figure 10–7. The order they arrive in or were sent in is unimportant, as Travis properly addressed and ordered all of them.

Figure 10–5

How do we move
the machine?

Figure 10–6
Breaking up the
machine

Figure 10–7
Hauling the boxes

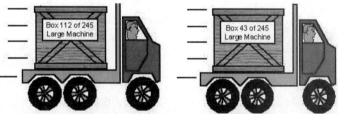

Compare this process of Travis and the boxes with the earlier analogy. The first system's transport protocol dismantles the machine while the first datalink protocol loads the boxes onto trucks and gets them to the other system. The second system's datalink protocol unloads the boxes and hands them to the second transport protocol, which then reassembles the machine. Figure 10–8 illustrates the whole process.

Protocols work in much the same way as Travis and his trucks and boxes, to allow communication among machines. First, the document or file must be broken down into smaller chunks that can be handled by the network. These chunks being transported across a network are known as packets—discreet units of information that can be passed across some kind of network cable. Rules define how the information is broken down to ensure that it can be reconstituted correctly when it reaches its destination. The package that the data is placed in must then have an address

Figure 10–8
Protocols in action

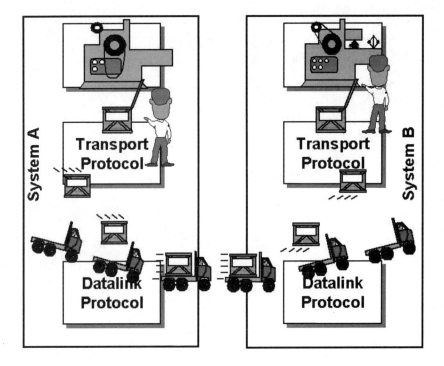

Figure 10–8
Protocols in action

for where it needs to go, as well as a return address. When the data reaches the destination, there must be instructions available for putting the file back into its original format so the recipient can use it. Rules need to be given to follow for the addressing and writing the instructions. This is especially important if the instructions and address are in a different language—the people at the receiving end will not be able to reassemble the machine if instructions aren't included. Networks use protocols or layers of protocols to do each of these tasks. The most important thing to remember is for a particular protocol to work correctly, both the sending and receiving machine have to use the same protocol.

As a general rule, it does not matter which protocol you use in your network, as long as every machine has at least one protocol in common with every other machine with which it needs to communicate. Microsoft Networking functions (File and Print Sharing, Logging on to an NT domain, etc.) all work fine with any combination of NetBEUI, IPX/SPX, or TCP/IP. Some applications, however, rely specifically on certain features of certain protocols. Utilities such as FTP or Web browsers such as Microsoft's Internet Explorer rely on features of TCP/IP that are not supported in other protocols. Similarly, Novell Netware File and Print Sharing relies on IPX/SPX.

NOTE: *The IPX/SPX protocol is called NWLink IPX/SPX in Microsoft Networking. In many cases, you will see the abbreviated version in the text, but be aware that NWLink is the Microsoft implementation of the IPX/SPX protocols.*

Protocols and the OSI Model

Networking protocols are designed to work in independent layers, each of which performs some of the required functions. Each layer must know something about the layer above it and the layer below it, but can remain blissfully ignorant of the other layers. These layers are not laws of physics —anybody who wants to design a network can do it anyway they want. But after many years of creating networks, the industry began to become aware of the fact that most networks followed the same basic procedures in the same layers. Up to this point there has only been two discrete layers described in this chapter: the Datalink and the Transport. Seven discrete layers, however, apply to network after network. The *International Standards Organization* (ISO) created a model of how to develop and describe networks that reflects real world implementations. This model is known as the *Open Systems Interconnection* (OSI) 7-layer model. Figure 10–9 lists the 7 layers of the OSI model.

NOTE: *Yes, the ISO created the OSI.*

THE OSI MODEL'S PURPOSE   The OSI model provides a set of conceptual tools—a model—that can be used to describe actual networks. The OSI model gives network designers and technicians a means to define the roles of the various tools used to build networks.

The OSI model allows developer to create different tools and utilities to fill the needs of the various layers of work that must be performed. One of the main tools is the protocol, or *protocol stack*. The term protocol is thrown about to refer to just about any technology or method for computers to communicate with each other over the network. As a working definition, however, a protocol is a set of standards designed to fulfill the requirements of one or more of the layers of the OSI model. The NetBEUI protocol, for example, only addresses a single layer's issues. TCP/IP, on the other hand, addresses as many as five layers; these types of protocols can be referred to as a protocol stack. (Both TCP/IP and NetBEUI are discussed in more detail below.) Unfortunately, because the breadth of issues

Figure 10–9
The OSI 7-layer
Model

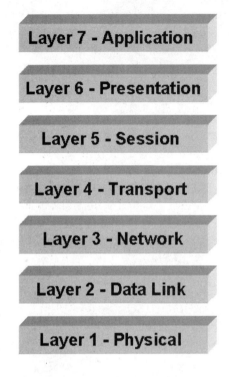

Figure 10–9
The OSI 7-layer
Model

covered by a particular protocol varies so much, the term protocol can be extremely confusing. The OSI 7-layer model gives developers a common way of talking about and understanding the different protocols and the layers of those protocols.

NOTE: *The following definitions and discussion of the OSI 7-layer model are abbreviated. The discussion is provided to allow common understanding of the protocols in the rest of the chapter. The information relating to layers and functions is not a specific element of the NT exams.*

The layers are described below in order from the lowest layer, which allows the physical movement of data, to the highest layer, which creates an interface for users and software to make network requests. This is the order that information would be received in on a destination machine. When sending data, the originating machine starts the information at the Application layer and it works its way down. Data will always traverse all the necessary layers on each machine in order. It will not skip any layers, although it may not travel all the way to the top of the model in all cases. Figure 10–10 shows two systems' OSI models in operation.

LAYER 1—PHYSICAL The Physical layer defines the physical transport of the data across the network cables, usually as electrical or optical pulses. This layer is a set of rules for translating binary data (1s and 0s) into a physical signal on the sending end, and back into the original binary data on the receiving end. The physical layer does not actually add any data. This layer also defines how the cable interfaces with the network card, and therefore what the correct electrical or optical impulse is for the particular network cable. Technology standards such as Token Ring and Ethernet include specifications for the Physical layer.

LAYER 2—DATA LINK The Data Link layer provides rules for accessing the physical layer. It allows data to be passed down from the Network layer (one layer above) to the Physical layer. It is this layer that packages the binary data into frames or packets. The Data Link layer also covers issues such as hardware addresses (e.g. MAC addresses) and rules for negotiating which machine should be allowed to access the physical media

Figure 10–10
Two OSIs working together.

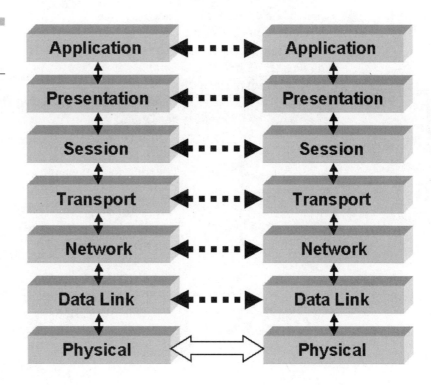

at any given moment (e.g. Ethernet's collision detection or Token Ring's token passing).

Ethernet and Token Ring were mentioned for both Layer 1 and Layer 2, as they cover specifications for both Physical and Data Link layer issues.

LAYER 3—NETWORK The Network layer provides the rules for routing traffic between networks. This layer provides addresses for the messages that will be sent. It includes rules for converting logical addresses (such as IP or IPX addresses) into physical addresses (such as MAC addresses). This layer also adds additional routing information, such as the path that the data should take. Finally, this is the layer that would be responsible for breaking down data into smaller pieces, so that the Data Link layer can place the data into frames. On the receiving end, the Network layer will recombine the pieces into data that the Transport layer can understand.

LAYER 4—TRANSPORT The Transport layer packages the data for transport, taking care of a wide variety of support issues, including but not limited to: Flow control, breaking data into small chunks on one end and recreating them on the receiving end, and providing reliable connections when needed. The Transport layer can be viewed as a catchall layer that guarantees smooth communication between the lower layers (1-3) and the upper layers (5-7). The lower layers concern themselves with moving data from point A to point B on the network, without regard for the actual content of the data. The upper layers concern themselves with dealing with specific types of requests from users and applications. This separation allows applications using the network to remain blissfully unaware of the underlying hardware.

LAYER 5—SESSION The Session layer controls the way in which machines on the network establish connections, keeping track of which information should be exchanged with which machine. Compare a network server to a short order cook, as shown in Figure 10–11. Just as the cook must keep track of which meals go to which table, the server has to keep track of what data should be sent to which client machine. The cook uses tickets; the server uses connections. The connections that are made between the applications on the different systems are called sessions. The Session layer allows these sessions to be established, allowing functions such as logon, security, communication timing, and control.

Figure 10–11
The short-order cook

LAYER 6—PRESENTATION   One of the jobs of a protocol is to ensure that the different languages spoken by various applications can be understood at lower levels of the OSI layers. This layer provides the rules and the ability to translate the formats from the Application layer into a format that the rest of the lower layers can understand and transport. In a Microsoft network, for example, server functions can run on top of a number of different operating systems, including MS LAN Manager, Windows for Workgroups, Windows 95, Windows 98, Windows NT 3.51, and Windows NT 4.0. Every Microsoft client should be able to access every Microsoft server, without regard to what operating system the server runs upon. At the protocol layer, a standard set of tools must be provided to hide these differences from the applications. In the Microsoft world, *Server Message Blocks* (SMBs) provide this layer's functions.

LAYER 7—APPLICATION   The Application layer provides an interface between applications and the network, allowing programmers to use a standard set of tools to access the network instead of having to concern themselves with network issues when designing an applications such as a word processor. The functions provided by Windows Explorer to other programs (such as the Save As dialogue box) operate at the Application layer. When a user saves a file in Microsoft Word to a network share, Word calls on functions provided by the Explorer interface to save the file to the network. In the TCP/IP world, a program such as CuteFTP or WS_FTP32 relies on the Application layer protocol FTP to access FTP servers on the Internet.

Each machine that uses the network to transport information has elements that correspond to the layers of this model. Each piece of data that travels between two machines traverses all of the layers of the model, undergoing translation and break down at each layer on the originating machine, and undergoing more translation and rebuilding at each layer on the receiving machine. Data cannot be handed off between machines at any layer except the physical layer; therefore, all data must first go all the way down the layers, being translated from application data to binary data. It can then be sent as electrical or optical physical pulses between machines. When it reaches its destination, it must then travel all the way up from the physical layer to the application layer, regaining the shape and format that was stripped away in order to send it in physical form.

Microsoft Networking Protocols

Once you have a basic understanding of the OSI model, you have a basic understanding of the functions that a protocol must perform to allow two machines to communicate. There must be some element that takes the text you type in an MS Word document, and translates and encapsulates that document into a data format that the network can understand. There must be an element that allows a session between the sending machine and the receiving machine. There must be an element that provides for error checking and reliable transportation of the data, so that data does not get lost during the passage of information. At the lowest layer, some element must be available to break the data down from binary into physical and actually send it out. Windows NT uses a variety of protocols to meet these requirements. The many layers sometimes require that more than one protocol or utility be involved, however, in order for the full translation in both directions to take place.

MICROSOFT NETWORKING AND OSI At this point, the term Microsoft Networking requires a deeper definition than simply a network based on Microsoft products. To gain this deeper definition, one must go back in time, back to the beginnings of networks on PCs. If one were to visualize the early years of PC networking (1980-1990), it might be tempting to visualize a world of government and industry working together, creating standards for network hardware and software in perfect compliance to the OSI 7-layer model. If one did make this visualization, one would be totally wrong. The reality of the early years of networking was a bunch of individual companies with totally proprietary network operating systems and hardware. At least hardware had some open standards with Ethernet, but even Ethernet was a smaller player compared to proprietary hardware like IBM's Token Ring. The OSI 7-layer model was ignored—it didn't even come out until 1985 so how could network operating system developers use it? For the most part, a company would create their NOS from the bottom up and then retroactively try to apply the OSI seven-layer model. Surprisingly, most would fit fairly nicely into the model.

Microsoft also made its own network software. They created, from the ground up, the top five layers of the OSI 7-layer model (actually they skipped one layer, Network) and put them into a DOS based networking product called Microsoft LAN Manager. Even though LAN Manager is long gone, the homemade protocols, including SMB, NetBIOS, and Net-BEUI, were incorporated into every successive Microsoft NOS, even the most advanced Microsoft NOSs—like Windows NT. These tightly knit, homegrown protocols are known collectively as Microsoft Networking.

Networking under the Microsoft Networking system corresponds to the OSI model, as shown in Figure 10–9. In Microsoft Networking, the Application, Presentation, and Session layers always use the same utilities and protocols: Explorer, SMB, and NetBIOS. Microsoft Networking uses three different options for the Transport and Network layers: NetBEUI, TCP/IP (actually TCP and UDP), and IPX/SPX (NWLink).

NOTE: *NetBEUI does not truly use the Network layer. It is sometimes impossible to map each element of Microsoft Networking directly to OSI layers—no one-to-one match usually exists, even though all the layers of OSI are represented in MS Networking.*

Microsoft Networking remains peacefully oblivious to the lower layers. As long as data packets are arriving at their intended destinations, Microsoft Networking does not concern itself with the details. It is a lot like how you probably think of the U.S. Postal Service. You probably do not care whether your letter is sent to its destination via air, land, or sea, as long as it gets to its destination in one piece and on time. In the same way, Microsoft Networking does not care whether you use Ethernet or Token Ring to handle the Data Link and Physical layer issues. Microsoft Networking can work with just about any lower layer protocols you wish, as long as they are working properly. Microsoft Networking does not concern itself with Network, Data Link, or Physical layer issues, as shown in Figure 10–12.

NOTE: *NetBIOS operates at the Session layer and is always used by Microsoft Networking. NetBEUI operates at the Transport layer and is not required for Microsoft Networking.*

THE TOP PROTOCOL LAYERS OF MICROSOFT NETWORKING
As mentioned before, the Application, Presentation, and Session layers of Microsoft Networking are always provided by the same elements. These elements are Explorer, the SMBs, and NetBIOS. To understand why these elements are important, think about what happens when a user at a workstation needs to access some files from a server. A user sits at his workstation (called \\ACCT1) and double-clicks a shortcut to a file on the server (\\ACCT2). When the user double-clicks this shortcut, Windows NT activates the Application layer (Explorer). Explorer needs a program at the Presentation layer to translate the request into a common format. That common format in Microsoft Networking is SMB. SMB formats the request from \\ACCT1 for the file on \\ACCT2. SMB needs an application or pro-

Figure 10–12
NT only uses the
higher layers of OSI.

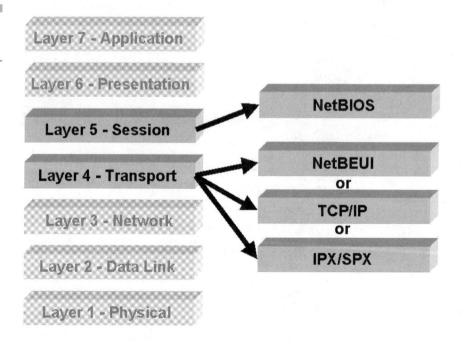

tocol to open communication with the remote machine, \\ACCT2. In Microsoft Networking, NetBIOS will open the lines of communication between the two machines, creating a session. Let's go through the process.

NOTE: *These layers are necessary to understanding the whole protocol stack used in Microsoft Networking, but do not expect to see questions on the Explorer or SMBs on the exams.*

EXPLORER—THE APPLICATION LAYER OF MICROSOFT NETWORKING When a user clicks on a network resource in Explorer, Explorer immediately launches the redirector. Redirector then sends along the request for the file or folder. Explorer and redirector combined essentially make up the Application layer in Microsoft Networking. NT Explorer refers not only to the user-interface with which you are no doubt familiar, but to the internal client and server elements of the operating system. Each NT machine has both a server portion and a client portion to allow both sharing and accessing of data.

While NT is capable of taking advantage of other Application layer protocols, such as FTP, the redirector and Explorer serve the application layer functions for Microsoft Networking. These elements (redirector and Explorer) are designed to tie-in completely to the server message blocks and NetBIOS, discussed below, as their Presentation and Session layers for Microsoft Networking functions.

SERVER MESSAGE BLOCKS (SMB) After the redirector sends out the request, that request must be formatted so that the other machine (as well as the other layers in the protocol model) can understand the request. Microsoft Networking relies on a message format called Server Message Blocks to handle the Presentation layer issues for all Microsoft Networking functions. SMBs provide a standard set of commands and requests for Application layer protocols to use when communicating via the network. SMB is so closely tied in to Microsoft Networking that it is not an optional choice in any Microsoft configuration, and SMBs are not covered heavily on the exams. They are included here for completeness.

SMBs are the most basic messages communicated back and forth between Microsoft clients and servers. The other layers exist to move these messages around the network. It is possible to make other network operating systems' servers operate as though they were Microsoft servers by giving them the ability to generate and receive SMBs. The most common example would be running SAMBA (SaMBa) on a UNIX or Linux based server. SMBs are the Microsoft Networking requests, such as requests for files, requests for printer functions, and requests to update folder contents using browsers, as shown in Figure 10–13.

The SMB cannot get to the shared resources until it establishes communication with the remote machine. NetBIOS—a Session layer protocol—establishes this communication. Microsoft designed SMB to work directly with NetBIOS. Each layer in the network, according to the OSI model, need only communicate with the layer immediately above and below itself. SMB, operating at the Presentation layer, for example, only needs to know what protocol is being used at the next layer, the Session layer. While it is theoretically possible to use SMB with other Session layer protocols, Microsoft currently has implemented support for only one, NetBIOS.

NETBIOS At the next layer, after the request has been made and formatted, communication needs to be started with the remote machine. Net-BIOS (Network Basic Input/ Output System), which provides the Session layer functions for Microsoft Networking, opens the communication session. The process of opening a communication session between two computers in the average network is similar to the process of starting a

Figure 10–13
Top NT Layers

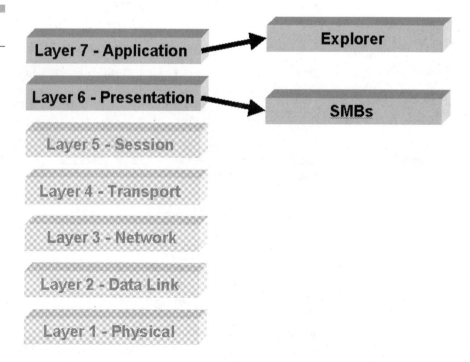

conversation between two people in a crowded room full of strangers. How do you determine people's names (computer names)? How do you tell who is willing to talk and who is just a listener (servers and clients)? If you have one more conversation going at the same time, how do you talk and listen to make sure the conversations aren't confused? NetBIOS handles all of these jobs.

Clearly, any orderly conversation must begin with some form of naming. In the Middle Ages, people often had a name that described *who* they were as well as *what* they *did*. Names like John the Archer or Peter the Blacksmith were very common. NetBIOS takes a very "Middle Aged" view of names in a network. Each computer gets a name that describes *who* they are as well as *what* they *do*. Unlike people, computers can have more than one name. They actually have one name for every function that they perform on the network. No communication can take place without the machines being able to address each other.

The base NetBIOS name for a given computer is determined by the Computer Name and the Workgroup Name entered in the Identification tab in the Network control panel applet. (For the purposes of NetBIOS names, Microsoft uses the term Workgroup to mean both Workgroups and Domains). NetBIOS names are limited to sixteen characters. Administrators can change the first fifteen characters of the computer names in Microsoft Networking, as shown in Figure 10–14, but the sixteenth is reserved for defining the function, and cannot be changed. An example of a base name would be SERVER1, ADMIN321, or JOHNSPC.

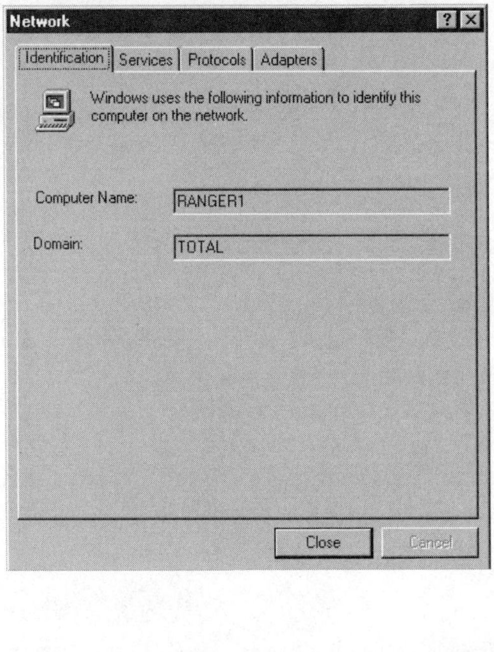

Figure 10–14
Identification tab in Windowns NT Network Control Panel applet

To get a complete NetBIOS name, a function must be added to the base name. NetBIOS names identify both the identity of a computer and the functions it can perform. Some typical roles of computers would be Server, Workstation, Member of a Workgroup, etc (There are more that will be described in a moment). Each of these functions are described by an assigned number, not words. The number assignment for a Workstation, for example, is <03>. Instead of saying JOHNSPC the WORKSTATION, NetBIOS will say JOHNSPC<03>. Remember each machine will have more than one name! JOHNSPC can be:

```
JOHNSPC<00> a workstation
JOHNSPC<20> a server
JOHNSPC  . . .  (whatever else he needs to be recognized
        as)
```

Each machine, by creating a list of names to which it will respond, defines its role within the network.

To determine the names NetBIOS has for the given computer, use the program NBTSTAT. This command—available only if you are using TCP/IP—displays the NetBIOS names in use by a particular machine. Use NBTSTAT from the command line with the -N switch to view the names in use for a machine for each necessary function. If the NBTSTAT -N command were run on a computer called \\ACCT2 in a workgroup (or domain) called STORE, it would give the following results:

```
NetBIOS Remote Machine Name Table
Name                    Type            Status
─────────────────
ACCT2              <00>  UNIQUE        Registered
STORE              <00>  GROUP         Registered
ACCT2              <03>  UNIQUE        Registered
ACCT2              <20>  UNIQUE        Registered
STORE              <1E>  GROUP         Registered
STORE              <1D>  UNIQUE        Registered
..__MSBROWSE__.  <01>  GROUP         Registered

MAC Address = 00-80-AD-11-AB-A8
```

The first column of the result screen displays the name, either of the machine or the workgroup (domain). The second column, the hexadecimal number enclosed within the angle brackets, represents the value for the sixteenth byte of each name. Table 10–1 shows the meaning of the various sixteenth bit extensions for Unique and Group names. The third column represents the two types of NetBIOS names: Unique and Group. A Unique name can only be registered by one machine on the entire network. There can only be one server with the name ACCT<20>, for example.

Table 10–1

NetBIOS Names
and Functions

Unique Names

16th Byte	Function
<00>	Workstation Service name. The name registered by clients on the network.
<03>	Messenger Service Name. Used by applications such as WINPOPUP and NET SEND to deliver messages
<1B>	Domain Master Browser
<06>	RAS server
<1F>	NetDDE Service
<20>	File Server
<21>	RAS client
<BE>	Network Monitor agent
<BF>	Network Monitor utility

Group Names

16th Byte	Function
<00>	Registers Machine as member of domain or workgroup
<1C>	Domain Controller
<1D>	Master Browser
<1E>	Potential Master Browser (used in Browser elections)
<20>	Special Internet Group that can be used for administrative purposes
MSBROWSE	Instead of individual 16th bit, "_MSBROWSE_" added to the end of the domain name is used to announce the domain master browser to other domain master browsers, allowing browsing between domains.

Multiple machines, on the other hand, can register Group names. Many machines can register the domain or workgroup name **STORE<00>**, for example. The final column shows that the chosen name has been successfully taken, or registered.

NOTE: *The term "messaging" is often used to refer to programs that provide email and groupware functions such as MS Exchange, cc:Mail, or Lotus Notes. The Messenger service referred to in Table 10–1 has nothing to do with e-mail or groupware functions. It is used primarily for administrative alerts and is a function of Microsoft Networking.*

The NetBIOS naming scheme provides a relatively simple means of managing connections. In the four-node network illustrated in Figure 10–15, the machine ACCT2 has been set up as both a Microsoft client and as a Microsoft server. Because it has a number of roles on the network, it has multiple NetBIOS names. Table 10–2 shows the NetBIOS names for

Figure 10–15

A small, four-node network

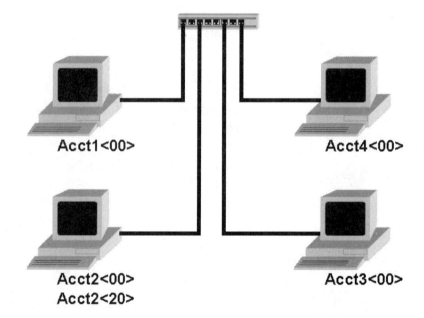

Acct1<00>

Acct4<00>

Acct2<00>
Acct2<20>

Acct3<00>

Table 10–2

Typical NetBIOS names

NetBIOS Name		Function
ACCT2	<00> UNIQUE	ACCT2 is a client that can access Microsoft Networking servers
STORE	<00> GROUP	Member of workgroup STORE
ACCT2	<03> UNIQUE	Will Accept messages from messenger service for ACCT2
ACCT2	<20> UNIQUE	ACCT2 is a file server that will service requests from Microsoft Networking clients
STORE	<1E> GROUP	ACCT2 is a potential master browser
STORE	<1D> UNIQUE	ACCT2 is the actual master browser
..__MSBROWSE__.<01> GROUP		Other master browsers can contact for ACCT2 its browse list.

ACCT2. (A *node*, by the way, is simply any machine connected to the network that can send or receive data.)

Machines use the NetBIOS names to connect to particular functions on another machine. If ACCT1—configured as a Microsoft client—wants to access a share on ACCT2, it would send out a message something like, "Hey, this is **ACCT1<00>** calling **ACCT2<20>**, can I connect with you?" The **ACCT1<00>** name for ACCT1 identifies it as a client, and the **ACCT2<20>** tells ACCT2 that, not only does ACCT1 want to connect with it, but also that ACCT1 needs ACCT2 to act in its capacity as a Microsoft file server, as shown in Figure 10–16. The NetBIOS names do not just identify the machines involved in the connection. They also identify the function those machines should perform.

In our example, ACCT3 is not configured as a server. In Figure 10–17, ACCT1 attempts to connect to ACCT3 as a file server using the name **ACCT3<20>**, but ACCT3 does not respond. Since it is not a server, it will not be using the NetBIOS name **ACCT3<20>**. ACCT3 ignores the message sent to **ACCT3<20>** because it does not have Microsoft File and Print sharing installed. It does not bother to respond to **ACCT1<00>**. ACCT1 will eventually time out, giving an error to the end user to the effect that "the server was not found." The error the user sees will vary depending on what application was in use.

Figure 10–16
Using NetBIOS names

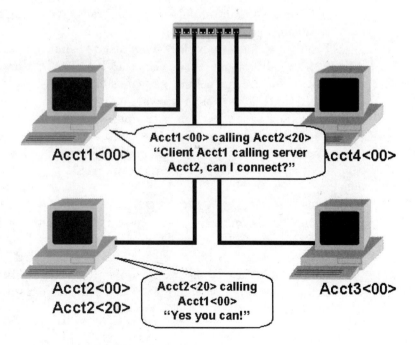

Acct1<00>

Acct1<00> calling Acct2<20>
"Client Acct1 calling server Acct2, can I connect?"

Acct4<00>

Acct2<00>
Acct2<20>

Acct2<20> calling
Acct1<00>
"Yes you can!"

Acct3<00>

Figure 10–17
ACCT3 ignores
ACCT1<00>.

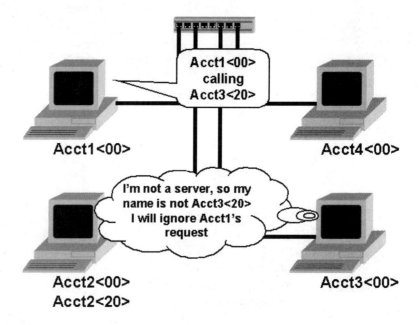

In some cases, the NetBIOS naming convention also allows for a Microsoft machine to connect with a machine whose specific name it does not know. Client machines logging into a domain, for example, do not have to know the name of the domain controller. Assuming the client knows the domain name, they simply log in to *domain name*<1C>. Only a domain controller machine will respond back to that name. Similarly, in Figure 10–18, all four machines belong to the STORE workgroup. ACCT4 does not know which machine is the master browser for the workgroup, but can still contact the master browser using the name **STORE<1D>**. ACCT 4 does not know which machine is the master browser for the workgroup, but can still contact the master browser using the name **STORE<1D>**. ACCT2 knows that it is the master browser of the STORE workgroup and will respond to the NetBIOS name **STORE<1D>**.

GETTING THE DATA FROM POINT A TO POINT B NetBIOS cannot create connections unless its messages can move from one machine to another. In the original Microsoft Networking scheme, making that connection was simple: NetBIOS hands off to NetBIOS Extended User Interface (NetBEUI). NetBEUI has two key jobs: Repackaging the messages so that they were small enough for the physical and data link layers to handle, and locating the destination machine.

Figure 10–18
Sending
a browse list

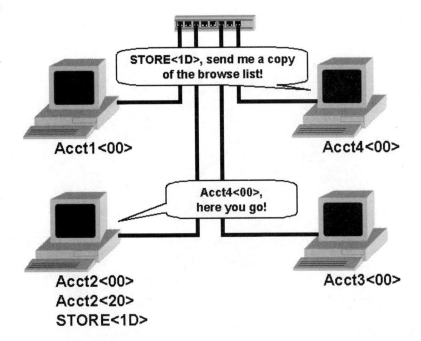

NetBEUI repackages the data, breaking large packages up into smaller units. For the receiving machine to reconstruct that data into its original form, NetBEUI adds extra information to each package. This additional information tells the receiving machine exactly how to reassemble the packets.

Before NetBEUI can transmit these packages, it must locate the destination machine. NetBEUI's technique for doing so is simple: It yells. If Phil's client PC, CLIENT15, needs to communicate with the server SERVER5, it broadcasts a message that says, "Hey SERVER5, are you out there?" If SERVER5 "hears" that message and responds, NetBEUI can transmit the data. The use of broadcast messages for finding other machines on the network has one key virtue: It requires no configuration on the part of the end user or the administrator.

To install and use the NetBEUI transport protocol in your Microsoft NT environment, open the Network applet in the Control Panel. On the Protocols tab, click the Add button. This displays the Select Network Protocol dialogue box, shown in Figure 10–19. Select NetBEUI, direct the applet to any necessary installation media, and NetBEUI is installed and ready to go.

Figure 10–19
Installing NetBEUI

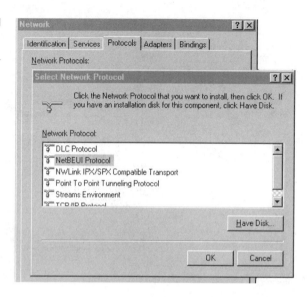

NetBEUI is great for small networks, but begins to break down as networks get larger. As the number of clients and servers grows, these broadcast messages eat up more and more time and bandwidth. This is bad. To solve the problem of excessive broadcasts and staggeringly slow networks, administrators of larger networks break their networks into smaller networks, joined together by specialized devices called routers. Routers cut the amount of traffic in the network as a whole by not transmitting any broadcasts from Network A to Network B. This feature limits NetBEUI to small networks without routers. Because it relies on broadcasts to send messages, NetBEUI cannot send data to the far side of a router. If John in Network A wants to access Jane's computer in Network B, their machines must use a routable protocol, such as IPX/SPX or TCP/IP. Let's look at broadcasts and routers, and then turn to the routable protocols.

BROADCASTS AND ROUTERS Within a LAN, every machine will "hear" every broadcast. The machines will ignore any broadcast message intended for another machine. In a small network, such as the three-node network shown in Figure 10–20, broadcast messages facilitate the flow of information.

A user sitting at the machine **RANDY** types in the command "**NET USE F: \\SALES\REPORTS**." RANDY needs to send a message to the server known as **SALES<20h>** (see the previous discussion of NetBIOS name 16th byte extensions). RANDY sends out a broadcast packet that all stations on the network must process, saying, "I need to get this message to SALES. If your NetBIOS

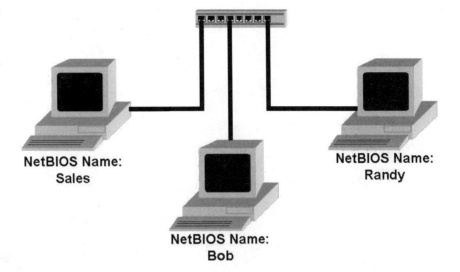

Figure 10–20

A small Ethernet LAN with 3 nodes.

NetBIOS Name:
Sales

NetBIOS Name:
Randy

NetBIOS Name:
Bob

name is SALES, please respond." BOB sees this broadcast and processes it, but does not respond. Despite the fact that BOB does not respond, however, BOB has to process the broadcast message all the way up to the session layer (layer 5) of the OSI model. None of the lower levels know that BOB's Net-BIOS name is not **SALES<20h>**. See Figure 10–21. Broadcast traffic increases the load on every machine on the network by requiring them to process data packets that are not intended for them.

Broadcast messages represent a challenge to network architects. On the one hand, they allow for a great deal of flexibility. Broadcasts allow machines to "discover" other machines on the network, avoiding the necessity for massive amounts of configuration. Excessive broadcast traffic, however, can slow down every machine on the network, because machines must process every broadcast, even if the broadcast has nothing to do with them. While many network functions rely on broadcasts to some degree, network architects place a premium on limiting broadcast traffic. A router can be a powerful tool in this battle.

A *router* is a device that connects distinct networks (LANs) into a larger inter- or intra-networks (WAN). Routers allow protocols such as IPX/SPX and TCP/IP to move data between machines even when those machines cannot "hear" each other's broadcasts.

Routers serve as both barriers and connections between networks. Figure 10–22 shows a router connecting two small networks. Unlike devices such as hubs and bridges, the router only forwards traffic from one network to the other when the destination for the traffic lies on the far side of the

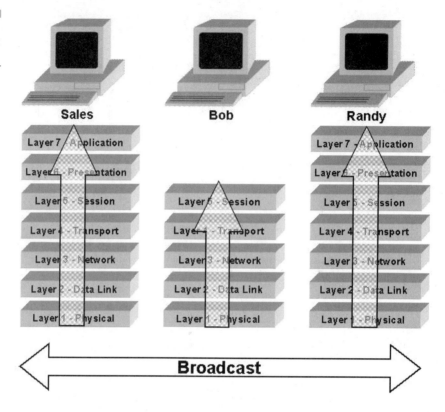

Figure 10–21
How Broadcast traffic affects the network

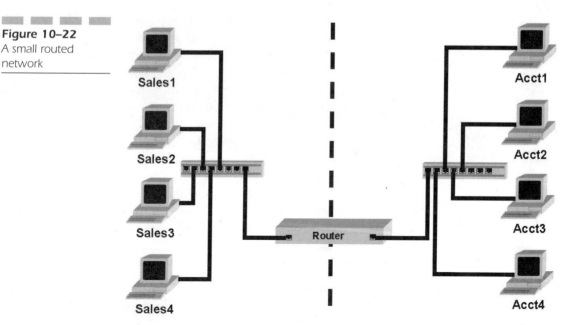

Figure 10–22
A small routed network

router, based on the destination network address included in routable protocols such as TCP/IP and IPX/SPX.

A router passes traffic to other networks only if the proper routing information is included in each packet. Since NetBEUI lacks such routing information, NetBEUI is not routable. Because TCP/IP and IPX/SPX packets do include routing information, they can be routed. While Microsoft Networking can run on top of IPX/SPX, Microsoft focuses on TCP/IP as its protocol of choice for routed networks. Microsoft does not cover IPX routing in detail on any of the current exams. Microsoft assumes an overall familiarity with TCP/IP for the three exams covered in this book, and has a separate (and wildly popular) TCP/IP elective exam.

ROUTABLE PROTOCOLS   In the modern world of networking, routers connect smaller networks into larger networks, allowing companies in one location to connect directly to their offices in other locations. To allow Microsoft Networking requests and connections to be sent over these routers, however, you must use a routable protocol in your environment. The two main routable protocols supported in a Microsoft Networking environment are NWLink (Microsoft's implementation of IPX/SPX), and TCP/IP.

IPX/SPX Compatible Transport, a.k.a. NWLINK   Microsoft Networking's reliance on the non-routable protocol NetBEUI put Microsoft at a competitive disadvantage with rivals such as Novell. Novell built their flagship networking product, NetWare, to run on top of their IPX/SPX protocol suite, which included a full-fledged Network layer. In order to compete with Novell, Microsoft engineered its own version of IPX/SPX and dubbed it NWLink (NetWare Link). NWLink can be used either to provide access to NetWare servers, or as a Transport and Network layer protocol for Microsoft Networking.

NOTE: *A protocol suite is a set of protocols intended to be used together to function at one or more layer of the OSI model. This is also referred to as a protocol stack.*

To install and configure NWLink IPX/SPX, open the Network Control Panel applet. On the Protocols tab, click the Add . . . button and select NWLink IPX/SPX compatible transport from the available list. After installing, you can click on the Properties button for this protocol to add in any specific configuration. This is not necessary in most networks, as the defaults will allow communication in most environments. For more information on configuring this protocol, refer to Chapter 12, "NT and Novell."

NOTE: *The terms NWLink and IPX/SPX compatible transport are used interchangeably in most Microsoft documentation and throughout this book. Most configuration screens, however, refer to the protocol as NWLink IPX/SPX compatible transport.*

The importance of IPX/SPX in Microsoft Networking has faded in recent years. While IPX/SPX provides a perfectly acceptable means of moving traffic across a LAN or WAN, the rise of the Internet has made TCP/IP the protocol of choice in most Microsoft networks. Microsoft has relegated IPX/SPX to two main roles: Support for legacy networks and connectivity to NetWare servers. For more information on connecting to Novell NetWare servers, refer to Chapter 12, "NT and Novell," which covers the role of IPX/SPX in connecting to Novell Networks in more detail.

NOTE: *The Microsoft exams do not stress an in-depth knowledge of IPX/SPX. The key pieces of knowledge expected of you on the exams are that IPX/SPX (a.k.a. NWLink) is required for connectivity with NetWare servers and that it is a routable protocol.*

TCP/IP The TCP/IP (Transmission Control Protocol/ Internet Protocol) protocol suite, which is the standard for Internet communications, allows routable communication among different clients and servers, both from Microsoft as well as from other vendors, such as servers and clients from the different flavors of UNIX, Novell, and Macintosh. Similarly to the IPX/SPX protocol stack, TCP/IP functions not only at the Transport layer, but also at the Network layer. The protocol accomplishes both the task of placing data into packets and the task of giving addresses to the machines in the environment. It is this addressing component, again, that allows the TCP/IP protocol to be routed among different networks.

TCP/IP originally had two barriers to its wide acceptance in internal networks—the size of the protocol stack and its slowness when compared to NetBEUI. With the common use of larger machines and more memory, the size of the TCP/IP stack has become less of an issue. In addition, Microsoft has implemented TCP/IP in a more integrated fashion, again reducing the importance of the size of the protocol stack. In terms of speed, the TCP/IP protocol allows similar speeds to IPX/SPX, while offering ability to route and the ability to connect with the Internet.

TCP/IP in Gory Detail

You will have noticed that there wasn't much to installing and configuring NetBEUI or IPX/SPX—you just install them and let them go. But TCP/IP is different—look at all the settings in the control panel that must be determined to set up a single network card (see Figure 10–23). Some might look at all these settings and say, "To heck with it, I'll just use Net-BEUI." But not you, you intrepid MCSE candidate! You know that TCP/IP, the protocol of the Internet, is both the present and the future of networking. Many advanced features of NT and other software rely on the TCP/IP protocol suite. In addition, Microsoft is moving to tie more and more features of the next version of NT, Windows 2000, ever more closely to TCP/IP and its related protocols. So let's dive right into the gory details.

While Microsoft has a separate exam covering TCP/IP in detail, the three core exams covered here require a strong general understanding of the TCP/IP settings available in the Windows NT control panel. Understanding the array of choices available in these screens requires a basic knowledge of the major parts of a TCP/IP-based network, including IP addressing, DNS, WINS, and DHCP.

Figure 10–23
TCP/IP settings can be accessed from the Network Control Panel's Protocol tab.

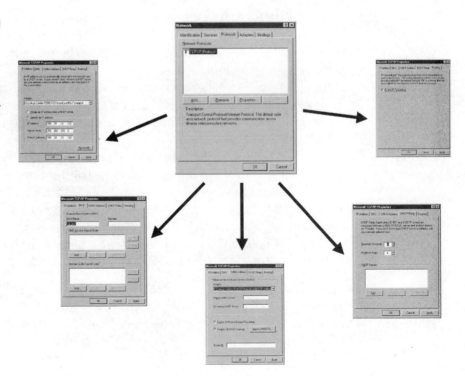

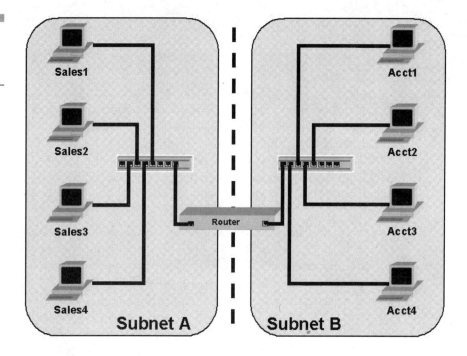

Figure 10–24
A small internetwork composed of two smaller subnets.

NETWORK ADDRESSING Any network address, whether an IP address or IPX address, must provide two pieces of information. It must uniquely identify the machine, and it must locate that machine within the larger network. Figure 10–24, for example, shows an internetwork composed of two smaller networks. In TCP/IP terminology, the two smaller networks are called *subnets*. In this example, the accounting and sales departments each have their own network, and these subnets connect through a router.

Any machine on the sales side of the router that needs to send data to a machine on the accounting side of the router must first send that data to the router. As mentioned earlier, a router is a device that connects distinct networks, allowing traffic to pass between them. In TCP/IP terminology, routers are sometimes referred to as gateways. The problem for the PC is determining when to deliver a packet locally and when to send it to the router. In this case, an IP address provides the answer.

NOTE: *Gateway is a dangerous term. Except in TCP/IP, the term "gateway" refers to a system that acts as a translator between dissimilar systems. The Gateway Services for NetWare (GSNW) discussed in the Chapter 12, "NT and Novell," for example, allows PCs with only the Microsoft Client installed to access files on a*

Novell NetWare server by using an NT server as an intermediary. In TCP/IP
terminology, however, the term gateway refers to routers. Unfortunately, both TCP/IP
gateways (i.e., routers) and gateways such as GSNW can exist in the same network.

IP ADDRESSING AND SUBNET MASKS   The IP Address tab, shown in Figure
10–25, requires three pieces of information about each network card installed in the system: Its IP address, its subnet mask, and its default gateway. Each of these entries provides information required by the IP
protocol for proper routing of packets. An IP address and subnet mask can
be entered either manually, or automatically set via DHCP by selecting
the "Obtain IP address automatically" radio button. (Hold that thought!
DHCP is discussed below.) IP addresses can be referred to as network addresses, because the IP protocol that requires them operates at the Network layer in the OSI model. To understand IP addressing requires you
to know what an IP address does in the network and how a machine gets
the various components of its IP address.

When a network node on the SALES network wants to communicate with
another PC on the sales network, it simply sends out a packet on the local
network cable with the appropriate hardware address and assumes that the
intended PC can "hear" the message. In the same way, a person might yell
out a message across a crowded office, assuming that the intended recipient

Figure 10–25
Critical IP settings

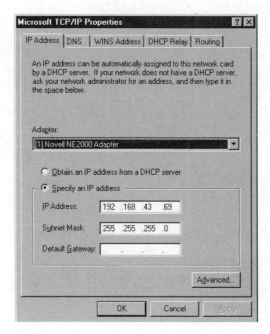

is present in the room. Most of the time, however, the destination computer is not in the same office. To ensure that the remote computer can receive the message, the networks require routers to forward the information.

Routers move data packets between networks. Think of a TCP/IP packet as a piece of interoffice mail. If Syd needs to send some paperwork to John Smith in the accounting department he can place the paperwork in an interoffice envelope, address the envelope, and send the information to John (see Figure 10–26). A data packet is similar to an envelope in many ways. The outside of the envelope contains addressing information, and the inside can hold a wide variety of contents.

If Syd works in the accounting department, he has the option of simply walking across the hall and handing the envelope to Mr. Smith. Similarly, the sending machine can deliver traffic bound for local addresses, just as an office worker can personally deliver an envelope to a coworker in the same department (see Figure 10–27).

On the other hand, what if Syd needs to send some information to Phil Jones in the Shipping department? In all likelihood, Syd does not even know where the shipping department is. At this point, Syd needs to rely on another person to get his message to its destination.

In this analogy, Syd might give the envelope to the "Mail Guy." As long as Syd trusts the Mail Guy to find the shipping department, Syd's job is

Figure 10–26
Data packet as envelope

John Smith
Accounting

Figure 10–27
Local messages can
be delivered directly.

Figure 10–27
Local messages can
be delivered directly.

Accounting Dept.

Figure 10–28
Remote messages
need intervention to
be delivered.

Accounting Dept.

done the moment he recognizes that shipping is not his department. Syd simply ensures the envelope is properly addressed and hands his data off to the Mail Guy (see Figure 10–28). Traffic bound for remote addresses must be delivered to the router for delivery, just as an office worker might give a package bound for a worker in a different department to the office Mail Guy.

The "Mail Guy" represents the router. It is Syd's job to know when he can deliver the package himself and to know when to pass it along to the router. In this analogy, the decision is easy. Syd works in the accounting office; therefore, if he creates anything for a coworker in accounting, he can obviously deliver the package himself. If its destination is any other department, however, he sends it on via the router, the "Mail Guy." Notice that Syd does not have to know where the shipping department is physically—that's the Mail Guy's job. All that must be clear is the address, so that the Mail Guy knows where to find the recipient.

TCP/IP networks handle routing in much the same way as our Mail Guy. Every host on a TCP/IP network must decide whether its outgoing packets should be delivered locally or sent to the router. Once the machine hands the packet to the router, it is the router's job to get the packet the rest of the way to its destination. TCP/IP answers the question "do I deliver it myself or send it to the router?" by using IP addresses and subnet masks.

NOTE: *In TCP/IP networks, any device that can be either the source or recipient of data is known as a "host."*

In TCP/IP, each host is assigned a unique 32-bit address. A machine's address, for example, might be:

11000000110101000011100101001000

No human being is ever going to be able to remember that number. In order to make these addresses manageable, it is necessary to find a shorthand method with which to express these addresses. While many other long binary strings are expressed in hexadecimal, the designers of TCP/IP decided to use "dotted decimal" notation. In order to translate the 32-bit address above into dotted decimal, break the 32-bit address into 4 sets of 8 bits each. These 8-bit values are called octets. When the address above, for example, is broken down, it looks like this:

11000000   11010100   00111001   01001000

There are 256 different combinations of eight ones and zeroes, from 00000000 to 11111111. They can be numbered into decimal equivalents, starting with 0, as follows:

00000000	0
00000001	1
00000010	2

all the way to the end

11111111	255

After breaking the address into octets, translate each octet into its decimal equivalent. You can use the Windows 95 or Windows NT calculator (in scientific mode) to do binary to decimal conversions, as shown in Figure 10–29. Set the calculator to binary mode (using the Bin radio button or hit <F8>). Then type in the binary address. To convert it to decimal, simply click the Dec radio button (or hit <F6>) and the calculator will convert it for you. For example, type in 01001000 and the calculator will translate it into its decimal equivalent: 72.

If you use the same process for each 8-bit value, 11000000 becomes 192; 11010100 becomes 212; 00111001 becomes 57; and, 01001000 becomes 72. The "dotted decimal" equivalent of 11000000110101000011100110001000, therefore, is 192.212.57.72. While at first glance 192.212.57.72 may not seem like the easiest setting that you have ever had to keep track of for a PC, it is clearly much easier to deal with than its binary equivalent.

The first rule of IP addresses is that they must be unique. No two hosts on a TCP/IP network can have the same IP address. If your network is directly connected to the Internet, your IP addresses must be unique across the entire Internet. IP addresses, however, must do more than just uniquely identify each host. IP addresses must contain enough information so that other machines can find your node. In a routed TCP/IP network, the network is broken up into smaller units called subnets. Part of the IP address is set aside as the address of the network (the Net ID) while the rest of the address identifies the individual host computer (the Host ID).

Figure 10–29
The Windows
calculator

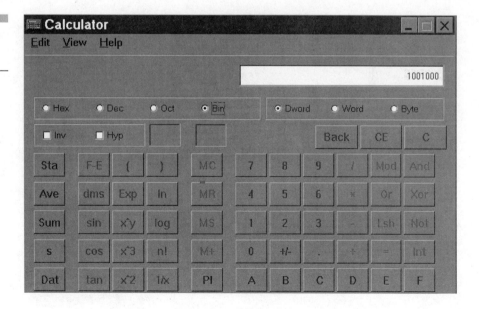

As an analogy for the IP address breakdown, think about a phone number. Total Seminars' phone number in Houston is 943-3888. "943" specifies a particular exchange of the Houston area telephone network, while "3888" specifies a particular phone. If someone at Total Seminars (943-3888) dials 943-8553, then the telephone network knows to keep the call within the 943 exchange, conserving circuits on the larger telephone network. IP addresses are broken up the same way, with part of the address referring to the particular network to which the host is connected and the rest referring to the individual host. If a host attempts to send to another host within the same subnet, it sends the packet without assistance. If a host needs to send to another machine outside the same subnet, it needs the assistance of a router (also known as a gateway) to move the message on toward its final destination.

With phone numbers, the division between the exchange (the Net ID) and the individual phone (the Host ID) is easy—just look for the dash. IP addresses will not be so easy. The division between the Net ID and the Host ID varies depending on another number: the subnet mask. The subnet mask is a 32-bit number, just like the IP address. Every TCP/IP host has both an IP address and a subnet mask. The system looks at its IP address, and compares it to the subnet mask to determine the Host ID and the Network ID. Sounds a little complicated but it is really a very simple concept. In binary, the subnet mask must have all ones on the left and all zeros on the right. The ones represent the Network ID portion and the zeros represent the Host ID. A common subnet mask is:

```
11111111 11111111 11111111 00000000
```

This is better known in its decimal format:

```
255.255.255.0
```

The subnet mask determines which part of the IP address refers to the network, and which part refers to the host.

To understand subnet masks, you have to do some more math. Renny's computer is configured with the IP address and subnet mask shown in Figure 10–30. The IP address is 196.76.141.58. The subnet mask, 255.255.255.0, determines which part of that address refers to the local network (i.e., the network to which his machine is attached) and which part refers to the host (the individual PC).

First, translate the IP address and subnet mask into their binary format:

```
IP address    11000100 1001100 10001101 00011101
Subnet mask   11111111 1111111 11111111 00000000
```

Figure 10–30
The IP address
configuration screen
for a Windows 95
host configured with
an IP address of
196.76.414.58 and a
subnet mask of
255.255.255.0.

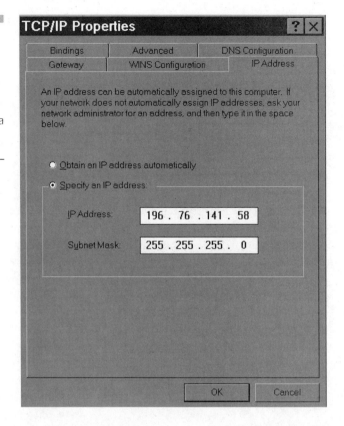

Any part of the IP address that corresponds to a one in the subnet mask is part of the Net ID; any part that corresponds to a zero in the subnet mask refers to the Host ID. In this example, the first 24 digits refer to the Net ID and the last 8 refer to the Host ID, which gives you the following results:

```
Net ID 11000100 1001100 10001101
Host ID         00011101
```

If you translate these binary numbers back into "dotted decimal" notation, you get the following results:

```
Net ID       196.76.141.0
Host ID      58
```

NOTE: *Net IDs normally get filled out with zeros. Computer speak would describe this network as "network 196.76.141.0," not as "network 196.76.141."*

IP addresses provide an excellent—but limited—way of describing the Host ID and the Net ID for a computer. With 32-bit addresses, 2^{32} unique addresses are possible (4,294,967,296 addresses). Four billion addresses sounds like a huge number, but today the Internet is close to running out of IP addresses. Why? Of the roughly four billion possible addresses, many cannot be used to identify individual machines. In the example above, there can be a limited number of hosts in the network 196.76.141.0. The subnet mask, 255.255.255.0, indicates that the first 24 bits are set aside to specify the Net ID, leaving the last 8 bits to specify the hosts on the network. Since $2^8 = 256$, there could be as many as 256 computers on that network, right? Actually, two of those addresses—196.76.141.255 and 196.76.141.0—cannot be used to represent individual machines. A Host ID containing all 1s indicates a broadcast message for all machines on the subnet. A Host ID of all 0s indicates that the message is for a network, not for an individual host. 196.76.141.0 already refers to the network as a whole, in other words, and 196.76.141.255 is the broadcast address for that network. A number reserved here and a number reserved there, still add up, even with 4 billion addresses!

NOTE: It is an important distinction to note that the binary Host IDs of all 1s or all 0s are reserved, not the decimal numbers 0 and 255. When dealing with subnet masks other than 255.255.255.0, that distinction becomes very important.

With a limited number of addresses, the powers-that-be of the Internet need to exercise care when assigning those addresses. Networks come in various sizes, and addresses need to be assigned with sensitivity to that fact. It would be wasteful, for example, to give Total Seminars and Coca-Cola the same number of addresses. Coca-Cola, with its huge organization, requires multiple thousands of addresses, while Total Seminars can get by with fewer than a hundred. IP addressing uses different subnet masks for different addresses to allow different size blocks of addresses to be assigned to different size organizations.

The IP addressing scheme allows for networks of various sizes. To supply addresses for a larger organization, for example, assign that organization the Network ID 188.25.0.0. The organization would use the subnet mask 255.255.0.0, giving them 16 bits to use for hosts (188.25.0.1 through 188.25.255.254). This gives them a little more than 65,000 different IP addresses.

To make it easier to manage the assignment of IP addresses to various organizations on the Internet, the governing body in charge of assigning addresses created several classes of "licenses" associated with networks of different sizes. Each class license has its own default subnet mask, which determines how many hosts can be part of the same network. The following are the three main classes:

Class A, with a subnet mask of 255.0.0.0, allows up to 16,777,214 ($2^{24}-2$) hosts in the network.

Class B, with a subnet mask of 255.255.0.0, allows up to 65,534 ($2^{16}-2$) hosts in the network.

Class C, with a subnet mask of 255.255.255.0, allows up to 254 ($2^{8}-2$) hosts in the network.

These licenses are not just used to assign addresses, but also to provide other hosts on the network with information about the address itself. The first few bits of any IP address determine to which class an address belongs. In the binary addresses, all Class A addresses begin with 0; all Class B addresses begin with 10; and, all Class C addresses begin with 110. Table 10–3 shows how the first few bits of an IP address divide all IP address into one of five classes. Class D and E addresses are never assigned to individual machines. Class D addresses are set aside for multicasting, and Class E addresses have been reserved for some future, as yet undetermined use.

MULTICASTING VERSUS UNICASTING: *Almost all TCP/IP traffic is unicast traffic, meaning that it is intended to go from one specific point on the network to another specific point on the network. Unfortunately, sending the same data to several hosts requires that a separate unicast message be sent, eating up precious bandwidth. Multicasting applications allow for a single host to send a message to multiple hosts, eliminating the need to send the same data multiple times. Multicast IP addresses are not covered on the three exams covered by this guide.*

Table 10–3

Class Licenses

First Octet (binary)	First Octet (decimal)	Class	Subnet Mask
0xxxxxxx	0-127	A	255.0.0.0
10xxxxxx	128-191	B	255.255.0.0
110xxxxx	192-223	C	255.255.255.0
1110xxxx	224-239	D	Multicast Addresses
1111xxxx	240-255	E	Experimental Addresses

Using the information about classes and IP addresses described above, each machine makes some assumptions about appropriate subnet masks for any address. When trying to send to 145.23.25.175, for example, the machine must decide where to send the data. Because all addresses with the form 145.x.y.z fall into the Class B range, the system can assume that the machine has a subnet mask of 255.255.0.0. (145 in binary is 10010001). When trying to send to a host with the IP address 145.23.25.175, therefore, the system knows to send that message to network 145.23.0.0.

The IP address and the subnet mask provide the two most vital pieces of information: a Host ID and a Network ID. When sending a packet to a host with the same Network ID, every machine delivers its own packet locally. When sending a packet to a host with a different Host ID, the packet is sent to the default gateway, otherwise known as the router.

THE DEFAULT GATEWAY The default gateway is simply the IP address of the router to which a host sends all traffic bound for other networks. When configuring the default gateway, remember that in order to reach the gateway, that gateway must have an address that is part of the same network as your host. Setting an incorrect default gateway is one of the more common configuration errors in TCP/IP networks. Figure 10–31 shows a small

Figure 10–31
A two-subnet IP
network

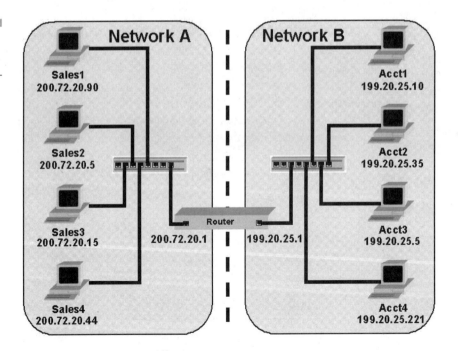

Network A

Sales1
200.72.20.90

Sales2
200.72.20.5

Sales3
200.72.20.15

Sales4
200.72.20.44

Router
200.72.20.1   199.20.25.1

Network B

Acct1
199.20.25.10

Acct2
199.20.25.35

Acct3
199.20.25.5

Acct4
199.20.25.221

TCP/IP-based network, divided into two smaller networks. Network A has a network address of 200.72.20.0 and Network B has a network address of 199.20.25.0.

Notice that the router actually has two addresses, one for each network. Hosts on Network A use the address 200.72.20.1 as their default gateway. They cannot reach the router's other address, 199.20.25.1 without going through a router. 199.20.25.1 cannot be their default gateway. The default gateway address must always be the address of the "near side" of the router, which has the same Network ID as the host being configured.

The most significant elements of the TCP/IP configuration screen are the IP address, the subnet mask, and the default gateway. In some environments, simple communication can take place with only these elements configured. For the more complex environments and the more complex needs of the network, however, the addressing needs to be taken a step further. Many applications require the use of a name, rather than an IP address. Resolving the IP address information into names is the next important element of the TCP/IP configuration.

THE CASE FOR NAME RESOLUTION   The discussion of IP addresses above assumed that the IP address of the destination host was known. The human beings and software applications that actually use the computers, however, rarely think of computers by their addresses. They do not want to use numbers like 129.168.43.3 to refer to the first server; they prefer to use a name like SERVER1. They don't want to access the Total Seminars Web site at 207.222.216.40; they want to type **http://www.totalsem.com** into their Web browsers. A method of "name resolution" needs to be developed to allow TCP/IP computers to use these names instead of numbers. To satisfy the demand for names instead of numbers when referring to systems in TCP/IP, a number of different methods have been developed. In a simple network, name resolution is trivial—a system can simply broadcast on the network to get the name of a particular system. When routing becomes involved, however, broadcasting is no longer an option—routers erase broadcasts. To handle names over routers, NT provides two totally separate name resolution tools: *Domain Name System* (DNS) and *Windows Internet Name Service* (WINS).

DNS and WINS essentially provide directory assistance for TCP/IP networks. Both DNS and WINS are manifested as DNS servers or WINS servers that store a list of names that refer to IP addresses. DNS and WINS servers are nothing more than systems running NT Server with special DNS server or WINS server services installed. They do not have to be dedicated NT servers. It is very common to see a PDC also act as a DNS server, for example. A client computer needing a name resolved simply queries a DNS or WINS server. The server then gets the information and sends it to the client. Just as Mary can dial "1411" and ask "what is John Robertson's phone number?" a TCP/IP host can access a DNS server to find out the IP address of `www.totalsem.com` or can access a WINS server to find out the IP address of SERVER1. The two different name services exist because Windows NT uses two very different types of applications: NetBIOS applications and Sockets applications.

NETBIOS APPLICATIONS NetBIOS applications are basically every program that has the word Microsoft in front of its name. These programs are aware of NetBIOS names and will use NetBIOS names when trying to talk to other computers. These programs are clueless about TCP/IP and must have some method of name resolution between NetBIOS names and IP addresses.

SOCKETS APPLICATIONS Knowing the IP address lets a user access a host, but there must be some way to tell that host what to do. This is where port numbers and sockets come in. A port number is simply a code assigned to a particular function a machine can perform. TELNET, for example, a program used to take control of another machine remotely, uses port 23 by default. A socket is the combination of the IP address and the port number that allows a machine to request a particular application on a particular machine. Sockets applications, such as FTP, TELNET, and Microsoft Internet Explorer, rely on the standard TCP/IP sockets interface for managing connections at the Session layer. In order to use TELNET from a Windows 95 or Windows NT machine, for example, open up a command prompt session and type in "TELNET w.x.y.z," where w.x.y.z represents the IP address of the host on which you want to establish a TELNET session. When the user types in this command, the TELNET program running on the host sends out a message saying, "Hey, host 199.21.212.25, give me a number 23!" When the client machine asks the server machine (199.21.212.25) for a number 23, the server machine understands that the client wants to open a TELNET session, as illustrated in Figure 10–32. The host is using the socket by combining the IP address and the port for the application.

A single host on a TCP/IP network can handle several incoming connections simultaneously, each one accessing a different function. The port numbers define the functions the machine can perform. Port numbers are essentially a list of predetermined options that act much like a menu at a drive in window—what is available is what you can get, as shown in Figure 10–33. When machines make connections, the host gives those connections

Figure 10–32
A socket combines the IP address and the port number.

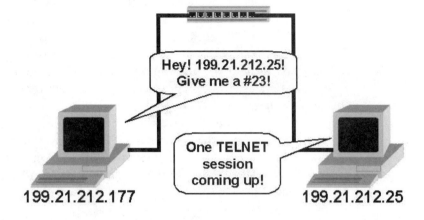

Figure 10–33
Port numbers are much like choices on a fast food menu—a list of numbers that correspond to the services offered by a TCP/IP host.

unique socket numbers to keep track of which connection uses which port. In Figure 10–32, for example, the socket number would be written 199.21.212.25: 23. Sockets provide a clear cut way for a TCP/IP host to track its connections with other hosts, identifying both the identity of the other host (its IP address) and the reason for the connection (the port number). Table 10–4 describes many of the common port numbers used in Sockets applications.

Applications do not need the name of the machine to define the socket —they only need the IP address. When a human being uses a name to specify the computer with which they wish to communicate, however, the application must resolve that name into an IP address. TCP/IP applications such as Web browsers, FTP clients, and email packages use DNS for this purpose.

Table 10–4

Some of the well-known TCP and UDP Port numbers

Port Number	Service	Description
20	FTP DATA	File Transfer Protocol—Data. Used for transferring files
21	FTP	File Transfer Protocol—Control. Used for transferring files
23	TELNET	Telnet, used to gain "remote control" over another machine on the network
25	SMTP	Simple Mail Transfer Protocol, used for transferring e-mail between e-mail servers
69	TFTP	Trivial File Transfer Protocol, used for transferring files without a secure login
80	HTTP	Hyper Text Transfer Protocol, used for transferring HTML (Hyper Text Markup Language) files (i.e. Web Pages)
110	POP3	Post Office Protocol, version 3 used for transferring e-mail from an e-mail server to an e-mail client
137	NETBIOS-NS	NetBIOS Name Service, used by Microsoft Networking
138	NETBIOS-DG	NetBIOS Datagram Service, used for transporting data by Microsoft Networking
139	NETBIOS-SS	NetBIOS Session Service, used by Microsoft Networking

DNS   TCP/IP networks don't need names like **www.totalsem.com** or **ftp.usgs.gov**. These user-friendly names, better known as "host names," provide a far easier method of accessing other hosts than using awful IP addresses. But there are millions of host names on the Internet—how can any one host determine the IP address for any other host on this massive network called the Internet? This titanic job of keeping track of the millions and millions of host names with the proper IP address is handled by thousands of special computers using Domain Name Service (DNS). DNS is powerful and complicated, requiring the understanding of certain terms such as the DNS name space.

The DNS Name Space   The first part of understanding how DNS resolves IP addresses into host names is understanding the DNS name space. DNS has a hierarchical name space. A name space is an imaginary structure of all possible names that could be used within a single system. In a flat name space, such as the NetBIOS name space, all names have to be absolutely unique. No two machines can ever share the same name under any condition. A flat name space can be extremely confining. A large organization with computers and networks spread among several cities, for example, would have to make sure that all of its administrators know all the names that are in use in the entire corporate network in order to ensure that no two machines have the same name.

A hierarchical name space offers a better solution. A hierarchical name space offers a great deal more flexibility by giving machines a longer, more fully descriptive name. The personal names people use every day are an example of a hierarchical name space. Most people address the town postman, Ron Samuels, as simply "Ron." When his name comes up in conversation, people usually refer to him as Ron. The town troublemaker, Ron Falwell, and Jim's son Ron who went off to New York, obviously share first names with the postman. In some conversations, people need to distinguish between the good Ron, the bad Ron, and the Ron in New York City. They could at that point use the more "Middle Ages" style of address, and refer to the Rons as Ron the Postman, Ron the Blackguard, or Ron the Lost; or, they could use a more typical address and include the Rons' surnames in their discussion. "That Ron Samuels; he is such a card!" "But that Ron Falwell: he is one bad apple." You might visualize the "People Name space" as shown in Figure 10–34. There is no confusion between the many people named Ron as long as their full names (or fully qualified names) differ.

Figure 10–34
Hierarchiacal names
are like people
names.

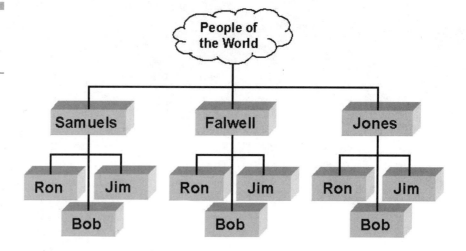

Figure 10–35
Hierarchical names
for files and
directories

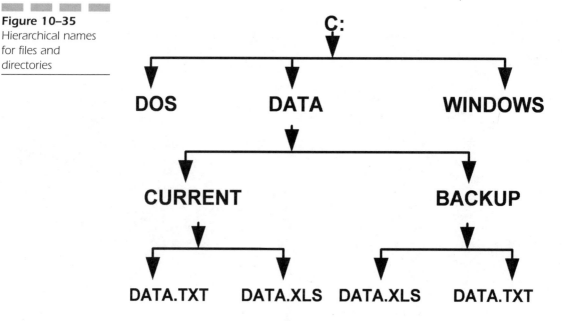

Another name space most of you already know is the hierarchical file name space used by FAT and NTFS volumes. Both NTFS and FAT use a hierarchical name space, allowing as many files named DATA.TXT as we wish as long as they exist in different paths. In the example shown in Figure 10–35, `C:\DATA\CURRENT\DATA.TXT` and `C:\DATA\BACKUP\DATA.TXT` can both exist on the same system, but only because they have been placed in different directories. While the files might both be called DATA.TXT, their fully qualified names are `C:\DATA\CURRENT\DATA.TXT` and `C:\DATA\BACKUP\DATA.TXT`.

If files were stored in a flat name space, where each file required a single unique name, naming files would quickly become a nightmare. Software vendors would have to avoid sensible descriptive names such as README.TXT, because they would almost certainly have been used already. In fact, an organization of some sort would probably have to assign names out of the limited pool of possible file names. With a hierarchical name space, such as that used by FAT and NTFS, naming is much simpler. The DNS name space works in the same fashion. The server name "www" exists in most organizations. If DNS used a flat name space, however, only the first organization with the name could have used it. Fortunately, however, because DNS naming appends domain names to the server names, the servers `www.totalsem.com` and `www.microsoft.com` can both exist.

DNS naming The DNS naming scheme is a hierarchical naming scheme that solves the challenge of assigning unique names in a large network. In a NetBIOS-based network, computer names must be unique. NetBIOS applications rely on the NetBIOS names to open connections with other NetBIOS-based machines. In a TCP/IP-based network, names are not generally as important. A TCP/IP host does not really need a name. Remember that a TCP/IP application opens a socket by specifying an IP address and a port number. Names are not truly needed by the applications; they are a convenience to the users. While unique names are not necessarily critical for the applications to function properly, however, they do help make the network more usable. The typical end user is much more comfortable typing in `www.microsoft.com` instead of 207.46.131.137. Providing DNS is functioning properly, the user is free to use either an address or a DNS name. Figure 10–36 shows that the same Web page comes up in Internet Explorer whether the user types in either `www.microsoft.com` or 207.46.131.137.

Programs like Internet Explorer (IE) accept names such as `www.microsoft.com` as a convenience to the end user. In order to work, however, they must use DNS or a HOSTS file to determine the IP address that corresponds to the name used. In Figure 10–36, IE displays the same Web page whether the IP address or the DNS name `www.microsoft.com` is used. In fact, even when you type in `www.microsoft.com`, Internet Explorer must resolve that name to the IP address 207.46.131.137 to make a connection to Microsoft's Web server.

DNS names such as `www.microsoft.com` must fit within a worldwide hierarchical name space, meaning that no two machines should ever have the same fully qualified name. The DNS name space must be managed

Figure 10–36
With DNS, you can
use IP addressses or
DNS names.

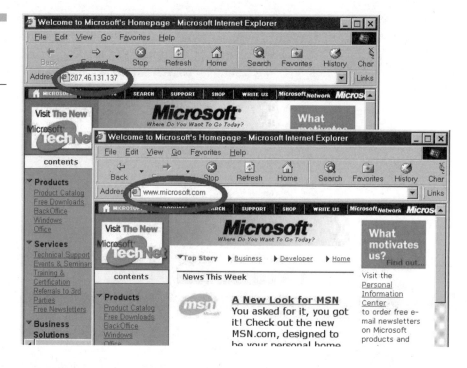

Figure 10–36
With DNS, you can use IP addressses or DNS names.

manually by network administrators. In order to allow decentralized administration, the DNS name space is broken up into domains.

DNS Domains   DNS domain names have nothing to do with NT domains. Instead they specify particular branches of the DNS name space tree, as shown in Figure 10–37. The DNS name space starts at the root, shown here as " " a set of empty quotation marks. The machine named ACCOUNTING has a fully qualified domain name of accounting.texas.microsoft.com.

The DNS name space is a hierarchical tree, similar in many respects to the file name space used by NTFS or FAT volumes. NTFS and FAT volumes can have several "trees," the roots of which have names such as "C:" or "D:" The DNS naming tree has a single root, usually left unnamed. The *Internet Network Information Center* (InterNIC) controls the root domain, sometimes referred to with a pair of empty quotation marks (" "). The InterNIC does not have to know the name of every computer in the world. Instead, the InterNIC delegates authority for particular subdomains to other organizations. InterNIC contracts with Network Solutions (**www.networksolutions.com**), for example, to maintain the .com subdomain.

Figure 10–37
DNS name space

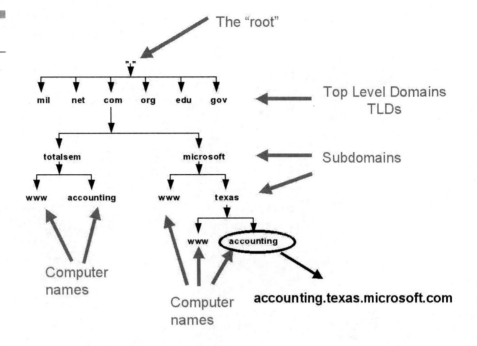

Table 10–5

Top level Domain
Names

Top level domain	Refers to:
.com	Originally intended for companies involved in commercial activities, but anyone can register a .com address.
.net	Companies involved in providing network access, such as Internet service providers (ISPs), but anyone can register a .net address.
.org	Organization not involved in commerce, especially non-profit organizations, but anyone can register a .org address.
.mil	United States military organizations
.edu	United States educational institutions, especially higher education
.gov	United States Federal government organizations

There are a variety of subdomains similar to .com in the Internet world. Table 10–5 shows the common top level subdomains used in the United States. This first level of subdomains, including the .com, .org, and .net domains, are often referred to as TLDs (top level domains).

In Figure 10–37, above, `accounting.texas.microsoft.com` specifies a particular host named accounting in the `texas.microsoft.com` domain. Although `texas.microsoft.com` in this example is technically a subdomain, the term domain and subdomain are commonly used interchangeably.

If you need to open a connection with `www.microsoft.com` using Internet Explorer or some other Web browser, some application must open a connection with the Web server at that address. Before a computer can attempt to open a socket connection with that Web server, it needs to determine the IP address of `www.microsoft.com`. In order to do so, the machine contacts its DNS server, requesting the IP address of `www.microsoft.com`, as shown in Figure 10–38.

The local DNS server may not know the address for `www.microsoft.com`, but it does know the address of a DNS root server. The root servers, maintained by the InterNIC, know all of the addresses of the top-level domain DNS servers. The root servers would not know the address of `www.microsoft.com`, but they would know the address of the DNS server in charge of all .com addresses. The ".com DNS server" would also not know the address of `www.microsoft.com`, but it would know the IP address of the microsoft.com DNS server. The microsoft.com DNS server may or may not know the address of `www.texas.microsoft.com`. The microsoft.com server would know the IP address of `www.microsoft.com`, and would send that informa-

Figure 10–38
A DNS client asks its DNS server for the IP address of
www.microsoft. com.

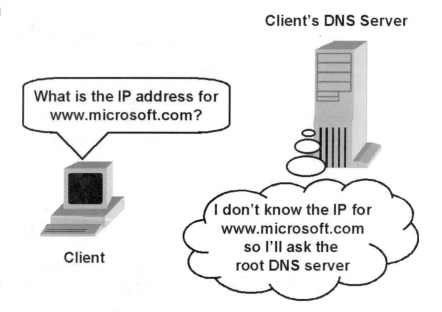

Client's DNS Server

What is the IP address for www.microsoft.com?

Client

I don't know the IP for www.microsoft.com so I'll ask the root DNS server

tion back to the local DNS server. Figure 10–39 shows the process of resolving a fully qualified domain name into an IP address.

No single machine needs to know every DNS name, as long as every machine knows who to ask for more information. The distributed, decentralized nature of the DNS database provides a great deal of flexibility and freedom to network administrators using DNS.

The DNS Tab   To further your understanding of DNS, it helps to look at the configuration for the DNS included with Windows NT. Access DNS by opening the Network applet in the Windows NT Control Panel, as shown in Figure 10–40. Each of the elements of this dialogue box is described in the following paragraphs.

Host Name   The Host Name entry specifies the host name for this machine. In TCP/IP, a host is any device that can either send or receive data. Sometimes a DNS server may not be available on the network. In that case, sockets-based applications will attempt to resolve host names to IP addresses by broadcasting within the local subnet. If the specified machine name belongs to a host that can hear the broadcast, that machine

Figure 10–39
A DNS server contacts oither DNS servers to determine the IP address requested by the DNS client.

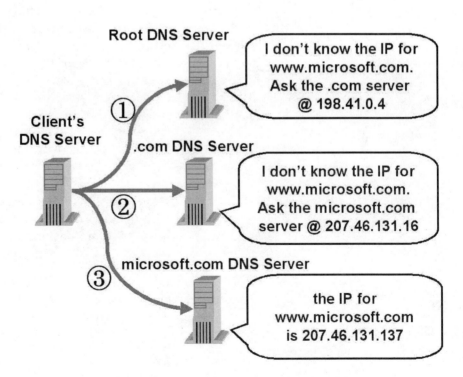

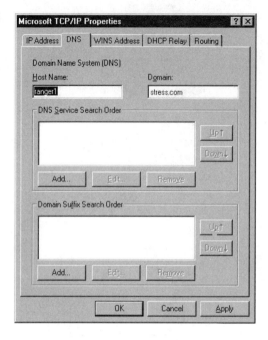

Figure 10–40
The DNS tab in the
Control Panel.

responds back with its IP address. The host name specifies the name to which this machine will respond via broadcasts. By default, the host name will be the same as the NetBIOS name specified in the Identification tab under the Network applet. In most cases, making the host name and Net-BIOS name the same makes sense and avoids confusion.

Typing in the Host name does not register the host's name and IP address with a DNS server. The DNS databases maintained on the DNS servers must be updated manually. The local machine only uses the Host name entered in the Network applet when deciding whether or not to respond to broadcast messages.

Domain The Domain field specifies a DNS domain name. Do not confuse DNS domain names with the domain names used in the NT security model. Although they both use the word domain, the two concepts have nothing to do with each other.

IMPORTANT: *DNS domains are used for name resolution; NT domains are used for security. The two uses of the word domain have nothing to do with each other.*

As with the Host name field, completing this field does not register the machine with a DNS server. Instead, when combined with the Host name entry it specifies the fully qualified domain name to which this machine responds when it receives broadcast requests. The host configured in Figure 10–40, would respond to broadcasts directed at either RANGER1 (its host name) or `ranger1.stress.com` (its fully qualified domain name).

DNS Service Search Order   The DNS service search order field is used to specify the IP addresses of the DNS servers that this client should use. Specifying multiple DNS servers provides redundancy in the event that a DNS server fails. If multiple DNS servers are specified, they will be queried in the order listed.

Domain Suffix Search Order   In some cases, it may be desirable for end users to use simple host names instead of fully qualified domain names. The domain suffix search order entry allows administrators to set up default domain names that will be used whenever a user types a domain name without a domain suffix (such as .com or .org). If you add .com and .org to the domain suffix search order list, for example, the computer tries to resolve the name Fred as three different possibilities: fred, fred.com, and fred.org. Because users have become increasingly comfortable typing in names such as `www.microsoft.com`, *little benefit comes from adding suffixes to this field.*

The fields on the DNS tab in the Network applet allow administrators to configure the manner in which the DNS clients in their environments will use DNS servers. While these specific fields are not usually directly tested on the exams, familiarity with them aids in the understanding of the DNS concept.

HOSTS: A Little Black Book for TCP/IP Host Names   In the absence of a DNS server, a file called HOSTS offers another means of resolving DNS host names to IP addresses. Each host machine can have a HOSTS file–its own directory of names and addresses. The HOSTS file is simply a text file with a list of IP addresses and their corresponding names. On a Windows NT server, the HOSTS file can be found in the `\WINNT\SYSTEM32\DRIVERS\ETC\` directory.

NOTE: *NT offers a sample HOSTS file called HOSTS.SAM in this directory. When implementing the HOSTS file, make sure that you remove the extension (.SAM). The HOSTS file should not have an extension when in use.*

The HOSTS file uses an extremely simply syntax. On each line, the IP address of a host is followed by its host name. If you want to comment on a particular line, add a pound sign (#) at the end of the line, followed by the comment. A sample entry might look like this:

```
199.20.25.35          account2      #the accounting FTP server
```

The HOSTS file is case sensitive. Microsoft follows the case-sensitive HOSTS file conventions established in UNIX.

NOTE: *Most TCP/IP utilities originated in UNIX. UNIX distinguishes between upper and lower case text. Most of the Microsoft equivalents of the UNIX TCP/IP utilities and programs, therefore, generally do so as well. Windows NT interprets, for example, the following commands differently:*

```
NBTSTAT -a
NBTSTAT -A
```

While most Microsoft Networking programs do not treat upper and lower case differently, most of the Microsoft TCP/IP utilities see both uppercase and lowercase characters and may respond in different ways.

Relying on the HOSTS file can lead to trouble. If the machine ACCOUNT2 physically moves to another network, for example, its name remains the same but its address probably changes. If each machine has its own HOSTS file, the system administrator must go to each machine every time an address changes (or come up with some kind of replication scheme to copy a new HOSTS file to each machine every time a change is required). By using DNS, the administrator only has a single place to make the change: the DNS database.

DNS Summary   DNS provides a naming scheme for TCP/IP applications to talk to hosts on remote subnets. DNS lets users access machines across the Internet, without having to remember the IP addresses for that machine. The core MCSE exams require only a basic understanding of DNS and how NT uses it as a client. The exams do not focus on the configuration of a DNS server, for example. Key points to remember include the following:

- DNS servers provide host name to IP address resolution, acting as a kind of "directory assistance" in a TCP/IP-based network.

- Not all applications use DNS. Applications that rely on the TCP/IP sockets interface (Web browsers, TELNET, FTP, PING, etc) require

DNS, while most Microsoft-specific applications (Windows Explorer, NET USE, etc.) rely on another name resolution mechanism: WINS (discussed below).

- DNS servers maintain a static database. Entries for new machines must be added manually by administrators.

- A HOSTS file can also be used to resolve host names to IP addresses.

WINS NetBIOS names serve the same function in a NetBIOS-based network that sockets perform in a TCP/IP socket-based network. To a sockets-based application, the Host name serves as a convenience for the human beings that use the network. These names have no real function as far as the computers are concerned. Without a name resolution process such as HOSTS files or DNS servers to translate a name into an address, the name has no meaning.

In a NetBIOS-based network, names play a more important function. In NetBIOS, a computer has many names, each one specifying a function the machine can perform, such as client, server, or master browser. The multiple names of a NetBIOS computer are made up of the name assigned to it in the Identification tab in the Network Control Panel applet, combined with the 16th-bit assigned, based on the functions the machine is performing.

Unfortunately, the design of NetBIOS assumes that every machine on the network can hear broadcast messages, which is true in the small, non-routed networks for which NetBIOS was designed. In Figure 10–41, SALES3 has no problem reaching SALES2 with a broadcast message. SALES3 establishes a NetBIOS connection to SALES 2 using a broadcast message.

The router in Figure 10–42 will prevent a similar broadcast from reaching ACCOUNT2 on the far side of the router. SALES3 cannot establish a NetBIOS connection with ACCOUNT2 because the router does not pass the broadcast message to the far side of the router.

In order to send a message from SALES3 to ACCOUNT2, SALES3 must first determine ACCOUNT2's IP address. Microsoft solves this dilemma with the Windows Internet Name Service (WINS). A WINS server maintains a centralized database of the NetBIOS names on a network and their corresponding IP addresses.

NOTE: *WINS servers keep track of NetBIOS names and IP addresses.*

DNS servers keep track of DNS host names and IP addresses.

Figure 10–41
NetBIOS broadcast
messages

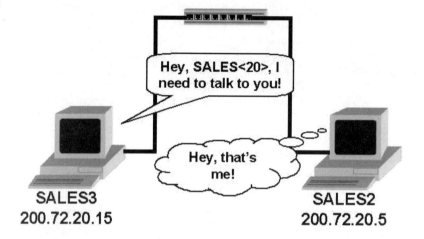

Figure 10–42
NetBIOS broadcast
messages are not
routed.

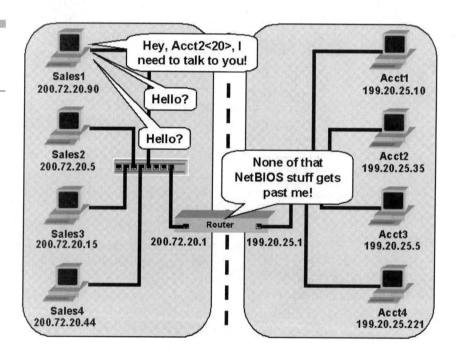

The WINS Address Tab   Similarly to DNS, configuring WINS is not the
main focus of the NT exams; however, it helps in understanding WINS to
look at the configuration for the WINS client. To configure Windows NT
as a WINS client, use the Network Control Panel applet. The WINS address tab, shown in Figure 10–43, asks for the IP address of a primary
and a secondary WINS server.

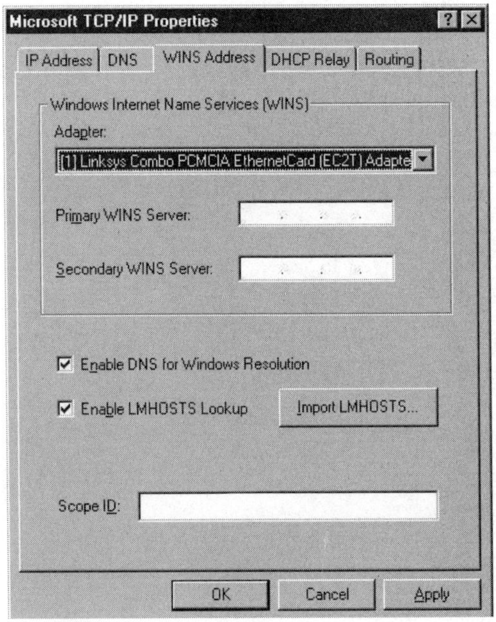

Figure 10–43
The WINS tab in the Networking applet

When a WINS client (i.e., any machine using WINS) boots up, it sends a message to the WINS servers listed in the Network applet and registers its name and IP address. In Figure 10–44, SALES1 and ACCOUNT2 register their addresses with their WINS server (SALES3). The WINS clients do not broadcast their registrations, they send them directly to the IP address of their WINS server: 200.72.20.15. Always specify the WINS server by its address, not its name. The WINS client does not care about the NetBIOS or host name of the WINS server. It just needs to know where to send the registration data.

After registering with the WINS server, the WINS clients have a means of determining the IP address that corresponds with a particular Net-BIOS name. They contact the WINS server. In Figure 10–45, SALES1, a WINS client, contacts the WINS server to determine the IP address that corresponds to the NetBIOS name ACCOUNT2.

Once SALES1 has the address, it no longer has to rely on a broadcast to reach ACCOUNT2. Remember that because ACCOUNT2 lies on the far side of the router, a broadcast would not work anyway. WINS allows Net-BIOS-based applications to direct their packets to specific IP addresses instead of depending on broadcasts, as shown in Figure 10–46.

The Scope ID field in the WINS tab refers to the NetBIOS scope for this machine. Leave this setting blank! Two machines with different Scope IDs

Figure 10–44
WINS clients register with the WINS server. Because the WINS server is specified in each hosts' IP configuration by its IP address, ACCOUNT2 has no problem registering with the WINS server even though the WINS server is on the far side of the router.

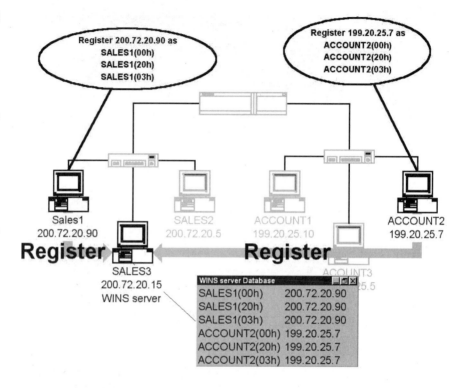

Figure 10–45
WINS clients can access the WINS server's database to determine the IP address that corresponds to a given NetBIOS name.

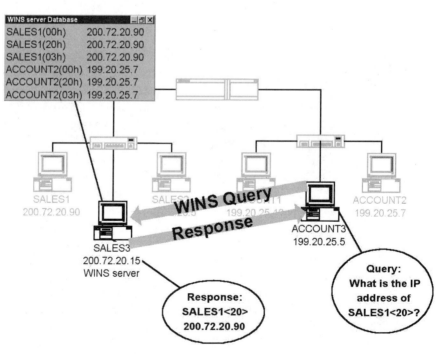

Figure 10–46
Once the IP address that corresponds to a particular IP address has been determined, there is no problem connecting to the machine, even if the destination machine lies on a remote subnet.

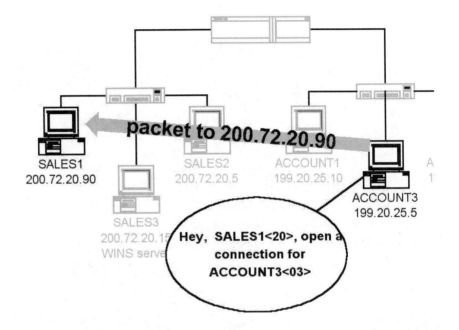

cannot connect to each other with NetBIOS. NetBIOS scopes are a primitive security feature, rarely used in modern networks.

Name Uniqueness WINS has another vital task on a NetBIOS-based network—ensuring name uniqueness. In a DNS-based network, applications manage connections using sockets, a combination of an IP address and a port number. The name of a computer has nothing to do with how the computers communicate, existing merely as a convenience to the user. While duplicate computer names might confuse the human beings using the network, they do not affect the computers because the computers do not identify other computers by name, only by IP address and port, or socket.

NetBIOS networks, however, rely on the NetBIOS names (and their 16th-byte extensions) to manage connections. If two computers share the same NetBIOS name, the computers themselves can become confused. To avoid this confusion, NetBIOS networks demand that all computers have unique names.

In a small, non-routed network, keeping names unique involves no challenge. Every machine running NetBIOS, upon booting up, broadcasts its name to the network. If another computer already uses that name, that computer will send a message to the new computer on the network, telling the new computer to get off the network, as shown in Figure 10–47. The user of the machine that has its name refused sees the error message shown in Figure 10–48.

Once the IP address that corresponds to a particular IP address has been determined there is no problem connecting to the machine, even if the destination machine lies on a remote subnet.

The broadcast will not reach machines on the far side of a router, leaving open the possibility of duplicate names on the network. Figure 10–49 shows two machines announcing themselves as SALES2. Because they sit on opposite sides of the router, however, they do not hear each other's announcements. Other machines on the network have no way to distinguish the two machines named SALES2. Although they have different IP addresses, NetBIOS does not use IP addresses to manage connections.

Figure 10–47

Within a local area network, broadcasts can guarantee that NetBIOS names are unique to each machine.

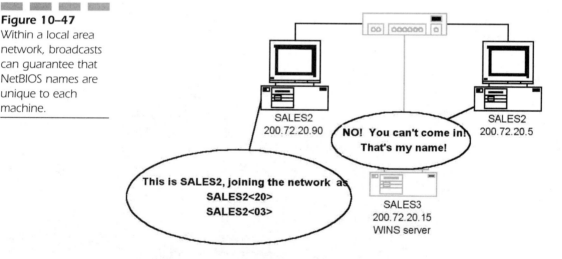

Figure 10–48

Should a machine detect another machine with the same NetBIOS name, the user will see this error message.

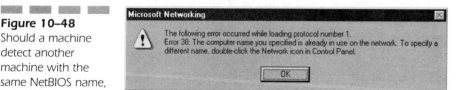

Figure 10–49
Broadcasts cannot
guarantee the
uniqueness of
NetBIOS names
across routed
networks.

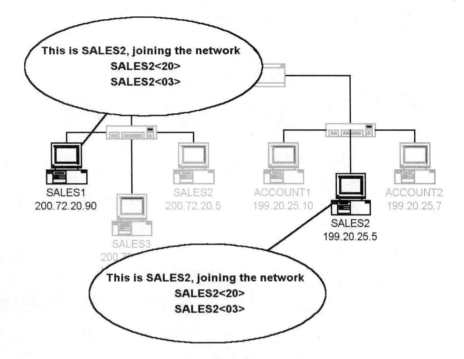

Figure 10–49
Broadcasts cannot guarantee the uniqueness of NetBIOS names across routed networks.

The best way to solve the problem of duplicate NetBIOS names on a routed network would be to install a WINS server. The WINS server will not allow a machine to register a NetBIOS name that is already in use anywhere on the network, as shown in Figure 10–50. The machine attempting to register a NetBIOS name that is already being used receives the same error message as was shown in Figure 10–48.

In TCP/IP-based networks using sockets applications, unique names are ensured by unique IP addresses and ports combined. The DNS applications use the IP addresses rather than the names. To allow for the same level of uniqueness in NetBIOS-based networks, use WINS.

LMHOSTS: A Little Black Book for NetBIOS Names   In the absence of a WINS server, a file called LMHOSTS offers another means of resolving names to IP addresses. This is very similar to the way that a HOSTS file functions for DNS host names. Where a WINS server acts much like directory assistance, the LMHOSTS file acts like a little black book of phone numbers. The WINS server provides a centralized database to which every machine can refer, while the LMHOSTS file exists on each machine's individual hard drive and exists for that machine's exclusive use.

Figure 10–50
WINS servers can guarantee the uniqueness of NetBIOS names across routed networks.

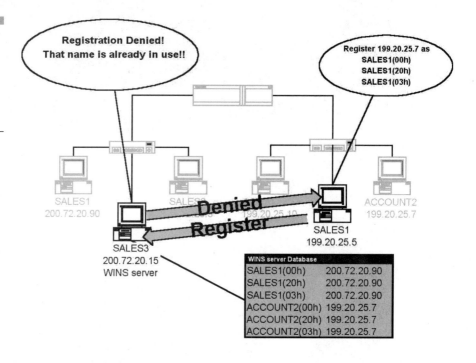

NOTE: *The LMHOSTS file can resolve NetBIOS names to IP addresses, but it cannot guarantee unique NetBIOS names across a routed network.*

The LMHOSTS file contains a simple list of NetBIOS names and their corresponding IP addresses. Microsoft supplies a sample file, LMHOSTS.SAM, in the **\WINNT\SYSTEM32\DRIVERS\ETC** directory, as shown in Figure 10–51.

To build an LMHOSTS file, simply begin each line with the IP address of a NetBIOS machine, followed by its IP address. Add comments explaining an entry by adding a pound sign (#), followed by the comment, at the end of the line.

Some comments, such as "#PRE" and "#DOM" have special meanings. The "#PRE" option preloads a name and address into the NetBIOS name cache, speeding up the name resolution process. The "#DOM" comment identifies the NetBIOS machine as a domain controller (PDC or BDC) of the specified domain. A "#PRE" entry must precede any "#DOM" entry. The special domain controller entry must exist to allow clients to log in to a domain controller on a remote network if a WINS server is not in use.

Figure 10–51

The LMHOSTS.SAM file provided by Microsoft explains the syntax of the LMHOSTS file with examples. Look for it in the **\WINNT\SYSTEM32 \DRIVERS\ETC** directory on a Windows NT machine, or in the **\WINDOWS** directory on a Windows 95 or 98 machine.

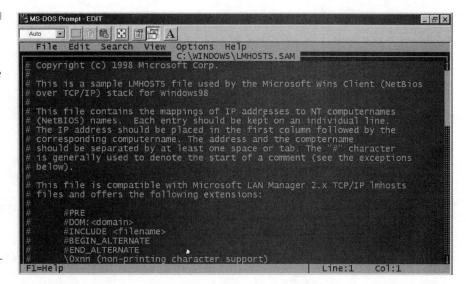

```
MS-DOS Prompt - EDIT                                          _ 8 X
 Auto        ▼   □ □ ▣ ▣ ▣ ▣ 🗗 A
     File  Edit  Search  View  Options  Help
                        C:\WINDOWS\LMHOSTS.SAM
# Copyright (c) 1998 Microsoft Corp.
#
# This is a sample LMHOSTS file used by the Microsoft Wins Client (NetBios
# over TCP/IP) stack for Windows98
#
# This file contains the mappings of IP addresses to NT computernames
# (NetBIOS) names.  Each entry should be kept on an individual line.
# The IP address should be placed in the first column followed by the
# corresponding computername. The address and the comptername
# should be separated by at least one space or tab. The "#" character
# is generally used to denote the start of a comment (see the exceptions
# below).
#
# This file is compatible with Microsoft LAN Manager 2.x TCP/IP lmhosts
# files and offers the following extensions:
#
#     #PRE
#     #DOM:<domain>
#     #INCLUDE <filename>
#     #BEGIN_ALTERNATE
#     #END_ALTERNATE
#     \0xnn (non-printing character support)
 F1=Help                                       Line:1      Col:1
```

IMPORTANT: *Adding an incorrect entry to the LMHOSTS file will prevent the machine from connecting to that NetBIOS name, even if a WINS server with the correct information exists on the network. A NetBIOS machine assumes that any preloaded options are correct and does not looks any farther. If an LMHOSTS entry does not have a #PRE option, the machine will still consult a WINS server if set up as a WINS client.*

Figure 10–52 shows the LMHOSTS file for the example network used in this section. All six PCs have entries, and ACCOUNT2 and SALES3 are designated as domain controllers. The router, however, has no entries. While it has its own IP addresses, routers do not typically run NetBIOS.

WINS servers are the preferred and recommended method for handling NetBIOS name resolution. While LMHOSTS files can be used, they cannot guarantee unique names. In addition, administrators must manually edit the LMHOSTS files of each machine should the network change. Typically, LMHOSTS files are used when a WINS server cannot easily be added to the network because of cost or other factors.

IMPORTANT: *Microsoft's LMHOSTS.SAM file warns that "the whole file is parsed including comments on each lookup, so keeping the number of comments to a minimum will improve performance. Therefore it is not advisable to simply add LMHOSTS file entries onto the end of this file." LMHOSTS files should contain as few comments as possible because a NetBIOS machine reads the comments every*

Figure 10–52
A properly
configured
LMHOSTS file

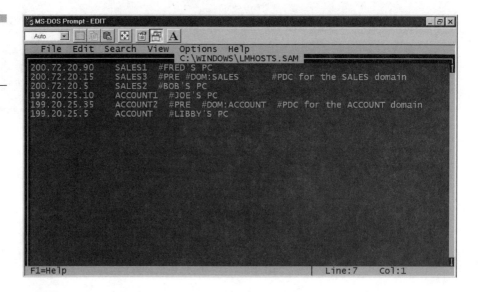

```
MS-DOS Prompt - EDIT                                                    _ ⊡ ✕
Auto    ▾  □ ▣ ▣ ▣ ▣ ▣ A
   File  Edit  Search  View  Options  Help
                            C:\WINDOWS\LMHOSTS.SAM
200.72.20.90    SALES1  #FRED'S PC
200.72.20.15    SALES3  #PRE #DOM:SALES        #PDC for the SALES domain
200.72.20.5     SALES2  #BOB'S PC
199.20.25.10    ACCOUNT1 #JOE'S PC
199.20.25.35    ACCOUNT2 #PRE  #DOM:ACCOUNT   #PDC for the ACCOUNT domain
199.20.25.5     ACCOUNT  #LIBBY'S PC




F1=Help                                           Line:7    Col:1
```

*time it uses the file. Since the file is used every single time the machine uses a
NetBIOS name to connect or reply to another machine on the network, this can have
significant impact on your environment.*

WINS Summary   WINS does the same thing for traditional Microsoft applications that DNS does for TCP/IP applications —it provides a way to discover the IP address of a machine running on a remote subnet. As with
DNS, the exams covered here do not require a detailed knowledge of WINS
server configuration. They do require a general understanding of the role
WINS plays in a network, however, particularly on the NT in the Enterprise exam. Key facts to remember about WINS include the following:

- WINS servers provide NetBIOS name to IP address resolution,
  acting as a kind of "directory assistance" in a TCP/IP-based
  network.

- Not all applications use WINS. Applications that rely on the
  NetBIOS interface, including most Microsoft-specific applications
  such as Windows Explorer and NET USE, rely on WINS.
  Applications that rely on the IP sockets interface (Web browsers,
  TELNET, FTP, PING) require DNS.

- WINS servers build and maintain their databases dynamically.
  WINS clients register with the WINS server each time they boot up.

■ WINS servers prevent two machines from using the same NetBIOS name, even when the two machines lie on opposite sides of a router.

■ The LMHOSTS file can also be used to resolve NetBIOS names to IP addresses, but does not guarantee the uniqueness of names.

DHCP   To configure a Microsoft TCP/IP host fully, the administrator may have to type in dozens of IP addresses. Multiply that number by hundreds of machines and the work involved in setting up a TCP/IP network can grow exponentially, not only during the initial setup but also when changes need to be made. To ease this burden, install a Dynamic Host Configuration Protocol (DHCP) server to distribute settings remotely to other machines on the network.

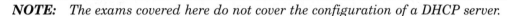

NOTE: *The exams covered here do not cover the configuration of a DHCP server.*

To use DHCP to assign TCP/IP settings to a Windows NT machine, select "Obtain an IP address automatically" in the TCP/IP address tab in the Network applet in the Control Panel. When a DHCP client boots up, it sends out a broadcast message requesting its configuration. If a DHCP server receives that message, it returns the appropriate values to the DHCP client, as shown in Figure 10–53. The DHCP server keeps track of the addresses it assigns to ensure that it does not assign the same address to two machines.

The DHCP client keeps its settings for the "lease duration," a variable set by default to 3 days. When the lease is fifty percent complete, the DHCP client begins attempting to renew its lease. If the client cannot renew its lease before it expires, the client "loses" its IP address and cannot communicate via TCP/IP until the DHCP server becomes available. The **IPCONFIG /ALL** command (run from the command line) allows you to see the current IP address configuration of any Windows NT host, including the DHCP lease information if applicable. The following is a sample result of the **IPCONFIG /ALL** command:

```
C:\>ipconfig /all
Windows NT IP Configuration
    Host Name . . . . . . . . . : sales2
    DNS Servers . . . . . . . . : 192.168.42.254
    Node Type . . . . . . . . . : Hybrid
    NetBIOS Scope ID. . . . . . :
    IP Routing Enabled. . . . . : No
    WINS Proxy Enabled. . . . . : No
    NetBIOS Resolution Uses DNS : Yes
```

Figure 10–53
A DHCP server
receives a broadcast
from the DHCP client
and sends the client
machine its IP
configuration.

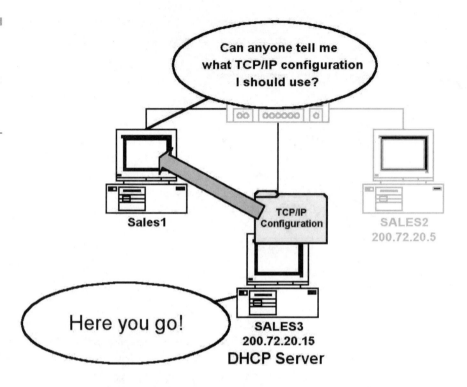

```
Ethernet adapter EC2T1:

    Description . . . . . . . . : PCMCIA Ethernet Card
    Physical Address. . . . . . : 00-E0-98-01-4A-19
    DHCP Enabled. . . . . . . . : Yes
    IP Address. . . . . . . . . : 192.168.42.10
    Subnet Mask . . . . . . . . : 255.255.255.0
    Default Gateway . . . . . . : 192.168.42.254
    DHCP Server . . . . . . . . : 192.168.42.254
    Lease Obtained. . . . . . . : Thursday, October 15, 1998
        10:16:02 AM
    Lease Expires . . . . . . . : Friday, October 16, 1998
        10:16:02 AM

C:\>
```

The **WINIPCFG** command run in Windows 95 and Windows 98 shows the same information in a GUI screen, as shown in Figure 10–54.

The DHCP server can automatically assign any value found within the TCP/IP configuration of the Network applet. Instead of having to enter dozens of values individually on each machine, simply specify the computer name, workgroup (or domain), and select "Obtain an IP address automatically."

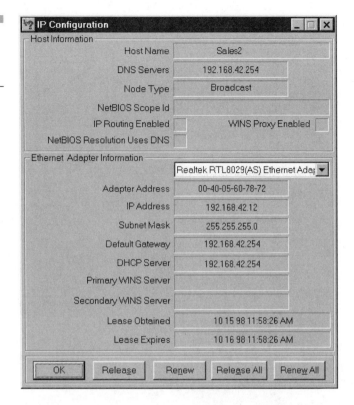

Figure 10–54
The WINIPCFG utility in Windows 95 and Windows 98

Unfortunately, routers can get in the way of this scenario. If the DHCP client does not lie on the same network as the DHCP server, the DHCP server will not "hear" the DHCP client's request for information. Remember that broadcasts are not routed. (See Figure 10–55) To avoid this problem, if DHCP is in use, install a DHCP server or DHCP relay (discussed below) on each subnet.

DHCP RELAY AGENTS Two options allow DHCP clients in routed networks to use DHCP servers. Either install a DHCP server in each subnet, or, in order to allow a DHCP server to meet the needs of DHCP clients that lie on other networks, install a DHCP relay agent on each network. The DHCP relay agent forwards DHCP broadcast requests to the specific IP address of a DHCP server, as shown in Figure 10–56.

THE DHCP RELAY TAB To make a Windows NT server act as a DHCP relay agent, specify the address of one or more DHCP servers in the DHCP relay tab in the Network Control Panel applet, as shown in Figure 10–57. Note that by default, a DHCP relay agent will not pass requests on to a DHCP server that lies more than 4 hops or 4 seconds away.

Figure 10–55
The DHCP client's broadcasts cannot reach a DHCP server on the far side of the router.

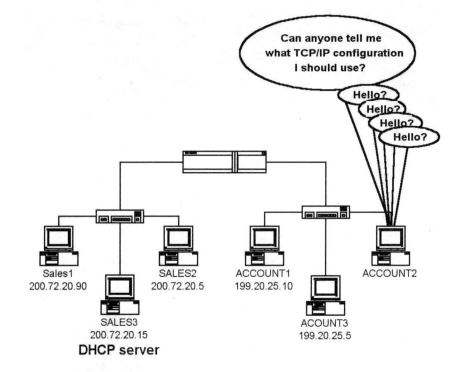

Figure 10–56
A DHCP relay agent can forward DHCP client requests to a remote DHCP server.

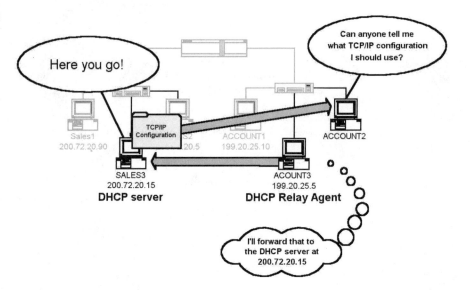

Figure 10–57
The DHCP relay tab
in the Control Panel

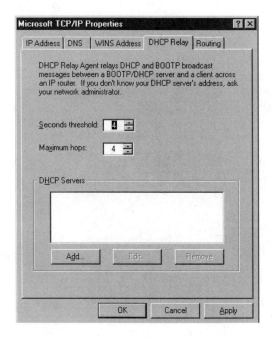

NOTE: *Every router a packet passes through is considered a hop. Each time a relayed DHCP packet passes through a router, the router subtracts one from the number of allowed hops. If the number of hops reaches zero, the packet is discarded.*

The "seconds threshold" sets another counter. Routers use this number to discard old packets that have been delayed too long to be useful. Because each router can decide how long a "second" is, the default of "4 seconds" should not be taken literally.

The DHCP relay agent runs as its own service. If the DHCP Relay Agent service has not been installed, Windows NT prompts you to install it as soon as you specify an IP address under "DHCP Servers" in the DHCP Relay tab in the Network applet.

THE ROUTING TAB Windows NT servers can function as TCP/IP routers. In order to do so, the server must have at least two network interfaces (NICs) installed, and the check box shown in Figure 10–58 must be enabled. These exams do not require an extensive knowledge of NT router configuration. You should know that an NT server can act as a TCP/IP router. (A Windows NT Server can also act as an IPX router.)

Figure 10–58
The Enable IP
Forwarding
checkbox under
Routing tab

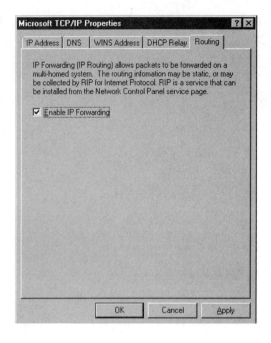

TCP/IP TROUBLESHOOTING UTILITIES Network administrators must also be network troubleshooters. It is important to understand the uses of the following basic TCP/IP configuration and troubleshooting utilities:

■ IPCONFIG displays the current TCP/IP configuration of an NT host. It can be used to renew or release DHCP leases with the **IPCONFIG /RELEASE** and **IPCONFIG /RENEW** commands. In a Windows 95 or Windows 98 machine, WINIPCFG provides the same functions as IPCONFIG, but with a graphical interface.

■ PING sends a test packet to a known IP address. It is used to test TCP/IP configuration and basic network connectivity. A successful PING confirms the proper IP address configuration on both ends of the connection.

■ TRACERT traces the route a packet takes from one machine to another. Like PING, it can be used to test connectivity. It also shows the exact route to the destination system. This command is especially useful for troubleshooting routing problems.

■ NBTSTAT shows statistics and information about NetBIOS functions running on top of TCP/IP. It supports many additional command line options, which NBTSTAT displays when you type the command with no options.

Troubleshooting is obviously a much larger topic than the few bullet points above, but these utilities give you a starting arsenal when you begin to verify connectivity and network functions. Keep in mind that any network troubleshooting should include verification of the hardware, connectivity, and drivers at a minimum.

TCP/IP SUMMARY   Microsoft is moving towards supporting TCP/IP as its protocol of choice. While Microsoft supports other protocols (IPX/SPX and NetBEUI), their bias in favor of TCP/IP shows up in the MCSE certification program. Questions about TCP/IP appear on all three of the core MCSE exams. The Workstation and Server exams require an understanding of the Network applet TCP/IP options, while the NT in the Enterprise exam tests your understanding of the roles and purposes of the various types of servers in a large TCP/IP network: DNS, WINS, and DHCP. Specific questions about the setup and configuration of those servers, however, are reserved for a test not covered here: Internetworking with Microsoft TCP/IP on Microsoft Windows NT 4.0, test #70-059.

DLC—A Special Case

DLC (Data Link Control) protocol is a non-routable protocol originally designed for communication with mainframe computers. Although it does not allow communication with the Windows NT redirector and server, it is included to allow NT to communicate with mainframes that might still be running the DLC protocol or with other network devices. Hewlett Packard uses DLC as its protocol for setting up stand-alone network printers over the network. Windows NT supports DLC as a protocol specifically for communicating with network printers from HP and other vendors. DLC is not installed with NT by default, but you can add it in the Network applet.

Questions

1. Craig must install a 15-node peer-to-peer Windows NT Workstation network for a small accounting firm. All the computers will be in the same physical location. No connectivity outside the LAN is required. What protocol should Craig use?

   a. IPX/SPX

   b. NetBEUI

   c. TCP/IP

   d. DLC

2. Which of the following is not a layer in the OSI Seven-layer model?

   a. Binding

   b. Data Link

   c. Session

   d. Transport

3. The Microsoft Networking component that handles the Session layer is called:

   a. NetBEUI

   b. NetBIOS

   c. SMB

   d. Explorer

4. Jung is upgrading his Windows NT Workstation network running NetBEUI to link into a large Windows NT network running TCP/IP. The administrator of the NT network has given his users' accounts privileges on the Domain. The administrator told him to use DHCP, but did not give him the name or IP address of the DHCP server. To allow his systems to log into the NT network he must (choose all that apply):

   a. Remove the NetBEUI protocol from all the NT Workstations.

   b. Add the TCP/IP protocol.

   c. Get the IP address of the DHCP Server and enter it in each system's IP configurations.

   d. Configure the systems to get an IP address automatically from the DHCP server.

5. Which protocol has nothing to do with any form of name resolution? (select all that apply)

   a. IP

   b. DNS

   c. WINS

   d. SMB

6. DLC protocol is most commonly used for:

   a. Print devices

   b. NetWare networks

   c. Routing networks

   d. DNS

7. Fred can successfully PING his domain PDC from his NT Workstation but is unable to find it under Start...Find...Computer. What could be the problem?

   a. The systems' DHCP lease is lost

   b. DNS is not configured properly

   c. WINS is not configured properly

   d. NetBIOS is not installed

8. Popo has been charged with installing the NT network for a new office. The users will want Internet access as well as access to the PDC. The network will have access to the Internet via a router. What TCP/IP information needs to be configured, either manually or automatically, on any system that wants to access the Internet? (choose all that apply)

   a. Gateway

   b. WINS Scope ID

   c. IP Address

   d. Subnet mask

9. Blanche has two totally separate NT networks. Each network is currently running TCP/IP (company policy prevents the use of any other protocol), has its own PDC, WINS, and DHCP server, and is not routed in any way. She would like to add a member server, with two network cards, to connect the networks and to allow the two networks to communicate through the member server. She must:

a. Set each NIC in the member server to use DHCP

b. Enable DHCP relay

c. Enable IP forwarding

d. Give each NIC the same IP address

10. The _____ file is to DNS what the _____ file is to WINS.

a. LMHOSTS, HOSTS

b. HOSTS, LMHOSTS

c. NBSTAT, HOSTS

d. NBSTAT, LMHOSTS

Answers

1. b—Craig should install NetBEUI. Because no connectivity outside the firm's LAN is required, the additional setup required by TCP/IP is not justified. No NetWare servers are mentioned, so IPX/SPX is not required. NetBEUI's simple configuration makes it the most attractive choice in this scenario.

2. a—Binding is not part of the OSI Seven-layer model.

3. b—NetBIOS is Session layer, NetBEUI is Transport layer, SMB is Presentation layer and Explorer is Application layer.

4. b, d—NetBEUI can easily co-exist with another protocol. The TCP/IP protocol must be loaded. You don't need the IP address of the DHCP server but you must configure the systems to use it.

5. a, d—IP is an addressing protocol, SMB is a messaging format. Neither has anything to do with any form of name resolution.

6. a—DLC is used almost exclusively for Print devices.

7. c—If DHCP were lost, he wouldn't be able to PING anything. DNS is not for NetBIOS names. WINS is for NetBIOS names and would prevent the system from being found. NetBIOS is always installed on NT systems.

8. a, c, d—The WINS Scope ID has nothing to do with Internet access. The systems must have a gateway, an IP address, and a subnet mask. These could all be configured automatically via DHCP.

9. c—The NICs in the server must have static IPs, not use DHCP. DHCP relay is not needed as each system has its own DHCP server. IP forwarding must be enabled. Each NIC must have a unique IP address.

10. b—HOSTS is used by DNS and LMHOSTS is used by WINS.

11

NT Server Clients

In today's "everything is connected to everybody" world, the idea that any two systems can communicate with each other is taken for granted. The problem here is the concept of "communication." Many levels of communication exist between systems. In all but the simplest communications between two systems, one system (the client) requests some aspect of a shared resource—while another system (the server) provides that resource. But even within this broad concept of client and server, some disparity will occur between one interpretation and another. In this chapter, we need a more specific definition that describes the deeper level of communication that occurs between Windows NT Servers and their clients. A client for Windows NT runs software designed to access the authentication mechanism of Windows NT Server. The server then recognizes the client and provides the client with a broad and intuitive cross-section of standard network resource offerings, such as file/directory and printer sharing.

Whew. That paragraph was a mouthful, but the information is important. As we progress through this chapter, we need to appreciate that there will be variances in how well different client programs can approach this definition. Some operating systems, such as Windows NT Workstation, totally and transparently achieve this goal. Other operating systems, however, such as all UNIX workstations, fall significantly short of this goal. (You cannot install an NT printer to your UNIX box, for example.) This chapter will describe the many NT clients available, including installation, use, and a portion of troubleshooting. While NT cannot boast perfect client software for every OS, NT is the closest that has yet been achieved in the entire history of microprocessors.

Types of Clients

Windows NT 4.0 can act as a server to some degree for client systems running every well-known OS. Machines running DOS, Windows for Workgroups, Windows 95, Windows 98, Windows NT 3.51, Windows NT Workstation 4.0, and Windows NT Server 4.0 can all act as clients on an NT network and are capable of logging into an NT Server or NT domain and accessing its resources via standard Microsoft networking. Services for Macintosh enables Macintosh clients to log into an NT Server (assuming the server has Services for Macintosh installed). Internet Information Server enables UNIX clients to access resources on an NT Server via FTP and HTTP. This flexibility makes NT an attractive choice for serving a network populated with a variety of operating systems. Not too surprisingly, the Microsoft clients tend to be far better than the non-Microsoft clients, requiring any client discussion to be broken into two basic groups: the Microsoft clients and the "other" clients.

Microsoft Clients

Microsoft supports all of its past and present operating systems as NT clients, including DOS, Windows for Workgroups, Windows 9X, Windows NT 3.51, and Windows NT 4.0.

DOS Although Microsoft DOS is not an NOS in and of itself, Microsoft offers several optional DOS network clients that can be used to log into an NT Server or Domain, including the Network Client version 3.0 included on the Windows NT 4.0 CD-ROM. Today, administrators often use the DOS client on DOS boot disks so they can install another OS over the network. (See the following section, Client Administrator, for more information.) While Microsoft offers only client software for DOS, other software vendors have offered server software for DOS in the past. Artisoft's LANtastic is one such example.

WINDOWS FOR WORKGROUPS   During the mid-1990s, Windows for Workgroups version 3.11 was the dominant Microsoft desktop OS. In addition to introducing numerous performance and stability enhancements to the Windows 3.X line, Windows for Workgroups shipped with both a network client and a server. Windows for Workgroups machines can operate either as a peer-to-peer network or as clients within an NT network. Although fading from the scene, Windows for Workgroups' modest hardware requirements (386 processor or better and 8MB of RAM) will ensure its survival in some environments for a few more years.

WINDOWS 95 AND 98   Windows 95 and 98 include both client and server software as well, enabling them to operate either in Windows workgroups or as part of an NT domain. With hardware requirements somewhat more stringent than Windows for Workgroups but less strict than Windows NT, Windows 95 and 98 systems will likely survive in corporate environments and thrive in the home market for several years to come. Windows 95 and 98 share the same user interface as Windows NT 4.0.

WINDOWS NT 3.51   The precursor to Windows NT 4.0, Windows NT 3.51 came in two versions: Windows NT 3.51, equivalent to Windows NT 4.0 Workstation, and Windows NT Advanced Server, equivalent to Windows NT 4.0 Server. NT 3.51 supports many of the same features as NT 4.0, including domain security and the NTFS file system. Windows NT 3.51 shares the same user interface as Windows for Workgroups.

WINDOWS NT 4.0   Windows NT 4.0 Workstation and Windows NT 4.0 Server can both act as clients on an NT network via the Workstation service, shown in Figure 11–1. Windows NT 4.0 shares the same user interface as Windows 95.

Other Clients

Windows NT machines can also act as servers for a variety of non-Microsoft clients, including NetWare, UNIX, and Macintosh. The level of

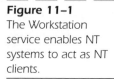

Figure 11–1
The Workstation service enables NT systems to act as NT clients.

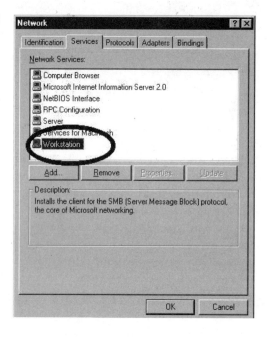

support for these clients tends to lag behind the Microsoft clients and usually lacks features and ease of use. In some cases, the clients are not built-in and may even cost additional money.

NETWARE   Client machines can access an NT Server using a NetWare client if the NT Server is running *File and Print Sharing for NetWare* (FPNW), an optional product offered by Microsoft. FPNW is not included on the NT 4.0 CD-ROM and is not covered on the Workstation, Server, or Enterprise exams. For more information about interoperability with NetWare, see Chapter 12, "Windows NT and Novell."

UNIX   Microsoft does not provide a client for UNIX. The only way for UNIX clients to access NT boxes is via standard TCP/IP protocols. The most common method for UNIX clients to access NT 4.0 servers is to access *Internet Information Server* (IIS) via the FTP, Gopher, or HTTP protocols. See Chapter 13, "Microsoft and the Internet," for more information about IIS.

APPLE MACINTOSH   Apple Macintosh computers can access NT Servers that have Services for Macintosh installed. Services for Macintosh will be covered in detail later in this chapter.

Because the NetWare client is outside the scope of the exams and the UNIX clients are no more than Internet connections, the rest of this chapter is really reduced to nothing more than Microsoft clients and Macintosh clients. Basically, Microsoft provides this support with two special programs: the Network Client Administrator for Microsoft clients and a few special Services for Macintosh for the Macintosh systems. So come along as we begin the happy journey into client software, beginning with the Microsoft clients' tool, the Network Client Administrator.

Network Client Administrator

Microsoft has a bit of a challenge in supporting the large number of Microsoft clients. Each Microsoft OS requires significantly different sets of installation files, configurations, Registry settings, etc. To facilitate this process, Microsoft has developed a special program called the Network Client Administrator. The *Network Client Administrator* (NCA) ships with Windows NT and is used to create floppy diskettes that enable clients to be installed on systems, to share special network administration tools, and to work with remote boot systems (see RPL in this chapter). Launch NCA from the Start Menu under Programs . . . Administrative Tools (Common). Figure 11–2 shows the main menu for NCA.

Creating Network Installation Startup Disks

Creating network installation disks with NCA is an extremely useful but underutilized feature of Windows NT. With a properly configured boot disk, a network administrator can install Windows 95 or a DOS client by simply inserting the boot disk into a new computer and rebooting. The

Figure 11–2
The main menu for NCA

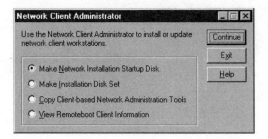

boot disks created by NCA contain enough DOS-based networking software to get on the network, connect to an NT Server, and install an OS from a shared folder on the network.

NOTE: *You can use network installation floppies combined with startup INF files to create a completely hands-free, "just put in the floppy and start the computer"-type of installation for Windows 95 and 98 or Windows NT. See Chapter 2, "Installing Windows NT," for details on hands-free installation.*

To create these diskettes, select Make Network Installation Startup Disk and click OK. The next screen enables an NT administrator to create a shared directory that will contain the contents of the **\CLIENTS** subdirectory from the NT Server CD-ROM, as shown in Figure 11–3.

Next, NCA asks for the type of floppy diskette, the type of *network interface card* (NIC), and which type of client to install (Windows 95 or DOS, as shown in Figure 11–4). An unfortunate flaw exists in the program, however—the lack of the "Have Disk" option that is available in many other programs. If the NIC installed in the new PCs does not appear on this list, you are seemingly out of luck. Go ahead and create the installation disk. In a moment, NT will give you a method to update the NIC driver on the diskette.

Next, specify how the new machine should connect to the NT Server. Figure 11–5 shows the Network Startup Disk Configuration dialog box, where you can specify the computer name, user account, domain name,

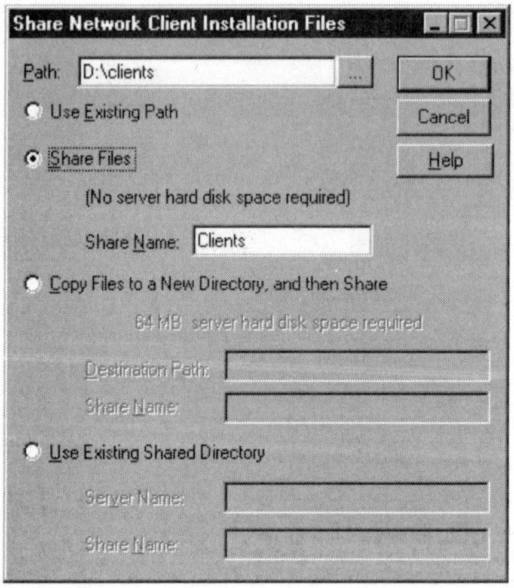

Figure 11–3

NCA creates a shared directory for the contents of the **\CLIENTS** directory of the NT Server CD-ROM.

```
Share Network Client Installation Files          _ □ ✕

 Path:  D:\clients                    ...      OK

 ○ Use Existing Path                          Cancel

 ● Share Files                                 Help

       [No server hard disk space required]

     Share Name:  Clients

 ○ Copy Files to a New Directory, and then Share

       64 MB  server hard disk space required

     Destination Path:

     Share Name:

 ○ Use Existing Shared Directory

     Server Name:

     Share Name:
```

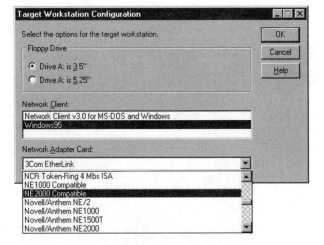

Figure 11–4
NCA needs to know the type of floppy, NIC, and OS.

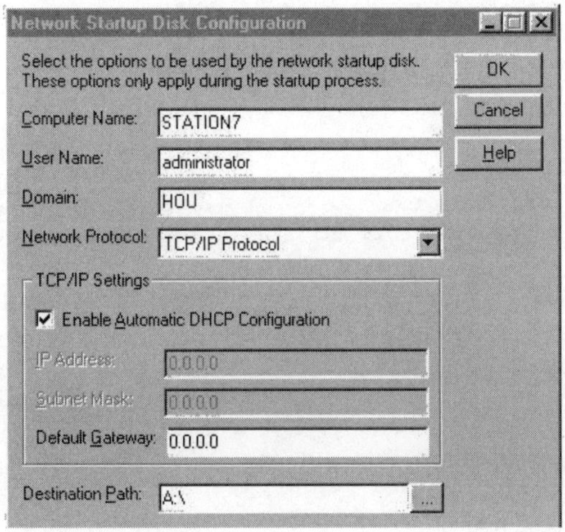

Figure 11–5
Specify the computer name, user account, domain name, and protocol.

and protocol to use. In addition, if using TCP/IP, you can specify the IP address, subnet mask, and default gateway, or you can select DHCP for automatic configuration. (For more information about TCP/IP settings, see Chapter 10, "Networking Protocols.")

NCA will then display a summary of the selected settings and prompt you for a formatted, bootable floppy disk, as shown in Figure 11–6.

The formatted diskette will boot up to a text prompt and load enough software to connect to the network and begin the installation of Windows 95 (or the Network Client version 3.0 for DOS). If the correct NIC driver was not available in NCA, you can manually update the **SYSTEM.INI** and

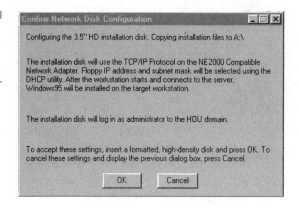

PROTOCOL.INI files in the **\NET** directory on the floppy disk to load the correct drivers. Most NIC cards will ship with a DOS driver on the installation disk that comes with the card. The NIC drivers used in DOS have the file extension *.DOS. Find the DOS driver for the NIC and copy the driver to the **\NET** directory on the boot diskette. Then, modify the following **\NET\SYSTEM.INI** file setting to point to the new NIC driver:

```
[network drivers]
netcard=ne2000.dos
; change ne2000.dos to the name of the new NIC driver
```

Next, change the **PROTOCOL.INI** file to reflect the new NIC driver, as seen in the following example. You need to make two changes. First, add a section named **[MS$drivername]** using the existing driver section as a guide. (Plug and Play cards usually do not require the INTERRUPT (IRQ) and IOBASE (I/O Base Address) settings, but be prepared to fiddle with these settings.)

```
[ms$ne2clone]
; drivername=MS2000$
; INTERRUPT=3
; IOBASE=0x300
; SlotNumber=1
; use this section as a guide to creating a [MS$drivername]
      section for
; the new card
```

Then, change the binding information for whichever protocol is to be used to bind to the new NIC driver:

```
[tcpip]
DriverName=TCPIP$
; BINDINGS=ms$ne2clone
; create a new BINDINGS= setting
;pointing to the new driver.
```

TIP: *The Workstation, Server, and Enterprise exams do not require detailed knowledge of* **PROTOCOL.INI** *and* **SYSTEM.INI** *settings. They are discussed here because NCA's network installation diskettes are worthless for newer machines with recent vintage NICs, unless the administrator can change the drivers on the diskette.*

In addition to their utility for installing new systems, NCA's network installation diskettes have another handy use not mentioned in the documentation: they make wonderful troubleshooting tools. Simply "remark out" the last three lines of the floppy's **AUTOEXEC.BAT** file:

```
REM net use z: \\TEST\Clients
REM echo Running Setup...
REM z:\win95\netsetup\setup.exe
```

Now the boot floppy will load the network client software without running setup. The resulting diskette can be handy for diagnosing network problems. If you can get on the network with the floppy disk but not from the system's regular NOS, you know that nothing is wrong with the physical connection to the network. If the boot disk does not connect you to the network, cabling problems might be a likely possibility.

Creating Installation Disk Sets

NCA does more than just create boot diskettes for LAN installations. When NT 4.0 came out, there was a big demand for the capacity to take existing DOS, Windows for Workgroups, and OS/2 systems and upgrade them so they could access an NT Server. To answer this demand, Microsoft designed NCA to create installation diskettes that contain all of the files necessary to install the NT clients to DOS and OS/2 systems. Additionally, NCA has TCP/IP drivers for Windows for Workgroups (WFW did not come with TCP/IP drivers). These five add-ons were called Network Client version 3.0 for MS-DOS and Windows, Remote Access version 1.1a for MS-DOS, TCP/IP 32 for Windows for Workgroups, LAN Manager version 2.2c for MS-DOS, and LAN Manager version 2.2c for OS/2. Again, these are not complete operating systems; rather, they are merely add-ons to existing DOS, Windows for Workgroups, and OS/2 installations.

NOTE: *The Installation Disk Sets option is basically obsolete.*

Copying Client-Based Network Administration Tools

The client-based Administration Tools enable NT administrators to administer NT Servers remotely from Windows 95, 98, and Windows NT Workstation machines. NCA copies the installation files from the NT CD-ROM and creates a shared copy of these files. They must still be installed on the client system. Actually, this process creates two separate network shares, one for administration tools that run under Windows NT workstation and another for administration tools to run under Windows 95 and 98. You do not need to use NCA for this process, because you can install the client-based Administration Tools directly from the Windows NT Server CD-ROM. Using NCA, however, makes for a handy, simple, installation of some the most popular and powerful NT administration tools. Figure 11–7 shows the following server management tools available for Windows NT Workstation:

- User Manager for Domains
- Server Manager
- Policy Editor
- Remote Access Admin
- RPL Manager
- DHCP Administrator
- WINS Manager

These tools enable an NT Administrator to handle most administrative tasks from an NT Workstation.

For Windows 95 and 98, a more modest set of three administrative tools is available:

- User Manager for Domains
- Server Manager
- Event Viewer

Figure 11–7
The server management tools available to NT Workstation.

Poledit   Rasadmin   Rplmgr   Dhcpadmn

Srvmgr   Usrmgr   Winsadmn

Figure 11–8 shows User Manager running on a Windows 95 system. Notice that programs such as User Manager for Domains function the same, whether they are run from a Windows 95, 98, or Windows NT machine. The Server tools available to Windows 95, 98, and NT machines enable NT administrators to handle most administrative tasks without having to go to the server.

The last option, View Remoteboot Client Information, displays the status of the Remoteboot service. *Remoteboot service* enables network systems to boot from the server. This option is ignored on the MCSE exams.

The NCA is a grab bag of useful utilities, because NCA can create shared directories for common installation files such as the Windows 95 installation files. NCA creates boot disks that install Windows 95 onto a new machine from a shared folder. NCA can also create a shared resource folder for client administration tools. Although a sharp administrator could do any of these things manually, NCA can reduce some of the administrative overhead involved in running an NT network.

Figure 11–8

A Windows 95 system running User Manager for Domains

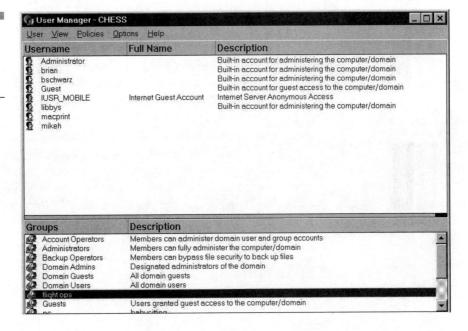

Macintosh

Despite the dominance of Intel x86-compatible, processor-based machines in most business environments, Apple Macintosh computers continue to maintain a strong presence as a desktop machine in many environments —especially in education and graphic design. Although Macintosh computers (commonly referred to as Macs) offer some advantages as workstation computers, the Macintosh OS was never designed for use as a server. The Macintosh OS has always been designed as a single-user system. When a dialog box in any application appears, everything stops until the user responds to the dialog box. This approach is vastly different from Windows NT's multi-tasking approach, which enables programs to run as services. A service continues to operate in the background, regardless of other processes that are running on the server. Because of this limitation of the Macintosh OS, Macintosh computers make poor servers. While Novell and UNIX servers can act as a server for Macintosh computers, Windows NT's GUI interface and ease of use make it the server of choice for Macintosh networks.

The process of enabling Macintoshes to act as NT Server clients is completely different from the process of making Microsoft operating systems NT clients. Microsoft programs have specialized client software, either already installed or imported via the NCA, that give the program the "smarts" to see the NT Server. The "smarts" of getting Macintoshes to see an NT Server are instead based on loading special network services on the NT Server—in essence, reversing the process. All of the services necessary for Macintosh NT Server clients are lumped together into one network service called Services for Macintosh. Like all network services, Services for Macintosh is installed from the Network Control Panel applet, as shown in Figure 11–9. For Services for Macintosh to operate, however, the NT Server must have the special AppleTalk network protocol installed.

AppleTalk

Services for Macintosh enables NT Servers to share resources to Macintosh clients using the Macintosh's native AppleTalk protocol. AppleTalk has significant differences from the other networking protocols used in Windows NT (IPX, TCP/IP, and NetBEUI) and does not show up in the Protocols tab of the Network Control Panel applet. Instead, configure the AppleTalk configuration of the NT Server through the properties of Client Services for Macintosh in the Network Control Panel applet.

Figure 11-9

Install Services for
Macintosh using the
Network Control
Panel applet.

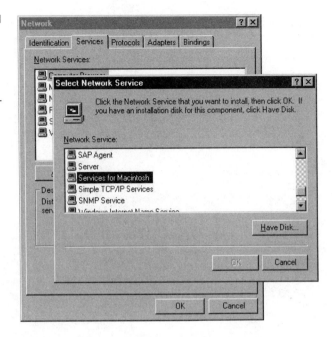

The properties for AppleTalk are divided into two tabs: General and
Routing. The Routing tab, shown in Figure 11–10, has two options:
Default Adapter and Default Zone. Selecting the Default Adapter binds
the AppleTalk protocol to that network card, enabling Macintoshes
attached to that network segment to communicate with the NT Server.
The Default Zone setting specifies the AppleTalk zone to which the NT
Server will belong. AppleTalk zones are similar to Microsoft workgroups
in that they organize the list of available servers on the network into
smaller lists, but they do not provide any security functions. Macintoshes
can connect to and communicate with servers in AppleTalk zones other
than their own. One difference between AppleTalk zones and Microsoft
workgroups is that an AppleTalk zone must already exist before a
machine can join the zone, whereas any machine can create its own
Microsoft workgroup by simply typing a new name in the Control Panel.

The Routing tab, shown in Figure 11–11, has options that control
AppleTalk routing. The term routing in AppleTalk is slightly different
than how TCP/IP describes routing. In an AppleTalk network, there will
always be one system that is called a seed router. A *seed router* specifies
the network addresses for other machines in an AppleTalk network—and
in some ways is analogous to a DHCP server in a TCP/IP network.

Figure 11–10
The first tab of the
Services for
Macintosh Control
Panel applet

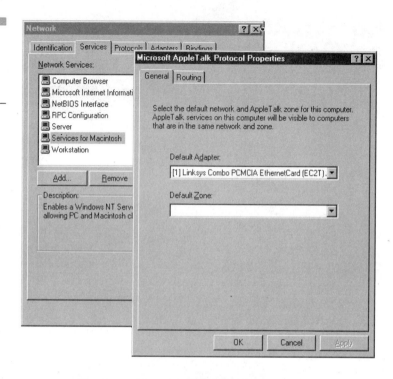

Figure 11–10
The first tab of the
Services for
Macintosh Control
Panel applet

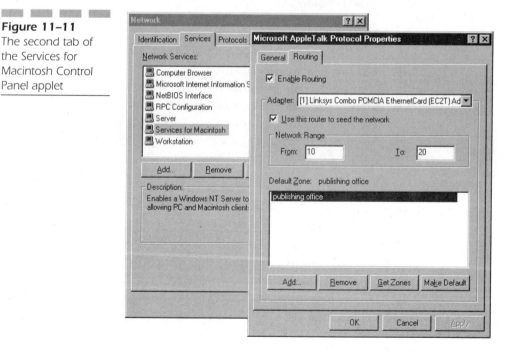

Figure 11–11
The second tab of
the Services for
Macintosh Control
Panel applet

In any routable protocol, each machine on the network must have a network address and an individual address. The network address specifies which network the machine is on, and the individual address stipulates which specific machine on the network it is. In TCP/IP networks, the network address is called the network ID, and the individual address is called the host ID.

In AppleTalk, the network address is the network number, and the individual address is the node number. The seed router specifies one or more network numbers, and the individual machines randomly choose their node numbers when they start up. A single network number can have up to 253 nodes, so a single physical network might contain more than one network number. When using the NT Server as a seed router, specify the network numbers to use in the Network Range box.

A seed router also creates AppleTalk zones for machines to join. To specify additional zones, click Add and type the name of the new zone.

NT Servers can act as servers for Macintosh clients without acting as an AppleTalk router, assuming some other system on the network is acting as a seed router. In those cases, the Enable Routing checkbox is left clear, disabling the other options on this tab. If you decide to use your NT Server as an AppleTalk router, select the "Use this router to seed the network" option, as shown in Figure 11–11.

Once you have properly configured the AppleTalk settings, you can configure the two key network functions prepared for Macintosh clients: file sharing and print sharing. Keep in mind that Macintoshes use a different set of rules to communicate with an NT Server than the rules used by Microsoft clients. Do not expect to use the same tools to share resources with users on the Macintosh clients as you would to share resources with users on Windows 95 or NT Workstation.

File Sharing with Macintosh Computers

Installing Services for Macintosh prepares the Windows NT system to share folders. Now, just for fun, guess which programs are used to administer shared folders to Macintoshes: Windows Explorer and User Manager? No. Windows Explorer and My Computer? Guess again. How about Server Manager and—here is a flash from the past—File Manager. No kidding—the old Windows 3.X File Manager is alive and well in Windows NT 4.0, and if you want to share folders for Macintoshes, you will need File Manager. Server Manager might not be the most intuitive choice either, but what about File Manager? What was Microsoft thinking? Well, for you youngsters out there who have never played with any version of Windows that did not have a task bar, let us introduce you to the Windows of Your Forefathers. But before the history lesson, Server Manager requires some configuration.

CONFIGURING SERVER MANAGER Services for Macintosh adds an option to the Server Manager called MacFile. This selection has three options: Properties, Volumes, and Send Message, as shown Figure 11–12.

Before you can share an NT volume to Macintoshes, you must give the volume a share name (which might or might not be different from the Windows share name), make the volume shareable, and deal with a number of small issues such as number of sessions, authentication, etc. Begin the configuration by selecting MacFile . . . Properties. This selection displays the MacFile Attributes dialog box, as shown in Figure 11–13.

By default, the Macintosh name for the NT Server will be the same as its computer name in the Network Control Panel applet. If you wish to use another name, click Change and specify the alternative name. You may also optionally specify a Logon Message that will appear when a Macintosh client connects to the NT Server, such as in Figure 11–14. This message is similar to the login message that can be used with Internet Information Server's FTP server. (See Chapter 13, "Microsoft and the Internet.")

Use care when installing Macintosh clients on an NT network. Macintosh clients cannot fully participate in the normal security features of NT. Users logging in through Services for Macintosh use their regular Windows NT user accounts, but they can only access resources explicitly shared through Services for Macintosh (see the following section for more details). One reason for this distinction between resources shared with more traditional NT clients (DOS, Windows for Workgroups, Windows 95 and 98, and Windows NT) is that Macintosh clients use a different mechanism to log into an NT Server.

Figure 11–12
MacFile options

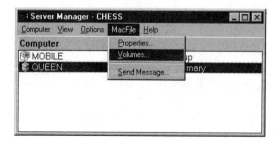

Figure 11–13
The MacFile . . .
Properties window in
Server Manager

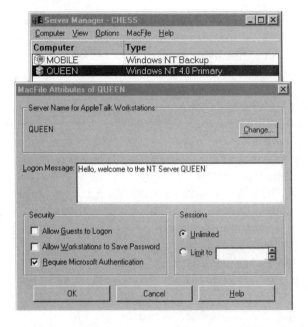

Figure 11–13
The MacFile . . .
Properties window in
Server Manager

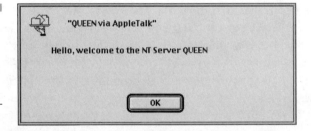

Figure 11–14
Macintosh client
displaying the
welcome message
specified in Server
Manager

Three checkboxes deal with security in the MacFile . . . Properties dialog box:

- Allow Guests to Logon
- Allow Workstations to Save Password
- Require Microsoft Authentication

The guest account can often be a source of security problems, and you should disable guest access unless there is a specific need for that type of access. Likewise, enabling workstations (i.e. the Macintosh clients) to save passwords can be a security risk and should not be enabled in most cases.

The "Require Microsoft Authentication" issue is more complex. Macintosh clients use a program called the *User Authentication Module* (UAM) to send login names and passwords to a server. Unfortunately, the default

Macintosh UAM has two problems. First, the UAM cannot be used if the passwords or usernames are longer than eight characters. Second, the UAM transmits usernames and passwords across the network in clear text, potentially enabling anyone with a packet sniffer and physical access to the network to steal the password for their own evil purposes. Microsoft offers a replacement UAM, the Microsoft UAM, that enables longer usernames and passwords and encrypts usernames and passwords sent over the network.

By default, an NT Server running Services for Macintosh will accept logins from Macintoshes using either UAM. Checking the Require Microsoft Authentication box causes the NT Server to reject the standard UAM's clear text login attempts and require clients to use the more secure Microsoft UAM. Unfortunately, that requires every Macintosh client to install the Microsoft UAM, creating more work for the administrator. The Microsoft UAM installation software is shared by default with Macintosh clients to make UAM easier to install. (See the following discussion of sharing files for more details.)

When a Macintosh client attempts to log into an NT Server, the login method determines which dialog box the Macintosh user sees. If the user logs in without installing the Microsoft UAM, they will see the dialog box shown in Figure 11–15. If the NT Server has been configured to Require Microsoft Authentication, then the Macintosh user will receive the error message shown in Figure 11–16. Once the Microsoft UAM has been installed on the Macintosh client, a user logging in to the NT Server from the Macintosh would see a choice of UAMs to use, as shown in Figure 11–17.

Determining which login method is being used by the Macintosh client is easy. If the Macintosh is using the standard clear text UAM, the words "clear text" will be displayed in the login dialog box. If the Microsoft UAM is in use, the dialog box will display "Microsoft authentication," shown in Figure 11–18.

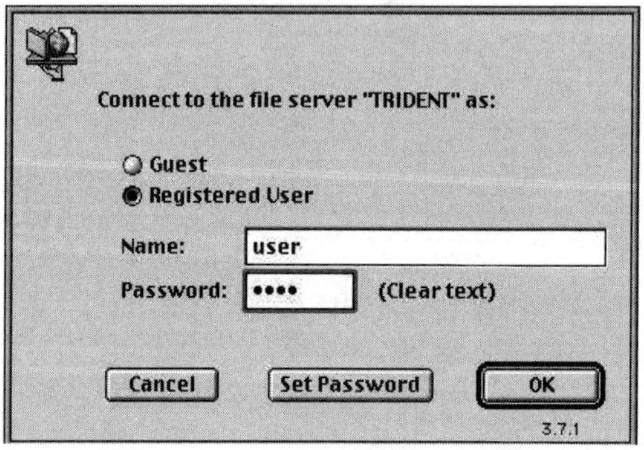

Figure 11–15

Macintosh clients use clear text by default for login names and passwords.

Figure 11–16
Clear text attempts to log into an NT Server set to require Microsoft Authentication to generate an error message.

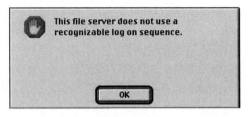

Figure 11–17
The Macintosh client chooses the log on method, once the Microsoft UAM has been installed.

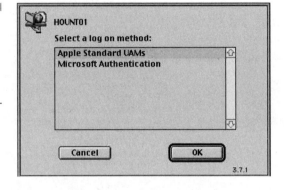

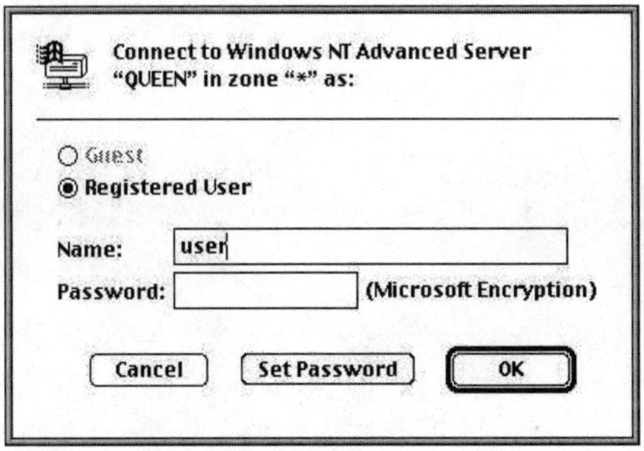

Figure 11–18
Logging in with the Microsoft UAM

When logging in to an NT Server running Services for Macintosh, Macintosh clients can use either the native Macintosh UAM or the encrypted Microsoft UAM. Using the native Macintosh UAM has the advantage of requiring no additional software on the Macintosh clients but can cause security problems—because the Macintosh UAM transmits passwords in clear text. The Microsoft UAM encrypts usernames and passwords but requires installation of additional software on the Macintosh client.

SHARING FILES   Sharing files with Macintosh clients using Services for Macintosh differs in two important ways from sharing files with traditional Microsoft clients. First, administrators use a different set of tools to create Macintosh-accessible, shared resources. Second, the capacity to create different levels of access for different users and groups is more limited.

TOOLS FOR SHARING RESOURCES   Services for Macintosh uses the old File Manager to administer shares. Administrators can create Macintosh-accessible shares, called volumes, using two tools: Server Manager and File Manager. The earlier deriding of File Manager is actually a little unfair. The good old file management utility from Windows for Workgroups 3.X and Windows NT 3.51 still exists and can actually do a few things that Windows Explorer cannot. While Server Manager is the more familiar tool for Windows NT 4.0 administrators, File Manager actually offers a more user-friendly interface for sharing resources with Macintosh clients.

NOTE: *Apple refers to shared resources on a network as volumes, while Microsoft calls them shares.*

Using Server Manager   To share a file using Server Manager, launch Server Manager from the Start Menu and Select the MacFile/Volumes menu option. This selection enables you to create or change the Macintosh-accessible file resources. The windows shown in Figure 11–19 should appear, showing a Macintosh-accessible volume called "Microsoft UAM Volume."

The "Microsoft UAM Volume" contains the installation files for the Microsoft UAM, making it easier to configure Macintosh clients to use the

Figure 11–19
Services for
Macintosh creates a
"Microsoft UAM
Volume" by default.

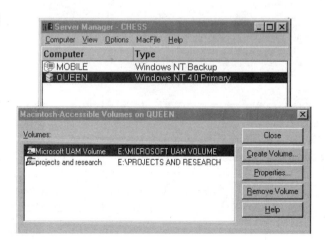

more secure login method. Unfortunately, this volume is no longer accessible once Services for Macintosh has been set to require Microsoft Authentication (as discussed earlier).

To create a new Macintosh-accessible volume, click the Create Volume button. This selection brings up the Create Macintosh-Accessible Volume dialog box. You can set permissions, as shown in Figure 11–20, by selecting the Permissions button. In addition to the Permissions button, this dialog box gives you five options:

- Volume Name—The volume name used here is analogous to the share name used to share resources with traditional Microsoft clients in Explorer. When Macintosh clients view the shared resources on the server running Services for Macintosh, this name is the name that they will see.

- Path—The path specifies where on the NT Server to find the files to be shared.

- Password—Services for Macintosh enables the administrator to set a password for access to a share that must be used in addition to a user's login password. Passwords must be typed exactly the same in both the Password and Confirm Password boxes.

- Volume Security—To provide additional security, a volume can be set as Read only, and guest access can be denied on a volume-by-volume basis.

- User Limit—Set a user limit on a particular volume to prevent access to the volume from monopolizing the server's resources or to comply with licensing restrictions.

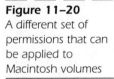

Figure 11–20
A different set of permissions that can be applied to Macintosh volumes

Directory Permissions on QUEEN

Path: e:\graphics

Permissions

		See Files	See Folders	Make Changes
Owner:	Administrators	☑	☑	☑
Primary Group:	CHESS\Domain Users	☑	☑	☑
Everyone:		☐	☐	☐

☐ Replace permissions on subdirectories
☐ Cannot move, rename, or delete

[OK]   [Cancel]   [Help]

Access to Macintosh volumes cannot be controlled as precisely as access to Windows NT shares. The Macintosh OS does not support the capacity to set different permissions for a wide variety of groups. In the Macintosh world, a file or folder can only distinguish between three types of users: the Owner, the Primary Group, and Everyone. In this example, the ADMINISTRATORS group (the owner of the volume) and the DIRECTORS global group from the CHESS domain (the Primary Group) both have full access, while the EVERYONE group has not been granted any access. Because the Macintosh OS does not permit granting permissions to multiple groups, there is no way to give another group, EDITORS, the right to SEE FILES. Although a useful tool, Services for Macintosh does not enable Macintosh clients to integrate fully with Windows NT security.

Fortunately, if the Macintosh volume exists on a drive formatted with NTFS, NTFS file permissions still apply. If MIKEH has full access (See Files, See Folders, and Make Changes) to a Macintosh-accessible volume but has only Read access to an NTFS file shared via that Macintosh-accessible volume, MIKEH will only have Read access to the file. Because of the limited restrictions that can be placed on access to a Macintosh-accessible volume, Macintosh-accessible volumes should only be used to share data on NTFS partitions.

Using File Manager   Creating Macintosh-accessible volumes with Server Manger has a serious drawback: no Browse option exists. To create the volume, the administrator needs to know the exact path to the directory to be shared on the NT Server. File Manager, that venerable tool from the Windows 3.X days of yore, provides a more user-friendly way of creating Macintosh-accessible volumes.

File Manager provides a more graphical interface for creating Macintosh-accessible volumes than the interface provided by Server Manager. Unfortunately, the NT gurus at Microsoft decided not to create a Start Menu option for File Manager. To launch File Manager, select Run from the Start menu and type "`WINFILE.EXE`" without the quotes, just like Figure 11–21. If Services for Macintosh has been installed, File Manager will open with an additional menu, a new menu choice—MacFile—and some additional icons, as shown in Figure 11–22.

Selecting MacFile . . . Create Volume brings up the same dialog box as Server Manager, but File Manager fills in the Path with a path to the currently selected directory and sets the Volume Name to the name of the directory being shared, as shown in Figure 11–23.

Figure 11–21
Launch File Manager
by running the
WINFILE.EXE
program.

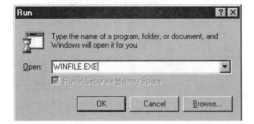

Figure 11–22
After installing
Services for
Macintosh, a new
menu and new icons
appear in File
Manager.

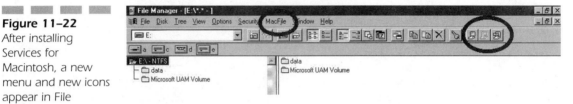

Figure 11–23
Using File Manager
instead of Server
Manager to create
Macintosh volumes
lets File Manager fill
in the Volume Name
and Path for you.

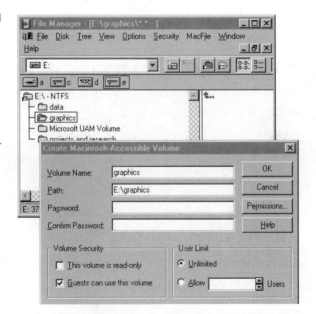

NOTE: *Remember that Windows Explorer cannot be used to create or manage Macintosh-accessible volumes.*

ACCESSING MACINTOSH-ACCESSIBLE VOLUMES FROM A MACINTOSH CLIENT

Macintosh clients access Macintosh-accessible volumes on an NT Server running Services for Macintosh in much the same way that they access files on Macintosh servers. To connect to a server, launch the Chooser application, shown in Figure 11–24.

After selecting a server and logging in, Macintosh-accessible volumes shared by the NT Server appear on the Macintosh desktop, just like any other Macintosh network drive—except for the addition of a small Microsoft flag, as shown in Figure 11–25. Double-clicking the network drive icon brings up the contents of the Macintosh-accessible Volume, as shown in Figure 11–26.

The Macintosh OS limits file and folder names to 31 characters. If a file or folder on a Macintosh-accessible volume is longer than 31 characters, the Macintosh truncates the name to six characters, a tilde (~), and a number, much the same way that DOS truncates Windows 9X or Windows NT filenames longer than eight characters. See Figure 11–27.

With the possible exception of installing the Microsoft UAM, Macintosh clients require no additional software to access Macintosh-accessible vol-

Figure 11–24
Use Chooser to select a server.

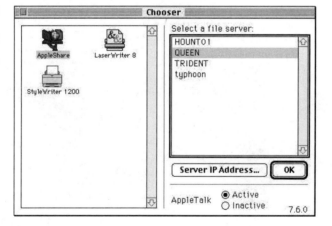

Figure 11–25
Macintosh-accessible Volumes on an NT Server look just like any other network drive, except for the Microsoft flag.

Figure 11–26
Double-clicking the
shared network drive
displays its contents.

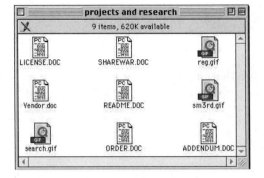

Figure 11–27
The Macintosh OS
truncates file and
directory names if
they are longer than
31 characters.

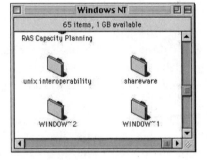

umes being shared by an NT Server through Services for Macintosh.
Users at Macintosh workstations can use files shared by the NT Server
running Services for Macintosh as though they were stored on another
Macintosh.

Printing with Macintosh Computers

Compared to the rather involved process of sharing folders, the process of
sharing printers to Macintosh clients is trivially easy. Surprisingly, sharing a printer with Macintosh clients is handled by right-clicking the icon
for the printer in the Control Panel's printers folder, the same application
used to share printers with Microsoft clients. Simply right-click the
printer icon, as shown in Figure 11–28.

Access to the printer can be controlled through the Security tab, enabling
an administrator to assign different degrees of control to different users.
Unfortunately, printing in the Macintosh world occurs without reference to
user accounts. The assumption is that every Macintosh client should be able
to print to every printer. No way exists for NT to determine which user is trying to access the printer. By default, every user logging in from a Macintosh

Figure 11–28
Share a printer by
right-clicking an
installed printer.

will be able to print, regardless of the permissions that have been set. Even a user who has been explicitly denied access (i.e. assigned the No Access permission) can still print if logged in to a Macintosh client.

Because there is no way to determine which user is attempting to print, all print jobs originating with a Macintosh client are printed by the Print Server for Macintosh itself. The reason this security loophole exists is that the Print Server for Macintosh logs in as the System Account by default. To restrict users of Macintosh clients to particular printers, create a user account for the Print Server for Macintosh and give that account the appropriate permissions for the printers that should be accessible to users accessing the network via Macintosh clients. To set the Print Server for Macintosh to log in using a particular user account, use the Services Control Panel applet as shown in Figure 11–29.

By setting the Print Service for Macintosh to log into a user account instead of the system account, you can achieve some measure of printing security. But remember that as far as NT is concerned, all Macintosh clients are the same user. Users connecting to the NT Server from a Macintosh client have the printing rights of the Print Server for Macintosh, not their own user account. A printer that needs tightly restricted access should not be shared via the Services for Macintosh because of these serious security limitations.

NOTE: *For more detail about printer security and other NT printing issues, see Chapter 15, "Printing in Windows NT."*

Services for Macintosh enables Macintosh clients to access resources on NT Servers as though they were resources on another Macintosh.

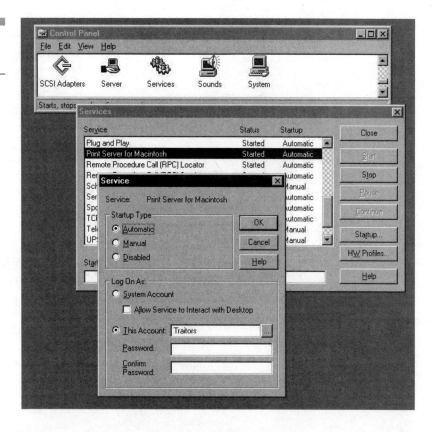

Figure 11–29
Services Control
Panel applet

Unfortunately, the Macintosh OS limits the ability of NT administrators to fully integrate Macintosh clients into the NT security model. When using Services for Macintosh, keep the following points in mind:

- Although Services for Macintosh uses the AppleTalk protocol for communicating with Macintosh clients, AppleTalk will not be listed as a protocol in the Network Control Panel applet.

- Macintosh clients transmit their usernames and passwords in clear text over the network. For more security, install the Microsoft UAM on each machine.

- Windows Explorer cannot be used to share files and folders with Macintosh clients. Administrators must use either Server Manager or File Manager instead.

- Share printers with Macintosh clients just as you would with Microsoft clients, but remember that NT grants users sitting at Macintosh clients access to printers based on the user account used by Print Server for Macintosh, not based on individual user accounts.

Services for Macintosh makes Windows NT an excellent server for a Macintosh network but requires extra caution on the part of administrators, because Services for Macintosh differs somewhat from traditional Microsoft networking.

Windows NT provides support for a wide variety of both Microsoft and non-Microsoft client operating systems. In some cases, such as Windows 95 and 98, the support requires little extra effort on the part of network administrators. In other cases, such as adding support for Macintosh clients, administrators must install extra software and plan carefully to take into account the differences between Windows NT and other operating systems.

Questions

1. Which of the following utilities can create Macintosh-accessible volumes on an NT Server? (Choose the best answer.)

   a. File Manager

   b. Windows NT Explorer

   c. Server Manager

   d. NCA

2. Allison, a user working at a Macintosh client, complains that every time she tries to log in, the Macintosh computer generates an error saying, "The file server does not use a recognizable log on service." How can you fix her problem?

   a. Restart the File Sharing for Macintosh service on the NT Server.

   b. Run User Manager for Domains and re-enable Allison's account.

   c. Install the Microsoft UAM on the Macintosh client.

   d. Install the Macintosh Security Module on the NT Server.

3. NCA can create boot disks to install which of the following? (Choose all that apply.)

   a. Novell NetWare

   b. Windows 95

   c. OS/2 Warp

   d. Network Client version 3.0 for DOS and Windows

4. Windows NT Server can act as a server for which the following types of network clients? (Choose all that apply.)

   a. Windows for Workgroups

   b. Macintosh

   c. Novell NetWare

   d. Windows NT Workstation

5. What advantages does the Microsoft UAM have over the default Macintosh UAM?

    a. The Microsoft UAM is faster.

    b. The Microsoft UAM uses TCP/IP.

    c. The Microsoft UAM encrypts usernames and passwords.

    d. The Microsoft UAM supports long filenames.

6. The user account TYLERC has been granted No Access to the printer LASER8. When TYLERC logs in from his Macintosh workstation, he discovers that he can successfully print documents on LASER8. This situation occurs because:

    a. TYLERC is a member of the ADMINISTRATORS global group, which can always use all printers.

    b. The Macintosh client is using the standard Macintosh UAM instead of the Microsoft UAM.

    c. The Printing Service for Macintosh is logged in as the system account.

    d. TYLERC is a member of another group that has been explicitly granted access to the printer LASER8.

7. Services for Macintosh uses which of the following networking protocols: (Choose all that apply.)

    a. NetBEUI

    b. DLC

    c. AppleTalk

    d. TCP/IP

8. Macintosh filenames are limited to _____ characters.

    a. 16

    b. 8

    c. 31

    d. 256

9. Ernie runs an NT network for a large architectural firm. The firm buys out a smaller firm, and Ernie is tasked to integrate the smaller firm's 20 Macintosh computers into his company's NT network. Required result: Enable every user in the design department to access files stored on the NT Server DRAWINGS1 in the NTFS folder **G:\CURRENT** while logged in to their Macintosh computers. They must be able to update the files stored in **G:\CURRENT** as needed. Optional results: 1. Install no additional software on the Macintosh computers. 2. Restrict access to the files stored on DRAWINGS1 according to NT user and group accounts. Proposed solution: Install Services for Macintosh on DRAWINGS1. Create a user account in the NT Domain for each Macintosh user. Assign those users to an NT global groups DESIGNERS. Create a local group on DRAWINGS1 called MACDESIGNERS. Put the global group DESIGNERS into the local group MACDESIGNERS. Use File Manager to create a Macintosh-accessible volume on DRAWINGS1 containing the relevant data, and grant the MACDESIGNERS local group See Files, See Folders, and Make Changes permissions to the Macintosh volume. Grant them the Change permission to the NTFS directory in which the data is stored. The proposed solution:

a. Achieves the required result and both optional results.

b. Achieves the required result and one of the optional results.

c. Achieves only the required result and neither of the optional results.

d. Does not achieve the required result and does not work.

10. A Macintosh-accessible volume is: (Select the best answer.)

a. A SCSI hard drive

b. An external data storage device

c. A shared network resource

d. A measure of available disk space

Answers

1. a, c—Only File Manager and Server Manager can create Macintosh-accessible volumes on an NT Server.

2. c—When setting up a Macintosh-accessible volume, administrators can require users to log in with the default Macintosh UAM or the more secure Microsoft UAM. If the administrator has selected the latter, all Macintosh clients must load the Microsoft UAM to access that shared resource.

3. b, d

4. b, c, d—Windows NT Server does not come with a server product for NetWare. Although File and Print Sharing for NetWare can be purchased separately from Microsoft, this software is not included with NT.

5. c—The Microsoft UAM encrypts usernames and passwords, making it more secure than the default Macintosh UAM.

6. c—The Printing Service for Macintosh logs in as the System account by default, which gives System account level permissions to any user who accesses the network through a Macintosh client.

7. c—Although Macintoshes support TCP/IP, Services for Macintosh works exclusively with the AppleTalk protocol.

8. c—Macintosh restricts filenames and folders to 31 characters.

9. a—None of the desired results required that passwords be encrypted, so the Microsoft UAM did not need to be installed on each machine.

10. c—Although Windows NT can share data on a SCSI hard drive with Macintosh clients, the term "Macintosh-accessible volume" refers specifically to files or folders shared with those clients.

12

NT and Novell

At this point, the intrepid MCSE candidate in you might be wondering why there is a big chapter on Novell sitting in the middle of a *Microsoft* Certified Systems Engineer study guide. Seems out of place, right? The truth is, no MCSE lives inside a vacuum. Every MCSE candidate must prepare for that evil day when he or she must make Novell NetWare and Microsoft Windows NT play well together.

Novell NetWare is Windows NT's chief rival for the corporate server market. NetWare has been around longer and has a large installed base. Microsoft requires MCSE candidates to demonstrate the skills needed either to integrate Windows NT into existing NetWare environments, or to convert existing NetWare networks into pure NT networks. Before looking at Microsoft's tools for integrating with and replacing NetWare, let's take a closer look at NetWare.

What is NetWare?

Novell NetWare offers a pure client and server model for file and print servers. Client and server means, in this context, that a client is just a client and a server is just a server. Clients can access resources stored on servers but cannot share their own resources, whereas servers can share their own resources but cannot access resources on other machines. In a pure NetWare network, administrators do little work at the server itself; rather, they accomplish almost all administrative tasks (creating users, sharing resources, etc.) while sitting at a client system and running remote administration utilities such as **SYSCON.EXE**, shown in Figure 12–1. Once the server is properly connected to the network, the server can normally be left in its closet, where the server will sit and happily serve up files for as long as its hardware functions properly.

The dedicated server idea differs considerably from Microsoft's approach with Windows NT. A Windows NT Server can also be used as a workstation, enabling a user to sit at that machine and run any program they wish, including administrative utilities such as User Manager for Domains or productivity applications such as Microsoft Word. You can even run games such as Quake II on an NT Server (of course, not that you would ever use the server that way). An NT Server is a Windows NT system with special server capabilities, but a Novell NetWare server is just a server. That is all NetWare does.

Figure 12–1
SYSCON.EXE

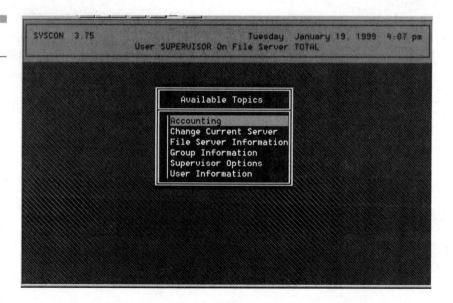

NetWare advocates argue that this dedicated server approach offers two key advantages: security and performance. Because no user should ever have to sit at the NetWare server's console, NetWare servers can be stored in a locked room—to which only a few administrators should have access. The fewer people with physical access to the server, the more secure the server. In addition, NetWare wastes no system resources providing a pretty, graphical user interface, which enables the server to dedicate more resources to improving system performance. Instead of providing resources for features such as sound and mouse support, the server can concentrate on being a server. NetWare uses dedicated servers to provide improved security and performance.

NT advocates counter that nothing stops them from using an NT Server as a dedicated server. While small organizations with limited budgets will sometimes use their NT Servers as workstations, most larger organizations use their NT Servers much as they would a Novell Server, dedicating it as a server and locking it in a secure server room. While these dedicated servers use some of their resources to maintain the Windows Explorer user interface, NT's defenders point out that with the power of today's machines, maintaining this interface costs little. In addition, many NT administrators enjoy the convenience of administering their NT servers directly from the server console, which is not possible with NetWare servers.

NOTE: *The Windows Explorer interface uses about 2.5MB of system RAM. With the cost of RAM hovering around $1 per megabyte, maintaining NT's user interface costs little.*

Versions of NetWare

Novell NetWare evolved significantly over the past decade. Unlike many desktop applications, where a new version quickly replaces earlier versions, organizations with different needs continue to use all three major releases of NetWare. NetWare 3.X works best for small organizations that require only a few servers, while NetWare 4.X works well for organizations that need to manage many servers. And NetWare 5.X supports large networks that require TCP/IP support.

NOVELL NETWARE 3.X   While earlier versions of NetWare exist, NetWare 3.X is the oldest version of NetWare that remains in widespread use

(NetWare 3.2 is the most current version). NetWare 3.X supports many features familiar to NT administrators, including the capacity to restrict access to files and folders to specific users and groups. Both systems have a "super user" who can create user accounts and assign them rights and permissions. NetWare 3.X calls the "super user" SUPERVISOR, while NT calls the "super user" ADMINISTRATOR. They both have menu-driven utilities that enable the "super user" to create and manage users (User Manager for Domains for NT and `SYSCON.EXE` for NetWare 3.X) and to share resources (Windows Explorer for NT and `SYSCON.EXE` for NetWare 3.X).

Aside from its GUI, Windows NT's clearest advantage over NetWare 3.X is its capacity to integrate multiple servers into a single, logical domain. NetWare 3.X requires each server to be administered separately, greatly increasing the burden on administrators. Each NetWare 3.X server holds a database called the Bindery. The Bindery serves roughly the same function in NetWare 3.X as a stand-alone server's SAM database in NT, storing all of the user and group account information. To access resources on multiple NetWare 3.X servers, a user needs an account on each NetWare 3.X server. No centralized database, analogous to the NT Domain SAM stored on the domain controllers in NT, exists for NetWare 3.X. In a network with more than a few servers, administering multiple user accounts for each user quickly becomes a nightmare.

NOVELL NETWARE 4.X   NetWare 4.X, in addition to numerous performance and stability enhancements, addresses the issue of managing multiple servers with a powerful tool: `NetWare Directory Services` (NDS). NDS provides a hierarchical database that can store all data about users, resources, and servers within the NDS tree, which is an organizational unit roughly analogous to Windows NT domains.

NOTE: *Any NDS expert or advocate who hears the NDS tree described as analogous to Windows NT domains will quickly transform into a 15-headed dragon and attack the foolish NT administrator who made such a ridiculous statement. In reality, NDS trees provide numerous functions and capabilities above and beyond those provided by Windows NT Domains. Administrators can use NDS, for example, to provide administrative functions for non-Novell products. The administration of routers and other devices can conceivably be integrated into the NDS tree, enabling all administrators to rely on a common security database. The true Microsoft competitor to NDS is Active Directory (AD), a directory services model that will be a crucial component of Windows 2000 (formerly known as Windows NT 5.0) when it ships.*

Because some older applications cannot function properly with NDS, NetWare 4.X supports "Bindery Emulation," which enables NetWare 4.X servers to "pretend" to have a Bindery database for backward compatibility to NetWare 3.X and 2.X products. While a full discussion of NDS is outside the scope of this book, a basic understanding of NDS is useful for comparison purposes.

NOVELL NETWARE 5.X   Novell NetWare 5.X builds on the NDS features of NetWare 4.X but includes additional support for TCP/IP. While older versions of NetWare can run TCP/IP as an optional protocol, they still require Novell's own IPX/SPX protocol for some functions. NetWare 5.X enables network designers to use TCP/IP exclusively, eliminating the need for running multiple protocols. NetWare 5.X even provides Java-based administration tools. NetWare 5.X shipped long after the writing of the current Workstation, Server, and Enterprise exams and is not discussed or mentioned on these exams.

NOTE: *For a more detailed look at Novell NetWare's features, visit* `http://www.novell.com/products`.

Both Microsoft Windows NT and Novell NetWare offer powerful file and print server capabilities. They can run on x86-compatible hardware and offer solid, user-level security. They both support DOS, Windows 3.X, Windows 95, Windows NT, and Macintosh clients. Hard-core advocates for both network operating systems exist, but either Windows NT or Novell NetWare can meet the needs of most organizations. When properly configured, the differences between the two systems should be largely invisible to the end user. This chapter will not argue the relative merits of NetWare and NT. The purpose here is not to decide between the two operating systems. Instead, this chapter concentrates on the tools that Microsoft provides with Windows NT to enable NT to operate within a NetWare network—and to replace NetWare servers with Windows NT Servers.

Tools in NT

Windows NT ships with four key tools for dealing with NetWare: IPX/SPX compatible transport (a.k.a. NWLink), CSNW, Gateway Services for NetWare, and Migration Tool for NetWare. On the MCSE exams, be prepared to choose the correct tool for any given situation.

IPX/SPX, a.k.a. NWLink

Microsoft supports IPX/SPX, NetWare's native protocol, with Microsoft's own version, NWLink. NWLink is sometimes referred to as IPX/SPX Compatible Transport, which can lead to confusion. Microsoft's own Control Panel screens use these terms interchangeably, expecting all NT gurus out there to know that they mean precisely the same thing. In fact, NWLink is often referred to as simply IPX.

IPX/SPX AS A ROUTABLE PROTOCOL Microsoft originally adopted IPX to give Microsoft products a routable protocol to use. In the days of Windows for Workgroups 3.X, Novell NetWare dominated the NOS market. Microsoft thought it made sense to adopt its routable protocol as the standard (at the time, TCP/IP was largely limited to UNIX-based computers). Today, a pure Microsoft network can run over IPX, but usually an NT administrator installs IPX only to provide connectivity with NetWare servers.

NOTE: *The current Workstation, Server, and Enterprise exams were written before NetWare 5.0 shipped. These tests assume that the default protocol used by NetWare servers is IPX. Even if you personally know of real-world examples of pure TCP/IP NetWare installations, remember that Microsoft assumes that NetWare uses IPX.*

IPX/SPX CONFIGURATION With one notable exception, NT administrators should find IPX/SPX simple to use. In most cases, simply install the protocol by using the Network Control Panel applet and clicking Add on the Protocols tab. At this point, IPX/SPX data can be sent over the network cable in several different formats called *frames*. The following list describes the available frame choices:

- Ethernet 802.2
- Ethernet 802.3
- Ethernet II
- Ethernet SNAP
- Token Ring 802.5
- Token Ring SNAP

Using NWLink IPX/SPX on a network with lots of IPX traffic can cause problems. If two machines on an IPX network want to communicate, they must use the same frame type. By default, Microsoft products "listen" to the network cable as they boot up and set the frame type to match the type being used by any traffic detected on the cable. Figure 12–2 shows the default setting.

In the rare instances where more than one type of IPX traffic exists on the cable during this process, the Microsoft machine might set itself to the wrong frame type. This situation is bad. To set the frame type manually, change the setting from the one shown in Figure 12–2 earlier to Manual, and select the correct frame type as shown in Figure 12–3.

At this point, an experienced MCSE candidate might say, "Wait a minute. I have used IPX/SPX hundreds of times and have never needed to mess with frame types." The default "Automatic" setting works 99 percent of the time. Unfortunately, that makes troubleshooting the remaining 1 percent even more difficult. For the exams, be ready to consider improperly set frame types as the cause of connectivity problems.

NetWare Clients

Connecting a Microsoft machine to NetWare servers requires IPX/SPX, but the protocol by itself does not provide all the components necessary for connectivity. Connectivity requires a client software component of

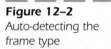

Figure 12–2
Auto-detecting the frame type

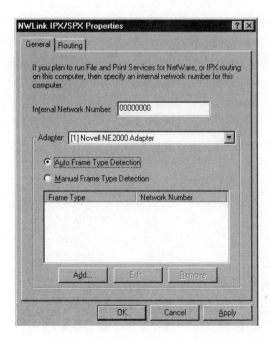

Figure 12–3
Select the correct
frame type from
the list.

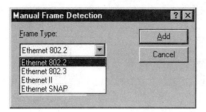

some type as well. Microsoft provides a different NetWare client for each of its network operating systems. For Windows 95 and 98 systems, the client is Client for NetWare Networks. Windows NT 4.0 Workstations use *Client Service for NetWare* (CSNW) as the NetWare client, while Windows NT 4.0 Servers use Gateway Services for NetWare—which includes all of CSNW's functions.

NOTE: *Do not look for CSNW in Windows NT 4.0 Server, because the program is not there. To access NetWare servers as a client, NT Servers must install the full Gateway Service for NetWare. If a scenario on the exam requires the use of an NT Server as a NetWare client, install GSNW.*

CSNW

On an NT Workstation, CSNW acts as the functional equivalent of Windows 95 and 98's Client for NetWare Networks. With CSNW, an NT Workstation can act as a client to NetWare, provided that the user logs in with a valid NetWare user account in addition to the user's valid NT user account.

The following items are key features to remember about CSNW:

- CSNW requires IPX (which will be installed automatically when CSNW is installed).
- CSNW requires that every user has two user accounts: one for NT and one for NetWare.
- CSNW only exists in NT Workstation. All of its functions are incorporated into Windows NT Server's GSNW.

GSNW

Windows NT Server's GSNW offers all the features of CSNW with the additional capacity to "reshare" data stored on NetWare servers with

Microsoft clients. The NT server can act as a gateway, enabling machines running a Microsoft client to access files stored on a NetWare server without directly accessing the NetWare server. The Microsoft clients do not have to run the NetWare client or have user accounts on the NetWare servers, but users can access resources on the NetWare server via the NT server that is running GSNW.

NOTE: *Gateway is another one of those jargon terms that can get you in trouble, because gateway can mean more than one thing. In Chapter 10, "Networking Protocols," the term was used to designate a router in a TCP/IP network. Remember the "Default Gateway" setting? The term gateway, as used here, has nothing to do with routers. Instead, gateway refers to a system that can act as a translator between servers and clients that do not speak the same language.*

Accessing files on the NetWare server using the Microsoft client involves four steps, as shown in Figure 12–4. First, the Microsoft client sends a request to the NT Server running GSNW. Second, the NT server running GSNW sends a request to the NetWare server. As far as the NetWare server is concerned, the server is dealing only with the NT Server. The NetWare server is not aware that the other Microsoft client exists. Third, the NetWare server

Figure 12–4
The four GSNW steps

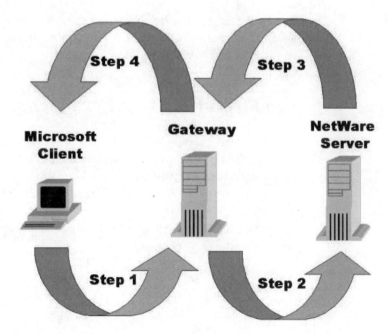

sends the requested data back to the NT Server. Fourth, the NT server forwards the requested data back to the Microsoft client.

Clearly, the use of the gateway generates more traffic than would occur if the client could directly access the NetWare server. Why not just install the appropriate NetWare client software on the Microsoft client PC (which would be CSNW for NT Workstation, or Client for NetWare Networks for Windows 9X)? Using GSNW enables the Microsoft client to access the NetWare server without the installation of any additional software. While installing CSNW on a single NT Workstation does not involve much effort, imagine installing CSNW on 400 machines. In addition, using the gateway makes administration easier—because the users sitting at their NT Workstations no longer need an account on the NetWare server. They simply log into their NT user accounts. Eliminating the need for multiple user accounts and additional software on every client on the network are the chief benefits of GSNW.

File and Print Sharing for NetWare

Microsoft sells an additional network service called *File and Print Sharing for NetWare* (FPNW), which enables an NT Server to share its resources as though the server were a NetWare server. NetWare clients can access resources on the FPNW NT server without running any Microsoft client software. Microsoft does not include FPNW on the Windows NT Server 4.0 CD-ROM, and the Workstation, Server, or Enterprise exams do not cover this topic.

The Migration Tool For NetWare

The Migration Tool for NetWare eases the conversion from NetWare to NT by transferring data and user accounts from existing NetWare servers to NT servers. Ideally, after using the Migration Tool, an NT administrator can remove any NetWare servers from service, resulting in a "pure" NT network. If used properly, users should quickly have access to all of the same resources on the new NT network that they had on the old NetWare network.

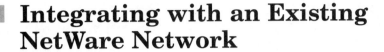

Integrating with an Existing NetWare Network

Many organizations have no interest in ridding themselves of their Net-Ware servers; rather, they prefer the NetWare approach to file and print sharing. Yet, these same organizations want to take advantage of NT as a desktop OS. To create a "mixed" environment by integrating NT into a NetWare environment, an administrator uses two of the tools discussed earlier: CSNW and GSNW. CSNW will integrate NT Workstations, while NT Servers require GSNW. Proper configuration of both tools will create a seamless and stable mixed NetWare and NT network. Let's look at each tool in detail.

CSNW

CSNW provides NT Workstations with access to resources on NetWare servers. Remember that CSNW can only be installed on NT Workstations. To access the same functions from an NT Server, use GSNW.

INSTALLATION   To install CSNW, bring up the Network Control Panel applet, select Services, and choose Add. Add the CSNW, as shown in Figure 12–5.

CSNW requires IPX/SPX-compatible transport. If the NT Workstation does not already have IPX/SPX installed, installing CSNW automatically adds the IPX/SPX protocol to the system. The Microsoft implementation of IPX/SPX is called NWLink IPX/SPX Compatible Transport.

Figure 12–5
Add CSNW.

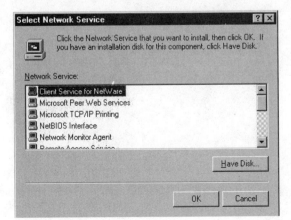

LOG IN   After rebooting, Julie logs in using her NT username and password. If she has the same password and username in both NT and NetWare, NT can pass her username and password to the NetWare server. Julie logs in once and has access to NT and NetWare resources. If her username is the same in both NT and NetWare but her passwords are different, however, NT will display the dialog box shown in Figure 12–6 when Julie logs in with her NT user account.

To avoid this prompt, users are free to set the same password manually for both their NT and NetWare accounts, but this process is not easily done. NT users, for example, cannot change their NetWare 3.X passwords with a graphical utility. Instead, they must use the **SETPASS.EXE** command line utility to change their NetWare passwords, as shown in Figure 12–7. **SETPASS.EXE** can be found in the **SYS:\PUBLIC** directory on a NetWare 3.X server.

NOTE: *NT's lack of an easy, automated way to synchronize NetWare and NT passwords has created a market for third-party applications that can synchronize these passwords without user intervention.*

ACCESSING NETWARE RESOURCES   NT Workstation accesses NetWare resources with the same techniques used to access resources on NT Workstations and NT Servers on the network. Double-clicking Network Neighborhood brings up a list of servers in the same workgroup or

Figure 12–6
Prompting for a
password

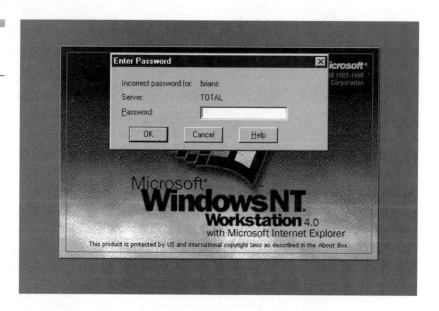

domain, with an additional icon labeled "Entire Network" to represent all machines outside of the local domain or workgroup. If CSNW has been installed, Windows Explorer divides the "Entire Network" into two lists: Microsoft Windows Network and NetWare or Compatible Network, as shown in Figure 12–8.

NOTE: *Windows 95 and Windows 98 behave differently when using their Client for NetWare Networks. In Windows 9X, NetWare servers show up in the same list as the servers in the Windows machine's own workgroup or domain.*

After the user double-clicks the NetWare Networks icon, NetWare servers appear and are available just like any other server on the network, as seen in Figure 12–9. The available file resources on the NetWare

Figure 12–7
SETPASS.EXE

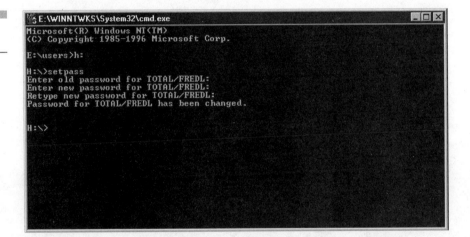

Figure 12–8
The "Entire Network" is divided into two pieces.

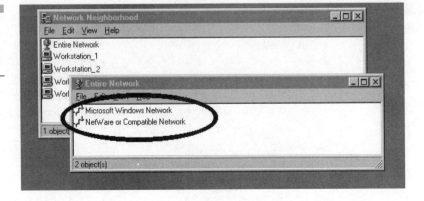

Figure 12–9
NetWare servers look like any other server on the network.

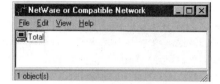

Figure 12–10
Shared NetWare volumes appear just like shares on an NT server.

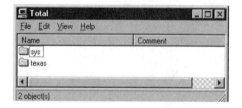

Figure 12–11
CSNW has its own Control Panel applet.

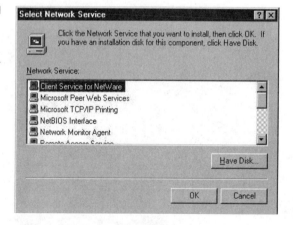

server also look just like shares on an NT server, as shown in Figure 12–10. NetWare refers to these shared folders as NetWare volumes.

CONFIGURING CSNW The work of configuring CSNW is fairly straight-forward for administrators. CSNW has only a few configuration options which are available through the CSNW Control Panel applet, as seen in Figure 12–11.

The most important choice to be made in the CSNW applet is the name of the NetWare server or tree to which the user should log in. NetWare 3.X servers, which each contain their own Bindery databases, require users to log into each server. To specify the login server for NetWare, enter the name of the NetWare server in the Select Preferred Server box. Although NetWare 4.X servers can emulate a Bindery database, NT users might also need to log into the NDS tree. As discussed earlier, the NDS tree serves roughly the same functions as an NT domain SAM. To log into the tree, the name of the tree is required but not the name of the server. The Context field refers to an organizational unit within the tree.

The remaining options cover NetWare printing and login scripts. For NetWare printing, the options control how cover sheets for print jobs—called banner pages in NetWare—will be handled. The login script option enables administrators to disable NetWare login scripts, which can be helpful for avoiding conflicts with NT login scripts.

CSNW enables NT Workstations to access resources shared by Net-Ware servers. CSNW requires NWLink IPX/SPX as a protocol and installs it by default. Users can enjoy access to NetWare servers and the benefits of NT as a desktop OS at the same time. From an administrator's view, CSNW has two key disadvantages. First, CSNW requires administrators to configure each client with two additional pieces of software: CSNW and IPX/SPX. Second, CSNW requires the IPX/SPX protocol in addition to any other protocols that might be required, such as TCP/IP. Running more than one protocol increases network traffic and requires additional network planning and maintenance. Administrators can avoid these pitfalls by installing GSNW on the NT Server instead.

GSNW enables Microsoft clients to access resources on NetWare servers without running a NetWare client or having a NetWare user account. Administrators must install GSNW on an NT Server machine. Once they accomplish that successfully, users can log into their NT domain (or stand-alone server) and connect to resources on the NetWare server. The shared resources from the NetWare server appear to the end user as though they were shares on the NT server.

NOTE: *A Microsoft client is any machine running client software that enables the machine to connect to Microsoft servers. Windows 3.X, Windows 9X, and Windows NT machines are examples of Microsoft clients.*

Using the GSNW has two main advantages over setting up the Microsoft clients with the NetWare client. First and foremost, Microsoft clients do not have to run any additional software. CSNW (or its equivalent) and IPX/SPX are not required. Second, an unlimited number of Microsoft clients can access resources on the NetWare server while only using a single connection on the NetWare server.

NetWare servers use a licensing scheme similar to NT's per server licensing mode. If you purchase a 50-user license for a server, only 50 clients can connect to that server. Other clients that attempt to connect will be refused. When using GSNW, the NT server running GSNW uses a single connection on the NetWare server, regardless of how many Microsoft clients are taking advantage of the gateway.

━━ ━━

NOTE: *Be careful. While the software enables a theoretically unlimited number of users to access resources on the NetWare server using a single connection, the software licensing issue is more complex. Double check with your local software-licensing guru to ensure that using GSNW does not violate your Novell licensing agreement.*

PREPARING THE NETWARE SERVER   To prepare the NetWare server, create both a user account and a group account on the NetWare server for use by the gateway. These accounts can have any name you wish, but most Microsoft documentation refers to the user account as NTUSER and the group account as NTGATEWAY. The NetWare supervisor must grant access to the NTGATEWAY group for any files or folders that will be shared with the Microsoft clients. Windows NT administrators use User Manager for Domains as a general-purpose tool for creating and managing user and group accounts. NetWare supervisors use **SYSCON.EXE** in NetWare 3.X and NETADMIN in NetWare 4.X for similar purposes.

To create the NTUSER user account on a NetWare 3.X server, log in as SUPERVISOR (equivalent to ADMINISTRATOR in NT) and run the **SYSCON. EXE** menu-driven, DOS-style utility. Figure 12–12 shows the **SYSCON.EXE**

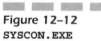

Figure 12–12
SYSCON.EXE

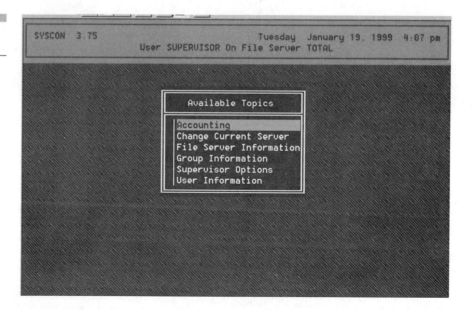

utility. **SYSCON.EXE** handles most of the administrative functions that User Manager for Domains handles in NT. Select the User Information menu to display a list of the user accounts on the NetWare server. Press **<INSERT>** to add the NTUSER account, as shown in Figure 12–13.

NOTE: *Navigating the NetWare utilities can be confusing for NT administrators raised in a Microsoft Windows environment. Most NetWare utilities do not support the use of the mouse and require different keystroke shortcuts than those commonly found in Windows. In most NetWare utilities, use the INSERT and DELETE keys to add and remove users and groups.*

Once the NTUSER account has been added, secure it. For the gateway to function properly, the NTUSER account will normally have full access to all of the files on the NetWare server. Take the time to secure the NTUSER account. First, select the account and press **ENTER** to bring up the Account Properties. Select Change Password to set a password for the user account. Because the NT Server running GSNW should be the only machine using this account, select Account Restrictions, change Limit Concurrent Connections to Yes, and set Maximum Connections to one. As long as the NT Server running GSNW is logged in, a hacker cannot use this account to access the NetWare server, even if the hacker has the correct password.

Figure 12–13
Add the NTUSER account using **SYSCON.EXE**.

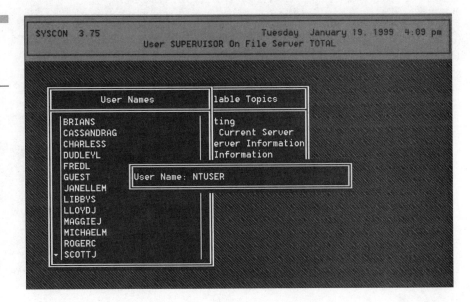

Next, create the NTGATEWAY group. From the main **SYSCON.EXE** menu, select Group Information. Press **INSERT** to add the new NTGATEWAY group, as shown in Figure 12–14.

Select the NTGATEWAY group, and choose Member List from the menu that appears, as shown in Figure 12–15. Press **INSERT**, select the NTUSER account, and press **ENTER** to add the account to the NTGATEWAY group.

Next, grant the NTGATEWAY group access to the resources on the NetWare server that GSNW will need to make available to Microsoft clients. From the Group Information menu, select Trustee Directory Assignments, as shown in Figure 12–16. Trustee Directory Assignments in NetWare 3.X are the equivalent of NTFS directory permissions in NT.

NetWare Trustee Rights are analogous to NTFS Special Permissions. The following items are the rights that can be assigned to a directory or file:

- Write, which enables the user to write to a file.

- Read, which enables the user to read from a file.

- Modify, which enables the user to modify a file's name or attributes.

- File Scan, which enables the user to list the contents of a directory.

- Access Control, which enables the user to change the access rights of other users to the specified resource.

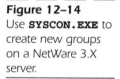

Figure 12–14
Use **SYSCON.EXE** to create new groups on a NetWare 3.X server.

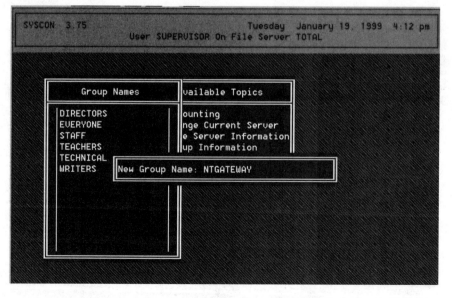

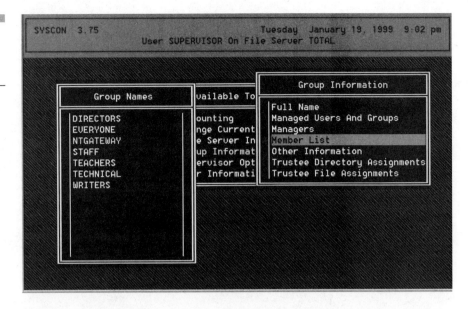

Figure 12–15
Add the NTUSER
account to the
NTGATEWAY group.

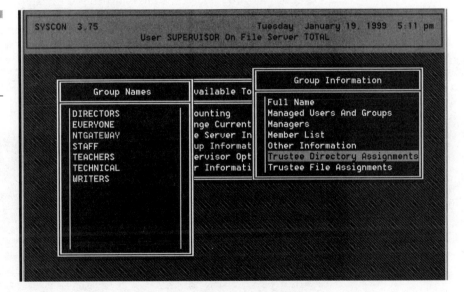

Figure 12–16
Give the
NTGATEWAY group
access to files on the
NetWare server.

- Create, which enables the user to create new files.
- Erase, which enables the user to erase files.
- Supervisory, which gives the user full control of the file or directory.

To give the NTGATEWAY group full access to all files on the SYS volume on the NetWare server, press **INSERT** and type **TOTAL/SYS:** (notice that **SYSCON.EXE** does not use UNC path names). By default, NetWare gives Read and File Scan access when initially granting access to a resource. To give a more complete set of rights, select the resource and press **ENTER**. Then press **INSERT** to add additional rights, as shown in Figure 12–17.

The NT Server running GSNW now has a user account that the server can use to access any file on the NetWare 3.X server. The next step is to install GSNW on the NT Server.

GSNW INSTALLATION   To install GSNW, launch the Network Control Panel applet, click Services, and select Add. As shown in Figure 12–18, GSNW is actually listed as "Gateway (and Client) Services for NetWare." GSNW includes all of the capabilities of CSNW, which does not exist as a separate feature in NT Server. To make an NT Server act as a NetWare client, install GSNW even if the gateway functions will not be used. As with CSNW, installing GSNW automatically installs NWLink IPX/SPX if it has not already been installed on the NT system.

TIP: *Remember that there is no CSNW in NT Server. To make an NT Server act as a NetWare client, use GSNW.*

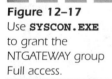

Figure 12–17
Use **SYSCON.EXE** to grant the NTGATEWAY group Full access.

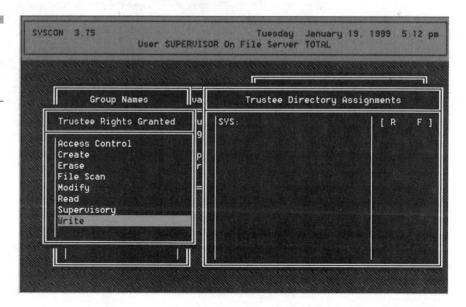

Figure 12-18
Install Gateway (and Client) Services for NetWare.

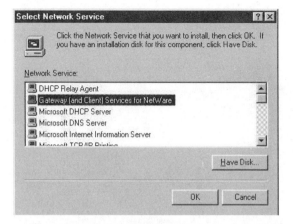

Figure 12-19
Be sure to log in using an account that exists on both the NT Server and the NetWare server to avoid this error message.

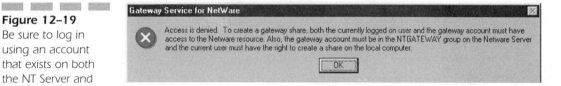

LOG IN   Logging in with GSNW is the same as logging in with CSNW. If the NT user account's name does not match a valid NetWare user account name, NetWare generates an error message. (See Figure 12–6.) To configure the GSNW, both the user account used to log into the NT Server and the gateway account (NTUSER) must be valid user accounts on the NetWare server. If not, the error message in Figure 12–19 appears when trying to configure GSNW.

CONFIGURING GSNW   To configure GSNW, launch the GSNW applet in the Control Panel. The initial screen, shown in Figure 12–20, looks similar to the CSNW Control Panel applet. To use the NT Server as a NetWare client, configure this screen exactly as though the screen were the CSNW configuration screen mentioned earlier. To configure the gateway features of GSNW, however, click Gateway to bring up the screen shown in Figure 12–21.

Specify the NTUSER account and the password previously specified in **SYSCON.EXE**. This action enables GSNW to log into the NetWare server. Now that GSNW has access to the NetWare volumes, the administrator has to tell GSNW which of the available resources it should share with the NT users. This process is commonly called creating GSNW shares.

Figure 12–20
The GSNW Control
Panel applet

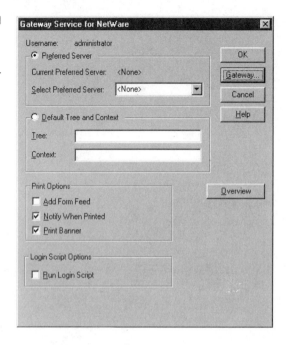

Figure 12–21
Enable the Gateway
and specify the
NetWare user
account.

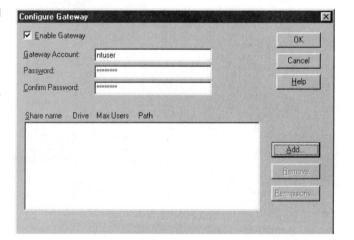

NOTE: *GSNW shares can only be administered from the GSNW Control Panel
applet, not from Windows Explorer.*

CREATING FILE SHARES USING GSNW To create GSNW shares,
use the GSNW Control Panel applet. Click the Add button to bring up the
window shown in Figure 12–22.

Figure 12–22
Create a new GSNW share.

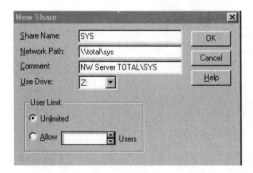

Complete the following steps in the GSNW applet to enable Microsoft clients to access file resources on the NetWare server via the gateway:

■ Specify the share name just as you would for a standard NT-shared folder.

■ Specify the network path to the NetWare resource using an UNC path name (**\\TOTAL\SYS**, in this example).

■ If desired, use a comment to describe the share.

■ Map a drive letter to the NetWare resource, such as a volume or a specific folder on the volume. For the NT server running GSNW to "reshare" the NetWare resource, the NetWare resource must be mapped to a drive on the NT Server.

Once the GSNW share has been created, the NT administrator must assign permissions for the new share to the NT users.

ASSIGNING PERMISSIONS Assign permissions to GSNW shares using the GSNW Control Panel applet. Click the Permissions button to specify which NT users and groups can have access to the share, as shown in Figure 12–23.

The share permissions that can be assigned to GSNW shares are the same as those that can be applied to any NT network share:

■ No Access

■ Read

■ Change

■ Full Control

Notice that while the GSNW account (NTUSER) on the NetWare server has full access to the entire NetWare volume, NT users accessing that volume through the GSNW share can be assigned more restricted access using these share permissions.

Figure 12–23
Specify the share permissions for the GSNW share.

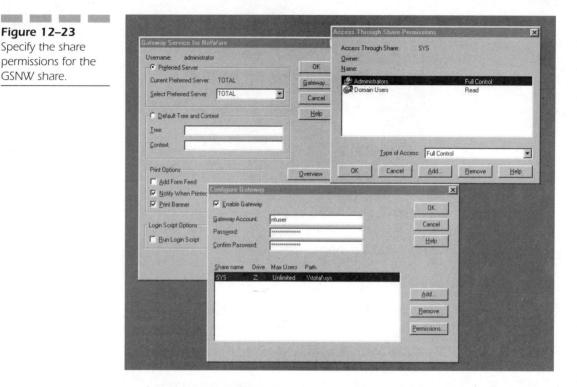

Figure 12–24
A Share is a Share is a Share.

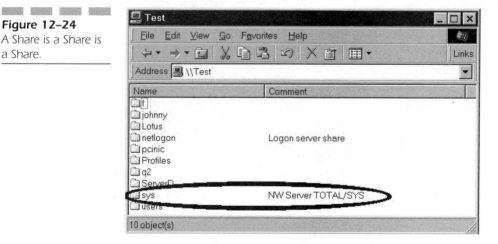

When a Microsoft client is ready to access them, GSNW shares look like any other shares on the NT server. Microsoft clients can create shortcuts, map drives, or use Network Neighborhood to access the shared resource as though the share resided on the NT servers, as shown in Figure 12–24.

SHARING NETWARE PRINT QUEUES Another resource available on a NetWare server that you might want to use in a mixed environment is a printer. While the NT server requires GSNW to enable the printer sharing, do not look in the GSNW Control Panel Applet to share NetWare print queues. The GSNW does not handle NetWare print queues. Instead, open the Printers folder in Control Panel. To share a NetWare print queue, first install a driver for the NetWare print queue on the NT server. In Network Neighborhood, double-click the NetWare printer. If a driver has not previously been installed, NT prompts you to install a driver for the NetWare print queue. Once the driver has been installed, the NT Server running GSNW can share the print queue as though the server were an NT printer. Right-click the Printers icon to see the sharing option, as shown in Figure 12–25.

NOTE: *NetWare print queues are analogous to NT printers. In NT, a single physical print device can serve multiple printers. In NetWare, a single physical printer can handle multiple print queues. See Chapter 15, "Printing in Windows NT," for more information about NT printing.*

CSNW or GSNW?

Many of the questions on the Workstation, Server, and Enterprise exams focus on choosing CSNW or GSNW as the appropriate tool for a given scenario.

Figure 12–25
Windows NT printer
sharing dialog box

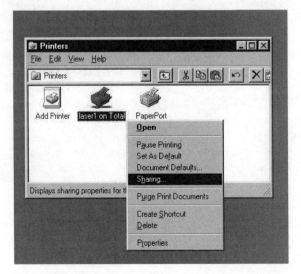

As a general rule, use CSNW when:

■ You want NT Workstations to use NetWare user accounts to directly access resources on NetWare servers.

■ Running the additional IPX protocol presents no problem.

As a general rule, use GSNW when:

■ You want NT Servers to use NetWare user accounts to directly access resources on NetWare servers. Remember, Gateway Services for NetWare is really Gateway (and Client) Services for NetWare.

■ You want to avoid running the NetWare client on your Microsoft clients (NT, Windows 9X, or Windows for Workgroups), but you still want to enable those clients to access resources on the Novell network.

■ You want to avoid running multiple protocols on any Microsoft clients that are already set up to use TCP/IP or NetBEUI.

Migration

Of course, Bill Gates would prefer that you use your NT Workstations the way He intended: to connect to NT servers organized into domains. Network administrators, on the other hand, tend to be a conservative lot. Their basic credo is, as the credo should be, "if it ain't broke, don't fix it." A NetWare supervisor, even if convinced of the benefits of upgrading to NT, will be reluctant to go through the pain and suffering of the transition. Remember that the key goal of a computer network is to help the end users get work done. If the transition from one NOS to another disrupts the lives of end users, that alone can be justification for sticking with the NOS that is already in place.

NOTE: Be careful. When talking to a loyal NetWare guru, calling a conversion from NetWare to NT an "upgrade" can incite brawls. Of course, when talking to a loyal NT guru, the reverse is equally true.

Migration Tool for NetWare addresses the need to make the conversion process as easy for the administrator and as transparent to the end user as possible. Migration Tool for NetWare, automatically installed with

GSNW, can transfer data from a NetWare server to an NT Server. This tool also transfers user account information from a NetWare Bindery to an NT Domain SAM database. The Migration Tool creates new accounts with NT account restrictions and group memberships that correspond to those that existed in the NetWare Bindery (the equivalent of the NT SAM). When copying data from the NetWare server to an NTFS partition, the Migration Tool sets NTFS permissions that correspond to the equivalent original NetWare file and directory trustee rights.

NOTE: *In NT, users are granted Permissions to files. In NetWare, users are granted Trustee Rights.*

To plan and implement a migration from NetWare to NT requires administrators to jump through five hoops. First, an administrator has to know what the Migration Tool for NetWare *cannot* do in a migration. This knowledge ensures that the Migration Tool is appropriate for use in your environment and that you have a plan in place to eliminate any issues created by the tasks the tool does not accomplish. After deciding that the good outweighs the gaps in the tool, an administrator must configure both the destination NT server and the Migration Tool for NetWare. After preparing the server and configuring the tool, the administrator decides precisely how to transfer the information stored both in the NetWare Bindery and on the NetWare server volumes to the NT world. Finally, after making all the configuration decisions and settings, the administrator should run a test or trial migration of both users and then the data, to ensure that all the elements are going to come together at the end.

What the Migration Tool for NetWare Cannot Do

The Migration Tool for NetWare, which is essential in any migration from a NetWare environment to a pure NT environment, has a few quirks that if not addressed beforehand can make a migration nightmare. Be aware of these issues before beginning a migration so that you have a plan for overcoming any issues.

Migration Tool for NetWare only works with Bindery databases and not with NDS. You might have noticed that the previous paragraphs have only referred to the way the Migration Tool for NetWare functions in relation to the NetWare Bindery. The Migration Tool for NetWare does not work with NDS; rather, the tool can only migrate users and data from NetWare servers that use a Bindery database to store their user account information. The Migration Tool for NetWare works well with NetWare 2.X and 3.X servers but cannot migrate users and data from NetWare 4.X servers unless the NetWare 4.X servers are operating in "Bindery Mode."

In addition, the Migration Tool for NetWare cannot migrate login scripts or user passwords from NetWare to NT. The incapacity to migrate the login script is inconvenient, but not critical. Login scripts in NetWare are often used for purposes that are better handled in NT with user profiles. When the user is created in NT, therefore, administrators should take advantage of the user profiles option to recreate the effect of the login script. The incapacity to migrate user passwords presents greater problems, potentially leaving the network vulnerable to hacker attacks immediately following the migration. The password issues in Migration Tool for NetWare are discussed in some detail later in this chapter.

NOTE: *If migrating to an NT Server running File and Print Sharing for NetWare, login scripts can be migrated to the NT server. Because FPNW is not included with Windows NT Server and must be purchased separately, however, this topic is not covered here or on the Workstation, Server, or Enterprise exams.*

Prepare the Destination NT Server

After deciding to do the migration, an administrator must configure the destination NT server(s) to receive the NetWare accounts and data. In addition, the server that is running the migration must have some specific elements installed and configured as well. The servers need the following elements to complete the migration successfully:

■ The destination server must be either a PDC or BDC for the domain. Remember that NetWare users log into individual servers, but NT users log into an NT domain. This requirement only exists for the server that is receiving user accounts. The server that is running the migration—and any servers only receiving files—does not need to be a domain controller machine.

■ Both the destination server and the server running the migration must have the NWLink IPX/SPX protocol installed. Although NetWare servers can run other protocols, including TCP/IP, the Microsoft tools assume that a NetWare server will be running IPX.

Both the destination server and the server running the migration must have GSNW installed. Without the Client side of Gateway (and Client) Services for NetWare, the destination NT server cannot communicate with the NetWare server.

The destination NT server should have an NTFS partition. If the Migration Tool for NetWare is used to transfer data from the NetWare server to a FAT volume on an NT server, all NetWare file and directory trustee rights are lost. If the administrator selects a FAT volume for migration, the Migration Tool for NetWare warns the administrator about the loss of the trustee rights information with the message shown in Figure 12–26.

An administrator should complete the earlier steps to prepare the NT servers involved for the migration. In addition, the administrator must do some configuration to the Migration Tool for NetWare.

Configuring The Migration Tool for NetWare

The next step in preparing to migrate users and data from NetWare to NT is to configure the Migration Tool itself. Before configuring the tool, ensure that you are using an account that has both administrative rights on the NT domain and supervisory rights on the NetWare server. Adding new user and group accounts to the Domain SAM requires administrative rights in the NT domain. Accessing the original user and group accounts in the NetWare server's Bindery database requires supervisor rights on the NetWare server.

To configure the Migration Tool, launch Migration Tool for NetWare from the Start Menu. Find its shortcut icon under Programs . . . Administrative Tools (Common), as shown in Figure 12–27.

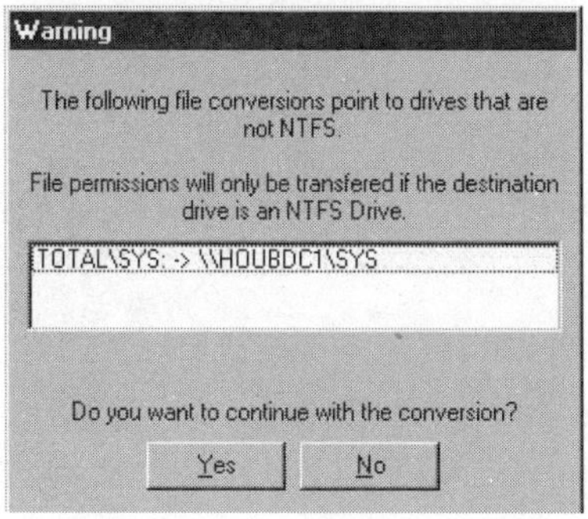

Figure 12–26
Do not use FAT.

> **Warning**
>
> The following file conversions point to drives that are not NTFS.
>
> File permissions will only be transferred if the destination drive is an NTFS Drive.
>
> TOTAL\SYS: -> \\HOUBDC1\SYS
>
> Do you want to continue with the conversion?
>
> Yes   No

Figure 12–27
The Migration Tool
for NetWare

Figure 12–28
Specify the NT and
NetWare server(s).

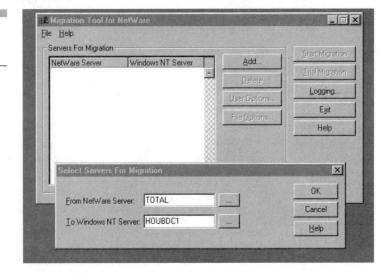

To begin configuring the Migration Tool, specify the servers involved in the migration. This action requires specifying both the NetWare and NT servers. The Migration Tool displays the Select Servers for Migration dialog box automatically when you open the tool. Alternatively, you can click the Add button to specify which NetWare server(s) to migrate to which NT server(s), as shown in Figure 12–28. Note that the NetWare server must be available on the network to complete the configuration.

After adding in at least one set of servers (a NetWare server and an NT server), you must specify how the Migration Tool will handle the users and files to be migrated. To specify how the Migration Tool for NetWare will handle converting the NetWare user and group accounts, click the User Options button. The Migration Tool displays the User and Group Options dialog box, as shown in Figure 12–29.

The checkbox labeled Transfer Users and Groups specifies whether Migration Tool for NetWare should migrate user and group accounts at all. If the Migration Tool is being used to transfer files only, clear the checkbox.

When migrating user accounts from a NetWare server, the administrator must decide how certain issues will be handled. Which passwords should the new NT domain accounts use? What should the Migration Tool

Figure 12–29

User options for the Migration Tool for NetWare

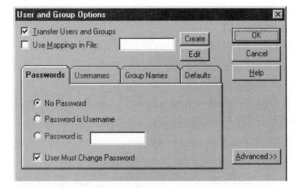

Figure 12–30

Create the Mappings File.

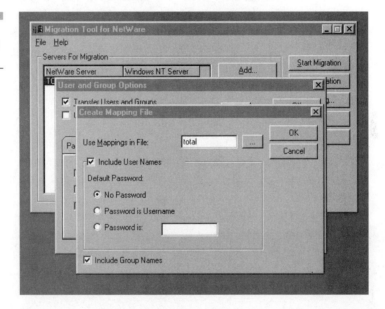

for NetWare do if a NetWare user or group has the same name as an NT user or group that already exists? The Migration Tool for NetWare offers two solutions: creating a text file that defines how each account should be handled (a "mappings" file), or letting the Migration Tool for NetWare decide for you.

MIGRATING WITH A MAPPINGS FILE   To take control of your own destiny and determine how the Migration Tool migrates each account, enable the Use Mappings in File checkbox. After enabling the checkbox, choose the Create button to display the Create Mapping File dialog box, as shown in Figure 12–30.

In the Use Mappings in File field in this dialog box, type in a name for the mappings file. The Migration Tool automatically adds the MAP extension to the file. Next, make a few basic decisions about the migration, including the following decisions:

▪ Use the Include User Names checkbox to determine whether the Migration Tool will add the user account names from the NetWare server to the mappings file.

▪ Use the Default Password radio buttons to determine how the Migration Tool deals with the fact that the NetWare password is encrypted, and is therefore not migrated. The choices include No Password, Password is Username, or, Password is: _____. Look for more details on these options later in this chapter.

▪ Use the Include Group Names checkbox to determine whether the Migration Tool will add the group account names from the NetWare server to the mappings file.

Migration Tool for NetWare creates a basic mappings file based on this information, listing all of the user accounts and/or group accounts specified, and fills in a password as specified under Default Password. When you click OK, the Migration Tool prompts you to edit the Mappings file, as shown in Figure 12–31. If you click Yes, Notepad opens the mappings file automatically.

The mappings file syntax is straight-forward. A semicolon (;) designates that a line is a comment and has no effect on the migration process. The file consists of two sections: [USERS] and [GROUPS]. In the [USERS] section, each line uses the following syntax:

```
NetWare user account name, new NT user account name,
     password
```

In the [GROUPS] section, each line uses the following syntax:

```
NetWare group name, new NT global group name
```

One of the benefits of creating a mappings file is the capacity to add unique passwords to each user account. By default, the Migration Tool fol-

Figure 12–31
Edit the File.

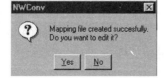

lows the rule specified above for passwords—leaving the password blank, using the username as the password, or using the same name as the password. In the mappings file, the administrator can override these choices. John, a wise NT administrator, created the following mappings file:

```
[USERS]
CASSANDRAG, CASSANDRAG, RACERX
DUDLEYL, DUDLEYL, DORIGHT
FREDL, FREDL, BULLWINKLE
JOHNS, JOHNS2, UMPIRE
; there is already an NT user account named johns
LIBBYS, LIBBYS, AUTHORGIRL
MAGGIEJ, MAGGIEJ, GOLDILOCKS
[GROUPS]
DIRECTORS, BOARD
; an NT group named DIRECTORS exists already.
; the NT group DIRECTORS is a group of users who direct
    video tapes.
; the NetWare group DIRECTORS is the Board of Directors
; in NT the Board of Directors group will be BOARD
STAFF, STAFF
TEACHERS, INSTRUCTORS
TECHNICAL, TECHNICAL
```

Notice that as a wise administrator, John realized that an account named JOHNS already exists in the NT domain, so he used the mappings file to specify a new name for the account, JOHNS2. Better yet, the administrator put a comment (designated by the semicolon) in the mappings file to document his actions to remind himself exactly why the changes were made. John also changed the name of a group and commented on his change.

The use of a mappings file is highly recommended, because this feature gives administrators lots of control over the migration process—especially the setting of passwords. As the next section illustrates, the automated methods of setting passwords leave much to be desired.

MIGRATING WITHOUT A MAPPINGS FILE Migrating without a mappings file enables the Migration Tool for NetWare to make decisions about how to handle migration issues. These issues include passwords, duplicate user and group account names, and default account policies. These issues will be handled according to preferences selected in the first three tabs of the User and Group Options dialog box.

THE PASSWORDS TAB As mentioned earlier, Migration Tool for NetWare cannot read NetWare passwords. Other than using a mappings file, Migration Tool for NetWare gives administrators three basic choices for how to handle the passwords of the newly created NT accounts.

■ No Password: This option is dangerous. Anyone who knows the username can log in using the account. If you use No Password, encourage users to log in as soon as possible and set their own NT password. This option should always be used with the User Must Change Password option.

■ Password is Username: This option is only slightly better than setting no password at all. The password for each imported account is set to match the account's username. Using the Password is Username option makes it easy for hackers to guess the password. As with the No Password option, encourage users to log in as soon as possible and change their password. Users should be forced to change their passwords at first login.

■ Password is _____: This option assigns the same password to every imported user account and is better than leaving the password blank or using the username for the password. But this option still enables employees who know the password to log into other users' accounts.

In addition, the administrator can change the default option of forcing the user to change their password immediately by removing the check mark from the User Must Change Password dialog box. In most cases, however, this option is a useful way to minimize the danger from using these highly unsecured passwords.

THE USERNAMES TAB The Usernames tab, shown in Figure 12–32, sets Migration Tool for NetWare's response to duplicate user account names. The options enable a variety of responses, although for complete flexibility, again, use the mappings file.

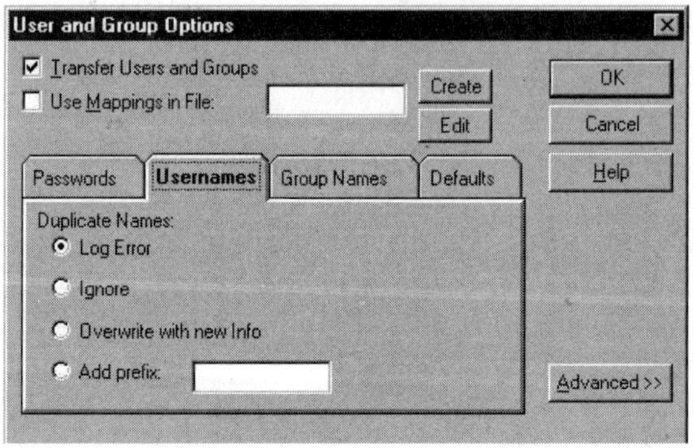

Figure 12–32
The Usernames tab

- Log Error: If duplicate usernames are found, the NetWare user account is not transferred, and a message is written to the error log. The administrator can manually create a new user account on the NT domain for the affected user(s).

- Ignore: If duplicate usernames are found, the NetWare user account is not transferred, and no error is written to the error log.

- Overwrite with new info: If duplicate usernames are found, the NetWare user account is transferred, overwriting the existing NT user account. Migration Tool for NetWare writes a message to the error log.

- Add prefix: Enables the administrator to specify a prefix to add to any NetWare account names that duplicate existing NT user account names. "NW-," for example, would specify that Migration Tool for NetWare should create a user account named NW_MAGGIEJ if an NT user with the name MAGGIEJ already existed.

THE GROUP NAMES TAB The Group Names tab, shown in Figure 12–33, sets Migration Tool for NetWare's response to duplicate group names. The following options are identical to those for dealing with duplicate usernames, except no "Overwrite with new Info" option is available:

- Log error
- Ignore
- Add prefix

THE DEFAULTS TAB The Defaults tab, shown in Figure 12–34, is the only tab in this dialog box that affects the operation of Migration Tool for NetWare—even when the Use Mappings File box is checked. The Use

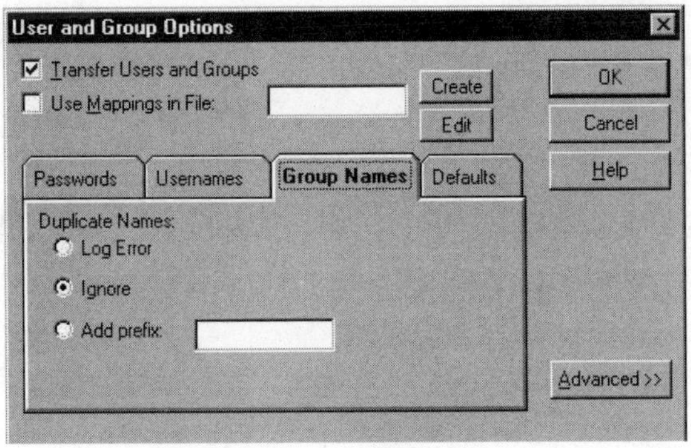

Figure 12–33
The Group Names tab

Figure 12–34
The Defaults tab

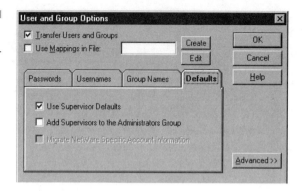

Supervisor Defaults option tells the Migration Tool for NetWare how to handle account policies for the new NT user accounts. Supervisor options should actually be called "NetWare Default Account Restrictions." If this box is checked, Migration Tool for NetWare preserves the account restrictions (login hours, account lock out, etc.) that were set for the accounts on the NetWare server. If the box is cleared, Migration Tool for NetWare uses the NT default account policy (set in User Manager for Domains) when creating the new NT user accounts. Despite all evidence to the contrary, this option has nothing to do with migrating the Supervisor account specifically; rather, this option is just an unhappy coincidence of menu and account names.

On the other hand, the Add Supervisors to the Administrators Group checkbox tells Migration Tool for NetWare how to deal with accounts that had administrative privileges on the NetWare server. If you enable this checkbox, these accounts will be added to the global Domain Adminstrators group. In most cases, users should be added to the Domain Administrators group manually to avoid careless mistakes. Letting the wrong people into the Domain Administrators group is, in technical terms, a "bad thing."

The Migrate NetWare Specific Account Information checkbox at the bottom of this tab is grayed, unless the NT server is running File and Print Sharing for NetWare (described earlier in this chapter).

THE ADVANCED BUTTON The Advanced button, which is also in effect whether or not a mappings file is in use, enables user accounts to be created in a trusted domain rather than in the current NT domain. The Migration Tool displays the Transfer Users to Trusted Domain option when you click this button. The option remains grayed, however, unless the current NT server's domain trusts another domain. In other words, this option is only available if trust has been previously configured for the current domain. For more information about trust relationships and master domains, see Chapter 9, "Microsoft Networking."

TRANSFERRING FILES   When you plan a migration from a NetWare server to an NT server, one of your main concerns should be volumes, folders, and files (or data) that need to be moved. A user with supervisory privileges on the NetWare server can simply copy any and all data from the NetWare server to the NT server using Windows Explorer. What benefit, you might ask, do you receive from using the Migration Tool for NetWare? The benefit comes because the Migration Tool for NetWare can convert the trustee file and directory assignments into equivalent NTFS permissions when copying the files. Using Windows Explorer, the files would simply inherit the default permissions of the directory to which they were copied.

To select the files to be transferred, select File Options. The Migration Tool displays the File Options dialog box. Click the Add . . . button to select a NetWare volume from which to transfer files and a destination share on the NT server. By default, the Migration Tool creates shares that correspond to the volumes on the NetWare server. You can, however, create additional shares as necessary. To select or exclude files and folders from the NetWare volumes, click the Files button. This action enables you to select files to transfer, either individually or by folder, as shown in Figure 12–35.

Do not automatically assume that you need to transfer all the files from the NetWare server to the new, clean, and pristine NT server. This situation can provide the perfect opportunity to force your users to clean up.

Migration Tool for NetWare Logging

While migrating files and/or user accounts, Migration Tool for NetWare generates three text files: **ERROR.LOG**, **LOGFILE.LOG**, and **SUMMARY.LOG**. These files enable the administrator to examine exactly what occurred during the migration process.

The **ERROR.LOG** file shows any errors that occurred during migration. If the same username existed on both the NT domain and the NetWare server, for example, the following message would appear in the **ERROR.LOG** file:

```
[LIBBYS]
Error: Duplicate User Name
```

Figure 12–35

Select the files for
Migration Tool for
NetWare to transfer.

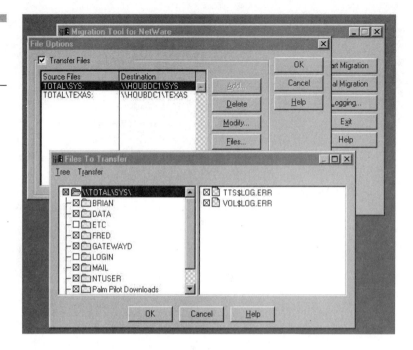

The **LOGFILE.LOG** lists detailed information about the migration process, including the following items:

■ A list of all user accounts that were migrated from NetWare to NT

■ A list for each user of every global group to which they were added on the NT domain

■ A list of all files migrated and their file attributes (Read only, Archive, System, Hidden)

■ A list of the NTFS permissions added to the ACL of each new NTFS file

The **SUMMARY.LOG** shows a simple summary of the migration process. The following is an example:

```
;+------------------------------------------------------------+
;| Migration Tool for NetWare Summary Log File                |
;+------------------------------------------------------------+
;| Created: Thursday, 01/01/1999 (12:02:3                     |
;| System : HOUBDC1                                           |
;| Admin   : Administrator                                    |
;| Version: 1.1                                               |
;+------------------------------------------------------------+
Number of Migrations = 1
```

```
[Servers]
From: TOTAL                  To: HOUBDC1
[TOTAL -> HOUBDC1]
Total Users Converted: 85
Total Groups Converted: 13
Copying Files From Volume: SYS
To Share: SYS
Total Files Converted: 451
Bytes Transferred: 13,519,895
Copying Files From Volume: TEXAS
To Share: TEXAS
Total Files Converted: 1
Bytes Transferred: 1,138
Conversion Finished: Thursday, 01/01/1999 (12:02:38)
```

The log files created by Migration Tool for NetWare help administrators debug the migration process and clean up any mistakes that occur during the process. A wonderful feature would be to see these log files, and their attendant, helpful messages, before the migration process starts, right? The Trial Migration feature enables an administrator to complete this action.

Trial Migration

Question: What should a hapless administrator do after accidentally wiping out an entire department's existing NT user accounts with the Migration Tool for NetWare? Answer: Begin updating his resume.

Fortunately, no worthy administrator should ever have to worry about that scenario. Migration Tool for NetWare offers a Trial Migration feature, which enables the administrator to run a simulated migration, generating the same log files that would have been generated in an actual migration. To run a trial migration, click the Trial Migration button. The Migration Tool simulates all the actions of the migration process and then displays the Transfer Completed dialog box. This dialog box displays basic, summary information about the migration that would have been performed and enables the administrator to click the View Log Files . . . button to launch the log viewer. Always run the trial migration and carefully examine the log files before running an actual migration.

Migration Tool for NetWare Summary

The Migration Tool for NetWare is a powerful tool for replacing NetWare servers with NT servers while preserving existing users, groups, and file permissions (called trustee rights in NetWare). Remember that powerful tools require careful use. Always run a trial migration before running the actual migration. Also remember that the Migration Tool is not perfect. To finish the migration successfully, the new NT user accounts need to be placed into the appropriate existing global groups on the NT domain.

Putting It All Together: The Migration Process

To lead their NetWare users out of the Novell wilderness and into the promised land of NT, a network administrator might need to use all of the NetWare connectivity tools provided by Microsoft: CSNW, GSNW, and the Migration Tool for NetWare.

The directors of the Bayland Widget Corporation decide that they need to incorporate NT into their existing NetWare environment. The Bayland Widget Corporation currently uses a Novell NetWare 3.12 network with a single server but recently purchased three new Windows NT Workstation PCs to run their new accounting software. Marty, the system administrator, needs to enable these new NT Workstations to access files stored on the NetWare server. Marty installs CSNW, making certain that the users have valid NetWare user accounts—and all is well.

Then the directors of the Bayland Widget Corporation decide that the company needs its own intranet web server. Marty decides to install an NT Server running IIS to fill that role. A user will sit at that NT Server, however, and will need access to files on the NetWare server. To enable the NT Server to act as a client to the NetWare server, Marty installs the GSNW. Although Marty does not currently need to use the NT Server as a gateway for other clients, he knows he must install GSNW in order to use that NT Server as a NetWare client.

The following week, the directors of the Bayland Widget Corporation, in their almighty wisdom, decide to buy out their competitors, the Highland Doohickey Corporation. The Highland Doohickey Corporation has a few dozen NT workstations configured as a workgroup. Marty becomes the manager in charge of integrating the Highland Doohickey Corporation's network into the existing Bayland Widget Corporation's network. Marty needs to enable the existing NT Workstations acquired from the old Highland Doohickey Corporation to access some databases on the Bayland Widget Corporation's NetWare server, but he decides not to add CSNW to the dozens of NT workstations from the Highland Doohickey

Corporation. Instead, Marty decides that now is the time to begin moving the Bayland Widget Corporation toward a pure NT network. Marty installs three new NT servers: a PDC, a BDC, and an NT member server. These servers will be responsible for running GSNW and providing a gateway to the NetWare server.

NOTE: *As a general rule, avoid running too many additional services on the domain controllers in an NT network. While not technically wrong, running additional services on the domain controllers can cause performance and security problems.*

Marty reasons that if the Bayland Widget Corporation is eventually going to run a pure, Windows NT domain-based network, he would waste time by creating NetWare user accounts for all of his new users from the Highland Doohickey Corporation. Presumably they are already comfortable with NT, and training them to work within a domain should be easier and more cost-effective than training them to deal with NetWare today and retraining them in 18 months or so to work within an NT domain.

Marty configures GSNW on the member server to provide access to the appropriate files on the NetWare server to the members of his new NT domain. At this point, all-important data is still stored on the NetWare server. The NT domain controllers and the member server running GSNW exist solely to provide a method for the NT Workstation users to log in securely and access data on the NetWare Server. All users now have access to the data on the original NetWare server, either directly (using NetWare client software), or indirectly (using the member server's GSNW gateway), as shown in Figure 12–36.

While Marty has provided every user access to the data on the NetWare server, he has also doubled his administrative workload. Marty has two separate user databases to manage: the NetWare 3.X Bindery and the NT Domain SAM database. Now that Marty has an NT domain running (and stable), he should take the plunge and migrate the data and user accounts from the NetWare server to the NT domain.

Of course, Marty is no fool. He runs a few trial migrations using the Migration Tool for NetWare before actually migrating his data and user accounts. After the first trial, Marty examines the **ERROR.LOG** file and notices that many of the NetWare user account names already exist in the NT domain. To prevent these errors from occurring during the actual migration, Marty creates a mappings file. In addition to dealing with the issue of duplicate names, creating the mappings file enables Marty to specify a new password for each new NT user account.

Figure 12–36
Accessing the data
on the original
NetWare server

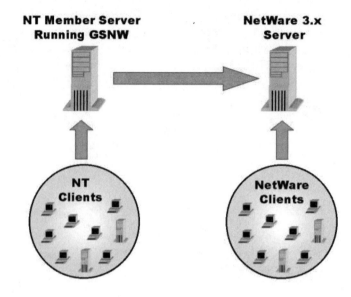

After running the Migration Tool for NetWare for real, Marty now has his ideal network. All of his users are using Windows NT Workstation to log into an NT domain, and the Bayland Widget Corporation stores all of its data on an NT Server. Now Marty can take the NetWare server offline, and enjoy the full benefits of a pure NT network.

Microsoft provides three key tools for working with NetWare: CSNW, GSNW, and Migration Tool for NetWare. These tools give NT administrators the flexibility needed either to integrate NT into an existing NetWare network, or to plan a smooth transition from NetWare to NT.

Questions

1. To sit at an NT Server and access files on a NetWare server, install (choose all that apply):

   a. CSNW

   b. GSNW

   c. IPX/SPX

   d. TCP/IP

   e. IIS

2. Marco, an assistant network administrator in a mixed NT and NetWare environment, is put in charge of granting access to a folder named DESIGN stored on the NetWare server RESEARCH7 to 35 NT users who access the network using Windows NT Workstation PCs. Their NT Workstations currently have no access of any kind to the NetWare server. Required result: Enable the 35 NT Workstation users to access the DESIGN folder on the NetWare server RESEARCH7. Optional results: 1. Control access to the DESIGN folder based on each user's NT user account. 2. Add no additional software to the NT Workstations. Proposed solution: Create a new user account for each of the 35 users on the NetWare server. Grant the new user account the appropriate rights to the DESIGN folder on the NetWare server. Install CSNW on each of the NT Workstations. The Proposed solution:

   a. Achieves the required result and both optional results

   b. Achieves the required result and one of the optional results

   c. Achieves only the required result and neither of the optional results

   d. Does not achieve the required result and does not work

3. The Migration Tool for NetWare can migrate which of the following from a NetWare server to an NT server? (Choose all that apply):

   a. User accounts

   b. Group memberships

   c. File permissions

   d. User passwords

   e. Account time restrictions

4. Marie is the administrator of the NT domain CHICAGO. Marie needs to grant Full access to a shared folder stored on a NetWare server to the NT global group ACCOUNTANTS. The ACCOUNTANTS global group accesses the NetWare server via an NT server running GSNW. To grant them Full access to the share, Marie should use (select the best answer):

a. Windows NT Explorer

b. Server Manager

c. Migration Tool for NetWare

d. The GSNW applet in Control Panel

e. Gateway Administrator

5. Fred, a user in a mixed NT and NetWare environment, realizes that someone else has guessed his NetWare user password. To change his NetWare password, Fred should:

a. Run Password Administrator

b. Press `<ctrl><alt><del>`, select Change Password, and click Change NetWare Password.

c. Run the NetWare command line utility `SETPASS.EXE`

d. Contact his NetWare administrator. End users cannot change their own passwords in NetWare.

6. Robert administers a network with 40 NT Workstations and five NetWare 4.X servers. To enable the users of the NT Workstations to log into the NDS tree, Robert should install _____ on each NT Workstation (select the best answer):

a. NWLink

b. GSNW

c. CSNW

d. TCP/IP

e. IIS

7. Ashley administers a mixed NT and NetWare network. She decides to remove the NetWare servers and give all of the NetWare users new accounts in her NT domain. She plans to use Migration Tool for NetWare to migrate all user and group accounts into her existing NT domain. To ensure that the new NT accounts have secure passwords, she should:

a. Do nothing. By default, the existing NetWare passwords will be used for the new NT user accounts.

b. Run NW Password Administrator and select Synchronize NetWare and NT Passwords from the options menu.

c. Create a mappings file for use with Migration Tool for NetWare, and specify a unique new password for each user. Use Migration Tool for NetWare to specify that each user must change their password the first time they log on. Inform each user of their new password.

d. Select Preserve NW Passwords in Migration Tool for NetWare.

8. Gateway Services for NetWare (choose all that apply):

a. Is an option for both NT Workstation and NT Server

b. Enables an NT server to act as an IP router

c. Enables Microsoft clients to access shared resources on NetWare clients without running additional NetWare client software

d. Synchronizes NT and NetWare passwords for user accounts with the same name

e. Requires IPX

9. To migrate files from a NetWare server to an NT server using Migration Tool for NetWare and preserve the existing file permissions (choose all that apply):

a. Both the NT server and the NetWare server must be running TCP/IP

b. The administrator must be logged in with a user account that has Full Control over the destination folders on the NT server and supervisory rights to the source folders on the NetWare server

c. The destination folder must be formatted as an NTFS partition.

d. The destination NT server must be running GSNW.

e. The destination NT server must be sharing the source folders on the NetWare server with GSNW.

10. Ishmael, administrator of the BALTIMORE NT domain, must
    configure his NT Server to act as a gateway, enabling members of
    the NT global group RESEARCHERS to access the DETAILS
    folder on the NetWare server MONTY. The RESEARCHERS
    global group should have Read Access to the DETAILS folder.
    Required result: Members of the RESEARCH global group must
    have Read Access to the data stored on the DETAILS folder on the
    NetWare server MONTY without installing any NetWare client
    software. Optional result: NT users do not require an account on
    the NetWare server. Proposed solution: Ishmael installs GSNW on
    an NT Server, and logs in using an account name that has
    administrative privileges on the NT Server and supervisory rights
    on the NetWare server. He creates a group called NTGATEWAY
    and a user called NTUSER using User Manager for Domains. He
    then configures the GSNW to log in using the NTUSER account.
    He creates a gateway share named NW_DETAILS using the
    GSNW applet in control panel and assigns the global group
    RESEARCH Read Access to the gateway share. The proposed
    solution:

    a. Achieves both the required result and the optional result

    b. Achieves only the required result

    c. Does not achieve the required result and does not work

Answers

1. b, c—CSNW does not exist as a separate service on NT Server. Its functions are folded into GSNW, a.k.a. Gateway (and Client) Services for NetWare.

2. c—The proposed solution gives the users access to the DESIGN folder, but requires administrators to control access based on a NetWare user account and requires additional software (CSNW) on each workstation.

3. a, b, c, e—The Migration Tool for NetWare cannot read NetWare passwords.

4. d—There is no Gateway Administrator program, and Windows NT Explorer cannot be used to administer the GSNW shares.

5. c

6. c—Although NWLink (a.k.a. IPX) is required, it will not in and of itself enable the users to log into NetWare. When Robert installs CNSW, NT will automatically install NWLink if has not already been installed.

7. c—NW Password Administrator does not exist. Because there is no way to read the existing NetWare passwords, answer A will not work. The option in answer D does not exist in Migration Tool for NetWare.

8. c, e

9. b, c, d—The NT server must be able to access files on the NetWare server, requiring the Client service included as part of GSNW.

10. c—The GSNW must be configured to log in using a valid NetWare user account. Because Ishmael used User Manager for Domains to create the NTUSER user account and the NTGATEWAY group account, these accounts would exist in the NT Domain, not on the NetWare server.

13

Microsoft and the Internet

The increasing importance of the Internet for exchanging information causes many companies to rethink their own networks. Network administrators now must think about how to structure their internal network to increase productivity and decrease retraining times, how to connect internal networks, and how to connect their internal networks with the big daddy—the Internet. Wouldn't it be cool if users could sit at their desks and use the same tools to access information on their own machines, on Jane's machine down the hall, on Roberta's computer in Oregon, and on Edgar's computer in London, all with a simple click of the mouse? Wouldn't it also be cool if Jane could tap into the company databases with ease, regardless of whether she accessed the databases from her office computer that connects directly to the company's local network or via cell phone and modem from a sidewalk cafe in Nairobi? With NT 4.0 Server, Microsoft provides the tools to make this idea a reality.

To rethink their networks to incorporate the excellent connectivity capacities of NT 4.0, administrators need four basic skills. They need to understand the terminology of internetworking, from the differences between internets and intranets to the various protocols that programs use to communicate. Furthermore, administrators should master NT's tools for accessing information across these internets—the client-side applications, such as Internet Explorer —and should know how to set up an NT Server to share resources using the various Internet protocols. Finally, to set up NT as an internet/intranet server requires knowledge of *Internet Information Server* (IIS), the one-stop application in NT that slices, dices, and runs HTTP, FTP, and Gopher.

Internet versus Intranet

What the heck does "Internet" mean? Generally, the lower-case term *internet* refers to any computer network composed of some number of smaller computer networks. If a private company connects its computer networks in Houston, Dallas, and Baltimore via dedicated phone lines and routers, for example, that company has its own internet, as illustrated in Figure 13–1. A private internet can run on any networking protocol, including TCP/IP, IPX, and others.

The upper-case term *Internet* refers to the global Internet that we all know and love: a public network that grew out of the ARPANET, a project

Figure 13–1
An internet is any network composed of smaller networks.

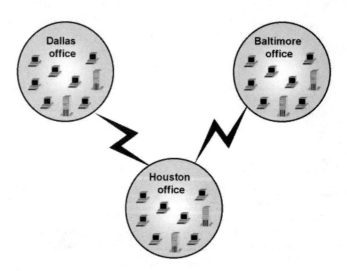

of the U.S. government. The Internet enables a person to sit at his or her home or office PC and exchange information with a huge number of other individuals and organizations. The Internet uses the TCP/IP protocol.

The Internet has spawned a number of exciting new technologies, with Web browsing and worldwide e-mail only the most prominent among them. Companies that run their own private internets often make use of these technologies. A company may put up an internal Web server, for example, available only to employees browsing on the company's internal network, with a copy of the company's policies and procedures. An internet that uses Internet technologies is called an *intranet*. Intranets make life easier for companies, because their employees have to master only a single tool—a browser, such as Netscape Navigator or Internet Explorer—and can then access data on both the internal network and the Internet.

NOTE: *An internet is a network made up of smaller networks. The Internet is a larger, public network that uses TCP/IP as its protocol. An intranet is an internet that uses technology originally developed for the Internet.*

Internet Protocols

Communicating on the Internet, just like on every other kind of network, requires that all machines share the same language, or protocol. A *protocol* is nothing more than a set of rules that enable communication between two parties. When people use the term protocol to refer to TCP/IP, NetBEUI, and IPX, they describe protocols that perform the "middle level" functions of the OSI 7 layer model, usually layers 3 (Network), 4 (Transport), and 5 (Session). Protocols such as TCP/IP help move data between two points in the network, but they do not usually concern themselves with the content of the data. The Internet uses TCP/IP to move data but relies on another level of protocols to translate that data into something useful. The names of many of these protocols may sound familiar: FTP, HTTP, SMTP, and POP3. Figure 13–2 shows a configuration screen in Microsoft Outlook Express requiring a user to modify the IP address of an SMTP and POP3 server.

NOTE: *The OSI 7-layer model is discussed in Chapter 10, "Networking Protocols."*

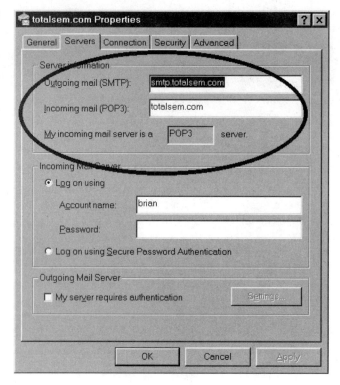

These additional Internet protocols deal with communications between applications running on different machines on the network. These protocols assume that the lower-level protocols are functioning. The *HyperText Transfer Protocol* (HTTP)—used for the World Wide Web—assumes that TCP/IP is doing its job and deals exclusively with communication between a client piece of software (your Web browser) and a server piece of software (the Web server). IIS version 2, which is included with NT Server, includes the server side software for three common Internet protocols: HTTP, FTP, and Gopher.

- *HTTP*: Used to transmit files from a server and a client—usually a Web browser such as Internet Explorer. HTTP can be used to transmit almost any kind of file but is generally used to transmit documents formatted in *HyperText Markup Language* (HTML).

- *FTP*: Used to transfer files between computers. Unlike HTTP, FTP can transfer files in either direction (the client can send files to the server). FTP proves especially useful for transferring data between UNIX and NT computers. FTP servers can enable anonymous access or can restrict access based on user accounts.

■ *Gopher*: An early alternative to the World Wide Web for organizing data and accessing data on the Internet. Available files are listed in text-based menus.

NOTE: *IIS version 4, the current version, has discontinued support for Gopher.*

The Internet protocols each define a method of "client-server communication," which is a fancy way of saying that one machine must act as server and the other must act as the client. The sending host is the server, while the receiving host is the client. IIS version 2 can act as the server for three of these protocols—HTTP, FTP, and Gopher. Competing products that support HTTP, and other protocols, include Apache Web Server (for Linux), Netscape Enterprise Server, and Lotus Domino.

NOTE: *In TCP/IP-based networks, any device that can either send or receive data is called a host.*

"Browsers" such as Internet Explorer or Netscape Navigator handle the client side for Internet protocols. While usually thought of as "Web browsers," these powerful client software packages can actually handle the client side of HTTP, FTP, Gopher, and many other protocols. Figure 13–3 shows Internet

Figure 13–3
Accessing an FTP site using Internet Explorer

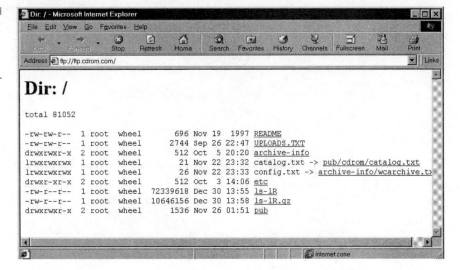

Figure 13–4
Accessing a Gopher
site using Internet
Explorer

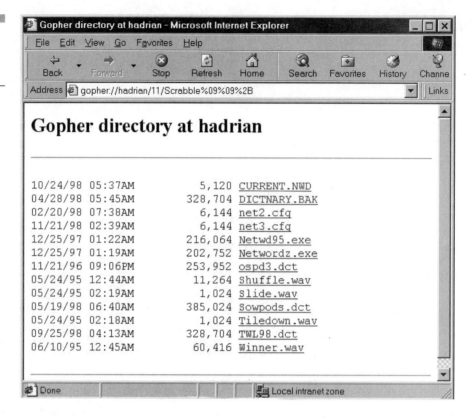

Explorer using the FTP protocol to access **ftp.cdrom.com**. In the event that they do not include support for a particular program, browsers can extend their capacities via add-on programs known as "plug-ins." The RealAudio and QuickTime plug-ins, for example, commonly grace actively used browsers to give users streaming audio and video off the Web. Both Internet Explorer and Netscape Navigator can also use the Gopher protocol to access Gopher sites, as shown in Figure 13–4.

Programs designed specifically to work with a particular protocol offer features unavailable in a more general-purpose product such as Internet Explorer or Netscape Navigator. Programs such as CuteFTP and WS_FTP Pro, for example, enable you to "drag and drop" files to and from Internet sites. Figure 13–5 shows CuteFTP accessing the same FTP site shown earlier in Figure 13–3.

The Internet protocols provide consistent sets of rules for communication, so it does not matter which server program and which client program actually do the communication. The files go where they are supposed to go.

Figure 13–5
CuteFTP accessing
an FTP site

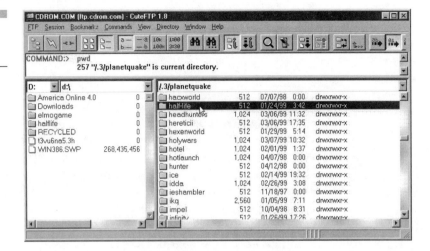

NOTE: *Anyone who has ever had trouble viewing a Web site designed specifically for Internet Explorer with the Netscape Navigator browser (or vice-versa) might argue this point. Some Web pages look great in one Web browser and are incomprehensible in another. The differences have nothing to do with the HTTP protocol; instead, the difference lies in the file format used to display Web pages: HTML. Both Internet Explorer and Netscape Navigator (as well as competing browsers such as Opera or Mosaic) handle the HTTP side just fine, transferring the actual data of the Web pages without difficulty. Their respective interpretations of how to display the HTML code of the documents can cause some Web pages to display differently.*

Other Internet Protocols

Many other protocols exist that are commonly used with TCP/IP—whose names pop up from time-to-time in configuration screens and error messages in Windows NT. Among the most important ones are SMTP, POP 3, SNMP, ICMP, and TFTP.

■ *Simple Mail Transfer Protocol* (SMTP)—SMTP is the standard protocol used for sending e-mail from one mail server to another. SMTP assumes that all hosts are connected to the network at all times. E-mail software packages such as Outlook Express or Eudora often refer to the SMTP server as the "outgoing mail server." The e-mail software can assume that the SMTP server is online at all times and sends outgoing mail to the SMTP server. Unfortunately, the mail server cannot make the same assumption about the host running the e-mail client software, requiring the use of another protocol for incoming mail, such as POP3. Sendmail (for UNIX/LINUX), Microsoft Exchange Server, and Lotus Domino are examples of server programs that can run the server side of SMTP.

■ *Post Office Protocol, version 3* (POP 3)—Most mail servers hold incoming mail for users, enabling users to retrieve that mail at their leisure. POP3 is the standard protocol used by e-mail client software to retrieve e-mail from a mail server. Software programs frequently refer to the POP3 server as the "incoming mail server." In many cases, the "mail server" acts as both an SMTP and a POP3 server. Microsoft Exchange Server and Lotus Domino are examples of server programs that can run the server side of POP3.

■ *Simple Network Management Protocol* (SNMP)—SNMP is a protocol used to exchange network monitoring and performance data between hosts on a TCP/IP network. (Do not confuse this with NT's Network Monitor, which relies on other protocols to perform a similar function on an NT network.)

■ *Internet Control Message Protocol* (ICMP)—ICMP is used for status messages. The PING and TRACERT utilities (discussed in Chapter 10, "Networking Protocols") send ICMP echo requests to another host on the network to determine whether that host is reachable.

■ *Trivial File Transfer Protocol* (TFTP)—TFTP, like its "big brother" FTP, is used to transfer files between machines. Unlike FTP, TFTP has no security whatsoever. If the client asks for something, the server sends out the information. TFTP requires no login procedure.

Windows NT Server 4.0 as an "Internet Client"

Microsoft bundles a number of tools in NT that enable users and administrators to interact with common Internet protocols, including both graphical tools and command line utilities. The graphical tools include a Web browser (Internet Explorer), an e-mail client (Internet Mail), and a Telnet front-end program. The command line utilities include file transfer utilities (FTP and TFTP), a variety of troubleshooting utilities (PING,

TRACERT, and NSLOOKUP), and a few UNIX connectivity tools (RSH and LPR).

The Graphical Tools

NT 4.0 comes with several graphical tools for using some of the more common Internet protocols, including HTTP, POP3, SMTP, and TELNET. These tools include Internet Explorer, a browser; Windows Messaging, for e-mail; and Telnet, a remote terminal.

- Internet Explorer version 2.0—Microsoft includes an adequate— but dated at the time of this writing—Web browser, *Internet Explorer 2.0* (IE 2.0), with Windows NT 4.0. As mentioned earlier, Internet Explorer is more than just a Web browser. Internet Explorer is a general-purpose client software, supporting HTTP, FTP, and Gopher out of the box and supporting many additional protocols through add-on programs called plug-ins. While IE 2.0 is adequate for viewing simple Web pages, many current Web sites rely on features found in newer browsers, such as Internet Explorer 4.0.

- Windows Messaging version 4, also known as "Internet Mail"— Microsoft includes an extremely limited e-mail client, called Internet Mail, with NT 4.0. Internet Mail is a part of Windows Messaging version 4. This e-mail client supports both POP3 and SMTP but lacks many of the features included with more complete packages such as Microsoft Outlook, Microsoft Outlook Express, Eudora, and Netscape Messenger. Microsoft includes Outlook Express with Internet Explorer 4.0.

- Telnet—Telnet is a command line interface for executing commands on a remote UNIX host. The Telnet application that ships with Windows NT displays this command line interface in a window within the GUI.

The Command Line Utilities

Unfortunately for those accustomed to working with pretty graphical tools, Microsoft has not yet created graphical utilities for all of the common Internet protocols. Instead, Microsoft supplies certain UNIX-style command line utilities for troubleshooting and connectivity to UNIX machines.

TROUBLESHOOTING UTILITIES   Windows tools such as the Network Neighborhood make networks easier to use but can hide the source of problems from network administrators. The command line troubleshooting utilities aid administrators in properly diagnosing trouble. They include PING, TRACERT, and NSLOOKUP.

■ PING—PING sends ICMP packets to another host on a TCP/IP network to determine whether the other host can be reached.

■ TRACERT—Similar to PING, the TRACERT utility uses ICMP packets to determine whether another host can be reached and by which route.

■ NSLOOKUP—The NSLOOKUP utility enables you to determine exactly which information about a particular DNS name or IP address a DNS server returns. NSLOOKUP can also trace the origin of invalid DNS information.

Familiarity with the proper use of these tools is crucial to maintaining the health of a TCP/IP-based network.

UNIX CONNECTIVITY TOOLS   The beauty of UNIX lies in the wide range of protocols that UNIX supports. In the UNIX world, many different protocols exist for both remote access and resource sharing. Although Windows NT does not support every protocol available in the UNIX world, Microsoft includes command line utilities to handle the client side of some of the most common UNIX protocols. These utilities include the following:

■ *File Transfer Protocol* (FTP)—As discussed earlier, FTP is used to transfer files between TCP/IP hosts. For help on using Microsoft's command line FTP client, type **"FTP -?"** without the quotation marks. Unlike most command line utilities, using a "/?" will not bring up helpful information. Instead, the FTP program will try to connect to an FTP server named "/?".

■ *Trivial File Transfer Protocol* (TFTP)—Use TFTP to transfer data between TCP/IP hosts when logging in is unnecessary. Windows NT 4.0 comes with the command line TFTP client but not a TFTP server. Type **"TFTP -?"** for more information.

■ *Remote Shell* (RSH)—RSH enables you to remotely execute commands on a UNIX machine running the RSH daemon. (Daemons in UNIX are equivalent to NT services.)

■ *Line Printer* (LPR)—LPR is a command line utility used to send print jobs to a UNIX machine running the *Line Printer Daemon* (LPD). See Chapter 15, "Printing in Windows NT," for more detail.

Microsoft provides these TCP/IP clients to enable Windows NT systems to connect to the Internet and to enable Windows NT systems to coexist with UNIX systems on corporate networks. Microsoft systems engineers should know and love these clients, and not surprisingly, the clients show up on the exams.

Windows NT Server 4.0 and IIS

IIS provides server-side support for three Internet protocols: Web (HTTP), FTP, and Gopher. Plus, IIS has the capacity to host multiple Internet sites simultaneously, creating "Virtual Servers." IIS makes setting up NT as an Internet server (or internal internet/intranet server) a snap. Microsoft includes IIS version 2.0 with NT Server 4.0 and even creates an icon on the desktop to encourage you to install the program. Although most administrators do *not* install IIS version 2 and prefer instead the advanced features of IIS 3 or IIS 4, version 2 can handle simple Web and FTP server needs adequately. From a more practical standpoint, the MCSE Server and Enterprise exams *test only on IIS version 2*. Microsoft has separate tests for IIS version 3 and IIS version 4 that cover these later versions of IIS in detail. Let's look at the installation process for IIS version 2 and then examine IIS settings for each of the three supported protocols.

Installing IIS Version 2

To install IIS, either click the shortcut icon created on the desktop during the initial NT Server 4.0 setup or select the Services tab in the Network Control Panel applet, as shown in Figure 13–6. Click the Add button, and the list of services shown in Figure 13–7 will appear. Select IIS version 2.0 from the menu and press **OK**. The installation program will prompt you to exit all other programs before continuing. Double-clicking the desktop icon will give you the same result.

The next screen prompts you to select individual components to install, as shown in Figure 13–8. Notice that IIS does not require you to run a Web, FTP, and Gopher server simultaneously. You are free to install only those components that you need. The following components are available at this point:

■■■■ ■■■ ■■■ ■■

Figure 13–6
Add new network services using the Network Control Panel applet.

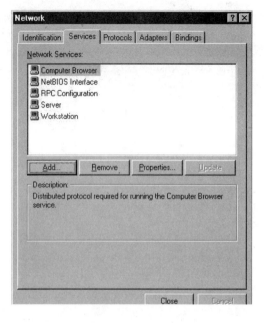

Figure 13–7
Select IIS version 2 from the menu.

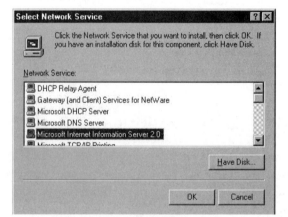

■ Internet Service Manager is the main graphical tool for managing the various services.

■ Internet Service Manager (HTML) gives you a Web browser interface for managing various services.

■ World Wide Web Service is the HTTP server itself.

■ WWW Server Samples installs a set of sample Web pages.

■ Gopher Service installs the Gopher server. Gopher is rarely used and should normally be disabled.

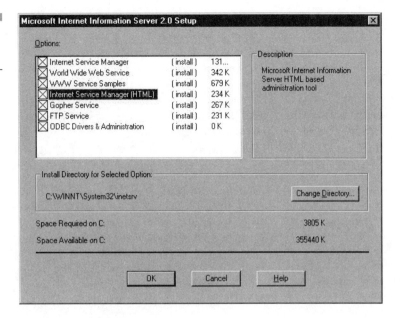

Figure 13–8
Selecting IIS
components

- FTP Service is the FTP server program.

- ODBC Drivers and Administration installs *Open Database Connectivity* (ODBC) drivers, which enable your Web pages to interact with certain types of databases. To enable visitors to your Web page to enter their names and contact information into an SQL Server database, for example, would require OBDC drivers.

Avoid the temptation to "select all." Installing and activating rarely used services such as Gopher can provide hackers with unexpected avenues into your network. If you are installing IIS to be your Web server, and you have no immediate plans to use FTP, do not install FTP. Administrators who do not use a service often forget to secure the service properly. Install only the services that you need.

NOTE: *Securing your Internet sites is beyond the scope of this book and is not covered in detail on the Workstation, Server, or Enterprise exams. The exams only cover NT internal security—user accounts, NTFS, etc.—which was discussed in previous chapters.*

The next screen asks you where you want to store the files that the server will "serve up" to its Web, FTP, and Gopher clients. By default, IIS creates a subdirectory named **\INETPUB** with four subdirectories: **\INETPUB\WWWROOT**,

`\INETPUB\FTPROOT`, `\INETPUB\GOPROOT`, and `\INETPUB\SCRIPTS`. These sub-directories will store the actual files that each service will serve. The installation enables you to specify the location of the subdirectories, as shown in Figure 13–9. If the directories do not already exist, the installation program will prompt you to create them.

NOTE: *Scripts are usually small programs or batch files used to handle repetitive tasks. The SCRIPTS subdirectory can store a variety of arcane tools for doing fancy tricks with Web pages. Scripts are beyond the scope of this book and are not covered on the Workstation, Server, or Enterprise Exams.*

A special user account, the IUSER_*servername* account, is created automatically for use by IIS when a user logs in anonymously. While you can set up a Web site so that logging in is required, most Web, FTP, and Gopher sites enable anonymous access. NT, however, hates anonymity. NT needs to identify each user that accesses its information. To reconcile the anonymous nature of these Internet protocols and the secure nature of NT, the IIS acts as a proxy. When a user logs in as "anonymous," IIS logs in as IUSER_*servername*, accessing the appropriate files and passing them along to the client. In the example shown in Figure 13–10, the IUSER_*servername* account for the server HADRIAN is called IUSER_HADRIAN.

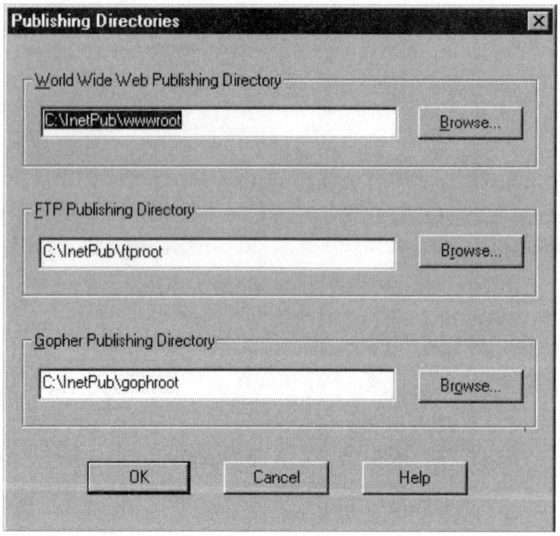

Figure 13–9
Specifying the directory names

Publishing Directories

World Wide Web Publishing Directory
C:\InetPub\wwwroot   [Browse...]

FTP Publishing Directory
C:\InetPub\ftproot   [Browse...]

Gopher Publishing Directory
C:\InetPub\gophroot   [Browse...]

[OK]   [Cancel]   [Help]

Figure 13–10
User Manager
showing the
IUSR_HADRIAN
account

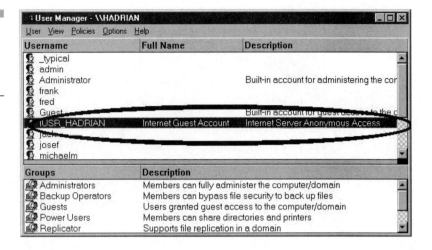

NOTE: *Be aware that the IUSER_servername account is a member of the GUESTS local group. While theoretically you should not be able to use IIS to access anything outside of the* `\INETPUB` *directory, do not take any unnecessary chances. Hackers often take advantage of default settings to do unexpected—and, well, exciting things. Either move the IUSER_servername account to its own group or disable your GUEST account and never add any additional users to the GUESTS local group.*

IIS version 2 Servers

IIS version 2 provides three types of Internet servers: Web (HTTP), FTP, and Gopher. Web and FTP are the most commonly used servers in NT internetworking environments, providing data on demand and even some security. Gopher, although rarely used today, provides a nice, text-based (and thus extremely fast) interface for resource access.

Microsoft provides one administrative tool to set up all three of the Internet servers: the Internet Service Manager. Three ways exist to run Internet Service Manager: locally, remotely from an NT Server, or remotely from any Web browser. To run Internet Service Manager locally, go to Start . . . Programs . . . Microsoft Internet Server (Common) . . . Internet Service Manager. This program provides a nice, clean interface to administer your Internet servers. In Figure 13–11, the Internet Service Manager displays the server VIENNA with all three Internet servers installed and running. To manipulate settings for the protocols, select one, and either double-click

Figure 13–11

Internet Service
Manager

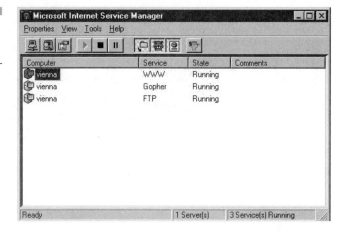

Figure 13–11

Internet Service
Manager

Figure 13–12

Internet Service
Manager accessing a
remote machine

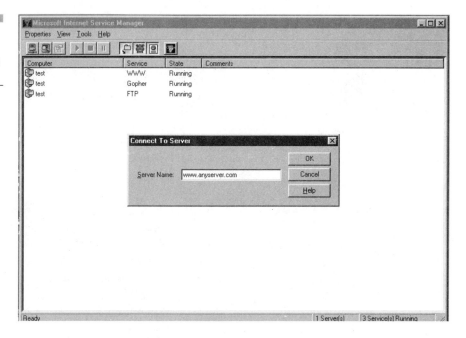

or right-click and select "Service Properties . . . ". This same screen enables
you to manipulate remote machines from your local NT server. Click the
network server icon (top left, with the "networked computer" graphic) and
type a name, as shown in Figure 13–12.

Microsoft also built Internet Service Manager so you can log in
remotely with any Web browser and manipulate settings. To run Internet
Service Manager from a remote browser, open a browser and type the

address for the server. This service requires that the server you want to log into has installed the Internet Service Manager (HTTP), which is disabled by default. Figure 13–13 shows Internet Explorer accessing Internet Service Manager on the intranet server VIENNA. You can use this same Web browser screen on a local machine (by selecting the browser from the Microsoft Internet Server tools), but the default local screen has a cleaner, more compact interface. Regardless of how you get there, the Internet Service Manager enables you to administer each Internet server process. Let's look at each option in turn.

WEB (HTTP)   IIS enables your NT server to act as a Web server, serving up Web pages to any client running a Web browser. In addition to enabling anonymous access to Web pages stored in the **\INETPUB\WWWROOT** directory, the Web server can be integrated with NT's security model. Figure 13–14 shows the three options for password authentication for use with the Web service:

- Allow anonymous—Enables anonymous access to the files in the **\INETPUB\WWWROOT** directory

- Basic—Requires users to log in with a valid account on the NT server. This option can cause security problems because usernames and passwords are sent through the network in clear text.

Figure 13–13
Running Internet Service Manager with a browser

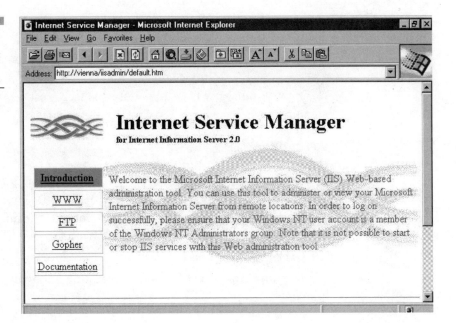

Figure 13-14
Web Server options

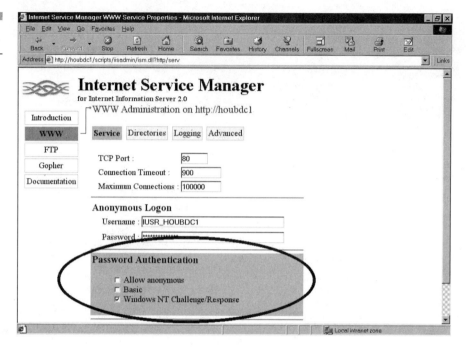

■ Windows NT Challenge/Response—Requires users to log in with a valid account on the NT server. This option is more secure than Basic because passwords are encrypted. Some older browsers do not support this feature, conceivably preventing some users from logging into the Web server.

The capacity to integrate the IIS Web server with an existing NT domain user account database (a.k.a. the Domain SAM), either through Basic or Windows NT Challenge/Response, represents one of the chief advantages of IIS over other Web server products.

FTP IIS can act as an FTP server, enabling clients running FTP client software to access the files stored in the **\INETPUB\FTPROOT** directory. Notice that the security options for FTP, shown in Figure 13–15, do not offer an option for Windows NT Challenge/Response. With FTP, all passwords are passed through the network in clear text, making the information more vulnerable to hackers than HTTP using Windows NT Challenge/Response. Only two options are offered here:

■ Allow anonymous connections—Enabling anonymous connections is appropriate for FTP sites that are used to distribute files that

Figure 13–15
No Challenge/
Response

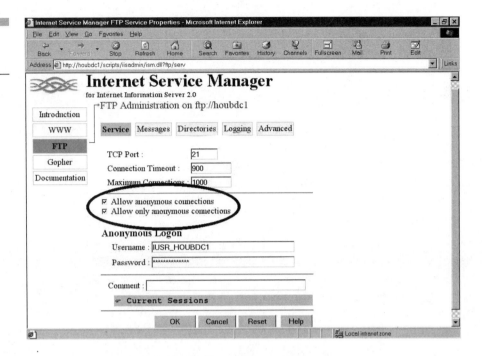

can be freely distributed to anyone. Anonymous FTP is an excellent way to distribute updates, patches, freeware, and shareware. Clearing this checkbox requires users to log in with a valid NT user account.

■ Allow only anonymous connections—Enabling only anonymous connections prevents users from logging in with valid NT user accounts. Instead, they must log in anonymously. This action prevents someone who has discovered the password for a powerful user account (such as the Administrator account) from logging in using FTP. Enabling only anonymous connections also discourages users from attempting to log in using their NT accounts, which can be dangerous because FTP sends username and password information in clear text.

Installing FTP can be especially useful for interacting with UNIX servers and workstations in a mixed NT and UNIX environment. FTP and most other Internet protocols are supported natively in UNIX. Installing an IIS FTP server on an NT server enables the UNIX server to access files on the NT server and send files to the NT server, without installing any additional software on the UNIX hosts.

NOTE: *Remember that the Workstation, Server, and Enterprise exams focus on Microsoft products. Even if there is a non-Microsoft solution to a particular problem, that solution will not be the correct answer on these exams. For example, at least two alternative methods exist for enabling UNIX hosts to access files on an NT host (and vice versa):*

1. *To install SAMBA on the UNIX hosts, enabling them to act as Microsoft clients and servers without any modification to the NT hosts.*

2. *To install a third-party NFS client (the native UNIX network client software) on the NT hosts, enabling them to act as UNIX clients and servers without any modification to the UNIX hosts.*

Although more involved to set up than FTP, in many cases these might be better solutions for transferring files between UNIX and NT. Because they are not Microsoft products, however, as far as the exams are concerned they do not exist. After taking the exams, many MCSE candidates express frustration at being limited to the answers that Microsoft provides on the test because they know of an even better answer.

GOPHER   Gopher was already on its last leg when IIS version 2.0 was released and is rarely used at all today. Gopher provides a text-based menu of available files. Gopher's only advantage over HTTP was its simplicity—no graphics, only text. The Gopher server in IIS version 2.0 was included purely as a backward-compatibility feature and is not emphasized on the Microsoft exams. Aside from remembering that IIS version 2.0 includes Gopher support, you can safely ignore this option.

IMPORTANT: *The most current version of IIS, Internet Information Server 4.0, no longer includes support for Gopher. When taking the Workstation, Server, and Enterprise exams, remember that the exams cover IIS version 2.0 only, which was included on the original Windows NT 4.0 Server CD-ROM.*

Virtual Servers

IIS has another powerful capacity: IIS can host multiple Internet sites on the same physical machine. Phil, the manager of a small business that hosts several companies' Web sites, has three customers with small, low-traffic sites. Rather than use an entire machine to handle each of their Web pages, Phil puts all three of their Web sites on the same machine. To make that single, physical machine appear to the network as three separate Web servers, Phil assigns the server's NIC three separate IP addresses, using the Advanced option in the Address tab of the TCP/IP Protocol's properties in Control panel, as shown in Figure 13–16.

Phil then launches Internet Service Manager and assigns each "virtual server" a home directory, as shown in Figure 13–17. For example, Phil sets the `C:\INETPUB\WWWROOT\LIBBY` directory as the home directory for 192.168.43.152 and the `C:\INETPUB\WWWROOT\TOTAL` directory as the home directory for 192.168.43.153. When a Web client connects to 192.168.43.152 and requests the `DEFAULT.HTML` file, IIS will send `C:\INETPUB\WWWROOT\LIBBY\DEFAULT.HTML` back to the client. When another Web client connects to 192.168.43.153 and requests the `DEFAULT.HTML` file, IIS will send `C:\INETPUB\WWWROOT\TOTAL\DEFAULT.HTML` back to the client. As far as the Web clients can determine, 192.168.43.153 and 192.168.43.152 are two different Web servers, although they exist on the same machine.

The capacity to create virtual servers gives IIS tremendous flexibility. If one of the Web servers that Phil hosts suddenly becomes busy, Phil can transfer the Web site's files to a new server and reassign that site's IP address to the new server. The busy Web site has a new, more powerful machine on which to run, and nobody but Phil needs to know about the change. The Web site continues to have the same IP address. IIS's Virtual Server feature is critical to organizations hosting multiple Web sites.

Figure 13–16
Assign multiple IP addresses to the server's NIC.

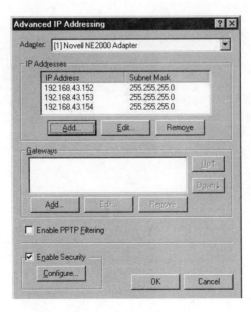

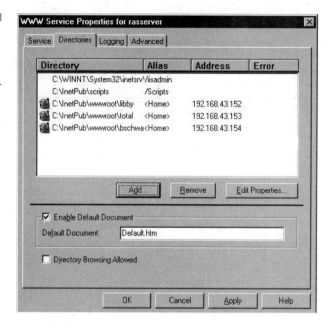

Figure 13-17
Set a home directory
for each virtual
server.

With IIS version 2.0, Windows NT Server 4.0 can host three Internet services—HTTP, FTP, and Gopher—and run those services in an internal intranet or internet or in the wild and wooly electronic roller-coaster that is the Internet. Running the Internet servers, even in an isolated intranet, enables powerful tools for your users such as Internet Explorer, command line FTP, PING, and more. Finally, IIS offers the capacity to integrate FTP and Web servers into your existing NT security structure, giving you powerful capacities without any dangerous security gambles.

NOTE: *The core MCSE exams assume you have a working understanding of the internetworking capabilities of NT 4.0, but do not test on TCP/IP or IIS in any detail. Other exams will test your knowledge of those areas.*

Questions

1. Abdul is the NT administrator of a TCP/IP-based network with both NT and UNIX servers and clients. Users sitting at the UNIX clients need to save data files on one of the NT servers. To enable the UNIX users to save files on the NT servers, Abdul should do the following:

   a. Install Gateway Services for UNIX on the NT Servers.

   b. Do nothing. The UNIX machines can access shared resources via Microsoft File and Print Sharing.

   c. Install IIS's FTP service, create a folder in the `\INETPUB\FTPROOT` folder called `\DATA`, and grant the UNIX users Write access to that folder.

   d. Install the Microsoft DNS Service on each NT server.

   e. Install the IIS's Web service, create a folder in the `\INETPUB\WWWROOT` folder called `\DATA`, and grant the UNIX users Write access to that folder.

2. Microsoft IIS includes support for which of the following Internet protocols (Choose all that apply):

   a. SMTP

   b. HTTP

   c. POP3

   d. FTP

   e. Gopher

3. Which of the following protocols would you use to share HTML documents with users connecting to your network via the Internet? (Select the best answer:)

   a. IPX/SPX

   b. FTP

   c. SMTP

   d. HTTP

   e. POP3

4. Stanley, a user in New York, complains to Blanche, his network administrator, that he cannot connect to the company's Web server in Dallas. Stanley can reach other company servers in Los Angeles and in Phoenix. Blanche suspects that one of the company's routers could be at fault. What would be the best tool for Blanche to use to test her hypothesis?

   a. NBTSTAT

   b. PING

   c. TRACERT

   d. IPCONFIG

5. NT's LPR command line utility enables users to do the following:

   a. Generate a report listing their group memberships and account rights.

   b. Send print jobs to a printer on a UNIX host.

   c. Access shared files and folders on a UNIX host.

   d. Determine the IP address that corresponds to a specific computer name.

6. Pippin worries about users sending their NT user account passwords as FTP passwords over the network in clear text. To prevent NT user passwords from being passed over the network in clear text, Pippin should set his FTP server to do the following:

   a. Use Windows NT Challenge/Response

   b. Enable only anonymous FTP connections

   c. Use MS-CHAP

   d. Use CHAP

7. Sam worries that users logging into his IIS version 2.0 Web site are sending their Windows NT passwords in clear text. Sam needs to require users to log in using their NT user accounts but also needs to prevent their passwords from being transmitted in clear text. What should Sam do?

   a. Use Windows NT Challenge/Response

   b. Enable only anonymous connections

   c. Use MS-CHAP

   d. Use CHAP

8. Bernice attempts to use her ancient but serviceable Mosaic 1.0 Web browser to log into an IIS server's Web site using her NT user account—and fails. While sitting at the same machine, she launches Internet Explorer 3.0 and logs in successfully using the same user account and password. Why did she fail to log in the first time?

   a. IIS Web sites can only be accessed by Microsoft's Web browser software.

   b. Bernice's default gateway is set incorrectly.

   c. The IIS Web server is set to use Windows NT Challenge and Response.

   d. Bernice's IP address is set incorrectly.

9. Alex needs to host three different companies' Web sites on his Window NT server: ACME Rockets, the Daily Bugle, and the Bayland Widget Corporation. Which of the following steps does Alex need to take to make these three Web sites appear as three different servers to users on the Internet? (Choose all that apply:)

   a. Assign the server's NIC three unique IP addresses using the Network Control Panel applet.

   b. Assign the server's NIC three unique IP addresses using Internet Service Manager.

   c. Assign a different home directory for the WWW service to each IP address using Server Manager.

   d. Assign a different home directory for the WWW service to each IP address using the Internet Service Manager.

10. FTP and TFTP are both used to transfer files between TCP/IP hosts. TFTP is different from FTP in that:

    a. TFTP requires both hosts to be on the same subnet.

    b. TFTP does not enable anonymous access.

    c. TFTP does not require users to log in.

    d. TFTP is not supported by Windows NT.

Answers

1. c—Answer a is incorrect because there is no such product as Gateway Services for UNIX. Answer b is incorrect because UNIX machines cannot access shared resources without running special additional software (such as SAMBA). Answer d is incorrect because DNS servers aid in name resolution (as discussed in Chapter 10, "Networking Protocols") and have nothing to do with transferring files. Answer e is incorrect because HTTP, the protocol used by the IIS Web server, supports file transfers from the server to the client but does not enable files to be sent from the client to the server.

2. b, d, e—IIS version 2.0 supports FTP, HTTP, and Gopher but does not support the e-mail-related protocols SMTP and POP3.

3. d—Answer d is correct because the HTTP protocol is specifically designed for transferring HTML documents across an intranet or the Internet. Answer a is incorrect because IPX/SPX is an alternative protocol to TCP/IP and has nothing to do with HTML documents. Answer b is incorrect. While you could transfer HTML files using FTP, FTP is a more general-purpose tool for transferring files of any type. Answer c is incorrect because SMTP is used for transferring e-mail messages between e-mail servers, not for transferring HTML documents. Answer e is incorrect because POP3 is used to transfer e-mail between e-mail servers and e-mail client software.

4. c—NBTSTAT is used to display information about NetBIOS and its interaction with TCP/IP and has nothing to do with routing. Therefore, answer a is incorrect. While PING can test whether or not Stanley's computer can reach the Web server, PING does not give any information about why the computer cannot reach the destination. Therefore answer b is incorrect. TRACERT is a better answer, because TRACERT does everything PING does—plus tracing the path to the destination. If a particular router fails to forward the data packets, TRACERT can help determine which router is the problem. The IPCONFIG utility shows the current machine's IP configuration and does not give any detailed information about the router. Because Stanley can reach other machines outside the local network, his default gateway (a.k.a. his router) setting must be correct. Therefore, answer d is incorrect.

5. b—The LPR utility enables NT users to send print jobs to printers shared by a UNIX host.

6. b—Answer a is incorrect, because IIS version 2.0 can only use Windows NT Challenge/Response for HTTP, not FTP. Answers C and D are security protocols used by RAS. See Chapter 14, "Remote Access Server," for more details. Answer b is correct. By enabling only anonymous connections with the FTP service, Pippin can prevent users from logging into the FTP server using their NT user accounts.

7. a—IIS version 2.0's Web server supports Windows NT Challenge/Response as a means of encrypting login information. While answer b would prevent passwords from being transmitted as clear text, answer b would also prevent users from logging in using their NT user accounts. Answers c and d are security protocols used by RAS. See Chapter 14, "Remote Access Server," for more details.

8. c—Answer a is incorrect because IIS uses the Internet standard HTTP protocol for sharing HTML documents over the Internet. Answer b is incorrect because an incorrect default gateway would prevent either Web browser from accessing the Web server. Older Web browsers do not support Windows NT Challenge and Response, so answer c is correct. If Bernice's IP address was set incorrectly, neither browser would be able to reach the Web server, so answer d is incorrect.

9. a, d—The Network Control Panel applet specifies the IP address(es) for each adapter under Protocols . . . TCP/IP . . . Properties . . . Address. To assign each IP address a different home directory for the WWW service, use Internet Service Manager, not Server Manager.

10. c—*Trivial File Transfer Protocol* (TFTP) does not require users to log in. TFTP does not require that the client and server reside on the same subnet, so answer a is incorrect. Because TFTP does not require users to log in, TFTP enables anonymous access by definition. Therefore, answer b is incorrect. Windows NT 4.0 comes with a TFTP command line utility, so answer d is incorrect.

CHAPTER **14**

Remote Access Server

Today's organizations are often far-flung affairs. Companies
have many coast-to-coast and even international locations.
Government and military entities are spread out to thousands of sites. Even if an organization has only one location,
it can have representatives, salespeople, or technicians fly-
ing to other cities for one reason or another. Despite this
mobility, as organizations become more physically divided,
the need to access centralized information becomes even
greater. An on-the-road salesperson needs to access a cus-
tomer's purchase history from the home office, while an
engineer needs to check specifications stored at the manufacturer's headquarters—or a manager needs to update critical employee information to the regional clearing center. To
do these jobs, people at remote locations need to be able to
access the network resources as though they were standing
at a PC in the other location. The process of providing this
capability to users is called "Remote Access."

Dedicated or Not

The concept of remote access can sometimes be a little fuzzy. Many different situations exist where a person can access another computer at a faraway location that would not be considered remote access. In a classic network, systems are connected together via some type of *dedicated* connection—usually a cable of some type. The system links, in essence, permanently with the network. When the computer starts, the computer logs onto the network. As long as the machine runs, the computer stays connected to the network. The user simply walks up to the machine and can access the network's shared resources. Even if the system has not logged on, a user can connect to the network simply by logging back on. An unusual situation would be for the system NOT to be connected to the network. Physically disconnecting the system creates an error scenario. A system can be far away and still fit within the criteria of a classic system. A system can access a distant LAN via a dedicated (never gets "unhooked") connection and still meet all of the above mentioned capacities. Regardless of whether the machine is in the office next door or in Topeka, if that system is moved away from its dedicated connection, the machine will immediately no longer have access to the network.

Although no completely agreed-upon definition for "Remote Access" exists, the Microsoft NT view—and thus the one that appears on Microsoft exams—defines remote access as the process of connecting to another network via a non-dedicated connection (i.e., through dial-up phone lines). Remote access requires two devices: a server and a client. First, remote access requires a "Remote Access Server," a system that has a dedicated connection to a LAN and some type of modem or modem equivalent, and thus can accept calls from other systems. In NT, the server software is called, quite appropriately, *Remote Access Server* (RAS). Second, remote access requires a "Remote Access Client"—a system not physically connected to the RAS but equipped with the necessary software, plus a modem or the equivalent, to dial the server and create a connection. In NT, the client software is *Dial-Up Networking* (DUN). Clearly, telephone systems and remote access are closely intertwined. To clarify remote access, we need to take a moment to understand the telephone system. In particular, we need to understand the different telephone transmission options and how they are—or are not—supported by Windows NT.

How Two Systems Connect: Telephony Options

The quickest way to turn a competent computer person into an incompetent, bumbling techno-babbler is to start talking about telephone systems. Because of the close integration of telephones to computers and networking, information technology people are often forced into the world of "telephony" with little—usually no—training at all. In this section, we will take a moment to understand the world of telephony and understand the many options available today for linking remote computers.

PLAIN OLD TELEPHONE SERVICE (POTS) The first and most common of phone connections is the classic *Plain Old Telephone Service* —better known as POTS—which is the phone line that runs into everyone's home telephone. POTS was designed long before computers were common and was designed to work with only one type of data: sound. POTS takes the sound you wish to transmit, which is usually your voice, picks up that sound, translates it into an electrical "analog" waveform by the microphone, and transmits your voice to another phone that then translates that signal into sound via a speaker. The important word to note here is analog. The telephone microphone converts the sounds into electronic waveforms that cycle 2,400 times a second. These cycles are known as "bauds." Pretty much all phone companies' POTS cycle up to 2400 baud.

V STANDARDS Modems utilize phone lines to transmit data, not just voice, at various speeds, which causes a world of confusion and problems for computer people. This situation is where a little bit of knowledge becomes dangerous. Most of us have dealt with modems to some degree. Today's modems have speeds up to 56Kbps, which is KiloBits per second—not baud. The problem here stems from the fact that most of us confuse the terms baud and bits per second. This confusion comes from the fact that for modems, the baud rate and the BPS are the same until the data transfer between the modems surpasses 2400 baud. Basically, a phone line can make analog samples of the sound at a rate of 2,400 times a second. This standard was determined a long time ago as an acceptable rate for sending voice over the phone lines. While 2400-baud analog signals are great for voice communication, they are a big problem for computers sending data. The thing to remember is that computers hate analog signals. For two computers to communicate over a POTS, one computer must have its digital (ones and zeros) signal changed into an analog signal that can be transferred over the telephone. Then, the other computer must take the analog signals and transform them into digital signals. This job is the responsibility of the modem (MOdulator DEModulator). Modems take incoming digital signals from the computer and then send these signals in an analog form using the baud cycles from the phone system. The earliest modem used four analog bauds just to send one bit of data—those we often erroneously called 300-baud modems. They were not 300-baud modems; rather, they were 300bps modems, but the name "baud" stuck for describing modem speeds. As technology progressed, modems became faster and faster. To get past the 2400 baud limit, modems would modulate the 2400 baud signal twice in each cycle, making 4800 bits per second. To get 9600, the signal would be modulated four times. That's why all POTS modem speeds are always a multiple of 2400. Look at the following speeds and see how many look like classic modem speeds:

2400 x 1 = 2400

2400 x 2 = 4800

2400 x 4 = 9600

2400 x 6 = 14400

2400 x 8 = 19200

2400 x 12 = 28800

2400 x 24 = 57600 (56K)

So, if someone comes up to you and says, "Is that a 56K baud modem?" Look them straight in the eye and say, "No, it is a 2400-baud modem. But its BPS is 57600." You will be technically correct, although you will have no friends.

For two modems to run at their fastest speeds, they must modulate signals in the same fashion. The two modems also must to be able to query, or negotiate with, each other to determine the fastest speed of each modem. The modem manufacturers themselves originally standardized these processes under what were known as "proprietary protocols." The down side to these protocols was that unless you had two modems from the same manufacturer, the two modems often would not work together. Quickly, the European standards body knows as the CCITT established standards for modems. These standards are known generically as the "V" standards and define the speeds at which modems can modulate. The most common speed standards are the following:

V.22   1200 bps

V.22bis   2400 bps

V.32	9600 bps
V.32bis	14400 bps
V.34	28000 bps
V.90	57600 bps

In addition to speed standards, the CCITT, now simply the ITT, has established standards that enable two modems to compress data and to perform error checking. These standards are the following:

V.42	Error Checking
V.42bis	Data Compression
MNP5	Both

The beauty of these standards is that there is no special work involved to enjoy their benefits. If you want 56K data transfers, for example, simply ensure that the modem in the local system and the modem in the remote system are both V.90 standard. Assuming good line quality, etc., the connections will run at 56K.

NOTE: *Many people get a little confused on the concept of port speed and modem speed. All versions of Windows give you the opportunity to set the port speed. This speed is the speed of the data between the serial port and the modem, not between the modems. As a rule, always set this speed to the highest rating of 115200bps.*

MODEM POOLS   One of the great powers of NT's RAS is that the RAS can accept up to 256 simultaneous connections. Administrators commonly use RAS to enable many people to connect to the network. Unfortunately, every connection needs a modem. Each modem needs a COM port, and every COM port needs an IRQ. Given that most PCs have only four or five extra COM ports, using standard external and internal modems is not an option. There are two common options to enable one PC to serve a large number of connections. The first and oldest method to get around this limit is to use "multi I/O boards." These are usually cards installed into the computer that have a number of serial connections. The card would enable all of the modems to share a common IRQ, enabling hundreds of connections—assuming that your wallet could afford an I/O card that could handle that many connections. These I/O cards were common in the early- to mid-'90s and are still available. The down side to multi I/O boards is that they are messy. Every port on the I/O board needs a modem, and all of those modems can make a cabling nightmare. For the most part, these cards have been relegated to small (less than eight) connections, due to the onset of the far more modern "modem pool" devices.

The term "modem pool" has been around for a long time. Back in the old days (any time before the WWW), a modem pool was known as a situation in which you had a bunch of modems working together in any fashion. Today, a modem pool describes a rack-mounted device of some sort to which many—hundreds maybe—of phone lines are connected. In essence, a modem pool can be considered a "super modem," which has the capacity to handle many phone lines simultaneously, eliminating the need for multi I/O cards with their separate modems. Modem pools usually manifest themselves as rack-mounted devices, connected directly to a serving computer through a high-speed connection and special card.

NULL MODEMS   A null modem is nothing more than two serial ports directly connected via a special "null modem" serial cable. This cable crosses the "send" wires of each serial cable to the receive wires of the other. Null modems are old, slow, and not useful anymore—with one big exception. Null modems are a really great way to teach yourself RAS without the expense and pain of two modems and two phone lines.

X.25   X.25 is an older type of data transmission, first invented in the '70s, and is considered the first attempt by the phone companies to create dedicated data transmission. X.25 is not actually a type of cabling, as X.25 can run on standard phone lines. Instead, X.25 is an analog method of "packetizing" data, a concept which is not too dissimilar to network packets such as Ethernet. X.25 manifests itself as a device called a *Packet Assembler/Deassembler* ("PAD") that takes the data coming from the computer and places the data into discrete packets. The phone company sends the packets through an X.25 network, and an X.25 PAD on the receiving side reassembles the packets.

In the '70s and '80s, X.25 was just about the only "game in town" for data transmissions and gathered quite a large following. X.25 was also a major money-maker for the phone companies. X.25 can work as a dial-up but is far more common as a "dedicated" (always connected) service. X.25 is fading away due to the onset of more powerful digital services, but this situation has actually made X.25 somewhat attractive. Some phone companies have slashed pricing to use the installed base of X.25 lines.

ISDN   There are many pieces to a POTS telephone connection. First is the phone line that runs from your phone, out the Network Interface Box (the little box on the side of your house), to a central switch. (In some cases, there are intermediary steps.) Standard metropolitan areas have a large number of central offices, each with a central switch. Houston, for example, has nearly 100 offices in the general area. These central switches connect to each other through high-capacity "trunk" lines. Before 1970, the entire phone system, from your phone to the other phone, was analog. Over time, phone companies began to upgrade their trunk lines to digital systems. Over time, the entire telephone system, with the exception of the line from your phone to the central office, has become digital.

During this same upgrade period, customers have continued to demand higher throughput from their phone lines. The old POTS was not expected to be able to produce more than 28.8Kbps. The 56K modems were a big surprise to the phone companies and did not come out until 1995, so the phone companies were motivated to come up with a way to generate higher capacities. The answer was actually fairly simple: Make the entire phone system digital. Using the same copper wires used by POTS and adding special equipment at the central office and at the user's location, the phone companies can achieve a throughput of up to 128K per line. This process of sending fully digital lines "end-to-end" is known as *Integrated Services Digital Network* (ISDN).

ISDN service consists of two types of channels known as "Bearer" or "B" channels and "Delta" or "D" channels. "B" channels carry data and voice information at 64Kbps. "D" channels carry setup and configuration information. Most providers of ISDN enable the user to choose between one or two B channels. The more common setup is the two B-one D, usually called a *Basic Rate Interface* (BRI).

The physical connections of ISDN bear some similarity to POTS modems. An ISDN wall socket is usually nothing more than what looks like a standard RJ-45 network jack. The most common interface is a device called a *Terminal Adapter* (TA). TA's look much like regular modems and come in external and internal variations.

 NOTE: *There is another type of ISDN, Primary Rate Interface (PRI), that is composed of 24 B channels and one D channel. PRI is rarely used with RAS.*

There are a number of telephony options with RAS. The most common by far are regular phone lines and ISDN. While this chapter will concentrate on these two types of connections, keep in mind that there are a number of other options that can be used with RAS. A proper discussion of these other telephony technologies, while fascinating, is unfortunately well outside the scope of this chapter—and the book. Instead, this chapter will concentrate on the proper configuration of RAS.

Now that we understand the basic telephony tools used to link far-flung systems, let's take a moment to clarify completely what is, and what is not, this tool called Microsoft Windows NT RAS.

What is RAS?

The goal of RAS is to enable an individual PC to link into a remote LAN. To understand the concept, we must understand an important pair of terms: "local" and "remote." Local and remote are terms relative to the user, as illustrated in Figure 14–1. A local machine is the machine at which the user physically works. The remote machine is the "faraway" computer to which the user would like to connect.

Remote access in NT consists of two separate products: a serving product and client software. A system installed with the serving product receives calls from remote systems and acts as the link between the remote system and the local network, as illustrated in Figure 14–2. The serving product—called simply RAS—is installed as a network service. A system that has RAS installed is usually referred to as an "RAS server." Both Windows NT Server and NT Workstation provide full support for RAS serving.

A system installed with the client software—known as *Dial-Up Networking* (DUN)—has the capability to dial out to and communicate with an RAS server, as illustrated in Figure 14–3. Windows NT Server and

Figure 14–1

Local and remote are relative statements.

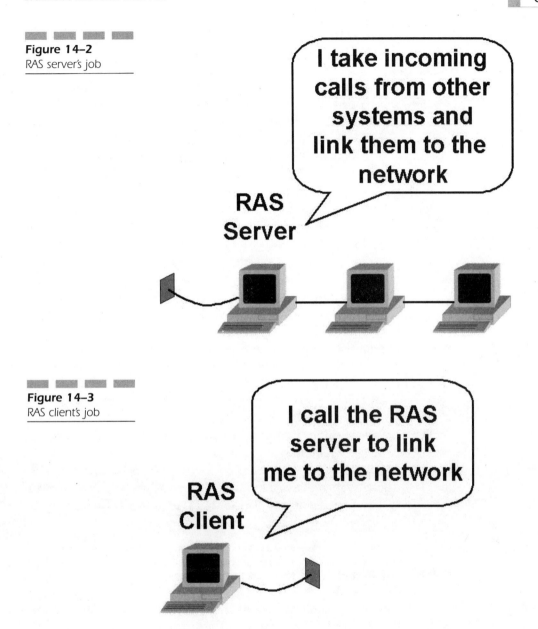

Figure 14–2
RAS server's job

Figure 14–3
RAS client's job

Workstation, as well as Windows 95 and Windows 98, have DUN available. DUN is not limited to linking into RAS exclusively and can also be used to remotely access a number of different dial-in servers.

THE ROLE OF RAS IN REMOTE ACCESS Microsoft developed RAS to fulfill a few specific roles in remote access. The key to understanding RAS is to appreciate what RAS can and cannot do in the network. The best way to visualize the roles of RAS is to display the classic uses of RAS.

Before we observe these classic uses of RAS, we should clear up a common misconception. NT administrators new to RAS always seem to expect a remote system, dialed in using RAS, to act in some way differently than a local system logged into the same network. In reality, a functioning RAS connection is really pretty boring. An RAS client that successfully logs into an RAS server is, in essence, nothing more than just another node on that network. Think of the telephone link as nothing more than a really long and really slow network cable. From a network standpoint, there is nothing special about the remote system. The remote system is subject to all of the same rules as a system on the local network. If the local network is domain-based, the remote system logs on with a valid domain account. The remote system can access all shared resources with the same ease as the systems on the local network, although more slowly. After understanding this point, let's look at the common uses for RAS, beginning with the most common use: accessing a standard NT network.

CONNECTING TO AN NT NETWORK The first and most common use of RAS is to connect a remote system to a local network. This action is performed using one system on the local network configured as an RAS server and a number of systems configured with DUN. The RAS server can be any machine on the network, but due to the risk of hacking, the RAS server is usually not the PDC, BDC, or any member server with particularly critical data. The RAS server can have a number of modems/terminal adapters installed, including a modem pool. Up to 256 remote users can dial in on known telephone numbers and access the network, as illustrated in Figure 14-4.

CONNECTING TO THE INTERNET The second most common use of RAS is to enable a system to access the Internet. There are two methods for using RAS to enable a system to access the Internet. The first and most simple method is to use DUN to access the Internet via an *internet service provider* (ISP), as illustrated in Figure 14-5. RAS server is not used. This method is the way millions of people access the Internet every day. The other method for connecting to the Internet is to dial into an RAS server that has an Internet link—in essence, making your own ISP, as illustrated in Figure 14-6.

Figure 14–4
RAS can accept
multiple links.

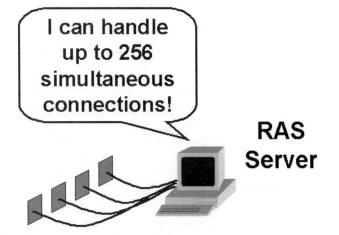

Figure 14–5
DUN for direct
Internet connection

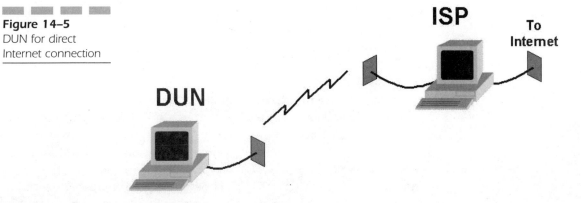

Figure 14–6
DUN for Internet
connection via a RAS
server

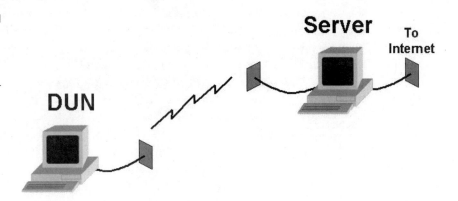

CONNECTING TO AN NT NETWORK VIA THE INTERNET The last and probably least-common use for RAS is to enable a remote system to access an NT network via the Internet. This process is known as a *Virtual Private Network* (VPN). A client accesses any local ISP, and through the Internet, creates the network link. To achieve this end, both the DUN client and the RAS server must both be configured with a special protocol, the *Point-to-Point Tunneling Protocol* (PPTP). (The next section discusses protocols.) VPNs are powerful tools that save a lot of money on transmission costs. Why use a long-distance call to the main office when you can just use a local ISP?

RAS PROTOCOLS All networks, even dial-up networks, need physical/datalink protocols. There is no way that a physical/datalink protocol such as Ethernet or Token Ring is going to work over a telephone line. Networking in general was never designed for operation over telephone lines. In the mid-'80s, demand by users to access the Internet via non-dedicated lines created a motivation for a new physical/datalink protocol to enable phone lines to be used for Internet access. This protocol was called *Serial Line Internet Protocol* (SLIP). By the early '90s, a far better protocol called *Point-to-Point Protocol* (PPP) replaced SLIP. PPP is a special form of PPTP that provides VPN functions.

SLIP was the first protocol to enable modems to access a network, but SLIP presented a serious challenge to configure. This difficulty certainly kept the Internet from growing until PPP came along. SLIP was usually a special program that ran in the background to provide a socket for the TCP/IP connection. The most famous of the stand-alone programs in the Windows world was the popular Trumpet Winsock. Trumpet Winsock was the first Windows application used to connect PCs to the Internet in Windows 3.X. Configuration of SLIP required that the user knew the IP address of the local system and the system into which they were dialing. Additionally, SLIP required the manual setting of a large number of special TCP/IP settings, such as MTU speed, etc. SLIP was further limited in that the program could only support the TCP/IP protocol.

PPP was developed to overcome the limits of SLIP. PPP is by far the most-used dial-up protocol, followed distantly by a few proprietary and unknown protocols. First of all, PPP is highly automated. PPP can query the serving systems for an IP address, DNS server, etc. This feature means that users do not have to use static IP addresses, nor must they enter all of the necessary details of TCP/IP. Also, PPP provides automatic logins, preventing the need for complex login scripts in most systems. PPP is not limited to any one type of protocol and can also support NetBEUI and IPX (called NWLink in NT), either singly or in combination. Last and possibly most importantly to RAS, PPP can handle a number of network aspects important to Windows. Through TCP/IP and IPX, PPP can support a Windows API. PPP also supports named pipes and Remote Procedure calls, both important for making RAS nothing more than an "extension of the wire."

PPTP has only one function: to provide virtual, private networking over the Internet. The Internet is an open area—by definition, a bad place for a secure network. Microsoft, working with other interested parties, however, has developed a special protocol called PPTP. First of all, PPTP does not replace PPP or SLIP. This protocol is designed to be run with PPP protocol to provide the necessary security to use the Internet to transmit data.

RAS is many different protocols, programs, and methods that can be brought together in different ways to perform one function: enabling remote systems to access a local network. RAS is two separate programs: RAS and DUN. You must appreciate, however, that RAS has some serious limitations. Now that we understand what RAS can do, let's look at some examples of what RAS is not designed to do.

RAS IS NOT A REMOTE CONTROL PROGRAM "Remote Control" programs, such as PC Anywhere or Remote Control, are a completely different class of programs than RAS. A remote control program literally takes control of a node on the network. Remote control programs do have server and client software, but the functions are completely different. When you successfully link on a remote control software, you actually control the I/O (keyboard, monitor, and mouse) of the serving system. Your local system has not become another node on the network; rather, your local system virtually becomes the serving system. Every icon on the desktop and every program on the Start menu is identical. Do not confuse remote control programs with RAS.

There seems to be a tendency today to dismiss remote control programs. Remote control programs, however, can fill a number of roles that RAS cannot. A critical point to remember about remote control programs is that they only pass I/O functions to the client. All programs continue to run on the server. This fact means that the client system does not need to have the software installed. (There are some limits here, depending on the brand of remote control software you use.) Remote control software is designed to run only with an identical brand of remote control software, making hacking virtually impossible.

RAS IS NOT A ROUTER This item is usually a shocker to someone just getting to know RAS. Logic would seem to dictate, at first glance, that if RAS can link one computer to a LAN, as in Figure 14–7, RAS should also be able to link one LAN to another, as illustrated in Figure 14–8.

Look at the diagrams for a moment. Notice that for the RAS server to enable the client to communicate, the RAS server must have basic packet forwarding. Any packet coming from the client must be forwarded to the rest of the network. That is fine—and that is what RAS is designed to do. In the lower figure, however, the DUN client would have to be able to forward the packets from the separate systems on the client side if this scenario is going to work. Basically, this process asks the RAS client to act as a router, forwarding the packets out through a determined port (the modem) to the other side of the network. RAS is not designed for routing. To do routing, you would want to purchase true routers, as illustrated in Figure 14–9.

Note that Microsoft has provided a free, add-on service to RAS called *Routing and Remote Access Service* (RRAS, often still referred to by its original Microsoft code name of "Steelhead"). RRAS provides the basic routing functions missing from RAS and can provide the configuration

Figure 14–7
If RAS lets me
do this . . .

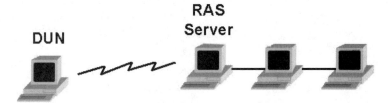

Figure 14–8
. . . then RAS should
let me do this, right?

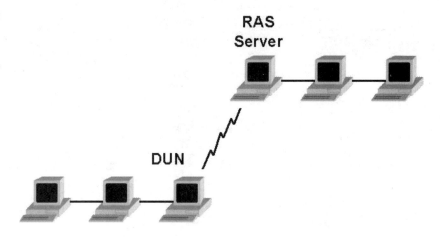

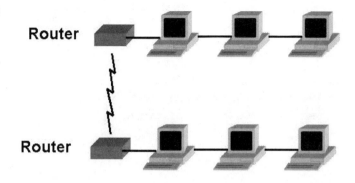

Figure 14–9
The right way:
router-to-router

shown earlier that RAS could not. RRAS is not covered on the exams, however, and is outside the scope of this book. RRAS is a product that you should consider trying, however. RRAS supports more advanced routing protocols, such as OSPF and RIP version 2 (which is cool if you are into routing), and enables you literally to make your own router from a PC with a modem and an NIC.

Now that we know what RAS is, which hardware it uses, what RAS is capable of, and what RAS cannot do, we now begin the process of installation. We will begin with the installation of the far more complex part of RAS: the RAS server programs and service.

Installing RAS for Serving

The process of installing RAS for serving takes three steps. These steps involve the following:

1. Installing modem, terminal adapter, etc.
2. Installing the RAS networking service
3. Configuring RAS dial-in options

INSTALL MODEMS You are not required to have the modem(s) installed before installing the RAS service. If RAS does not detect a modem or TA, RAS will simply prompt for the installation of one. You should always, however, install the hardware before this process, because the hardware will enable you to test whether the modem/TA works. The initial install of RAS is almost always a pain, requiring plenty of little tweaks to get the system running. Knowing that the modem actually works when something goes wrong removes a lot of work from the diagnostic process.

The process of installing a modem in NT will always be simple as long as you remember that NT is not a Plug and Play OS. Be sure to configure your modem manually to an unused I/O address and IRQ. Windows 95 and 98 users gleefully install Plug and Play devices, but until that glorious day when we can replace every copy of NT 3.5 and 4 with Windows 2000, we will still be playing with jumpers or software configuration floppies. For those who need a brush up, here are the default COM ports:

COM1 is I/O Address 3F8 and IRQ4.

COM2 is I/O Address 2F8 and IRQ3.

COM3 is I/O Address 3E8 and IRQ4.

COM4 is I/O Address 2E8 and IRQ3.

Watch out for built-in COM ports and any devices that you have installed that may have taken any of these I/O addresses or IRQs. If the modem is installed on the system with I/O address conflicts, NT will not be able to find the modem.

NOTE: *Have you forgotten, or never bothered to learn, all the defaults for COM ports? Well, the MCSE core tests do not seem too interested in your skills here, either. But in the real world, this knowledge is considered basic stuff everyone knows.*

Once you have properly configured the modem (set the jumpers and physically installed the card into the machine or connected the external serial cable), go to the Modem applet in the Control Panel. Assuming that there are no modems installed, the Modem applet will automatically prompt you to enable it to search for the modem. You should always enable NT to search for the modem unless the modem's documentation says otherwise. If NT finds the modem, you can rest assured that you have a good, non-conflicting COM port and that the modem is probably in good working order. Assuming all is well, the dialog box in Figure 14–10 will appear.

You can install a modem manually in cases where NT cannot find the modem—or in the situation that NT finds the modem but thinks the modem is the wrong kind—or if the modem manufacturer tells you to install manually. NT comes with a broad number of drivers and also has the ubiquitous "Have Disk" button for those special drivers. You can also install a null modem in this applet, if desired, as shown in Figure 14–11.

Once you have installed a modem, opening the Modems applet will display all of the currently configured modems, as shown in Figure 14–12.

Figure 14–10

NT finding a modem

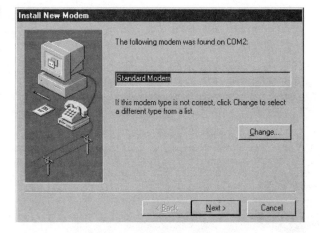

Figure 14–11

Installing a null modem

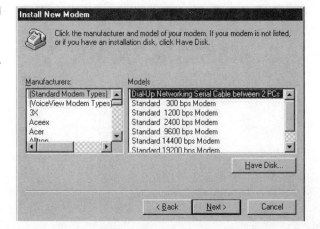

By selecting a modem and then selecting Properties, you can configure any configuration options specific to the modem itself. The General tab (Figure 14–13) enables the configuration of the speaker volume, a darn handy tool for answering questions such as, "Did the modem answer the line?" and the maximum COM port speed.

The Connection tab (Figure 14–14) sets a few other options, such as the Data, Stop, and Parity bits, as well as a few preferences. The INF file that comes with the modem sets the initial settings. Ninety-nine percent of the time, you never need to touch these settings. Some settings, such as the Data, Stop, and Parity bits, are so standardized on the defaults (8, N, 1) that it is amazing these are still even displayed as options. (Certainly, there

Figure 14–12
Installed modems

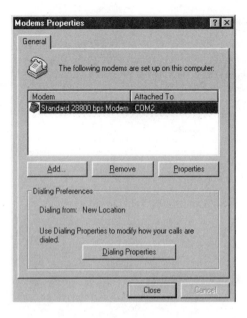

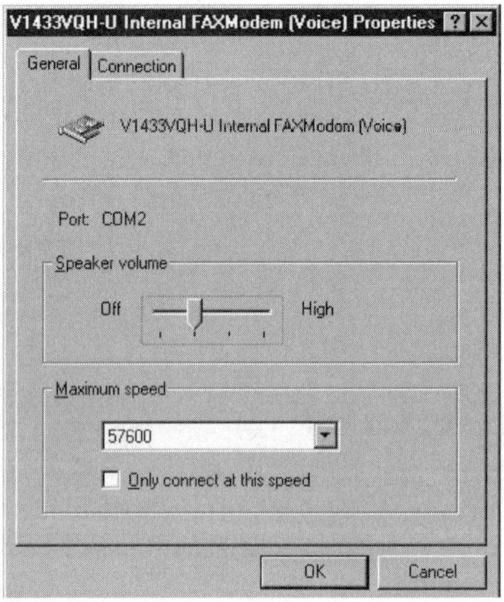

Figure 14–13
General Properties
tab

must be some dial-ups that would need settings other than 8, N, 1, although we have not seen one since the heyday of Bulletin Boards.

Figure 14–14
Connection
Properties tab

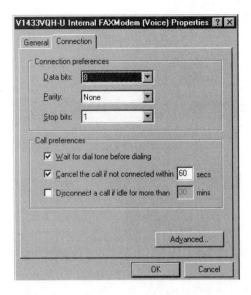

NOTE: *Watch out for ISDN terminal adapters. They always come with their own driver and often a complete setup program. Use these features. Windows NT 4 is basically clueless about terminal adapters. Also, many TAs will add their own Control Panel applet. These custom applets work great—but sometimes we do not think to look for them.*

INSTALL RAS SERVICE Once you have installed the hardware driver, you can add the RAS service. RAS is a network service, so access the Network properties, select the Services tab, and press the **Add** button. Just select RAS, as shown in Figure 14–15.

NT will prompt for the installation CD and begin to add the necessary files. After the files are installed, NT will show a list of modems installed on the system. You can then select your modem, or if for some reason you were the type who does not add his or her modem, you will be prompted to install at that time. We hope you have the modem physically installed, or you will be aborting the installation at this point. After selecting the modem, you will see the screen displayed in Figure 14–16. Click the Configure button.

You can configure each modem to accept only incoming calls, only dial out, or both, as shown in Figure 14–17. Choose the setting most appropriate to your configuration. "Dial out only" is fairly rare, but "Dial out and Receive calls" is a common setting. Do not forget that this must be done for every installed modem, or you will get the default of "Receive calls only."

Figure 14–15
Adding RAS network
service

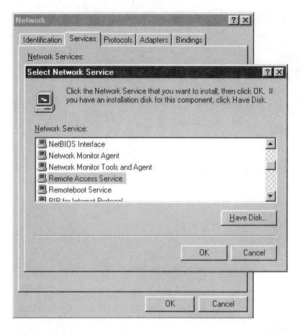

Figure 14–16
Modem selected
(RAS dialog)

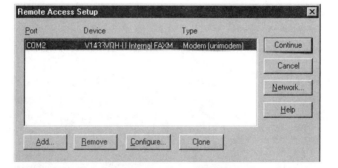

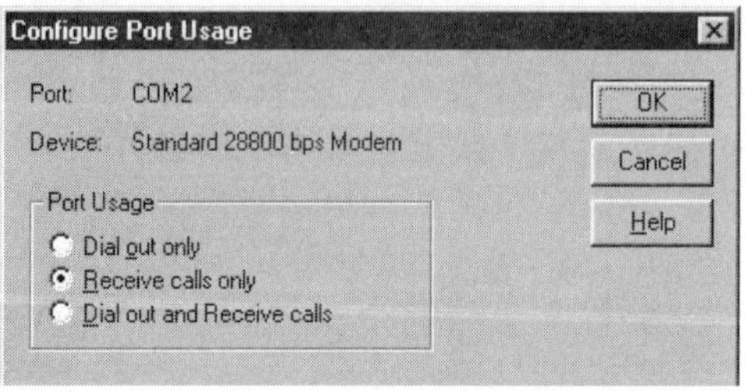

Figure 14–17
Configuring Port
usage

Now that RAS knows what hardware to use, you must determine what network protocols to support. Clicking the Network button brings up the Network Configuration dialog box, as shown in Figure 14–18. Note that in this example, the top Dial out Protocols checkboxes are active. These become active by default when you select Dial out and Receive calls. Selecting Receive calls only, in contrast, would gray these options. Check all protocols desired for the dial out/receive that your configuration needs.

NOTE: *RAS is a slow "pipe." No real-world RAS installation is EVER going to have more than one protocol. Multiple protocols will slow down a 10MB network and will bring a 56K-phone line to its knees. Use just one protocol if you want anything even partially tolerable.*

Each protocol will have special configurations. You can click the configure buttons now or simply wait until the Remote Access dialog is closed and the screens will be forced upon you. We will do the latter and move down to the Encryption settings.

When a user log into an RAS server, the user will enter their username and a password. A good hacker could monitor the connection as the user is logging in and determine the username and password. Sound hard? This process is really simple and is done all the time. To prevent others from discovering passwords, RAS supports a number of different encryption options,

Figure 14–18
Selecting dial-in/
dial-out protocols

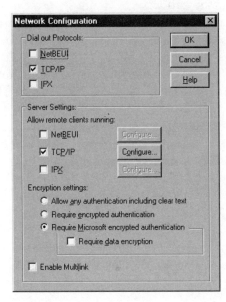

including the common *Password Authentication Protocol* (PAP), and the *Challenge Handshake Authentication Protocol* (CHAP). In addition, RAS also supports Microsoft's own MS-CHAP encryption. Here is where you tell RAS how to handle encryption. There are three choices. First, "Enable any authentication including clear text" says what the phrase means: this option will take anything—including clear text. The second, "Require encrypted authentication," takes anything other than PAP. These first two options are only selected when systems other than Windows NT, Windows 95 and 98, and Windows 3.1 are used. The third option, "Require Microsoft encrypted authentication," is the default and is the most common. This option uses the MS-CHAP for authentication. This method is a pretty good protection and does not require any special moves on the part of the DUN folks upon login. MS-CHAP is transparent and darn safe.

If you really want to get paranoid (and there are times when you need to), selecting the "Require data encryption" checkbox will encrypt all data over the course of the connection. Again, it is transparent to the users and really does a pretty good job of protecting your data moving back and forth. This option is particularly popular for those folks who like to do VPNs over the Internet.

Selecting "Enable Multi-link" enables more than one line to work as a single connection—in essence, doubling the throughput of the data. Refer to Multi-link later in this chapter for details.

The RAS installation sees what protocols are installed and gives a screen for each one. While all of these protocols will have different options, there is one that they all have in common. You can limit clients using a particular protocol to have access to either the entire network or to just the RAS server. This tool is powerful. As mentioned earlier, any proper RAS network will only use one protocol, such as TCP/IP. A common security trick is not to let RAS clients access the entire network. Therefore, the TCP/IP protocol will be set to "This computer only." Suddenly, an administrator wants to access something on the broader network. They can set another protocol, usually NetBEUI, as Entire network, giving them broader access without messing with the settings for normal clients. Be sure to turn off that extra protocol when you have finished doing whatever required the extra access. Configuring NetBEUI is the easiest of all the protocols, as NetBEUI only has the access option, as shown in Figure 14–19. IPX and TCP/IP, however, require a bit more tweaking.

The IPX configuration screen, as shown in Figure 14–20, has a few more options than NetBEUI, but fortunately, the defaults are almost always used. To appreciate the details of this screen requires a deeper understanding of the IPX protocol than is necessary for either passing the

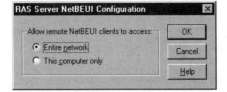

Figure 14–19
NetBEUI
configuration

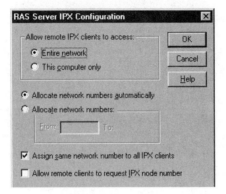

Figure 14–20
IPX configuration

core MCSE exams or for the average day-to-day use of RAS. Suffice it to say that every time an IPX client accesses an IPX-based RAS server, a special 32-bit IPX network number must be assigned. By default, RAS will assign any available IPX network number to the link. This option is the "Allocate network numbers automatically" option. If, for some reason, you want to give a range of IPX network numbers, the "Allocate network numbers" can be used. You only need to enter the beginning network number in the "From" box. RAS will then automatically calculate the number of available ports and enter the "End" number.

The "Assign same network number to all IPX clients" is checked by default. This tells RAS to give all RAS clients the same IPX network number, reducing overall network traffic.

The "Enable remote clients to request IPX node number" is unchecked by default and will almost always stay that way. Enableing remote clients to specify their own node number is somewhat dangerous. If one system can use the same network number as another, it is "spoofing"—impersonating—another connected client and will have all of the same rights and privileges of the other client.

The TCP/IP dialog box has a large number of configuration details, as shown in Figure 14–21. Fortunately, most of these are amazingly straight forward, assuming that you read the pertinent TCP/IP information in

Figure 14–21
TCP/IP configuration

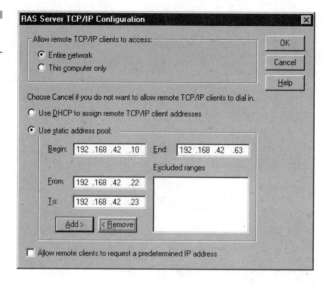

Chapters 9, "Microsoft Networking," Chapter 10, "Networking Protocols," and Chapter 16, "Managing and Monitoring NT Server."

The big issue with TCP/IP configuration is, "What IP address does the client receive?" The bottom line is that you either use DHCP, or you set a static pool of IP addresses. This situation is similar to setting up a DHCP pool with a range of addresses and adding any excluded addresses as needed. There is also an option to enable clients to request a predetermined IP address, which is somewhat obsolete in today's world of allocated IP addresses.

ADMINISTERING RAS   Once the protocols are configured, the RAS server is basically ready. The primary maintenance/administration tool for RAS serving is the *Remote Access Admin* (RAA) application, shown in Figure 14–22. The RAA tool enables administrators to handle the day-to-day functions of RAS.

There are five menu options for RAA. The View only updates the view, and Help is a standard help screen, however—leaving only the Server, Users, and Options worthy of detail. The Server option enables the administrator to start, stop, or pause the RAS service, see who is logged on (active users), and verify the status of the RAS ports. Figure 14–23 shows RAA selecting a domain.

The User menu has two options. First, the menu is used to set which users have permission to log into the particular RAS server and whether or not they have Call Back, as shown in Figure 14–24. A user must have dial-in permission or they will not be able to access the RAS server.

Figure 14–22
RAA in action

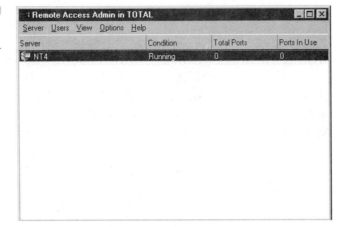

Figure 14–23
Selecting a domain

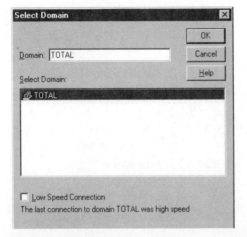

Figure 14–24
Setting dial-in
permissions

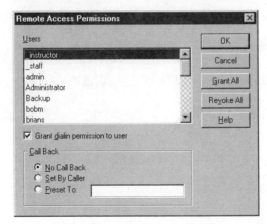

Call Back is an excellent security feature. When a user calls in, the RAS server will hang up and then dial the client to ensure that someone is not trying to hack. This method is also a great way to keep long-distance call costs down. Either the caller can give the number to call, or the number is preset.

The second User option, Active Users, enables the administrator to deal with individual active users, as shown in Figure 14–25. An administrator can send a message to all active users or to just one active user. Furthermore, you can also disconnect an active user—always a fun thing to do to users who you have an urge to "smite."

Installing and configuring RAS is not too complicated. The biggest trick is to understand the underpinnings of your network and provide what the network needs in terms of hardware, protocols, and access. Some configuration issues do become a little more complex, but to appreciate these issues, we need first to take a look at the client side of RAS: DUN.

Installing DUN

The RAS client DUN is a common sight on most PCs today, given that versions of DUN can be found on NT Server, NT Workstation, Windows 95, and Windows 98. This powerful tool enables systems to link not only into RAS servers, but also into almost every type of RAS used today, including virtually all ISPs. DUN is a phone book-based system, enabling one system to store many different dial-up settings. Each phone book entry stores the pertinent information of that particular server, including phone numbers, logins, and network addressing details. This section will concentrate on linking DUN to RAS servers, looking first at the NT version of DUN, followed by a quick peek at the Windows 95 and 98 version.

Figure 14–25
Checking active users

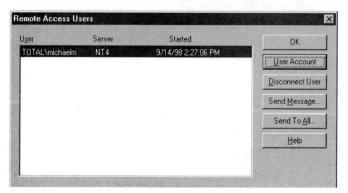

DUN IN WINDOWS NT To install DUN, go to the Start . . . Programs . . . Accessories and select Dial-Up Networking. Installation begins with a greeting screen and then attempts to locate a modem, as shown in Figure 14–26. If the installer cannot find a modem, the computer will prompt you to install one.

After the modem is installed, NT displays the Remote Access Setup dialog box, the same one seen in RAS, as shown in Figure 14–27. The same options, Configure (for receive calls, dial out, and both) and Network (for configuring protocols), need to be handled. Because DUN is really only dial out, this process is usually a fairly simple one. Many of the RAS options simply do not have any meaning in DUN.

NOTE: *Gee, that screen sure looks a lot like RAS. Well, that screen should, because RAS and DUN are really just different ways to look at the same product. DUN is really nothing more than RAS set for dial out only by default.*

After DUN is installed, or if RAS is already installed, DUN will simply prompt for the name of the dial-up connection, as shown in Figure 14–28. Give the connection a good, descriptive name.

Figure 14–26
Locating a modem in DUN

Figure 14–27
RAS

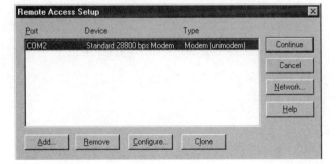

Figure 14–28
Setting up a new
phone book entry

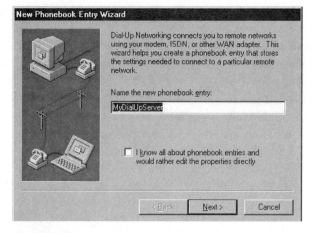

Figure 14–29
Setup Wizard options

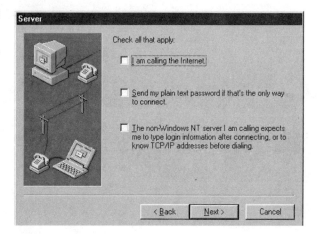

The new dial-up connection will then prompt for information to help it configure itself, as shown in Figure 14–29. If you select the "I am calling the Internet," you will get TCP/IP installed and will be prompted for account name and password. Clicking the "Send my plain text password if that's the only way to connect" option is actually setting the authentication protocol options seen earlier under RAS. The last option, the one that starts with "The non-Windows NT server I am calling . . . " is for login scripts. Some UNIX systems require the user to log in from a terminal screen. A login script simply reads the prompts from the login screen and automatically responds. Failure to select or not select the proper checkbox here simply means that something will have to be edited manually later—no big deal.

Finally, the dial-up prompts for the phone number, as seen in Figure 14–30. You can enter a telephone number here, or you can require the system to use telephony-dialing properties and then enter a number. The Alternates button enables for alternate phone numbers to be used on failure of the main number or to add Multi-link numbers. Click **OK**, and the phone book entry is done.

To dial or edit a phone book entry, select Dial-Up Networking from the Start menu as shown earlier or from My Computer. This action brings up the DUN dialog box, shown in Figure 14–31.

The More button on the DUN dialog box enables you to set all of the configuration options. This pulldown button has a number of options that break down into three groups: modem properties, Monitor status, and

Figure 14–30
Phone numbers

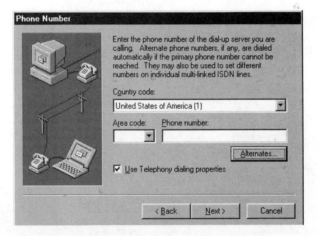

Figure 14–31
Editing a phone book entry

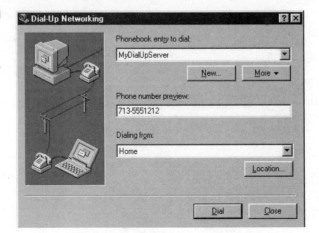

user/logon preferences, as shown in Figure 14–32. The Monitor status is actually a handy tool called DUN Monitor and will be covered later. For now, let's look at the Modem properties and the user/logon preferences.

Modem Properties   DUN supports multiple phone book entries. The modem properties options enable you to edit, clone (i.e., copy), or delete entries in the phone book. The add, delete, and copy options are obvious. The "Edit entry and modem properties," shown in Figure 14–33, is big, powerful, and a little complicated.

Note that there are five tabs: Basic, Server, Script, Security, and X.25. The Basic tab, shown earlier, enables changes to the name, telephony options, telephone number, and modem. The Server tab (Figure 14–34) defines the type of server, the protocols used, and any special TCP/IP settings.

Figure 14–32
DUN configuration menus

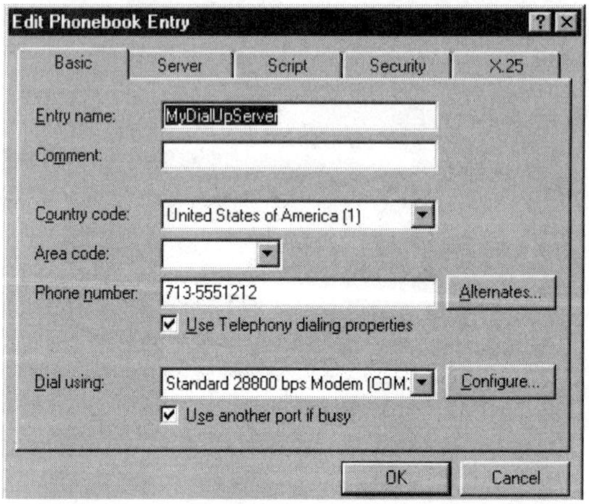

Figure 14–33
Phone book Edit—General tab

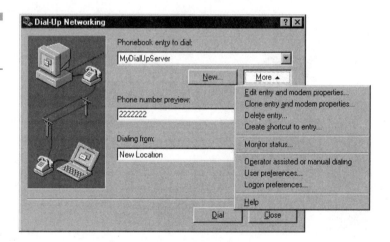

Figure 14–34
Phone book Edit—
Server tab

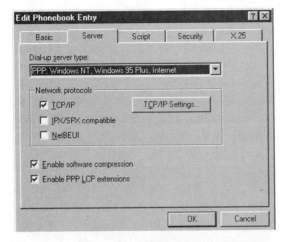

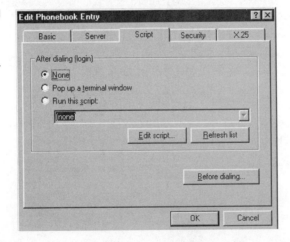

Figure 14–35
Phone book Edit—
Script tab

The Scripts tab (Figure 14–35) enables the creation of logon scripts. Logon scripts are never used for NT RAS but will be needed for a few other types of servers.

The Security tab should be called the Authentication tab, because this tab does nothing more than define the type of authentication used by the system. The settings are identical to the authentication options in RAS. The last tab, X.25, is for X.25 settings.

Preferences The More button also includes two options: User and Logon preferences. Both of these dialog boxes are identical. The Logon dialog box is for an individual user. The Logon preference is for when the system prompts for DUN. Either way, there will be four tabs: Dialing, Callback, Appearance, and Phone Book. Dialing (Figure 14–36) is the AutoDial feature of DUN. A shared resource is mapped to the method of access. If a system accesses a shared resource, say a shared directory called **FRED****DOG**, AutoDial will remember that, to access that resource, the program must use a particular phone entry in DUN. If the user clicks that shared resource, AutoDial will automatically dial out using the proper phone book entry. The dialing tab also determines redial options (number of attempts, wait time between attempts, etc.)

NOTE: *For AutoDial to operate, the Remote Access AutoDial Manager service must be started.*

The next tab, Callback (Figure 14–37) gives the user the capacity to set callback information. If RAS callback Remote Access Permissions is set to Set by Caller, the server will read these settings to determine its handling of callback options. These are basically the same options seen in RAS.

The Appearance tab (Figure 14–38) enables the user to customize the look of DUN and how certain applets react to dialing. The Phone book tab lets the user choose the phone book to use for dial-ups.

Once everything is properly configured, DUN, like RAS, is a fairly transparent feature of Windows NT. Only the occasional slowdown and the squeals of linking modems give clues that DUN is working hard in the background, giving your system links to the remote servers.

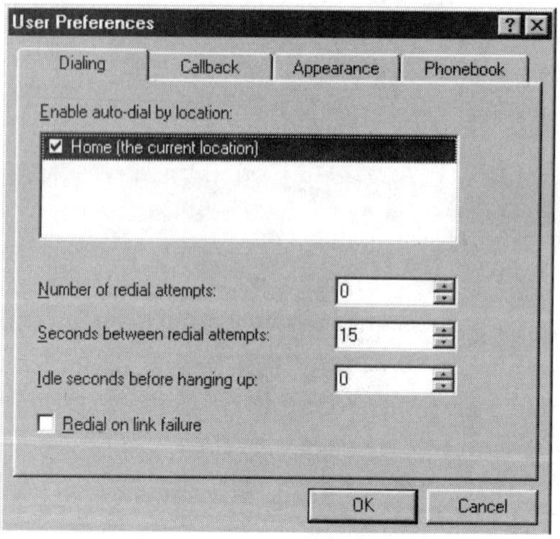

Figure 14–36
Preferences Edit—
Dialing tab

User Preferences

Dialing | Callback | Appearance | Phonebook

Enable auto-dial by location:

☑ Home (the current location)

Number of redial attempts: 0

Seconds between redial attempts: 15

Idle seconds before hanging up: 0

☐ Redial on link failure

OK   Cancel

Figure 14–37
Preferences Edit—
Callback tab

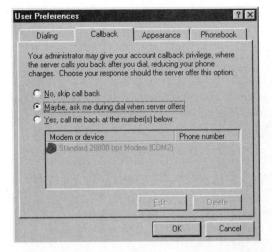

Figure 14–38
Preferences Edit—
Appearance tab

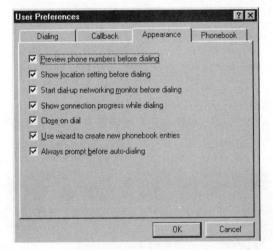

DUN MONITOR   Just as RAS has the Remote Access Administrator, DUN also has a tool for administering existing links, called the DUN Monitor. You can start the DUN Monitor through its own Control Panel applet. Dial-Up Monitor has three tabs: Status, Summary, and Preferences.

The Status tab (Figure 14–39) is the first place to turn for those "how long, how many"-type questions that tend to crop up during the course of a dial-up connection. Of particular note is the Line BPS information. This information is the actual speed between the modems, not the speed of the serial ports, and is a great gauge of the actual throughput of the system.

Figure 14–39
DUN Monitor—
Status tab

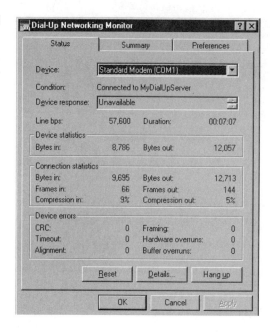

The Summary tab shows all of the dial-ups (networks) available and the device used to access the network. Usually, there is a one-to-one correlation of network to device. If there are any Multi-linked devices, however, they are visible here as two devices connected to one network. Figure 14–40 shows a simple modem connected to one network.

The Summary tab is also a great place for protocol-specific details (such as, "What is the IP address right now?"). Just click the Details button. This feature sure beats typing **IPCONFIG** from a C: prompt.

The last and least important tab is the Preferences, shown in Figure 14–41. This enables the user to determine when sounds are played. If you are into torturing people, just click the "Play a sound when data is sent or received" checkbox. This feature is a real crowd-pleaser. Seriously, the one thing that is handy here is to have the DUN Monitor on the taskbar, as shown in Figure 14–42. If you need to access the DUN monitor, you can just click the icon. The blue bars that appear on the top and bottom of the icon show incoming and outgoing data.

DUN IN WINDOWS 95 AND 98 DUN in Windows 95 and 98 is in some ways similar and in other ways quite different from the RAS/DUN combination in Windows NT. First, there are two components: a DUN client software and a DUN server. The DUN server originally only came with the Windows 95 Plus! pack but comes as part of the OS in Windows 98.

Figure 14–40
DUN Monitor—
Summary tab

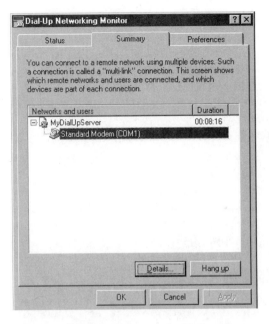

Figure 14–41
DUN Monitor—
Preferences tab

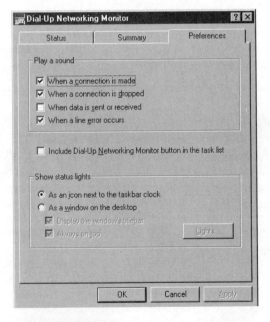

Figure 14–42
DUN Monitor on
Taskbar

The MCSE core exams ignore this DUN server, so forget about it for the exams. While you are at it, forget about the server for the real world, also, because it is a poor substitute for the power, reliability, and convenience of the Windows NT RAS. If you need a system to act as a RAS, install Windows NT and use RAS.

The Windows 95 and 98 DUN client (simply "DUN" for the remainder of this small section) has undergone a number of small changes from the original Windows 95 through Windows 98. This example is from Windows 95 OSR2, generally the version of Windows 95 most commonly referred to in the MCSE core exams.

As a client, the Windows 95 DUN is similar in function to the Windows NT DUN. The interface is somewhat different and may actually be superior to the Windows NT DUN interface. In particular, the 95 DUN opens as a group of different connections, each one with a separate icon, as shown in Figure 14–43.

Of course, the NT DUN also supports multiple dial-ups but is not nearly as obvious as the 95 and 98 version, relying on a combination box with only the default phone book option shown. (See Figure 14–44.) Selecting another phone book entry in NT requires you to press a separate pulldown button.

The Windows 95 DUN is not nearly as difficult to configure as the NT DUN, because there is nothing in the Windows 95 DUN that hints to the fact that it can also be an RAS, as it can under NT. The properties of each dial-up show a simple three-tab display: General, Server Types, and Scripting. (Windows 98 DUN adds a Multi-link tab). The General tab sets the phone number and the device to be used to make the connection, as shown in Figure 14–45. The Server Types tab handles all of the protocol issues. The 95 client supports NetBEUI, IPX and TCP/IP—same as in NT—but tends to be much simpler, because the client has no pretense of being anything more than a good client software, as shown in Figure 14–46.

Figure 14–43
DUN in Windows 95

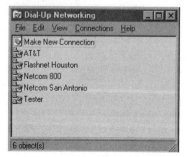

Figure 14–44
DUN in Windows NT

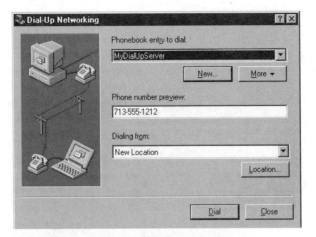

Figure 14–45
DUN for Windows
95—General tab

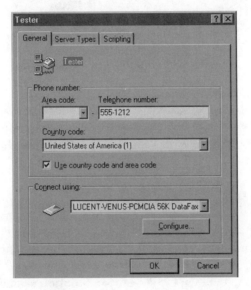

 NOTE: *One of the biggest security issues in RAS is the fact that client machines continue to load unnecessary protocols (such as NetBEUI) on a TCP/IP network and enable total access to their system via file sharing. This feature is part of the power and flexibility of Microsoft networking and is also a huge invitation to hack. You will want to turn off file sharing in Windows 95 and 98 dial-up clients.*

You have got to hand it to Microsoft for taking an excellent path in the "Big Picture" of networking. The snug fit between the Windows NT, Windows 95, and Windows 98 RAS applications really makes fitting these

Figure 14–46
DUN for Windows
95—Server types tab

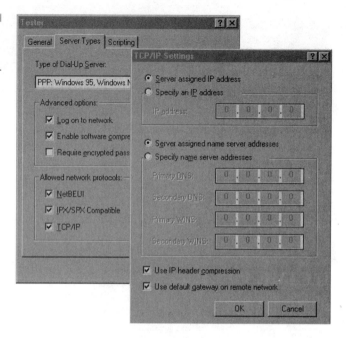

pieces together in your LAN/WAN a real no-brainer. The rest of this chapter will deal with some of the exceptions to the ease of use of RAS under Windows NT, starting with the powerful Multi-link function.

Multi-Link

Multi-link simply means to enable two or more phone lines to act as one big data pipeline, thereby doubling or tripling throughput on the RAS connection. Certainly, everybody wants to go faster on his or her RAS connections, so on first swipe the Multi-link option seems attractive—and it is. But there are a few limitations to Multi-link that most technicians do not realize until they ask Multi-link to do something the program was never created to do—and after they have spent *beaucoup* bucks setting up something. Let's try to prevent this situation from happening to you.

The single most important rule of Multi-link is that you must have Multi-link support on the other side. If the system is RAS, then it must have clients that can perform Multi-link. If this client is a Multi-link client, then the server must accept Multi-link. While this information may seem obvious, almost all systems that do not support Multi-link will support one line, giving you the impression that all is well—when in reality, only one-half the pipe is being used.

For all practical purposes, Multi-link is relegated to ISDN 128K links. The only exception to this statement might be in-house (where you control the server and the clients) RAS setups. While Multi-link will, in theory, work with POTS, ISDN, or a combination, the only real support is for ISDN 128K Multi-link. If you are thinking about Multi-link, think ISDN (or have an in-house RAS setup).

Forget about using the Callback feature with Multi-link. NT is not designed to do callback on two lines. If you want callback, you cannot use Multi-link.

Almost all ISDN adapters must have Multi-link turned on in their setup program. Do not assume that they call it Multi-link, either. In fact, simply telling an ISDN TA to do Multi-link can be a serious hair-puller. The best idea is to assume that Multi-link is turned off, and dive through the setup to find how to turn it on.

Many ISDN devices are designed to provide the second channel on demand only. There will be situations where the Multi-link is perfectly configured but only one line is being used, due to low network demand.

When connecting a Multi-link to someone else's systems (usually an ISP), do not assume that you are the problem if the Multi-link fails. ISPs can do some strange things with their routers that may prevent your system from working properly. If you think you have everything correct, call the ISP and make them verify their side of the setup.

Multi-link is a great way to increase data throughput, as long as you are willing to take the time to make Multi-link work. Take the time. The extra speed is worth it.

TCP/IP and RAS

TCP/IP and RAS go together like jalapeño peppers and cold beer—they work great together, but you need to be mentally prepared. Seriously, Microsoft definitely had TCP/IP in mind when it developed RAS. Both the server and client portions fully support TCP/IP, making it generally an easy configuration issue, assuming that you understand TCP/IP. Let's look at a few issues that can make TCP/IP and RAS unnecessarily painful— and how to avoid these problems.

First of all, do not let the fact that the machine uses RAS confuse you. TCP/IP is TCP/IP, whether it is a piece of Ethernet, a phone line, or bongo drums. The standard tools should always work. If there are any problems linking to shared resources, try the standard tools. Use IPCONFIG to verify a good IP address, DNS, WINS, etc. Use PING to see whether you can find other machines on your subnet. If you can, your network problem probably is not due to TCP/IP.

Second, try to keep things as automated as possible. Take advantage of DHCP, DNS, and WINS as needed by your configuration. Do not start thinking of the remote systems as "something" special, requiring their own TCP/IP configuration that is different from the rest of the LAN. If the LAN uses DHCP, so should the remote systems. If the LAN is using DNS and/or WINS, then the remote systems should also. Plus, remember that the remote systems will need their own HOST and LMHOSTS files if you do not use DNS and WINS respectively.

Questions

1. John wants to set up DUN clients so they only have access to the RAS server. The RAS server is NT Workstation, running NetBEUI and TCP/IP, as are all of the other machines on the network. Can he do that?

   a. Yes, but he will have to set up each user's dial-in permissions to "This Machine Only"

   b. No, only if they are all members of the same Global group

   c. Yes, but he will have to set the remote users to one protocol and set the access to "This Machine Only"

   d. No, this level of security only works under a domain model.

2. How many channels are used in BRI ISDN?

   a. Three

   b. Two

   c. One

   d. Four

3. RAS under NT server can handle a maximum of _____ simultaneous connections.

   a. One

   b. 16

   c. 256

   d. 65,536

4. RAS supports which network protocols? (Choose all that apply):

   a. NetBEUI

   b. Ethernet

   c. IPX

   d. TCP/IP

5. RAS supports which authentication protocols? (Choose all that apply):

   a. PAP

   b. MS-PAP

   c. CHAP

   d. MS-CHAP

6. Which hardware device is not supported by RAS?

   a. POTS modem

   b. Null modem

   c. ISDN terminal adapter

   d. Ethernet card

7. John has set aside five IP addresses for remote dial-ups. He can assign them via:

   a. The DNS server

   b. The DHCP server

   c. The WINS server

   d. The RAS server

8. Which is not a callback option?

   a. No callback

   b. Callback in a certain time

   c. Callback a certain number only

   d. Prompt for callback number

9. Joyce has two networks that she would like to connect together to make a WAN. She should use _____ on one side and _____ on the other.

   a. DUN, RAS

   b. A router, a router

   c. A router, DUN

   d. A router, RAS

10. Boyd is using DUN to connect to a remote LAN on his system running NT Workstation. He would like to know his IP address on the dial-up. He could (Choose all that apply):

    a. Run WINIPCFG.

    b. Run IPCONFIG.

    c. Run DUN Monitor.

    d. Run PING.

Answers

1. c—RAS enables access (entire network/this machine only) to be handled by protocol used.
2. a—BRI ISDN consists of two B channels and one D channel.
3. The correct answer is C. RAS enables 256 simultaneous connections.
4. a, c, d—NetBEUI, IPX, and TCP/IP. Ethernet is a data-link protocol.
5. a, c, d—There is no such authentication protocol as MS-PAP.
6. d—Ethernet cards are not supported by RAS. They are not telephony devices.
7. d—The RAS server can be given a pool of static IP addresses. The DHCP server cannot reserve IP addresses just for remote dial-ups.
8. b—There is no callback option based on time.
9. b—To have full WAN function, there must be a router on both sides.
10. b, c—WINIPCFG is a Windows 95 utility. PING will not give your IP address.

Printing in Windows NT

Windows NT provides simple, easy, and intuitive network OS support for printing. Most network operating systems before Windows NT controlled network printing through complicated, text-based menus and command line controls. They were difficult to configure, difficult to troubleshoot, and not particularly intuitive. Windows NT provides a superior alternative (see Figure 15–1).

In this chapter, we will take a detailed tour of the broad concept of Windows NT printing, starting with the understanding of printing in a stand-alone environment and then proceeding to network printing—the real power of Windows NT. Although Windows NT printing is quite simple, Microsoft uses a few terms that might be a little confusing. Let's take a moment to understand how Windows NT sees the printing process.

Figure 15–1
Print king

Figure 15–2
Hey! Print this
document!

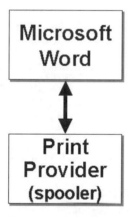

The Windows NT Printing Process

The Windows NT printing process has four components: the application that generates a print job, the GDI (which is a series of calls used by the application to create the print job), the spooler (print provider) that holds, controls, and maintains the print job until the printer is ready, and the printer itself (known in Microsoft parlance as the "Print Device").

Everything begins with the application that needs to print. For example, Veronica has written a memo with Microsoft Word and decides to print her document. She clicks the Print button, which starts the print process by sending a generic print request to the print spooler, as illustrated in Figure 15–2.

The print request does not go directly to the spooler. First, the print request runs through the GDI, as illustrated in Figure 15–3. The GDI is a group of programs that create "Print Jobs." The beauty of Windows printing is that programs that send print jobs do not care about things

Figure 15–3
GDI is the first step.

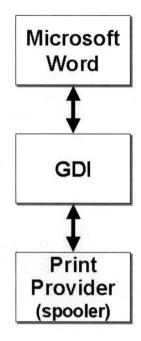

such as printer resolution, color depth, and the thousands of other items that plagued applications in other operating systems. In Windows, the GDI takes care of all of the details for the application, creating a print job that is specific to a certain type of printer.

Microsoft uses the terms "Printer" and "Printer Device" to designate specific aspects of the print process. These terms are not synonymous. The *printer* is the software necessary for controlling a physical *printing device*. Several different hardware devices can be considered print devices. In the world of Windows printing, for example, a fax device is just another type of print device. Instead of outputting the print job to paper, the print job goes to the fax machine. Laser printers, inkjet printers, dot-matrix printers, and fax machines are all known as print devices. The relationship between printers and print devices is usually one-to-one. In other words, for each printer there is one print device. While this case is the most common, this situation is not the only one. For example, you might have a printer—say a Hewlett-Packard LaserJet—which has the capacity to print in both its native PCL format and in Postscript. Most of the time, the office uses the standard PCL language. On occasion, however, Bob, the resident artist, needs to use the Postscript language. To enable users to choose between these functions, an administrator needs to create two printers, both pointing to the same print device. Figure 15–4 shows a single print device being serviced by two printers.

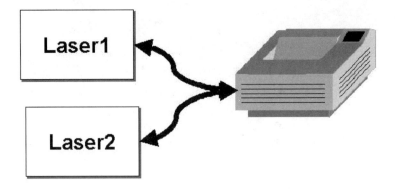

Figure 15–4
Some single print devices can handle both PCL and Postscript printers.

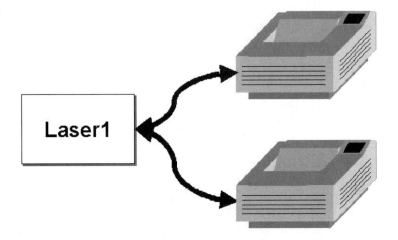

Figure 15–5
One printer can send jobs to many print devices.

Windows NT can also support one printer connected to multiple print devices. This term is known as "Printer Pooling" and is usually done in an environment where lots of printing happens. One printer connects to a number of identical print devices. As print jobs come to the printer, printer pooling determines which print device is inactive and sends the print job to that print device. Figure 15–5 shows a single printer servicing two print devices.

NOTE: *The concept of print pooling requires identical print devices in the print pool. A single printer driver must be able to run all the print devices.*

Conceptually, the Windows NT printing process is quite simple. Due to its flexibility and power, however, the actual installation, configuration, and troubleshooting of Windows NT printing can challenge nearly any administrator. Let's examine the process of installing and configuring a printer within a stand-alone environment.

Stand-Alone Printing

If you are familiar with printers in Windows 95 and Windows 98, the process of working within Windows NT on a stand-alone system will seem extremely similar. The primary difference is that in Windows NT, the person installing the printer must have an account with the right to install a printer on that system. The two default groups in Windows NT that have this right are Administrators and Power Users. After logging on to the systems with the proper account, the first step in installing a printer is the "Add Printer" Wizard in the "My Computer/Printers" folder, as shown in Figure 15–6.

The first screen of the Add Printer Wizard (Figure 15–7) asks whether you want to install the printer locally on the machine or attach to a printer already created on another machine in the network. For a stand-alone system, select the "My Computer" radio button.

After selecting the My Computer option, Windows NT needs to know how the printer or print device attaches to the computer. Most printers attach via the computer's parallel ports—often referred to as LPT ports. To let Windows NT know how the printer attaches to the system, simply click the appropriate checkbox, as shown in Figure 15–8.

By default, Windows NT installs three LPT ports, four COM (serial) ports, and a File port for printing directly to a file. Many years ago, printing to serial ports was common. Due to their low speed (compared to parallel ports), almost no one uses a serial port for printing today. Microsoft's motive for giving serial port options was not for backward compatibility with ancient printers (although the equipment is perfectly capable of doing so), but rather to support print devices other than paper printers. In particular, fax devices use serial ports.

Figure 15–6
Add Printer Wizard

Figure 15–7
Local or remote printer?

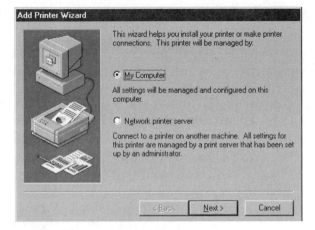

Figure 15–8
So many ports, so little time.

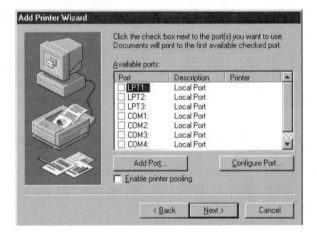

NOTE: *A serial or parallel port is not a COM or an LPT port. The serial or parallel port is the physical attachment, which is the connector in the back that you can hold in your hand. The COM or LPT port is really nothing more than an I/O Address and an Interrupt Request (IRQ) that is preassigned to that parallel device. LPT1, for example, is actually I/O Address 378/IRQ 7, while COM1 is I/O Address 3F8/IRQ 4. The assignments for I/O Addresses and IRQs for LPT and COM ports were developed a long time ago by IBM and are still respected today. You can more easily tell someone to click a checkbox that says "LPT1" or "COM1" than to have someone select a confusing I/O Address and IRQ combination.*

Printer Pooling

To set up printer pooling on a stand-alone machine, open the Printers folder just as you did previously, and add a local printer. When Windows NT asks for port information, make sure to select "Enable printer pooling." The checkboxes used for selecting ports act like radio buttons by default. If LPT1 is selected, clicking LPT2 will check the LPT2 port and will simultaneously remove the checkbox from the LPT1 port. This action makes perfectly good sense, because for most systems, one printer will attach to only one port. With printer pooling enabled, however, you can select multiple ports for print devices.

Print pools are not perfect. Once a print job goes to a particular print device, the job will stay with that device. This feature is a problem only if one print device fails. If one printer in a print pool runs out of toner, for example, the print job will wait for the printer to come back online. No method exists to take a print job from one print device and send that job to another print device.

In print pooling, the printer decides which print device gets a particular print job. Windows NT does not provide any controls that enable the separate print devices to take certain print jobs. Simply put, you can never tell which device in a print pool is going to be printing a print job. As a result, you should have all print devices in a print pool physically close to each other, so that users can easily find their printouts.

After selecting a port for your stand-alone printer or setting up multiple ports for a printer pool, click the "Next" button to continue. Windows NT prompts you for the necessary print drivers.

Print Drivers

Windows NT comes "out of the box" with the drivers for hundreds of printers. The left half of the screen lists the manufacturer names, and the right half shows the different models for the selected manufacturer. Figure 15–9 shows a Hewlett-Packard LaserJet 5 selected. If the driver for the printer being installed is not listed on this screen, click the "Have Disk" button and the Print Wizard will then prompt for a location for the print drivers. By default, the Have Disk will look on the A:\ drive for the print drivers. While most print drivers do come on floppy disks, you will commonly find them on a CD-ROM, a local hard drive, or on another machine in a network. "Have Disk" includes a standard "Browse" button that enables you

Figure 15–9

Selecting the proper
printer driver

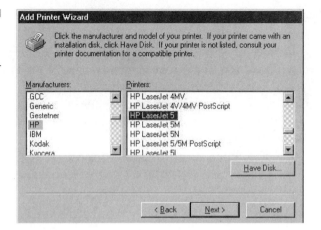

to locate the printer drivers on any storage device. Although Windows NT does come with many print drivers, you really should use the supplied print drivers that come with the printer—assuming that the printer came with Windows NT print drivers and that the print drivers are more recent than August 9, 1996 (the date of the Windows NT 4.0 drivers).

Once the print drivers are installed, the Wizard prompts you for a "friendly name" for the printer. This name will show when referring to the printer in applications. Keep the name to 31 characters or fewer. Longer names can cause some programs to roll over and die. The default friendly name is based on the driver name, as shown in Figure 15–10. While this default name is usually acceptable in a stand-alone environment, the default name can cause trouble in networked situations (see the Network Printing section).

This same window gives you the option to make the printer the default. Select "Yes" if you want all applications to use this printer by default. Applications can use other print devices by selecting an alternative device at the time of printing.

Once you have set the friendly name, the Print Wizard asks a few questions about sharing. The default option for sharing is "Not Shared," as shown in Figure 15–11. We will return to this screen in the Network Printing section to clarify sharing options.

The last screen prompts for printing a test page. While Windows NT does not require you to print a test page, this option gives you an easy and handy way to verify that the newly installed printer is working properly. The printer then installs a few more support files, and the new printer now appears in the Printers folder, as shown in Figure 15–12.

Figure 15–10
The friendly name
defaults to the driver
name.

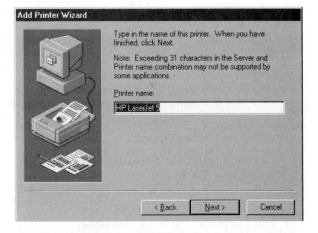

Figure 15–11
Printers, by default,
are not shared.

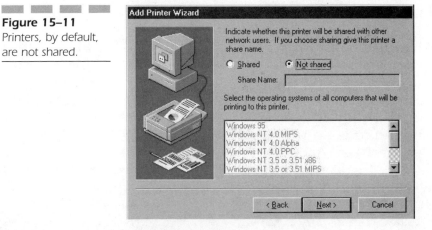

Figure 15–12
Success

Network Printing

Networked printers give organizations much more bang for their buck. Although Windows NT provides all the tools for stand-alone printers—and printers have dropped dramatically in cost—the day has not yet come when Julia, Ralph, and Veronica can each cost-effectively have their own printers. Networked printers, in contrast, enable many users to share the same print device. Microsoft designed Windows NT from the ground-up for printing in a network environment. Let's look at the many ways a printer can physically connect to a network and then repeat the process of installing a printer—this time concentrating on creating a printer accessible to many other PCs on the network.

The Print Server Model

The cornerstone of Windows NT printing is the concept of the "Print Server." The *print server* machine actually runs the printer. Remember that a printer in Windows NT is the software, not the physical printer. The print serving process is quite flexible. Any Windows NT machine on the network can be a print server. In small networks, the PDC often has the duty of acting as the print server. As the network grows, administrators often dedicate one machine as the print server, giving that machine nothing to do other than take care of print jobs. In many cases, the print server will also have the printer physically installed. All other PCs access that print server for printing, as shown in Figure 15–13.

Today, printers are commonly attached directly to the network as opposed to being attached to the LPT port of a print server. This task is accomplished in two ways. First, a hardware network print server is attached to the network. These hardware print servers are usually little more than a small box with a network connection and an LPT and/or a serial port. Figure 15–14 shows a typical network printing device.

Printers, in particular laser printers, can also be equipped with a network card. The most famous of all these is the Hewlett-Packard Jet Direct card. This card is inserted into a LaserJet, enabling the printer to become a network device. Figure 15–15 shows a classic network printer configuration. Keep in mind that even though the network printer is directly connected to the network, Windows NT still needs a PC to act as the print server.

Windows NT enables multiple print servers. You will commonly have multiple print servers in a network environment, with each print server

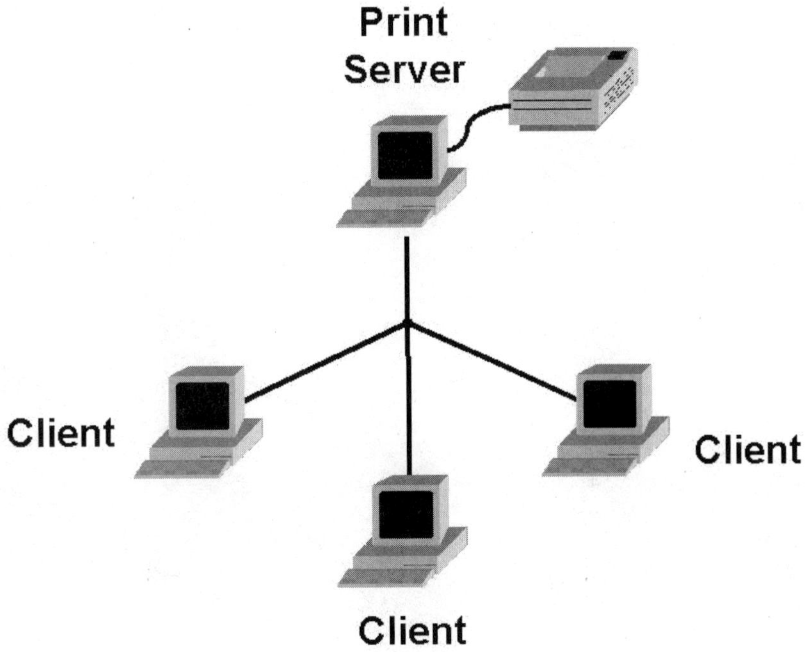

Figure 15–13
You wanna print?
You gotta talk to me.

**Print
Server**

Client

Client

Client

Figure 15–14
Network printing
device

handling the needs for a particular group, location, or function within the network infrastructure, as described in Figure 15–16.

Making a PC a print server requires little more that simply installing and sharing a printer. Let's look at this process by installing some printers with the explicit goal of sharing them in a network environment. We can begin with the classic scenario of a printer hooked directly to the server.

NOTE: *Both Windows NT Workstation and Windows NT Server systems can act equally well as print servers. Windows NT Workstation has one limitation not shared by Windows NT Server, however: Windows NT Workstation can only accept 10 simultaneous network connections. If more than 10 print jobs are sent to a Windows NT Workstation print server, the system will cause the 11th print job to fail. When anticipating more than 10 systems printing at a time, use Windows NT Server.*

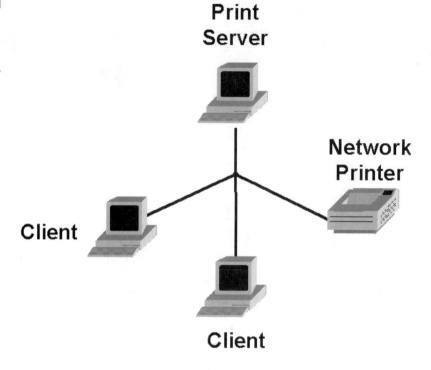

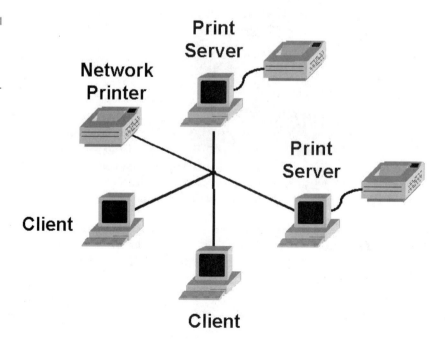

Installing a Printer for Networks

The process of installing a printer directly connected to the PC for network use is similar to the process of installing a stand-alone printer. Let's repeat the HP LaserJet example used in the stand-alone example. The first four screens are identical. Note that you will still install to My Computer. The Network Print Server option is only to install a printer to connect to a printer on another machine.

The big change takes place in the name of the print device and the sharing options. In a network, the naming of the print device becomes critical. The name of the print device should include clear information about at least one of the following items: the printer's location, who the printer is designed to serve, and what type of printing the job performs. If each floor of a network has one printer, the printer's name should reflect its floor, such as "Laser 1st" or "Printer 3." If the printers in the network are separated to serve separate groups, some good names might be "Accounting Laser" or "Sales 2" (Sales has more than one printer). If there are many types of printers—color inkjet, low-end and high-end lasers, maybe a plotter or two —the printer name should reflect those capabilities. A name such as "Epson Stylus" may mean something to the person installing the printer but will mean little to the person who wishes to use that printer. A better name might be something such as, "Color Inkjet" to reflect its capabilities. Like a shared folder, you can use a dollar sign ($) on the end of a share name to make a hidden share for the printer. If the printer has a hidden share, the user will have to know the name of the printer to connect to that printer. This action is a handy way to keep undesired users from accessing a shared printer—unless the user knows the share name.

The one danger with descriptive network printer naming is the 31-character name limit. The limit applies not just to the name of the printer but also includes the name of the print server. If the *combined* print server and printer name exceeds 31 characters, the printer will not be visible on the network. Make sure that the entire UNC name of \\(**Print Server Name**)\\(**Shared Printer Name**)—including the slashes—does not exceed 31 characters.

The actual sharing of the printer takes place in the sharing window. Figure 15–17 shows a sharing window being configured for sharing. The Shared As radio button has been pressed, activating the sharing options. Note that its name reflects the printer's function—Accounting Laser. If this network were composed completely of Intel-based, Windows NT 4.0 PCs, the job of installing a shareable printer would be complete. In the real world, however, we need to understand one more big piece of the printing puzzle: printer drivers.

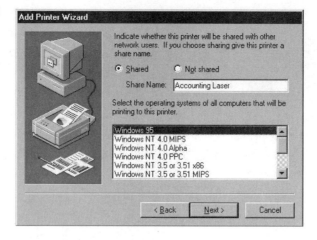

Drivers, Drivers, Drivers

When a Windows NT machine tries to access a remote printer, the print server verifies whether the PC trying to access the printer has the proper print drivers. If the printer does not, the print server will automatically send to that PC the proper drivers for the printer. This handy function means no more manual printer updates for Windows NT machines. A Windows NT print server can also be designed to provide the same function for Windows 95, Windows 98, Windows NT 3.5/3.51 (x86, Alpha, PPC, and MIPS processors), and Windows NT 4.0 (Alpha, PPC, and MIPS processors) machines. To provide this "automatic driver download" function, the print server needs to be able to supply the drivers for those types of systems. The lower part of the sharing window enables you to install the drivers for those operating systems, so that when they try to access the printer, the drivers will automatically install. You can select as many of the drivers as necessary. The Wizard then prompts you for your installation disks/CD-ROM to copy the drivers. Make sure to have these items handy before you choose to install the drivers for other operating systems.

Configuring an Installed Printer

Both stand-alone and network printers have a broad selection of configuration options. Opening the Printers folder, right-clicking the desired printer and selecting Properties enables access to all configuration options.

This screen has six tabs: General, Ports, Scheduling, Sharing, Security, and Device Settings. Figure 15–18 shows the default General tab selected.

General Tab

The General Tab enables access to some of the more commonly changed settings. The Command and Location fields are self-explanatory. They provide for special commentary and location information that may be helpful for users and support personnel. The Print Driver shows the print driver used by the printer. You can change the printer driver from here, if necessary.

The three buttons at the bottom of the General tab—Separator Page, Print Processor, and Print Test Page—provide three totally different functions. The Separator Page button enables each print job to be separated by a separator page. If many print jobs come out of the printer, separator pages can be a life-saver for users trying to find their printouts. Separator Pages are text files with the extension SEP that must be designed for the type of printer being used. Windows NT provides three default separator pages: **PCL.SEP** for the Hewlett-Packard PCL language printers; **SYSPRINT.SEP**, which is compatible with Postscript printers; and **PSCRIPT.SEP**. **PSCRIPT.SEP** is not really a separator page, because **PSCRIPT.SEP** only switches the printer to its Postscript mode. The Print Processor button enables Windows NT to support

Figure 15–18
General tab

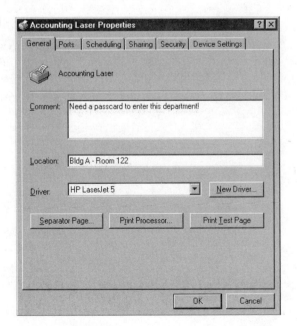

print jobs from other operating systems, such as Macintosh or UNIX. The defaults of "winprint" for the Print Processor and "RAW" for the Default Datatype, shown in Figure 15–19, are the most common. The last button, Print Test Page, is handy for answering those "Is the printer working?" questions—and will generate a test page that includes a small Windows graphic and a listing of the printer drivers used by the printer.

Ports Tab

The Ports tab is identical to the Ports settings when a printer is being installed. Here again, you can set the port to which the printer is physically connected, configure and add ports, and establish printer pooling. We will look at this screen in more detail when we discuss connecting to a remote printer later in this chapter.

Scheduling Tab

The Scheduling tab sets the availability of the printer, sets the printer's priority, and determines spooler settings (Figure 15–20). Set the availability of the printer by giving a stop and start time. Any print jobs sent to a printer at an unavailable time will be spooled until the printer available start time is reached. This option is nice for keeping large print jobs from dominating printers used during the day.

The Priority slider bar is used when there is more than one printer assigned to a print device. The Engineering LaserJet can handle both PCL and Postscript printing. To take advantage of both functions, Veronica, the administrator, installs two printers: one with PCL drivers and another with Postscript. While the engineers rarely use the Postscript drivers, their doc-

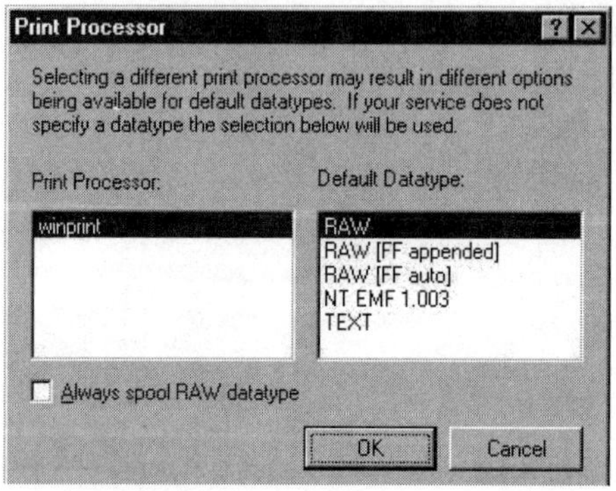

Figure 15–19
Print Processor
defaults

Print Processor	? X

Selecting a different print processor may result in different options being available for default datatypes. If your service does not specify a datatype the selection below will be used.

Print Processor: Default Datatype:

winprint	RAW
	RAW [FF appended]
	RAW [FF auto]
	NT EMF 1.003
	TEXT

☐ Always spool RAW datatype

[OK]   [Cancel]

Figure 15–20
Scheduling tab

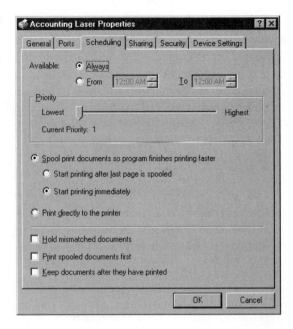

uments need to be printed quickly when they do use those drivers. By adjusting the print priority to a number larger than one, Veronica ensures that any Postscript print jobs will be handled before the PCL print jobs.

Priorities are handy in many other ways. Another trick is to give one print device two printers, and then set one printer with a high priority and another with a low priority. Let users who need high priorities access the high-priority printer, and let everyone else use the lower-priority printer to ensure that the "high-priority" users are not waiting for their printouts.

In most printing scenarios, the print job is spooled to the hard drive and is then sent to the printer. Print spooling can be turned off by clicking the "Print directly to the printer" radio button—usually not a good idea, because the computer will put users in "hourglass land" until the printer is ready to print. The default of "Spool print documents so program finishes printing faster" has two options. The spooler can store the entire print job before sending the job to the printer, or the spooler can begin immediately sending the print job to the printer before the entire print job is spooled ("Start printing immediately"). The initial reaction might be to accept the default "Start printing immediately," and that is usually the fastest option. A few situations exist, though, where it would be better to wait until the job is spooled—especially with a large print job. Imagine trying to print 300 pages, or at least the first 150 out of 300 pages, only to discover an error or print failure. By waiting until the entire print job is spooled, you can be sure that the application has handled the job correctly. Then, you can send the known good job to the printer, giving the user a much higher probability of success. Just make sure that the system has plenty of hard drive space to store that large job. A good rule of thumb is to have three to four times the size of the files being printed in available hard drive space.

The three checkboxes on the bottom of the Scheduling tab are useful in some situations. The "Hold mismatched documents" option helps, in heavy printing situations, to prevent a print job from coming out of the printer in pieces. "Print spooled documents first" gives all spooled documents priority over non-spooled print jobs. The last option, "Keep documents after they have printed," is rather interesting. After a print job is printed, the spooled job is normally deleted. By selecting this option, the job will be kept in the spooler. If the job needs to be printed again, the job will be printed quickly. You do not even need to be in the application. This feature is often used in organizations that constantly generate standard forms, information sheets, etc. This feature is handy when printing to fax devices, as fax jobs seem to take a bit longer than most print jobs. The down side is that "Keep documents after the have printed" is a hard drive space-eating monster. Print jobs tend to be big, and storing just a few will take a significant amount of drive space. Use this feature with care, and always keep a eye on remaining hard drive space.

Sharing Tab

Like the Ports tab, the Sharing Tab is identical to the sharing options in the Install Printer Wizard. This tab is handy for stopping the share on a printer that is temporarily being taken offline for maintenance or repair. The printer remembers all of its share information when sharing is turned back on after the maintenance or repair. More auto-loading drivers can also be installed for any new systems coming online to the network that would need them.

Security Tab

Users and Groups need permissions to access printers, just as they need permissions to access folders and files. All of the standard rules of sharing exist with printers, except that the permissions themselves are different. Printers have four levels of permissions:

1. No Access

2. Print

3. Manage Documents

4. Full Control

Unfortunately, these permissions are not totally descriptive of the functions of printing. Sure, common sense tells you that the "Print" permission will let the user print, and "Full Control" will probably let the user do anything he or she wants—including deleting the printer. But what about all those little things users like to do? What if a user wants to abort his or her print job? What if the user wants to pause someone else's print job? Table 15–1 is useful for determining which permissions are necessary to perform those functions.

The Security tab enables you to set the permissions for the printer. In Figure 15–21, which shows the printer permissions being configured, note the high degree of similarity to the permissions for any other resource. Note that the administrator in this case created a Local group called "Printer Users." This task follows the Windows NT Mantra of, "Users go into global groups, which go into local groups, which get rights and permissions." You should always create a local group for the printer, because

Table 15–1

Functions versus permissions for printers

Function	No Access	Print	Manage Documents	Full Control
Print documents	No	Yes	Yes	Yes
Purge, Pause, Restart their own documents	No	Yes	Yes	Yes
Purge, Pause, Restart other user's documents	No	No	Yes	Yes
Purge, Pause, Restart all document print settings	No	No	Yes	Yes
Change Permissions	No	No	Yes	Yes
Share a Printer	No	No	No	Yes
Change Printer Properties	No	No	No	Yes
Delete a Printer	No	No	No	Yes

Figure 15–21
Printer Permissions
look mighty familiar.

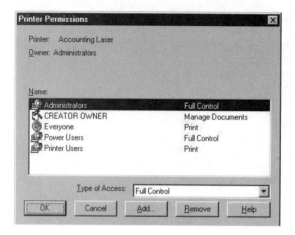

administration will be easier. Sadly, many administrators skip the creation of the local group, because by default all users have access to a printer. In addition, some of the built-in local groups have special default permissions. Administrators and Power Users, for example, are given Full Control of the printer by default. Also, the Creator Owner special user account has the Manage Documents permission by default.

If you can raise your right hand and guarantee that everyone will always have access to the printer, skipping the creation of the local group is probably acceptable. But consider the following scenario. Assume that a printer has given the Print permission to a global group called Accounting, Manage Documents permission to a global group called Managers, and Full Control permission to a global group called Techs. The print device is removed and replaced with a far better print device. The Administrator (or equivalent) will then have to rebuild all of these permissions—and heaven forbid that any other permissions need to be changed. The administration of the global groups is too much trouble. Why not just make a local group and add the global groups to the local group? If a print device needs to be replaced, the only permission that needs to be added is the one local group you created—which is much easier.

Device Settings

The Device Settings tab is specific to the type of print device being used and will vary tremendously. Figure 15–22 shows the settings for the Hewlett-Packard LaserJet 5. Administrators can use this area to set printer defaults,

Figure 15–22
Device Settings tab

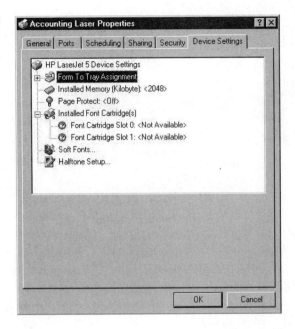

such as paper trays, print quality, and memory usage. Sadly, many administrators forget about the Device Settings tab for printers. That is too bad—and this forgetfulness is probably due to the fact that most applications enable the user to change defaults at run time. One of the best tricks is to reduce the default resolution to speed up printing. If the users need to print in higher-quality, let them change the defaults. Depending on the printer, reducing the default resolution will greatly decrease printer time and will definitely lengthen the life of toner or ink cartridges.

With the printer installed and carefully tested, and with shares and permissions configured, the next step is to go to the other PCs in the network and have them access the printer. Accessing a printer on another machine requires installation of a "remote" printer.

NOTE: *Be comfortable with the concept of "Local" and "Remote" printers. A "Local" printer is installed on the machine where the user is physically located. A "Remote" printer is physically attached to the network someplace other than at the machine where the user is sitting.*

Installing Remote Printers

Windows NT makes the process of printing to remote printers extremely easy. Many ways exist to access a remote printer, depending on the OS of the PC accessing the remote printer and the applications that are in use by the system. If the system is another Windows NT 4.0 system, this process is almost trivial. If the system is Windows NT 4.0 non-Intel, Windows NT 3.51 (Intel or non-Intel), or Windows 95 or Windows 98, the process is also trivial—assuming that drivers have been installed on the print server for those systems. If the accessing system is Windows 3.X, print drivers will have to be installed on the system first before the printer can be accessed. Last, if the system is a DOS system (gasp), the printer will have to be "redirected" to an LPT port. Let's look at some examples of remote printer installation to appreciate how easy—and how hard—it can be to access a remote Windows NT printer. All of the following examples assume that the print server holds print drivers for all operating systems that can take advantage of automatic driver installation.

Installing a Remote Printer on Windows NT 4.0

Users can access remote printers in three different ways. The most common method to access a remote printer from a Windows NT machine is to install the printer. Once again, use the Add Printer Wizard to accomplish this task. In fact, the process of installing a remote printer is much simpler than having to install a local printer, because the user installing the remote printer should not have to deal with options such as share name, permissions, ports, etc. As Figure 15–23 shows, the user simply clicks the Network Print Server radio button to tell the Wizard to look around the network for an already installed printer.

The Wizard will query the network and show a listing of all available printers, as illustrated in Figure 15–24. The printer must be shared for the printer to appear on this list. Figure 15–24 shows a LaserJet 5 installed on the NOTES01 machine.

The system automatically installs the necessary drivers and displays the new printer in the Printer folder, as shown in Figure 15–25. This process is way too easy. If the logged-on user has the proper permissions, he or she can right-click the printer's icon and select Properties, enabling him or her to make configuration settings as though sitting at the local machine.

Figure 15–23
Just click, and the
Wizard will fly.

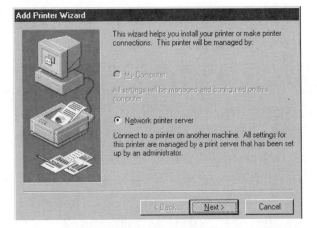

Figure 15–24
Look. The Wiz found
a LaserJet 5.

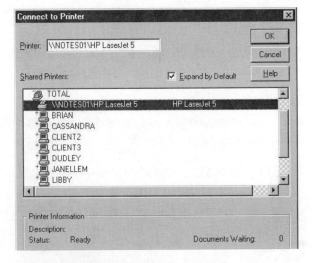

Figure 15–25
Success again

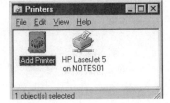

Another way to install a remote printer in Windows NT is to install the
printer locally, then redirect the port. This is accomplished by selecting the
printer's Properties ... Ports ... Add Port ... Local Port, as displayed in Figure 15–26, and typing in the UNC name for the shared printer. While this

Figure 15–26
Just type a UNC
name to install a
remote printer.

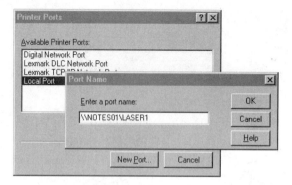

Figure 15–26
Just type a UNC
name to install a
remote printer.

Figure 15–27
Point and Print in
action

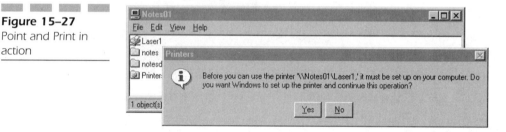

method is not a common way to add a printer, it is an extremely handy way to take a printer offline temporarily without completely disrupting the users. The domain ACCOUNTING does a lot of printing. One system, Server1, has an HP LaserJet 5N printer. The printer is installed on LPT1 and is shared as PrinterA. To keep up with demand, and to reduce walk time for users, administrators install another system, Server2. Server2 also has an HP LaserJet 5N printer. The LaserJet is on LPT1 and is shared as PrinterB. Half of the users print to Server1 and half print to Server2. Suddenly, Printer A breaks and needs to go offline for a few days to get serviced. An administrator could go to Server1 and from the Ports tab, redirect all print jobs sent to PrinterA to PrinterB. All print jobs that used to go to PrinterA now redirect to PrinterB—without the need to make any changes to the user machines.

The last common method of accessing a printer is via the Network Neighborhood. A shared, but uninstalled, printer is visible. When the user clicks the printer, the screen in Figure 15–27 appears. If the user clicks Yes, the printer installs automatically. Microsoft calls this capacity "Point and Print." You can get the same results simply by dragging a file to be printed onto a share name of a network printer.

Windows 95 and 98

The process of accessing a remote Windows NT printer from a Windows 95 and 98 machine is very similar to the process of accessing a Windows NT printer from another Windows NT machine. All of the above methods of attaching a printer, also work in Windows 95 and 98, including the Add New Printer Wizard, automatic downloading of drivers (assuming that the drivers are pre-installed on the print server), the redirection of a printer port, and the Network Neighborhood methods. The big difference is in the properties for the printer after it is installed. A Windows 95 and 98 machine has a completely different Properties window and does not enable the user to change most of the configurations that could be achieved on a Windows NT machine. Security features, for example, only exist on the Windows NT side and can only be configured on the Windows NT machines. Windows NT gives administrators the capacity to change permissions on a remote printer, just like they would with a local printer. 95 and 98 gives no capacity whatsoever to set permissions locally or change permissions remotely. Compare Figure 15–28 with Figure 15–29 to appreciate the differences.

Figure 15–28
Windows NT Security tab

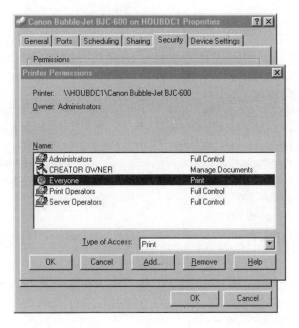

Figure 15–29
Windows 95 and 98
—no security here

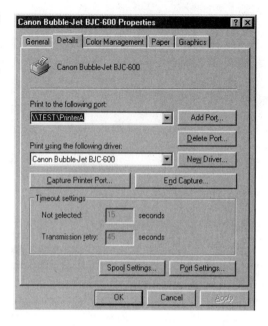

Windows 3.X

Windows 3.X has very few of the automatic features of printing that are shared by Windows NT and Windows 95 and 98. A Windows 3.X machine must first install the print drivers locally for the remote printer. After installing the printer, the user must redirect—by typing in its UNC name —the printer to the Windows NT print server.

Keep in mind that both Windows 3.X and Windows NT 3.X use the old Windows Print Manager. The 16-bit Print Manager, although roughly equivalent to the spooler settings in today's 95/98/NT4 printers, had far fewer functions. To keep a printer shared on the network, for example, Print Manager had to run continuously. This drained precious resources needed by applications.

DOS Clients

Setting up a DOS client to print remotely in Windows NT requires resolution of two separate issues. First, the DOS machine must have the capacity to attach to a remote Windows NT printer. Second, DOS applications running under Windows NT or Windows 95 and 98 must be able to access a shared Windows NT printer. Because DOS provided little support for printers, most DOS applications dealt directly with the printers. Word and WordPerfect, for example, had different internal drivers for accessing a Panasonic dot-matrix printer. To work in Windows NT, DOS applications usually need a defined port, usually an LPT port, and must use their own printer drivers. To attach a true DOS machine to a Windows NT printer, first load DOS-based networking software, such as Microsoft's Network Client for DOS or LAN Manager. These programs provide the necessary software to enable a DOS machine to access any Microsoft Windows network, but will not enable the DOS system to provide any sharing functions. The DOS program can then "Map" network printers using menus or the NET USE command. An example of mapping a network drive would look something like this:

```
NET USE LPT3: \\NOTES01\LASER4
```

Then, it is up to the DOS applications to output to the mapped LPT port.

The slow death of true DOS machines, combined with the excellent support for DOS applications within Windows 95 and 98 and Windows NT, has made the goal of having a true DOS machine accessing a remote Windows NT printer a rare situation. Far more common is to have a DOS application—running on a Windows NT system—that needs to access a remote printer. Windows NT uses UNC names to access network resources, but DOS applications cannot support a UNC directed printer—they need LPT ports. DOS applications running under Windows NT access a remote printer identically to the way a DOS machine accesses a remote printer: via the NET USE command. Windows NT (and 95 and 98) has complete support for all of the NET commands first used by Microsoft's LAN Manager (Microsoft's first networking program). A DOS application can use a printer shared on a Windows NT network by running the NET USE command to map the proper port.

NOTE: *Understanding the NET commands is not stressed on the Windows NT exams, but is something that you should take the time to understand. These commands are often helpful in diagnosing network problems. Go to a command prompt and type* **NET** */?* *to get help on the many powerful tools of the net command.*

Printing Protocols

The concept of protocols is a non-issue in most situations involving Windows NT printing. When a print device is directly attached to a Windows NT machine, it will use the same protocol used by all of the other network traffic. Some situations require special protocols. Many manufacturers of network printing devices may use a special printing protocol. The most common example of this is HP Jetdirect network printer cards. These devices invariably call for the DLC (*Data Link Control*) protocol. If one of these types of devices is installed on the printer attached to the network, every machine that wants to access that print device must have the DLC protocol installed. Accessing printers controlled by other operating systems, in particular Novell NetWare and Macintosh machines, also require their native protocols—NWLink (IPX/SPX) and AppleTalk, respectively. Connecting to NetWare and Macintosh printers requires adding special services. For NetWare, the service is called Gateway Services for NetWare and for Macintosh it is called Services for Macintosh. These services are required to access printers on these systems and will also install the required protocols. Make sure that you know the required protocols for the different types of systems. See Chapter 12, "Windows NT and Novell," for more information about Gateway Services for NetWare; and see Chapter 11, "Windows NT Server Clients," for information about Macintosh support in Windows NT.

Printing in TCP/IP

For the most part, Windows NT does not give a hoot about protocols. The NetBIOS functions of Windows NT hide the majority of the detailed protocol issues that drove network administrators crazy in the past. In printing, for example, it does not matter whether the network is using NetBEUI or TCP/IP—all of the steps of sharing and accessing a printer are identical. NetBIOS shields the administrator and the user from the many details of the protocol. While this makes networking in Windows NT a real breeze, it can also sometimes create great confusion for Windows NT administrators who are not clear about some of the "lower level" aspects of protocols. The ultimate example of this situation is TCP/IP. In a pure Windows NT environment, TCP/IP is just another protocol and is invisible to the installation and configuration of printers. What many administrators forget, however, is that TCP/IP has both features in Windows NT and its own non-

OS specific functions to share printers and to access other machines' shared printers. Let's take a moment to understand these functions and then see how they can be configured for Windows NT.

Remember that TCP/IP defines more than just how the lower-end network functions, such as IP addresses, gateways, DNS, etc. TCP/IP also defines a number of rules for applications. For example, if you want to send and receive e-mail, you must make programs that use the set of rules known as SMTP. If you want to look at or let people look at Web pages, you must create programs based on the set of rules known collectively as HTTP. These rules, better known as application protocols, run on top of the TCP/IP protocols, as illustrated in Figure 15–30. These applications rely on specific functions provided by the TCP/IP suite of protocols, without regard to the OS being used—Windows NT, UNIX, Windows 95, etc.

TCP/IP has a number of special application protocols that are designed to deal with printing. The first application protocol, called LPR, handles all printing functions in TCP/IP. The LPD is the server function and must be running on the machine that controls the print device. The LPR is the program used to send print jobs to a machine running LPD. In the UNIX world, both of these protocols manifest themselves as executable files. There is also a third executable called LPQ that is used to determine the current state of a printer queue running under LPD.

Figure 15–30
TCP/IP supports many application protocols.

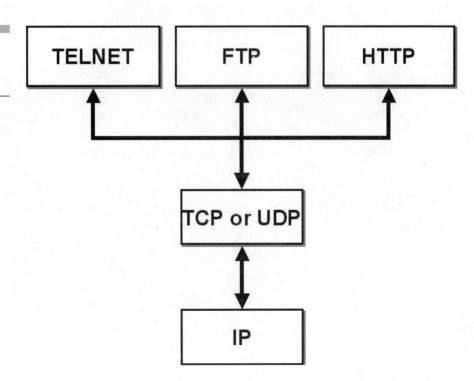

Windows NT supports the use of LPR, LPD, and LPQ under the Windows NT environment to enable UNIX machines to access Windows NT printers and to enable Windows NT machines to access printers shared by UNIX boxes using LPD. It is important to note that not all versions of UNIX support LPD/LPR and may not be compatible with Windows NT for printing.

NOTE: *You do not need to use LPD/LPR in a pure Windows environment. The NetBIOS features of Windows NT know how to talk to TCP/IP and can handle printing functions. You only need LPD/LPR to work with UNIX systems.*

To set up LPD/LPR sharing, first install the Microsoft TCP/IP Printing service, as shown in Figure 15–31. Windows NT does not install this service by default. The Microsoft TCP/IP Printing service installs all of the files necessary for LPD, LPR and LPQ functionality. Microsoft TCP/IP Printing must be installed on every machine that wants to share an LPD printer or to access a shared LPD printer with LPR. The system must first have TCP/IP protocol installed before the TCP/IP Printing service can be installed.

Figure 15–31
Install TCP/IP Printing service before LPD/LPR.

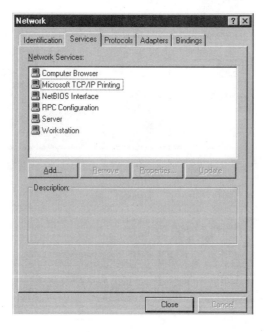

NOTE: *To all of you UNIX people: There is no LPD executable file. To share printers under LPD, just start the TCP/IP printing service. LPR and LPQ are executable files. To access (LPR) or to query (LPQ) shared LPD printers, use the command prompt.*

Make sure to start the TCP/IP Printing service by running the Services applet in the Control Panel. Set the service's Startup Type to Automatic, as shown in Figure 15–32, to make sure it starts every time the system is started.

Do not bother starting the TCP/IP Printing service on machines that will only access other printers. The only reason this service was installed on those machines was to get the required files needed to access those remote printers.

After the Microsoft TCP/IP Printing service is installed and started, the PC can then accept any LPR calls from any PC. The process of getting a system to print to a remote machine running LPD is a little more complicated. In its most basic format, use the LPR program to print to an LPD system. The LPR program is designed to print only text files, but can print pre-formatted PRN files, assuming that they are in a format that the printer can understand. In order to use LPR, the user must know the IP address of the LPD system, the shared printer name, and the local file they wish to print. If a user wants to print a file called **JOB.TXT** to a printer called LASER1 on a machine with the IP address of 192.168.42.10, the command would be:

```
LPR -S 192.168.42.10 -P LASER1 JOB.TXT
```

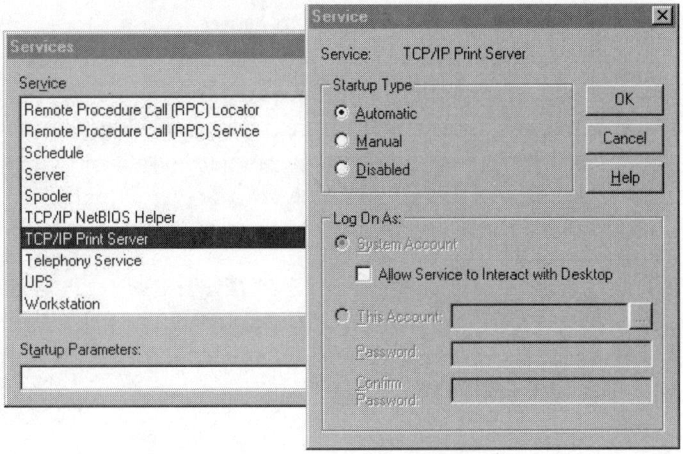

Figure 15–32
Set the service's
Startup Type to
Automatic.

The -S option gives the IP address of the LPR printer. The -P option sets the name of the printer (or in the case of UNIX systems, the print queue). The last option is the name of the file to print—you can use paths if needed. The LPR command does not return any information if the print job is successful.

The LPQ program lets you query the status of a remote printer. Like the LPR program, it is run from the C: prompt. To query the earlier example, the LPQ command would be run as follows:

```
LPQ -S 192.168.42.10 -P LASER1
```

This command would return the following text:

```
Windows NT LPD Server
                                        Printer laser4

Owner           Status              Jobname             Job-Id
        Size    Pages     Priority
_____
admin (192. Waiting    c:\boot.ini                 4
        0       0         1
```

Note that in this case, LPQ shows a waiting print job. This can of course vary greatly depending on the status of the printer queue that is being queried.

While the manual use of LPR to print to an LPD printer works, it is hardly practical. The far more common use would be to install a printer on a Windows NT machine that redirects its output to an LPD device. Remember that the LPD printer is not a Windows NT printer. An LPD device does not have drivers or any security, and is not visible to the network. Installing a printer to redirect to an LPD system takes care of all of these problems. Users printing to a Windows NT printer that redirects to an LPD system get all of the benefits associated with all Windows NT printers, plus the printer does not have to be installed on the system that has the LPD service. This is particularly handy for enabling Windows NT users to access a UNIX box with an LPD printer.

NOTE: *Be careful with Microsoft's TCP/IP Printing. There are no security functions included with this service. If a system has the TCP/IP Printing service running, any computer anywhere will be able to print to any printer on that machine—even if the printer is not shared.*

The process of installing a Windows NT printer and associating it with an LPD printer is roughly similar to the installation of any other printer. Install the printer as if it were a local printer and then redirect the printing to an LPR port. Assume that an HP LaserJet 4 is installed on a UNIX box, and you would like to make that printer available to all users on the Windows NT domain. Designate a Windows NT machine as the print server, and install the Microsoft TCP/IP Printing service. Then, install a LaserJet 4 on the print server as a local machine. After installing the printer, access the Properties . . . Ports for the printer, select Add Port, and click LPR Port, as shown in Figure 15–33. If LPR Port is not an available option, the Microsoft TCP/IP Printing service is not installed. After selecting the LPR Port, click Add Port and enter the IP address and the printer name, as shown in Figure 15–34.

Figure 15–33
I will take LPR Ports for $200, please.

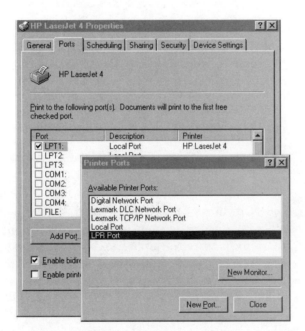

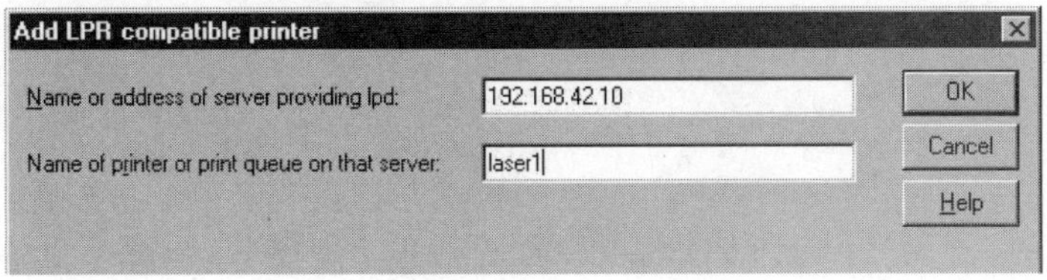

Figure 15–34
Type a printer name.

Auditing Printers

Printers can be audited for printer-specific actions. Before printer auditing can take place, the system to which the printer is attached must have File and Object Auditing turned on using the User Manager. Once auditing is enabled, a printer can have the following events audited for failure or success:

- Print
- Full Control
- Delete
- Take Ownership
- Change Permissions

Auditing printers can be helpful for tracking usage and security. Just remember to keep track of the auditing file sizes and be sure to keep them at a manageable size.

Troubleshooting Windows NT Printers

This section will cover some of the more classic problems involved with Windows NT printing. This section is more than just troubleshooting. The goal here is to be aware of some of the better ways to optimize, as well as "fix" common Windows NT problems.

Bad Drivers

Incorrect or corrupted drivers can make printing in Windows NT a nightmare. Until Windows NT becomes a true Plug and Play OS, there will always be the problem of installing incorrect print drivers. An equally bad situation is when print driver files sometimes become corrupted. Usually you can tell quite easily which has happened. First, the printouts will come out as ASCII gibberish—useless nonsense and crazy characters with lots of wasted paper. This result is due to the print device trying to read the incompatible data as a series of commands. If the driver has just been installed, the driver is probably incorrect; if the printer was doing fine before, the drivers are probably corrupt. In either case, delete the printer and reinstall.

Printer Device Failures

Printer device failures happen all too frequently. They are certainly the most common of all printer problems. Printers get paper jams, run out of toner or paper, get unplugged, and sometimes die horrible deaths that require completely replacing the device. When these things happen, the first and best thing to do is to redirect the print jobs to another printer—as discussed earlier in this chapter. Of course, the printer to which you redirect the print jobs must be identical—or at least close enough to have the capacity to understand the print jobs from the printer it is taking the redirection from. If there is no other printer to redirect to, the print jobs will stay in the spooler until the printer comes back online. After fixing the problem, you can simply go to the Printer folder, open the printer and choose Restart from the Document menu option.

The Evil Spooler

The Spooler program holds print jobs before they are sent to the printer. Double-clicking the printer icon in the Printers folder will open the Spooler window and display each job currently being handled by the Spooler, as shown in Figure 15–35. Assuming that the user has the proper permissions, print jobs can be paused, restarted, and deleted in this window.

While the spooler is usually an invisible, dependable program, there are many situations where the spooler is a big problem. One big problem is when a print job becomes jammed. Sometimes even an Administrator

Figure 15–35
Spooler window

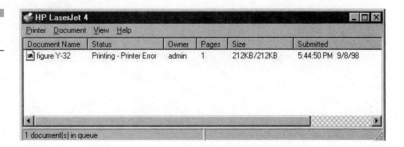

cannot delete a print job. In this case, the only fix is to stop and restart the Spooler service. This is done in the Services window, as shown in Figure 15–36—simply stop and restart the Spooler to get rid of the problem print job. Remember that when the Spooler is stopped, no one can print to the printer.

The Spooler can also be a big problem if the hard drive becomes low on space. Corrupted print jobs in the spooler can rapidly devour disk space. These print jobs are files, by default stored in the **\SYSTEM32\SPOOL\PRINTERS** directory. It's a good idea to shut down the spooler occasionally to determine whether the directory contains any files, and to delete any files that do appear. If the spooler directory is empty but the drive upon which it is installed is running out of space, you can move the spooler directory to another drive by opening the Printers folder, selecting File . . . Server Properties, and choosing the Advanced tab. A Window appears to let you select a new folder location, as shown in Figure 15–37. Always remember to put the spooler in a folder and not to let the spool files fill up a root directory. This graphical capacity to change the spooler folder is a major improvement over Windows NT 3.51—you used to have to hack the registry. There is a chance that you may run into a question that gives editing the Registry as the only real option. You can still do it with Windows NT 4.0, but that is the old-fashioned way to do it.

Figure 15–36
Services window

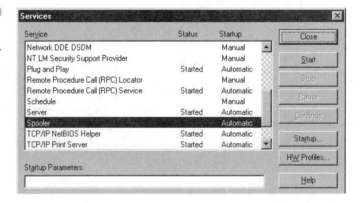

Figure 15–37
Advanced tab

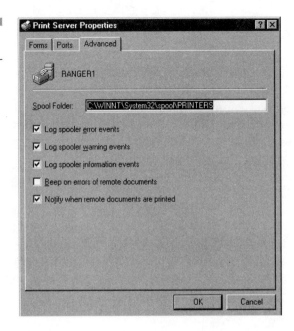

Questions

1. True or False: "You can attach many print devices to one printer, but you can have only one printer on a print device."

2. The process of having one printer serve more than one print device is known as _____.

3. Windows version _____ must still have the print drivers installed locally.

4. There is only one difference between Windows NT Server and Windows NT Workstation that may affect printing. What is that difference?

5. Two identical printers with identical print devices have different print priorities: eight and 88. Which printer has the higher priority?

6. How do you configure a printer's scheduling so that it can only be accessed on weekdays?

7. The four levels of printer permissions are what?

8. How do you update the print drivers on client Windows NT machines?

9. LPR is used by Windows NT to do what?

10. True or False: You need to edit the Registry to turn off the Spooler.

Answers

1. False. You can have many printers on one print device.

2. Printer Pooling

3. 3.X (Windows 3.1 and 3.11, Windows for Workgroups 3.1 and 3.11) still must have print drivers installed on each machine.

4. Windows NT Workstation can only accept up to 10 simultaneous connections.

5. The printer with the 88 priority has the higher priority.

6. You cannot. Scheduling is only based on time of day.

7. No Access, Print, Manage Documents, Full Control

8. Just update the drivers on the print server. The client systems will be automatically updated next time they attempt to print.

9. LPR is designed to enable Windows NT systems to interact with other LPR printers on non-Windows NT operating systems under TCP/IP.

10. False. You can turn off the spooler by turning off the Spooler service.

16

Monitoring and Maintaining NT Server

You might be shocked by this fact, but Windows NT networks can have problems. What is even worse is that sometimes—for no obvious reason whatsoever—they can suddenly grab themselves by the throat and keel over dead. Windows NT administrators live for these moments. When your server crashes for no apparent reason, or when your users complain of problems with logon or slow access, you must find ways to diagnose and fix the problems and then tune and optimize your servers to avoid such problems in the future. Diagnosing any problem often requires you to decide which one element of your system caused the problem. One bad part or protocol, after all, can rock your server's world in a most negative way. Most Windows NT administrators are not sure whether to look at hardware or software first when something goes wrong. Windows NT has several diagnostic techniques and tools to help you determine whether a slow access time is due to a lack of RAM, a slow processor, or bad virtual memory configuration. Once you have determined which element of your system (be it hardware, software, or configuration) has caused your problem, the data you have gained should tell you how to fix this problem. The solution might be to add more RAM, buy a faster processor, or move or enlarge your page file. Finally, after you have diagnosed and fixed issues for a particular server, you may want to reuse the data you obtained to plan for the future growth of your environment and to configure other systems so that they will not give you the same problems. Keeping a Windows NT network strong and stable requires you to monitor and maintain your servers to determine which resources cause slow work or bottlenecks, how to relieve these bottlenecks, and how to maximize the throughput and work of your servers.

Windows NT provides three tools to make the tasks of monitoring and maintaining servers easier: Performance Monitor, Network Monitor, and Event Viewer. The NT *Performance Monitor* (sometimes abbreviated as Perf-Mon) enables you to track and monitor information about the hardware and system elements of your Windows NT machines, both local and remote. Performance Monitor, a flexible applet that touches most parts of a Windows NT machine, provides your first diagnostic tool—especially with hardware. Performance Monitor will help you determine, for example, whether you should add RAM or buy a new processor. *Network Monitor* (sometimes abbreviated as NetMon) can capture and analyze data flowing across your network. Network Monitor enables you to pinpoint problem areas and problem machines. Finally, Event Viewer enables you to access several log files to see information about your system, security, and applications to understand what errors, if any, have occurred on your system. We will discuss each tool in detail, giving you the information needed to pass a Microsoft exam—and, more importantly, giving you the knowledge you need to succeed as a network administrator.

Performance Monitor

Administrators use Performance Monitor to view the behavior of hardware and other resources on their Windows NT machines, either locally or remotely. Performance Monitor—available with both Windows NT Server and Windows NT Workstation—can monitor both real-time and historical data about the performance of your system. To access the Performance Monitor applet, choose Start . . . Programs . . . Administrative Tools . . . Performance Monitor. This action launches Performance Monitor, shown in Figure 16–1.

Figure 16–1
Performance Monitor

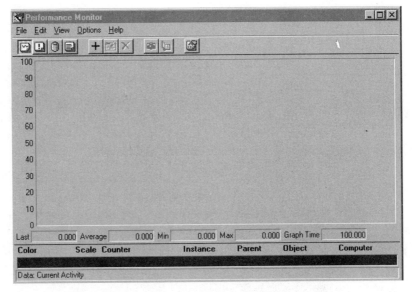

Once you access Performance Monitor, you need to configure the program to display data. The process of configuring Performance Monitor requires you to understand the concept of objects, counters, and views. An *object* in Performance Monitor relates directly to the component of your system that you want to monitor, such as the processor or memory. Each object has different measurable aspects called counters. *Counters*, in other words, are the portions of an object that you want to track. A large number of available counters exist in Performance Monitor. The number of device interrupts each second on a processor, for example, (displayed as Processor: Interrupts/sec), is a processor counter. As you decide which object(s) to monitor in your system, select one or multiple counters for each object. Add these counters to whichever view you need to use. Performance Monitor can display selected counter information in a variety of views, with each view imparting different types of information. The Chart view, for example, will enable you to graphically visualize current values for the counters you selected. Let's look at each component of Performance Monitor—objects, counters, and views—and then put these elements into practical use to create a baseline for a system (and an excellent diagnostic tool for Windows NT).

Objects

The objects available in Performance Monitor enable you to track and monitor the behavior of your system by tracking the behavior of each of its elements. This feature helps you isolate the component of the server that is causing the slow work, crashes, or inefficiency. The objects also provide the grouping, or classification, for the counters that will be added to the views in Performance Monitor. Each Windows NT system will have different objects available for viewing, based on the software and hardware installed in the system—although all Windows NT systems share certain core objects. To view the available objects for your system, select Edit . . . Add to Chart (or Log, Report, or Alert). The Add to Chart dialog box is displayed, as shown in Figure 16–2.

NOTE: The available views (Chart, Log, Report, and Alert) are each configured similarly. The Chart view is the default when you first begin working with Performance Monitor. The following examples, therefore, use the Chart view unless otherwise noted. The configuration and dialog boxes will be similar for the other views, which will be discussed later in the chapter.

In the Add to Chart dialog box, you should first select the computer to monitor. You can choose the local machine (the default) or a remote machine. To monitor a remote machine, type the computer name using UNC. To monitor a machine named ACCOUNTINGDC, for example, you would type **ACCOUNTINGDC** in the "Computer" field. You can also use the Select Computer button (at the right end of the Computer field) to view the available machines and select the one you want to monitor, as shown in Figure 16–3.

While monitoring a machine locally is often easiest, monitoring the machines remotely is often more accurate. Performance Monitor running

Figure 16–2
Add to Chart dialog box

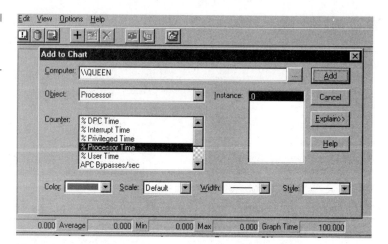

Figure 16–3
Select Computer
dialog box

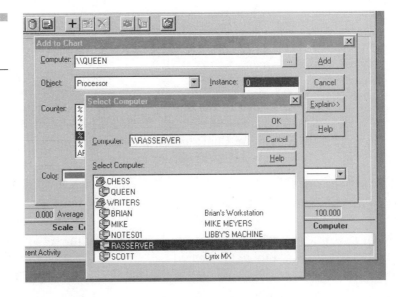

on a machine uses a certain amount of resources to take the measurements and display the data graphically. Especially when you troubleshoot issues with disk performance, memory and paging, or processor use, you should not corrupt your results by monitoring locally. Some cases exist where monitoring locally is preferred or required. If you are monitoring network access or networking protocol objects, for example, monitoring locally will affect the readings less than if monitoring remotely. Similarly, you must monitor a system locally if you cannot access that system over the network. Finally, when you monitor objects created by a specific application, such as Microsoft Exchange, you should monitor locally. The objects related to this application are only created locally and will not be available from another system.

Once you have selected a system to monitor, either locally or remotely, you must select the object to monitor. Click the drop-down arrow in the "Object" field. This list indicates all the system objects available that you have chosen to monitor, as shown in Figure 16–4.

Certain objects, as mentioned earlier, will appear on all Windows NT systems that you choose to monitor. The following list describes these core objects:

- Cache, which enables you to monitor activity in the area of RAM that holds the data currently in use

- LogicalDisk, which enables you to monitor activity on the disk partitions in the system

Figure 16–4
Selecting an object
to monitor

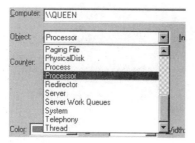

- Memory, which enables you to monitor activity in the system RAM
- Objects, which enables you to monitor some of the central elements of the system software
- Paging File, which enables you to monitor activity in the file that is used to create virtual memory
- PhysicalDisk, which enables you to monitor activity on the hardware used for storage in the system
- Process, which enables you to monitor activity in the software element that is running an application or program
- Processor, which enables you to monitor the activity in the hardware element that runs the application or program instructions
- Redirector, which enables you to monitor the activity in the portion of the file system that acts as the client, sending requests to the server
- System, which enables you to monitor general activity in the hardware and software of the system
- Thread, which enables you to monitor the activity in the element of the process (described earlier) which is using the processor (described earlier)

Other objects are visible in the list based on the hardware or software installed in the machine. Commonly, these other objects that will appear on the list can be the networking objects for protocols such as TCP/IP, Net-BEUI, or others.

When you select an object from the drop-down list, you will notice in some cases that the "Instance" field contains more than the single object you have selected. Some of the objects in your machine will have more than one instance, because there are more than one of the instances in the machine. The Processor, PhysicalDisk, and LogicalDisk objects, for example, all may

Figure 16–5

Multiple LogicalDisk
object instances

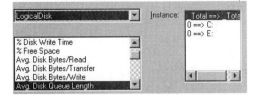

have more than one instance. In the case of the LogicalDisk object, a machine might have a hard drive partitioned into three or four partitions. In this case, there would be multiple LogicalDisk object instances for each of the drive letters, as shown in Figure 16–5. When multiple instances are available, you can add one or more of these instances. In most cases, you can also add a total for the instances.

Counters

When you select an object from the drop-down list, you must then select a counter for the object. Each object has multiple counters that enable you to measure specific elements of that object. If you want to measure the LogicalDisk object, for example, you could choose counters such as the Current Disk Queue Length, which would tell you how many requests are outstanding or waiting. This particular counter and object combination would be written as LogicalDisk: Current Disk Queue Length, combining both the object and counter. This notation is important, because some objects have similar counters. When you select a counter, be aware that Performance Monitor is collecting data for all the counters for that object. Performance Monitor, however, will only display the data for the counter you selected. If you selected the LogicalDisk: Current Disk Queue Length, for example, Performance Monitor will gather data for all the LogicalDisk counters but will only display the data for the Queue Length, as specified. While this feature does add some overhead to the process by only displaying the requested data, the performance hit is not too great.

As you begin to select counters for monitoring, the huge number of counters available might overwhelm you. To help reduce this overwhelming feeling, be aware that there are three types of counters: instantaneous, averaging, and difference counters. *Instantaneous* counters will always display the most current readings. The *averaging* counters will take the last two measurements, add them together, and divide by two to give a reading. This one causes a delay when you begin to take readings, because Performance Monitor waits until the counter has taken two readings to display the average. Finally, the *difference* counters take the most current reading, subtract that value from the previous reading, and display the values only if they are positive. The difference counters are limited in use and will not be available with the core objects discussed here.

Do not panic trying to learn the function of every counter. One of the most convenient features of Performance Monitor and its counters is that you do not need to memorize all of their functions. Certain widely used counters—and thus the ones likely to be on the exams—will be covered here. When you need to learn about a specific counter, select the counter from the list and then click the Explain button. Performance Monitor displays a counter definition field on the dialog box. This description discusses the use of the counter as well as information about the type, as shown in Figure 16–6.

While you can find information about the counters from Performance Monitor itself and therefore have no need to memorize the counters and their uses, there are certain counters that you should know—both for the exams and for optimizing certain specific elements of your system. Table 16–1 describes some of the most pertinent counters, both recommended by Microsoft and found in real, enterprise environments.

The "LogicalDisk" and "PhysicalDisk" counters mentioned earlier require additional configuration before you will see data from them. If you simply open Performance Monitor and add any disk monitoring counters to a view, you will have a consistent zero value. Disk counters increase disk access time overhead by a significant percentage. For this reason, the disk counters are disabled by default in Windows NT. To use any disk counters for either the PhysicalDisk object or the LogicalDisk object, first type the command **diskperf -y** at a command prompt, as shown in Figure 16–7. Then, reboot the system. The disk performance counters will start at boot time. You will then be able to see values form the disk performance counters

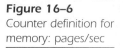

Figure 16–6
Counter definition for memory: pages/sec

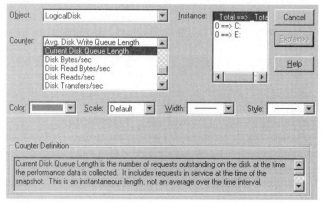

Table 16–1

Common counters

Counter	Definition/Recommendations
Memory: Available bytes[1]	This counter displays the amount of free virtual memory. On Windows NT workstations and Windows NT application servers, this value should remain larger than 4MB. If the value regularly falls below that number, usually too much paging is occurring. When you have an indication that too much paging is occurring, the usual recommendation is to add more RAM.
Memory: from Pages/Sec	This counter measures the number of pages written to or read disk. If the average of this counter over time is greater than 10, you are probably paging too much. Again, this value indicates that you probably need more RAM. You should also measure Memory: Cache Faults and Memory: Page Faults. More faults would usually indicate high paging and would again be indicative of the need for more RAM.
Processor: %Processor	This counter determines how busy the processor is while carrying out system requests and application threads. Occasionally, you may see the processor percentage peak at 100 percent. This situation is normal, providing the processor does not stay at 100 percent all of the time. The processor utilization should be a constant up-and-down action between zero and 80 percent. If you do see the processor at or near 100 percent on a more-or-less constant basis, the processor is more than likely the problem—or bottleneck—on the system. Finally, you have an excuse to buy that new, supercharged processor that just arrived.
Processor: Interrupts/Sec	This counter tracks the rate of service requests, or device interrupts, from I/O devices. A high value here, especially when this value is more than 100, indicates a hardware problem—potentially with a disk controller or NIC.
PhysicalDisk: % Disk Time or LogicalDisk: % Disk Time	This counter measures how busy the physical disk is or while servicing waiting reads and writes. If this number is consistently high—more than 60–70 percent—the physical disk is likely to be your problem. To solve this problem, you might obtain a faster disk or faster I/O controller. Other solutions include disk striping or mirroring.
PhysicalDisk: Disk Queue OR LogicalDisk: Disk Queue Length	This counter, mentioned earlier, measures the number of requests waiting to be serviced by the physical disk. If this number is more than two on a regular basis, the physical disk is not servicing the requests quickly enough. To solve this problem, you might obtain a faster disk or faster I/O controller. Other solutions include disk striping or mirroring.

[1]Paging is the process of writing portions of active processes occurring on the system to the hard disk, to reclaim some of the physical memory (RAM). This process occurs when the active processes or applications on the system require more memory than is physically available on the system. Too much paging slows processes because of the disk access time. In general, you want to use physical memory as efficiently as possible and minimize paging.

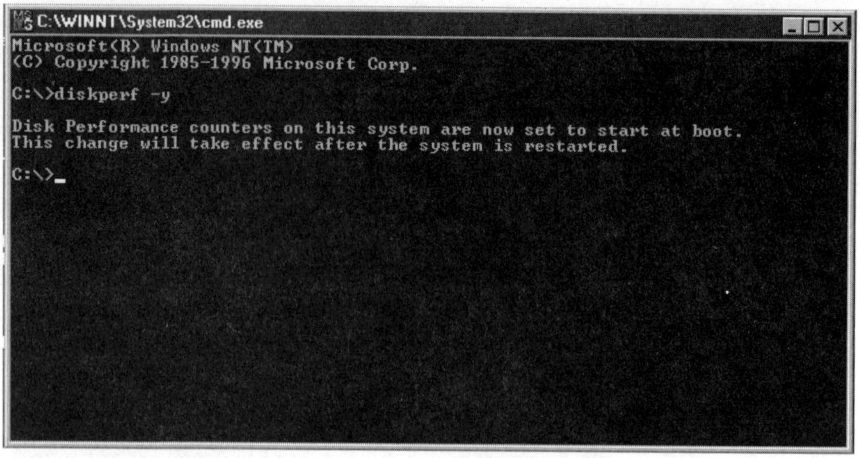

Figure 16–7
Loading Diskperf -y

Figure 16–7
Loading Diskperf -y

when you add them to a view in Performance Monitor. When you are finished taking disk performance measurements, you should turn the counters off again by typing the command **diskperf -n** and rebooting again. As a final note, remember that you must be logged in as a member of the Administrators group to have the right to start these counters.

Views

After you have selected appropriate counters for the objects that you need to monitor, you will look at them by default in the Chart view, as shown in Figure 16–8. The Chart view is one of the four available views in Performance Monitor. The other available views are Log, Alert, and Report. Each view is independent of the other views, so if you add the PhysicalDisk: Current Disk Queue Length counter to the Chart view, for example, and then switch to the Report view, the counter data will not be visible. Similarly, because each view is independent, the overhead increases as you use more than one view.

Each view has a different purpose, shows different data in different formats, and has different options. You should use the view or combination of views which is most appropriate to your current monitoring needs. To select a view, either use the View menu or use the buttons available on the toolbar. Select the Chart view when you need a graphical representation of your data over time. As you add counters to the Chart view, they are represented by different color lines on a line chart. The line chart displays the most current activity, overwriting previous data each minute.

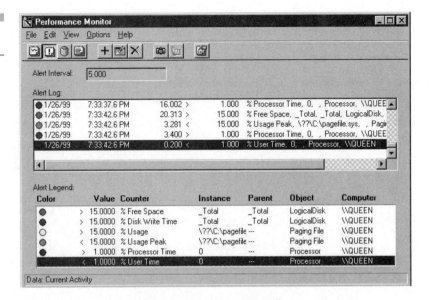

Figure 16–11
Alert view

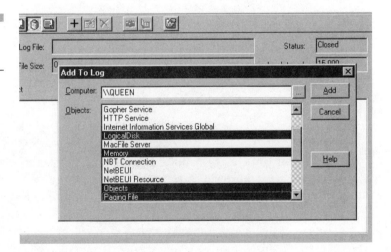

Figure 16–12
Add to Log
dialog box

After you have configured the Log to save to a particular file, you can see the log filename, status of the logging process, log interval, and file size of the log in the Performance Monitor dialog box. To stop collecting data in a log, open the Log Options dialog box again and click Stop Log. You can then choose to create a new Log file and begin logging again if necessary. You will also have the capacity to view data from one of these saved log files by selecting Options . . . Data From. In the Data From dialog box, shown in Figure 16–14, you can choose to continue obtaining data from the current activity or to obtain data from a particular log file.

Figure 16–13
Log Options
dialog box

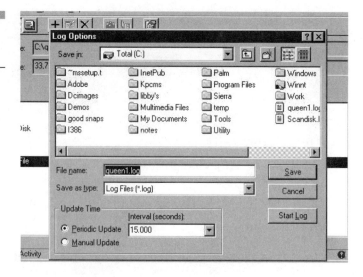

Figure 16–13
Log Options
dialog box

Figure 16–14
Data From
dialog box

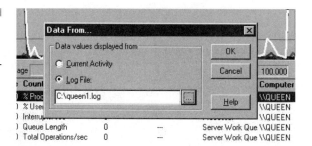

When you choose to obtain data from a saved log, you go back to that frozen moment in time and add counters to the other views for the objects you chose to save in the log. In our Log options, we selected to store data for the LogicalDisk object, for example. After we have loaded that particular log file, we can change to the Chart view, add counters for the LogicalDisk object, and view a static chart for that moment in time, as shown in Figure 16–15. You might want to select a wide variety of objects so that when you open the log to display in any of the other views (Chart, Alert, and Report), you can add any counters necessary.

The final view available in Performance Monitor is the Report view. The Report view functions similarly to the Chart view in that you see the most current settings for the selected counters. To create a report, switch to the Report view. Add counters to the report by selecting Edit . . . Add to Report. In the Add to Report dialog box, shown in Figure 16–16, select the necessary counters.

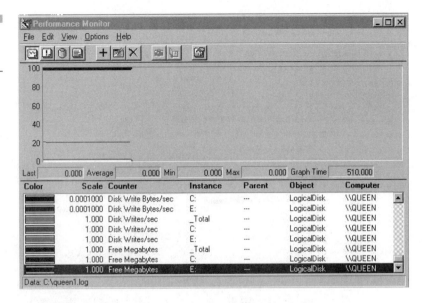

Figure 16–15
Displaying a saved
log in Chart view

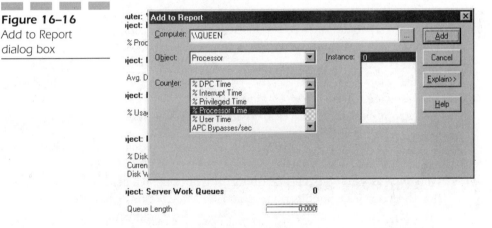

Figure 16–16
Add to Report
dialog box

When you have added the preferred counters, use Options . . . Report options to determine whether the update will occur periodically or manually—and how often—for periodic updates. After adding the report counters, you can view the report information, as shown in Figure 16–17.

Many times, you will find it useful to save the data that you have obtained from Performance Monitor. One of the ways you can save this data is in the log file, as described earlier. You also have the option of exporting the data from any of the views as either a *Comma-Separated* file (CSV) or a *Tab-Separated* file (TSV). You can then import these formats into Microsoft Access, Microsoft Excel, and other programs. In addition, you can use the Print

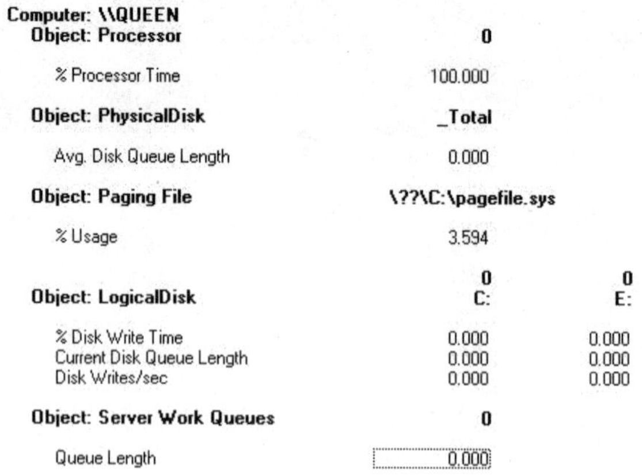

Figure 16–17
Report view

Computer: \\QUEEN		
Object: Processor	**0**	
% Processor Time	100.000	
Object: PhysicalDisk	_Total	
Avg. Disk Queue Length	0.000	
Object: Paging File	\??\C:\pagefile.sys	
% Usage	3.594	
	0	**0**
Object: LogicalDisk	**C:**	**E:**
% Disk Write Time	0.000	0.000
Current Disk Queue Length	0.000	0.000
Disk Writes/sec	0.000	0.000
Object: Server Work Queues	**0**	
Queue Length	0.000	

Screen button on your keyboard (or other screen capture utilities) to copy an image of the data and store that image as a bitmap or other graphics file. Finally, you can choose to store the settings for a view or for the entire workspace. If you have selected counters and options that are particularly useful to you in monitoring your system, you may save these settings for any view so that you do not have to create them again each time you use Performance Monitor. To save the settings for a single view, choose File . . . Save Settings for the Chart, Alert, Log, or Report view. These files will either be *chart files* (PMC), *alert files* (PMA), *log files* (PML), or *report files* (PMR). If you want to save settings for all the views simultaneously, choose File . . . Save Workspace to save a *workspace file* (PMW) containing selected objects, counters, and options for all of the views.

Create a Baseline

In many cases, the best way to monitor your servers over the long term is to create a measurement baseline when servers are healthy and functioning normally—so that you have comparison data. This process will also enable you to analyze how the changes you make to the system affect performance. Baselining also gives you the capacity to use comparisons over time to predict future needs. Creating a baseline uses the techniques described earlier for saving Performance Monitor data to store measurements in a database. First, select some core objects and counters that you will track over time. These counters will usually be for the Memory, Processor, System, Server Work Queues, PhysicalDisk, LogicalDisk, and Server objects. After selecting the objects and counters for each view, export the data to an external file. Then, import the data into a database or spreadsheet such as Access or Excel. Make sure to save the workspace so that you can repeat the same readings over time. As you repeat the readings and build a database, you can make comparisons based on the state of the system at any time. This feature will enable you to predict needs as you make changes in the environment or add more users and applications.

Identify Performance Bottlenecks

Once you have created a baseline and database for normal data, you can use this information to troubleshoot bottlenecks. A *bottleneck* is the location in the system where a slowdown is occurring. If you have problems with slow user connections, for example, the problem could stem from many elements of the system—from the NIC to not having enough RAM. Use the historical data as a comparison to new charts to determine where the bottleneck might be. Some of the places that bottlenecks are most common are in the memory, the processor, the disk, and the network. Armed with this information, you can troubleshoot these bottlenecks. First, create the baseline and measurement database mentioned earlier. Then, when the bottlenecks begin occurring, use the following list of counters, as well as the Counters table earlier in this chapter, to take readings. Compare the readings to determine where the bottleneck is occurring. Be aware that the nature of bottlenecks in computer systems means that you will discover and fix one bottleneck, only to discover another one beneath or behind that bottleneck. Tuning, optimizing, and troubleshooting your system is an ongoing process, because the use of the system is also a continuously changing process.

Use the counters in Table 16–2 as a suggested list when trying to locate a bottleneck. You should usually start at the Chart view with these counters and then delete the counters that appear to behave normally.

Using the earlier list of counters, you should be able to identify the major element of your system that is causing or is being affected by the bottleneck. Use application-specific counters to track down this information. In addition, your system will have additional counters that are specific to your system based on hardware, software, or protocols installed. Use the core counters with the application-specific counters to determine any additional bottlenecks or problems. After you have determined what is causing the bottleneck or other performance problem, you will need to solve the problem. The earlier table mentions some solutions for each type of bottleneck; however, you should also search Microsoft's TechNet or contact your hardware vendor for additional information on specific problems.

Table 16–2

Commonly used
counters

Counters for Memory Bottlenecks	
Memory: Pages/Sec	Look for values larger than 0–20, which will indicate high paging rates. Add RAM to fix the problem, and find the process or application that is causing the paging.
Memory: Available Bytes	Look for values smaller than 4MB, which indicates that there is too little physical memory (RAM) available for applications. Again, add RAM—but also look for the process or application causing the high rate of paging.
Memory: Committed Bytes	Look for a value larger than the amount of RAM in the system. If the system has 256MB of RAM, the value of this counter should be less than 256; otherwise, you need more RAM.
Memory: Pool Nonpaged Bytes	This counter represents the RAM used for the OS. If you notice an increase in this counter while the system is doing the same amount of work, there is probably a process or application with a memory leak. Reboot the system, and start applications one-at-a-time to attempt to isolate the problem.
Counters for Processor Bottlenecks	
Processor: % Processor Time	If the processor is busy more than 75 percent of the time, the processor is probably the bottleneck. In this case, you can add another processor or add a faster processor.
Processor: % Privileged Time	If the processor is busy working for the OS more than 75 percent of the time, again, the processor is probably the bottleneck. In this case, you can add another processor or add a faster processor.
Processor: % User Time	If the processor is busy working for a user process (such as running e-mail or word-processing software) more than 75 percent of the time, the processor is probably the bottleneck. In this case, you can add another processor or add a faster processor.
Processor: Interrupts/Sec	The number of interrupts per second is the number of interrupt requests for service that the processor is receiving from hardware or applications. While the acceptable range varies based on the type and speed of your installed processor(s), if the counter gets too high the processor is probably causing a bottleneck. On a Pentium processor, the number of interrupts should be fewer than 3,500/sec. If the counter is regularly higher than this number, you can add another processor or add a faster processor.
System: Processor Queue Length	The processor queue length is the number of requests waiting for processor time (or waiting in the queue). If this number stays larger than two, your processor might be overworked. You should determine whether there is a particular application or piece of hardware causing the bottleneck and consider adding an additional or faster processor.

Counters for Processor Bottlenecks

Server Work Queues: Queue Length	Similarly to the processor queue length, the server work queue length is the number of requests waiting for processor time (or waiting in the queue). If this number stays larger than two, your processor might be overworked. You should determine whether there is a particular application or piece of hardware causing the bottleneck and consider adding an additional or faster processor.

Counters for Disk Bottlenecks[1]

PhysicalDisk: % Disk Time LogicalDisk: % Disk Time	On either counter, if the percentage is consistently more than 50, the disk is busy servicing read and write requests too much of the time. To improve disk performance, find out what is using the disk and consider upgrading to a faster controller or adding more disks in a RAID array.
PhysicalDisk: Disk Queue Length LogicalDisk: Disk Queue Length	Similarly to other queue length counters, if the disk queue length consistently gets higher than two, too many requests are waiting to be serviced. This situation suggests that the disk is a bottleneck and that you should find out what is using the disk and consider upgrading to a faster controller or adding more disks in a RAID array.

Counters for Network Bottlenecks

Server: Bytes Total/sec	If the number of bytes the server has sent and received falls too low, depending on the type and number of NICs and protocols, the network adapter may be the bottleneck. Adding another (or better) NIC or improving other network infrastructure components, such as bridges and routers, can solve network problems.
Server: Logon/sec and Server: Logon Total	Use these counters to determine the amount of logon validation that is occurring on domain controller servers. The value should be high. If the value is not high and users are complaining about problems logging on, add more domain controllers.
Network Segment: % Network Utilization[2]	This counter, which measures the amount of the available bandwidth in use on the local network segment, should be lower than 30 percent. If the value is higher than this number, you might choose to limit the number of protocols or segment the network in a greater amount.

[1]To use disk counters, remember to load `diskperf -y` (or `diskperf -ye` when using RAID) at a command prompt.

[2]Network segment counters must be enabled using the Network applet in the Control Panel. Open the Network applet by double-clicking. Select the Services tab. Click the Add ... button. Choose Network Monitor Agent from the list of services. This service forces the NIC to accept and examine all network traffic on its segment, rather than just the traffic intended for NIC. Only use this agent when troubleshooting or diagnosing, because this agent will downgrade the performance on the machine on which it is running.

Network Monitor

Besides using the Performance Monitor tool to determine the health of your system, you have other monitoring tools at your disposal. One of the areas in which Performance Monitor's capabilities are more limited is in tracking the networking elements of your system. While Performance Monitor does have networking counters that are available when you add the Network Monitor Agent (as described earlier), if you install the Network Monitor Tools and Agent—or simply Network Monitor—you have an actual packet sniffer at your disposal, which is a tool that collects and analyzes individual packets on a network to determine bottlenecks or security breaches.

A *packet sniffer* or *packet analyzer* captures and examines the packets that go through your network segment. A *network segment* is a discrete portion of the network that is not separated by routers, where all machines hear all the traffic. Machine A speaks, in other words, and Machine Z hears, although the message was not meant for Machine Z. Both machines reside in the same network segment, as seen in Figure 16–18. Serious network techno-geeks will often call segments "collision domains," but these techno-geeks do not have any friends.

Data going through a network segment must be broken into small pieces called *packets*, or *frames*. These packets have specific elements that can be commonly recognized, such as a source address and a recipient address, as well as the data. Packets are built and sized differently depending on the protocol being used on the network. An example of the components of a packet is shown in Figure 16–19.

Figure 16–18
Two computers on the same network segment

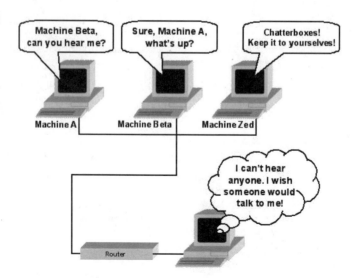

Figure 16–19
Packet components

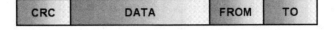

| CRC | DATA | FROM | TO |

Packet analyzers grab some or all of the packets on the network. These packets are then filtered and viewed in various ways to determine information. Packet analyzers can be hardware-based, software-based, or a combination of the two. Network Monitor, as a function of the OS, is obviously software-based.

NOTE: *Packets and frames are terms used interchangeably in this chapter to refer to the containers for data passing across the network.*

Network Monitor can capture these packets as they go through your system. Once the packets have been captured, this tool can determine the contents of the packet, the protocol used to create and send the packet, and the sending and receiving machines. In the case of this version of Network Monitor, you can capture the following types of packets:

- Any packets sent to your system
- Any packets sent from your system
- Any broadcast frames
- Any Multicast frames

The Network Monitor provides a powerful tool for troubleshooting network problems—much more powerful than merely running a Network Monitor Agent under Performance Monitor. With the Monitor Agent, you could only add Network Segment counters to Performance Monitor or enable another machine to view network data about your system. When you install Network Monitor, however, you have installed a simple version of a network packet analyzer. Furthermore, an agent running under Performance Monitor requires an NIC that supports Promiscuous mode. Network Monitor does not. *Promiscuous mode* enables an NIC to capture all data packets on the network segment, regardless of the sender or recipient indicated in the packet. An NIC that enables this type of capturing is required for a Monitor Agent. In Network Monitor, however, the card does not need to support Promiscuous mode. Note that the capability to monitor the network without using Promiscuous mode on the NIC will improve performance on the system.

NOTE: *The version of Network Monitor installed with Windows NT is not as fully functional as the version of Network Monitor installed with Microsoft Systems Management Server (SMS). Both versions enable you to capture data packets traveling across the network, although the simple version captures only packets sent to-and-from the computer that is actually running the Network Monitor tool. The full-featured version includes the capacity to monitor any packets on the entire network. The SMS version also has additional features that enable you to determine which protocol is using the most bandwidth, which devices on the subnet are routers, and to capture network packets remotely. While this full version is not included with NT4, the version can be installed on Windows NT, Windows 95, or Windows 98 by accessing the application from the SMS CD.*

Install and Configure Network Monitor

The Network Monitor tool, although included with Windows NT 4, does not install automatically with the OS. To install Network Monitor, first uninstall the Network Monitor Agent if you have previously installed this agent to enable Network Segment counters to be displayed in Performance Monitor. To uninstall the Network Monitor Agent, open the Network Control Panel applet. In this applet, select the Services tab. On the Services tab, select the Network Monitor Agent from the Network services list, as shown in Figure 16–20. After selecting the Network Monitor Agent, click the Remove button. After Windows NT has removed the service, restart your machine.

After restarting your Windows NT machine, you can install the more powerful option—Network Monitor Tools and Agent (although this agent is still less powerful than the version included with SMS). To install this service, open the Control Panel and double-click the Network applet. Click the Services tab of the Network applet, and click the Add button. From the Select Network Service dialog box, shown in Figure 16–21, choose the Network Monitor Tools and Agent and click OK to install the agent. Windows NT will prompt you for the location of your installation files. Point the way to the Windows NT Server CD, allow the files to copy, and then reboot to complete the process. To use Network Monitor after installing the agent, go to Start . . . Programs . . . Administrative Tools . . . Network Monitor.

Capturing Network Data

When you start Network Monitor, you will first see the Capture window shown in Figure 16–22. You can use this window to configure the captur-

Figure 16–20
Remove the Network
Monitor Agent
service

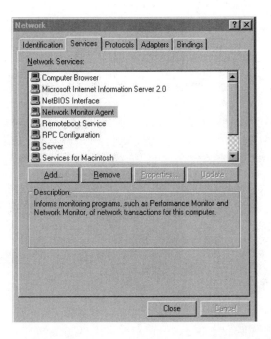

Figure 16–21
Install the Network
Monitor Tools and
Agent.

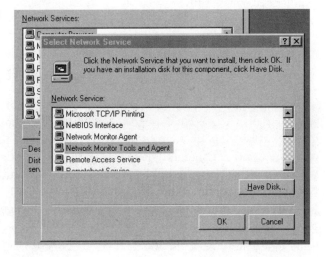

ing of the network packets and to watch while capturing occurs. To start
a capture, choose Capture . . . Start from the menus, or press the F10 key.

The Network Monitor Capture window has four panes: Graph, Session
Statistics, Station Statistics, and Total Statistics. You can focus on a specific
pane by clicking that pane, or you can toggle specific panes on and off using
the Window menu. In addition, the panes are adjustable in size. The top-left

Figure 16–22
Network Monitor
Capture window

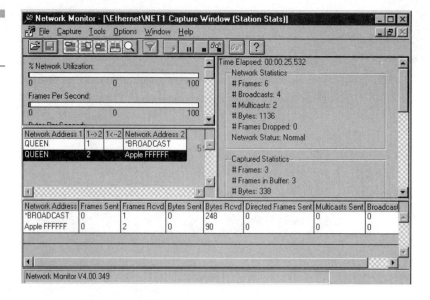

corner contains the Graph pane. This pane shows the network activity happening during the capture process. The measurements shown in this window include the following: % Network Utilization, Frames per second, Bytes per second, Broadcasts per second, and Multicasts per second. The pane immediately below this pane is called the Session Statistics pane. This pane shows the summary of the communications occurring during the capture process. Included in this pane are the names or network addresses of the hosts that are communicating, as well as the types of communication—including broadcasts and Multicasts. Of course, this feature will include only communications originating from or destined for your current system, based on the limitations of the Windows NT version of Network Monitor. Below this pane is the Station Statistics pane, which displays summary information for a specific host based on network address or name, in terms of frames and bytes sent and received as well as Multicasts and broadcasts sent. The right-hand pane is the Total Statistics pane. The Total Statistics pane, as its name suggests, shows data related to the total amount of data sent across the network and captured by Network Monitor.

The Dedicated Capture Mode, available from the Capture menu on the Network Monitor Capture window, enables capturing to progress while the Network Monitor application is minimized. The main purpose for this type of capturing is to provide Network Monitor with the resources necessary for capturing all frames. In some cases, frames will be dropped because of a lack of resources on the capturing machine. The buffer size also affects

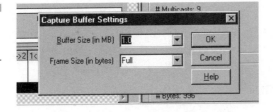

Figure 16–23
Capture Buffer
Settings dialog box

the amount of resources available for capturing. By default, Network Monitor reserves 1MB of RAM as a buffer space to hold the captured frames, as shown in Figure 16–23. In the Capture Buffer Settings dialog box, available by choosing Capture . . . Buffer Settings, you can change this buffer size as well as change the number of bytes captured for each frame. Be careful not to set the buffer size higher than the amount of available RAM on your system, or the paging will cause the process to drop frames. In addition, if you need to reserve resources, reduce both the buffer size and the number of bytes per frame captured.

Capture Triggers

While Network Monitor is capturing data, you will occasionally want a process to occur based on the data you are capturing. If the buffer space for frame captures reaches a certain point, or if a frame matching a certain pattern is captured, you might want to run a batch file or stop the capturing. You can cause these events to occur by using a Capture Trigger. To create and activate capture triggers, select Capture . . . Trigger. The option is only available when there is no capturing occurring. While the default setting for the Capture Trigger dialog box is to trigger based on Nothing, you will add triggers based on pattern matches or buffer space, as shown in Figure 16–24. The following trigger options are also available.

- Select the "Pattern match" button to trigger an action based on matching an ASCII or HEX pattern in the frame.

- Select the "Buffer space" button to trigger an action based on the capture buffer being filled to a specified percentage.

- Select the "Pattern match then buffer space" button to trigger an action based on having a pattern match first, and then reaching the specified threshold. The specified action will only occur if both triggers are found.

Figure 16–24

Capture Trigger
dialog box

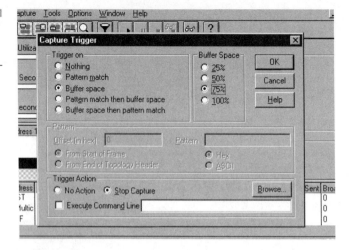

■ Select the "Buffer space then pattern match" button to trigger an action based on first reaching a specified space threshold in the capture buffer, and then matching a pattern. The specified action will only occur if both triggers are found.

After selecting a trigger, you must specify the pattern to match, the buffer space percentage, or both. To specify a pattern to match, use the following fields:

■ Use the "Offset (in hex)" field to indicate whether Network Monitor should look for the pattern at the beginning of the packets or farther into the packet. Use "Hex" to complete this field. The default is zero, which enables Network Monitor to look only at the beginning of the frame for the pattern.

■ Use the "From Start of Frame" radio button to indicate that Network Monitor should start looking for the pattern at the beginning of the frame. In addition, this radio button will enable Network Monitor to begin counting the offset from the beginning of the frame (if necessary).

■ Use the "From end of Topology Header" radio button to indicate that Network Monitor should start looking for the pattern, or should start counting the offset, from the end of the header data.

■ Use the "Pattern" field to type the pattern to match. This value can be in either Hex or in ASCII.

■ Use the "ASCII" and "Hex" radio buttons to indicate to Network Monitor which format was used in the Pattern field.

To specify a percentage of buffer space, use the radio buttons to select 25 percent, 50 percent, 75 percent, or 100 percent. This action tells Network Monitor to activate the triggered action when the capture buffer reaches that percentage. After selecting the triggers, you must also select an action for Network Monitor to perform. By default, the No Action radio button is selected. Use the following fields and buttons to select an alternative action:

■ Use the "Stop Capture" radio button to force Network Monitor to stop the capturing process when the trigger is activated.

■ Use the "Execute Command Line" field to type a command for Network Monitor to activate when triggered. This command line can be any command or executable file. If selecting an executable file, you can use the Browse button.

Use the options available in the Capture Triggers dialog box to enable Network Monitor to run without supervision. Capture triggers will enable you to stop Network Monitor automatically if the capture buffer becomes full. Capture triggers also will enable you to run an executable in response to a full capture buffer—or to a specific pattern match.

Displaying Network Data

A capture can be paused or stopped at any time to enable you to view and analyze the captured packets. To stop a capture, either select Capture . . . Stop from the menus or press the F11 key. After you have stopped the capture, you can view the data in the Capture Summary window by pressing the F12 key or by selecting Capture . . . Display Captured Data from the menus. This option displays the Network Capture Summary window, as shown in Figure 16–25. Similar to the capture window, this window is broken into multiple, adjustable panes. The top pane is the Summary pane. This pane shows a list of all the captured packets. For each packet, the list includes the following information: the source and destination address (listed by hardware or MAC address), information about the protocol used to send that packet, a description of the packet, and any other addresses available for the source and destination, such as an IP address. In some cases, this window will be the only one visible when you open the Display view. To obtain more information about a particular packet and to see the other available panes, double-click a packet. (If the other panes are visible, this action will toggle them off.)

The Detail pane, directly below the Summary pane, describes the protocol layers of the captured frame. Each frame may contain multiple

Figure 16–25
Network Capture
Summary window

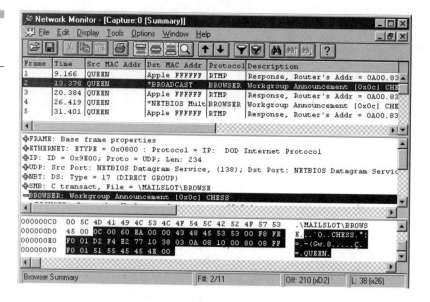

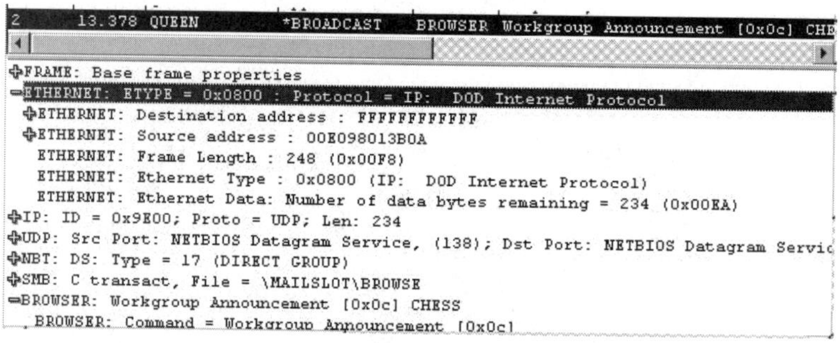

Figure 16–26
Detail pane

protocol layers as defined by the OSI seven-layer model (described in Chapter 10, "Networking Protocols"). The Detail pane lists each of these layers, as shown in Figure 16–26. To see more information about each layer in the frame, click the plus (+) sign to the left of the text lines, or press **Enter** to expand the data about each portion of the frame.

As you select and examine portions of the frame, the bottom pane (Hexadecimal pane) is displayed. The portion of the hexadecimal data that corresponds to the layer or data you have selected in the Detail pane is selected and highlighted, as shown in Figure 16–27.

Viewing the information displayed in the capture summary enables you to understand the type of traffic going to-and-from your computer. In some cases, you may notice that you have a certain type of network problem—perhaps a slowdown or bottleneck. The Network Monitor can help deter-

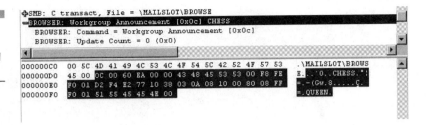

Figure 16–27
Hexadecimal frame showing highlighted data

mine what type of traffic, if any, crosses the network card while this slow-down occurs. You might find a broadcast storm, for example. You can also use the capability to examine the hexadecimal representation of the data to see patterns in the frames. This feature will enable you to match a particular pattern in a frame for use in capture triggers or filters.

Filtering Network Data

Capture and Display filters enable you to limit both the data you capture and the data you display after capturing. As mentioned earlier, the capture buffer has a limited size and can fill quickly when you are capturing all the data that goes across a busy network card. A Capture filter can limit the data Network Monitor captures based on protocol, addresses, or patterns in the packets. This feature enables the capture to continue longer without filling up the capture buffer. A Display filter, on the other hand, helps you slog through the captured data to find precisely what you need. Once all the packets have been captured, you can create a filter that only displays certain packets—again based on protocol, addresses, or patterns in the packets.

CAPTURE FILTERS The Capture Filter dialog box, shown in Figure 16–28, enables you to select which frames you want to capture. Access the Capture Filter dialog box by selecting Capture . . . Filters from the pull-down menu or by hitting **F8**. The image shown in the Capture Filter dialog box is called the *decision tree*, which is a graphical representation of the AND and OR statements that include or exclude frames from capture. You can limit capture based on protocol, address, and patterns in the frames.

To edit the decision tree to include or exclude a particular protocol, select the **SAP/ETYPE** line in the decision tree and then click the Edit Line . . . button. By default, Network Monitor captures packets from all available protocols. Choosing to edit the **SAP/ETYPE** line displays the Capture filter SAPs and ETYPEs dialog box, which provides you the opportunity to enable or disable

Figure 16–28
Capture Filter
dialog box

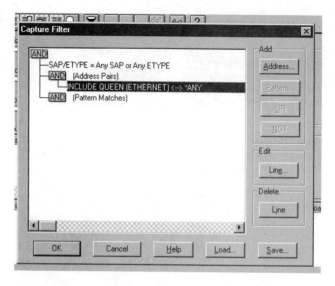

Figure 16–29
Capture Filter SAPs
and ETYPEs
dialog box

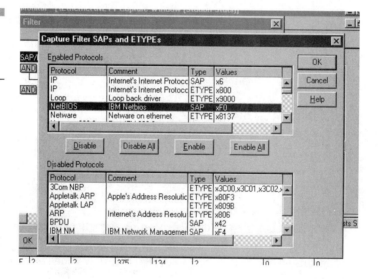

protocols, as shown in Figure 16–29. Enabling or disabling a protocol helps Network Monitor decide which packets to capture. To disable the capturing of packets sent using a particular protocol, for example, select that protocol from the Enabled Protocols list and then click the Disable button. If you want to exclude any frames that are not TCP or IP protocol frames, for example, select each of the other protocols listed and click Disable. This action causes Network Monitor to capture only packets created and sent using the TCP and IP protocols, thus limiting the number of packets captured and the information displayed for you.

Besides limiting captures by type of protocol, you can also limit the capture by selecting address pairs or by matching patterns in the frames. By default, Network Monitor captures all frames sent to-or-from your local machine. To limit captures based on the systems sending and receiving from your system, click the line below Address Pairs. You can then edit this line using the Edit Line . . . button, remove the limitation by clicking the Delete Line . . . button, or add an address by clicking the Add Address . . . button. The addresses that you use to limit the capturing can be hardware addresses (MAC addresses) or software addresses (such as IP or IPX).

In addition, you can filter captures by comparing patterns in the packets. If you have used the display portion of Network Monitor to discover a particular pattern in a type of frame that you do not need to capture, you can add this item to the filter by editing the Pattern Match line. You can also decide how the protocols, address pairs, and patterns are related to each other by editing the AND, NOT, and OR connectors. Keep in mind that AND is more restrictive than OR—because AND arguments require both elements to be met.

DISPLAY FILTERS   A Display filter limits the information displayed after a capture has occurred. Running a Capture filter followed by a Display filter can help refine a search for information (and increase the speed, lower the size, etc.). To create or apply a Display filter, choose Display . . . Filter from the menus or press **F8**. For either method, you must be in Display mode rather than the capture mode. Network Monitor shows the Display Filter dialog box, as shown in Figure 16–30.

By default, Network Monitor displays all captured packets. Similarly to the Capture filter, you have the capacity to use the decision tree in the dialog box to limit the packets that are displayed to the user based on protocol, address, or pattern-matching.

With both types of filters, you have the capacity to save filters that you create for later use. To save a filter, click the Save . . . button available from either dialog box. Capture filters will be saved with a CF extension, while Display filters will be saved with a DF extension. When you want to reuse a saved filter, enter the appropriate filter dialog box and click the Load . . . button. Then, select any saved filter to apply the filter.

In Network Monitor, Windows NT provides an excellent and necessary network troubleshooting tool. Network Monitor can analyze packets sent within a segment to determine the locations of bottlenecks, slowdowns, bad NICs, and more. Through various filters, you can refine Network Monitor's data gathering to focus only on certain protocols, addresses, or patterns. Network Monitor can make an administrator's life much easier.

Figure 16–30
Display Filter
dialog box

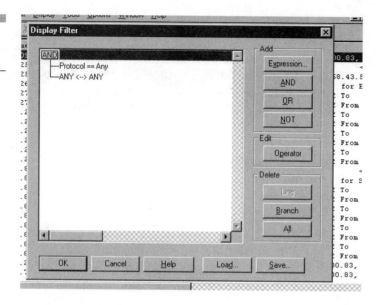

Event Viewer

The Event Viewer displays all the significant happenings on your system, including errors, warnings, informational messages, and security audit information. The Event Log service, which by default runs automatically at startup, captures the events. Performance Monitor and Network Monitor enable you to take an active role in monitoring your Windows NT environment. Event Viewer, on the other hand, gives you an excellent monitoring tool that requires little effort on your part.

NOTE: *If you want to stop logging events on a machine, open the Services Control Panel applet. Select the Event Log service and stop the event log. The service will start again automatically when the machine is rebooted, or you can click Start to resume logging.*

Viewing the Event Logs

To access the Event Logs, choose Start . . . Programs . . . Administrative Tools . . . Event Viewer. In the Event Viewer tool, you have access to three types of logs: System, Security, and Application. Each of these logs contains data on a different aspect of your system. To switch between the three types of logs, use the Log menu.

The System Log records events that occur in the system itself. Examples of system events include driver failures, low memory or disk space, and browser election information, as shown in Figure 16–31.

The Security Log, which can only be viewed by system administrators, logs events based on the elements of the system selected for auditing. User Manager, described in Chapter 8, "Managing Users in Windows NT," enables administrators to configure auditing for events such as logging on or changing account information. In addition, on NTFS drives you can configure auditing of the exercising of NTFS permissions on files and folders. When these audited events occur, they are written to the Security Log. Figure 16–32 shows an example of a Security Log.

The Application Log displays events recorded about applications on the system. Some internal applications, such as the Directory Replicator service and the Network Monitor application, write events to the Application Log. In addition, if an error has occurred in an application such as Microsoft Exchange or Lotus Notes, for example, the error would be written to the Application Log. Servers used primarily for file and print services rarely write anything to the application log. Figure 16–33 shows an example of an Application Log.

CONFIGURING AUDITING To use the Security Log effectively, first you must have configured auditing on your Windows NT system. Auditing enables Windows NT to monitor the use of user privileges, access to files, log

Figure 16–31
System Log

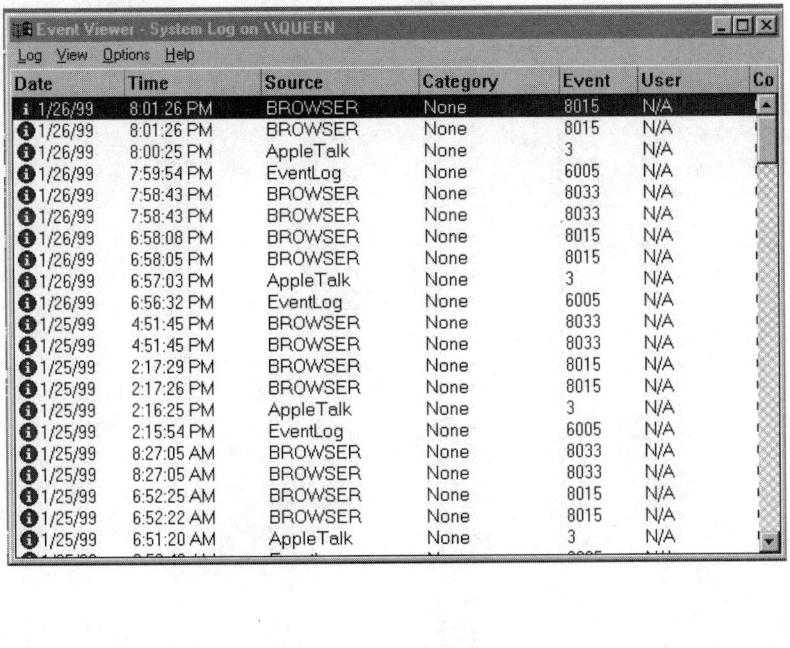

Date	Time	Source	Category	Event	User	Co
1/26/99	8:01:26 PM	BROWSER	None	8015	N/A	
1/26/99	8:01:26 PM	BROWSER	None	8015	N/A	
1/26/99	8:00:25 PM	AppleTalk	None	3	N/A	
1/26/99	7:59:54 PM	EventLog	None	6005	N/A	
1/26/99	7:58:43 PM	BROWSER	None	8033	N/A	
1/26/99	7:58:43 PM	BROWSER	None	8033	N/A	
1/26/99	6:58:08 PM	BROWSER	None	8015	N/A	
1/26/99	6:58:05 PM	BROWSER	None	8015	N/A	
1/26/99	6:57:03 PM	AppleTalk	None	3	N/A	
1/26/99	6:56:32 PM	EventLog	None	6005	N/A	
1/25/99	4:51:45 PM	BROWSER	None	8033	N/A	
1/25/99	4:51:45 PM	BROWSER	None	8033	N/A	
1/25/99	2:17:29 PM	BROWSER	None	8015	N/A	
1/25/99	2:17:26 PM	BROWSER	None	8015	N/A	
1/25/99	2:16:25 PM	AppleTalk	None	3	N/A	
1/25/99	2:15:54 PM	EventLog	None	6005	N/A	
1/25/99	8:27:05 AM	BROWSER	None	8033	N/A	
1/25/99	8:27:05 AM	BROWSER	None	8033	N/A	
1/25/99	6:52:25 AM	BROWSER	None	8015	N/A	
1/25/99	6:52:22 AM	BROWSER	None	8015	N/A	
1/25/99	6:51:20 AM	AppleTalk	None	3	N/A	

Event Viewer - System Log on \\QUEEN
Log View Options Help

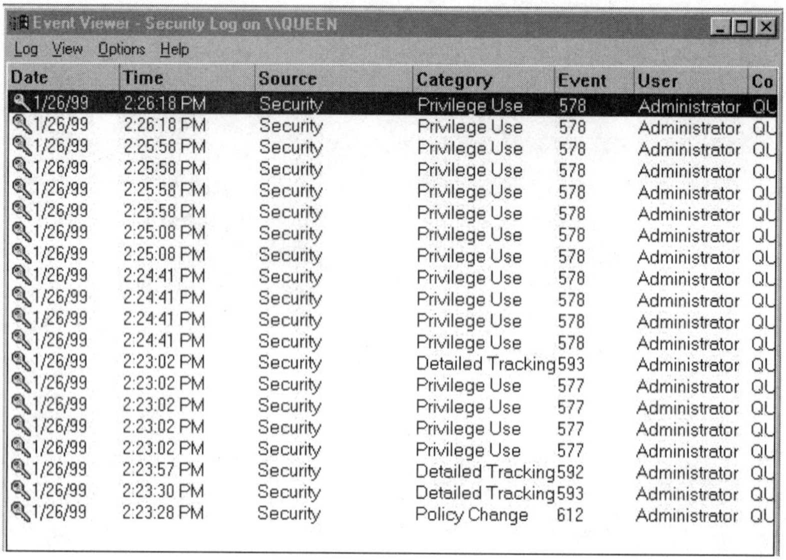
Event Viewer - Security Log on \\QUEEN
Log View Options Help

Date	Time	Source	Category	Event	User	Co
1/26/99	2:26:18 PM	Security	Privilege Use	578	Administrator	QU
1/26/99	2:26:18 PM	Security	Privilege Use	578	Administrator	QU
1/26/99	2:25:58 PM	Security	Privilege Use	578	Administrator	QU
1/26/99	2:25:58 PM	Security	Privilege Use	578	Administrator	QU
1/26/99	2:25:58 PM	Security	Privilege Use	578	Administrator	QU
1/26/99	2:25:58 PM	Security	Privilege Use	578	Administrator	QU
1/26/99	2:25:08 PM	Security	Privilege Use	578	Administrator	QU
1/26/99	2:25:08 PM	Security	Privilege Use	578	Administrator	QU
1/26/99	2:24:41 PM	Security	Privilege Use	578	Administrator	QU
1/26/99	2:24:41 PM	Security	Privilege Use	578	Administrator	QU
1/26/99	2:24:41 PM	Security	Privilege Use	578	Administrator	QU
1/26/99	2:24:41 PM	Security	Privilege Use	578	Administrator	QU
1/26/99	2:23:02 PM	Security	Detailed Tracking	593	Administrator	QU
1/26/99	2:23:02 PM	Security	Privilege Use	577	Administrator	QU
1/26/99	2:23:02 PM	Security	Privilege Use	577	Administrator	QU
1/26/99	2:23:02 PM	Security	Privilege Use	577	Administrator	QU
1/26/99	2:23:02 PM	Security	Privilege Use	577	Administrator	QU
1/26/99	2:23:57 PM	Security	Detailed Tracking	592	Administrator	QU
1/26/99	2:23:30 PM	Security	Detailed Tracking	593	Administrator	QU
1/26/99	2:23:28 PM	Security	Policy Change	612	Administrator	QU

Figure 16–32
Security Log

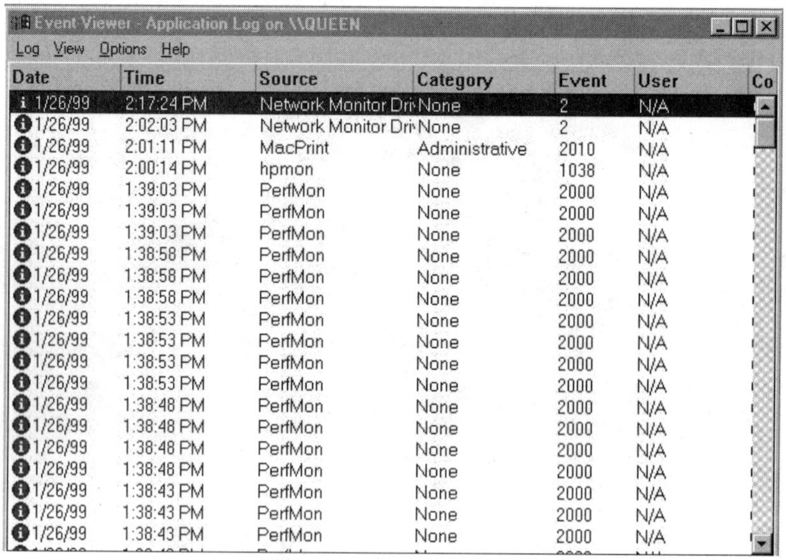
Event Viewer - Application Log on \\QUEEN
Log View Options Help

Date	Time	Source	Category	Event	User	Co
1/26/99	2:17:24 PM	Network Monitor Dri	None	2	N/A	
1/26/99	2:02:03 PM	Network Monitor Dri	None	2	N/A	
1/26/99	2:01:11 PM	MacPrint	Administrative	2010	N/A	
1/26/99	2:00:14 PM	hpmon	None	1038	N/A	
1/26/99	1:39:03 PM	PerfMon	None	2000	N/A	
1/26/99	1:39:03 PM	PerfMon	None	2000	N/A	
1/26/99	1:39:03 PM	PerfMon	None	2000	N/A	
1/26/99	1:38:58 PM	PerfMon	None	2000	N/A	
1/26/99	1:38:58 PM	PerfMon	None	2000	N/A	
1/26/99	1:38:58 PM	PerfMon	None	2000	N/A	
1/26/99	1:38:53 PM	PerfMon	None	2000	N/A	
1/26/99	1:38:53 PM	PerfMon	None	2000	N/A	
1/26/99	1:38:53 PM	PerfMon	None	2000	N/A	
1/26/99	1:38:53 PM	PerfMon	None	2000	N/A	
1/26/99	1:38:48 PM	PerfMon	None	2000	N/A	
1/26/99	1:38:48 PM	PerfMon	None	2000	N/A	
1/26/99	1:38:48 PM	PerfMon	None	2000	N/A	
1/26/99	1:38:48 PM	PerfMon	None	2000	N/A	
1/26/99	1:38:43 PM	PerfMon	None	2000	N/A	
1/26/99	1:38:43 PM	PerfMon	None	2000	N/A	
1/26/99	1:38:43 PM	PerfMon	None	2000	N/A	

Figure 16–33
Application Log

on and log off attempts, and other user access events. Auditing is configured in two main areas: the User Manager and resource (such as File or Printer) properties. In User Manager, you configure whether the system does any auditing as well as whether events such as log on and log off, file and object access, and system restarts should be audited. This portion of auditing was

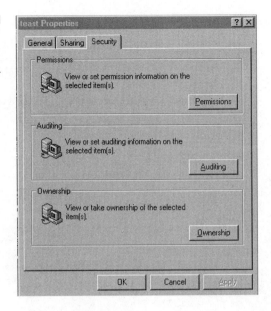

Figure 16–34
File Properties dialog box, Security tab

described in Chapter 8, "Managing Users in Windows NT." Auditing must first be enabled and configured in User Manager before the Security log will begin to track and display audit successes and failures. If you have enabled auditing of File and object access auditing in User Manager, you have the additional capacity to enable auditing on specific resources, such as files, folders, and printers. You can configure this auditing by opening the properties of the specific resource, usually by right-clicking and choosing Properties. In the Properties dialog box, select the Security tab. On the Security tab, click the Auditing button, as shown in Figure 16–34.

NOTE: *Note that file and object access auditing for specific files and folders will only be available when those files and folders reside on NTFS partitions. NTFS is required for auditing, sharing, and other security for files and folders.*

In the File Auditing dialog box, shown in Figure 16–35, use the Add . . . button to configure auditing for users and groups that try to access the resource. For each user and group that you add, you can audit the success or failure of the following file events:

- Read
- Write
- Execute

Figure 16–35
File Auditing
dialog box

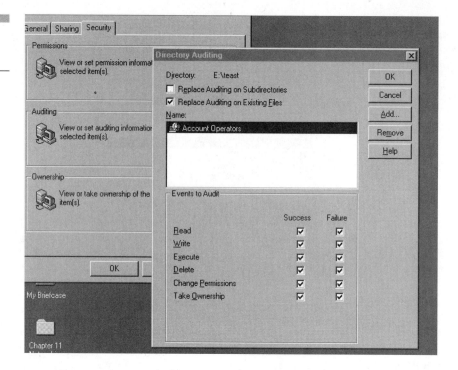

- Delete
- Change Permissions
- Take Ownership

When you choose to audit the success or failure of these file access events (similar audit events are also available for folders and printers), events are written to the security log indicating when one of the selected events has occurred or has been attempted.

Choosing a Computer to View

Some situations exist when you will want to view the Event Logs from a remote computer. Any Windows NT machine can open the Event Logs for any other Windows NT computer. To choose another computer's Event Logs, select Logs . . . Select Computer from the menus. This choice will only be available when you are logged on as the administrator of the system. Event Viewer displays the Select Computer dialog box, shown in Figure 16–36. Use the Computer field to type the UNC name (discussed in Chapter 9, "Microsoft Networking") of the remote computer, such as \\NERO. You can

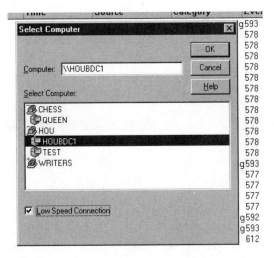

Figure 16–36
Select Computer
dialog box

also use the Select Computer window to browse through available computers and select the appropriate machine. Use the Low Speed Connection checkbox if you do not have a high-speed connection to the remote machine.

Event Types

The Application and System logs display three types of events. The *Information Event*, indicated by a blue circle with the letter "i" inside, gives messages that relate to the functioning of the system. These messages do not necessarily indicate any type of problem. Next, the *Warning Event*, indicated by a yellow circle, relates messages that did not cause the system to stop functioning but did cause a problem or error. Finally, the *Error Event*, indicated by a red, stop sign-type icon, relates messages for errors that might have caused a portion of the system to cease functioning.

The Security Log displays Success Audits and Failure Audits. These audit events are indicated either by a key icon or a padlock icon. These items indicate the success or failure of a logon, file use, or privilege use.

Each of these types of events contains the following details for each event: date, time, source, category, event, user, and computer. The date and time stamps indicate when the event occurred. The Source detail indicates which element of the system recorded the event that caused the message. This element can be part of the Windows NT OS or part of an application, such as security, Browser, and Service Control Manager. The Category detail is a category imposed by the element of the system that recorded the event. The System Log displays few categories. The Security

Log, on the other hand, displays several categories—including log on and log off, privilege use, and object access. The Event detail is a numerical event code. Jot down this number before you call Microsoft support, because Microsoft often has a key to explain the message based on this code. The User detail indicates the logged in user or the user attempting to use a particular element of the system. The Computer detail indicates which system is reporting the message.

To see another level of detail about each event, you can double-click the event. This action displays the Event Detail dialog box, shown in Figure 16–37. The Event Dialog box shows the same details shown in the Event Viewer window. The dialog box then displays a text description of the event, which can be used to understand and troubleshoot the event. In addition, some events also display a binary event description, which can be used by programmers and Microsoft Technical Support when troubleshooting. Use the Previous and Next buttons on this dialog box to navigate through the events.

Viewing the Logs

To make the Event Logs easier to read, there are times when you may choose to alter the display of the events. The two most common changes

Figure 16–37
Event dialog box

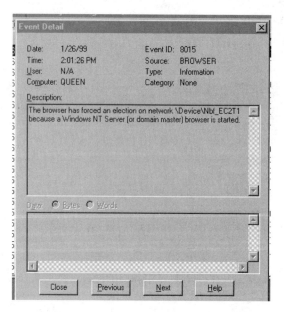

that you can make are filtering the events and sorting the events. When you filter the events, you select certain types of events, based on severity or other details, to display. To create a filter for the Event log, choose View . . . Filter events. Event Viewer displays the Filter dialog box, shown in Figure 16–38. Use the View From and View Through sections to choose Events to view based on date. You can use the fields in these sections to view from the first event to the last event—and to view events at specific dates and times. Use the Types checkboxes to select events to view based on the Event type. In addition, you can create filters based on the other details available for an event, including source, category, user, computer, and Event ID. The Source filter, for example, would enable you to limit your display to events reported by the Service Control Manager or any other element that you are troubleshooting.

After you apply a filter to the Event Viewer window, the window title indicates that you are viewing the specific log in filtered mode. This feature helps remind you that the visible events are not necessarily all of the available events. By default, Event Viewer displays all events. To remove the filter and go back to this state, either choose View . . . All Events or click the Clear button on the Filter dialog box.

The Event Viewer window also enables you to sort events. The only sort options are Newest First and Oldest First and are available from the View menu. This window enables the administrator to view events in the format he or she prefers. To set a default sort order, use the Options . . . Save Settings on Exit menu choice to maintain your choices.

Figure 16–38
Filter dialog box

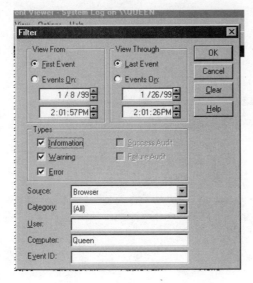

Besides changing the appearance of the events in the logs, you also have the capability to search the logs for particular types of events. Use the View . . . Find menu choice to search for events based on type, source, category, user, computer, Event ID, or description. The Find dialog box, which is similar to the Filter dialog box, is shown in Figure 16–39.

Log Settings

As time passes and more events occur on your system, the logs can fill up. Unfortunately, full Event logs can prevent you from being able to see and troubleshoot new events as they arise. To avoid this problem, use the Log Settings available by selecting Log . . . Log Settings. The Log Settings dialog box, shown in Figure 16–40, enables you to create separate settings

Figure 16–39
Find dialog box

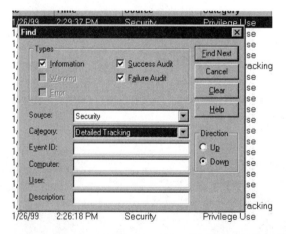

Figure 16–40
Log Settings
dialog box

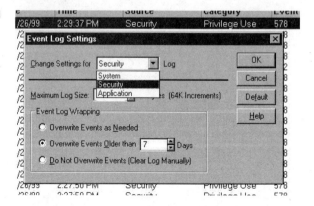

for each of the logs. To change settings for a particular log, click the drop-down arrow at the top of the dialog box and select System, Application, or Security.

The two main settings available for each log are the maximum log size and the log wrapping settings. The maximum log size defaults to 512KB and can be changed in increments of 64KB. The log will only grow to the indicated size. If more events occur after the log reaches this size, the log wrapping settings determine what happens to the events currently in the log. The following choices are available at this point:

- The "Overwrite Events as Needed" radio button enables all new events to be written to the log as they occur. If the maximum log size has been reached, the oldest events are rewritten by the newest events. This setting requires the least configuration and maintenance and is therefore the default.

- The "Overwrite Events Older than 7 Days" radio button enables events older than seven days to be removed from the log to make room for newer events. The days can be changed to anywhere from one to 365, with seven as the default.

- The "Do Not Overwrite Events" radio button keeps all events in the log and does not permit any events to be overwritten. When the log reaches the maximum size limit, events are no longer written to the log. To clear the log to enable new events to be written, use the Log . . . Clear All Events option from the menus. Note that using this option will prompt you to save all the current events to an archive file before clearing the log. If you want a record of the previous events, choose Yes to save all events before clearing the log. The log can be saved as an EVT file, which can be read later by Event Viewer or as a text file (either normal text or comma-separated), which can be opened and read in other applications.

Used in tandem, Performance Monitor, Network Monitor, and Event Viewer give you an excellent suite of tools for monitoring and maintaining your Windows NT servers. Each tool helps you troubleshoot and optimize different areas of the Windows NT network, from hardware utilization to packet transfer rates.

Performance Monitor, Network Monitor, and Event Viewer are not the only tools available to you for monitoring or troubleshooting your system, however. Task Manager, for example, can monitor the active applications and processes on your system. This tool is described in more detail in Chapter 5, "NT Application Support." In addition, the ERD can restore accounts or overcome boot problems. The ERD is described in more detail in Chapter 4, "The

NT Boot Process." When troubleshooting problems that may be hardware-related, you will also want to remember basic techniques such as verifying IRQ and I/O settings and resolving device conflicts. Within Windows NT, the SCSI Control Panel applet may assist with this process, although much of this type of maintenance or troubleshooting will be completed at the hardware and CMOS level. In all cases where logons or permissions are the problem, you will want to verify settings in User Manager for Domains or on particular resources. Finally, you may also want to investigate other tools included with the Windows NT Resource kit and third-party products that may help you with the immense task of monitoring and maintaining your Windows NT system and network.

Questions

1. Fidel is using Network Monitor to capture packets on his EtherNet network. He runs the capture for 15 minutes and has captured 400 packets. Fidel is overwhelmed by the amount of information and only wants to see packets sent using IP or NetBIOS. What should he do?

   a. Create a Capture filter. Configure the **SAP/ETYPE** line to disable all protocols except IP and NetBIOS.

   b. Create a Capture filter. Add two Protocol = Lines connected with the AND operator. One protocol line should be IP, and the other should be NetBIOS.

   c. Create a Display filter. Configure the **SAP/ETYPE** line to disable all protocols except IP and NetBIOS.

   d. Create a Display filter. Edit the Protocol = Any line to disable all protocols except IP and NetBIOS.

2. Timmy selects some LogicalDisk counters in Performance Monitor and adds them to the Chart view. He notices, however, that they are staying at zero. What did Timmy forget to do?

   a. Run **diskperf -n** before using LogicalDisk counters.

   b. Run **diskperf -y** before using LogicalDisk counters.

   c. Run **logicaldisk -n** before using LogicalDisk counters.

   d. Run **logicaldisk -y** before using LogicalDisk counters.

3. Raoul wants to run PerfMon for a week on his three new servers to create a baseline. Which view should he use?

   a. Chart view

   b. Alert view

   c. Log View

   d. Report view

4. What can Matilda do to receive an alert any time the free disk space on her Windows NT server falls below 30 percent?

   a. She can configure the Alert Options in Performance Monitor to send a network alert message when that counter is reached.

   b. She can configure the System Events log to send an alert to her workstation each time an event related to low free disk space on her server is recorded.

   c. She can configure Task Manager to send a network alert message when that counter is reached.

   d. She can configure NetMon to send a network alert message when that counter is reached in PerfMon.

5. Skippy is experiencing significant system slowdowns. He thinks the problem may be due to excessive paging. Which object should he add to a Performance Monitor view to find out whether he is correct?

   a. LogicalDisk

   b. Memory

   c. Browser

   d. ServerWorkQueues

6. If Skippy finds that he is having excessive paging. What is his best course of action?

   a. Add a faster I/O controller or a second controller to his system.

   b. Add disk mirroring to his system.

   c. Add more RAM to his system.

   d. Add a faster or second hard disk to his system.

7. When Gilly looks at her Security Log, it is empty. How can she cause events to be written to this log?

   a. She must enable Auditing in Server Manager before any Security events will be written.

   b. She must enable Auditing using User Manager for Domains before any Security events will be written.

   c. She must enable Security Alerts in Performance Monitor before any Security events will be written.

   d. She must enable Security Alerts in User Manager for Domains before any Security events will be written.

8. When creating a baseline for comparing the performance of your system, which tools are you likely to use? (Select any that apply):

   a. Performance Monitor, Log view

   b. Performance Monitor, Chart view

   c. Microsoft Excel

   d. Microsoft Word

9. Lenny wants to add network segment counters to the Chart view in Performance Monitor, but none are currently available. What should he do to enable these counters?

   a. Use the **diskperf -y** command from a command prompt.

   b. Use the **netperf -y** command from a command prompt.

   c. Use the Network applet to add Network Monitor tools and agent
      to the system.

   d. Use the Network applet to add Network Monitor agent to the system.

10. Zane is trying to capture all of the EtherNet packets that pass through his segment of the network. What does he need to do?

    a. Use the Network applet to install Network Monitor Tools and Agent.

    b. Configure his NIC to be in Promiscuous mode.

    c. Install the version of Network Monitor available with SMS.

    d. You can only do this task with a hardware-based packet sniffer.

Answers

1. d—After a capture has already been completed, use the Display filter, not the Capture filter. The **SAP/ETYPE** line is available in the Capture filter, not in the Display filter.

2. b—LogicalDisk counters are disabled by default and must be disabled by using the **diskperf -y** command from a command prompt. **Use diskperf -n** to disable the counters when finished to avoid using too many resources on the capturing machine.

3. c—Only the Log view enables you to collect data and save the data to be compared later.

4. a—The Alert view in Performance Monitor enables you to use Alert Options to forward network messages related to counters being reached.

5. b—Both the Memory: Pages/sec and the Memory: Available Bytes counters will give an administrator information on the amount of paging occurring on the system.

6. c—The usual reason for excessive paging is too little physical memory.

7. b—Auditing is enabled using User Manager for domains. You can also enable auditing for specific printers or files and folders that reside on NTFS volumes using the properties for the specified resource.

8. a, c—The Log view enables data from Performance Monitor to be saved and reviewed later. You should also export that data into Microsoft Excel or Microsoft Access to create a database for comparing readings at different times.

9. d—Install the Network Monitor agent to enable Performance Monitor to capture performance counter statistics for the Network segment counters. **Diskperf -y** installs the disk performance counters, and the Network Monitor Tools and Agent installs the full-fledged Network Monitor on the system. **Netperf** does not exist.

10. c—The version of Network Monitor included with Windows NT does not support Promiscuous mode and only captures packets directed to-or-from your specific system. While a hardware-based packet sniffer will work for this task, the best answer is to install the full-featured version of Network Monitor available with SMS.

Index

Note: Boldface numbers indicate illustrations.

AUTHOR'S BIOGRAPHY

Brian Schwarz realized sometime in the early-'90s that playing with computers was more fun than his real job, and so he leapt into the computer training and course development field with both feet. Fortunately, he was not wearing his in-line skates at the time. As a member of the Total Seminars team, Brian has taught classes all over the United States for clients ranging from Lucent Technologies to the United States Army. Practicing what he teaches, Brian is a *Microsoft Certified Systems Engineer* (MCSE) and an A+ Certified Technician. E-mail Brian at **brian@totalsem.com**.

Other Members of the Writing Team

Mike Meyers is the President of Total Seminars and the Head Keeper of the Total Seminars creative group. He is also the ultimate computer nerd. Mike is the author of McGraw-Hill's *A+ Certification Exam Guide*. E-mail Mike at **michaelm@ totalseminars.com**.

Libby Ingrassia Schwarz has been in the computer industry doing technical writing, training, course development, and consulting in Lotus Notes, Windows NT, and other technologies since 1994. Although she would rather be writing poetry for a living, little things like food and a roof over her head have turned her into a Jill of All Trades—and mistress of several trades—in the industry. She has planned and implemented installations, taught classes, developed applications, and even slung cable through the bowels of major office buildings. E-mail Libby at **LibbyS@ totalseminars.com**, and maybe she will send you some Domino haiku.

Libby has so many certifications that she needs a higher ceiling on her office walls. She is a MCSE, a Certified Lotus Professional in both Application Development and System Administration for R4 and R5, a Microsoft Certified Trainer, a Certified Lotus Instructor, and a Certified Technical Trainer.

Scott Jernigan wields a mighty red pen as Chief Technical Editor for Total Seminars. With a master of arts degree in medieval history, Scott feels as much at home in the musty archives of London as he does in the warm CRT glow of Total Seminars' Houston headquarters. After fleeing a purely academic life, Scott has spent the last couple of years teaching computer hardware seminars around the United States, including stints at the FBI Academy and the United Nations, among others. E-mail Scott at **scottj@totalseminars.com**.

Total Seminars is a unique group of teachers, authors, and presenters who all share one common trait: we love computers. Total Seminars has many venues that enable us to display that love of computers, including seminars, videos, CD-ROMs, and books such as the one you are reading right now. We have trained thousands of people from every level, including individuals as well as corporate, federal, state, and local government employees. Visit our Web site at **http://www.totalseminars.com**.